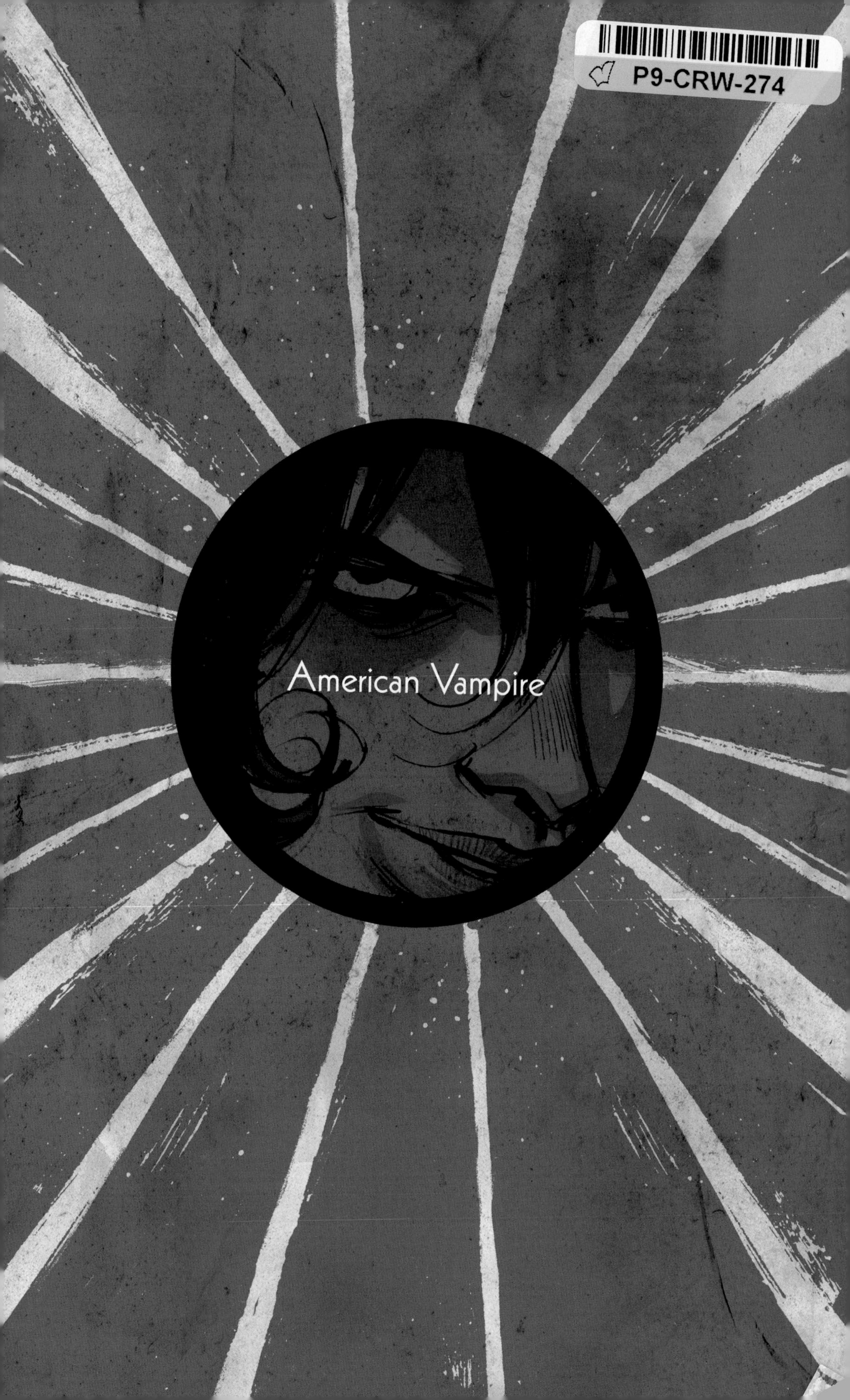
American Vampire

AMERICAN

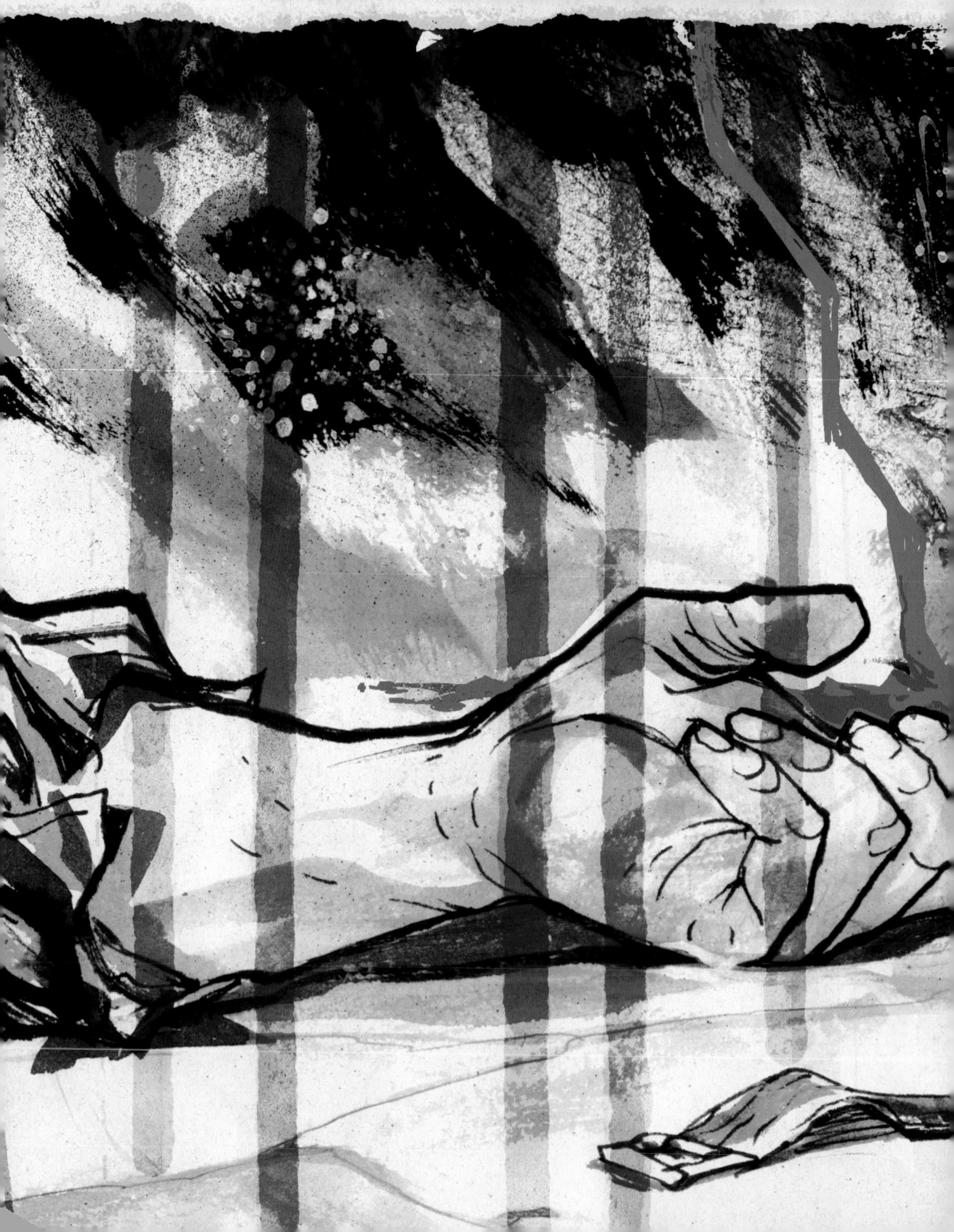

VAMPIRE

VOLUME THREE

Scott Snyder Writer

Rafael Albuquerque Sean Murphy Danijel Zezelj Artists

Dave McCaig Dave Stewart Colorists

Steve Wands Pat Brosseau Letterers

Rafael Albuquerque Cover Artist

American Vampire created by Scott Snyder and Rafael Albuquerque

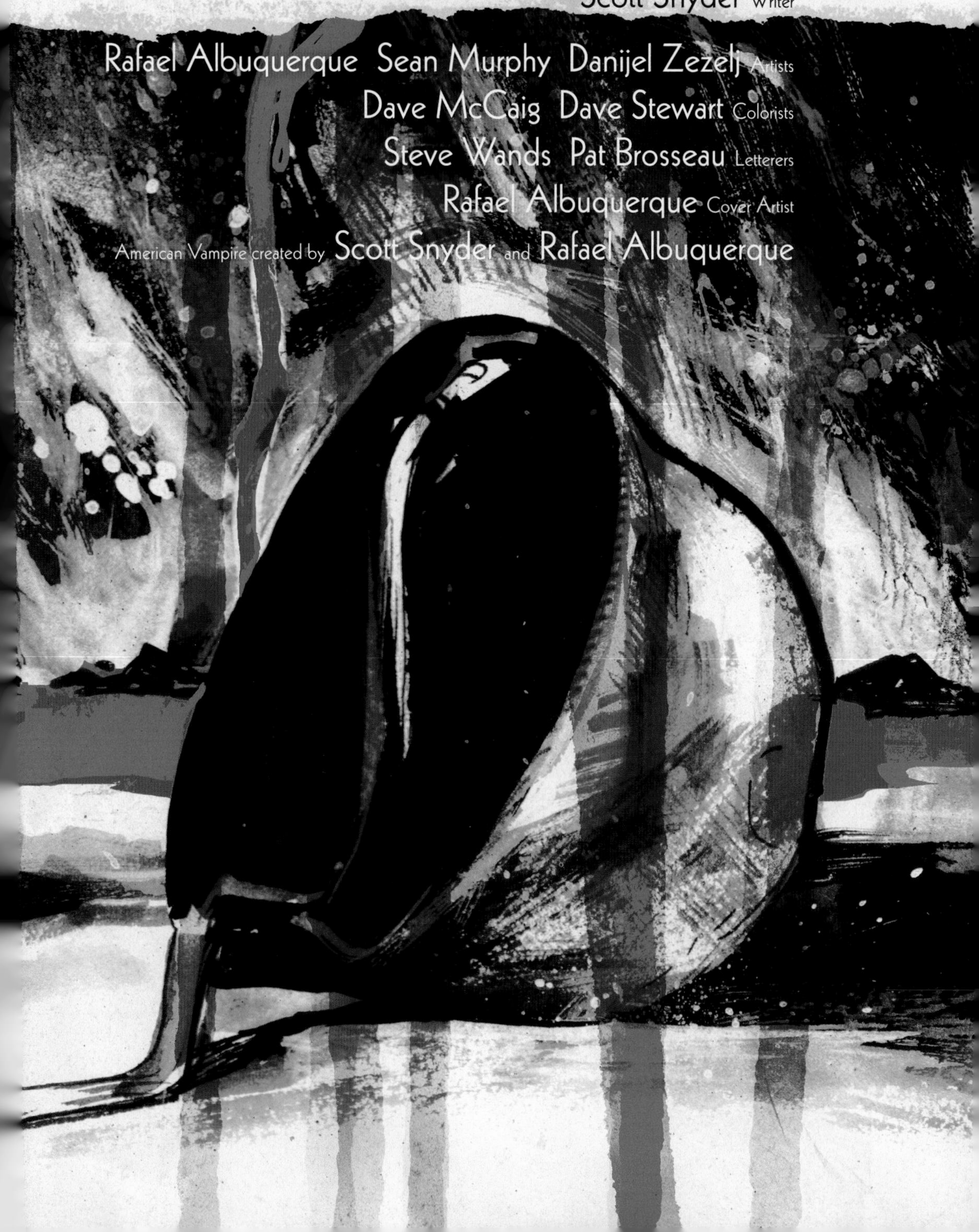

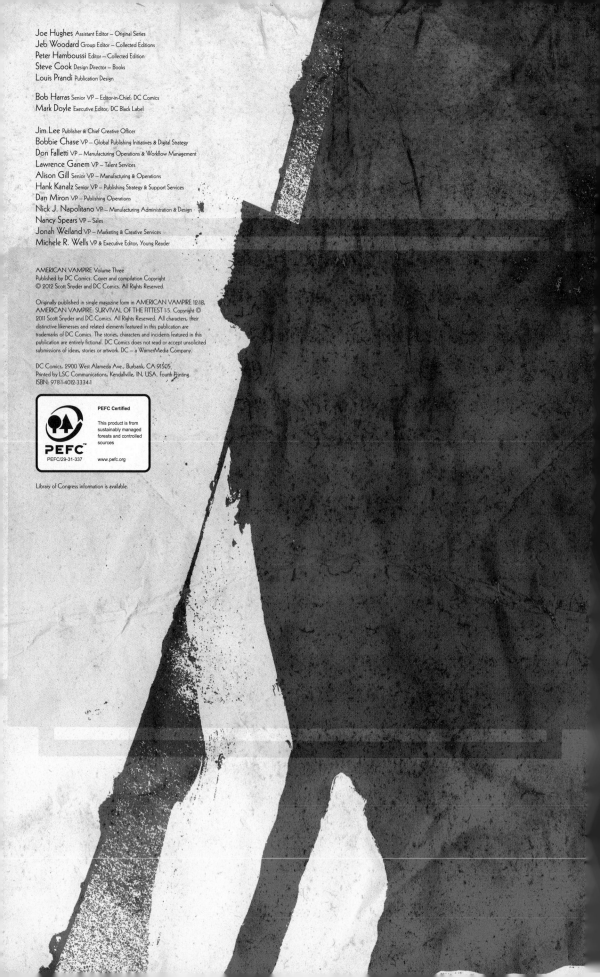

Joe Hughes Assistant Editor – Original Series
Jeb Woodard Group Editor – Collected Editions
Peter Hamboussi Editor – Collected Edition
Steve Cook Design Director – Books
Louis Prandi Publication Design

Bob Harras Senior VP – Editor-in-Chief, DC Comics
Mark Doyle Executive Editor, DC Black Label

Jim Lee Publisher & Chief Creative Officer
Bobbie Chase VP – Global Publishing Initiatives & Digital Strategy
Don Falletti VP – Manufacturing Operations & Workflow Management
Lawrence Ganem VP – Talent Services
Alison Gill Senior VP – Manufacturing & Operations
Hank Kanalz Senior VP – Publishing Strategy & Support Services
Dan Miron VP – Publishing Operations
Nick J. Napolitano VP – Manufacturing Administration & Design
Nancy Spears VP – Sales
Jonah Weiland VP – Marketing & Creative Services
Michele R. Wells VP & Executive Editor, Young Reader

AMERICAN VAMPIRE Volume Three
Published by DC Comics.

DC Comics, 2900 West Alameda Ave., Burbank, CA 91505.
Printed by LSC Communications, Kendallville, IN, USA. Fourth Printing.
ISBN: 978-1-4012-3334-1

PEFC Certified

This product is from sustainably managed forests and controlled sources

PEFC/29-31-337

www.pefc.org

Library of Congress information is available.

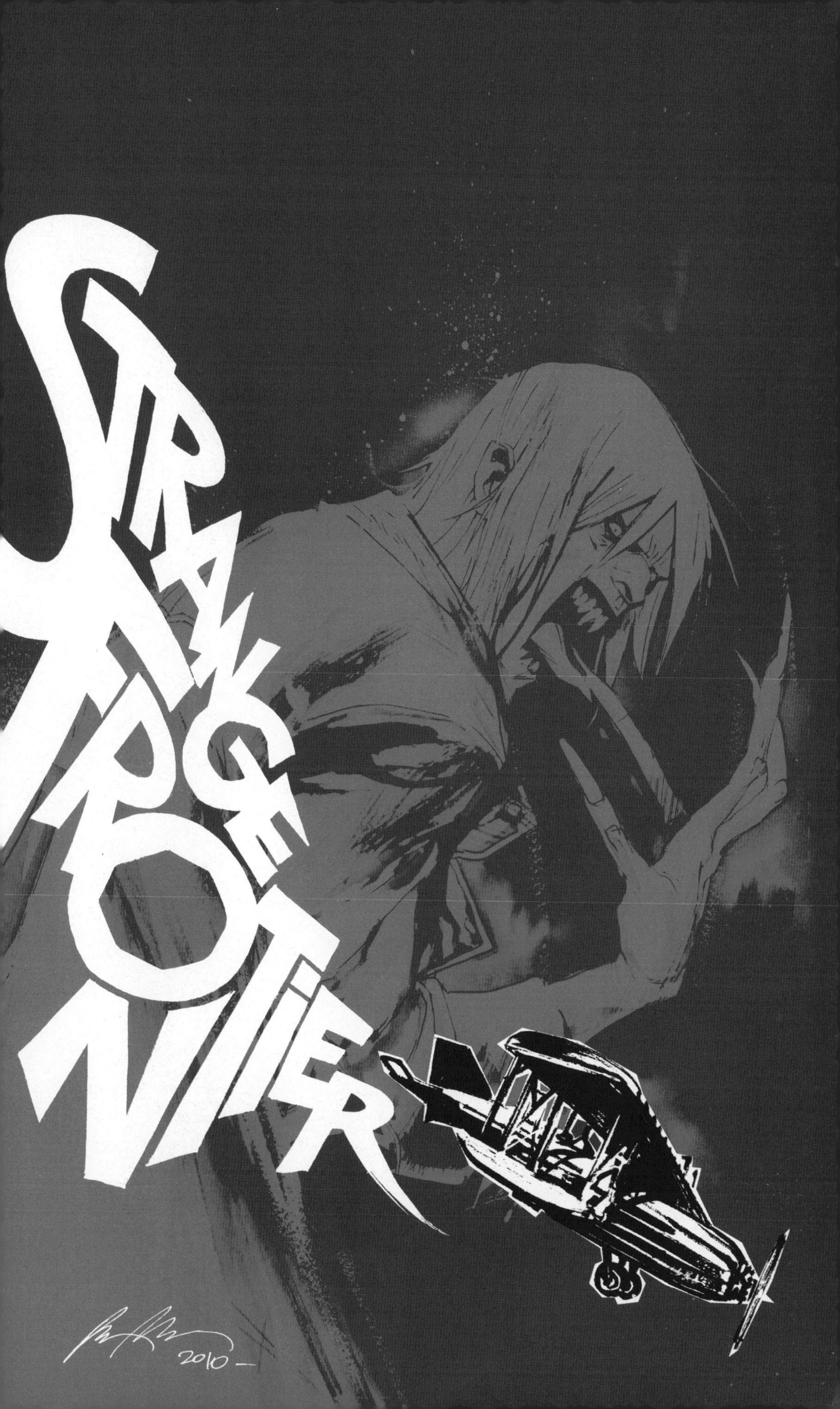
STRANGE FRONTIER
2010

Strange Frontier

Danijel Zezelj
Artist

Rafael Albuquerque
Cover

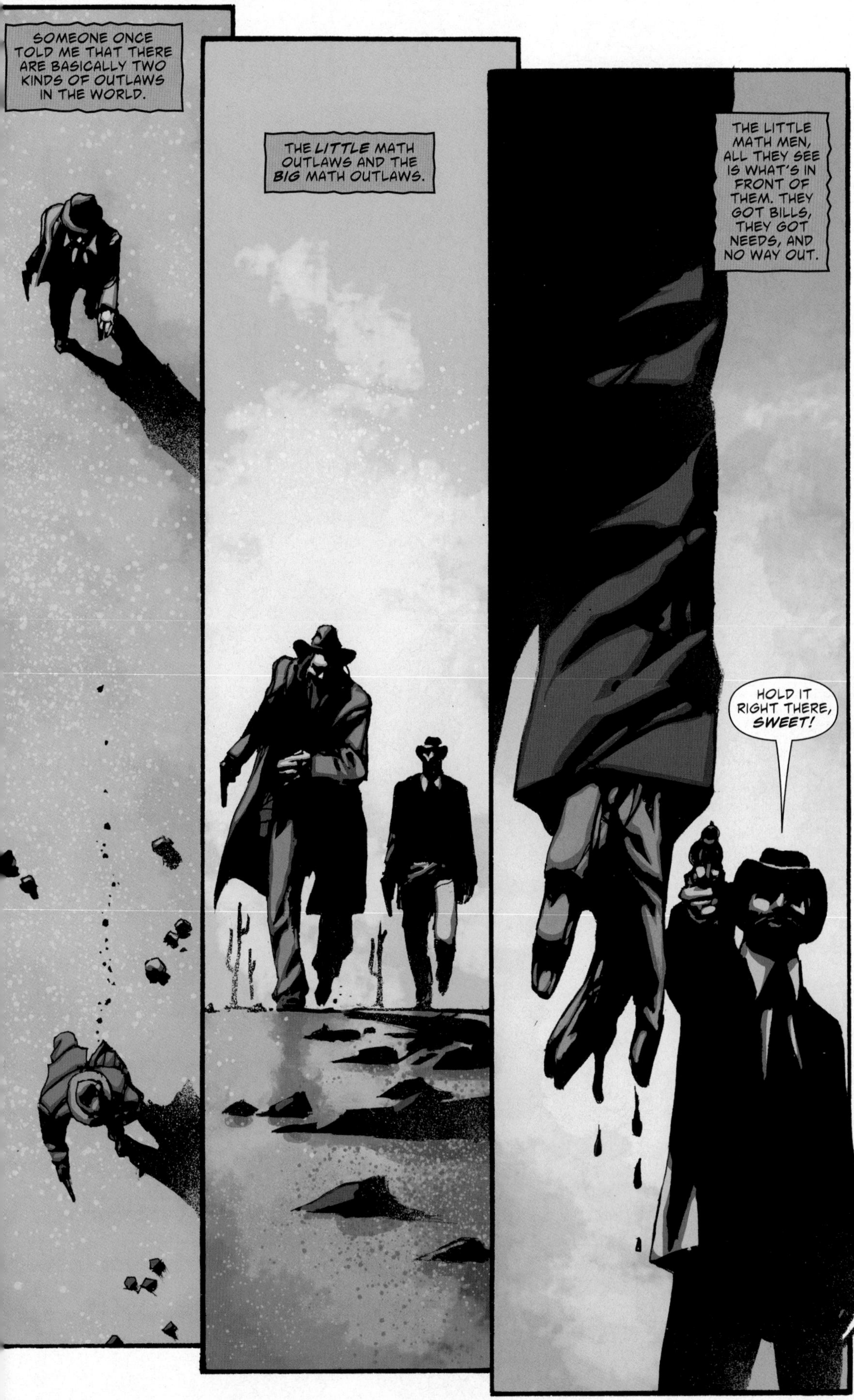
SOMEONE ONCE TOLD ME THAT THERE ARE BASICALLY TWO KINDS OF OUTLAWS IN THE WORLD.
THE *LITTLE* MATH OUTLAWS AND THE *BIG* MATH OUTLAWS.
THE LITTLE MATH MEN, ALL THEY SEE IS WHAT'S IN FRONT OF THEM. THEY GOT BILLS, THEY GOT NEEDS, AND NO WAY OUT.
HOLD IT RIGHT THERE, ***SWEET!***

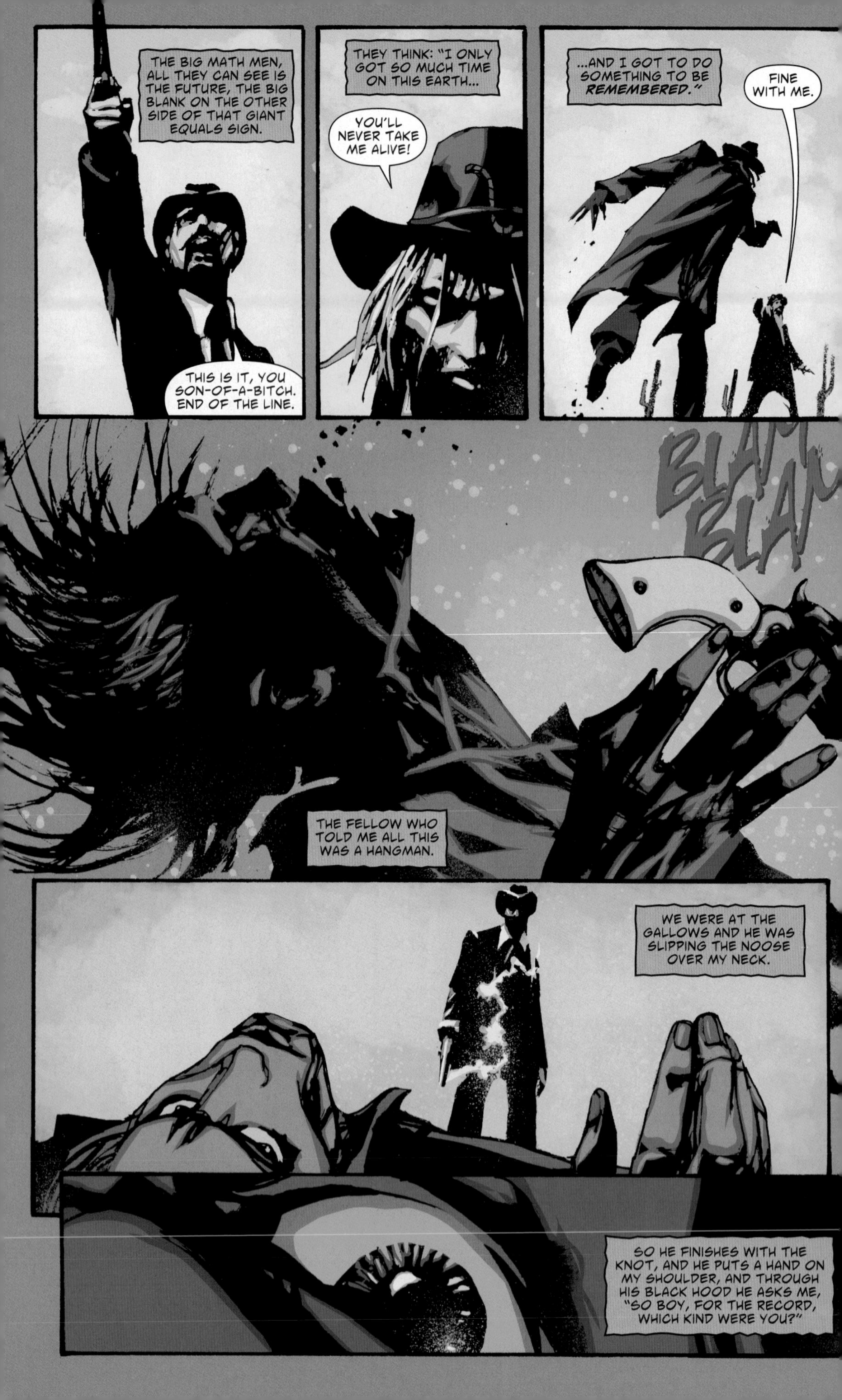
THE BIG MATH MEN, ALL THEY CAN SEE IS THE FUTURE, THE BIG BLANK ON THE OTHER SIDE OF THAT GIANT EQUALS SIGN.
THIS IS IT, YOU SON-OF-A-BITCH. END OF THE LINE.
THEY THINK: "I ONLY GOT SO MUCH TIME ON THIS EARTH...
YOU'LL NEVER TAKE ME ALIVE!
...AND I GOT TO DO SOMETHING TO BE *REMEMBERED.*"
FINE WITH ME.
BLAM
BLAM
THE FELLOW WHO TOLD ME ALL THIS WAS A HANGMAN.
WE WERE AT THE GALLOWS AND HE WAS SLIPPING THE NOOSE OVER MY NECK.
SO HE FINISHES WITH THE KNOT, AND HE PUTS A HAND ON MY SHOULDER, AND THROUGH HIS BLACK HOOD HE ASKS ME, "SO BOY, FOR THE RECORD, WHICH KIND WERE YOU?"

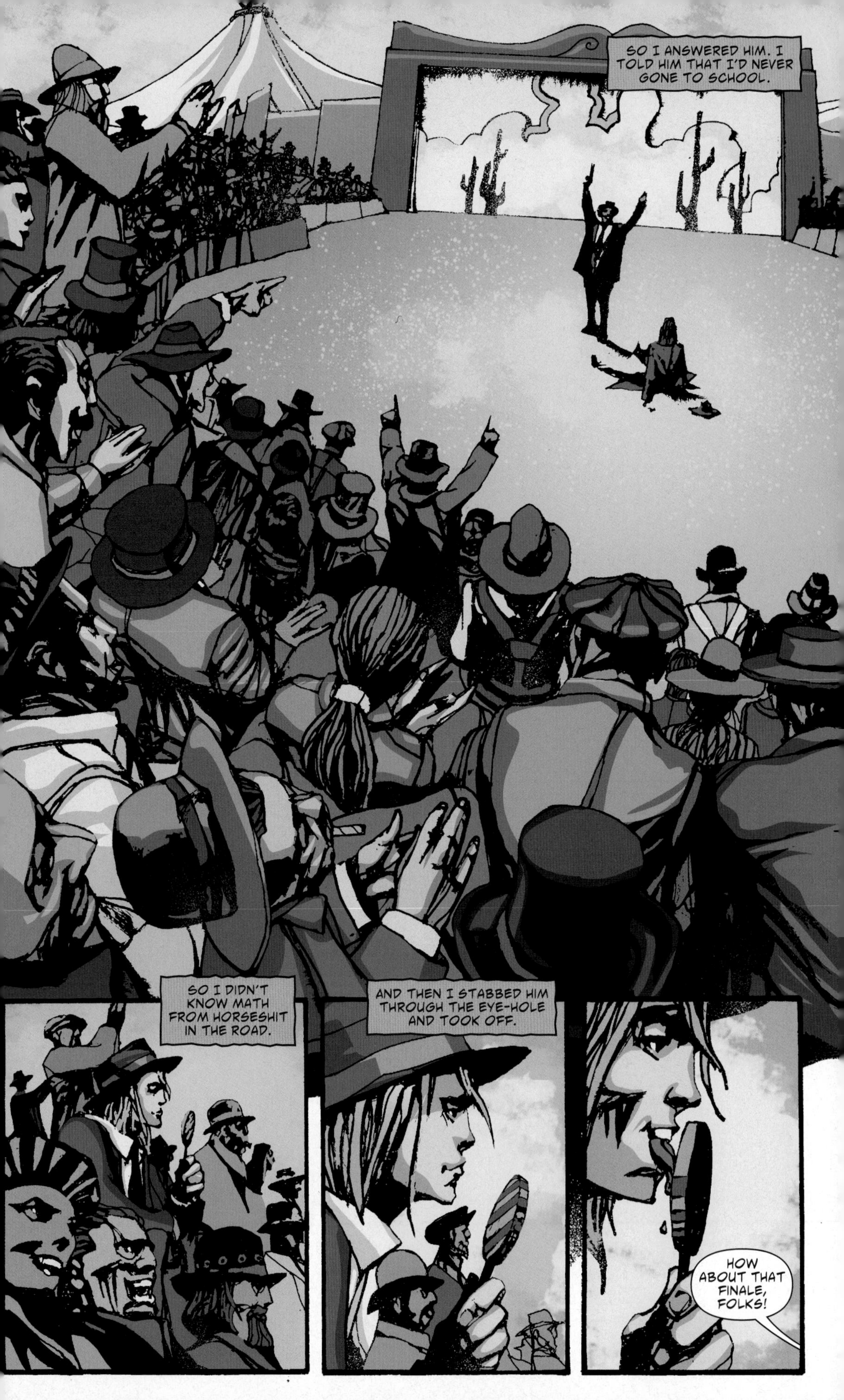
SO I ANSWERED HIM. I TOLD HIM THAT I'D NEVER GONE TO SCHOOL.
SO I DIDN'T KNOW MATH FROM HORSESHIT IN THE ROAD.
AND THEN I STABBED HIM THROUGH THE EYE-HOLE AND TOOK OFF.
HOW ABOUT THAT FINALE, FOLKS!

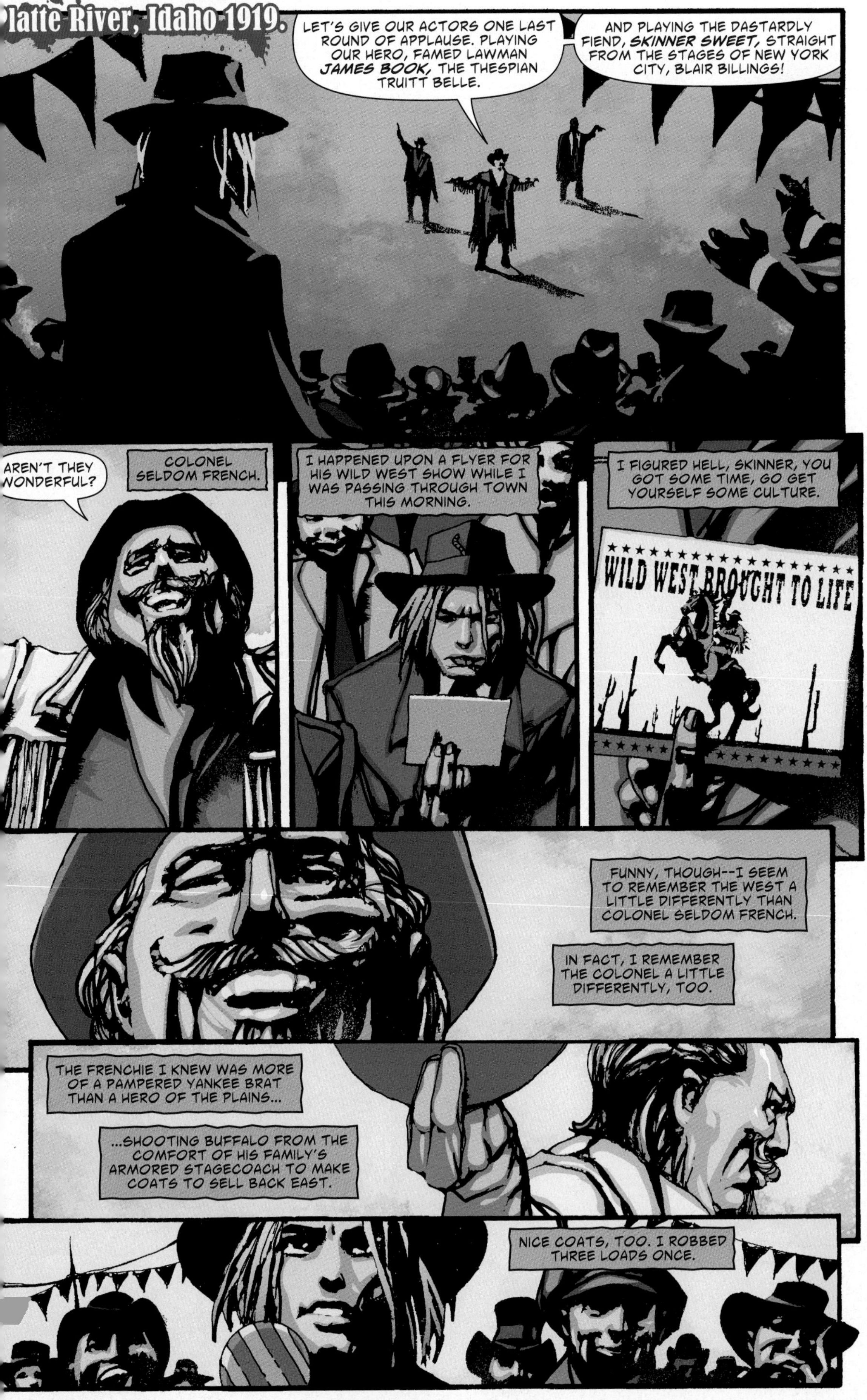
latte River, Idaho 1919.
LET'S GIVE OUR ACTORS ONE LAST ROUND OF APPLAUSE. PLAYING OUR HERO, FAMED LAWMAN JAMES BOOK, THE THESPIAN TRUITT BELLE.
AND PLAYING THE DASTARDLY FIEND, SKINNER SWEET, STRAIGHT FROM THE STAGES OF NEW YORK CITY, BLAIR BILLINGS!
AREN'T THEY WONDERFUL?
COLONEL SELDOM FRENCH.
I HAPPENED UPON A FLYER FOR HIS WILD WEST SHOW WHILE I WAS PASSING THROUGH TOWN THIS MORNING.
I FIGURED HELL, SKINNER, YOU GOT SOME TIME, GO GET YOURSELF SOME CULTURE.
WILD WEST BROUGHT TO LIFE
FUNNY, THOUGH--I SEEM TO REMEMBER THE WEST A LITTLE DIFFERENTLY THAN COLONEL SELDOM FRENCH.
IN FACT, I REMEMBER THE COLONEL A LITTLE DIFFERENTLY, TOO.
THE FRENCHIE I KNEW WAS MORE OF A PAMPERED YANKEE BRAT THAN A HERO OF THE PLAINS...
...SHOOTING BUFFALO FROM THE COMFORT OF HIS FAMILY'S ARMORED STAGECOACH TO MAKE COATS TO SELL BACK EAST.
NICE COATS, TOO. I ROBBED THREE LOADS ONCE.

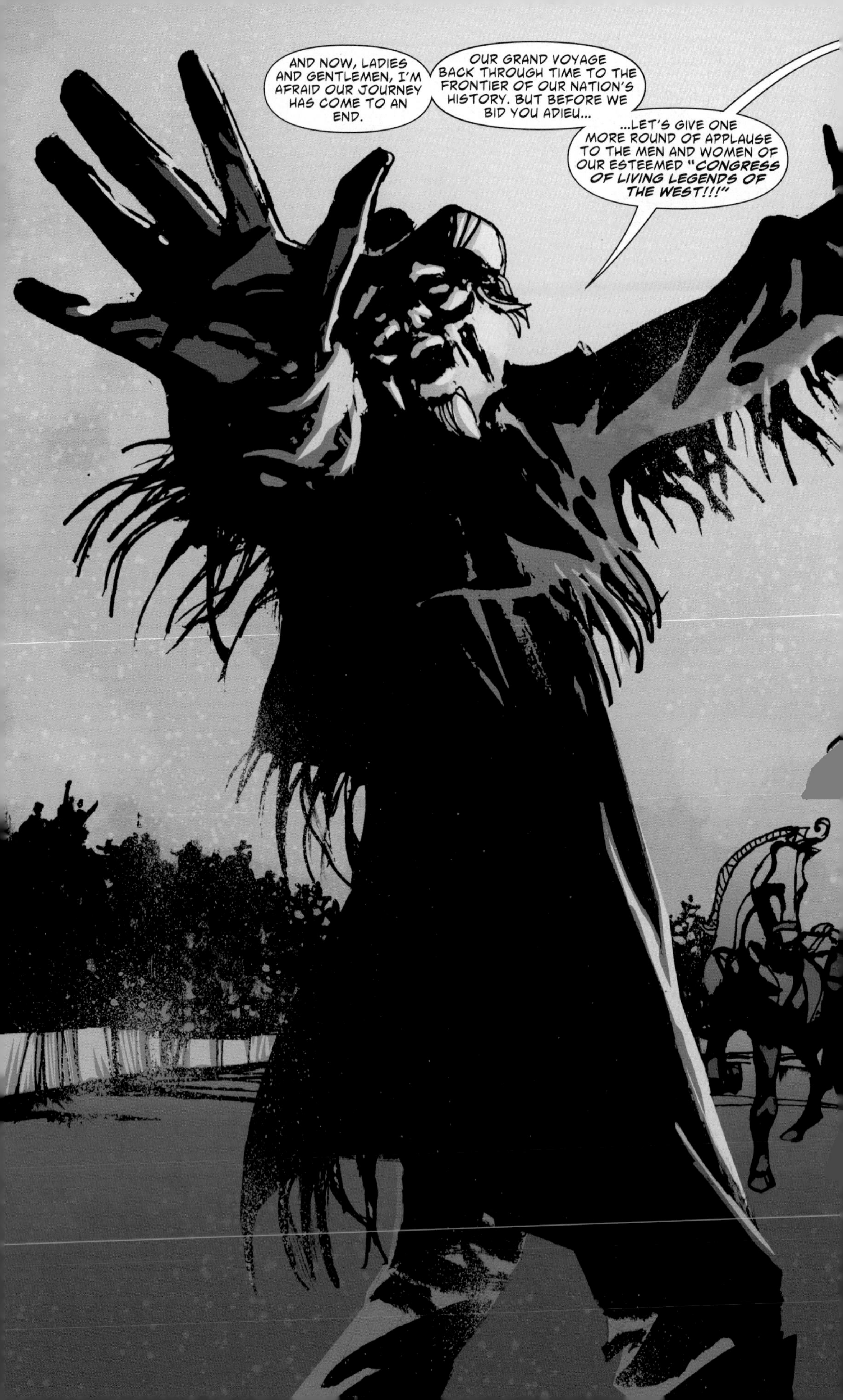
AND NOW, LADIES AND GENTLEMEN, I'M AFRAID OUR JOURNEY HAS COME TO AN END.
OUR GRAND VOYAGE BACK THROUGH TIME TO THE FRONTIER OF OUR NATION'S HISTORY. BUT BEFORE WE BID YOU ADIEU...
...LET'S GIVE ONE MORE ROUND OF APPLAUSE TO THE MEN AND WOMEN OF OUR ESTEEMED "CONGRESS OF LIVING LEGENDS OF THE WEST!!!"

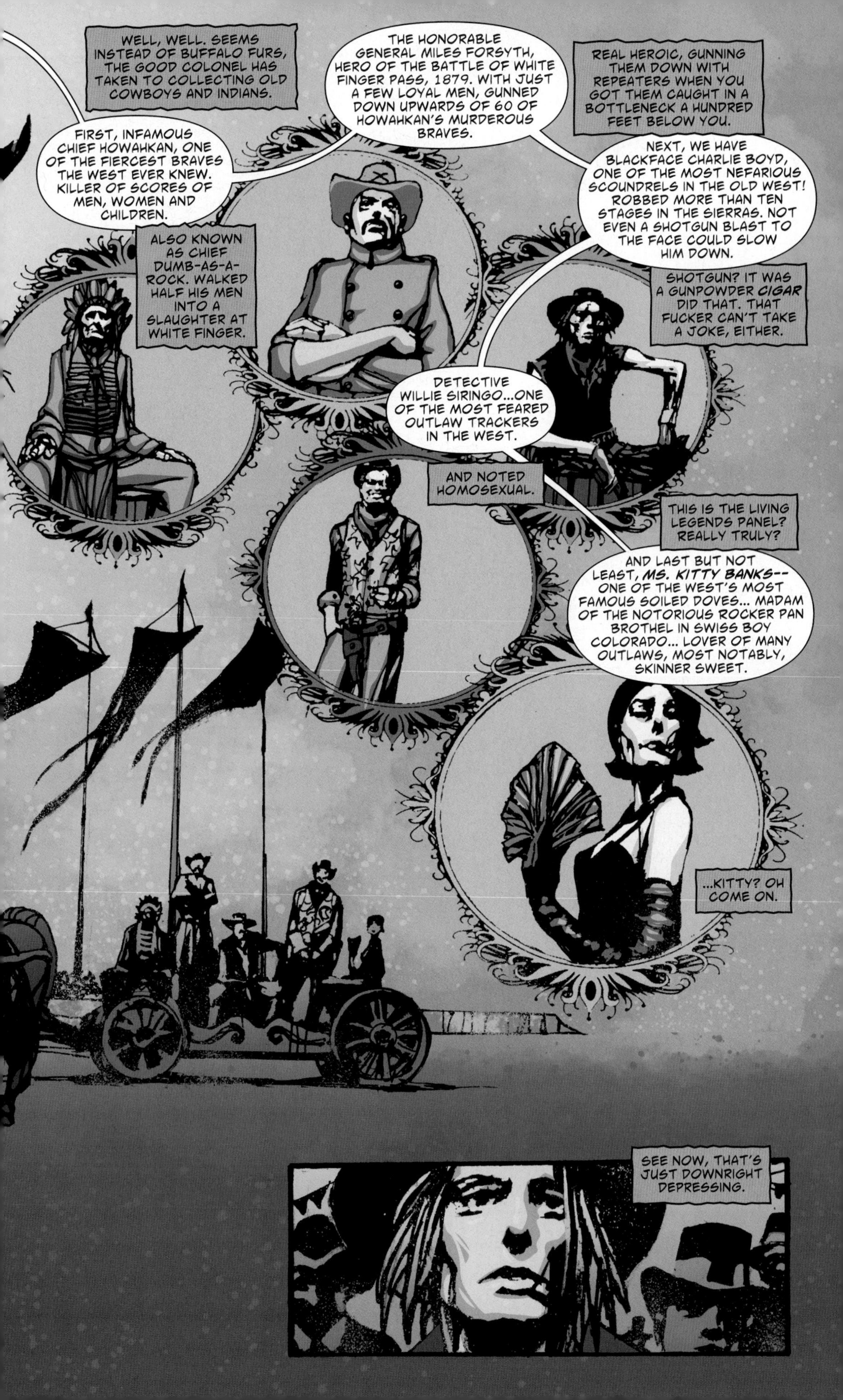
WELL, WELL. SEEMS INSTEAD OF BUFFALO FURS, THE GOOD COLONEL HAS TAKEN TO COLLECTING OLD COWBOYS AND INDIANS.
FIRST, INFAMOUS CHIEF HOWAHKAN, ONE OF THE FIERCEST BRAVES THE WEST EVER KNEW. KILLER OF SCORES OF MEN, WOMEN AND CHILDREN.
ALSO KNOWN AS CHIEF DUMB-AS-A-ROCK. WALKED HALF HIS MEN INTO A SLAUGHTER AT WHITE FINGER.
THE HONORABLE GENERAL MILES FORSYTH, HERO OF THE BATTLE OF WHITE FINGER PASS, 1879. WITH JUST A FEW LOYAL MEN, GUNNED DOWN UPWARDS OF 60 OF HOWAHKAN'S MURDEROUS BRAVES.
REAL HEROIC, GUNNING THEM DOWN WITH REPEATERS WHEN YOU GOT THEM CAUGHT IN A BOTTLENECK A HUNDRED FEET BELOW YOU.
NEXT, WE HAVE BLACKFACE CHARLIE BOYD, ONE OF THE MOST NEFARIOUS SCOUNDRELS IN THE OLD WEST! ROBBED MORE THAN TEN STAGES IN THE SIERRAS. NOT EVEN A SHOTGUN BLAST TO THE FACE COULD SLOW HIM DOWN.
SHOTGUN? IT WAS A GUNPOWDER *CIGAR* DID THAT. THAT FUCKER CAN'T TAKE A JOKE, EITHER.
DETECTIVE WILLIE SIRINGO...ONE OF THE MOST FEARED OUTLAW TRACKERS IN THE WEST.
AND NOTED HOMOSEXUAL.
THIS IS THE LIVING LEGENDS PANEL? REALLY TRULY?
AND LAST BUT NOT LEAST, ***MS. KITTY BANKS***--ONE OF THE WEST'S MOST FAMOUS SOILED DOVES... MADAM OF THE NOTORIOUS ROCKER PAN BROTHEL IN SWISS BOY COLORADO... LOVER OF MANY OUTLAWS, MOST NOTABLY, SKINNER SWEET.
...KITTY? OH COME ON.
SEE NOW, THAT'S JUST DOWNRIGHT DEPRESSING.

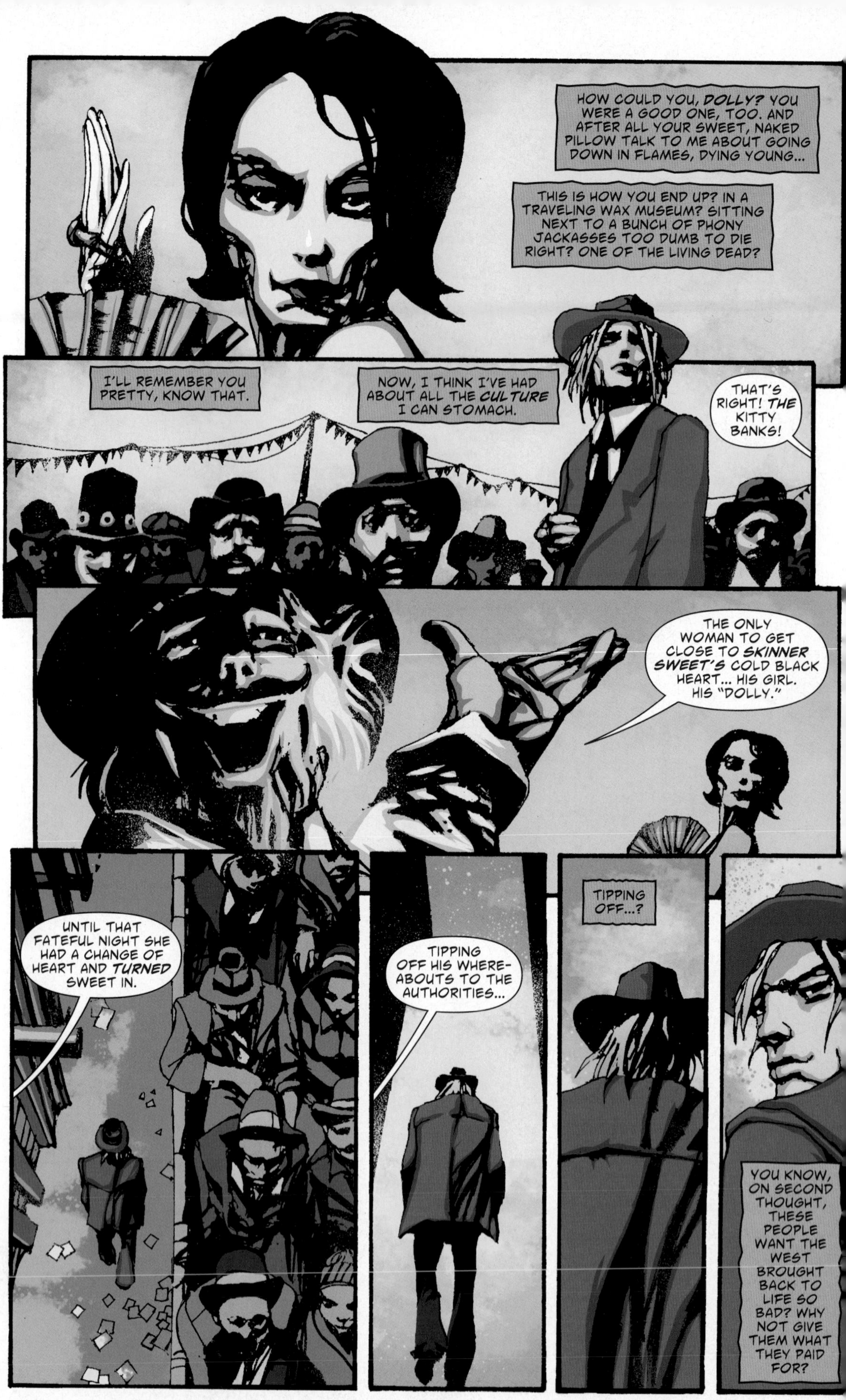
HOW COULD YOU, DOLLY? YOU WERE A GOOD ONE, TOO. AND AFTER ALL YOUR SWEET, NAKED PILLOW TALK TO ME ABOUT GOING DOWN IN FLAMES, DYING YOUNG...
THIS IS HOW YOU END UP? IN A TRAVELING WAX MUSEUM? SITTING NEXT TO A BUNCH OF PHONY JACKASSES TOO DUMB TO DIE RIGHT? ONE OF THE LIVING DEAD?
I'LL REMEMBER YOU PRETTY, KNOW THAT.
NOW, I THINK I'VE HAD ABOUT ALL THE CULTURE I CAN STOMACH.
THAT'S RIGHT! THE KITTY BANKS!
THE ONLY WOMAN TO GET CLOSE TO SKINNER SWEET'S COLD BLACK HEART... HIS GIRL. HIS "DOLLY."
UNTIL THAT FATEFUL NIGHT SHE HAD A CHANGE OF HEART AND TURNED SWEET IN.
TIPPING OFF HIS WHERE-ABOUTS TO THE AUTHORITIES...
TIPPING OFF...?
YOU KNOW, ON SECOND THOUGHT, THESE PEOPLE WANT THE WEST BROUGHT BACK TO LIFE SO BAD? WHY NOT GIVE THEM WHAT THEY PAID FOR?

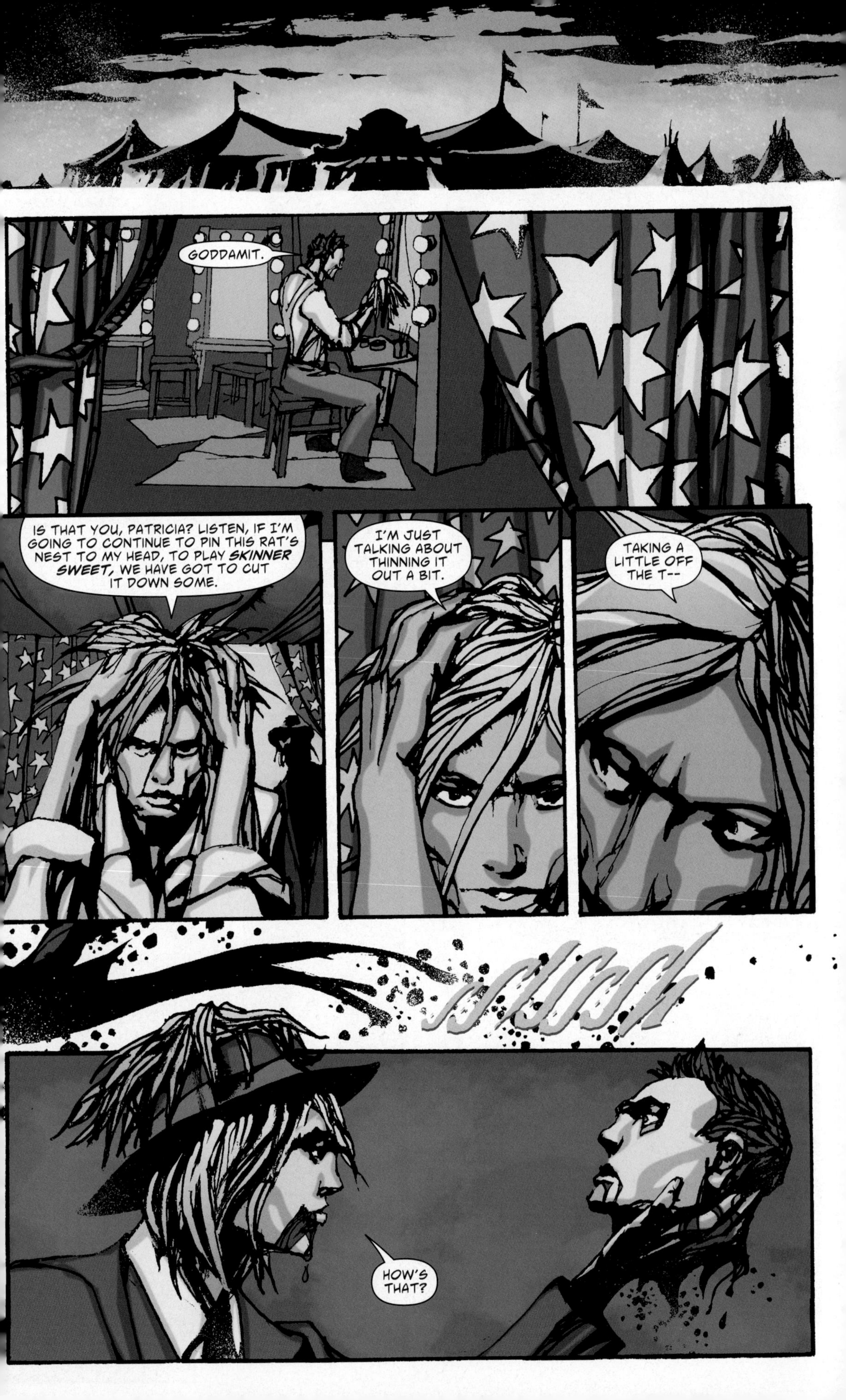
GODDAMIT.
IS THAT YOU, PATRICIA? LISTEN, IF I'M GOING TO CONTINUE TO PIN THIS RAT'S NEST TO MY HEAD, TO PLAY *SKINNER SWEET,* WE HAVE GOT TO CUT IT DOWN SOME.
I'M JUST TALKING ABOUT THINNING IT OUT A BIT.
TAKING A LITTLE OFF THE T--
SSSCCHHH
HOW'S THAT?

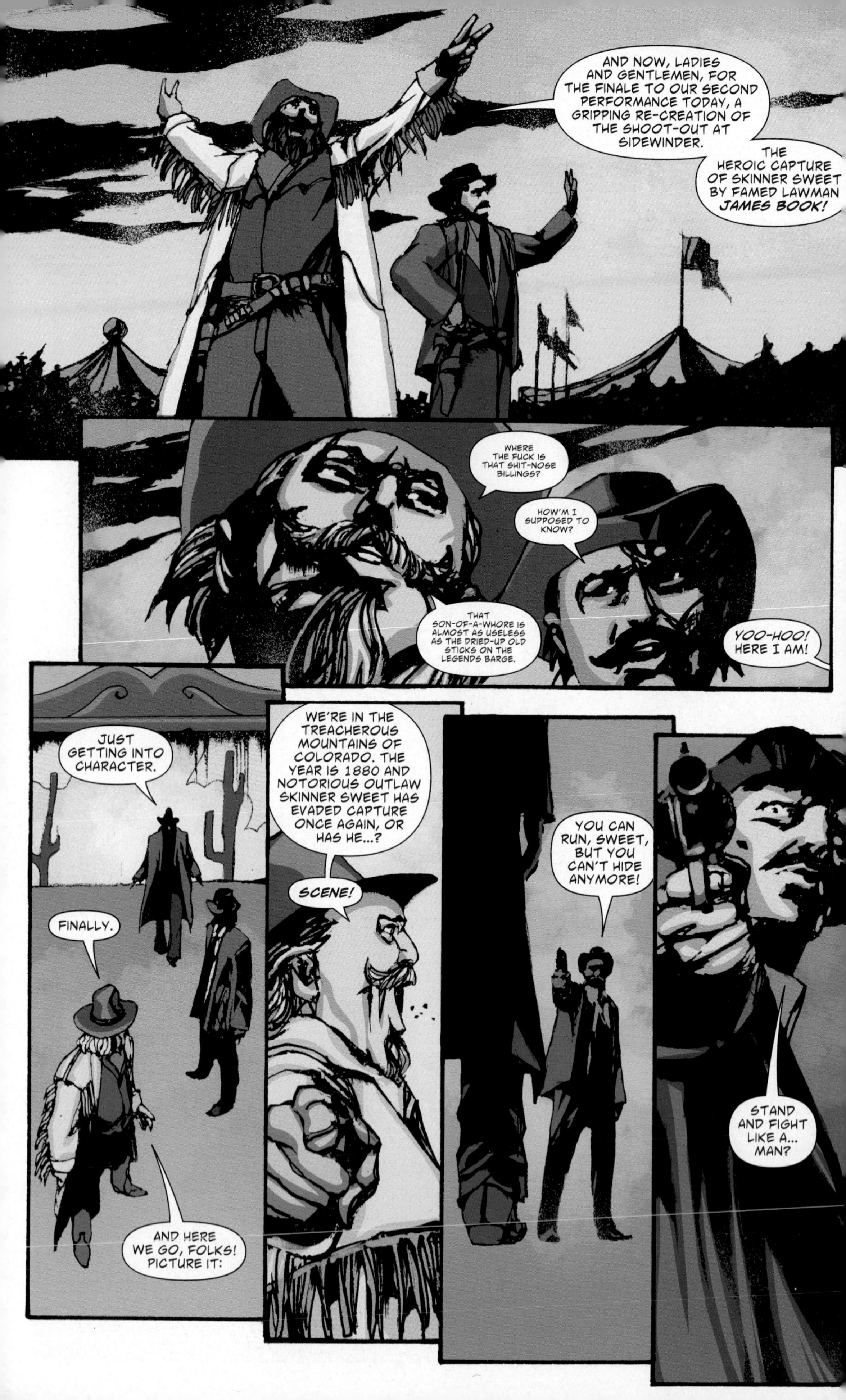
AND NOW, LADIES AND GENTLEMEN, FOR THE FINALE TO OUR SECOND PERFORMANCE TODAY, A GRIPPING RE-CREATION OF THE SHOOT-OUT AT SIDEWINDER.
THE HEROIC CAPTURE OF SKINNER SWEET BY FAMED LAWMAN JAMES BOOK!
WHERE THE FUCK IS THAT SHIT-NOSE BILLINGS?
HOW'M I SUPPOSED TO KNOW?
THAT SON-OF-A-WHORE IS ALMOST AS USELESS AS THE DRIED-UP OLD STICKS ON THE LEGENDS BARGE.
YOO-HOO! HERE I AM!
JUST GETTING INTO CHARACTER.
FINALLY.
AND HERE WE GO, FOLKS! PICTURE IT:
WE'RE IN THE TREACHEROUS MOUNTAINS OF COLORADO. THE YEAR IS 1880 AND NOTORIOUS OUTLAW SKINNER SWEET HAS EVADED CAPTURE ONCE AGAIN, OR HAS HE...?
SCENE!
YOU CAN RUN, SWEET, BUT YOU CAN'T HIDE ANYMORE!
STAND AND FIGHT LIKE A... MAN?

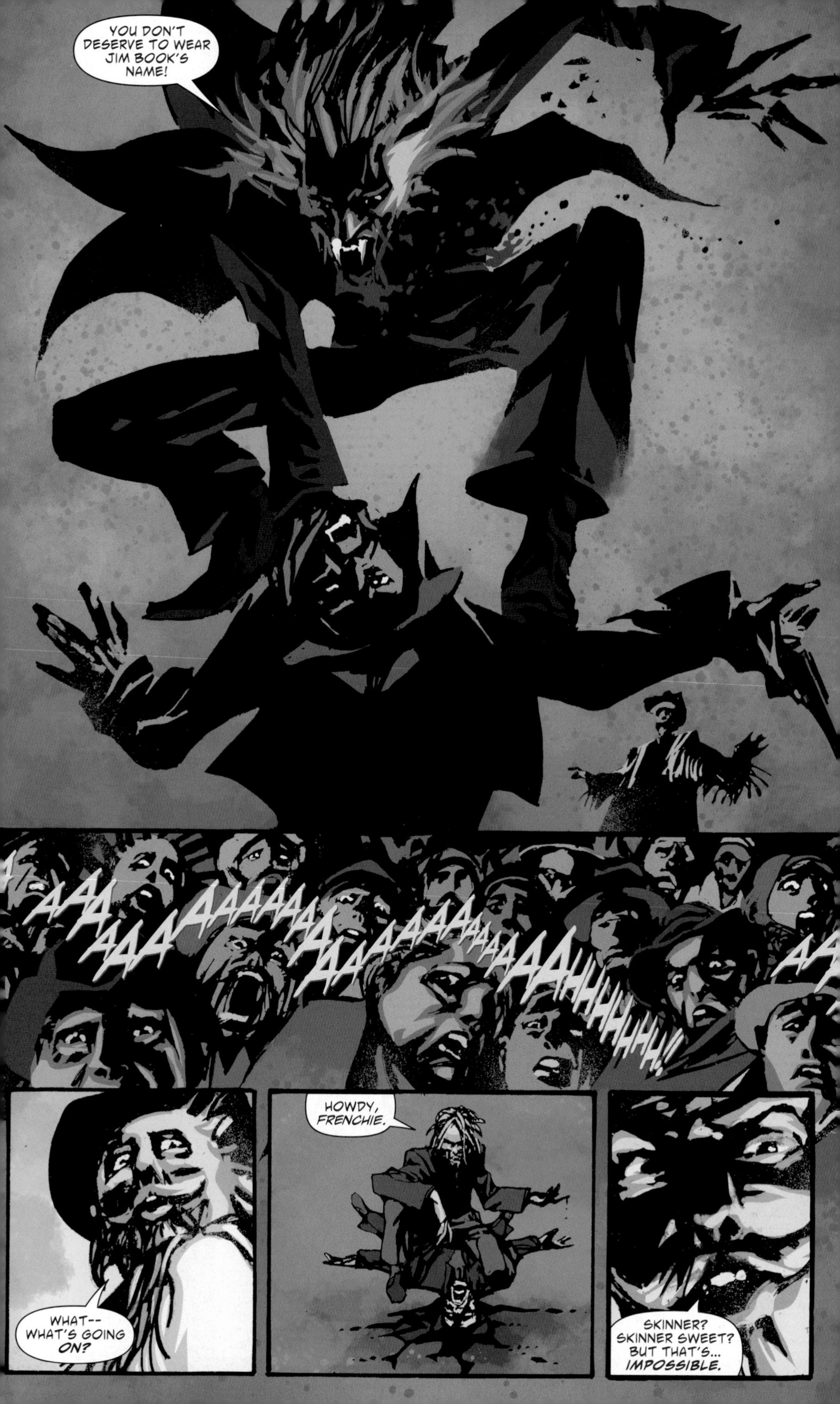
YOU DON'T DESERVE TO WEAR JIM BOOK'S NAME!
AAAAAAAAAAAAAAAAAAAAAAAAAAHHHHHHHH!!
WHAT-- WHAT'S GOING *ON?*
HOWDY, FRENCHIE.
SKINNER? SKINNER SWEET? BUT THAT'S... *IMPOSSIBLE.*

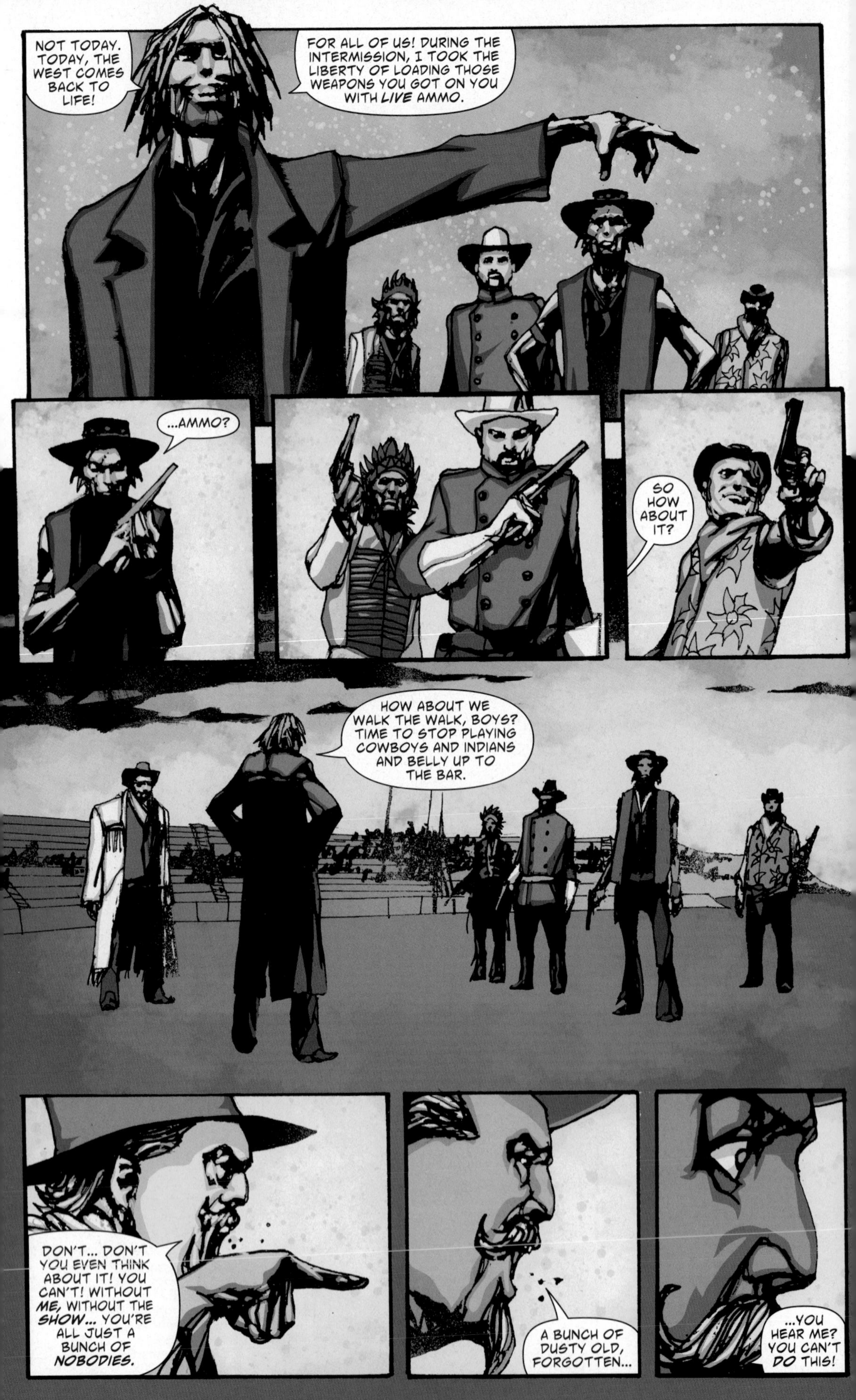
NOT TODAY. TODAY, THE WEST COMES BACK TO LIFE!
FOR ALL OF US! DURING THE INTERMISSION, I TOOK THE LIBERTY OF LOADING THOSE WEAPONS YOU GOT ON YOU WITH LIVE AMMO.
...AMMO?
SO HOW ABOUT IT?
HOW ABOUT WE WALK THE WALK, BOYS? TIME TO STOP PLAYING COWBOYS AND INDIANS AND BELLY UP TO THE BAR.
DON'T... DON'T YOU EVEN THINK ABOUT IT! YOU CAN'T! WITHOUT ME, WITHOUT THE SHOW... YOU'RE ALL JUST A BUNCH OF NOBODIES.
A BUNCH OF DUSTY OLD, FORGOTTEN...
...YOU HEAR ME? YOU CAN'T DO THIS!

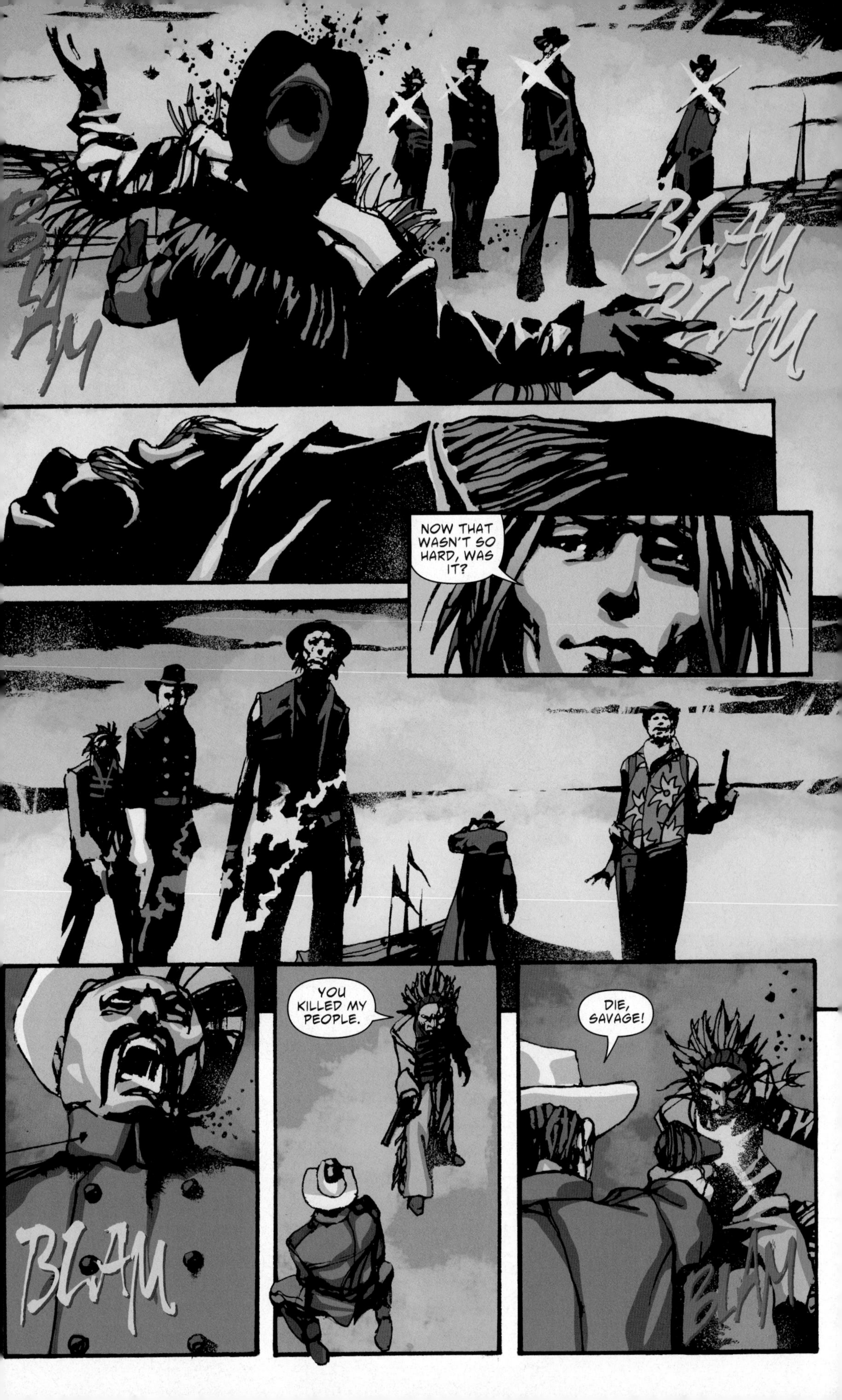
BLAM
BLAM
BLAM
NOW THAT WASN'T SO HARD, WAS IT?
BLAM
YOU KILLED MY PEOPLE.
DIE, SAVAGE!
BLAM

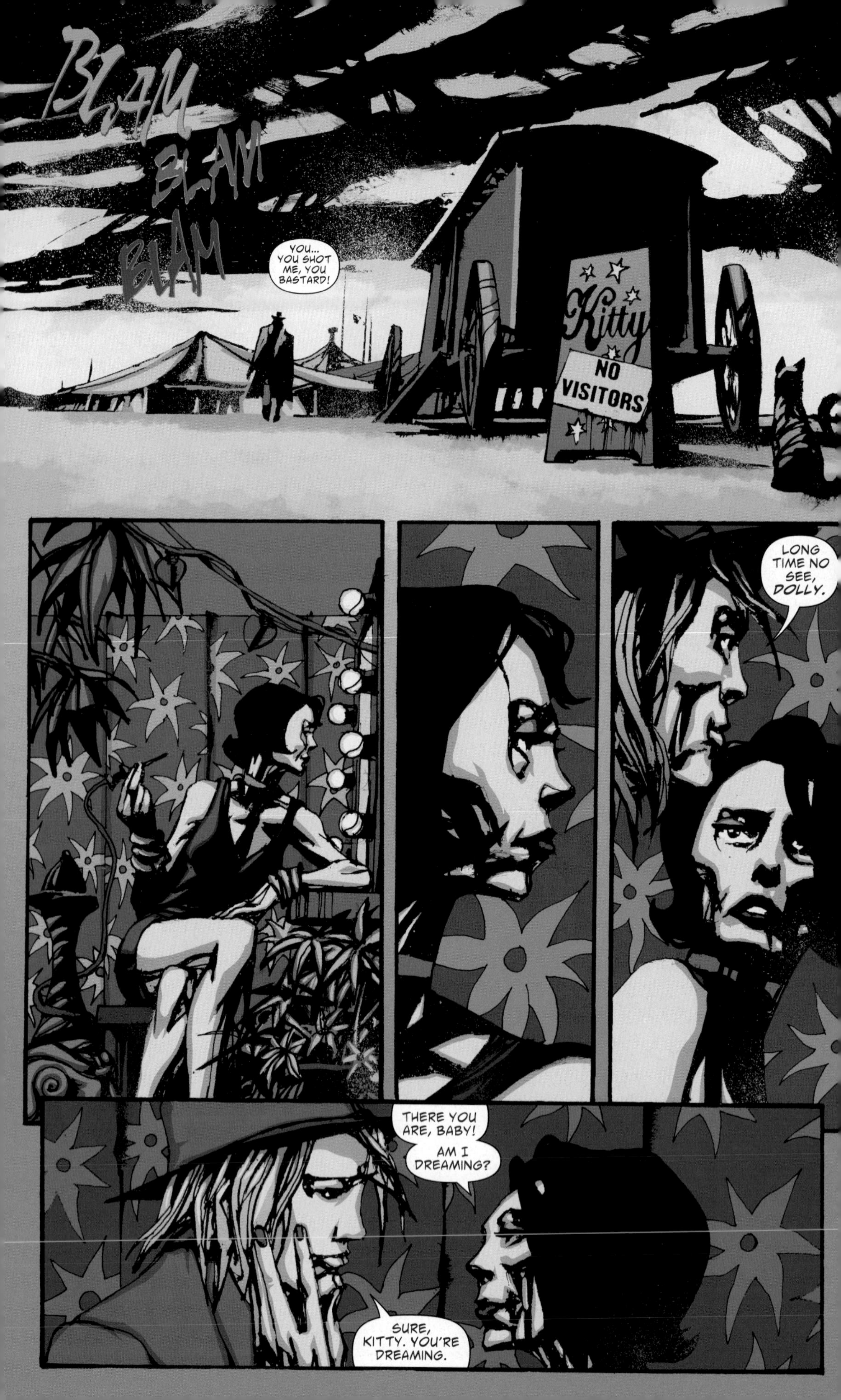
BLAM
BLAM
BLAM
YOU... YOU SHOT ME, YOU BASTARD!
Kitty
NO VISITORS
LONG TIME NO SEE, DOLLY.
THERE YOU ARE, BABY!
AM I DREAMING?
SURE, KITTY. YOU'RE DREAMING.

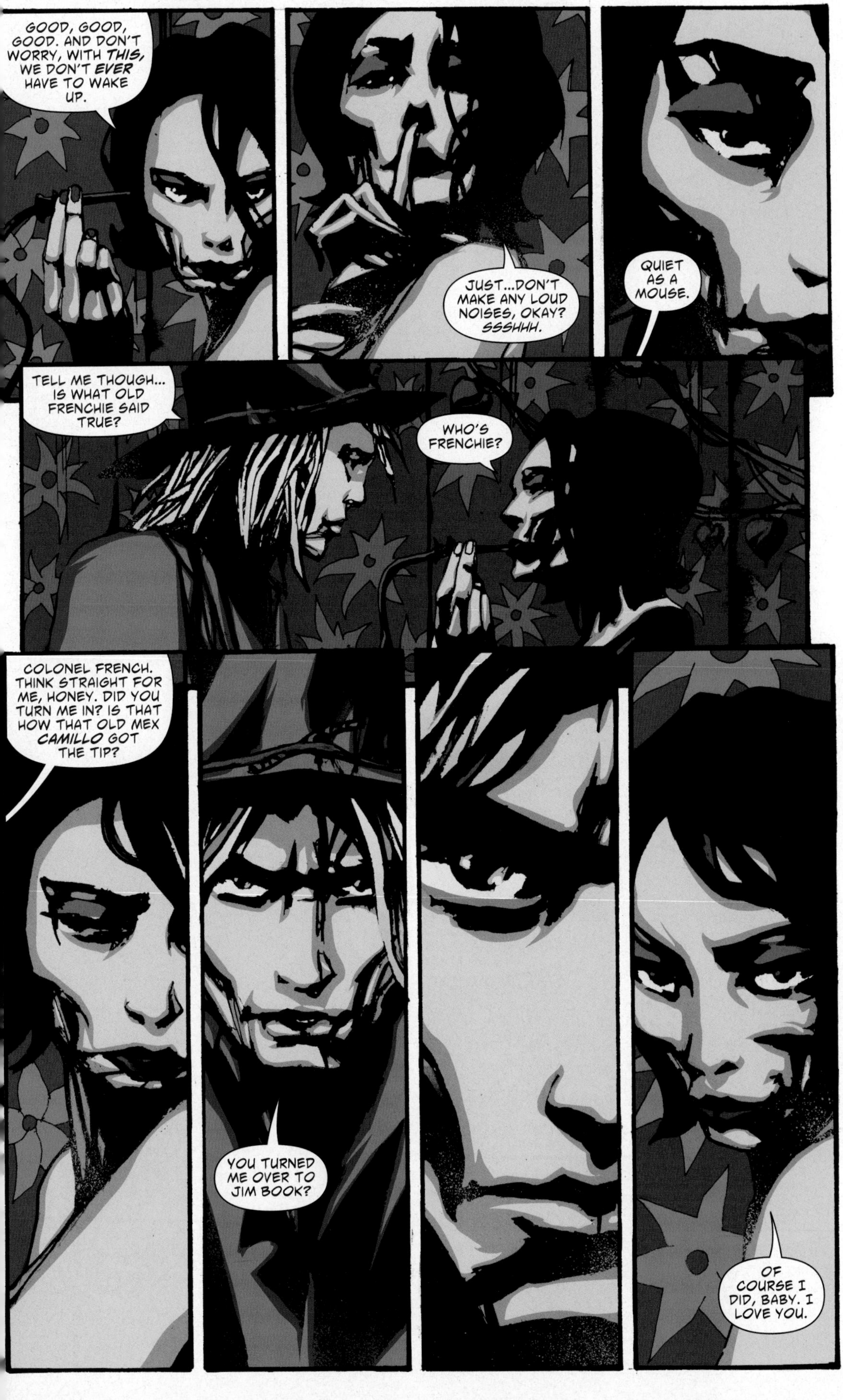
GOOD, GOOD, GOOD. AND DON'T WORRY, WITH THIS, WE DON'T EVER HAVE TO WAKE UP.
JUST...DON'T MAKE ANY LOUD NOISES, OKAY? SSSHHH.
QUIET AS A MOUSE.
TELL ME THOUGH... IS WHAT OLD FRENCHIE SAID TRUE?
WHO'S FRENCHIE?
COLONEL FRENCH. THINK STRAIGHT FOR ME, HONEY. DID YOU TURN ME IN? IS THAT HOW THAT OLD MEX CAMILLO GOT THE TIP?
YOU TURNED ME OVER TO JIM BOOK?
OF COURSE I DID, BABY. I LOVE YOU.

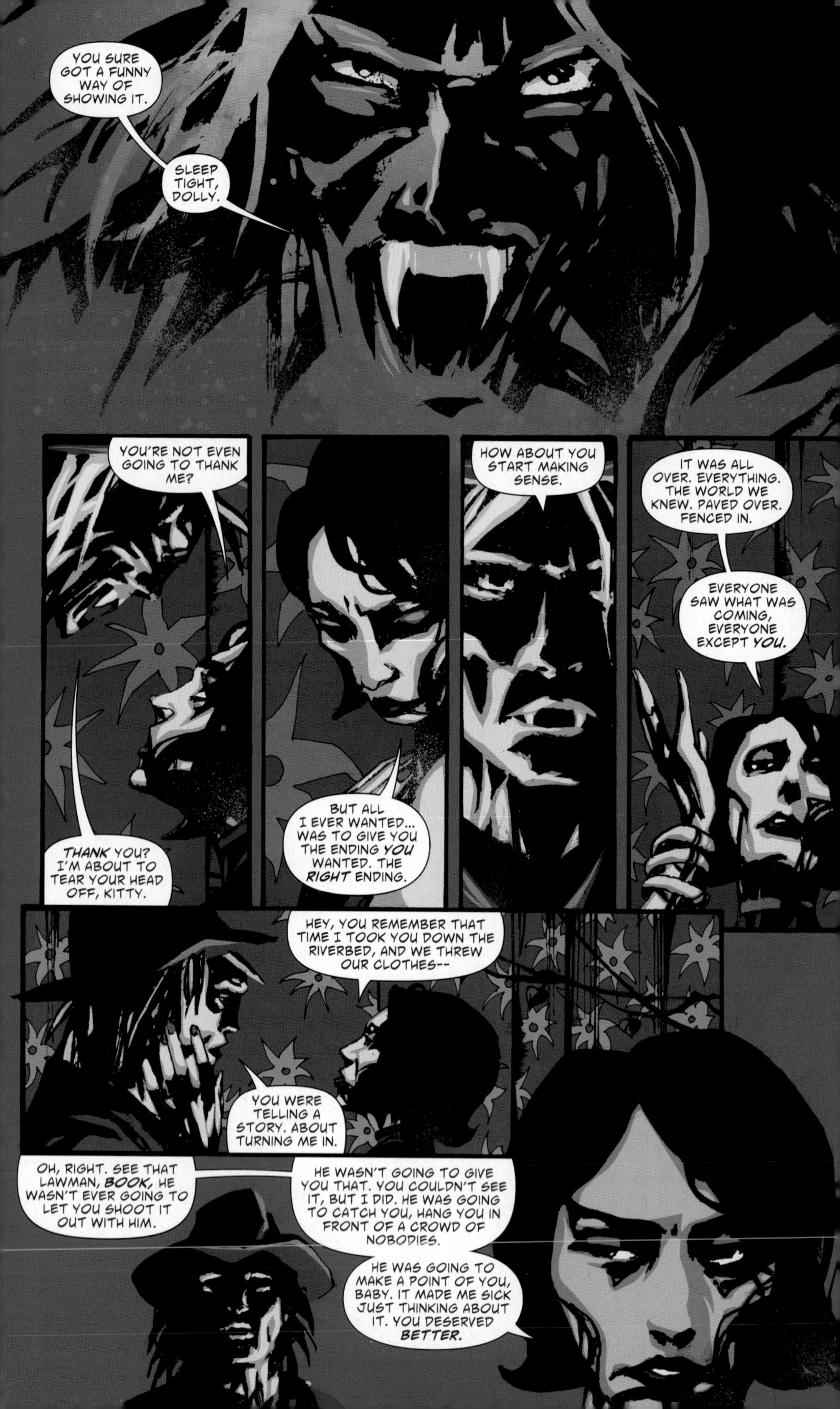
YOU SURE GOT A FUNNY WAY OF SHOWING IT.
SLEEP TIGHT, DOLLY.
YOU'RE NOT EVEN GOING TO THANK ME?
THANK YOU? I'M ABOUT TO TEAR YOUR HEAD OFF, KITTY.
BUT ALL I EVER WANTED... WAS TO GIVE YOU THE ENDING YOU WANTED. THE RIGHT ENDING.
HOW ABOUT YOU START MAKING SENSE.
IT WAS ALL OVER. EVERYTHING. THE WORLD WE KNEW. PAVED OVER. FENCED IN.
EVERYONE SAW WHAT WAS COMING, EVERYONE EXCEPT YOU.
HEY, YOU REMEMBER THAT TIME I TOOK YOU DOWN THE RIVERBED, AND WE THREW OUR CLOTHES--
YOU WERE TELLING A STORY. ABOUT TURNING ME IN.
OH, RIGHT. SEE THAT LAWMAN, BOOK, HE WASN'T EVER GOING TO LET YOU SHOOT IT OUT WITH HIM.
HE WASN'T GOING TO GIVE YOU THAT. YOU COULDN'T SEE IT, BUT I DID. HE WAS GOING TO CATCH YOU, HANG YOU IN FRONT OF A CROWD OF NOBODIES.
HE WAS GOING TO MAKE A POINT OF YOU, BABY. IT MADE ME SICK JUST THINKING ABOUT IT. YOU DESERVED BETTER.

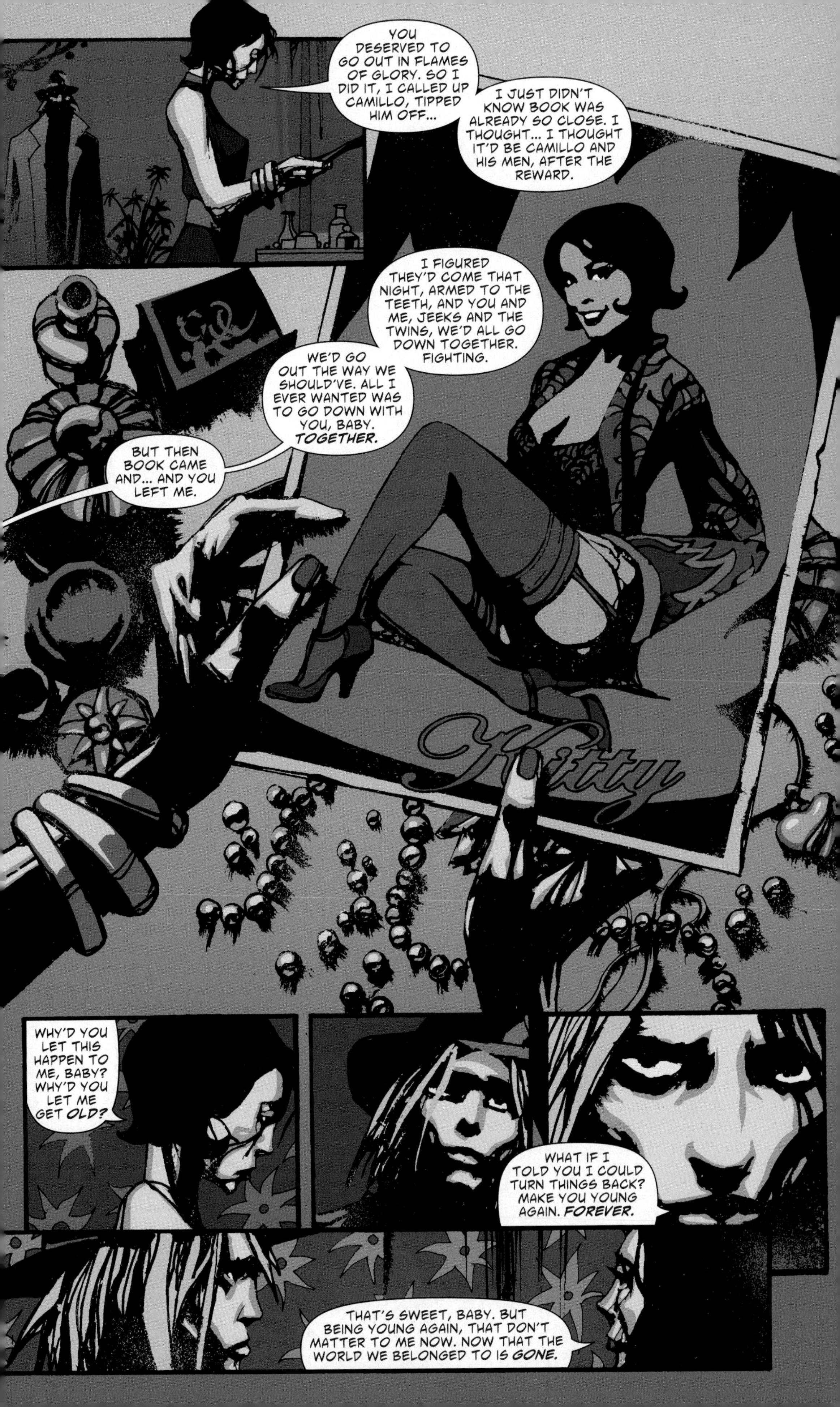
YOU DESERVED TO GO OUT IN FLAMES OF GLORY. SO I DID IT, I CALLED UP CAMILLO, TIPPED HIM OFF...
I JUST DIDN'T KNOW BOOK WAS ALREADY SO CLOSE. I THOUGHT... I THOUGHT IT'D BE CAMILLO AND HIS MEN, AFTER THE REWARD.
I FIGURED THEY'D COME THAT NIGHT, ARMED TO THE TEETH, AND YOU AND ME, JEEKS AND THE TWINS, WE'D ALL GO DOWN TOGETHER. FIGHTING.
WE'D GO OUT THE WAY WE SHOULD'VE. ALL I EVER WANTED WAS TO GO DOWN WITH YOU, BABY. **TOGETHER.**
BUT THEN BOOK CAME AND... AND YOU LEFT ME.
Kitty
WHY'D YOU LET THIS HAPPEN TO ME, BABY? WHY'D YOU LET ME GET **OLD?**
WHAT IF I TOLD YOU I COULD TURN THINGS BACK? MAKE YOU YOUNG AGAIN. **FOREVER.**
THAT'S SWEET, BABY. BUT BEING YOUNG AGAIN, THAT DON'T MATTER TO ME NOW. NOW THAT THE WORLD WE BELONGED TO IS **GONE.**

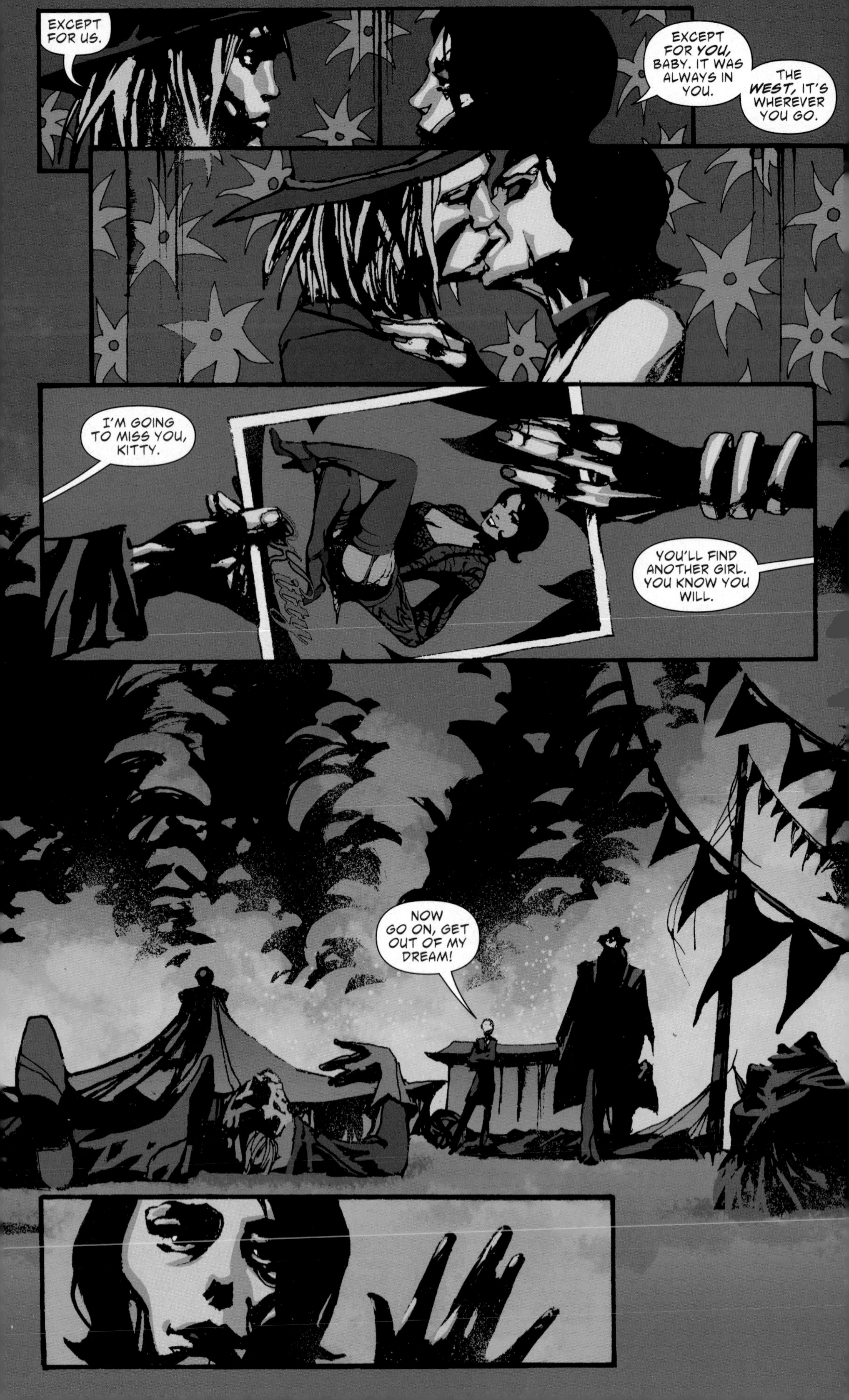
EXCEPT FOR US.
EXCEPT FOR YOU, BABY. IT WAS ALWAYS IN YOU.
THE WEST, IT'S WHEREVER YOU GO.
I'M GOING TO MISS YOU, KITTY.
YOU'LL FIND ANOTHER GIRL. YOU KNOW YOU WILL.
NOW GO ON, GET OUT OF MY DREAM!

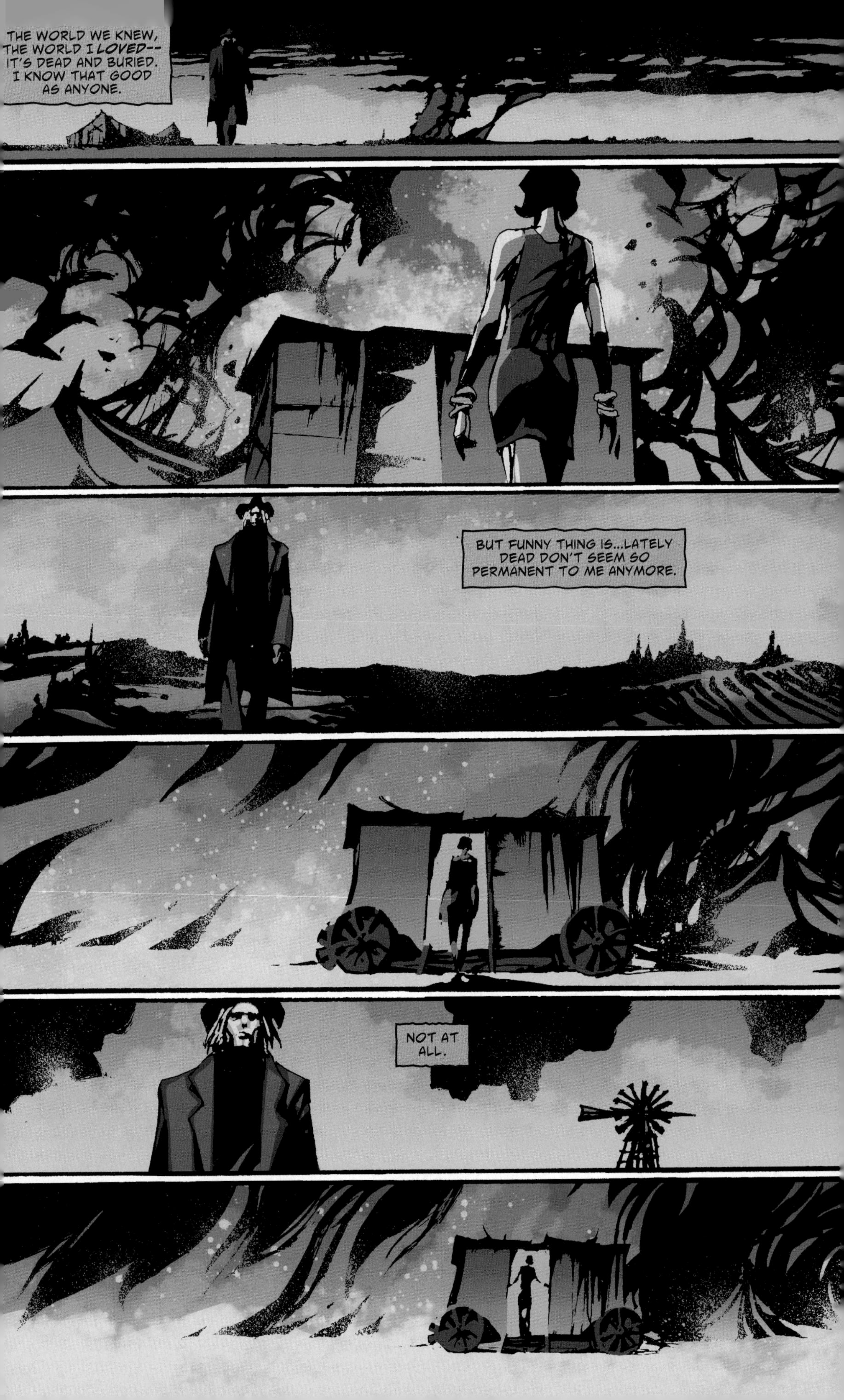
THE WORLD WE KNEW, THE WORLD I *LOVED*-- IT'S DEAD AND BURIED. I KNOW THAT GOOD AS ANYONE.
BUT FUNNY THING IS...LATELY DEAD DON'T SEEM SO PERMANENT TO ME ANYMORE.
NOT AT ALL.

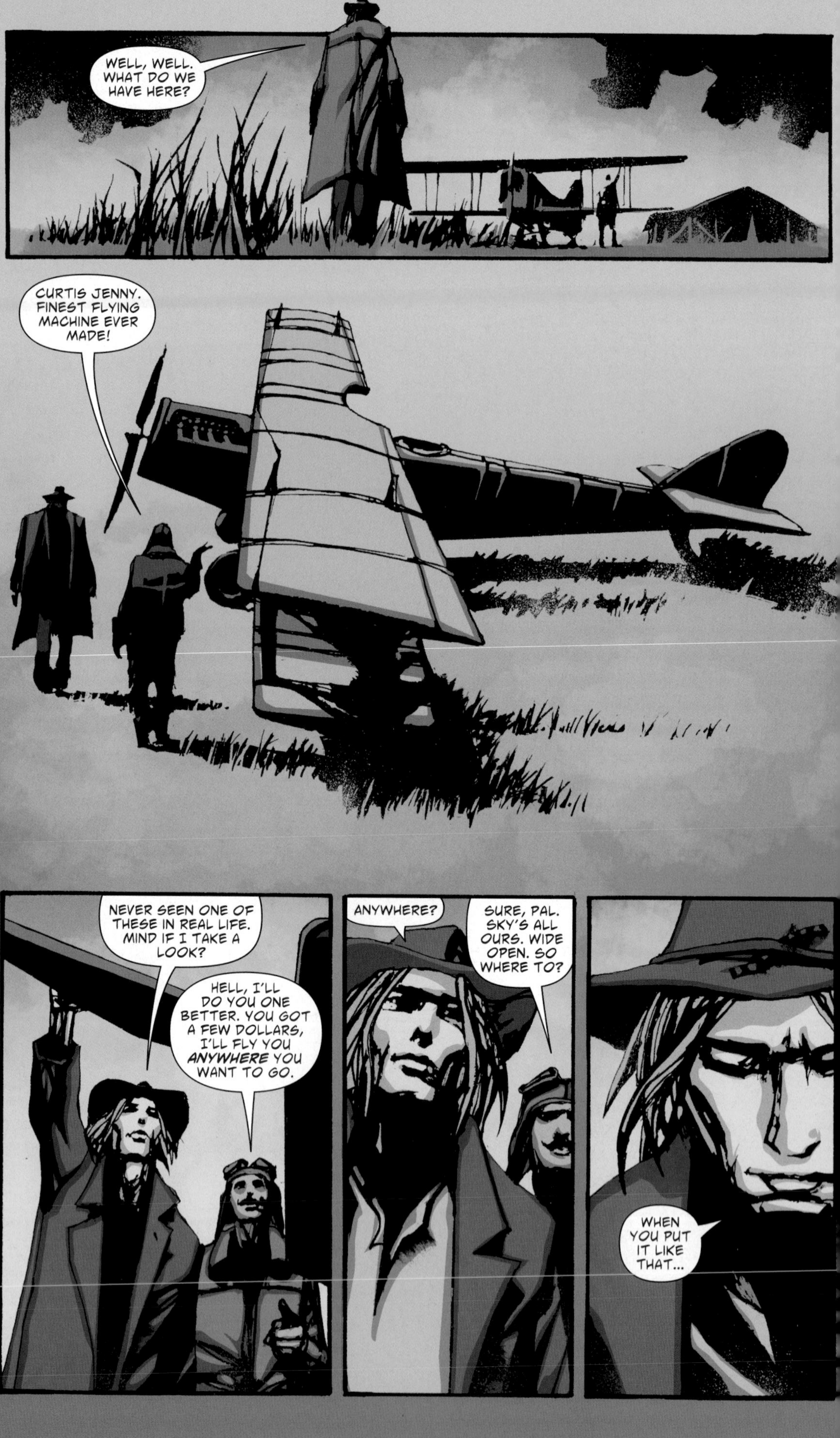
WELL, WELL. WHAT DO WE HAVE HERE?
CURTIS JENNY. FINEST FLYING MACHINE EVER MADE!
NEVER SEEN ONE OF THESE IN REAL LIFE. MIND IF I TAKE A LOOK?
HELL, I'LL DO YOU ONE BETTER. YOU GOT A FEW DOLLARS, I'LL FLY YOU *ANYWHERE* YOU WANT TO GO.
ANYWHERE?
SURE, PAL. SKY'S ALL OURS. WIDE OPEN. SO WHERE TO?
WHEN YOU PUT IT LIKE THAT...

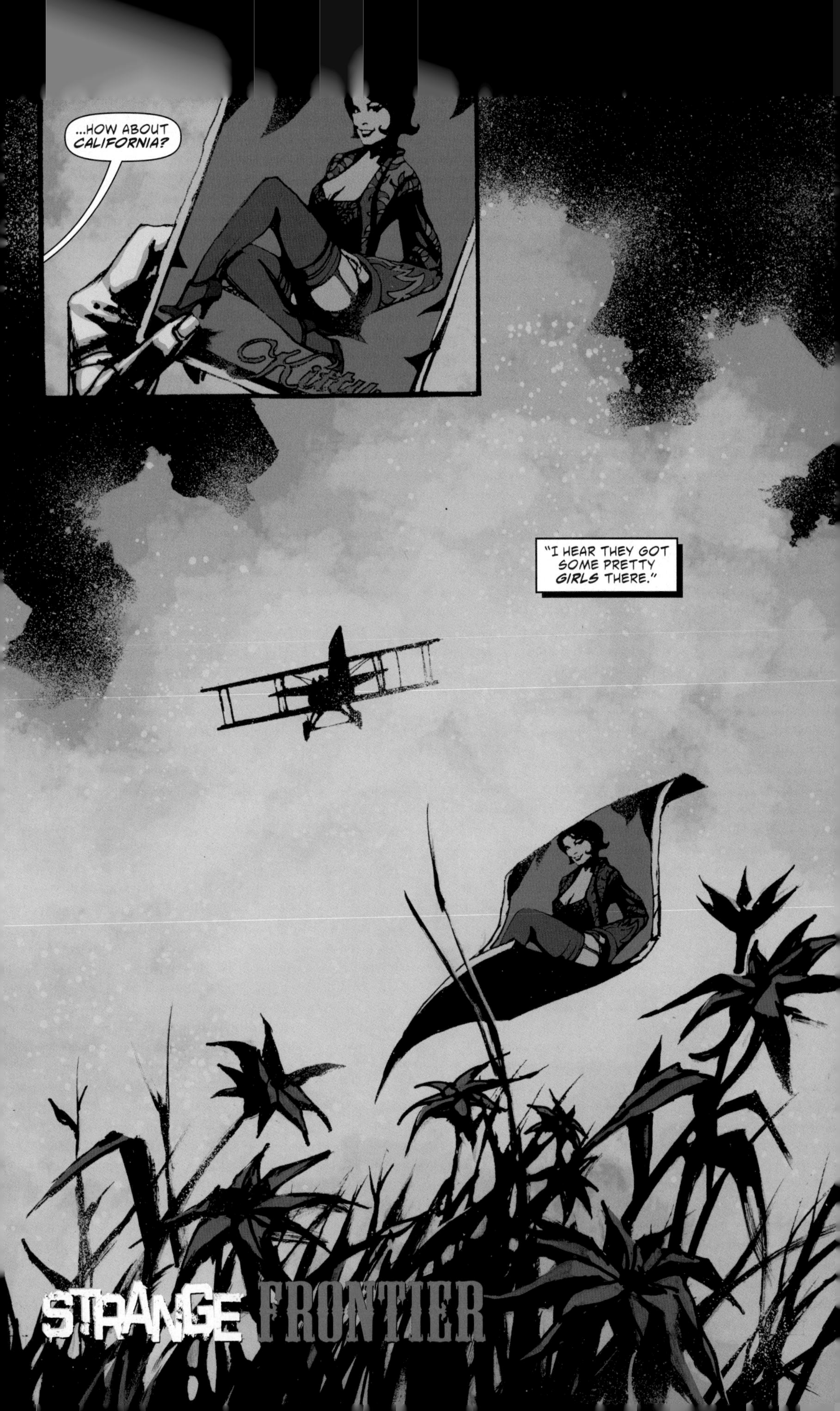
...HOW ABOUT CALIFORNIA?
"I HEAR THEY GOT SOME PRETTY GIRLS THERE."
STRANGE FRONTIER

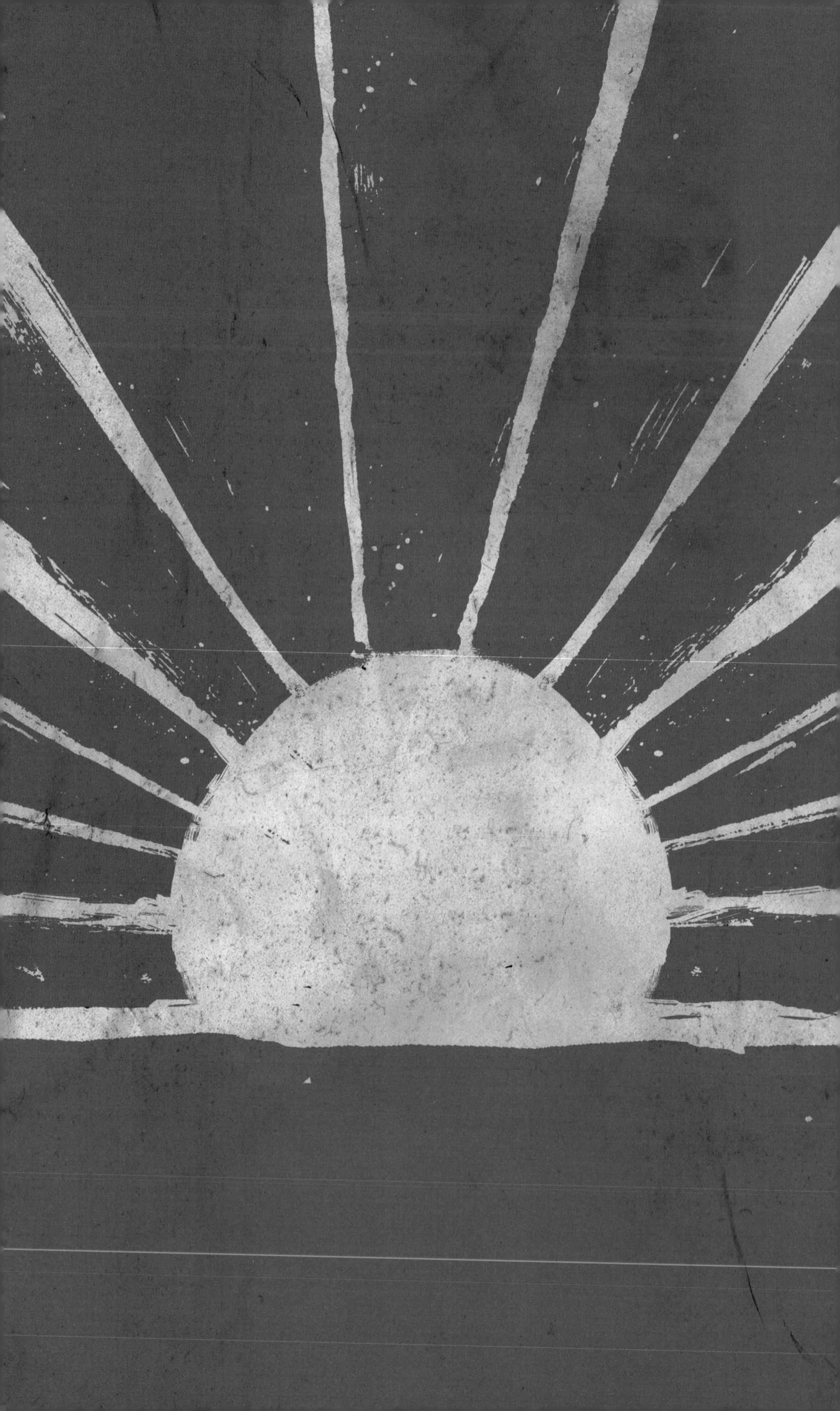

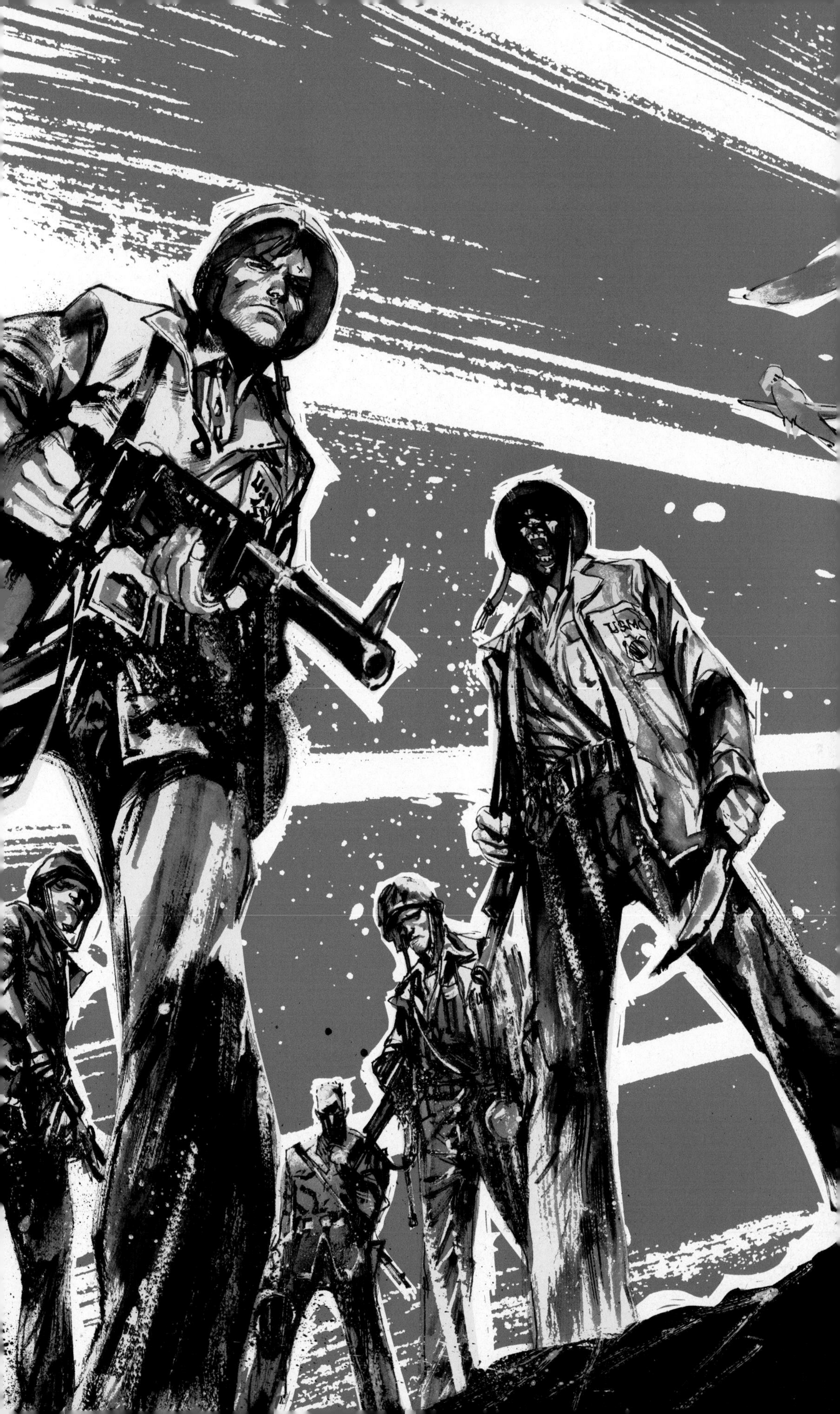
USMC

Ghost War

Part One

Rafael Albuquerque
Artist and cover

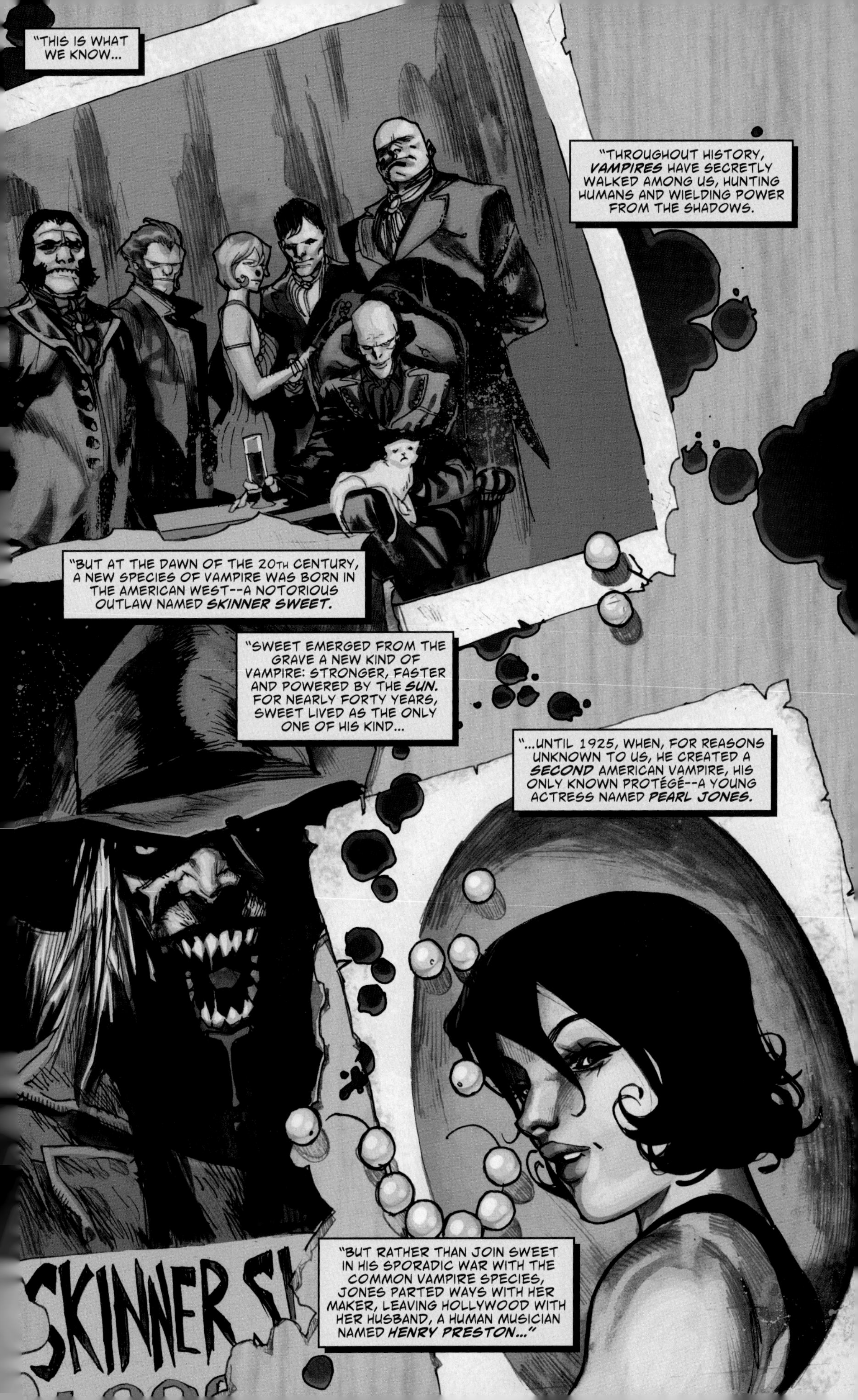
"THIS IS WHAT WE KNOW...
"THROUGHOUT HISTORY, VAMPIRES HAVE SECRETLY WALKED AMONG US, HUNTING HUMANS AND WIELDING POWER FROM THE SHADOWS.
"BUT AT THE DAWN OF THE 20TH CENTURY, A NEW SPECIES OF VAMPIRE WAS BORN IN THE AMERICAN WEST--A NOTORIOUS OUTLAW NAMED SKINNER SWEET.
"SWEET EMERGED FROM THE GRAVE A NEW KIND OF VAMPIRE: STRONGER, FASTER AND POWERED BY THE SUN. FOR NEARLY FORTY YEARS, SWEET LIVED AS THE ONLY ONE OF HIS KIND...
"...UNTIL 1925, WHEN, FOR REASONS UNKNOWN TO US, HE CREATED A SECOND AMERICAN VAMPIRE, HIS ONLY KNOWN PROTÉGÉ--A YOUNG ACTRESS NAMED PEARL JONES.
"BUT RATHER THAN JOIN SWEET IN HIS SPORADIC WAR WITH THE COMMON VAMPIRE SPECIES, JONES PARTED WAYS WITH HER MAKER, LEAVING HOLLYWOOD WITH HER HUSBAND, A HUMAN MUSICIAN NAMED HENRY PRESTON..."
SKINNER S

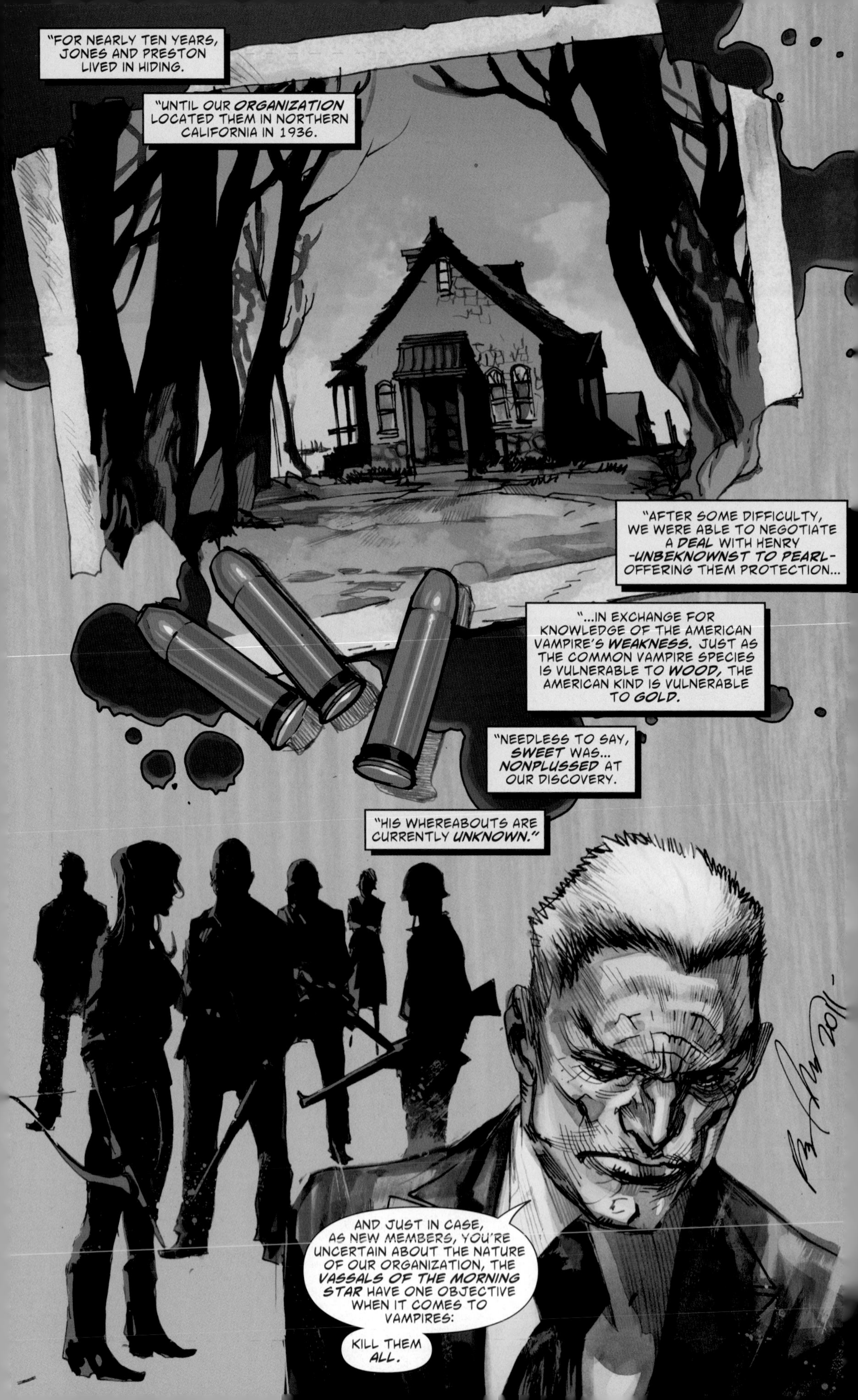
"FOR NEARLY TEN YEARS, JONES AND PRESTON LIVED IN HIDING.
"UNTIL OUR *ORGANIZATION* LOCATED THEM IN NORTHERN CALIFORNIA IN 1936.
"AFTER SOME DIFFICULTY, WE WERE ABLE TO NEGOTIATE A *DEAL* WITH HENRY *-UNBEKNOWNST TO PEARL-* OFFERING THEM PROTECTION...
"...IN EXCHANGE FOR KNOWLEDGE OF THE AMERICAN VAMPIRE'S *WEAKNESS.* JUST AS THE COMMON VAMPIRE SPECIES IS VULNERABLE TO *WOOD,* THE AMERICAN KIND IS VULNERABLE TO *GOLD.*
"NEEDLESS TO SAY, *SWEET* WAS... *NONPLUSSED* AT OUR DISCOVERY.
"HIS WHEREABOUTS ARE CURRENTLY *UNKNOWN.*"
AND JUST IN CASE, AS NEW MEMBERS, YOU'RE UNCERTAIN ABOUT THE NATURE OF OUR ORGANIZATION, THE *VASSALS OF THE MORNING STAR* HAVE ONE OBJECTIVE WHEN IT COMES TO VAMPIRES:
KILL THEM *ALL.*

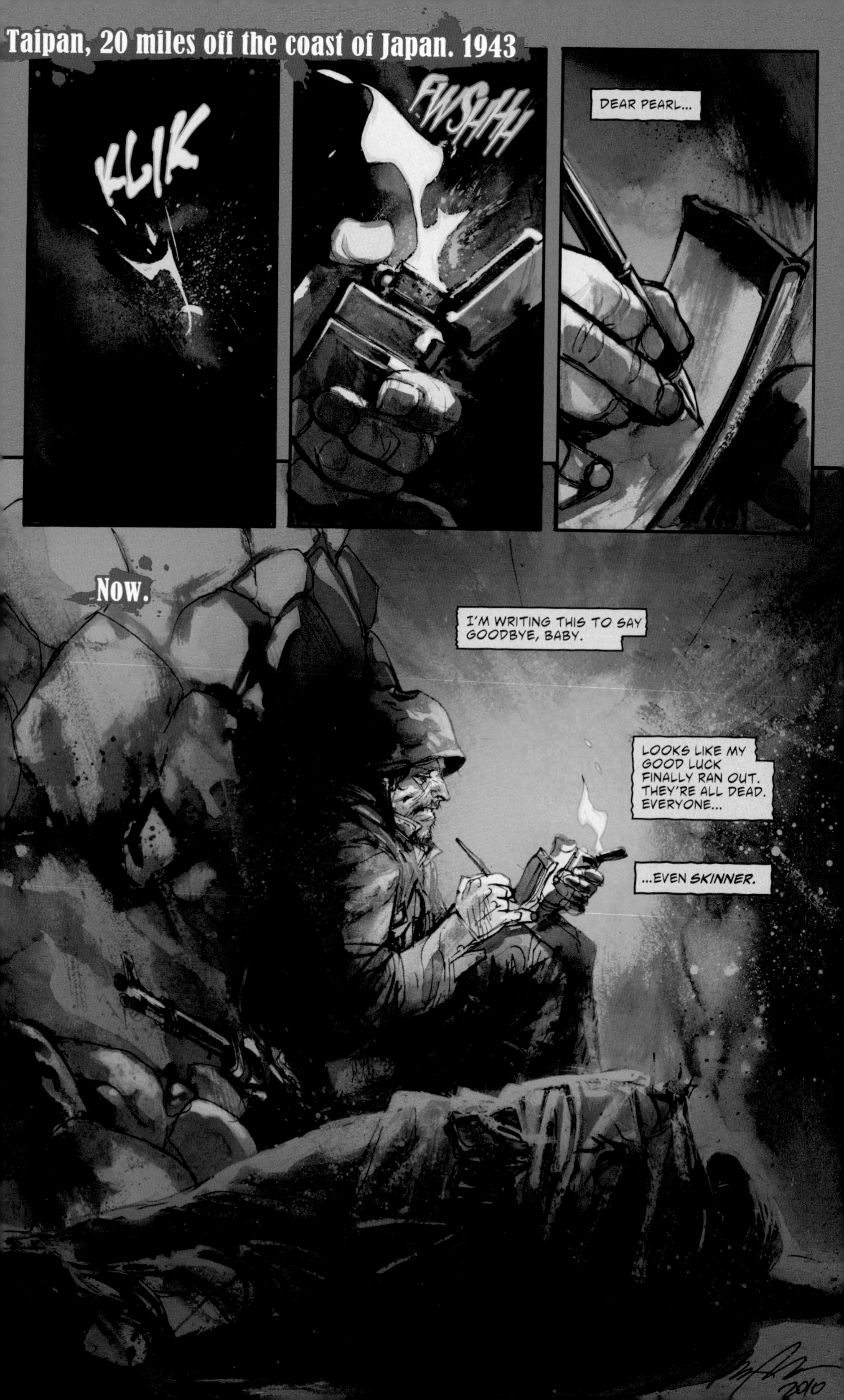

Taipan, 20 miles off the coast of Japan. 1943
KLIK
FWSHHH
DEAR PEARL...
Now.
I'M WRITING THIS TO SAY GOODBYE, BABY.
LOOKS LIKE MY GOOD LUCK FINALLY RAN OUT. THEY'RE ALL DEAD. EVERYONE...
...EVEN SKINNER.

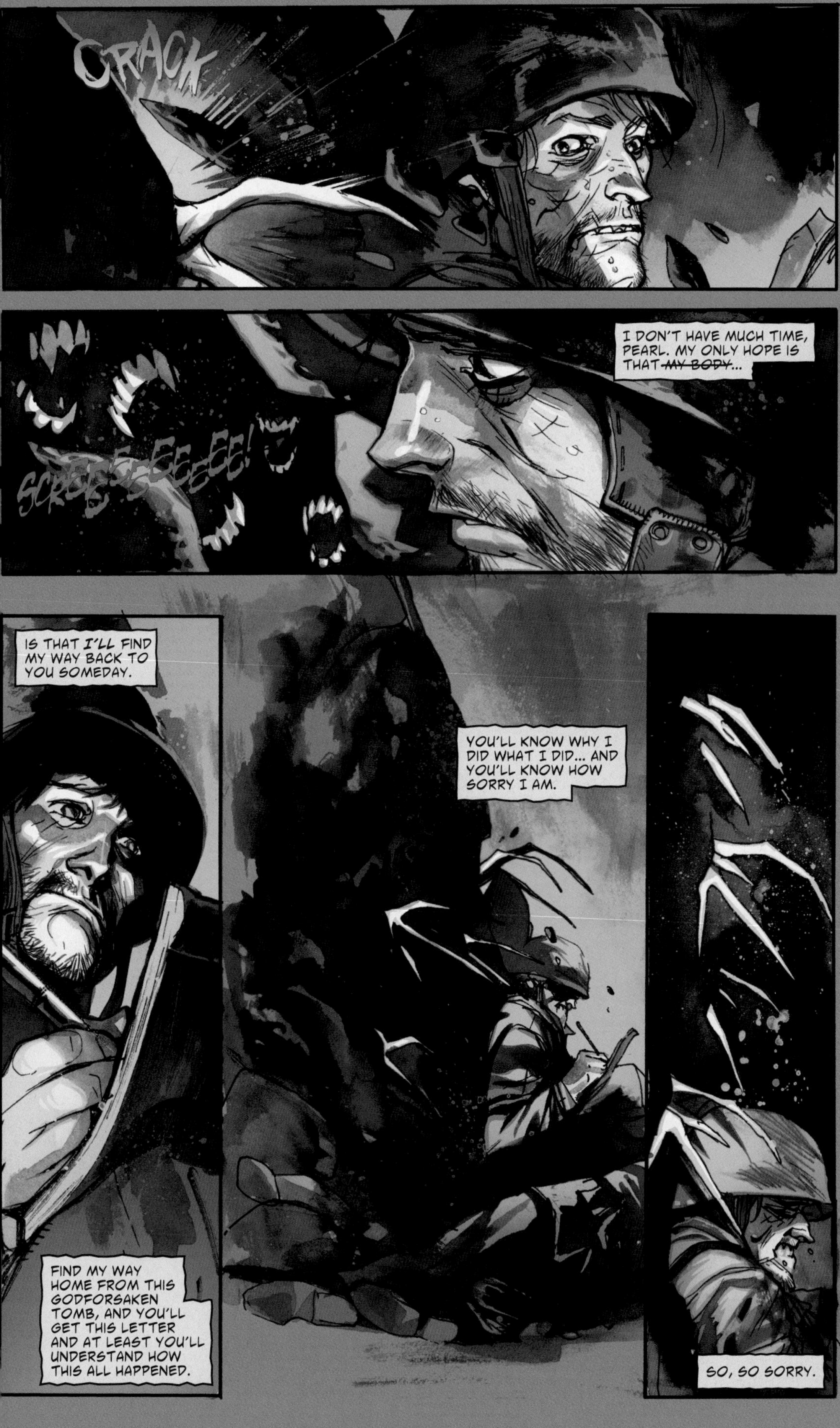
CRACK
I DON'T HAVE MUCH TIME, PEARL. MY ONLY HOPE IS THAT ~~MY BODY~~...
SCREEEEEEEEE!
IS THAT *I'LL* FIND MY WAY BACK TO YOU SOMEDAY.
YOU'LL KNOW WHY I DID WHAT I DID... AND YOU'LL KNOW HOW SORRY I AM.
FIND MY WAY HOME FROM THIS GODFORSAKEN TOMB, AND YOU'LL GET THIS LETTER AND AT LEAST YOU'LL UNDERSTAND HOW THIS ALL HAPPENED.
SO, SO SORRY.

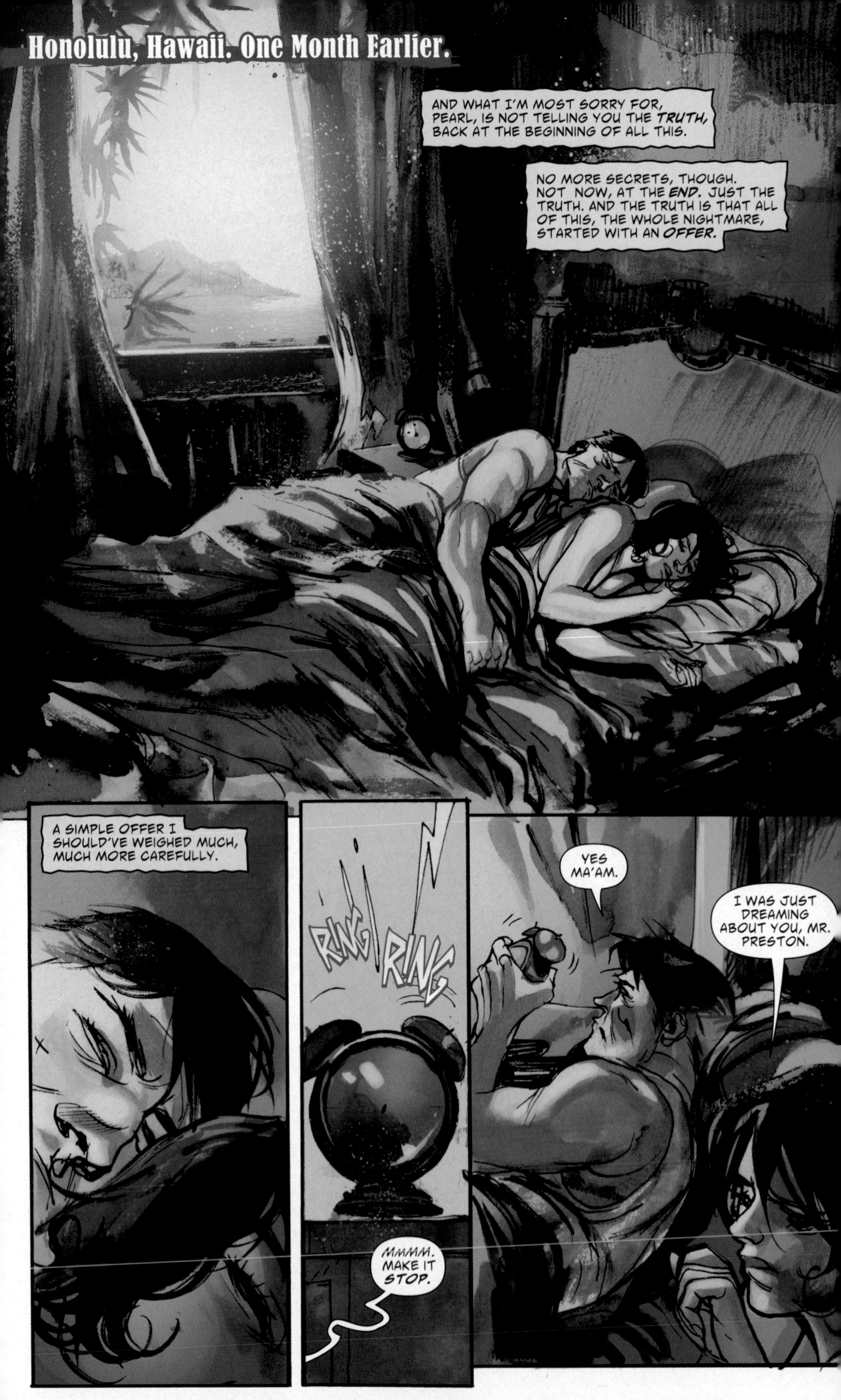
Honolulu, Hawaii. One Month Earlier.
AND WHAT I'M MOST SORRY FOR, PEARL, IS NOT TELLING YOU THE TRUTH, BACK AT THE BEGINNING OF ALL THIS.
NO MORE SECRETS, THOUGH. NOT NOW, AT THE END. JUST THE TRUTH. AND THE TRUTH IS THAT ALL OF THIS, THE WHOLE NIGHTMARE, STARTED WITH AN OFFER.
A SIMPLE OFFER I SHOULD'VE WEIGHED MUCH, MUCH MORE CAREFULLY.
RING RING
MMMM. MAKE IT STOP.
YES MA'AM.
I WAS JUST DREAMING ABOUT YOU, MR. PRESTON.

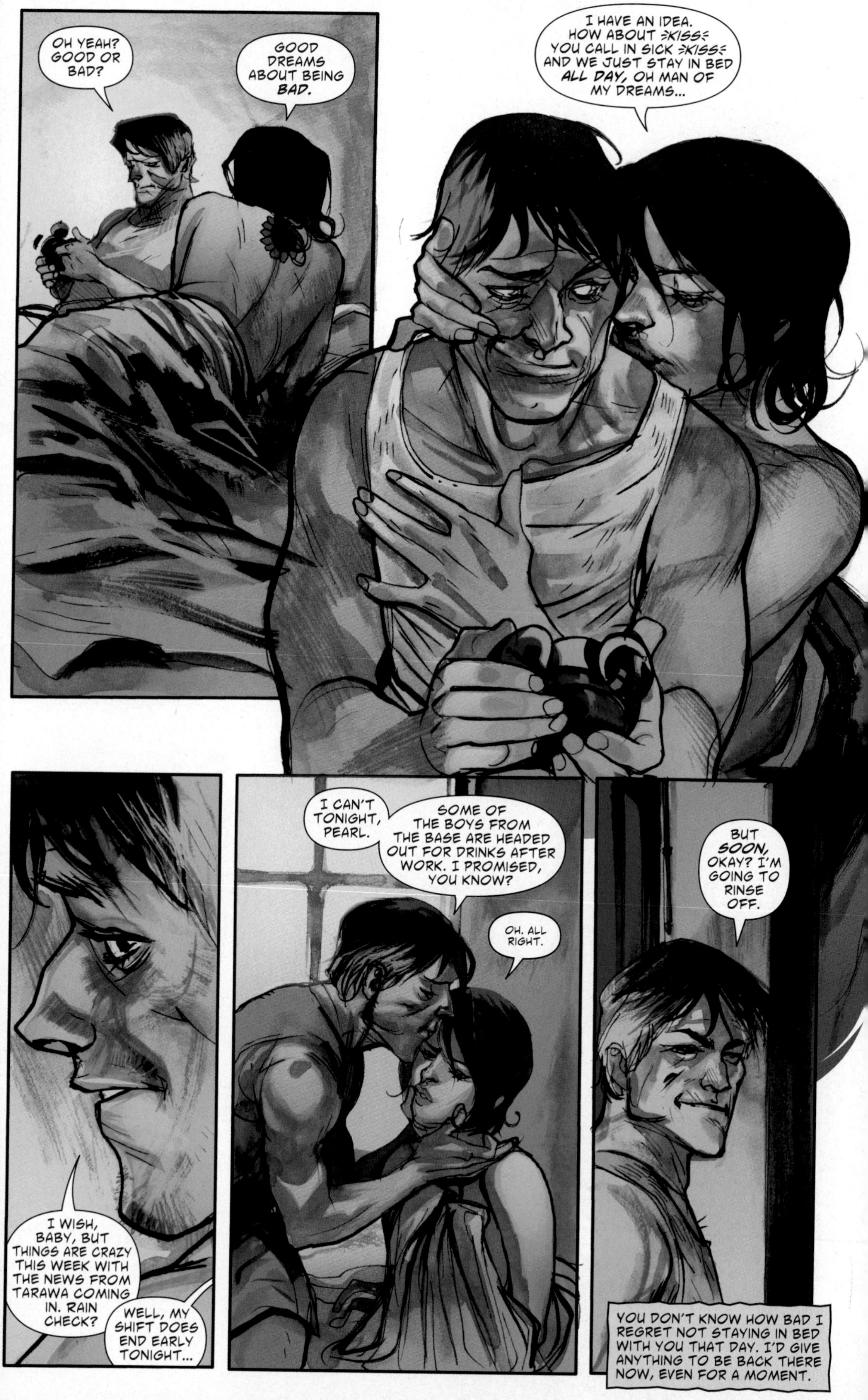
OH YEAH? GOOD OR BAD?
GOOD DREAMS ABOUT BEING BAD.
I HAVE AN IDEA. HOW ABOUT ≶KISS≶ YOU CALL IN SICK ≶KISS≶ AND WE JUST STAY IN BED ALL DAY, OH MAN OF MY DREAMS...
I WISH, BABY, BUT THINGS ARE CRAZY THIS WEEK WITH THE NEWS FROM TARAWA COMING IN. RAIN CHECK?
WELL, MY SHIFT DOES END EARLY TONIGHT...
I CAN'T TONIGHT, PEARL.
SOME OF THE BOYS FROM THE BASE ARE HEADED OUT FOR DRINKS AFTER WORK. I PROMISED, YOU KNOW?
OH. ALL RIGHT.
BUT SOON, OKAY? I'M GOING TO RINSE OFF.
YOU DON'T KNOW HOW BAD I REGRET NOT STAYING IN BED WITH YOU THAT DAY. I'D GIVE ANYTHING TO BE BACK THERE NOW, EVEN FOR A MOMENT.

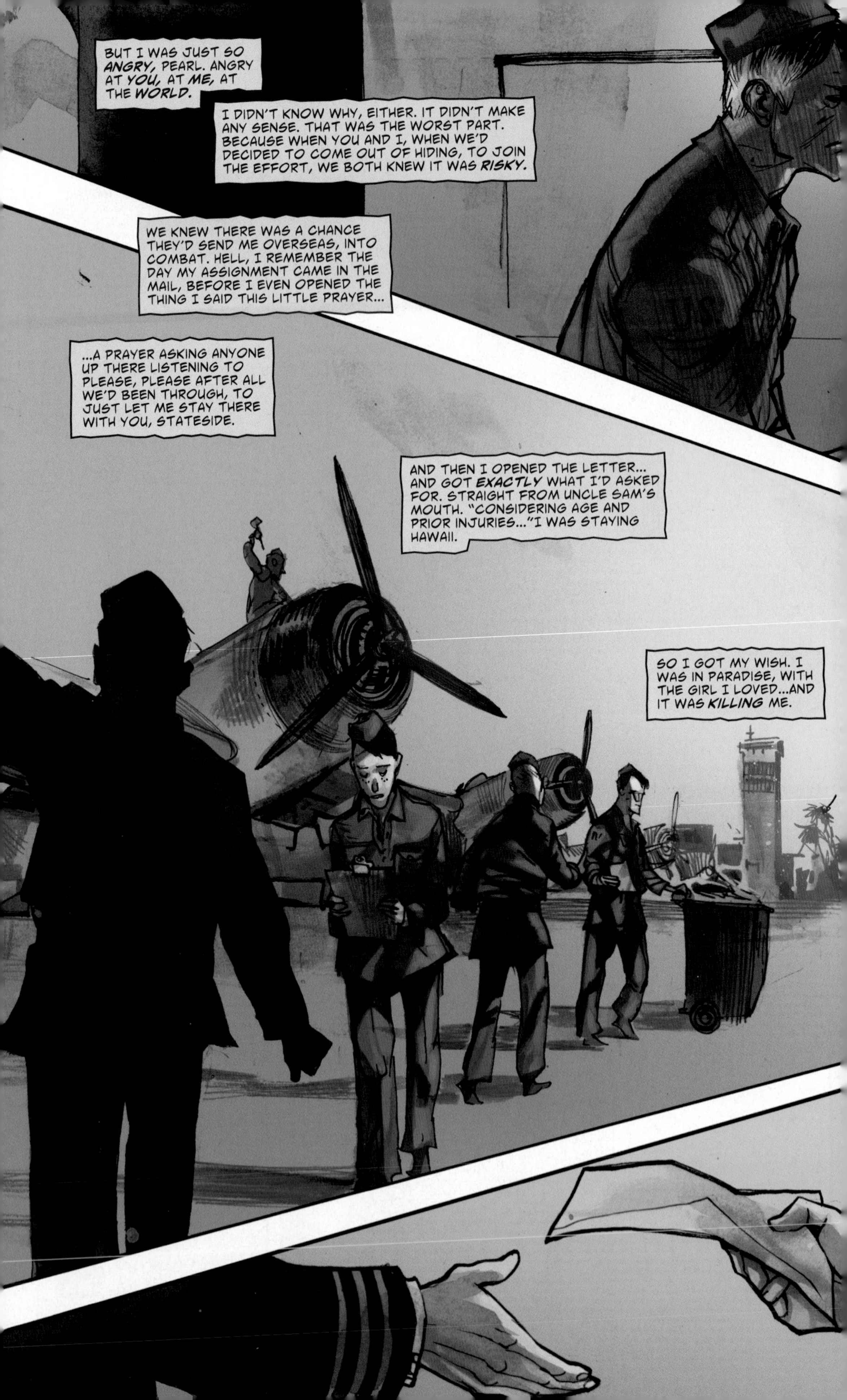
BUT I WAS JUST SO ANGRY, PEARL. ANGRY AT YOU, AT ME, AT THE WORLD.
I DIDN'T KNOW WHY, EITHER. IT DIDN'T MAKE ANY SENSE. THAT WAS THE WORST PART. BECAUSE WHEN YOU AND I, WHEN WE'D DECIDED TO COME OUT OF HIDING, TO JOIN THE EFFORT, WE BOTH KNEW IT WAS RISKY.
WE KNEW THERE WAS A CHANCE THEY'D SEND ME OVERSEAS, INTO COMBAT. HELL, I REMEMBER THE DAY MY ASSIGNMENT CAME IN THE MAIL, BEFORE I EVEN OPENED THE THING I SAID THIS LITTLE PRAYER...
...A PRAYER ASKING ANYONE UP THERE LISTENING TO PLEASE, PLEASE AFTER ALL WE'D BEEN THROUGH, TO JUST LET ME STAY THERE WITH YOU, STATESIDE.
AND THEN I OPENED THE LETTER... AND GOT EXACTLY WHAT I'D ASKED FOR. STRAIGHT FROM UNCLE SAM'S MOUTH. "CONSIDERING AGE AND PRIOR INJURIES..."I WAS STAYING HAWAII.
SO I GOT MY WISH. I WAS IN PARADISE, WITH THE GIRL I LOVED...AND IT WAS KILLING ME.

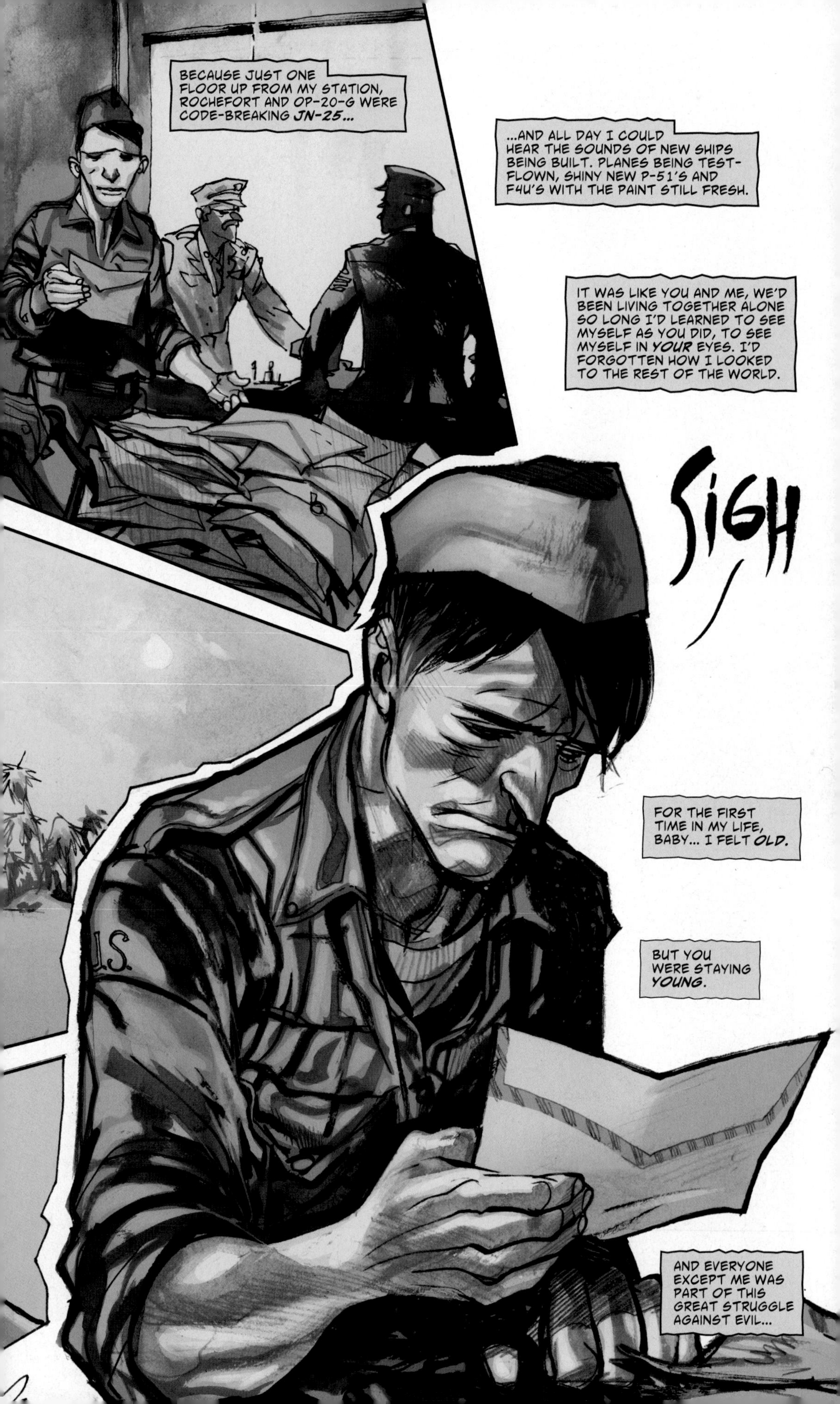
BECAUSE JUST ONE FLOOR UP FROM MY STATION, ROCHEFORT AND OP-20-G WERE CODE-BREAKING *JN-25*...
...AND ALL DAY I COULD HEAR THE SOUNDS OF NEW SHIPS BEING BUILT. PLANES BEING TEST-FLOWN, SHINY NEW P-51'S AND F4U'S WITH THE PAINT STILL FRESH.
IT WAS LIKE YOU AND ME, WE'D BEEN LIVING TOGETHER ALONE SO LONG I'D LEARNED TO SEE MYSELF AS YOU DID, TO SEE MYSELF IN *YOUR* EYES. I'D FORGOTTEN HOW I LOOKED TO THE REST OF THE WORLD.
SIGH
FOR THE FIRST TIME IN MY LIFE, BABY... I FELT *OLD*.
BUT YOU WERE STAYING *YOUNG*.
AND EVERYONE EXCEPT ME WAS PART OF THIS GREAT STRUGGLE AGAINST EVIL...

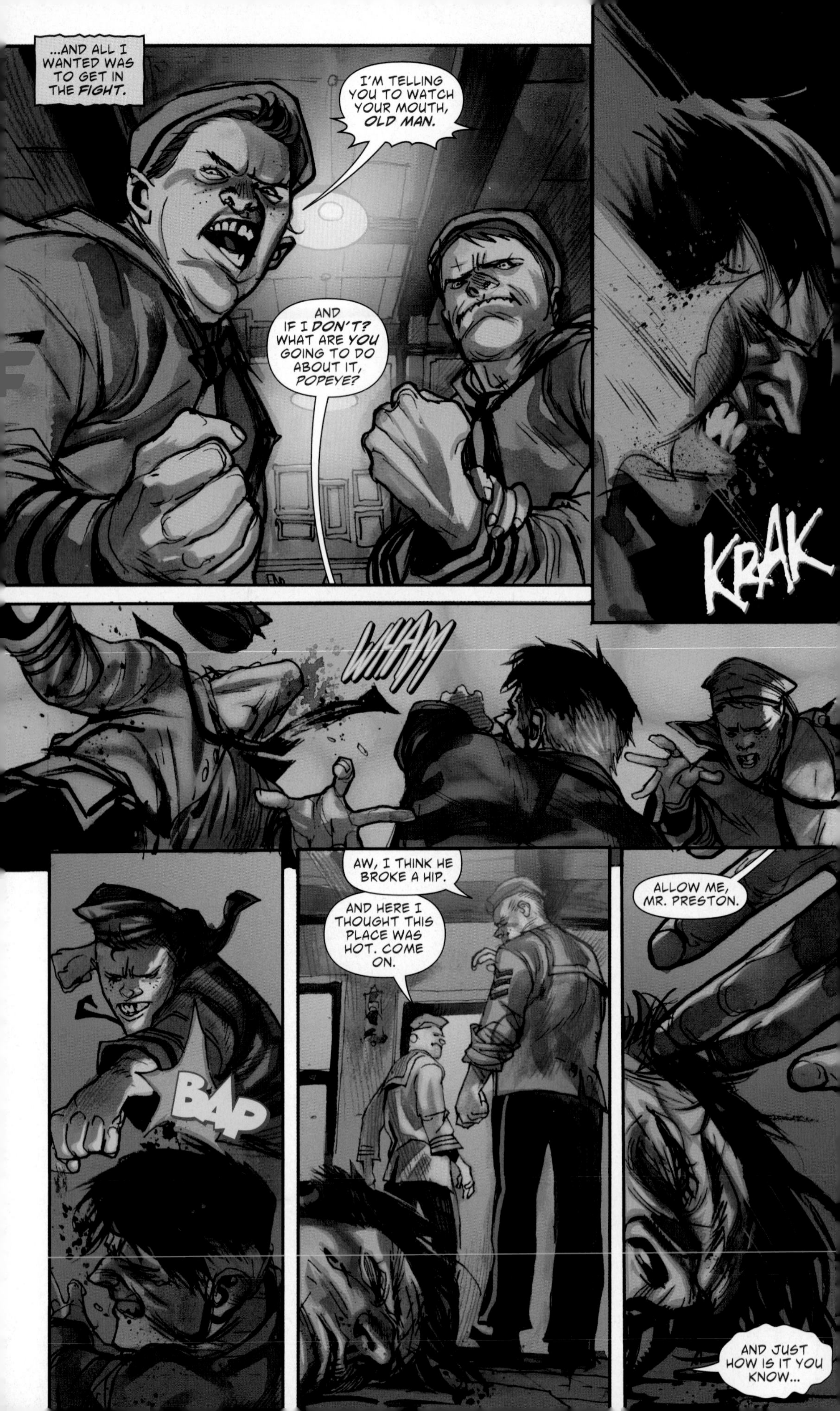
...AND ALL I WANTED WAS TO GET IN THE FIGHT.
I'M TELLING YOU TO WATCH YOUR MOUTH, OLD MAN.
AND IF I DON'T? WHAT ARE YOU GOING TO DO ABOUT IT, POPEYE?
KRAK
WHAM
BAP
AW, I THINK HE BROKE A HIP.
AND HERE I THOUGHT THIS PLACE WAS HOT. COME ON.
ALLOW ME, MR. PRESTON.
AND JUST HOW IS IT YOU KNOW...

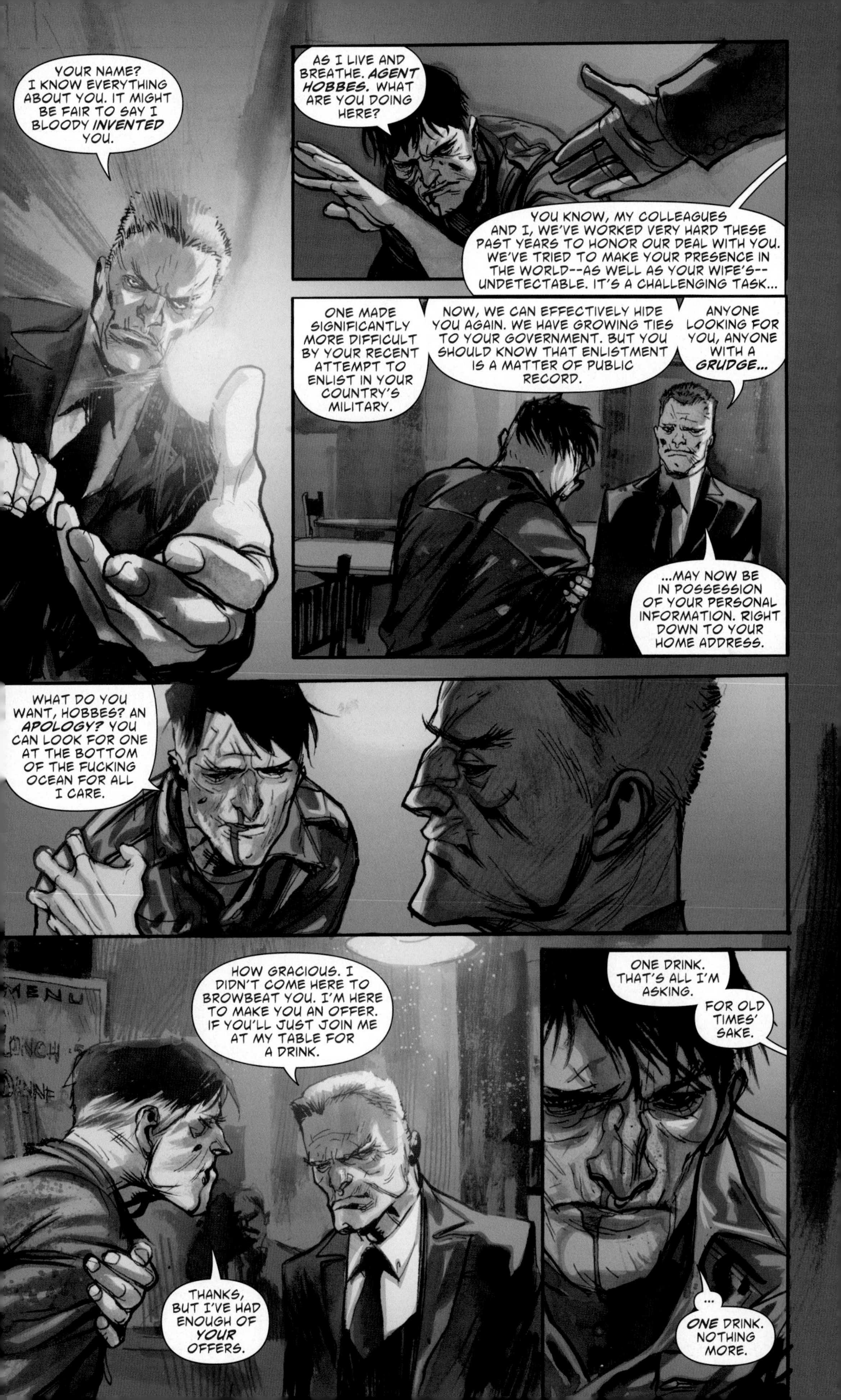
YOUR NAME? I KNOW EVERYTHING ABOUT YOU. IT MIGHT BE FAIR TO SAY I BLOODY *INVENTED* YOU.
AS I LIVE AND BREATHE. *AGENT HOBBES.* WHAT ARE YOU DOING HERE?
YOU KNOW, MY COLLEAGUES AND I, WE'VE WORKED VERY HARD THESE PAST YEARS TO HONOR OUR DEAL WITH YOU. WE'VE TRIED TO MAKE YOUR PRESENCE IN THE WORLD--AS WELL AS YOUR WIFE'S--UNDETECTABLE. IT'S A CHALLENGING TASK...
ONE MADE SIGNIFICANTLY MORE DIFFICULT BY YOUR RECENT ATTEMPT TO ENLIST IN YOUR COUNTRY'S MILITARY.
NOW, WE CAN EFFECTIVELY HIDE YOU AGAIN. WE HAVE GROWING TIES TO YOUR GOVERNMENT. BUT YOU SHOULD KNOW THAT ENLISTMENT IS A MATTER OF PUBLIC RECORD.
ANYONE LOOKING FOR YOU, ANYONE WITH A *GRUDGE...*
...MAY NOW BE IN POSSESSION OF YOUR PERSONAL INFORMATION. RIGHT DOWN TO YOUR HOME ADDRESS.
WHAT DO YOU WANT, HOBBES? AN *APOLOGY?* YOU CAN LOOK FOR ONE AT THE BOTTOM OF THE FUCKING OCEAN FOR ALL I CARE.
MENU
HOW GRACIOUS. I DIDN'T COME HERE TO BROWBEAT YOU. I'M HERE TO MAKE YOU AN OFFER. IF YOU'LL JUST JOIN ME AT MY TABLE FOR A DRINK.
THANKS, BUT I'VE HAD ENOUGH OF *YOUR* OFFERS.
ONE DRINK. THAT'S ALL I'M ASKING.
FOR OLD TIMES' SAKE.
...
ONE DRINK. NOTHING MORE.

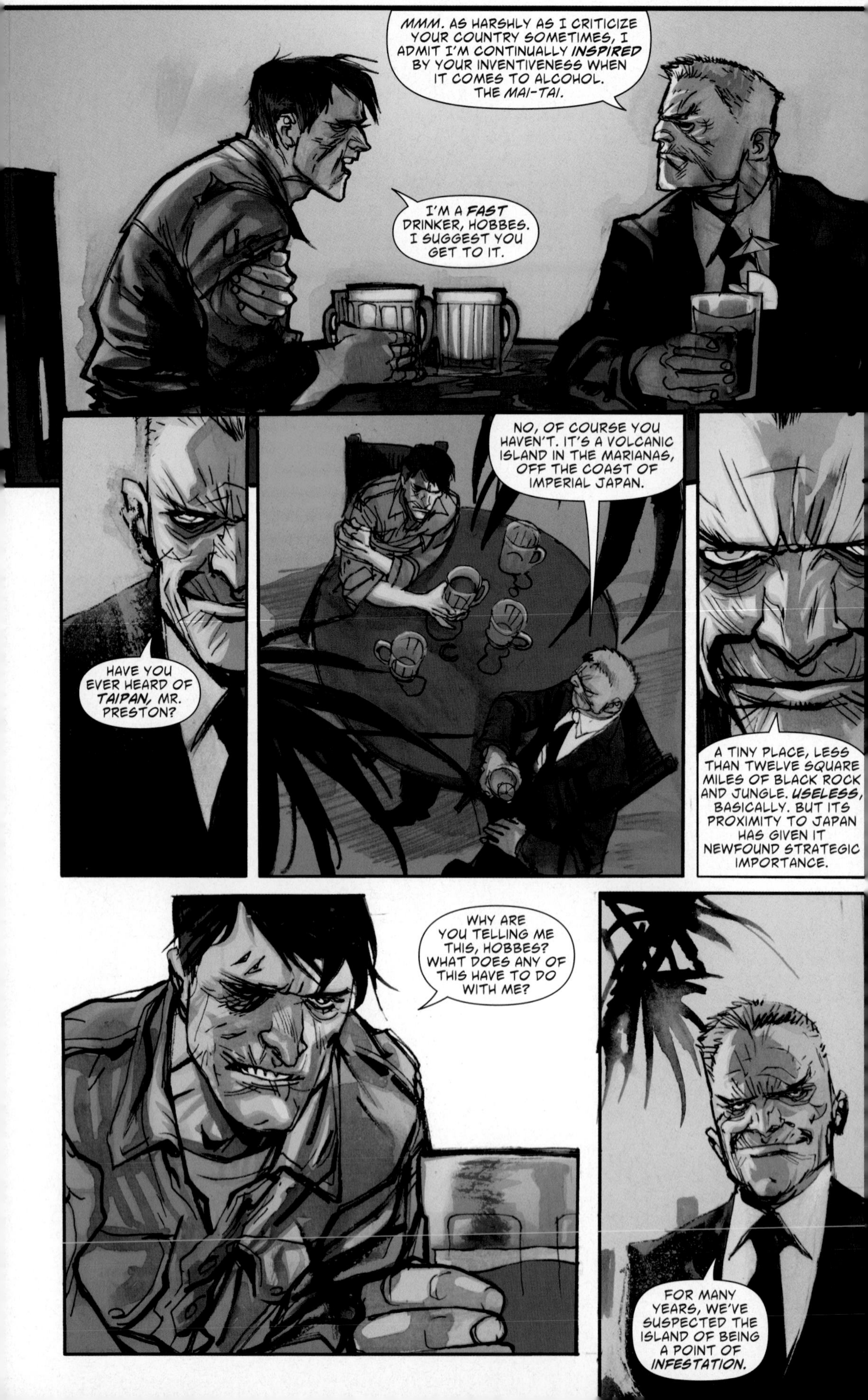

MMM. AS HARSHLY AS I CRITICIZE YOUR COUNTRY SOMETIMES, I ADMIT I'M CONTINUALLY INSPIRED BY YOUR INVENTIVENESS WHEN IT COMES TO ALCOHOL. THE MAI-TAI.
I'M A FAST DRINKER, HOBBES. I SUGGEST YOU GET TO IT.
HAVE YOU EVER HEARD OF TAIPAN, MR. PRESTON?
NO, OF COURSE YOU HAVEN'T. IT'S A VOLCANIC ISLAND IN THE MARIANAS, OFF THE COAST OF IMPERIAL JAPAN.
A TINY PLACE, LESS THAN TWELVE SQUARE MILES OF BLACK ROCK AND JUNGLE. USELESS, BASICALLY. BUT ITS PROXIMITY TO JAPAN HAS GIVEN IT NEWFOUND STRATEGIC IMPORTANCE.
WHY ARE YOU TELLING ME THIS, HOBBES? WHAT DOES ANY OF THIS HAVE TO DO WITH ME?
FOR MANY YEARS, WE'VE SUSPECTED THE ISLAND OF BEING A POINT OF INFESTATION.

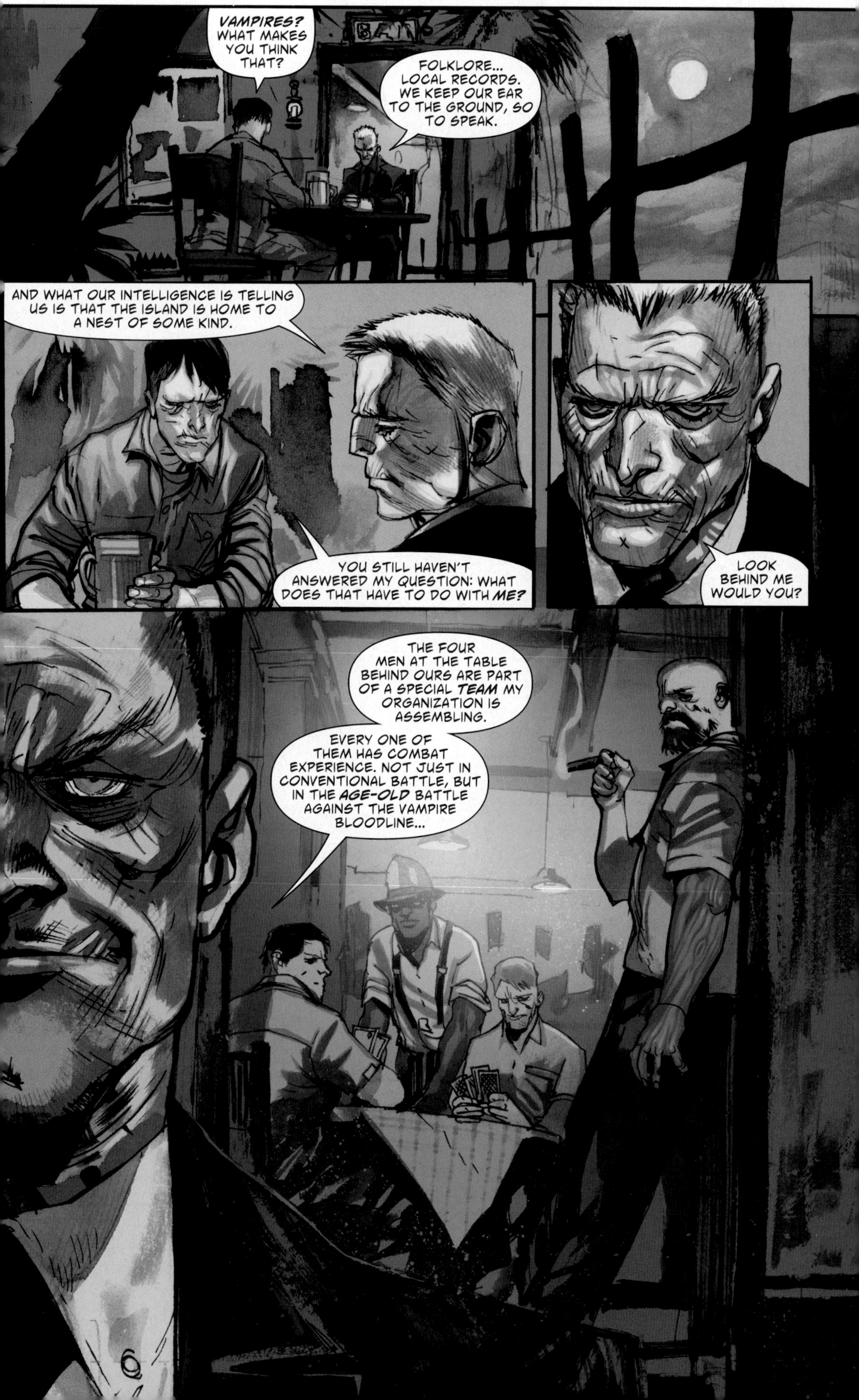

BAR
VAMPIRES? WHAT MAKES YOU THINK THAT?
FOLKLORE... LOCAL RECORDS. WE KEEP OUR EAR TO THE GROUND, SO TO SPEAK.
AND WHAT OUR INTELLIGENCE IS TELLING US IS THAT THE ISLAND IS HOME TO A NEST OF SOME KIND.
YOU STILL HAVEN'T ANSWERED MY QUESTION: WHAT DOES THAT HAVE TO DO WITH ME?
LOOK BEHIND ME WOULD YOU?
THE FOUR MEN AT THE TABLE BEHIND OURS ARE PART OF A SPECIAL TEAM MY ORGANIZATION IS ASSEMBLING.
EVERY ONE OF THEM HAS COMBAT EXPERIENCE. NOT JUST IN CONVENTIONAL BATTLE, BUT IN THE AGE-OLD BATTLE AGAINST THE VAMPIRE BLOODLINE...

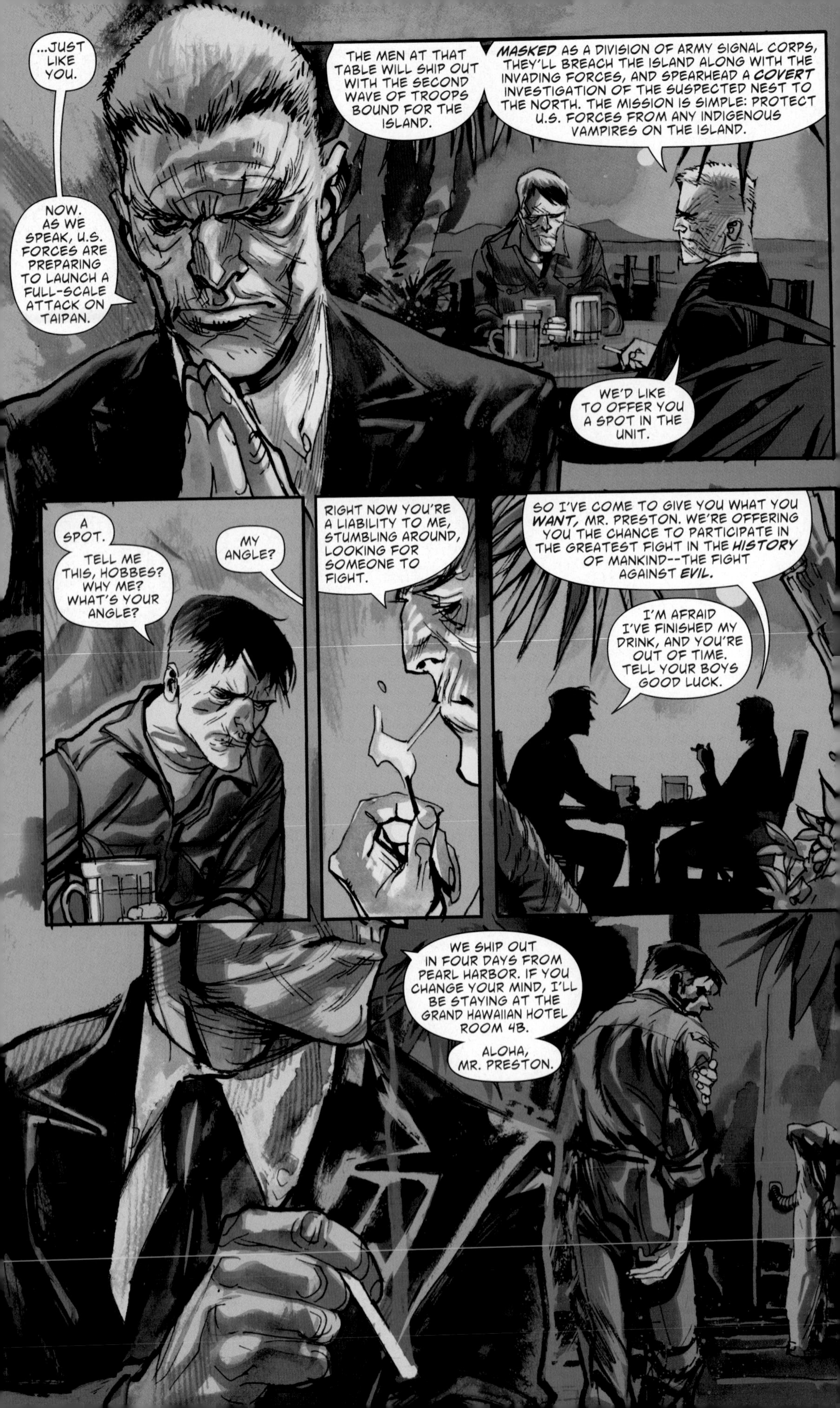

...JUST LIKE YOU.
NOW. AS WE SPEAK, U.S. FORCES ARE PREPARING TO LAUNCH A FULL-SCALE ATTACK ON TAIPAN.
THE MEN AT THAT TABLE WILL SHIP OUT WITH THE SECOND WAVE OF TROOPS BOUND FOR THE ISLAND.
MASKED AS A DIVISION OF ARMY SIGNAL CORPS, THEY'LL BREACH THE ISLAND ALONG WITH THE INVADING FORCES, AND SPEARHEAD A COVERT INVESTIGATION OF THE SUSPECTED NEST TO THE NORTH. THE MISSION IS SIMPLE: PROTECT U.S. FORCES FROM ANY INDIGENOUS VAMPIRES ON THE ISLAND.
WE'D LIKE TO OFFER YOU A SPOT IN THE UNIT.
A SPOT.
TELL ME THIS, HOBBES? WHY ME? WHAT'S YOUR ANGLE?
MY ANGLE?
RIGHT NOW YOU'RE A LIABILITY TO ME, STUMBLING AROUND, LOOKING FOR SOMEONE TO FIGHT.
SO I'VE COME TO GIVE YOU WHAT YOU WANT, MR. PRESTON. WE'RE OFFERING YOU THE CHANCE TO PARTICIPATE IN THE GREATEST FIGHT IN THE HISTORY OF MANKIND--THE FIGHT AGAINST EVIL.
I'M AFRAID I'VE FINISHED MY DRINK, AND YOU'RE OUT OF TIME. TELL YOUR BOYS GOOD LUCK.
WE SHIP OUT IN FOUR DAYS FROM PEARL HARBOR. IF YOU CHANGE YOUR MIND, I'LL BE STAYING AT THE GRAND HAWAIIAN HOTEL ROOM 4B.
ALOHA, MR. PRESTON.

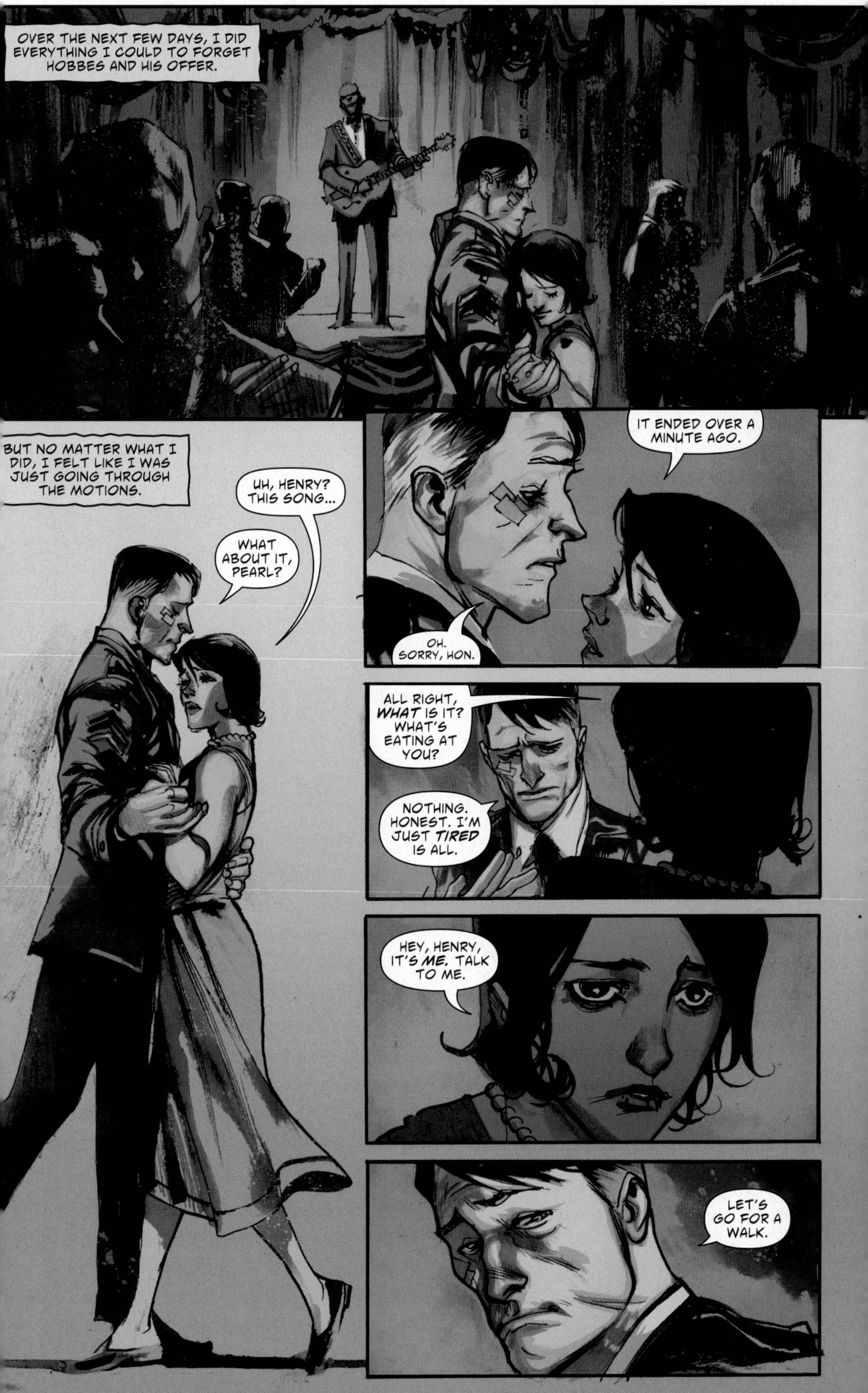
OVER THE NEXT FEW DAYS, I DID EVERYTHING I COULD TO FORGET HOBBES AND HIS OFFER.
BUT NO MATTER WHAT I DID, I FELT LIKE I WAS JUST GOING THROUGH THE MOTIONS.
UH, HENRY? THIS SONG...
WHAT ABOUT IT, PEARL?
IT ENDED OVER A MINUTE AGO.
OH. SORRY, HON.
ALL RIGHT, WHAT IS IT? WHAT'S EATING AT YOU?
NOTHING. HONEST. I'M JUST TIRED IS ALL.
HEY, HENRY, IT'S ME. TALK TO ME.
LET'S GO FOR A WALK.

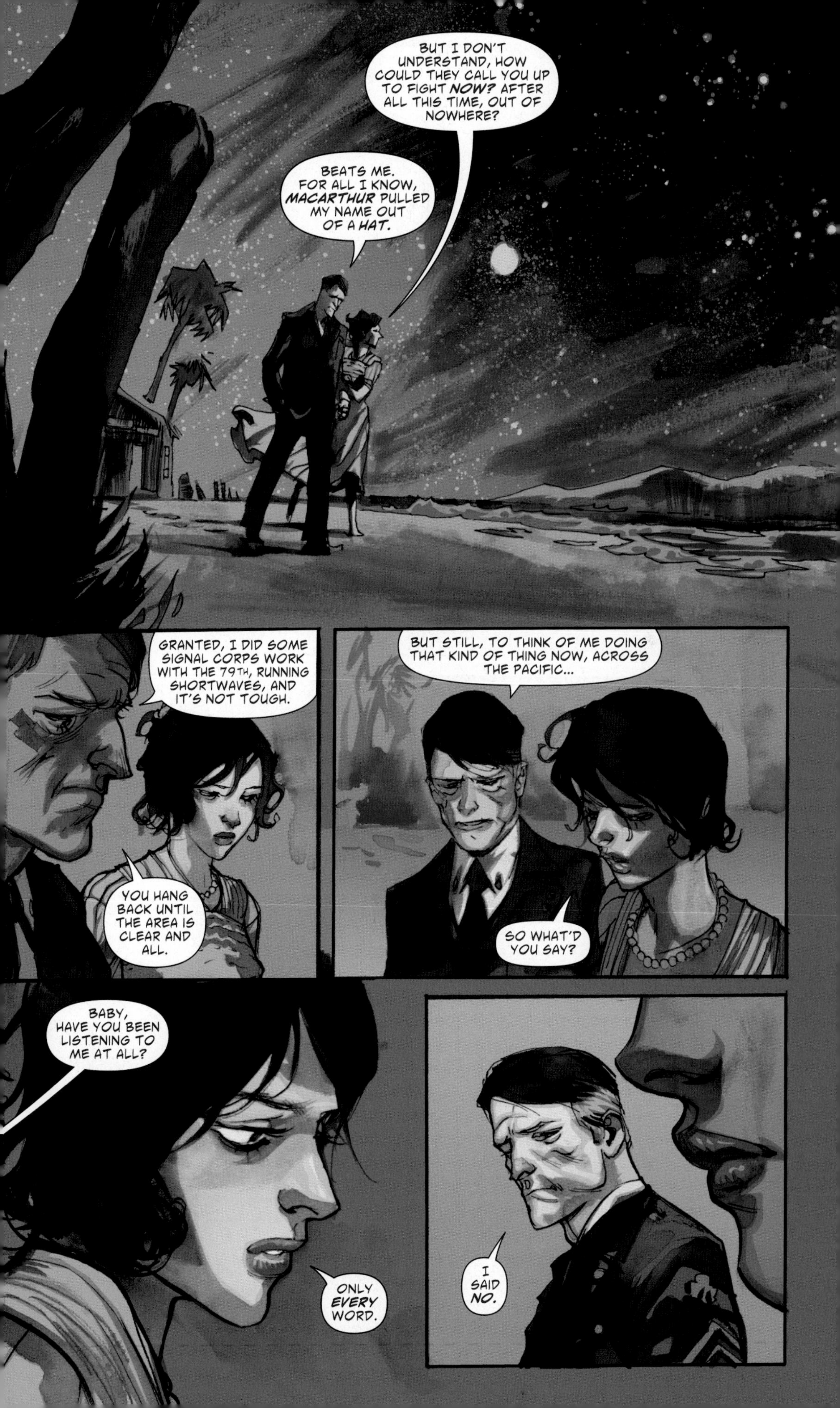
BUT I DON'T UNDERSTAND, HOW COULD THEY CALL YOU UP TO FIGHT NOW? AFTER ALL THIS TIME, OUT OF NOWHERE?
BEATS ME. FOR ALL I KNOW, MACARTHUR PULLED MY NAME OUT OF A HAT.
GRANTED, I DID SOME SIGNAL CORPS WORK WITH THE 79TH, RUNNING SHORTWAVES, AND IT'S NOT TOUGH.
YOU HANG BACK UNTIL THE AREA IS CLEAR AND ALL.
BUT STILL, TO THINK OF ME DOING THAT KIND OF THING NOW, ACROSS THE PACIFIC...
SO WHAT'D YOU SAY?
BABY, HAVE YOU BEEN LISTENING TO ME AT ALL?
ONLY EVERY WORD.
I SAID NO.

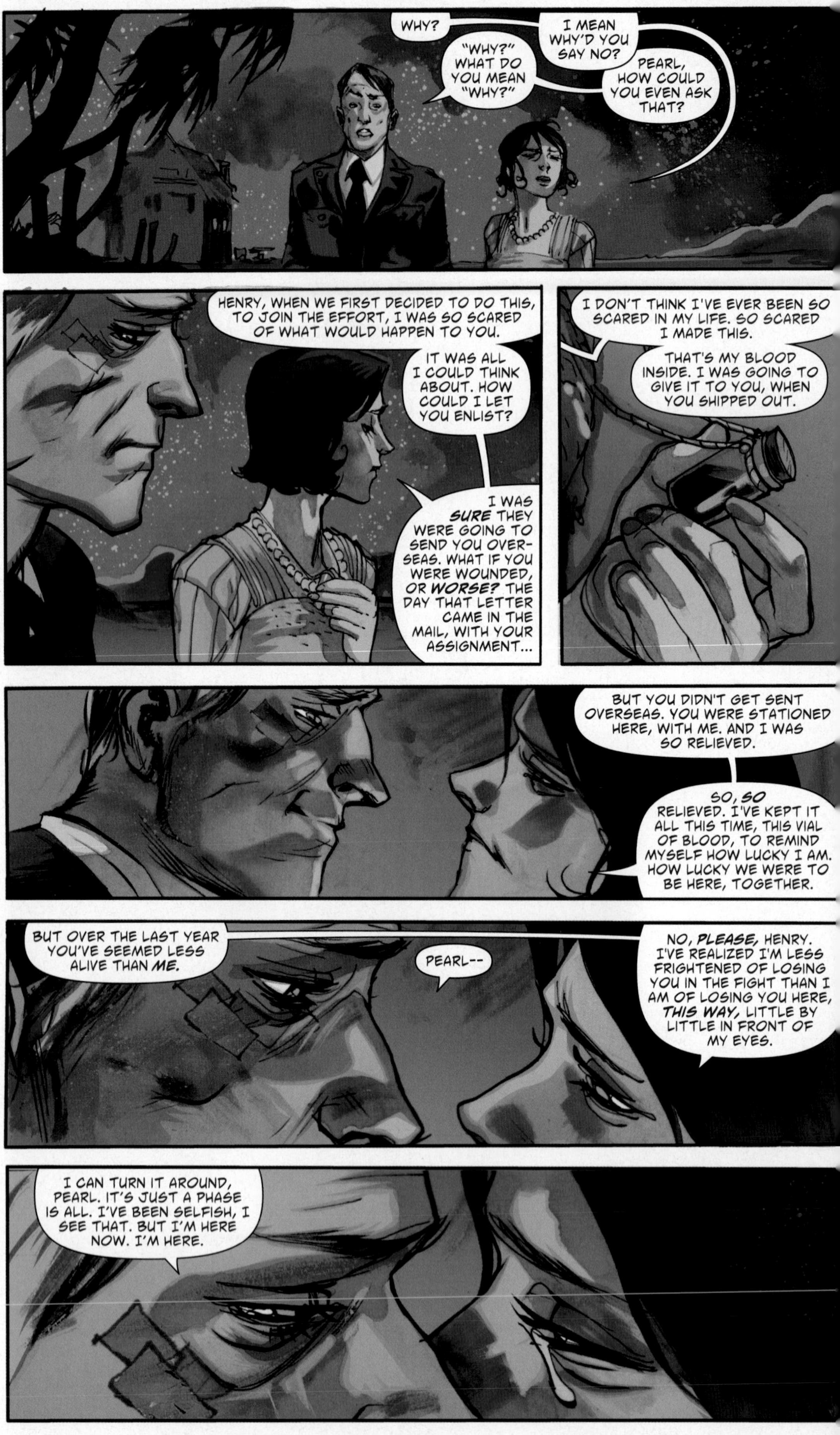
WHY?
I MEAN WHY'D YOU SAY NO?
"WHY?" WHAT DO YOU MEAN "WHY?"
PEARL, HOW COULD YOU EVEN ASK THAT?
HENRY, WHEN WE FIRST DECIDED TO DO THIS, TO JOIN THE EFFORT, I WAS SO SCARED OF WHAT WOULD HAPPEN TO YOU.
IT WAS ALL I COULD THINK ABOUT. HOW COULD I LET YOU ENLIST?
I WAS *SURE* THEY WERE GOING TO SEND YOU OVER-SEAS. WHAT IF YOU WERE WOUNDED, OR *WORSE?* THE DAY THAT LETTER CAME IN THE MAIL, WITH YOUR ASSIGNMENT...
I DON'T THINK I'VE EVER BEEN SO SCARED IN MY LIFE. SO SCARED I MADE THIS.
THAT'S MY BLOOD INSIDE. I WAS GOING TO GIVE IT TO YOU, WHEN YOU SHIPPED OUT.
BUT YOU DIDN'T GET SENT OVERSEAS. YOU WERE STATIONED HERE, WITH ME. AND I WAS SO RELIEVED.
SO, *SO* RELIEVED. I'VE KEPT IT ALL THIS TIME, THIS VIAL OF BLOOD, TO REMIND MYSELF HOW LUCKY I AM. HOW LUCKY WE WERE TO BE HERE, TOGETHER.
BUT OVER THE LAST YEAR YOU'VE SEEMED LESS ALIVE THAN *ME.*
PEARL--
NO, *PLEASE,* HENRY. I'VE REALIZED I'M LESS FRIGHTENED OF LOSING YOU IN THE FIGHT THAN I AM OF LOSING YOU HERE, *THIS WAY,* LITTLE BY LITTLE IN FRONT OF MY EYES.
I CAN TURN IT AROUND, PEARL. IT'S JUST A PHASE IS ALL. I'VE BEEN SELFISH, I SEE THAT. BUT I'M HERE NOW. I'M HERE.

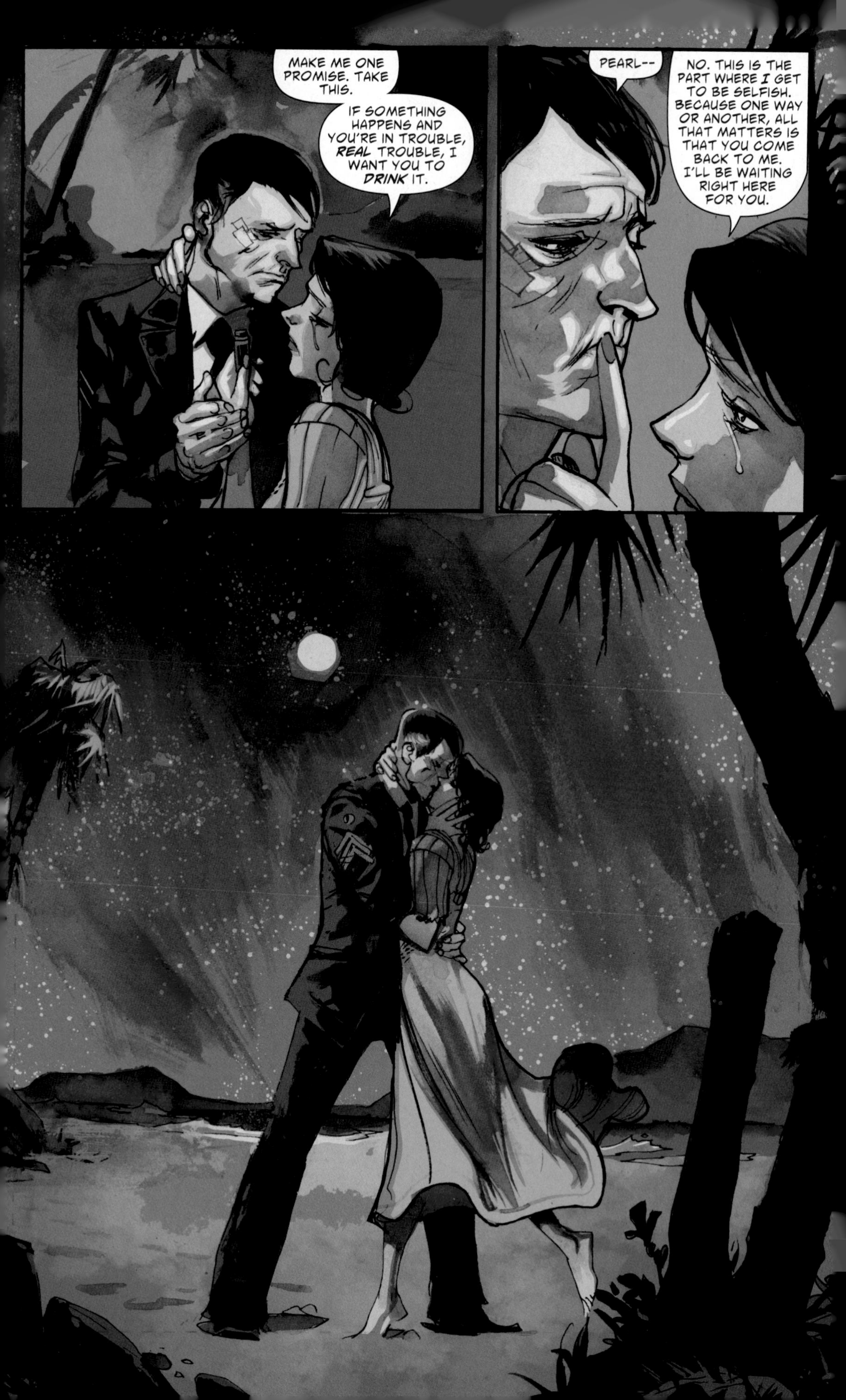
MAKE ME ONE PROMISE. TAKE THIS.
IF SOMETHING HAPPENS AND YOU'RE IN TROUBLE, *REAL* TROUBLE, I WANT YOU TO *DRINK* IT.
PEARL--
NO. THIS IS THE PART WHERE *I* GET TO BE SELFISH. BECAUSE ONE WAY OR ANOTHER, ALL THAT MATTERS IS THAT YOU COME BACK TO ME. I'LL BE WAITING RIGHT HERE FOR YOU.

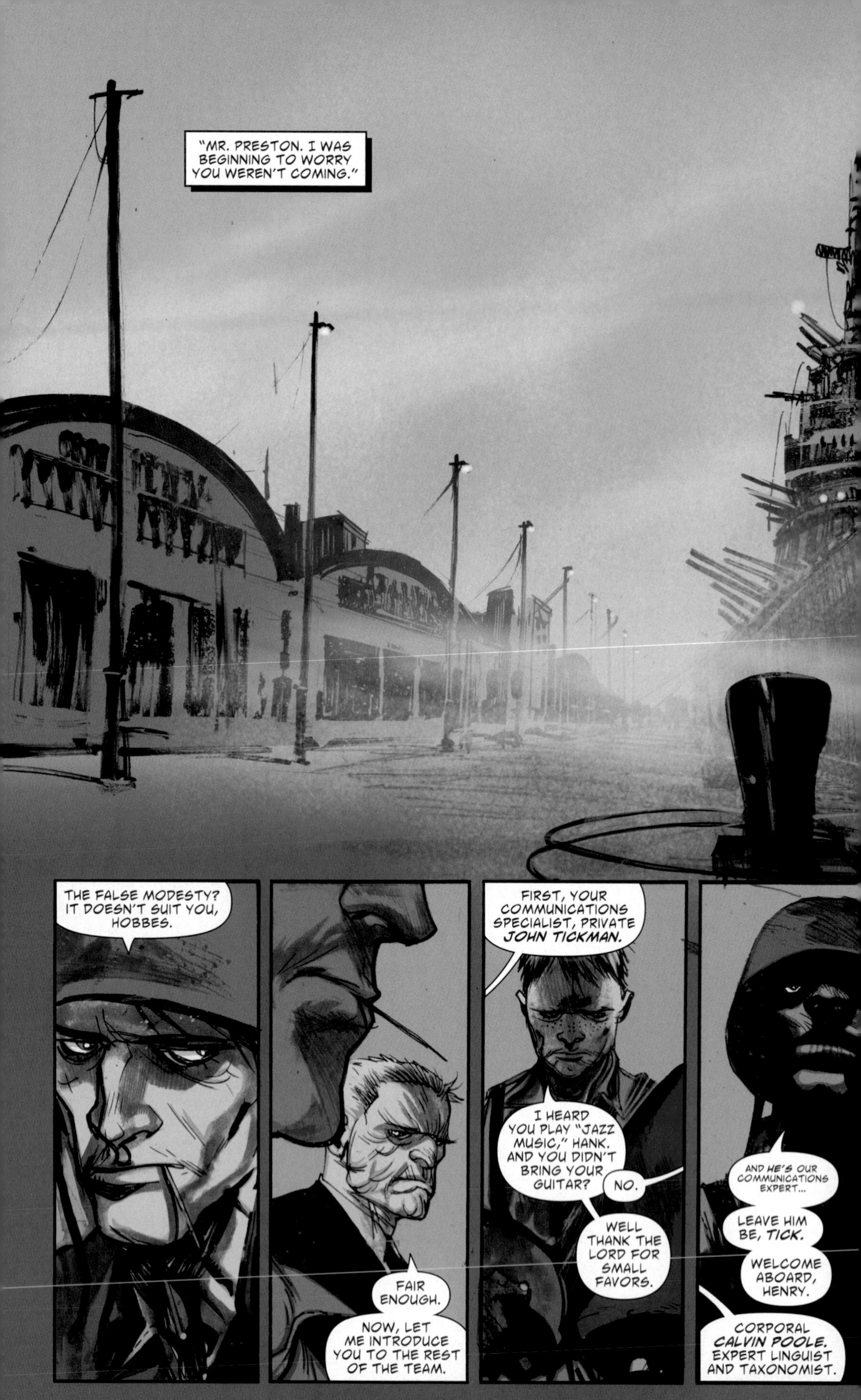
"MR. PRESTON. I WAS BEGINNING TO WORRY YOU WEREN'T COMING."
THE FALSE MODESTY? IT DOESN'T SUIT YOU, HOBBES.
FAIR ENOUGH.
NOW, LET ME INTRODUCE YOU TO THE REST OF THE TEAM.
FIRST, YOUR COMMUNICATIONS SPECIALIST, PRIVATE JOHN TICKMAN.
I HEARD YOU PLAY "JAZZ MUSIC," HANK. AND YOU DIDN'T BRING YOUR GUITAR?
NO.
WELL THANK THE LORD FOR SMALL FAVORS.
CORPORAL CALVIN POOLE. EXPERT LINGUIST AND TAXONOMIST.
WELCOME ABOARD, HENRY.
LEAVE HIM BE, TICK.
AND HE'S OUR COMMUNICATIONS EXPERT...

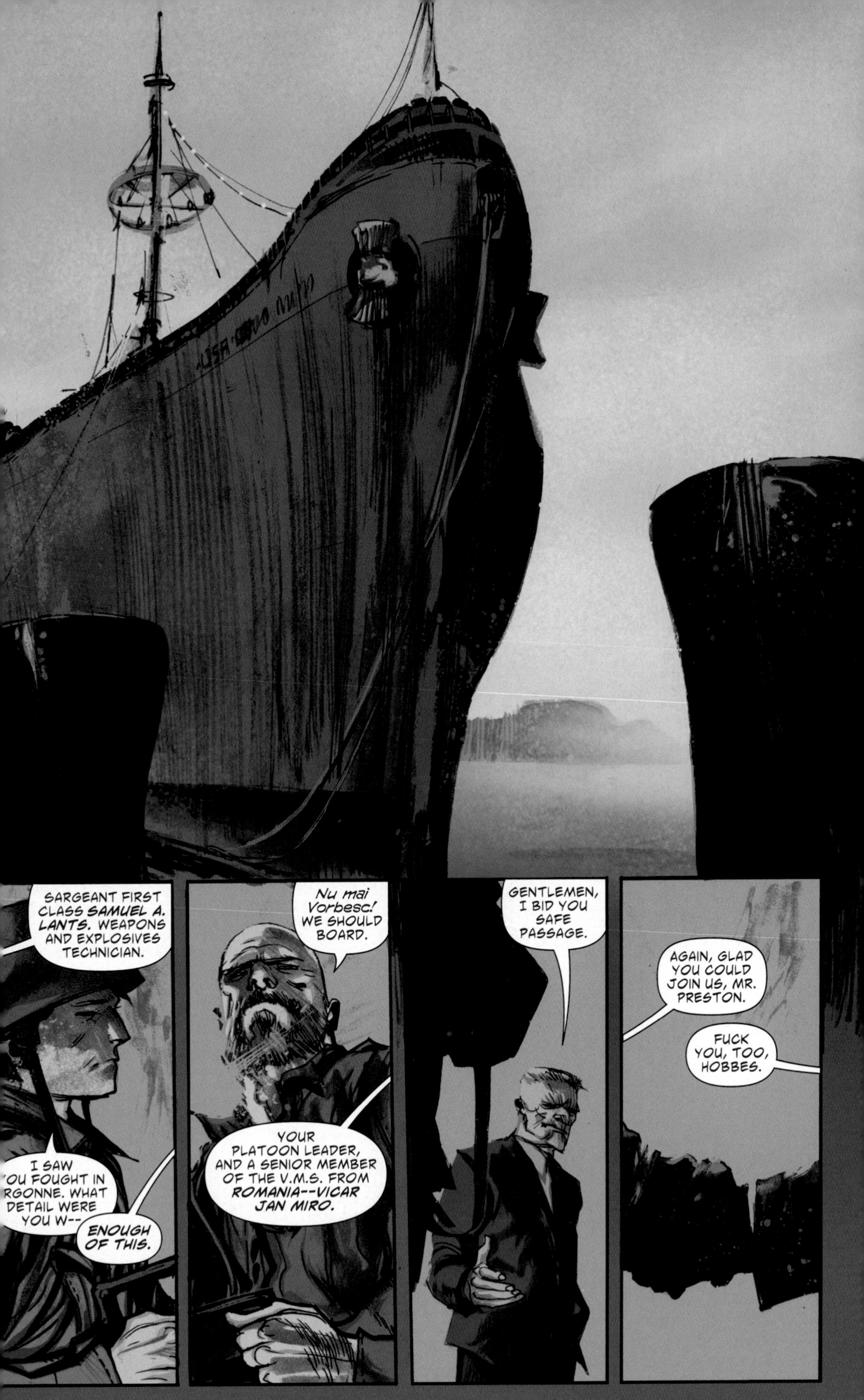
SARGEANT FIRST CLASS SAMUEL A. LANTS. WEAPONS AND EXPLOSIVES TECHNICIAN.
I SAW YOU FOUGHT IN ARGONNE. WHAT DETAIL WERE YOU W--
ENOUGH OF THIS.
Nu mai Vorbesc! WE SHOULD BOARD.
YOUR PLATOON LEADER, AND A SENIOR MEMBER OF THE V.M.S. FROM ROMANIA--VICAR JAN MIRO.
GENTLEMEN, I BID YOU SAFE PASSAGE.
AGAIN, GLAD YOU COULD JOIN US, MR. PRESTON.
FUCK YOU, TOO, HOBBES.

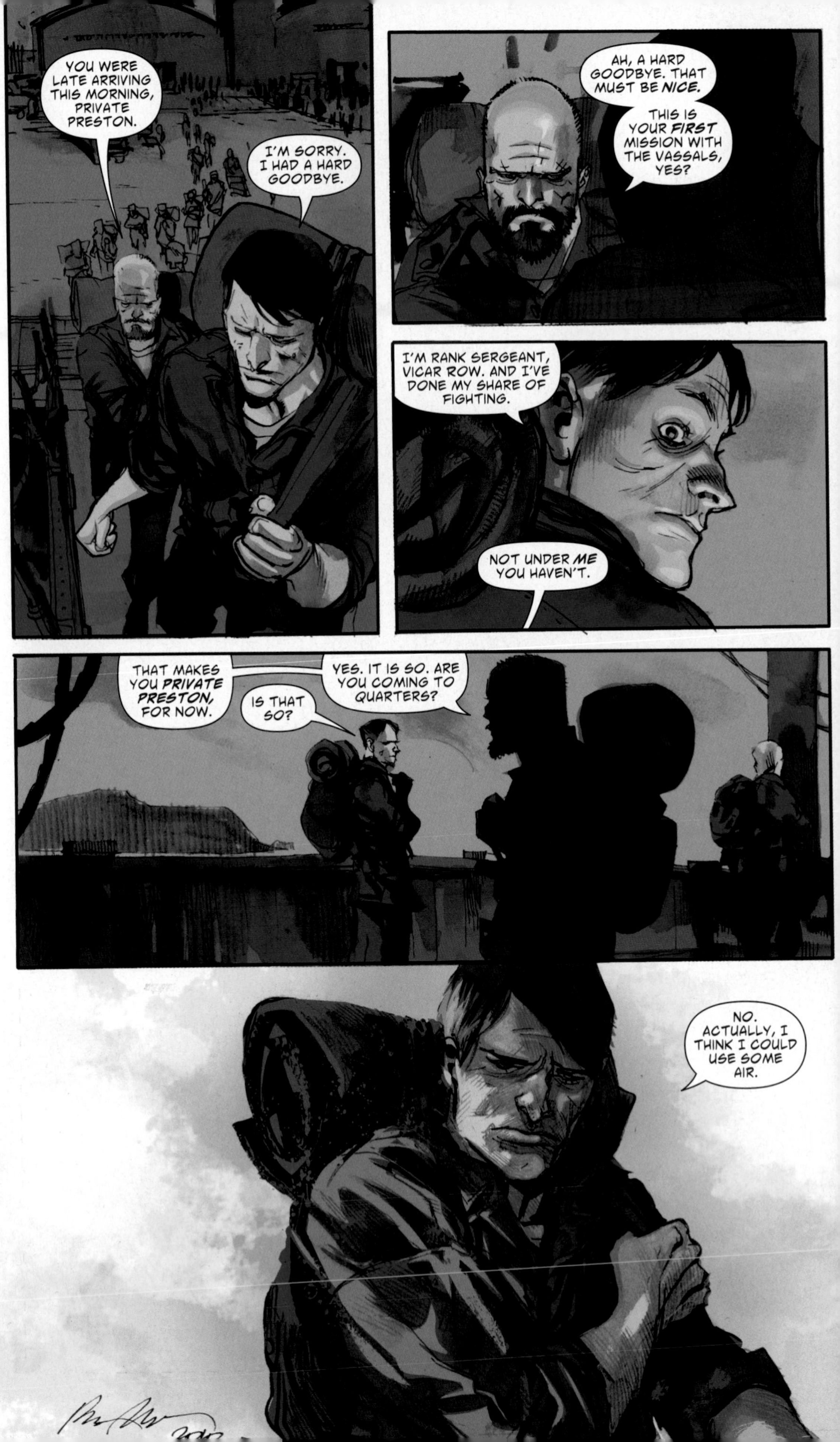
YOU WERE LATE ARRIVING THIS MORNING, PRIVATE PRESTON.
I'M SORRY. I HAD A HARD GOODBYE.
AH, A HARD GOODBYE. THAT MUST BE *NICE.*
THIS IS YOUR *FIRST* MISSION WITH THE VASSALS, YES?
I'M RANK SERGEANT, VICAR ROW. AND I'VE DONE MY SHARE OF FIGHTING.
NOT UNDER *ME* YOU HAVEN'T.
THAT MAKES YOU *PRIVATE PRESTON,* FOR NOW.
IS THAT SO?
YES. IT IS SO. ARE YOU COMING TO QUARTERS?
NO. ACTUALLY, I THINK I COULD USE SOME AIR.

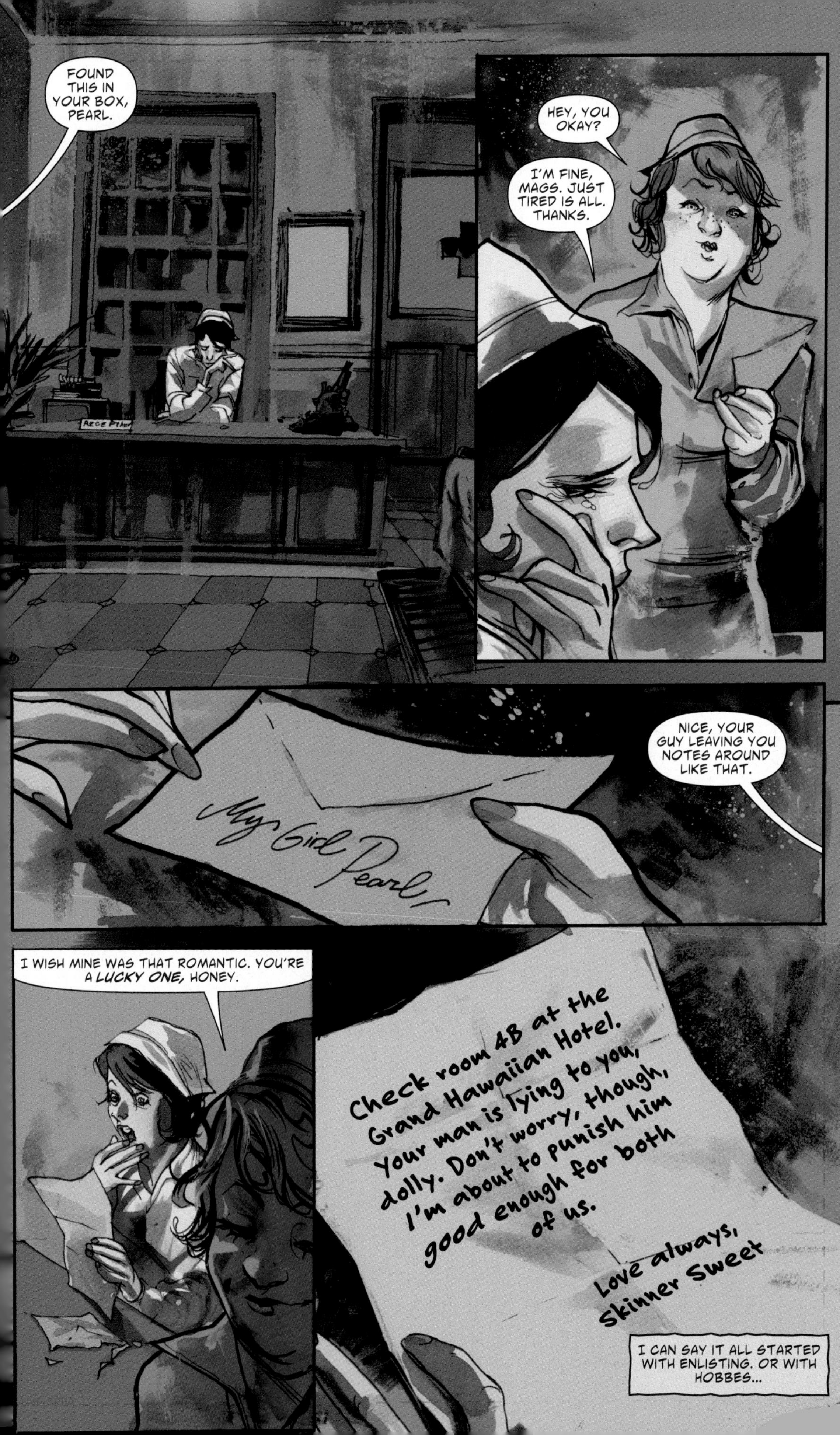
FOUND THIS IN YOUR BOX, PEARL.
HEY, YOU OKAY?
I'M FINE, MAGS. JUST TIRED IS ALL. THANKS.
My Girl Pearl
NICE, YOUR GUY LEAVING YOU NOTES AROUND LIKE THAT.
I WISH MINE WAS THAT ROMANTIC. YOU'RE A LUCKY ONE, HONEY.
Check room 4B at the Grand Hawaiian Hotel. Your man is lying to you, dolly. Don't worry, though, I'm about to punish him good enough for both of us.
Love always, Skinner Sweet
I CAN SAY IT ALL STARTED WITH ENLISTING. OR WITH HOBBES...

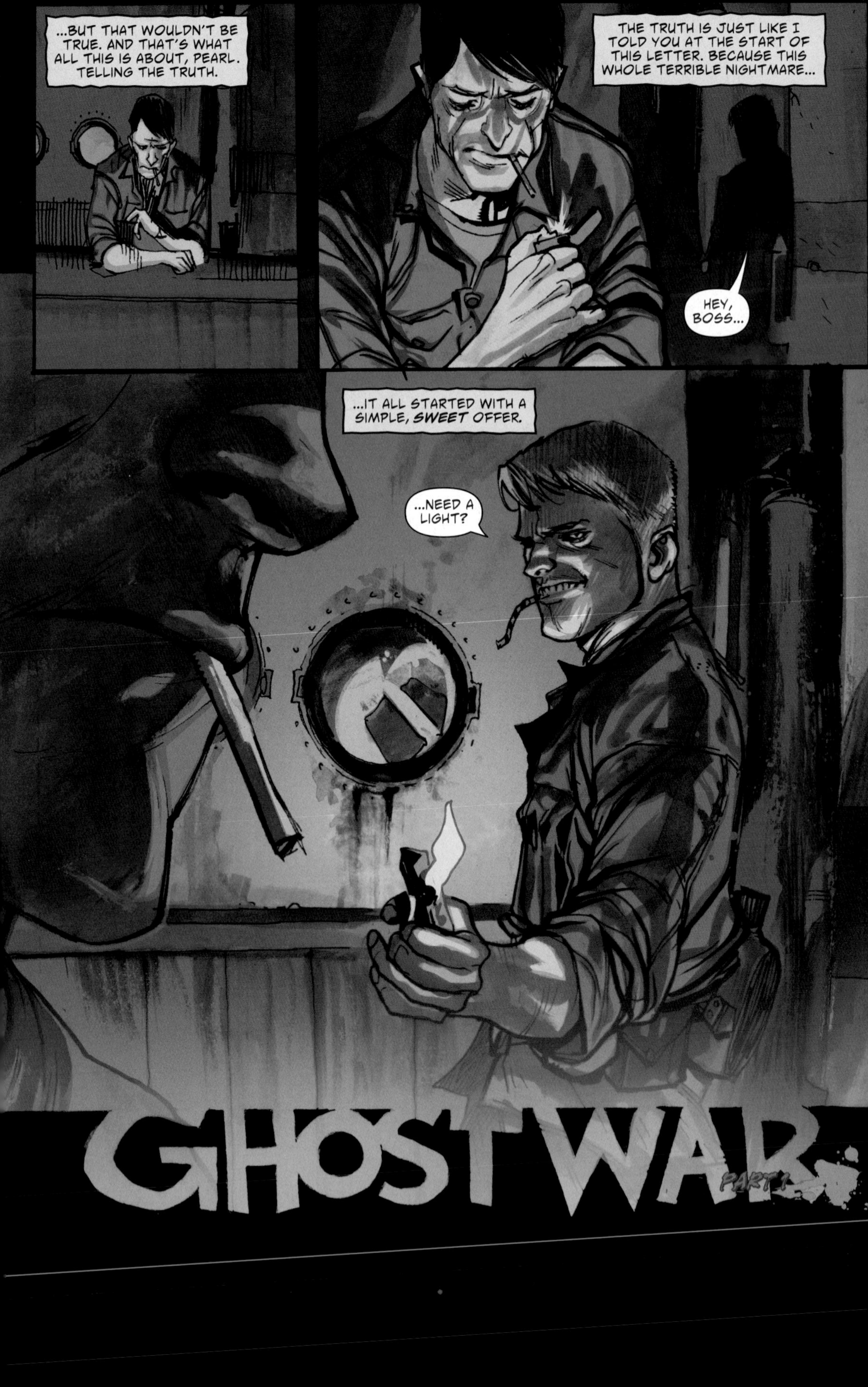
...BUT THAT WOULDN'T BE TRUE. AND THAT'S WHAT ALL THIS IS ABOUT, PEARL. TELLING THE TRUTH.
THE TRUTH IS JUST LIKE I TOLD YOU AT THE START OF THIS LETTER. BECAUSE THIS WHOLE TERRIBLE NIGHTMARE...
HEY, BOSS...
...IT ALL STARTED WITH A SIMPLE, SWEET OFFER.
...NEED A LIGHT?
GHOST WAR
PART 1

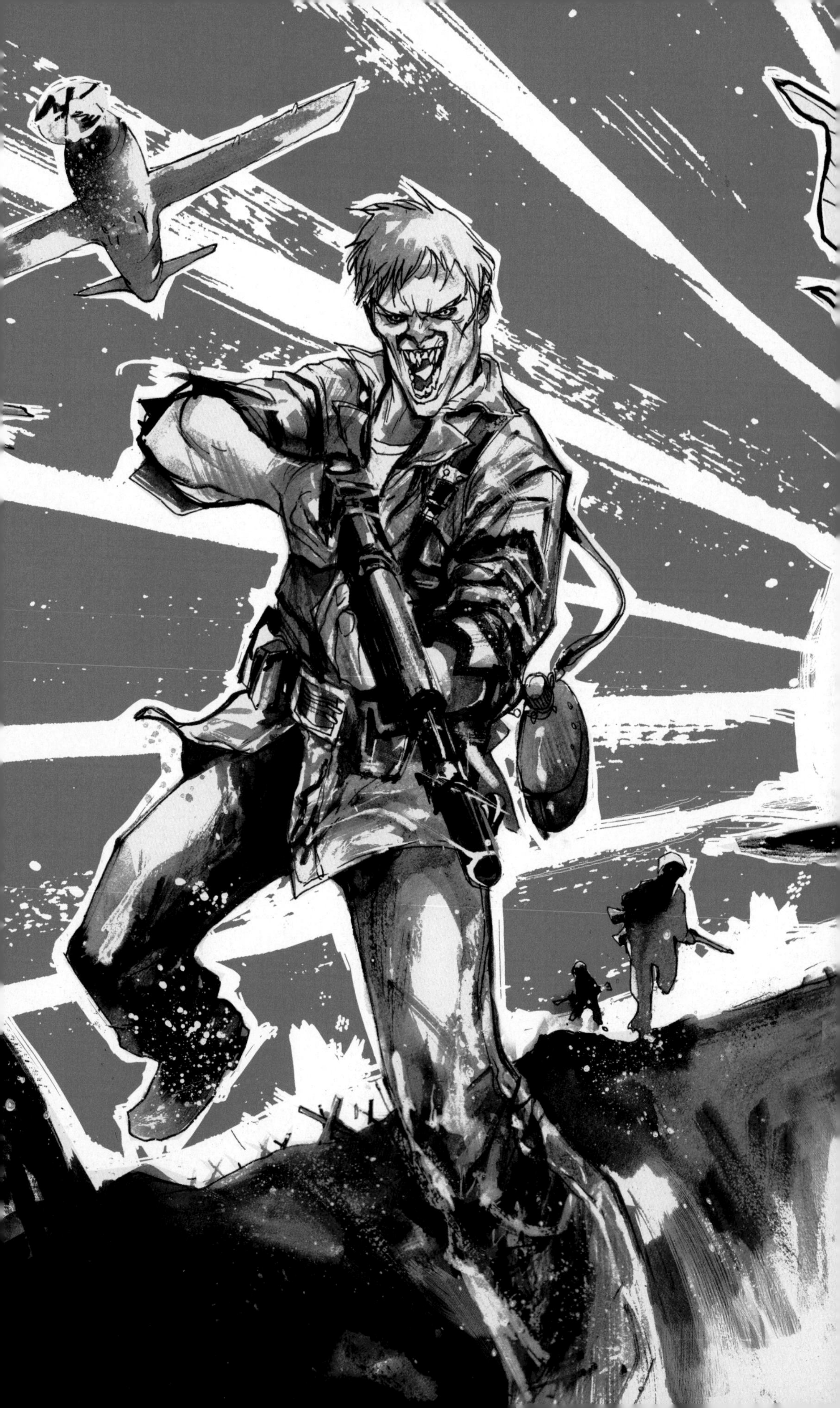

Ghost War
Part Two

Rafael Albuquerque
Artist and cover

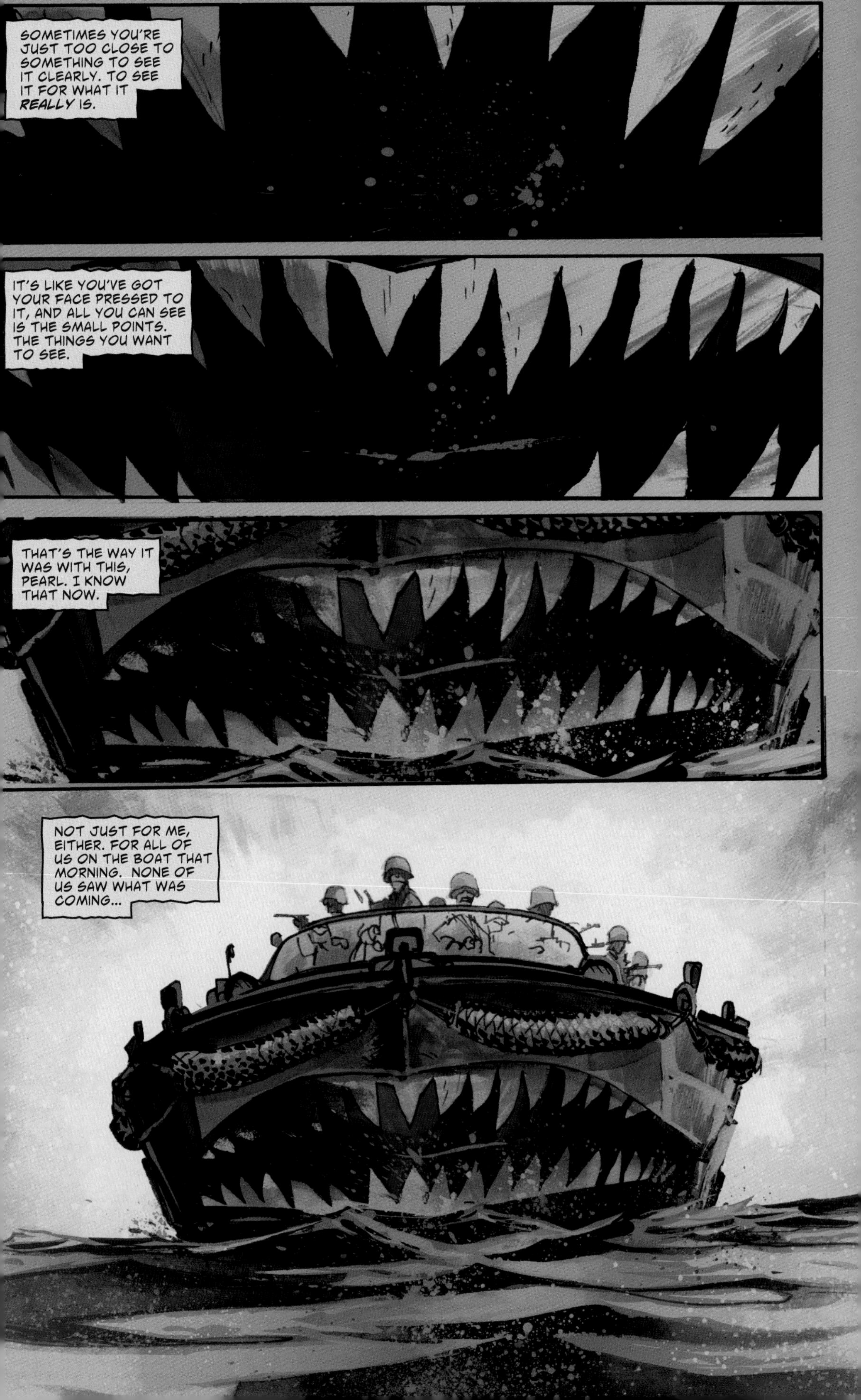
SOMETIMES YOU'RE JUST TOO CLOSE TO SOMETHING TO SEE IT CLEARLY. TO SEE IT FOR WHAT IT *REALLY* IS.
IT'S LIKE YOU'VE GOT YOUR FACE PRESSED TO IT, AND ALL YOU CAN SEE IS THE SMALL POINTS. THE THINGS YOU WANT TO SEE.
THAT'S THE WAY IT WAS WITH THIS, PEARL. I KNOW THAT NOW.
NOT JUST FOR ME, EITHER. FOR ALL OF US ON THE BOAT THAT MORNING. NONE OF US SAW WHAT WAS COMING...

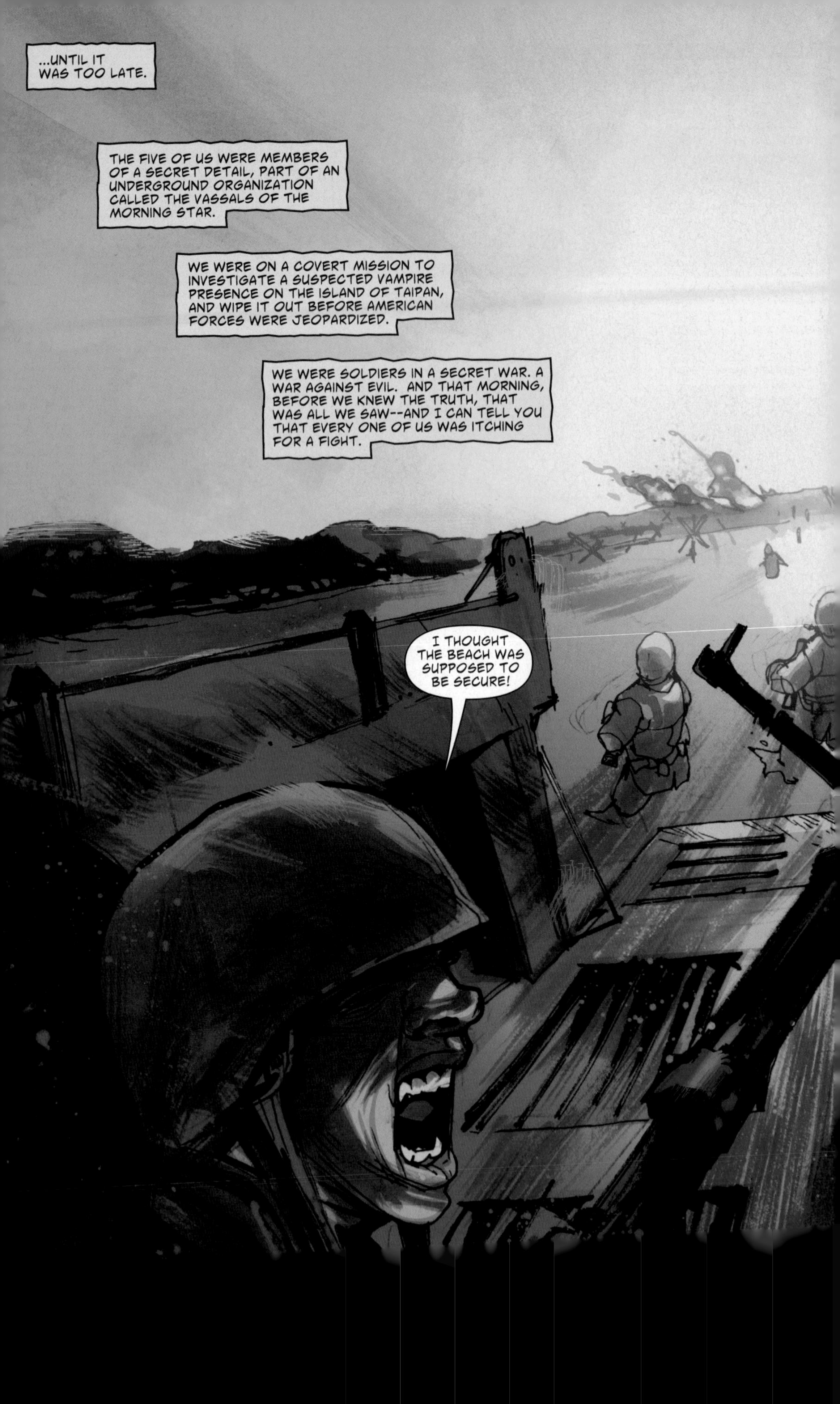
...UNTIL IT WAS TOO LATE.
THE FIVE OF US WERE MEMBERS OF A SECRET DETAIL, PART OF AN UNDERGROUND ORGANIZATION CALLED THE VASSALS OF THE MORNING STAR.
WE WERE ON A COVERT MISSION TO INVESTIGATE A SUSPECTED VAMPIRE PRESENCE ON THE ISLAND OF TAIPAN, AND WIPE IT OUT BEFORE AMERICAN FORCES WERE JEOPARDIZED.
WE WERE SOLDIERS IN A SECRET WAR. A WAR AGAINST EVIL. AND THAT MORNING, BEFORE WE KNEW THE TRUTH, THAT WAS ALL WE SAW--AND I CAN TELL YOU THAT EVERY ONE OF US WAS ITCHING FOR A FIGHT.
I THOUGHT THE BEACH WAS SUPPOSED TO BE SECURE!

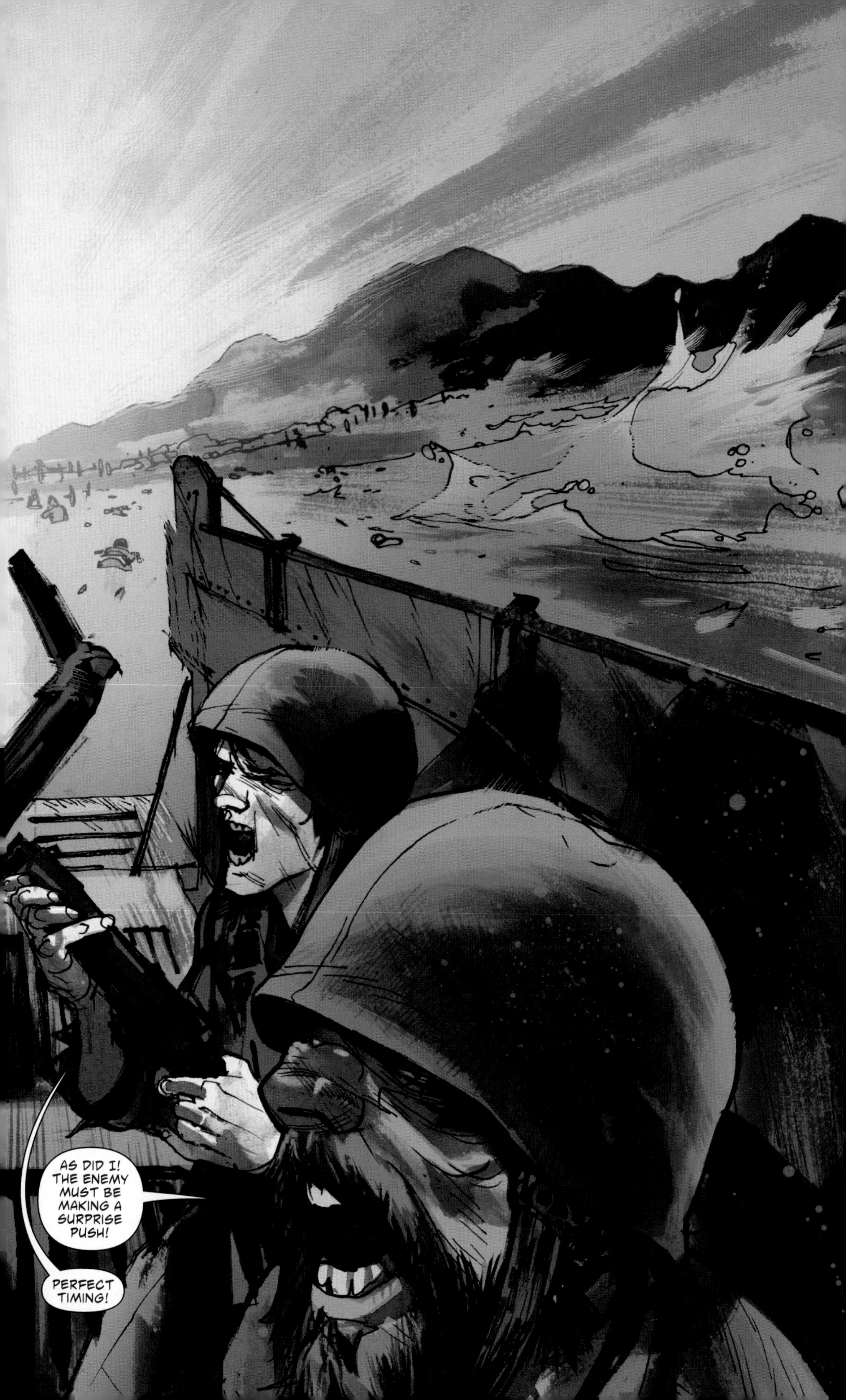
AS DID I! THE ENEMY MUST BE MAKING A SURPRISE PUSH!
PERFECT TIMING!

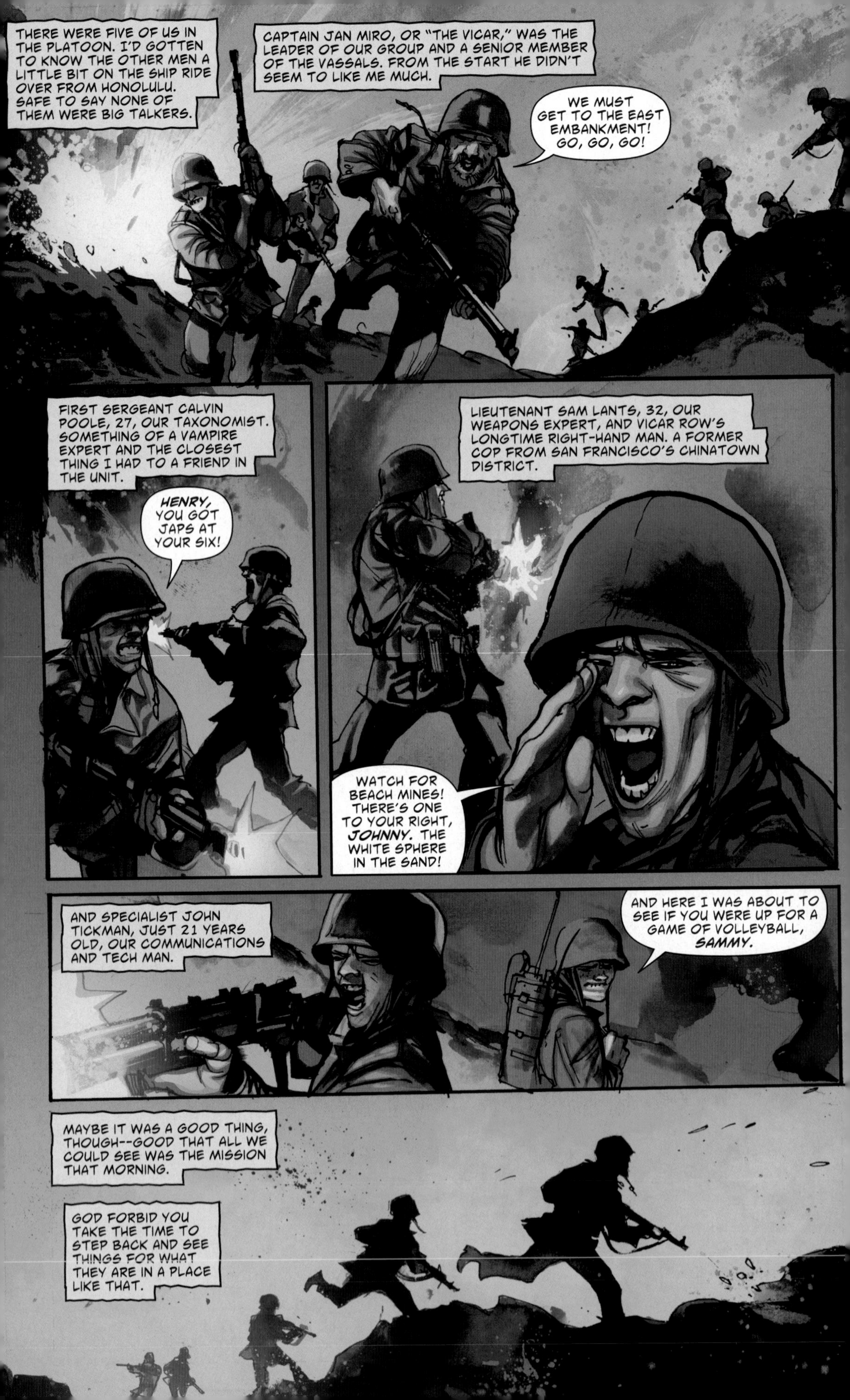
THERE WERE FIVE OF US IN THE PLATOON. I'D GOTTEN TO KNOW THE OTHER MEN A LITTLE BIT ON THE SHIP RIDE OVER FROM HONOLULU. SAFE TO SAY NONE OF THEM WERE BIG TALKERS.
CAPTAIN JAN MIRO, OR "THE VICAR," WAS THE LEADER OF OUR GROUP AND A SENIOR MEMBER OF THE VASSALS. FROM THE START HE DIDN'T SEEM TO LIKE ME MUCH.
WE MUST GET TO THE EAST EMBANKMENT! GO, GO, GO!
FIRST SERGEANT CALVIN POOLE, 27, OUR TAXONOMIST. SOMETHING OF A VAMPIRE EXPERT AND THE CLOSEST THING I HAD TO A FRIEND IN THE UNIT.
HENRY, YOU GOT JAPS AT YOUR SIX!
LIEUTENANT SAM LANTS, 32, OUR WEAPONS EXPERT, AND VICAR ROW'S LONGTIME RIGHT-HAND MAN. A FORMER COP FROM SAN FRANCISCO'S CHINATOWN DISTRICT.
WATCH FOR BEACH MINES! THERE'S ONE TO YOUR RIGHT, JOHNNY. THE WHITE SPHERE IN THE SAND!
AND SPECIALIST JOHN TICKMAN, JUST 21 YEARS OLD, OUR COMMUNICATIONS AND TECH MAN.
AND HERE I WAS ABOUT TO SEE IF YOU WERE UP FOR A GAME OF VOLLEYBALL, SAMMY.
MAYBE IT WAS A GOOD THING, THOUGH--GOOD THAT ALL WE COULD SEE WAS THE MISSION THAT MORNING.
GOD FORBID YOU TAKE THE TIME TO STEP BACK AND SEE THINGS FOR WHAT THEY ARE IN A PLACE LIKE THAT.

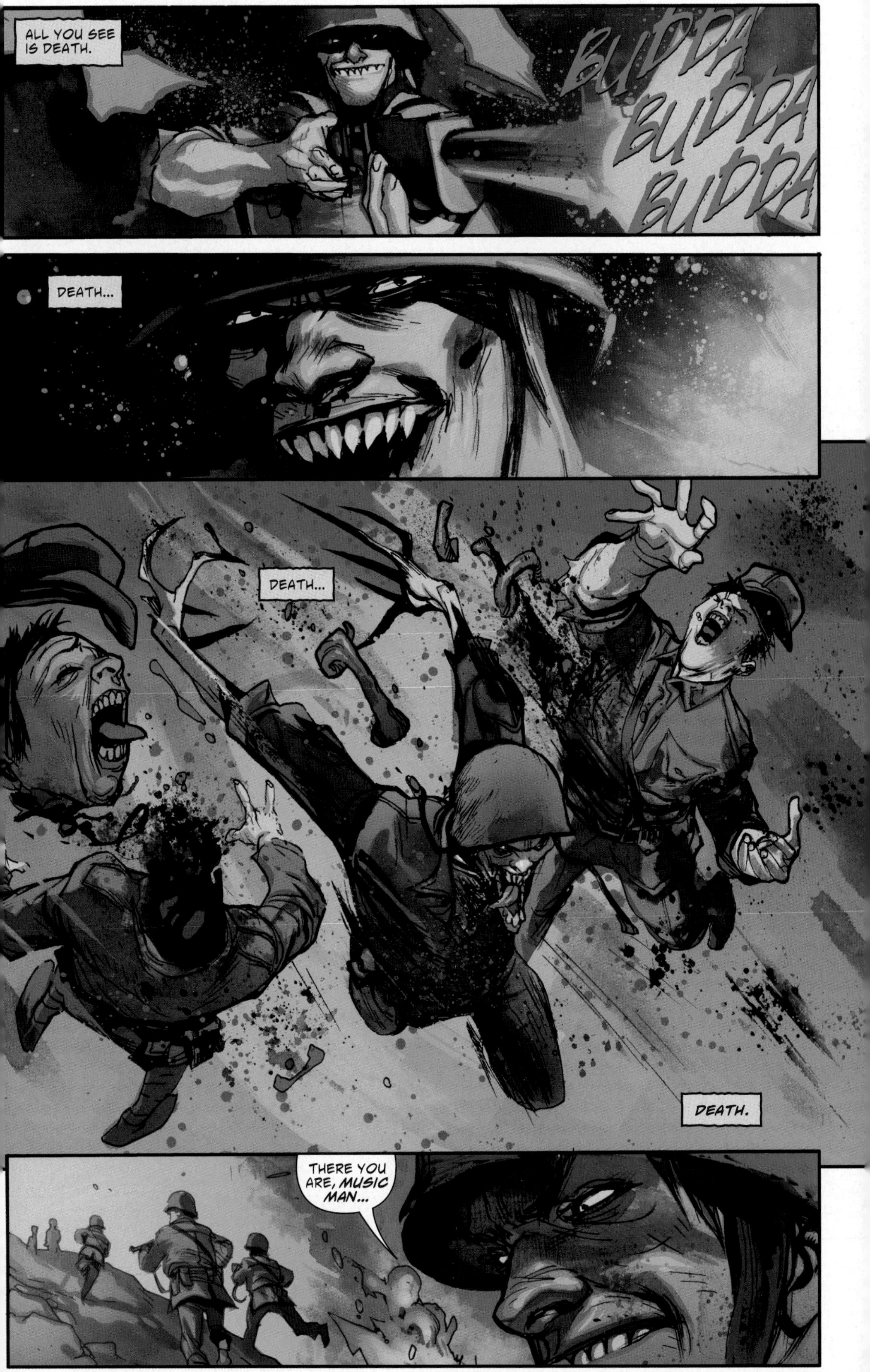
ALL YOU SEE IS DEATH.
BUDDA BUDDA BUDDA
DEATH...
DEATH...
DEATH.
THERE YOU ARE, MUSIC MAN...

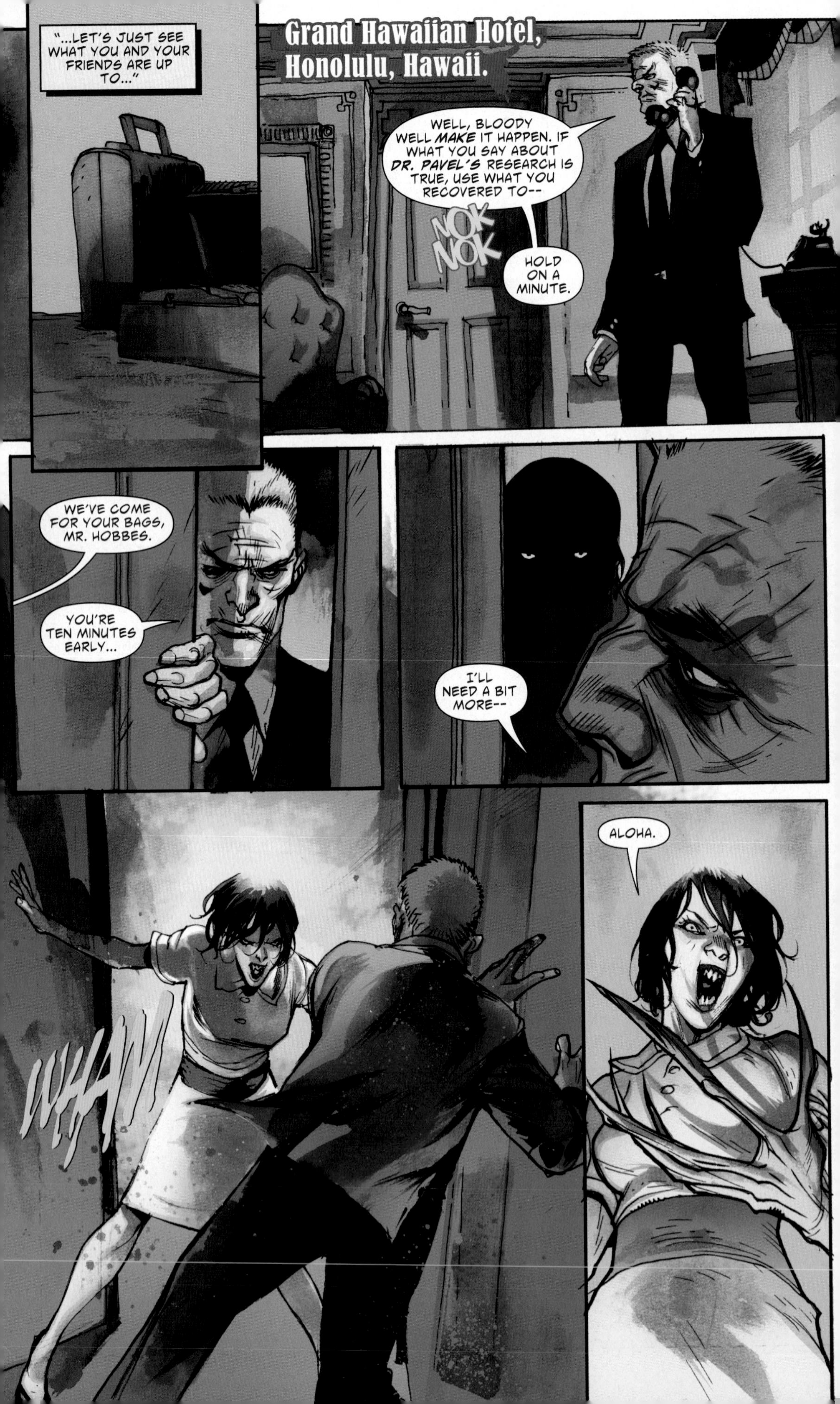
"...LET'S JUST SEE WHAT YOU AND YOUR FRIENDS ARE UP TO..."
Grand Hawaiian Hotel, Honolulu, Hawaii.
WELL, BLOODY WELL MAKE IT HAPPEN. IF WHAT YOU SAY ABOUT DR. PAVEL'S RESEARCH IS TRUE, USE WHAT YOU RECOVERED TO--
NOK NOK
HOLD ON A MINUTE.
WE'VE COME FOR YOUR BAGS, MR. HOBBES.
YOU'RE TEN MINUTES EARLY...
I'LL NEED A BIT MORE--
WHAM
ALOHA.

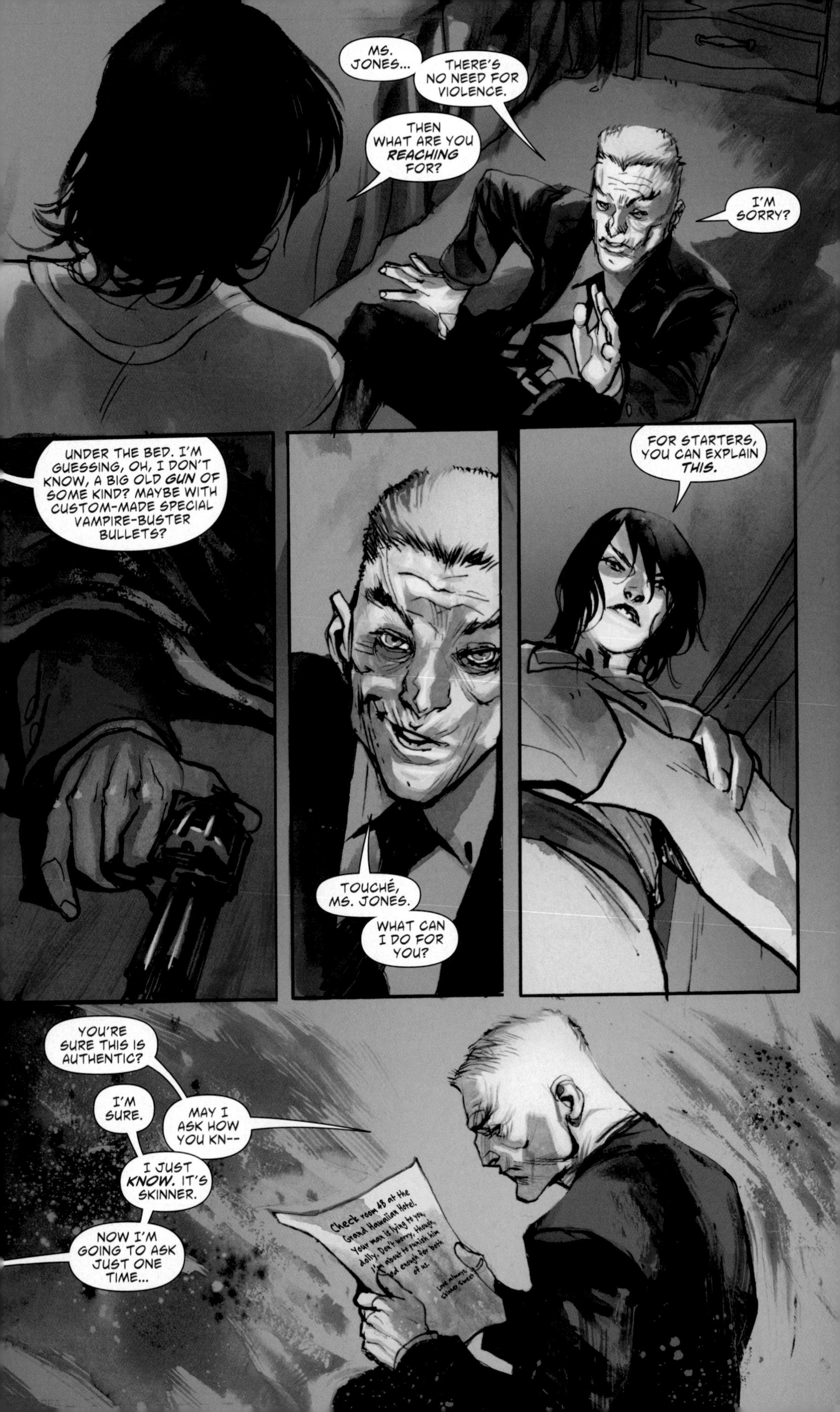
MS. JONES...
THERE'S NO NEED FOR VIOLENCE.
THEN WHAT ARE YOU *REACHING* FOR?
I'M SORRY?
UNDER THE BED. I'M GUESSING, OH, I DON'T KNOW, A BIG OLD *GUN* OF SOME KIND? MAYBE WITH CUSTOM-MADE SPECIAL VAMPIRE-BUSTER BULLETS?
TOUCHÉ, MS. JONES.
WHAT CAN I DO FOR YOU?
FOR STARTERS, YOU CAN EXPLAIN ***THIS.***
YOU'RE SURE THIS IS AUTHENTIC?
I'M SURE.
MAY I ASK HOW YOU KN--
I JUST ***KNOW.*** IT'S SKINNER.
NOW I'M GOING TO ASK JUST ONE TIME...
Check room 48 at the Grand Hawaiian Hotel. Your man is lying to you, dolly. Don't worry, though, I'm about to punish him od enough for both of us.
Love always, Skinner Sweet

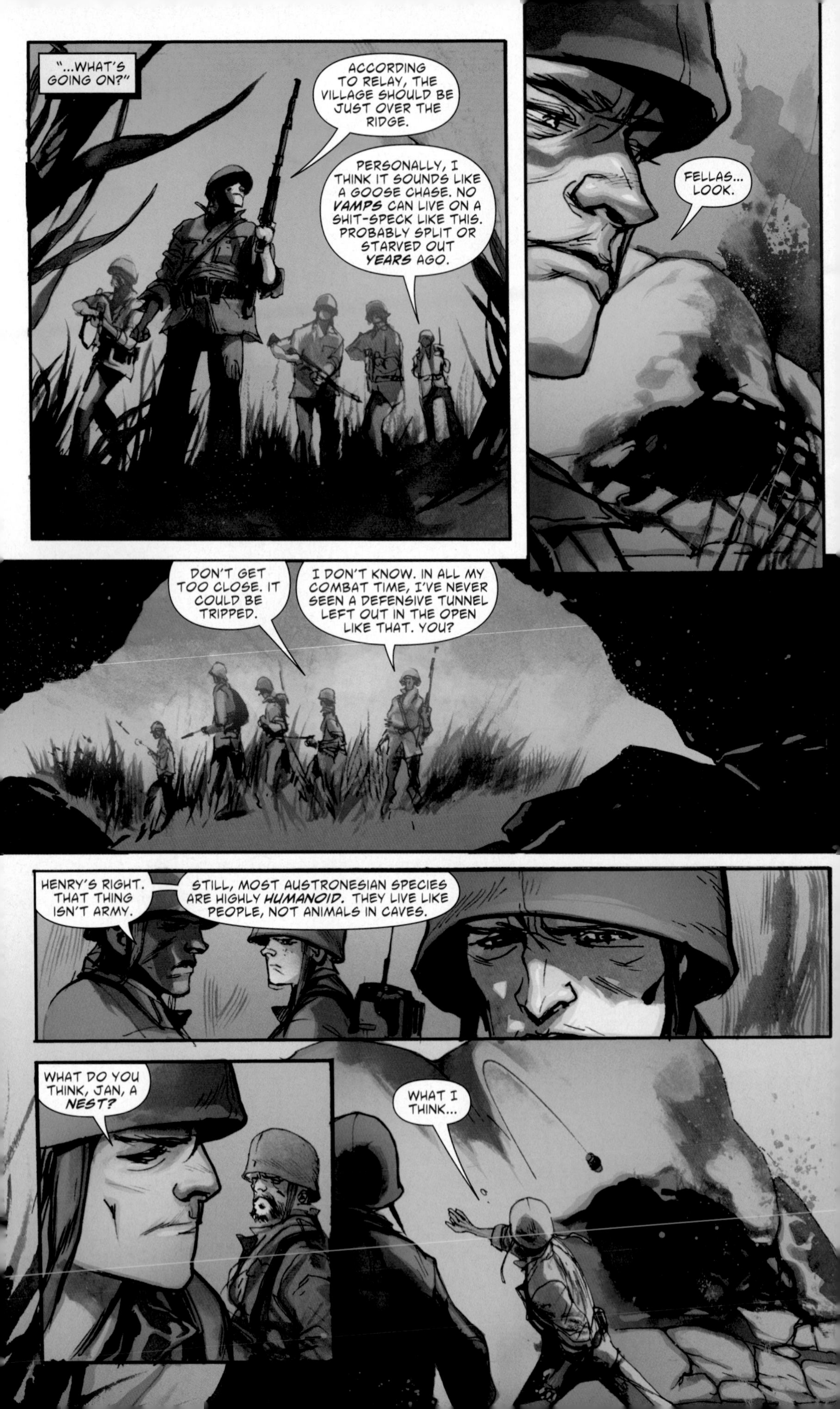
"...WHAT'S GOING ON?"
ACCORDING TO RELAY, THE VILLAGE SHOULD BE JUST OVER THE RIDGE.
PERSONALLY, I THINK IT SOUNDS LIKE A GOOSE CHASE. NO VAMPS CAN LIVE ON A SHIT-SPECK LIKE THIS. PROBABLY SPLIT OR STARVED OUT YEARS AGO.
FELLAS... LOOK.
DON'T GET TOO CLOSE. IT COULD BE TRIPPED.
I DON'T KNOW. IN ALL MY COMBAT TIME, I'VE NEVER SEEN A DEFENSIVE TUNNEL LEFT OUT IN THE OPEN LIKE THAT. YOU?
HENRY'S RIGHT. THAT THING ISN'T ARMY.
STILL, MOST AUSTRONESIAN SPECIES ARE HIGHLY HUMANOID. THEY LIVE LIKE PEOPLE, NOT ANIMALS IN CAVES.
WHAT DO YOU THINK, JAN, A NEST?
WHAT I THINK...

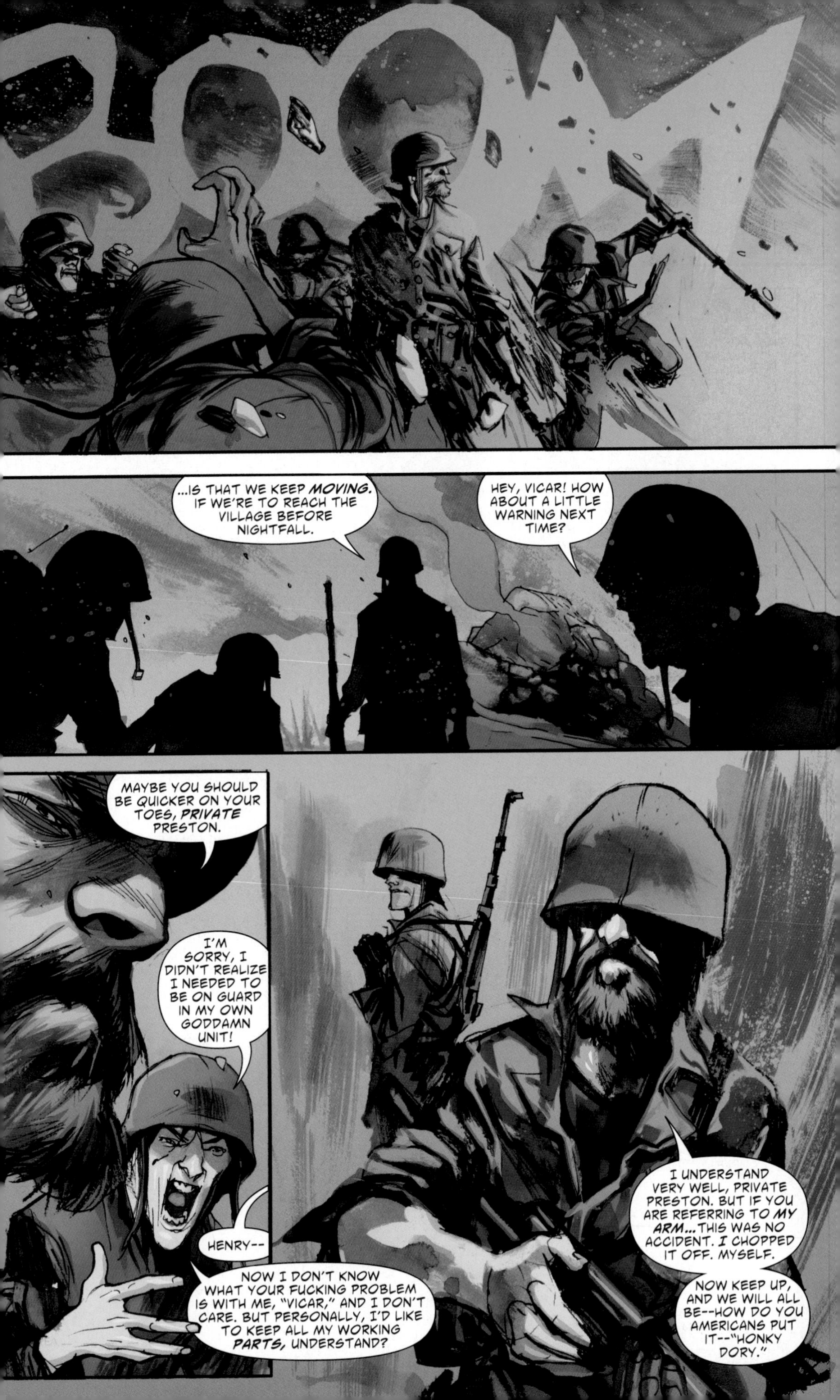
...IS THAT WE KEEP *MOVING.* IF WE'RE TO REACH THE VILLAGE BEFORE NIGHTFALL.
HEY, VICAR! HOW ABOUT A LITTLE WARNING NEXT TIME?
MAYBE YOU SHOULD BE QUICKER ON YOUR TOES, *PRIVATE* PRESTON.
I'M SORRY, I DIDN'T REALIZE I NEEDED TO BE ON GUARD IN MY OWN GODDAMN UNIT!
HENRY--
NOW I DON'T KNOW WHAT YOUR FUCKING PROBLEM IS WITH ME, "VICAR," AND I DON'T CARE. BUT PERSONALLY, I'D LIKE TO KEEP ALL MY WORKING *PARTS,* UNDERSTAND?
I UNDERSTAND VERY WELL, PRIVATE PRESTON. BUT IF YOU ARE REFERRING TO *MY ARM...* THIS WAS NO ACCIDENT. *I* CHOPPED IT OFF. MYSELF.
NOW KEEP UP, AND WE WILL ALL BE--HOW DO YOU AMERICANS PUT IT--"HONKY DORY."

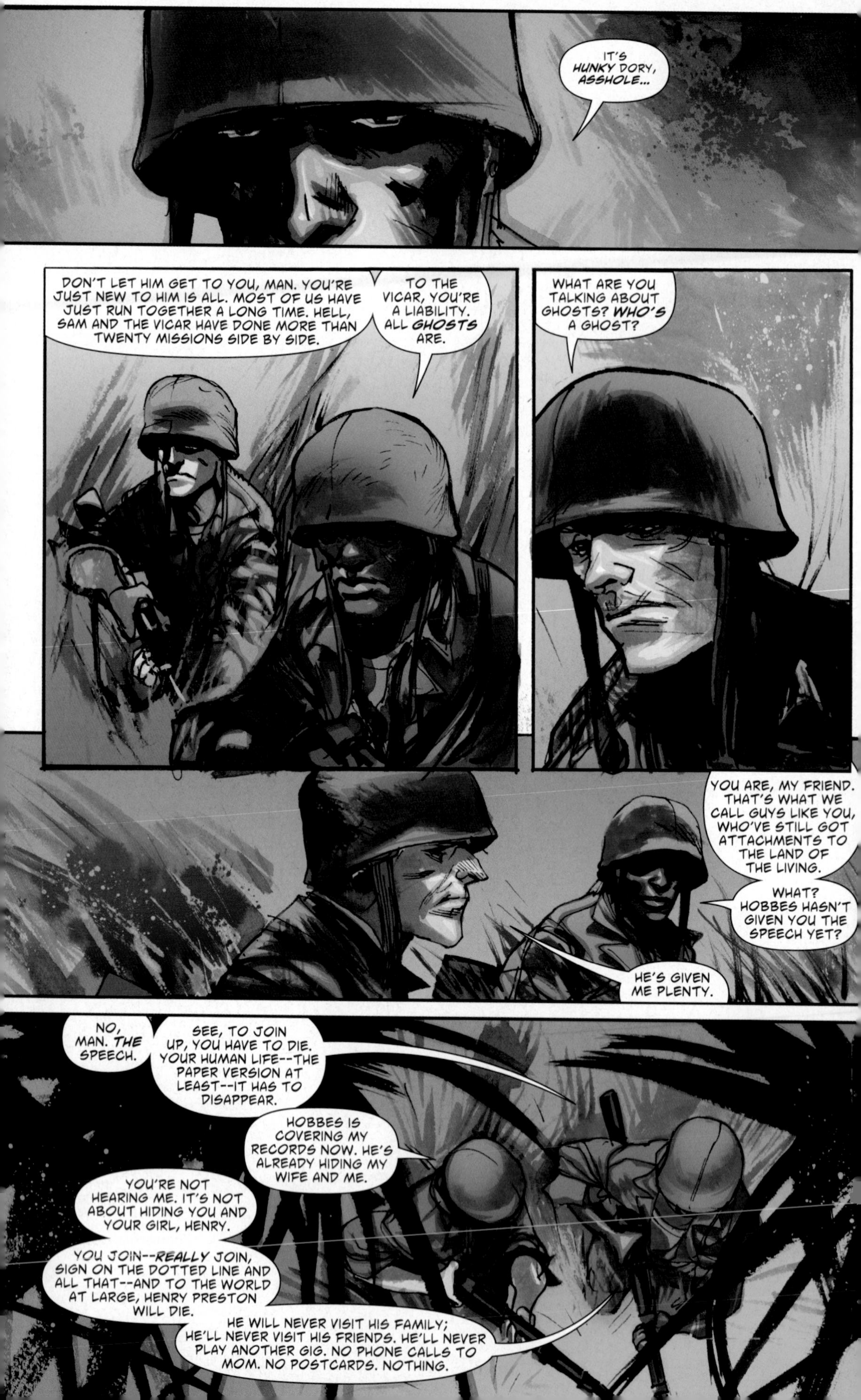

IT'S HUNKY DORY, ASSHOLE...
DON'T LET HIM GET TO YOU, MAN. YOU'RE JUST NEW TO HIM IS ALL. MOST OF US HAVE JUST RUN TOGETHER A LONG TIME. HELL, SAM AND THE VICAR HAVE DONE MORE THAN TWENTY MISSIONS SIDE BY SIDE.
TO THE VICAR, YOU'RE A LIABILITY. ALL GHOSTS ARE.
WHAT ARE YOU TALKING ABOUT GHOSTS? WHO'S A GHOST?
YOU ARE, MY FRIEND. THAT'S WHAT WE CALL GUYS LIKE YOU, WHO'VE STILL GOT ATTACHMENTS TO THE LAND OF THE LIVING.
WHAT? HOBBES HASN'T GIVEN YOU THE SPEECH YET?
HE'S GIVEN ME PLENTY.
NO, MAN. THE SPEECH.
SEE, TO JOIN UP, YOU HAVE TO DIE. YOUR HUMAN LIFE--THE PAPER VERSION AT LEAST--IT HAS TO DISAPPEAR.
HOBBES IS COVERING MY RECORDS NOW. HE'S ALREADY HIDING MY WIFE AND ME.
YOU'RE NOT HEARING ME. IT'S NOT ABOUT HIDING YOU AND YOUR GIRL, HENRY.
YOU JOIN--REALLY JOIN, SIGN ON THE DOTTED LINE AND ALL THAT--AND TO THE WORLD AT LARGE, HENRY PRESTON WILL DIE.
HE WILL NEVER VISIT HIS FAMILY; HE'LL NEVER VISIT HIS FRIENDS. HE'LL NEVER PLAY ANOTHER GIG. NO PHONE CALLS TO MOM. NO POSTCARDS. NOTHING.

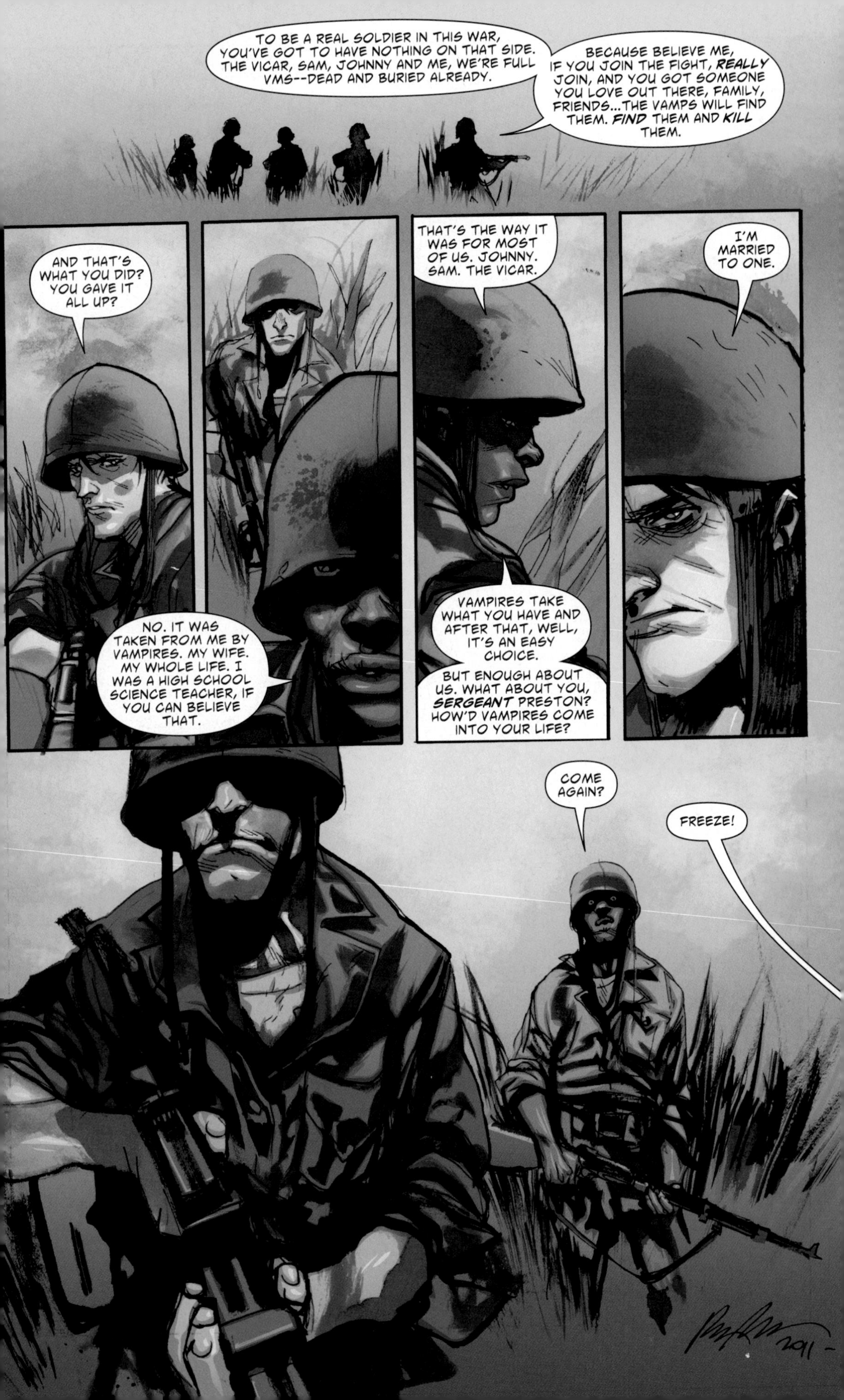
TO BE A REAL SOLDIER IN THIS WAR, YOU'VE GOT TO HAVE NOTHING ON THAT SIDE. THE VICAR, SAM, JOHNNY AND ME, WE'RE FULL VMS--DEAD AND BURIED ALREADY.
BECAUSE BELIEVE ME, IF YOU JOIN THE FIGHT, REALLY JOIN, AND YOU GOT SOMEONE YOU LOVE OUT THERE, FAMILY, FRIENDS...THE VAMPS WILL FIND THEM. FIND THEM AND KILL THEM.
AND THAT'S WHAT YOU DID? YOU GAVE IT ALL UP?
NO. IT WAS TAKEN FROM ME BY VAMPIRES. MY WIFE. MY WHOLE LIFE. I WAS A HIGH SCHOOL SCIENCE TEACHER, IF YOU CAN BELIEVE THAT.
THAT'S THE WAY IT WAS FOR MOST OF US. JOHNNY. SAM. THE VICAR.
VAMPIRES TAKE WHAT YOU HAVE AND AFTER THAT, WELL, IT'S AN EASY CHOICE.
BUT ENOUGH ABOUT US. WHAT ABOUT YOU, SERGEANT PRESTON? HOW'D VAMPIRES COME INTO YOUR LIFE?
I'M MARRIED TO ONE.
COME AGAIN?
FREEZE!

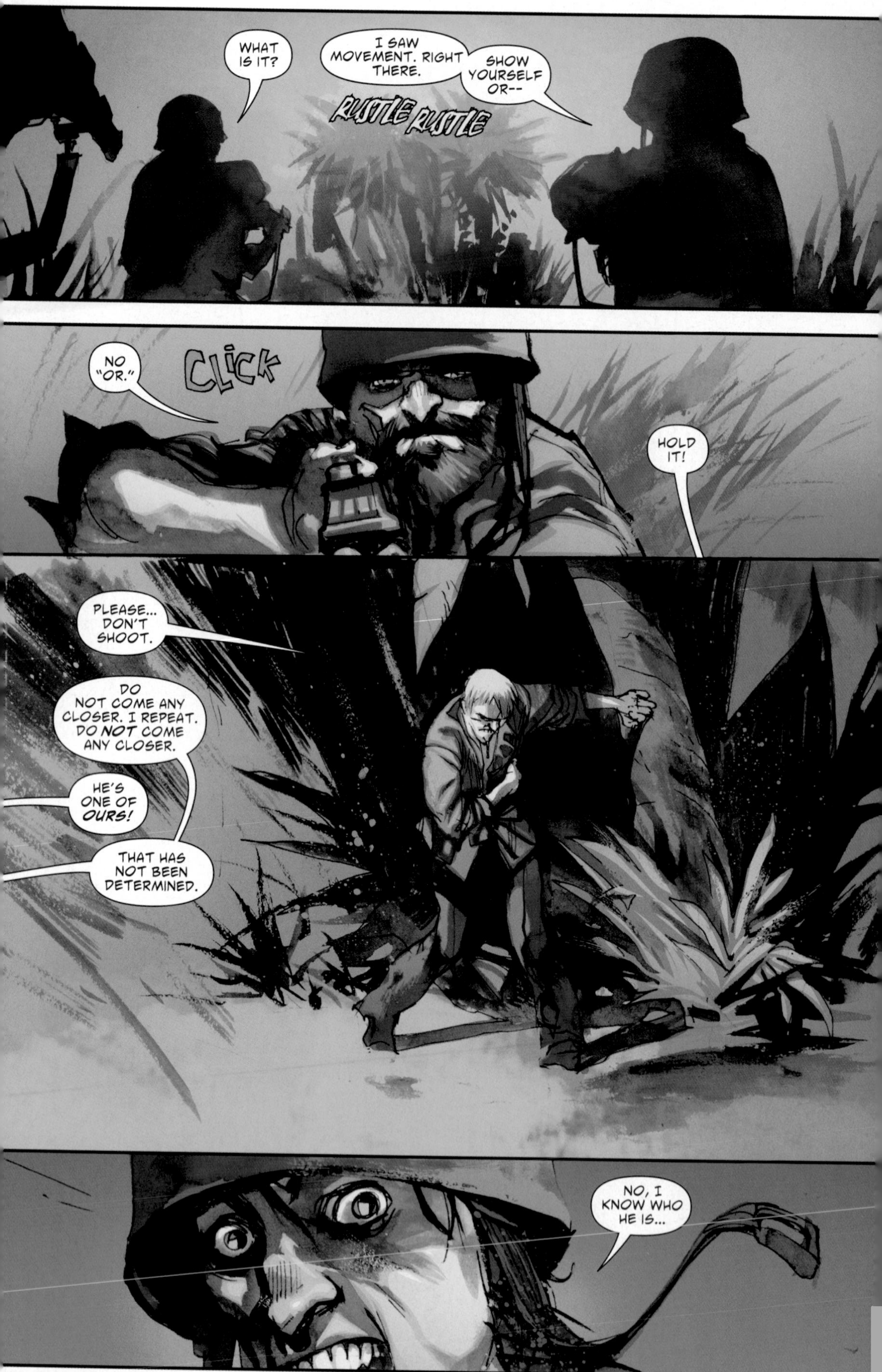
WHAT IS IT?
I SAW MOVEMENT. RIGHT THERE.
SHOW YOURSELF OR--
RUSTLE RUSTLE
NO "OR."
CLICK
HOLD IT!
PLEASE... DON'T SHOOT.
DO NOT COME ANY CLOSER. I REPEAT. DO NOT COME ANY CLOSER.
HE'S ONE OF OURS!
THAT HAS NOT BEEN DETERMINED.
NO, I KNOW WHO HE IS...

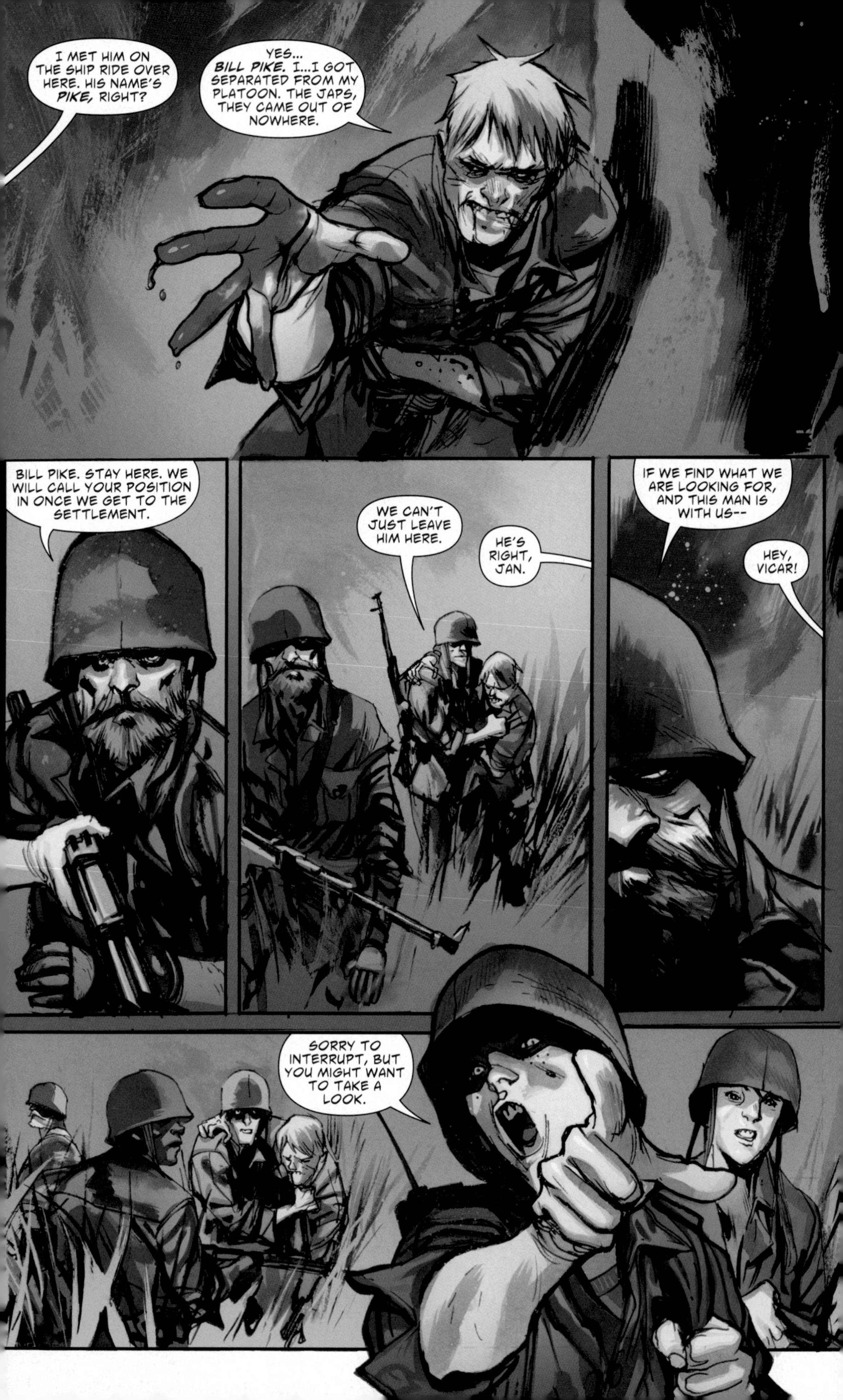
I MET HIM ON THE SHIP RIDE OVER HERE. HIS NAME'S *PIKE,* RIGHT?
YES... *BILL PIKE.* I...I GOT SEPARATED FROM MY PLATOON. THE JAPS, THEY CAME OUT OF NOWHERE.
BILL PIKE. STAY HERE. WE WILL CALL YOUR POSITION IN ONCE WE GET TO THE SETTLEMENT.
WE CAN'T JUST LEAVE HIM HERE.
HE'S RIGHT, JAN.
IF WE FIND WHAT WE ARE LOOKING FOR, AND THIS MAN IS WITH US--
HEY, VICAR!
SORRY TO INTERRUPT, BUT YOU MIGHT WANT TO TAKE A LOOK.

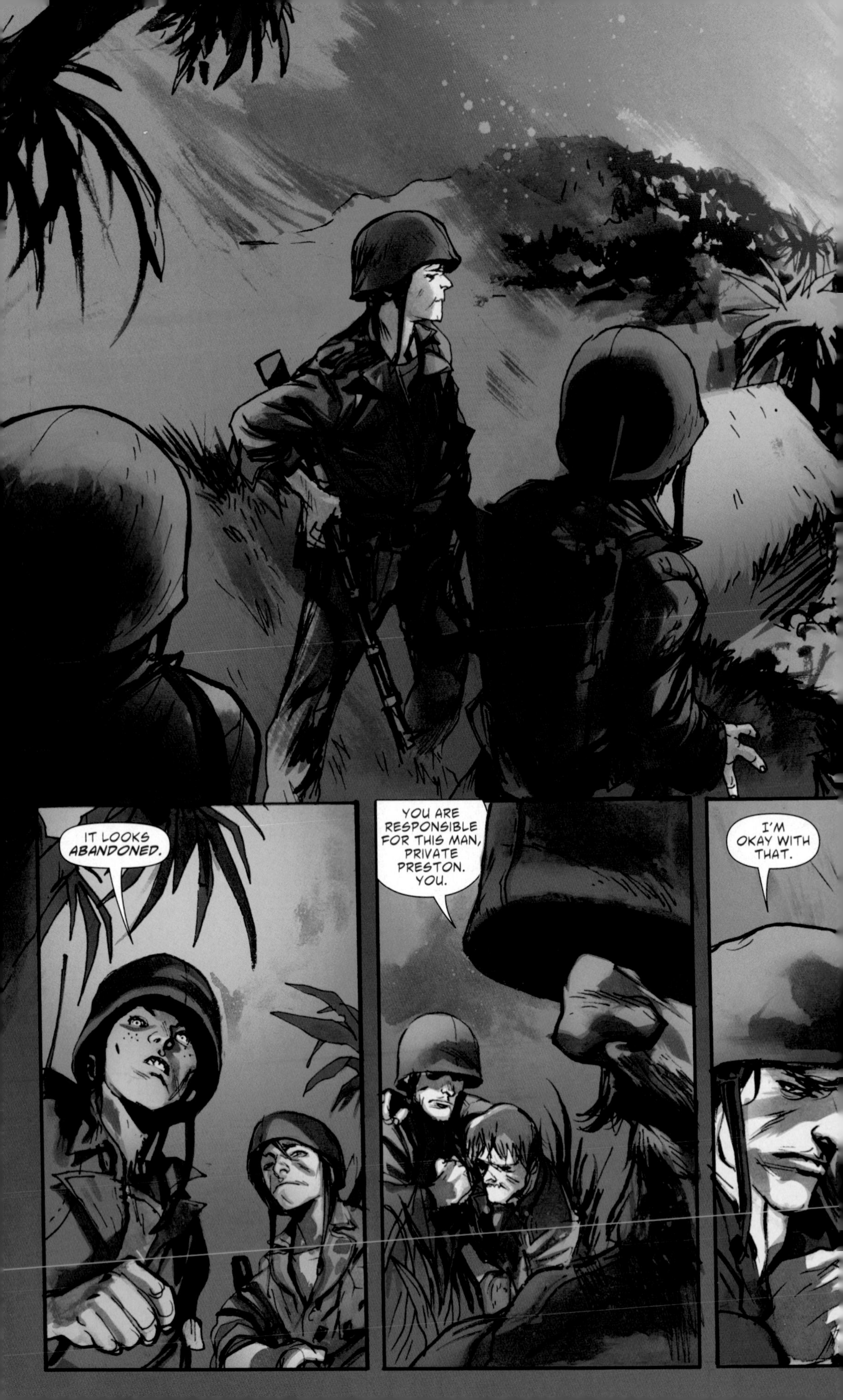
IT LOOKS ABANDONED.
YOU ARE RESPONSIBLE FOR THIS MAN, PRIVATE PRESTON. YOU.
I'M OKAY WITH THAT.

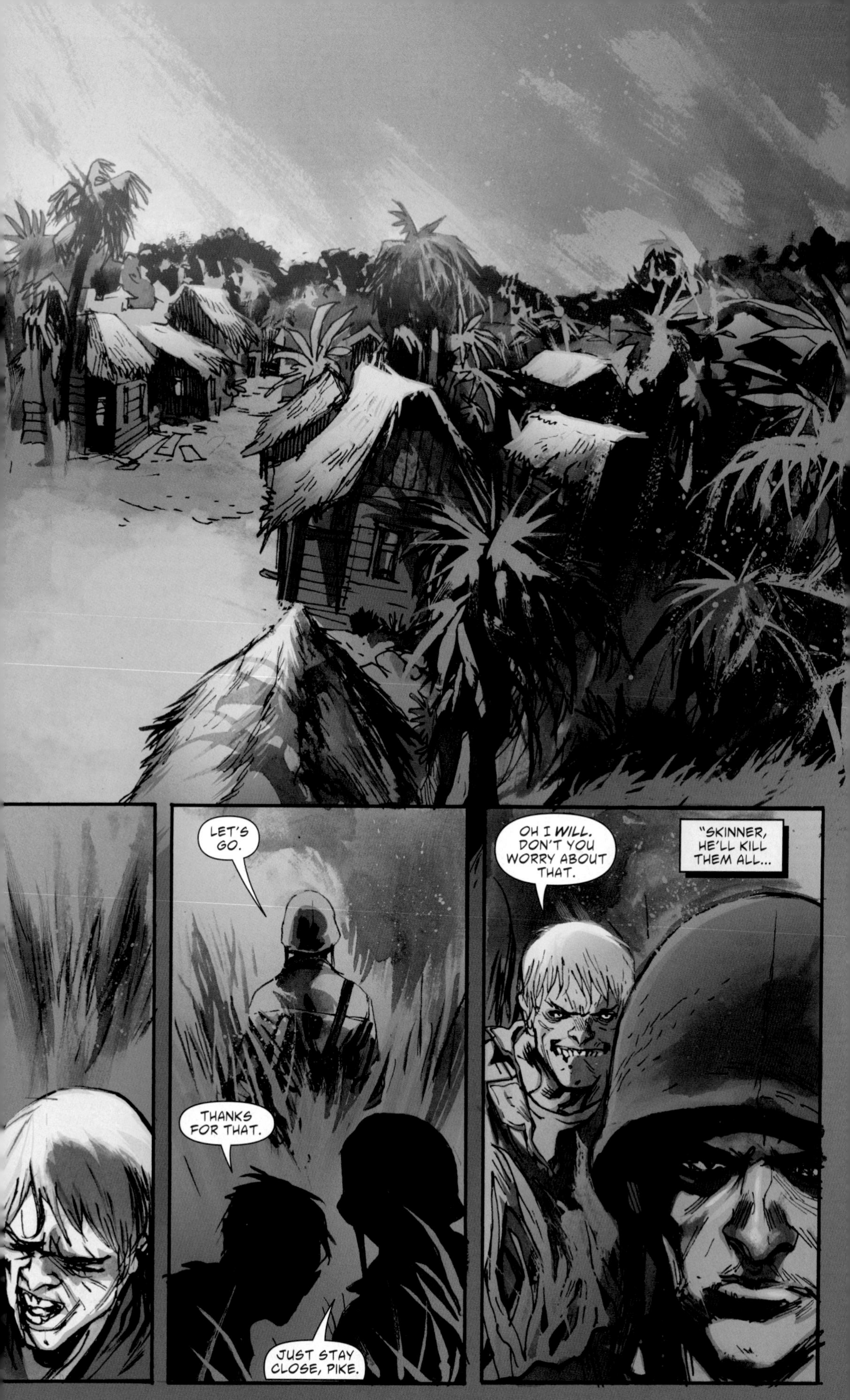
LET'S GO.
THANKS FOR THAT.
JUST STAY CLOSE, PIKE.
OH I *WILL*. DON'T YOU WORRY ABOUT THAT.
"SKINNER, HE'LL KILL THEM ALL...

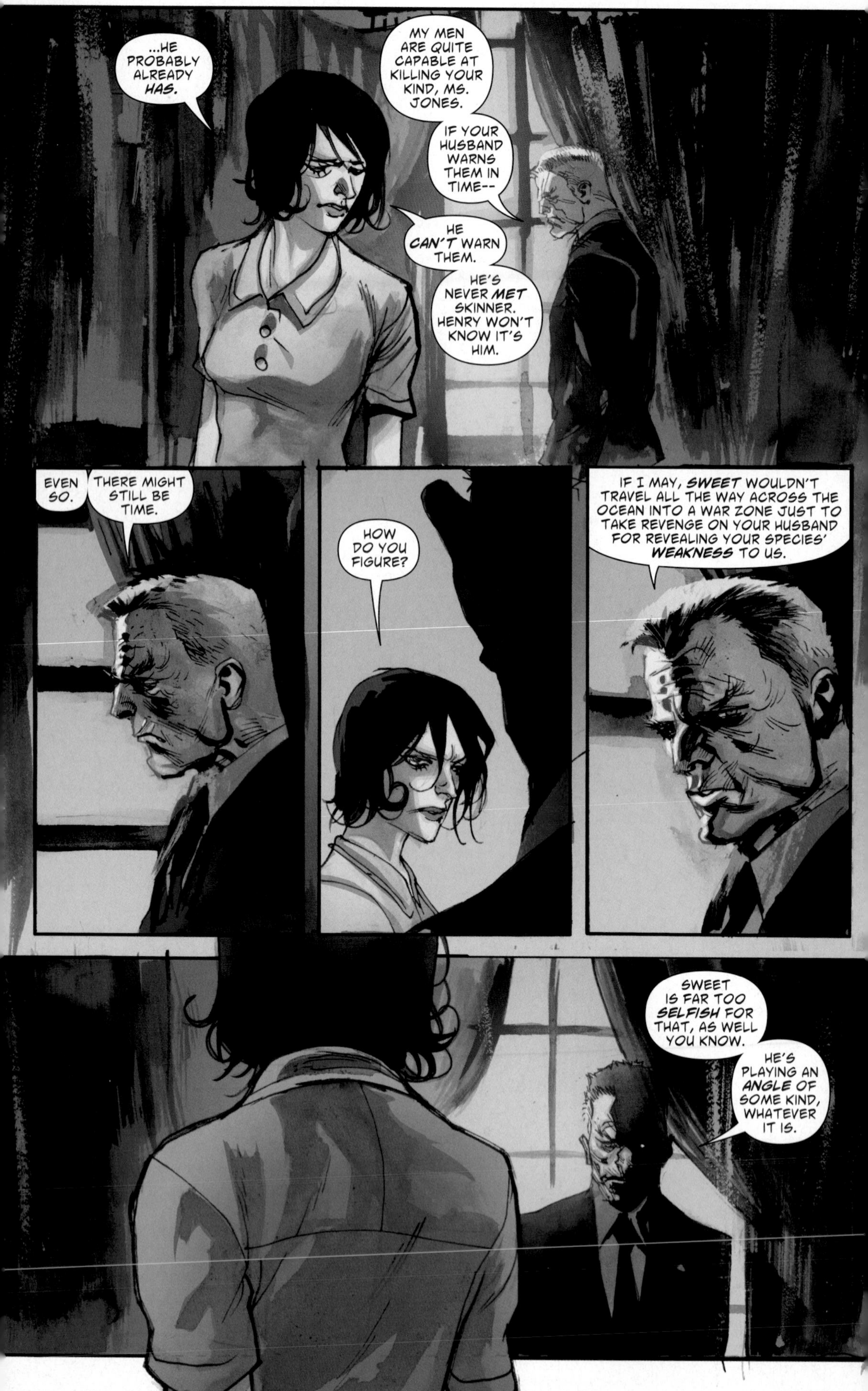
...HE PROBABLY ALREADY HAS.
MY MEN ARE QUITE CAPABLE AT KILLING YOUR KIND, MS. JONES.
IF YOUR HUSBAND WARNS THEM IN TIME--
HE CAN'T WARN THEM.
HE'S NEVER MET SKINNER. HENRY WON'T KNOW IT'S HIM.
EVEN SO.
THERE MIGHT STILL BE TIME.
HOW DO YOU FIGURE?
IF I MAY, SWEET WOULDN'T TRAVEL ALL THE WAY ACROSS THE OCEAN INTO A WAR ZONE JUST TO TAKE REVENGE ON YOUR HUSBAND FOR REVEALING YOUR SPECIES' WEAKNESS TO US.
SWEET IS FAR TOO SELFISH FOR THAT, AS WELL YOU KNOW.
HE'S PLAYING AN ANGLE OF SOME KIND, WHATEVER IT IS.

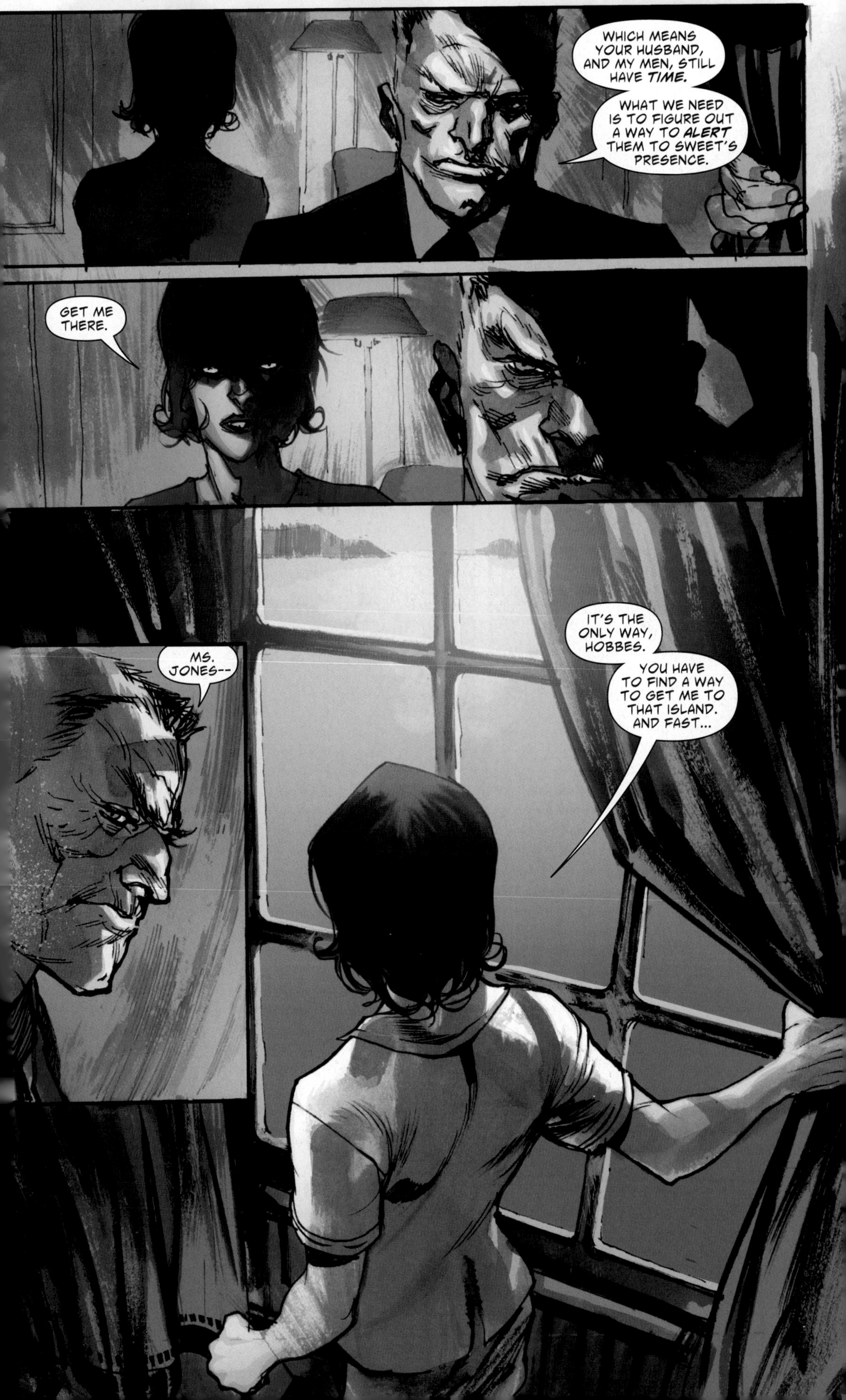
WHICH MEANS YOUR HUSBAND, AND MY MEN, STILL HAVE *TIME.*
WHAT WE NEED IS TO FIGURE OUT A WAY TO *ALERT* THEM TO SWEET'S PRESENCE.
GET ME THERE.
MS. JONES--
IT'S THE ONLY WAY, HOBBES.
YOU HAVE TO FIND A WAY TO GET ME TO THAT ISLAND. AND FAST...

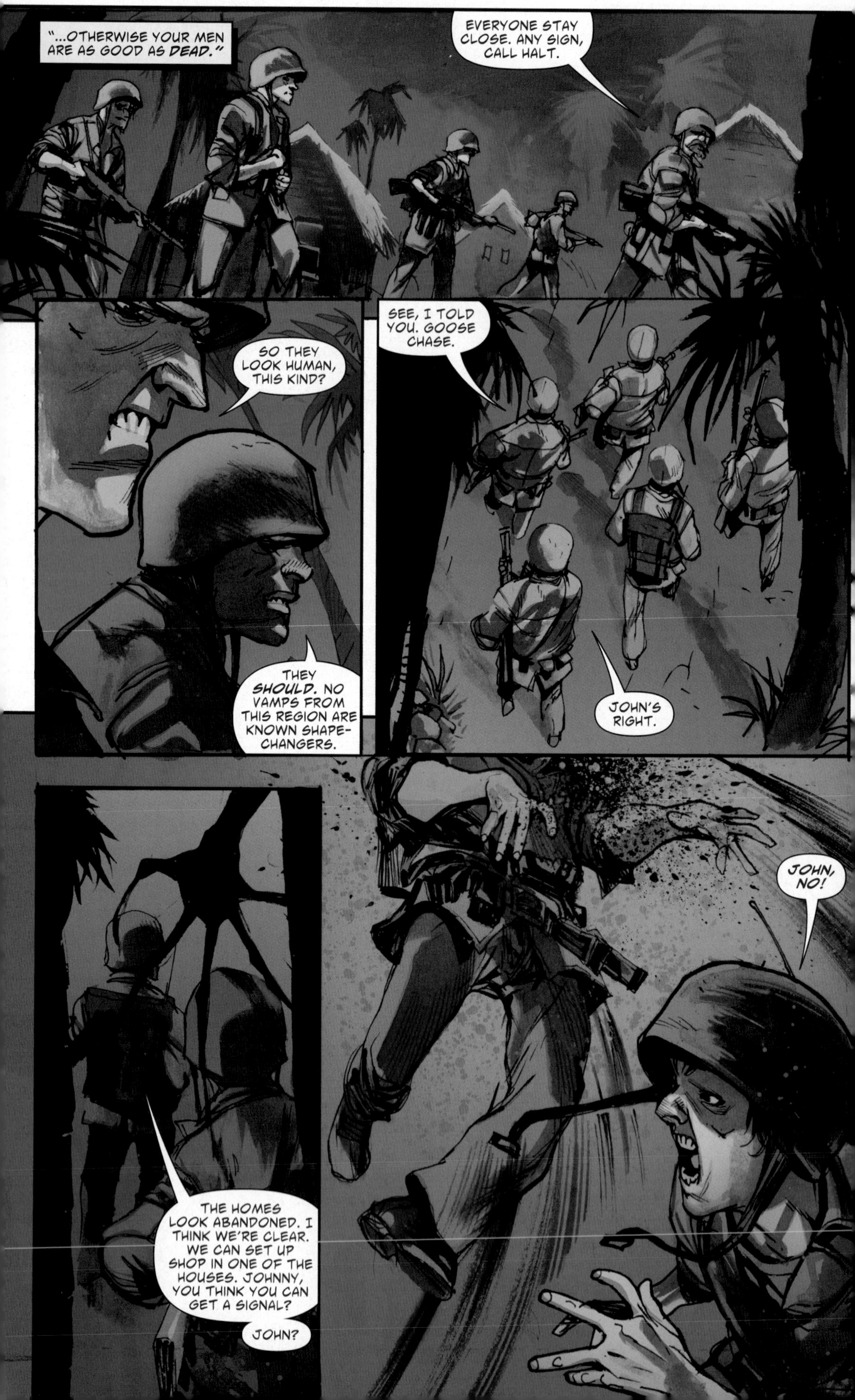
"...OTHERWISE YOUR MEN ARE AS GOOD AS DEAD."
EVERYONE STAY CLOSE. ANY SIGN, CALL HALT.
SO THEY LOOK HUMAN, THIS KIND?
THEY SHOULD. NO VAMPS FROM THIS REGION ARE KNOWN SHAPE-CHANGERS.
SEE, I TOLD YOU. GOOSE CHASE.
JOHN'S RIGHT.
THE HOMES LOOK ABANDONED. I THINK WE'RE CLEAR. WE CAN SET UP SHOP IN ONE OF THE HOUSES. JOHNNY, YOU THINK YOU CAN GET A SIGNAL?
JOHN?
JOHN, NO!

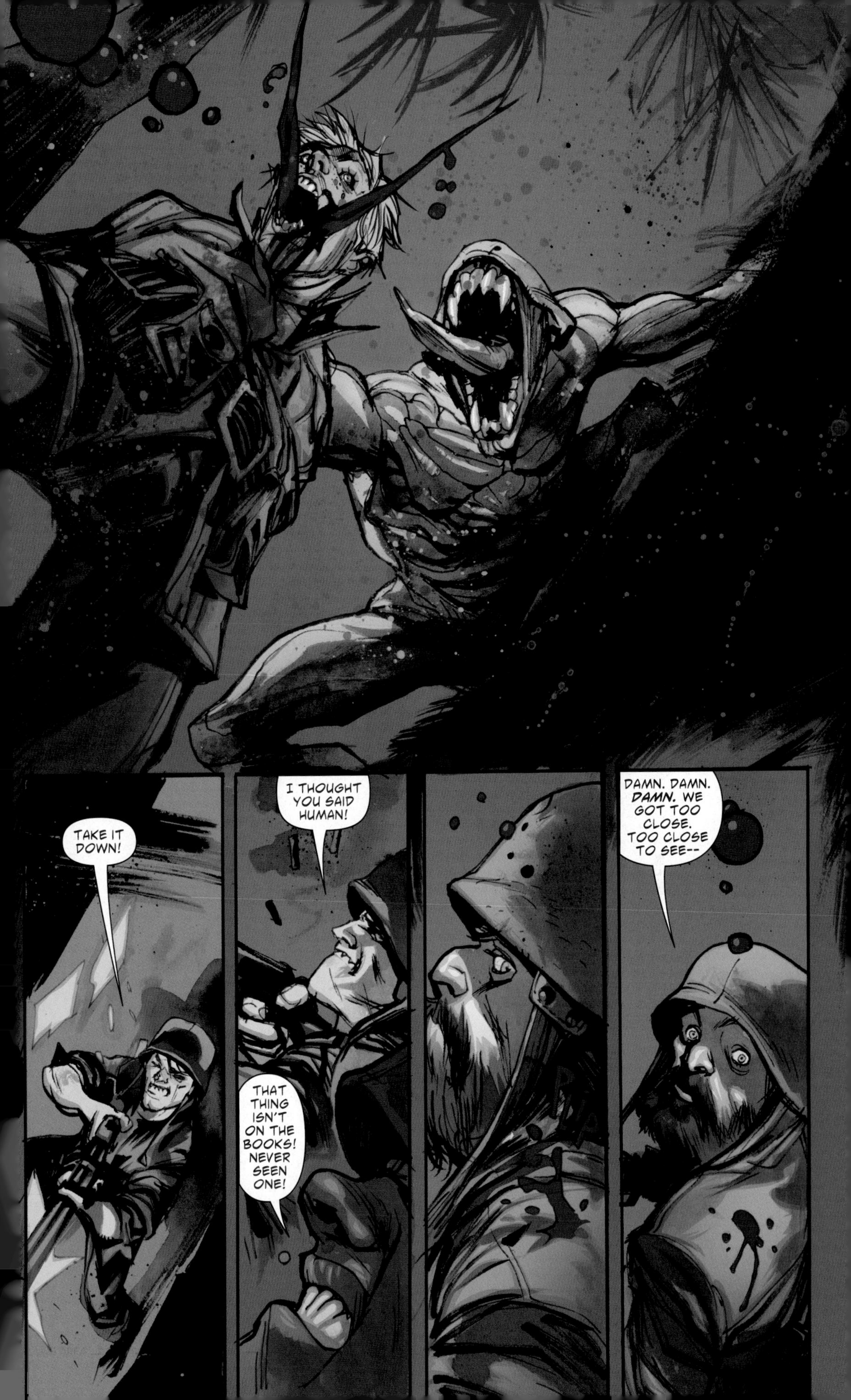
TAKE IT DOWN!
I THOUGHT YOU SAID HUMAN!
THAT THING ISN'T ON THE BOOKS! NEVER SEEN ONE!
DAMN. DAMN. DAMN. WE GOT TOO CLOSE. TOO CLOSE TO SEE--

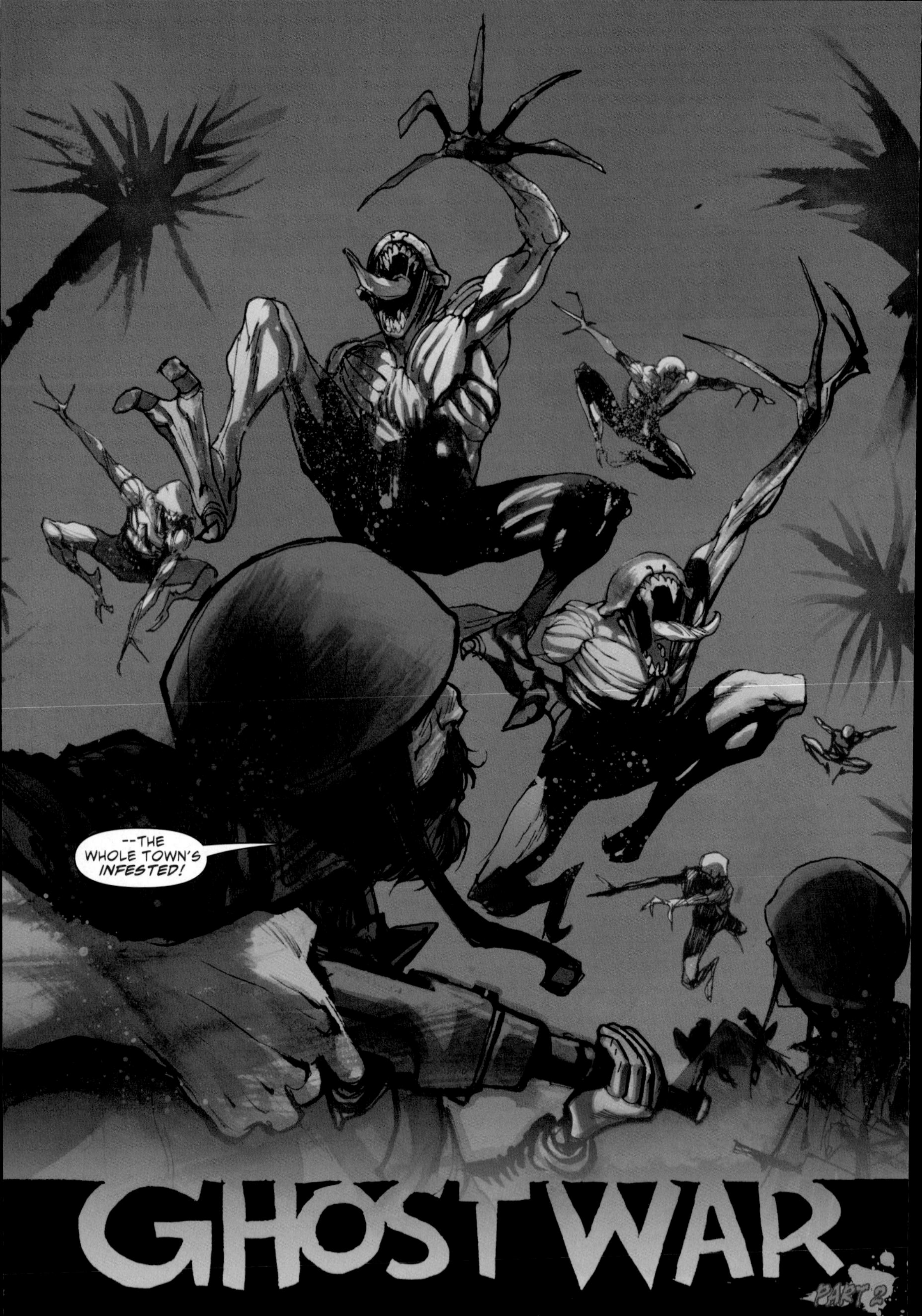
--THE WHOLE TOWN'S INFESTED!
GHOST WAR
PART 2

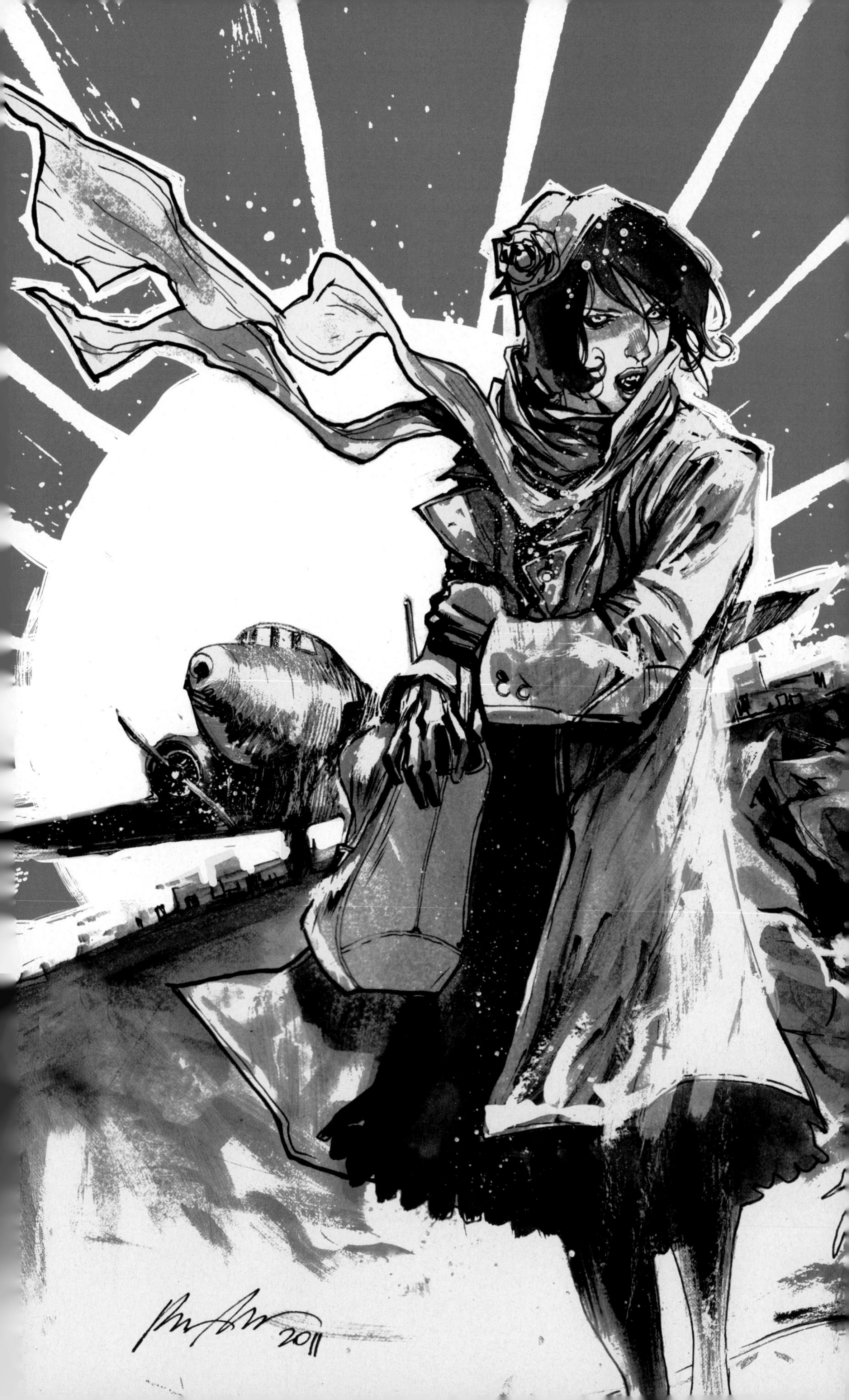
2011

Ghost War

Part Three

Rafael Albuquerque

Artist and cover

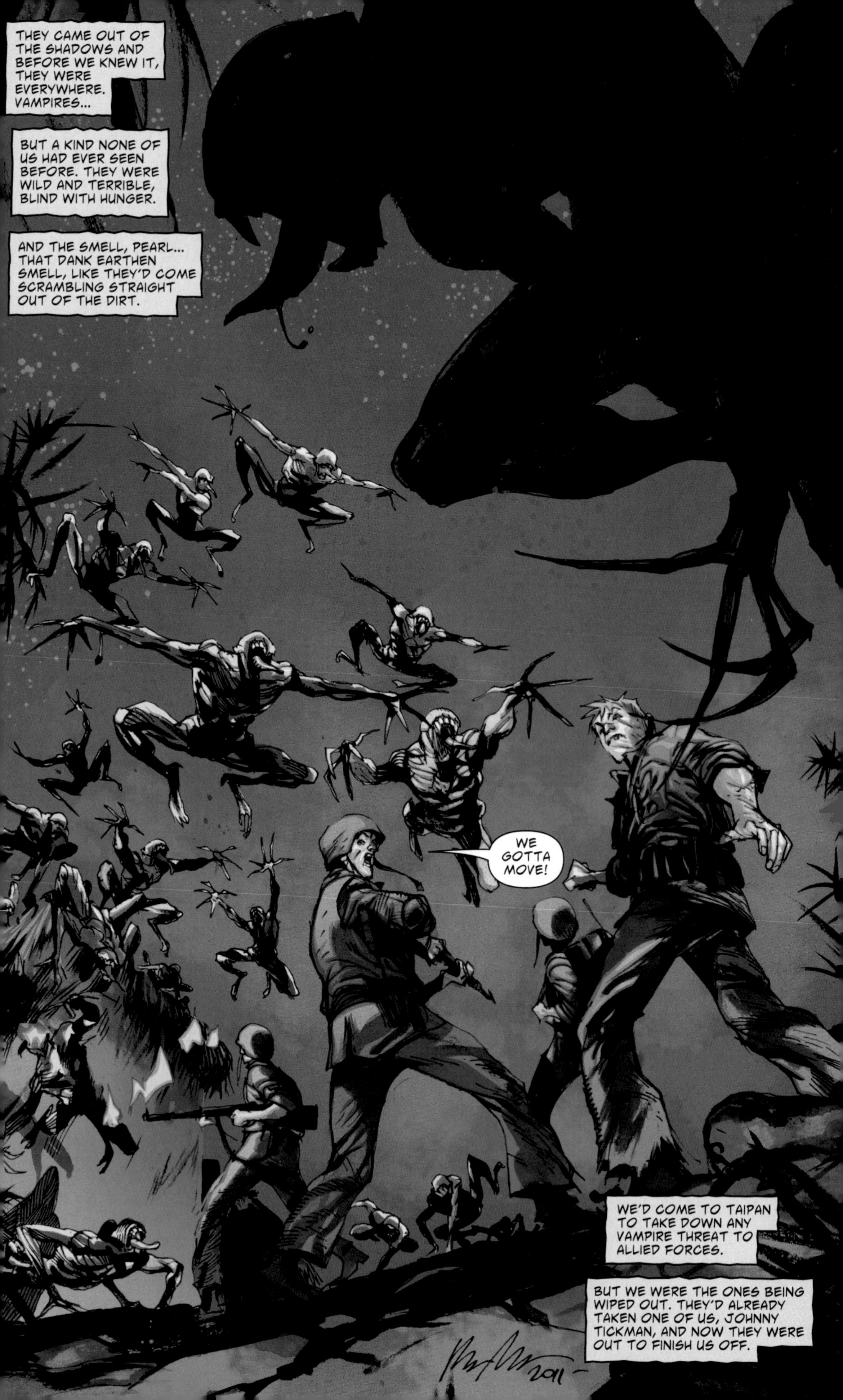

THEY CAME OUT OF THE SHADOWS AND BEFORE WE KNEW IT, THEY WERE EVERYWHERE. VAMPIRES...
BUT A KIND NONE OF US HAD EVER SEEN BEFORE. THEY WERE WILD AND TERRIBLE, BLIND WITH HUNGER.
AND THE SMELL, PEARL... THAT DANK EARTHEN SMELL, LIKE THEY'D COME SCRAMBLING STRAIGHT OUT OF THE DIRT.
WE GOTTA MOVE!
WE'D COME TO TAIPAN TO TAKE DOWN ANY VAMPIRE THREAT TO ALLIED FORCES.
BUT WE WERE THE ONES BEING WIPED OUT. THEY'D ALREADY TAKEN ONE OF US, JOHNNY TICKMAN, AND NOW THEY WERE OUT TO FINISH US OFF.

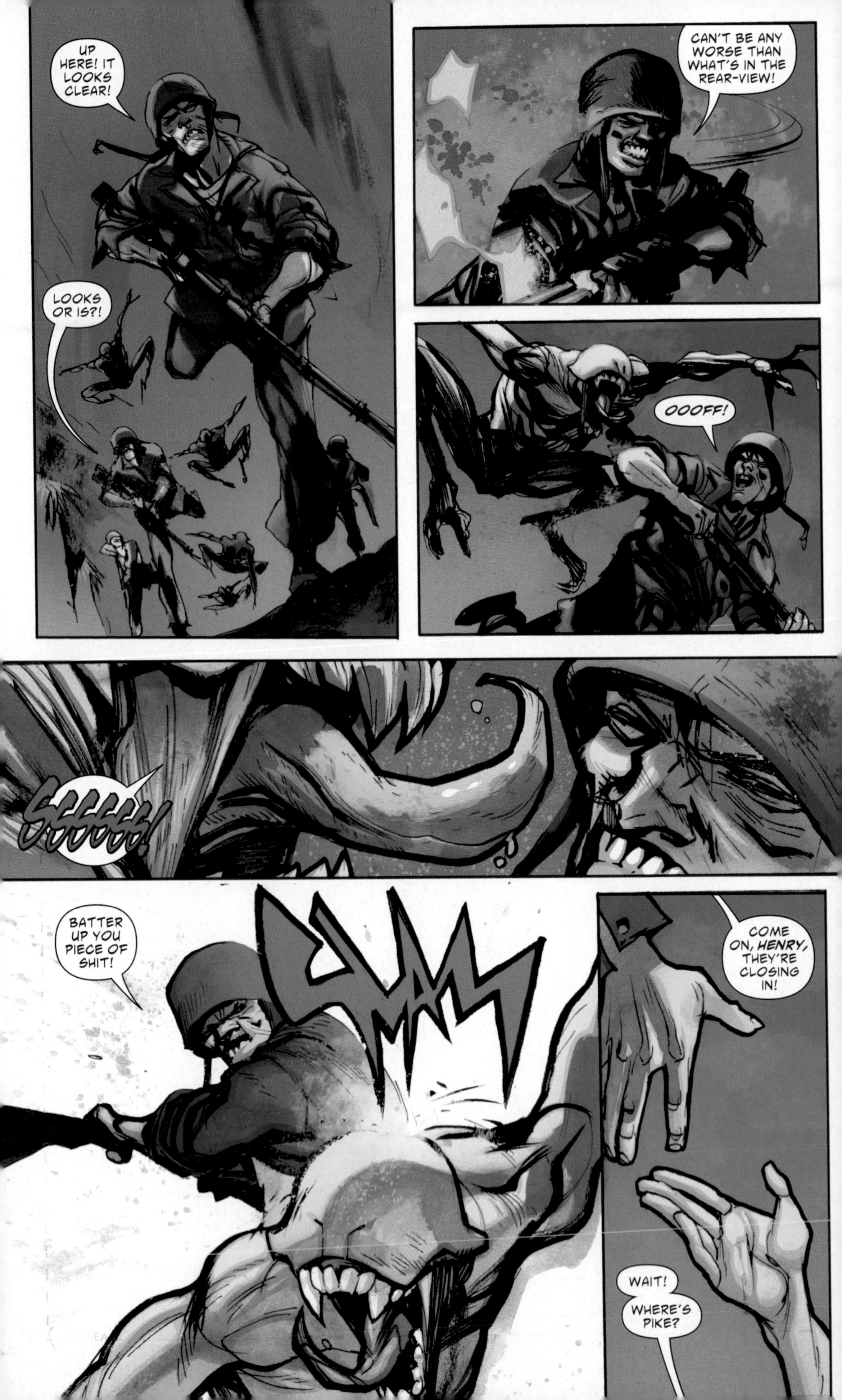

UP HERE! IT LOOKS CLEAR!
LOOKS OR IS?!
CAN'T BE ANY WORSE THAN WHAT'S IN THE REAR-VIEW!
OOOFF!
SSSSSS!
BATTER UP YOU PIECE OF SHIT!
CHAK
COME ON, HENRY, THEY'RE CLOSING IN!
WAIT!
WHERE'S PIKE?

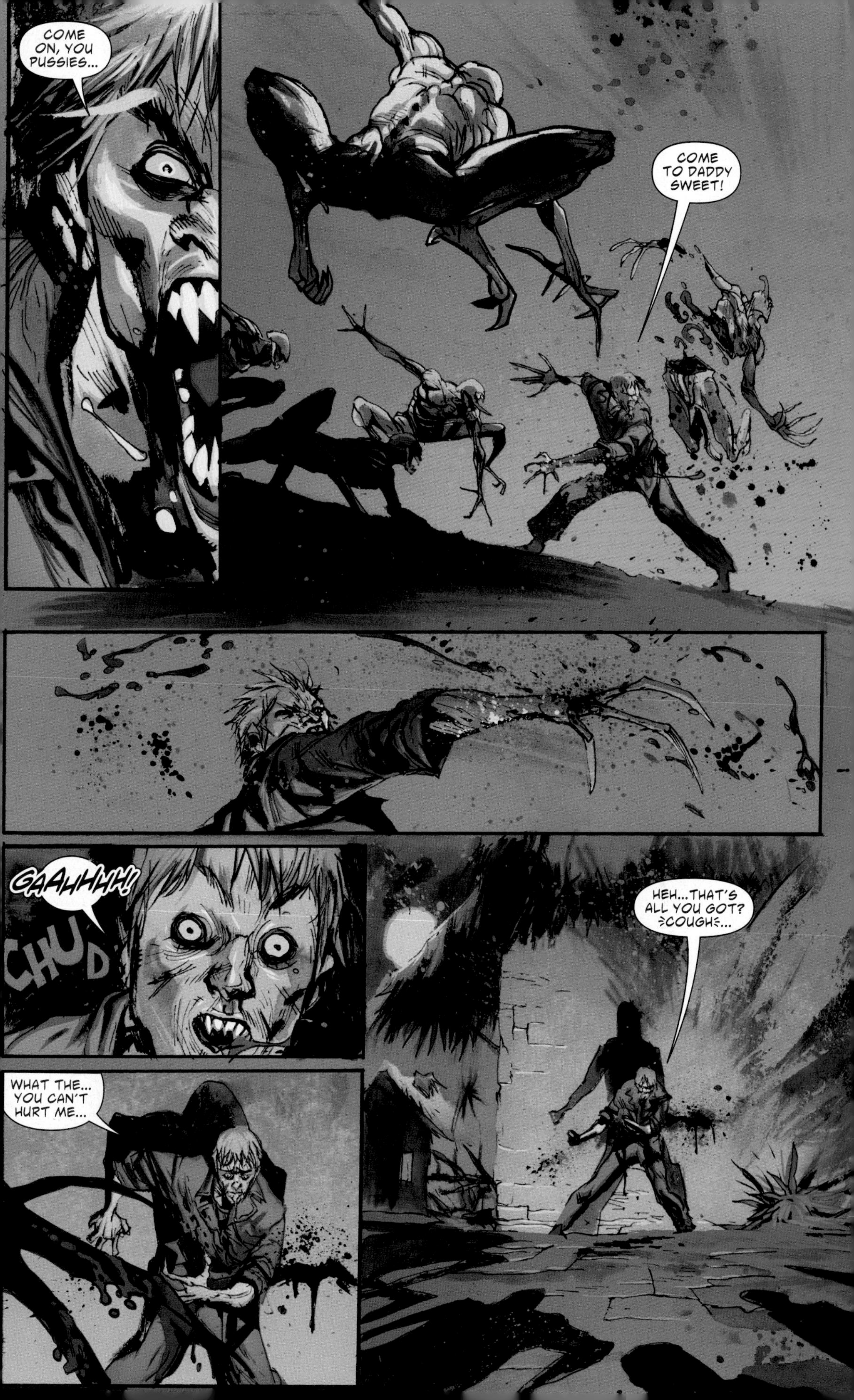
COME ON, YOU PUSSIES...
COME TO DADDY SWEET!
GAAHHHH!
CHUD
WHAT THE... YOU CAN'T HURT ME...
HEH...THAT'S ALL YOU GOT? ≷COUGH≶...

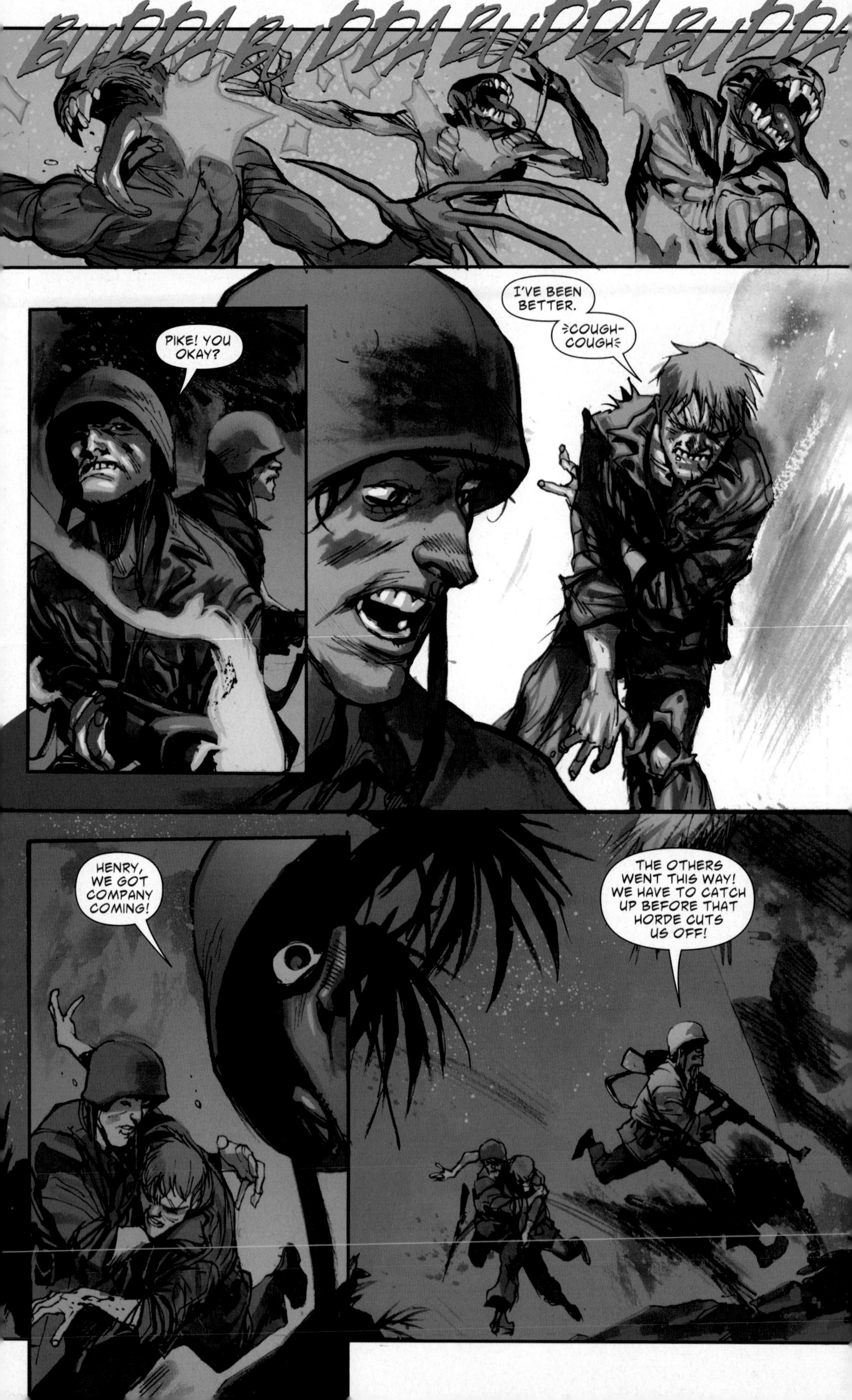
BUDDA BUDDA BUDDA BUDDA
PIKE! YOU OKAY?
I'VE BEEN BETTER.
COUGH-COUGH
HENRY, WE GOT COMPANY COMING!
THE OTHERS WENT THIS WAY! WE HAVE TO CATCH UP BEFORE THAT HORDE CUTS US OFF!

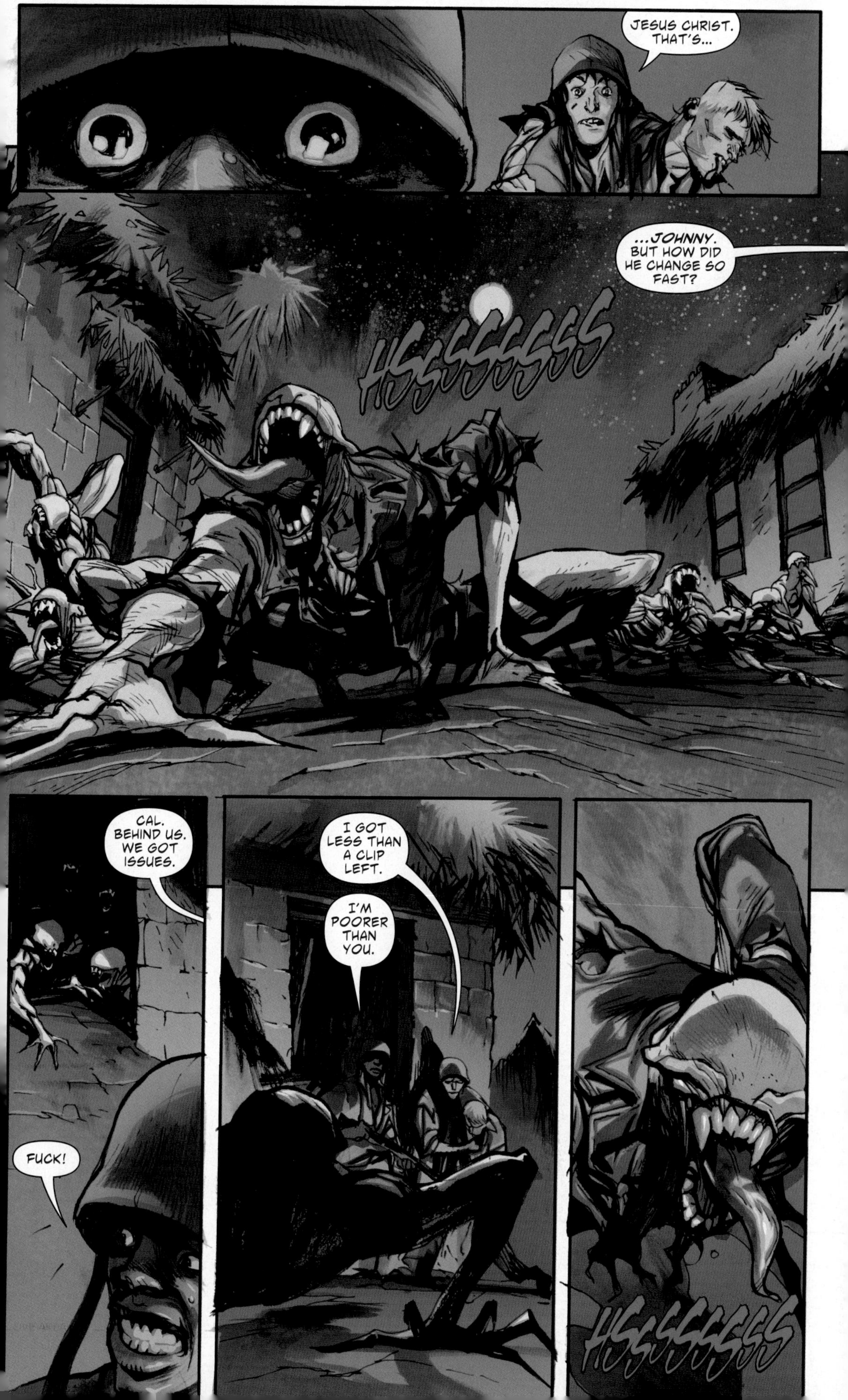
JESUS CHRIST. THAT'S...
...JOHNNY. BUT HOW DID HE CHANGE SO FAST?
HSSSSSSSS
CAL. BEHIND US. WE GOT ISSUES.
FUCK!
I GOT LESS THAN A CLIP LEFT.
I'M POORER THAN YOU.
HSSSSSSS

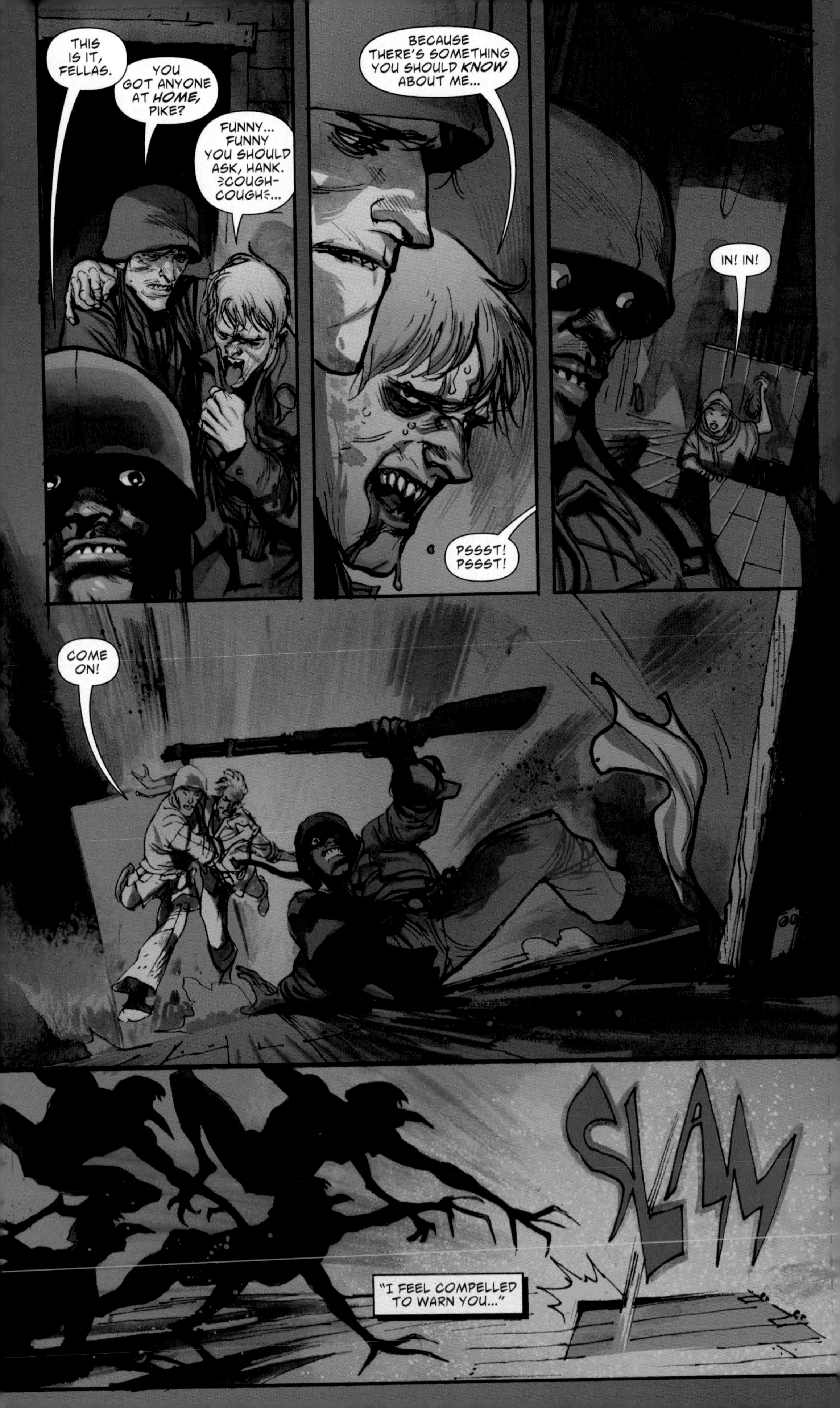
THIS IS IT, FELLAS.
YOU GOT ANYONE AT HOME, PIKE?
FUNNY... FUNNY YOU SHOULD ASK, HANK. ≥COUGH-COUGH≤...
BECAUSE THERE'S SOMETHING YOU SHOULD KNOW ABOUT ME...
PSSST! PSSST!
IN! IN!
COME ON!
SLAM
"I FEEL COMPELLED TO WARN YOU..."

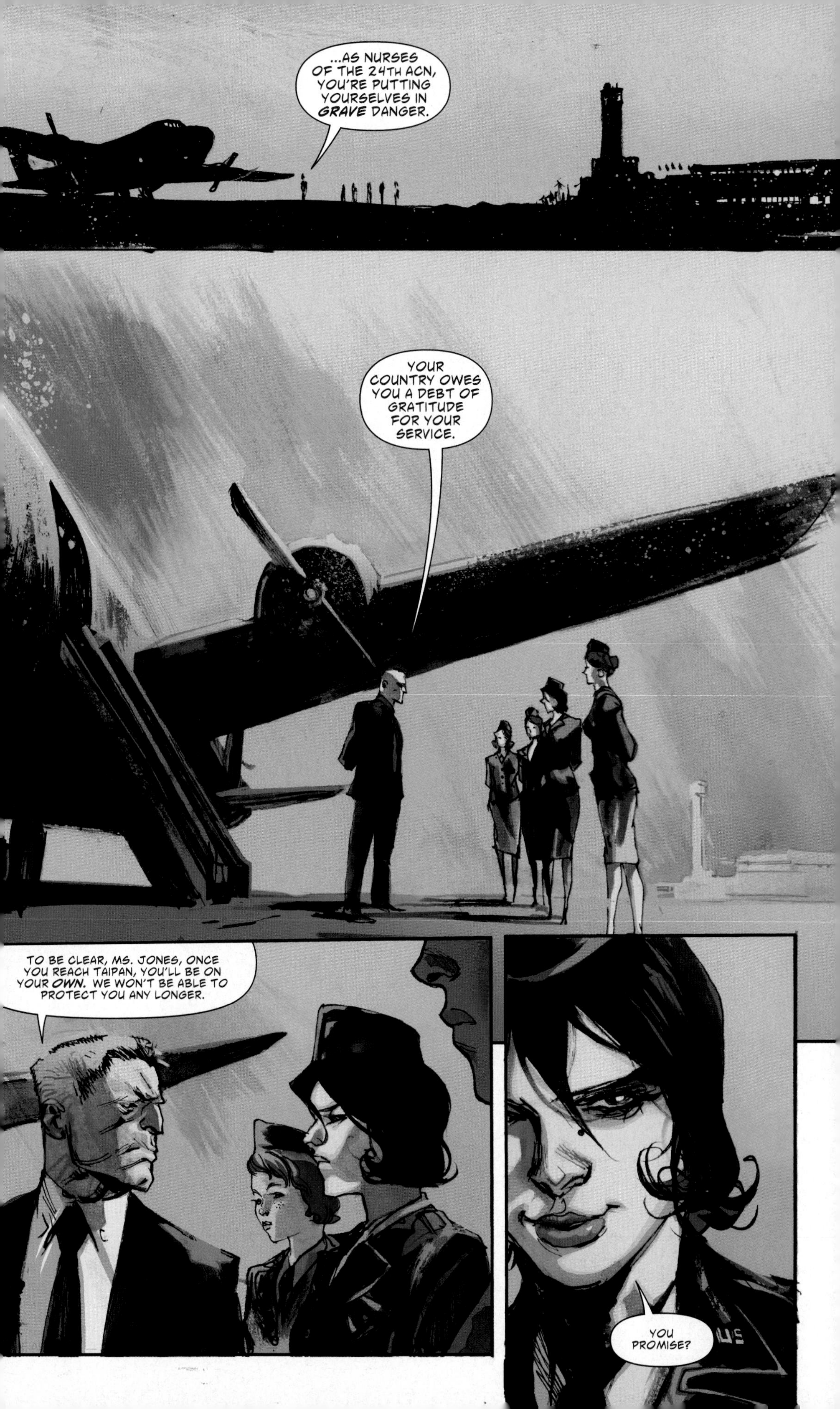
...AS NURSES OF THE 24TH ACN, YOU'RE PUTTING YOURSELVES IN GRAVE DANGER.
YOUR COUNTRY OWES YOU A DEBT OF GRATITUDE FOR YOUR SERVICE.
TO BE CLEAR, MS. JONES, ONCE YOU REACH TAIPAN, YOU'LL BE ON YOUR OWN. WE WON'T BE ABLE TO PROTECT YOU ANY LONGER.
YOU PROMISE?

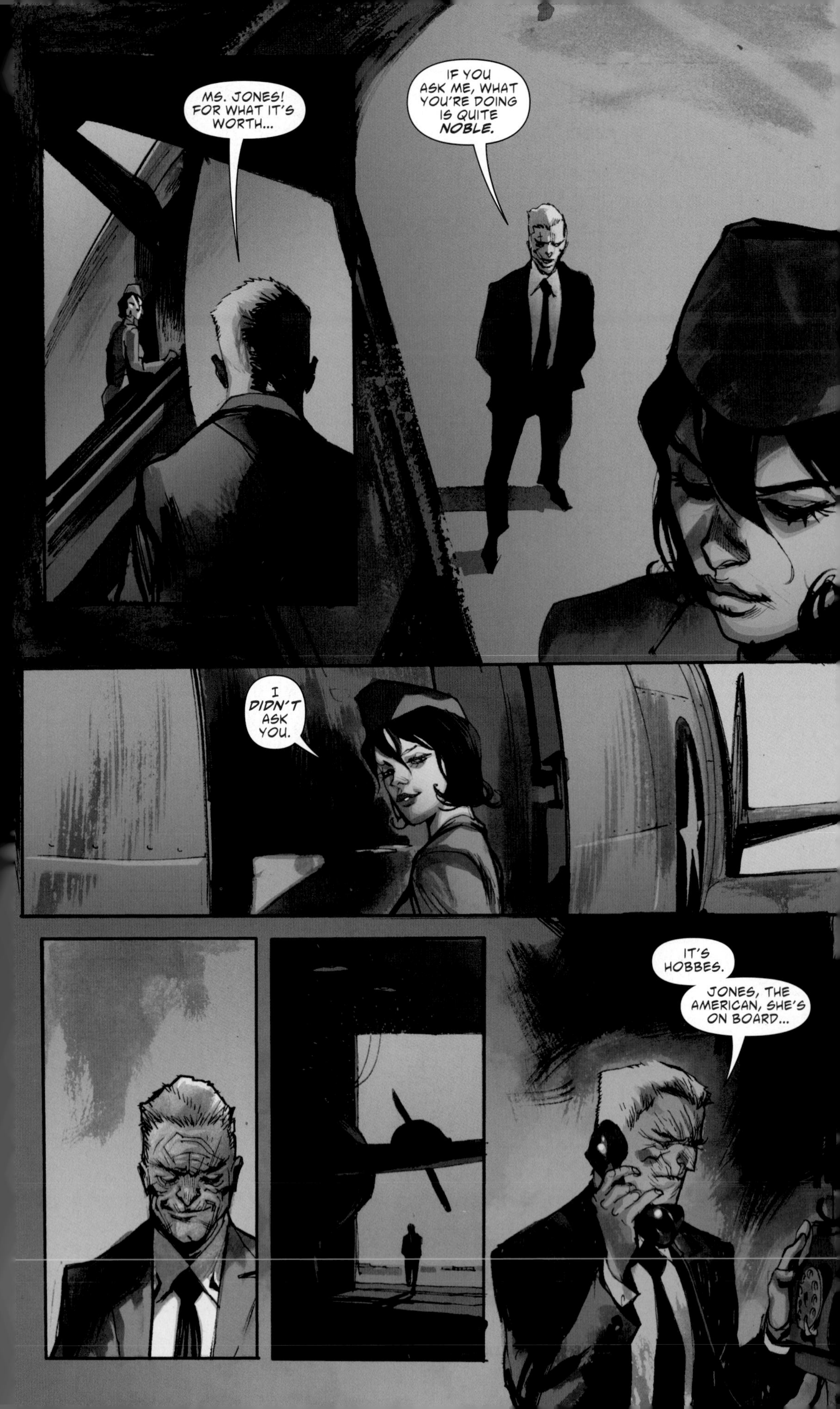
MS. JONES! FOR WHAT IT'S WORTH...
IF YOU ASK ME, WHAT YOU'RE DOING IS QUITE NOBLE.
I DIDN'T ASK YOU.
IT'S HOBBES.
JONES, THE AMERICAN, SHE'S ON BOARD...

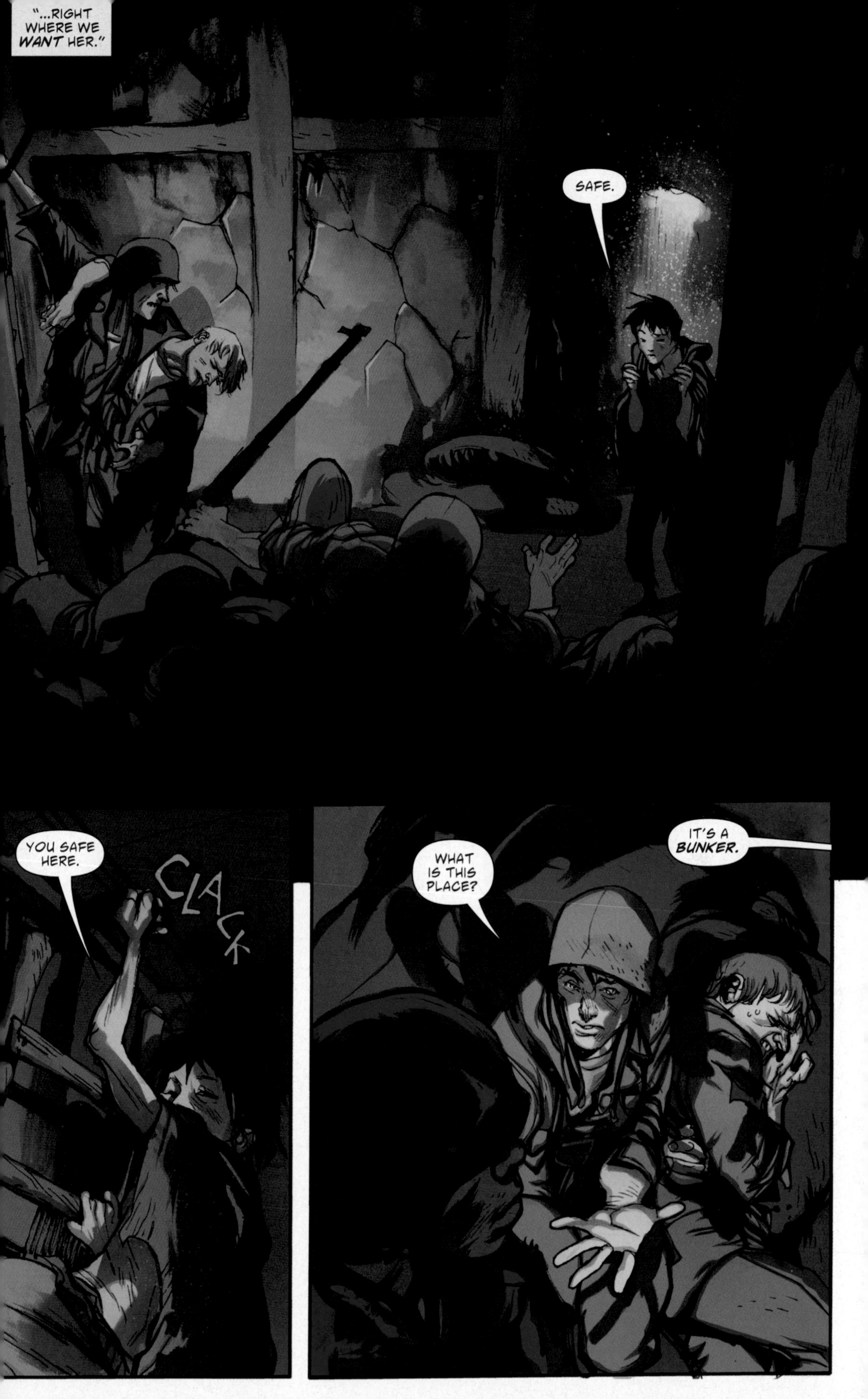
"...RIGHT WHERE WE *WANT* HER."
SAFE.
YOU SAFE HERE.
CLACK
WHAT IS THIS PLACE?
IT'S A *BUNKER.*

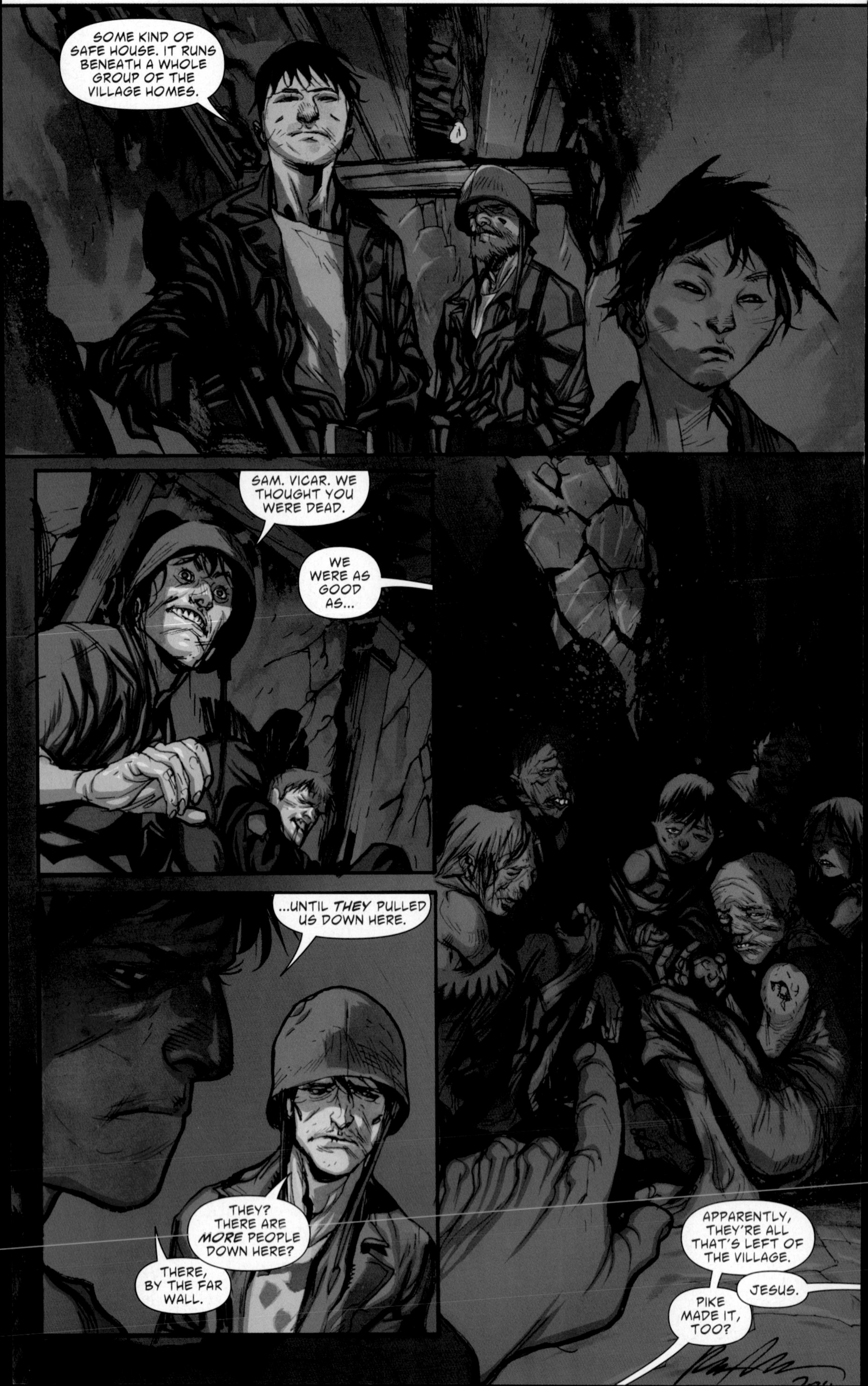
SOME KIND OF SAFE HOUSE. IT RUNS BENEATH A WHOLE GROUP OF THE VILLAGE HOMES.
SAM. VICAR. WE THOUGHT YOU WERE DEAD.
WE WERE AS GOOD AS...
...UNTIL *THEY* PULLED US DOWN HERE.
THEY? THERE ARE *MORE* PEOPLE DOWN HERE?
THERE, BY THE FAR WALL.
APPARENTLY, THEY'RE ALL THAT'S LEFT OF THE VILLAGE.
JESUS.
PIKE MADE IT, TOO?

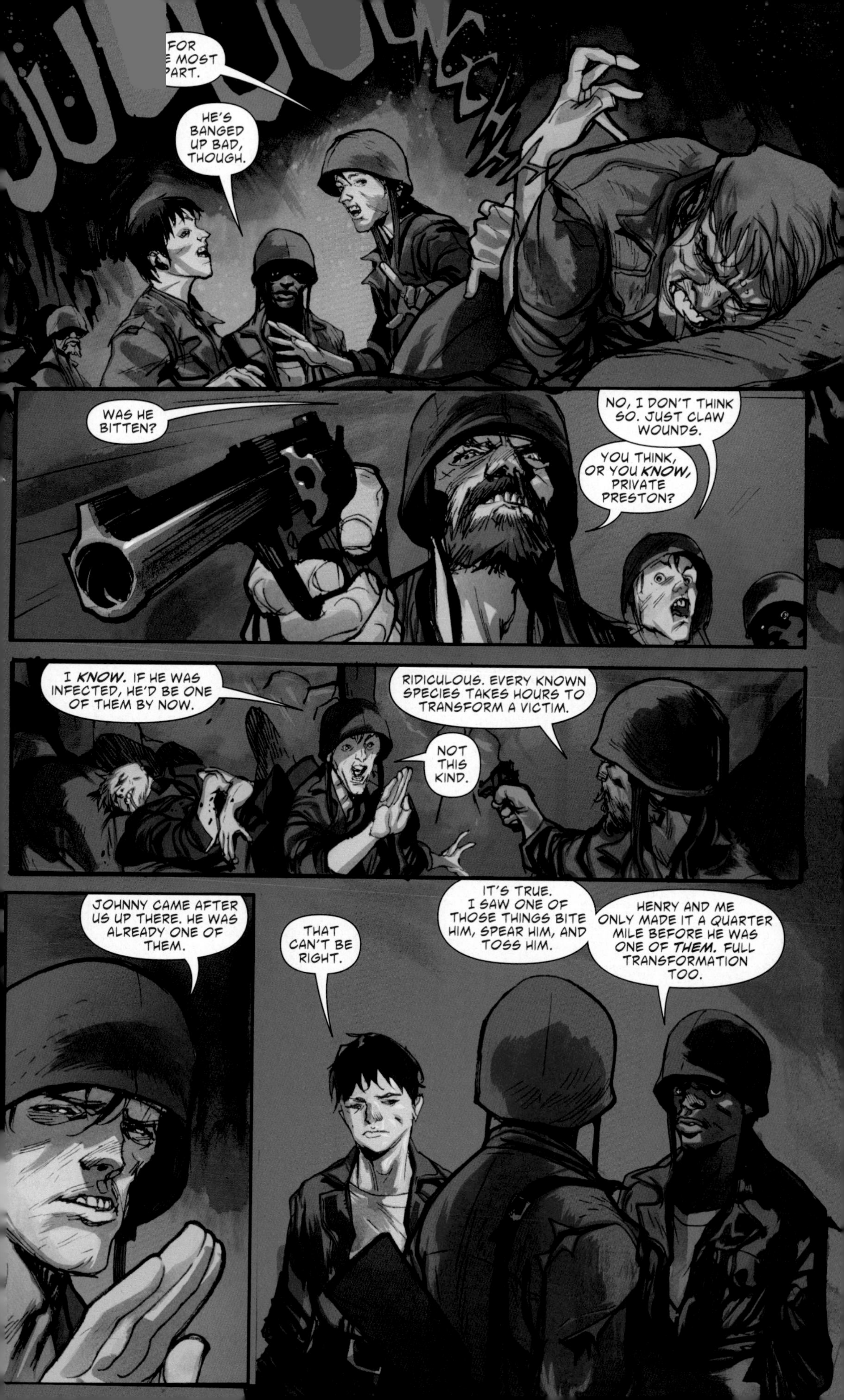
FOR
E MOST
PART.
HE'S BANGED UP BAD, THOUGH.
WAS HE BITTEN?
NO, I DON'T THINK SO. JUST CLAW WOUNDS.
YOU THINK, OR YOU *KNOW*, PRIVATE PRESTON?
I *KNOW*. IF HE WAS INFECTED, HE'D BE ONE OF THEM BY NOW.
RIDICULOUS. EVERY KNOWN SPECIES TAKES HOURS TO TRANSFORM A VICTIM.
NOT THIS KIND.
JOHNNY CAME AFTER US UP THERE. HE WAS ALREADY ONE OF THEM.
THAT CAN'T BE RIGHT.
IT'S TRUE. I SAW ONE OF THOSE THINGS BITE HIM, SPEAR HIM, AND TOSS HIM.
HENRY AND ME ONLY MADE IT A QUARTER MILE BEFORE HE WAS ONE OF *THEM*. FULL TRANSFORMATION TOO.

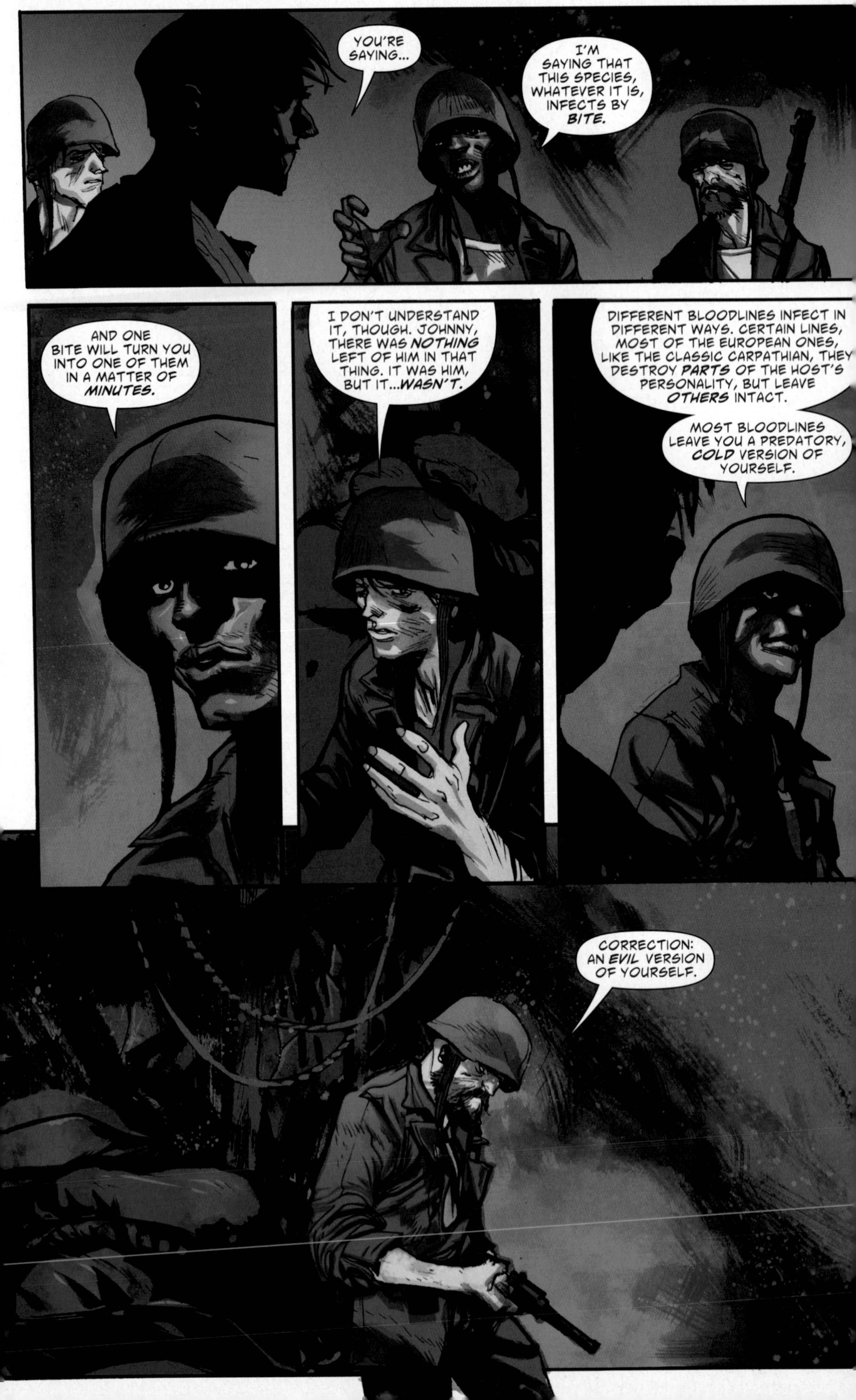
YOU'RE SAYING...
I'M SAYING THAT THIS SPECIES, WHATEVER IT IS, INFECTS BY BITE.
AND ONE BITE WILL TURN YOU INTO ONE OF THEM IN A MATTER OF MINUTES.
I DON'T UNDERSTAND IT, THOUGH. JOHNNY, THERE WAS NOTHING LEFT OF HIM IN THAT THING. IT WAS HIM, BUT IT...WASN'T.
DIFFERENT BLOODLINES INFECT IN DIFFERENT WAYS. CERTAIN LINES, MOST OF THE EUROPEAN ONES, LIKE THE CLASSIC CARPATHIAN, THEY DESTROY PARTS OF THE HOST'S PERSONALITY, BUT LEAVE OTHERS INTACT.
MOST BLOODLINES LEAVE YOU A PREDATORY, COLD VERSION OF YOURSELF.
CORRECTION: AN EVIL VERSION OF YOURSELF.

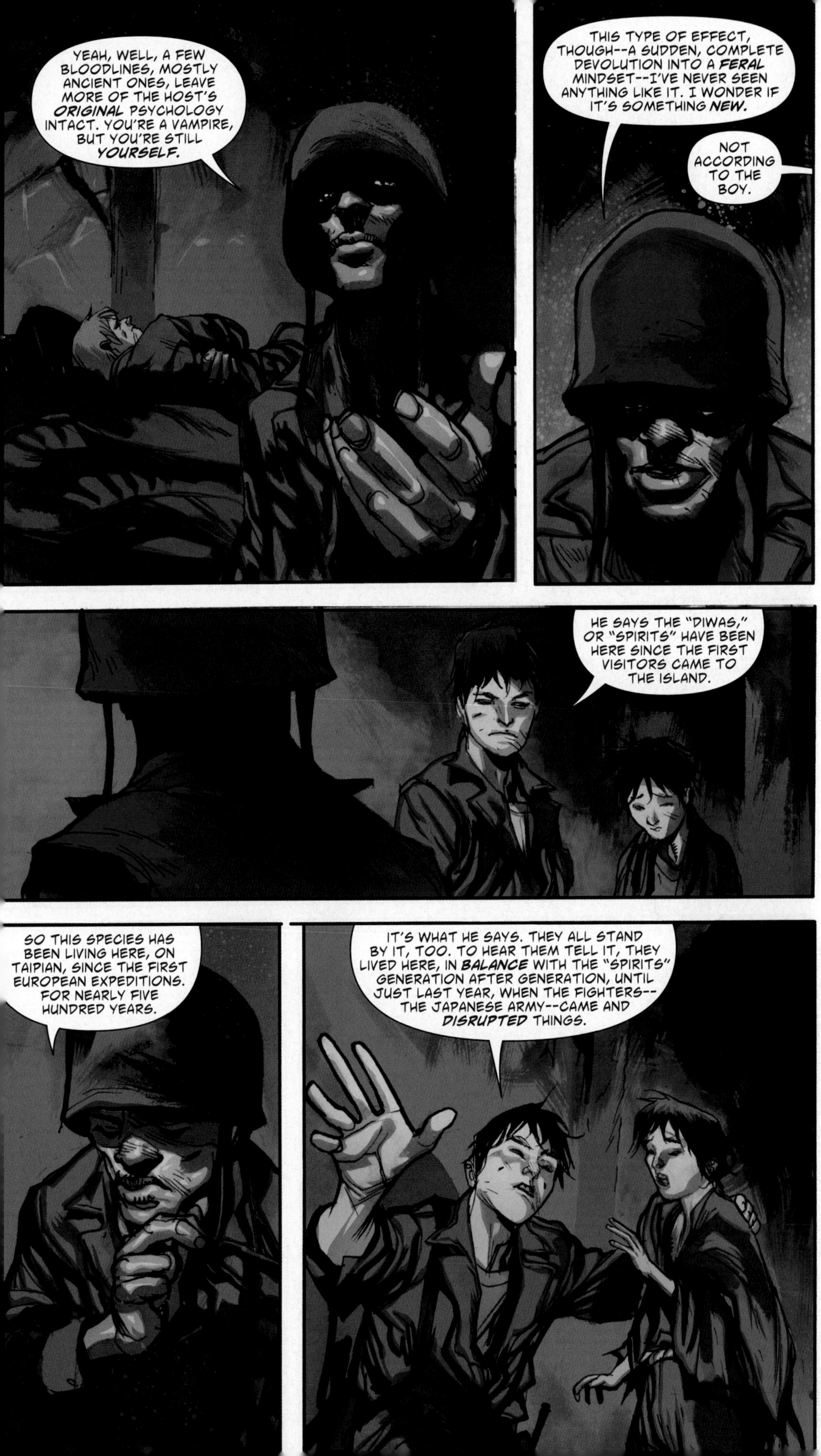
YEAH, WELL, A FEW BLOODLINES, MOSTLY ANCIENT ONES, LEAVE MORE OF THE HOST'S ORIGINAL PSYCHOLOGY INTACT. YOU'RE A VAMPIRE, BUT YOU'RE STILL YOURSELF.
THIS TYPE OF EFFECT, THOUGH--A SUDDEN, COMPLETE DEVOLUTION INTO A FERAL MINDSET--I'VE NEVER SEEN ANYTHING LIKE IT. I WONDER IF IT'S SOMETHING NEW.
NOT ACCORDING TO THE BOY.
HE SAYS THE "DIWAS," OR "SPIRITS" HAVE BEEN HERE SINCE THE FIRST VISITORS CAME TO THE ISLAND.
SO THIS SPECIES HAS BEEN LIVING HERE, ON TAIPIAN, SINCE THE FIRST EUROPEAN EXPEDITIONS. FOR NEARLY FIVE HUNDRED YEARS.
IT'S WHAT HE SAYS. THEY ALL STAND BY IT, TOO. TO HEAR THEM TELL IT, THEY LIVED HERE, IN BALANCE WITH THE "SPIRITS" GENERATION AFTER GENERATION, UNTIL JUST LAST YEAR, WHEN THE FIGHTERS-- THE JAPANESE ARMY--CAME AND DISRUPTED THINGS.

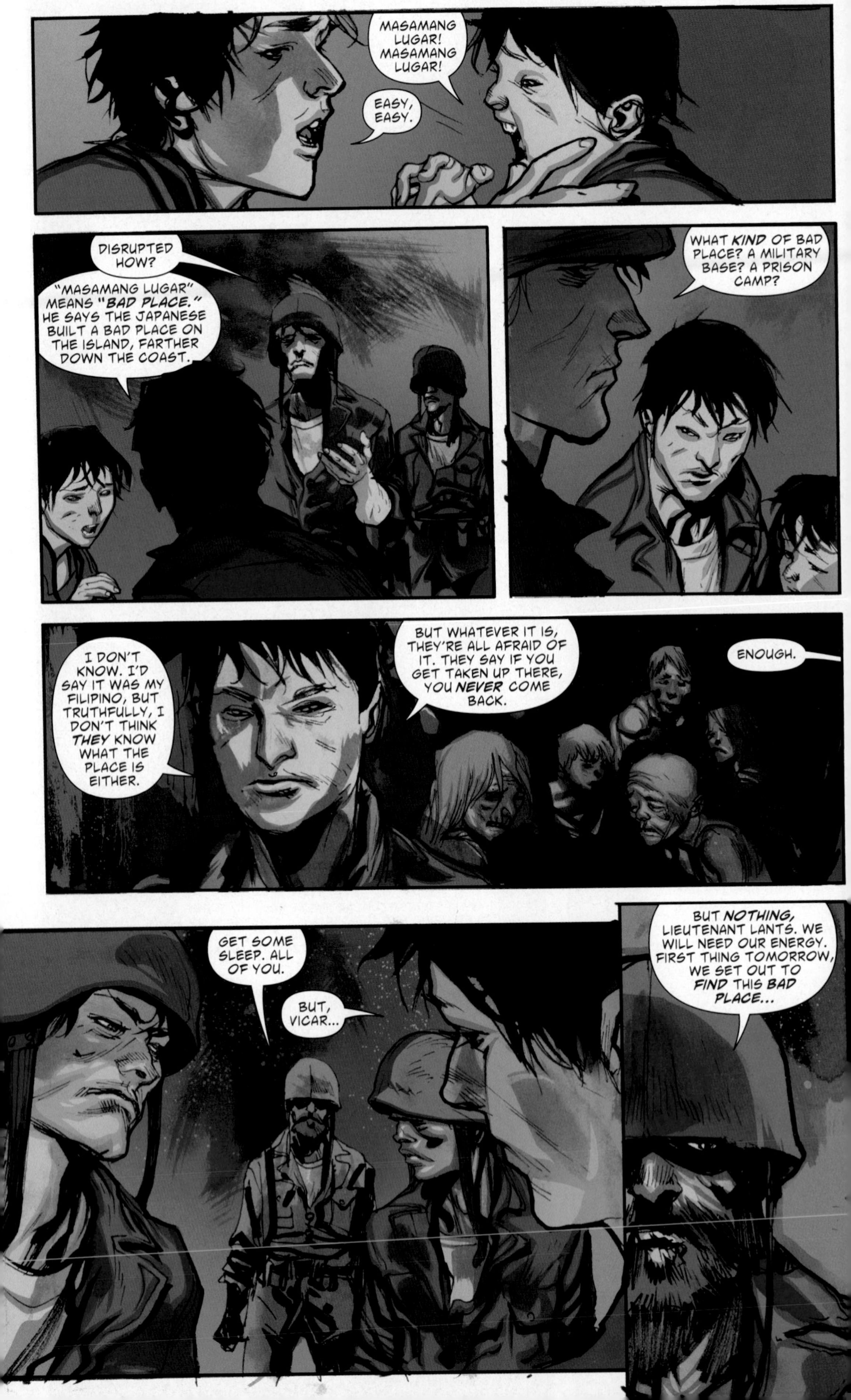
MASAMANG LUGAR! MASAMANG LUGAR!
EASY, EASY.
DISRUPTED HOW?
"MASAMANG LUGAR" MEANS "BAD PLACE." HE SAYS THE JAPANESE BUILT A BAD PLACE ON THE ISLAND, FARTHER DOWN THE COAST.
WHAT KIND OF BAD PLACE? A MILITARY BASE? A PRISON CAMP?
I DON'T KNOW. I'D SAY IT WAS MY FILIPINO, BUT TRUTHFULLY, I DON'T THINK THEY KNOW WHAT THE PLACE IS EITHER.
BUT WHATEVER IT IS, THEY'RE ALL AFRAID OF IT. THEY SAY IF YOU GET TAKEN UP THERE, YOU NEVER COME BACK.
ENOUGH.
GET SOME SLEEP. ALL OF YOU.
BUT, VICAR...
BUT NOTHING, LIEUTENANT LANTS. WE WILL NEED OUR ENERGY. FIRST THING TOMORROW, WE SET OUT TO FIND THIS BAD PLACE...

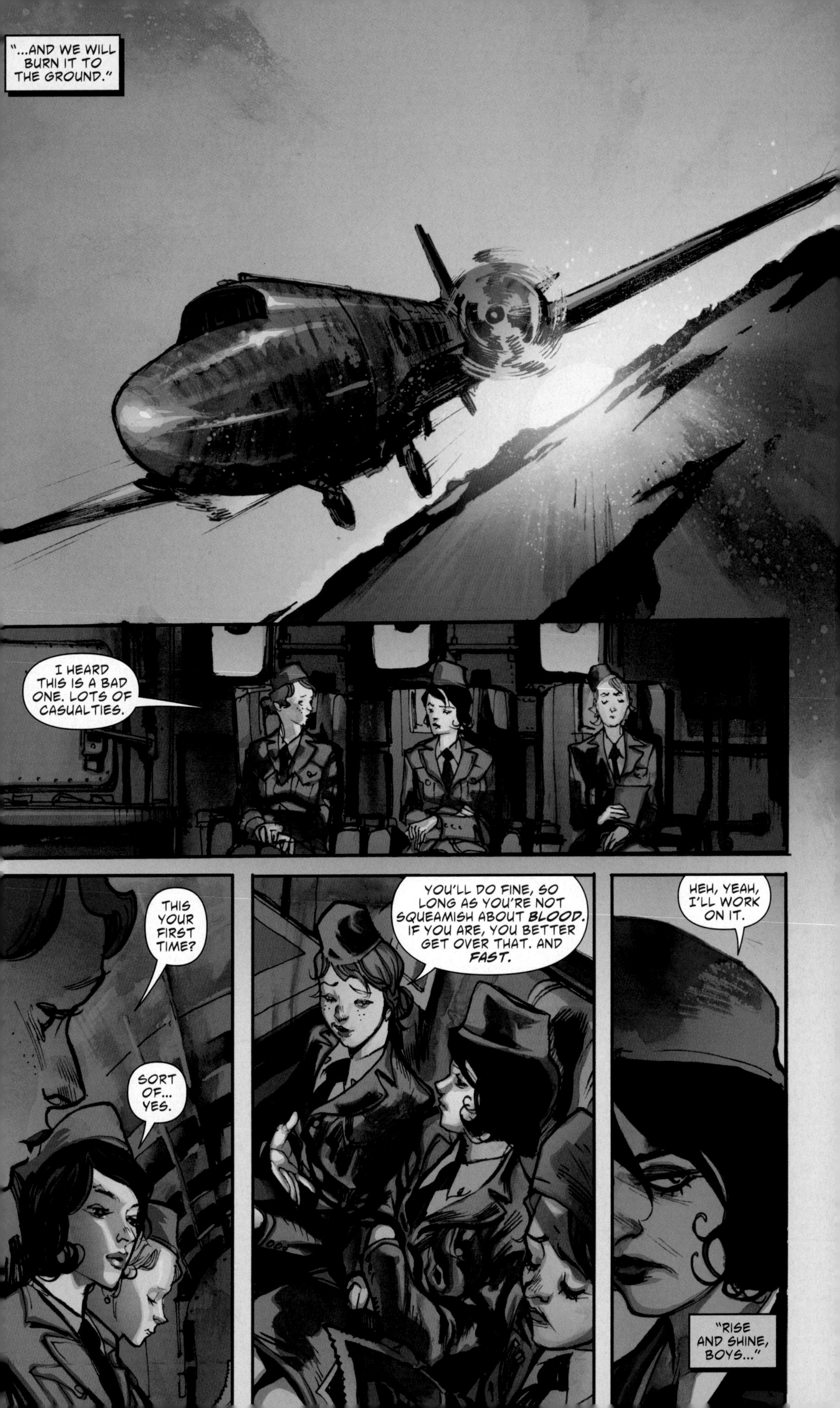
"...AND WE WILL BURN IT TO THE GROUND."
I HEARD THIS IS A BAD ONE. LOTS OF CASUALTIES.
THIS YOUR FIRST TIME?
SORT OF... YES.
YOU'LL DO FINE, SO LONG AS YOU'RE NOT SQUEAMISH ABOUT BLOOD. IF YOU ARE, YOU BETTER GET OVER THAT. AND FAST.
HEH, YEAH, I'LL WORK ON IT.
"RISE AND SHINE, BOYS..."

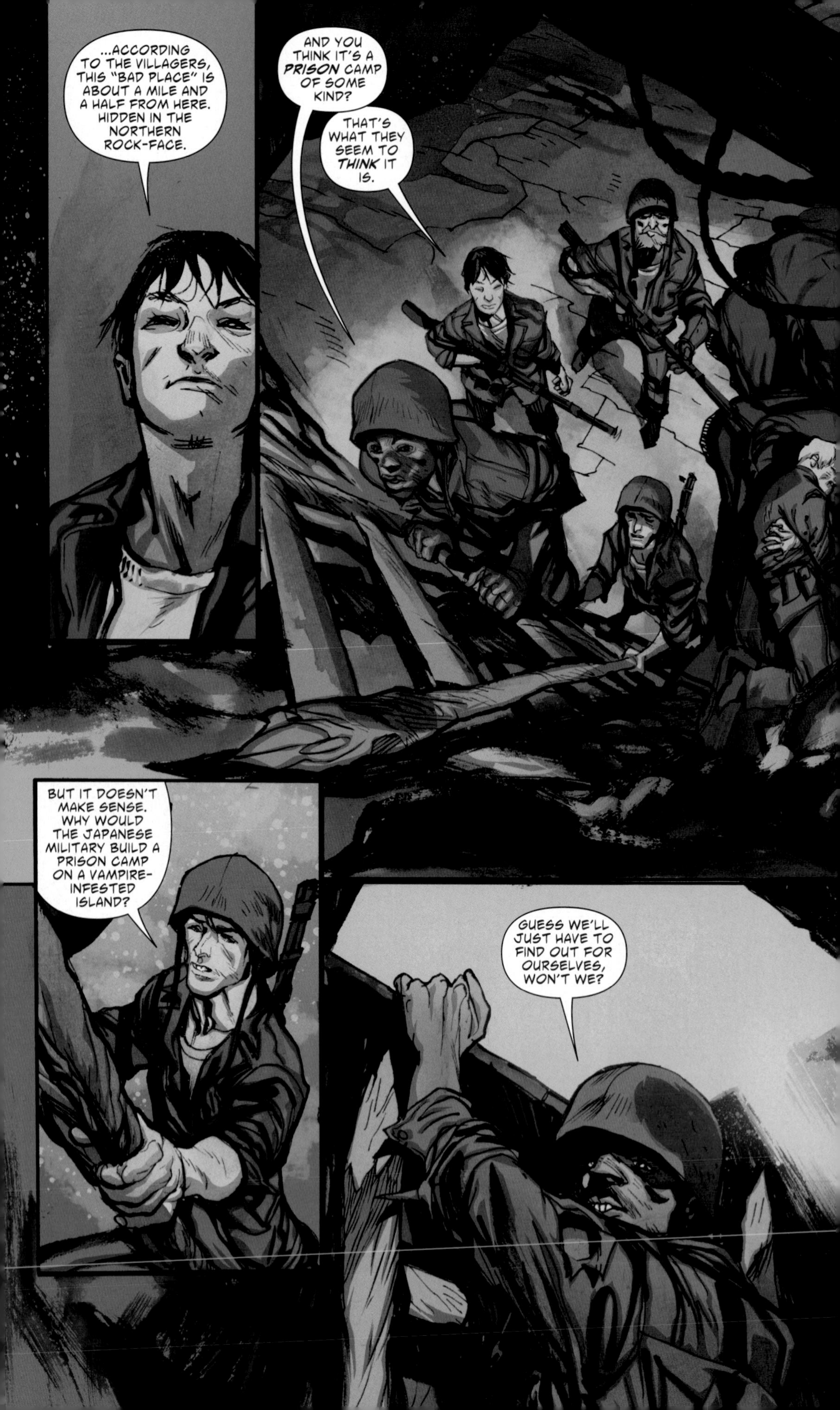
...ACCORDING TO THE VILLAGERS, THIS "BAD PLACE" IS ABOUT A MILE AND A HALF FROM HERE. HIDDEN IN THE NORTHERN ROCK-FACE.
AND YOU THINK IT'S A PRISON CAMP OF SOME KIND?
THAT'S WHAT THEY SEEM TO THINK IT IS.
BUT IT DOESN'T MAKE SENSE. WHY WOULD THE JAPANESE MILITARY BUILD A PRISON CAMP ON A VAMPIRE-INFESTED ISLAND?
GUESS WE'LL JUST HAVE TO FIND OUT FOR OURSELVES, WON'T WE?

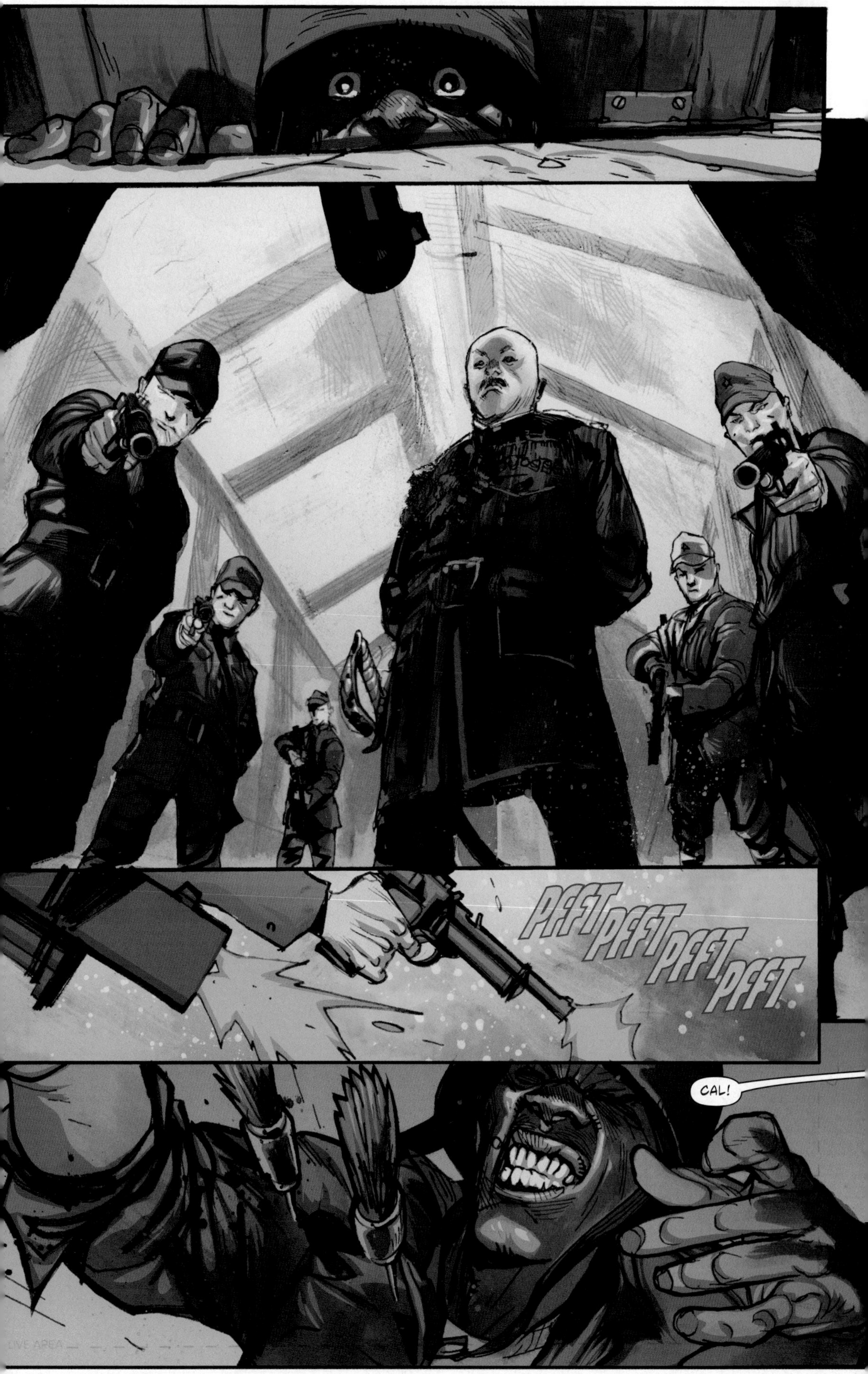
PFFT PFFT PFFT PFFT
CAL!
LIVE AREA

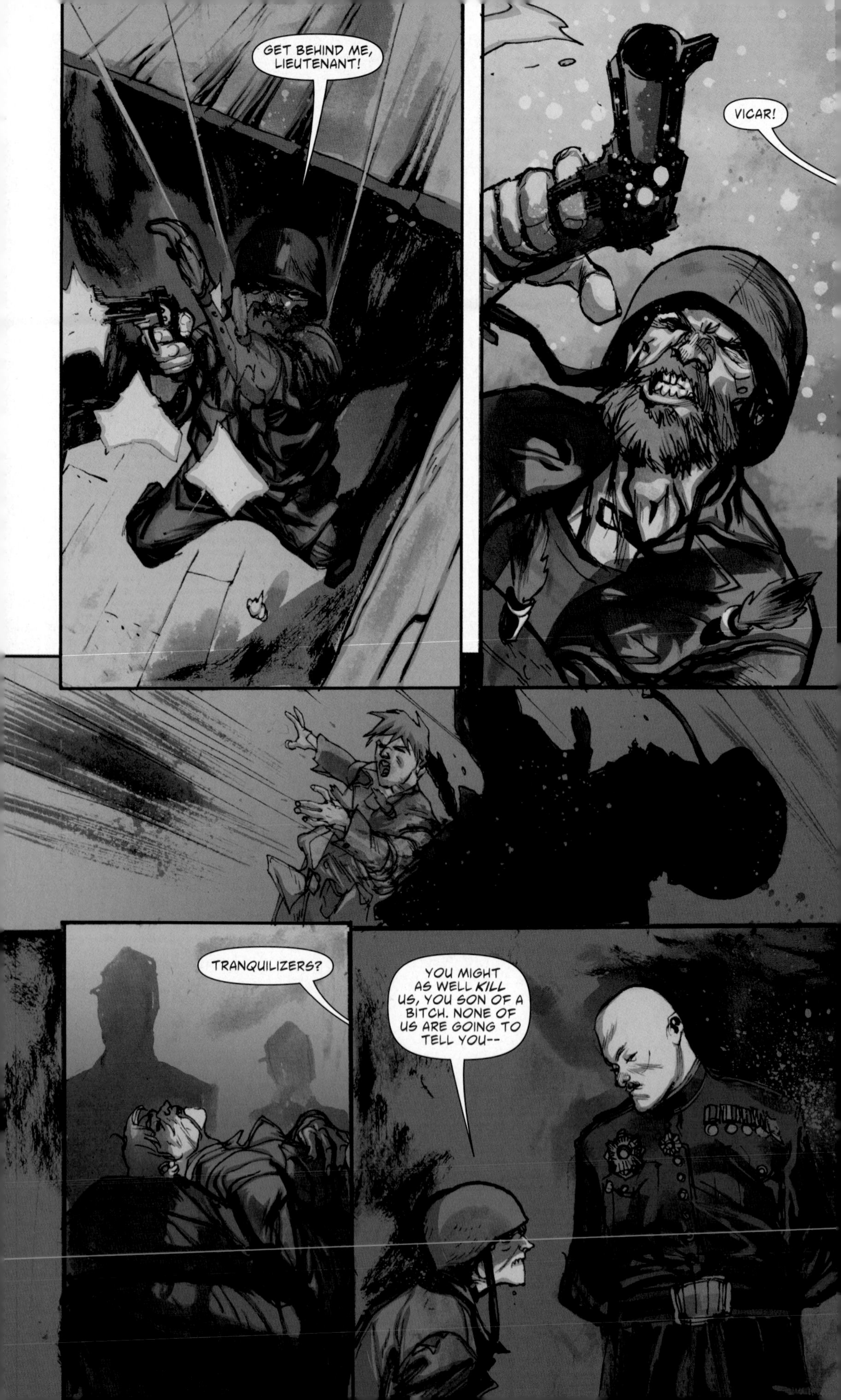
GET BEHIND ME, LIEUTENANT!
VICAR!
TRANQUILIZERS?
YOU MIGHT AS WELL *KILL* US, YOU SON OF A BITCH. NONE OF US ARE GOING TO TELL YOU--

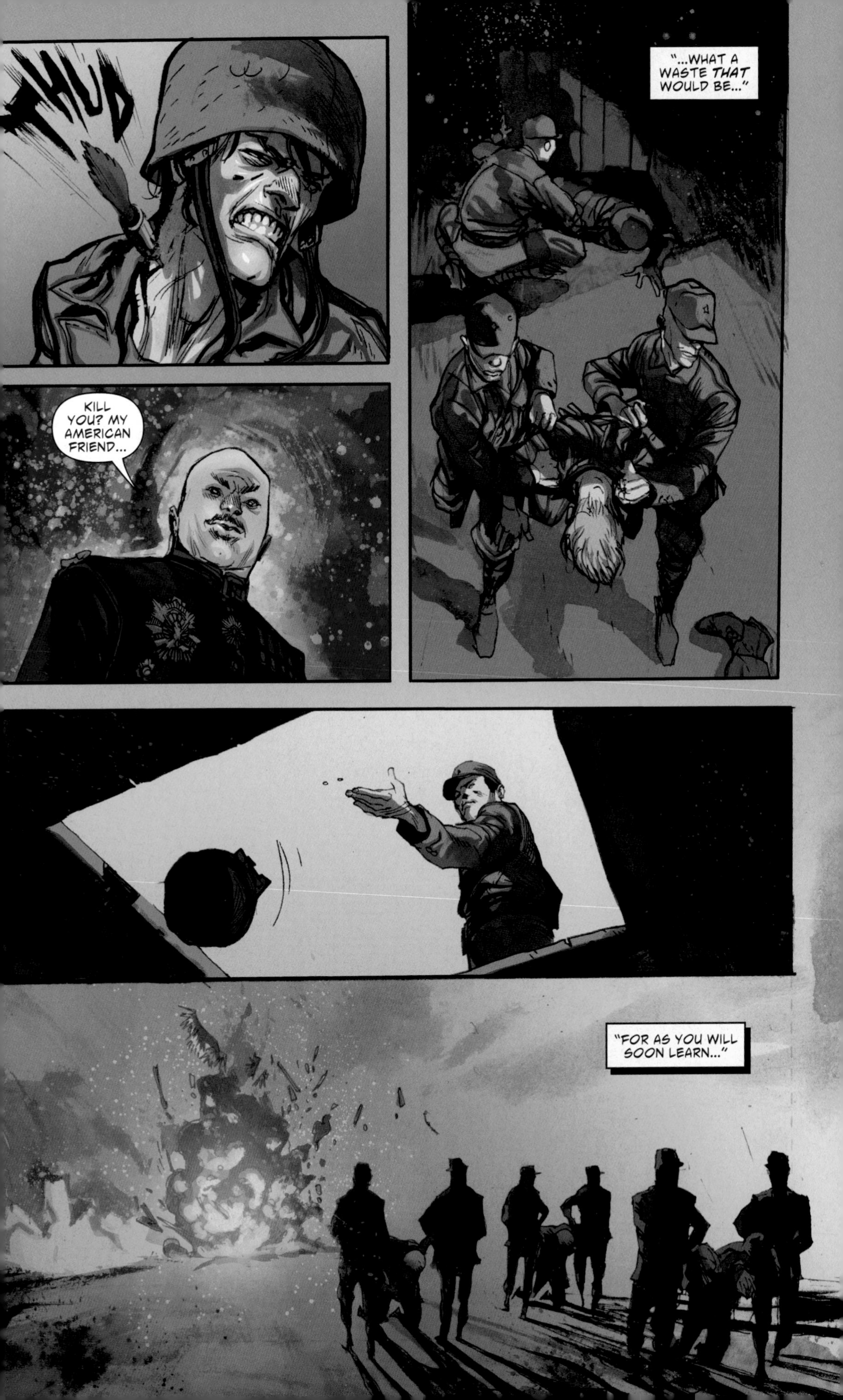
THUD
"...WHAT A WASTE THAT WOULD BE..."
KILL YOU? MY AMERICAN FRIEND...
"FOR AS YOU WILL SOON LEARN..."

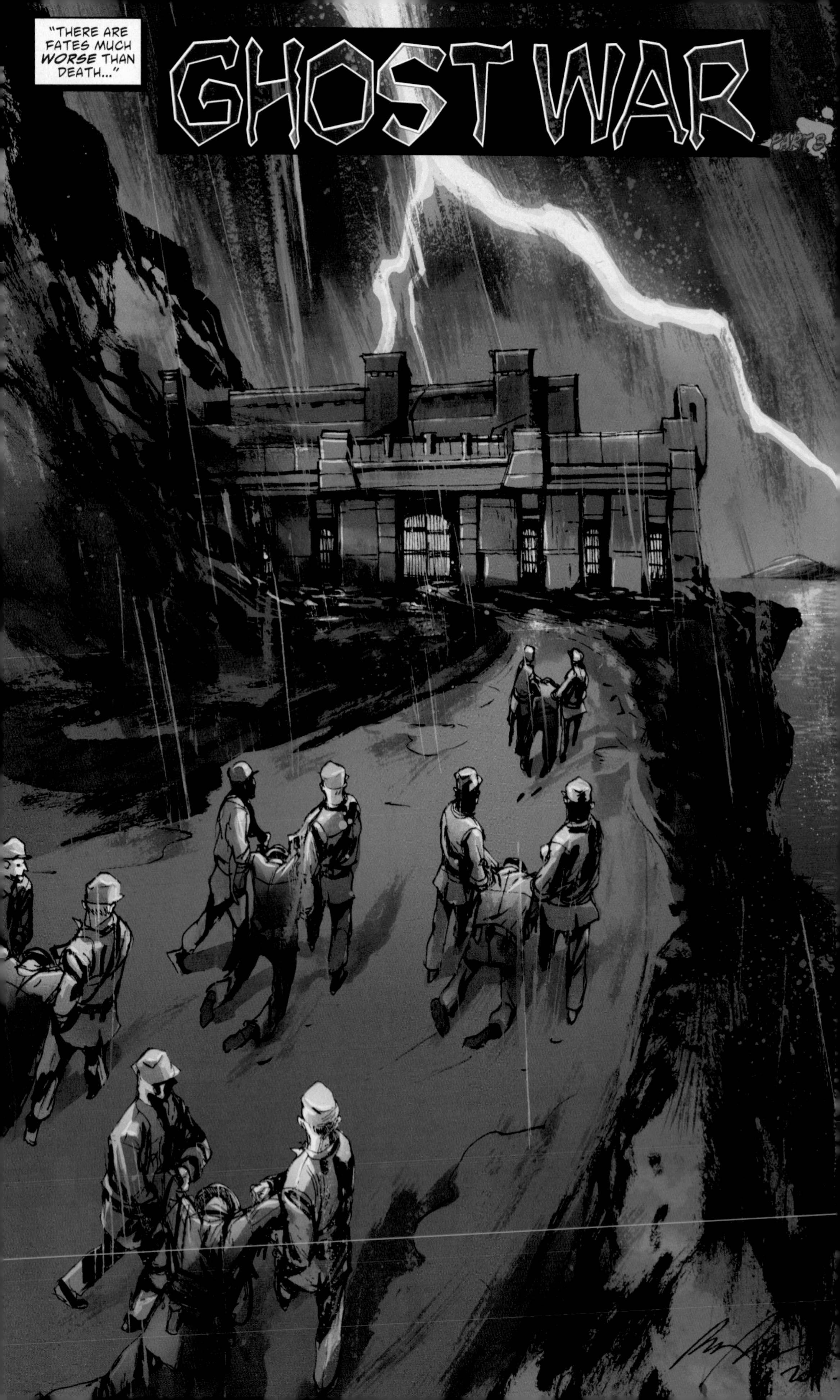
"THERE ARE FATES MUCH WORSE THAN DEATH..."
GHOST WAR
PART 3

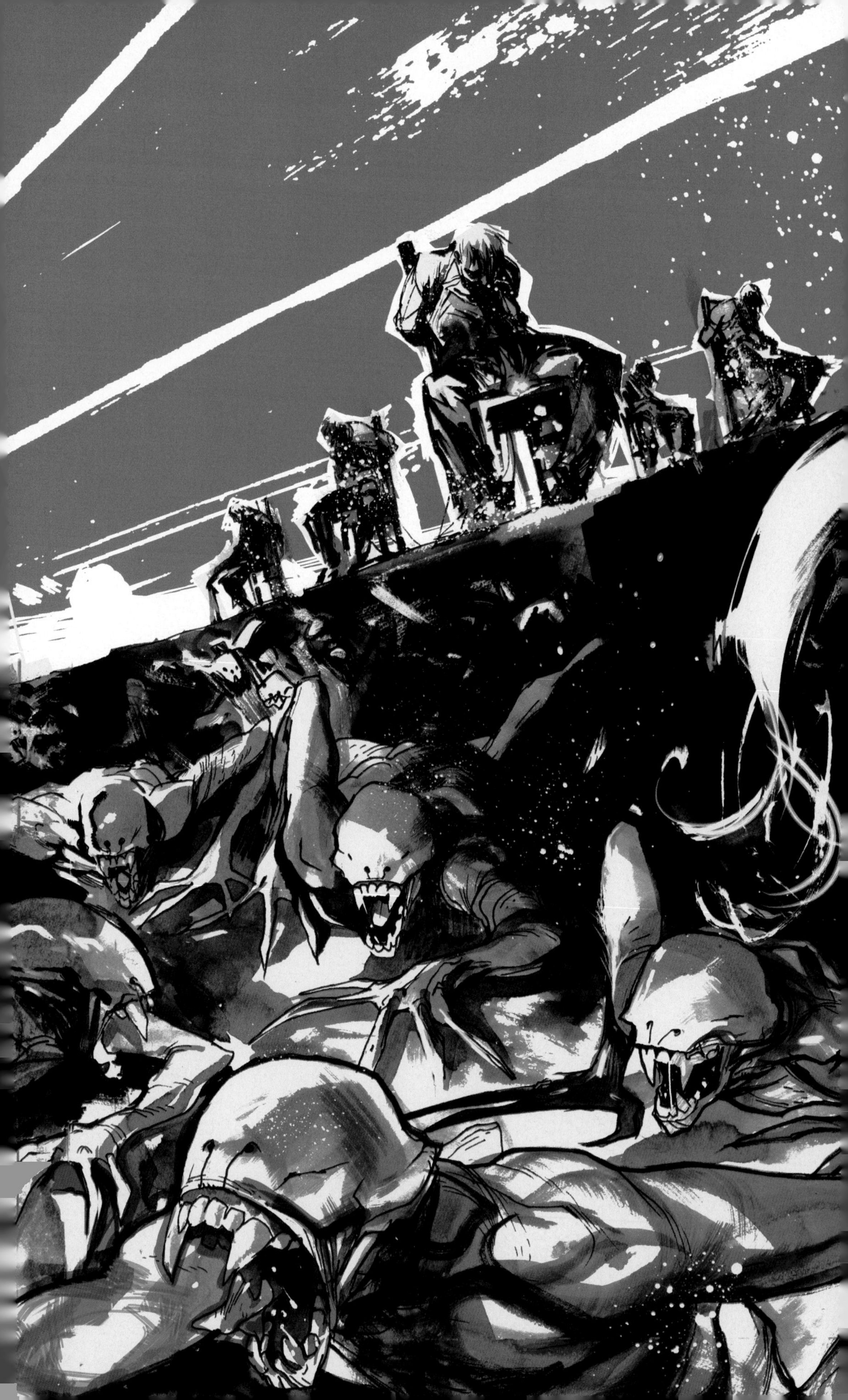

Ghost War

Part Four

Rafael Albuquerque
Artist and cover

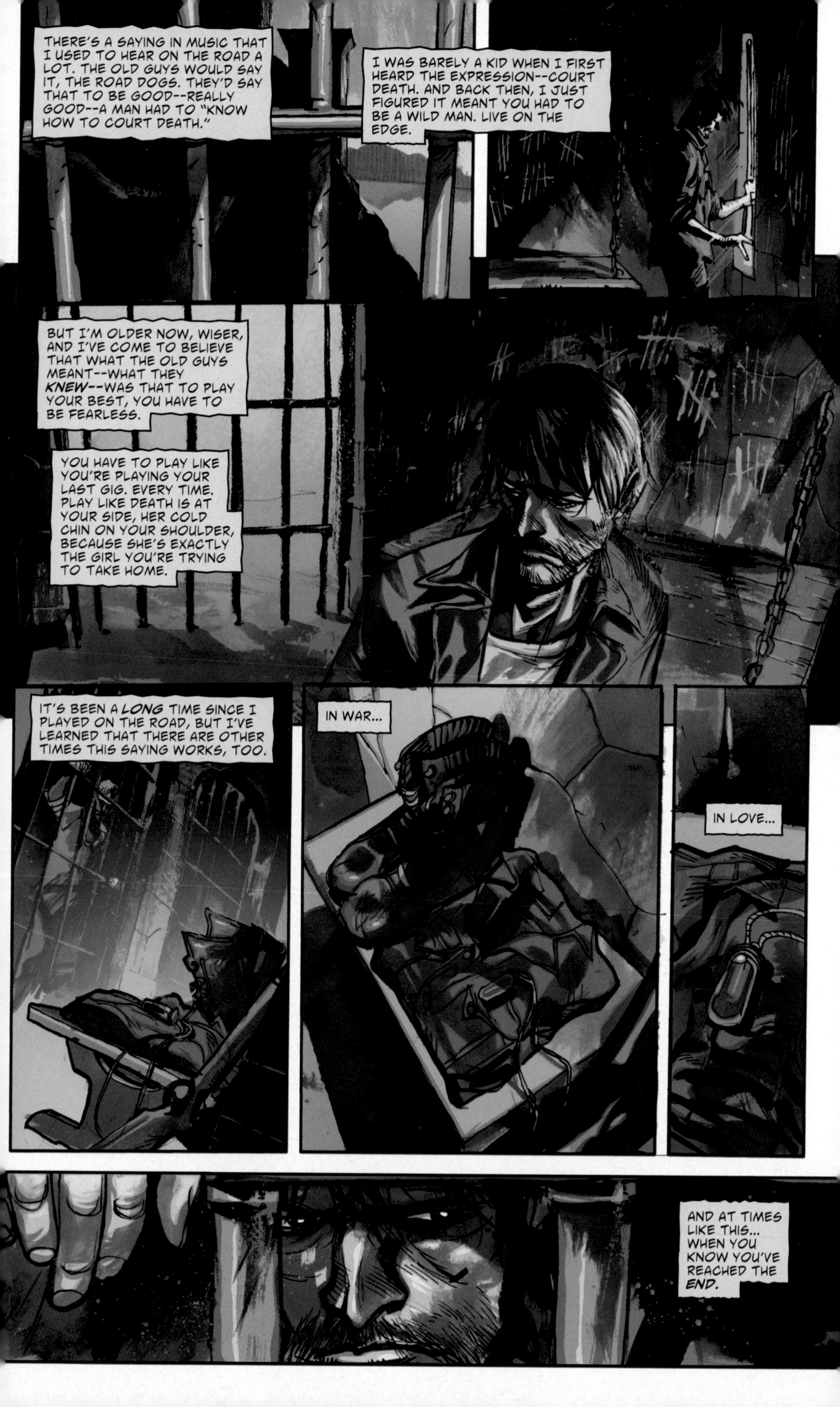
THERE'S A SAYING IN MUSIC THAT I USED TO HEAR ON THE ROAD A LOT. THE OLD GUYS WOULD SAY IT, THE ROAD DOGS. THEY'D SAY THAT TO BE GOOD--REALLY GOOD--A MAN HAD TO "KNOW HOW TO COURT DEATH."
I WAS BARELY A KID WHEN I FIRST HEARD THE EXPRESSION--COURT DEATH. AND BACK THEN, I JUST FIGURED IT MEANT YOU HAD TO BE A WILD MAN. LIVE ON THE EDGE.
BUT I'M OLDER NOW, WISER, AND I'VE COME TO BELIEVE THAT WHAT THE OLD GUYS MEANT--WHAT THEY *KNEW*--WAS THAT TO PLAY YOUR BEST, YOU HAVE TO BE FEARLESS.
YOU HAVE TO PLAY LIKE YOU'RE PLAYING YOUR LAST GIG. EVERY TIME. PLAY LIKE DEATH IS AT YOUR SIDE, HER COLD CHIN ON YOUR SHOULDER, BECAUSE SHE'S EXACTLY THE GIRL YOU'RE TRYING TO TAKE HOME.
IT'S BEEN A *LONG* TIME SINCE I PLAYED ON THE ROAD, BUT I'VE LEARNED THAT THERE ARE OTHER TIMES THIS SAYING WORKS, TOO.
IN WAR...
IN LOVE...
AND AT TIMES LIKE THIS... WHEN YOU KNOW YOU'VE REACHED THE *END*.

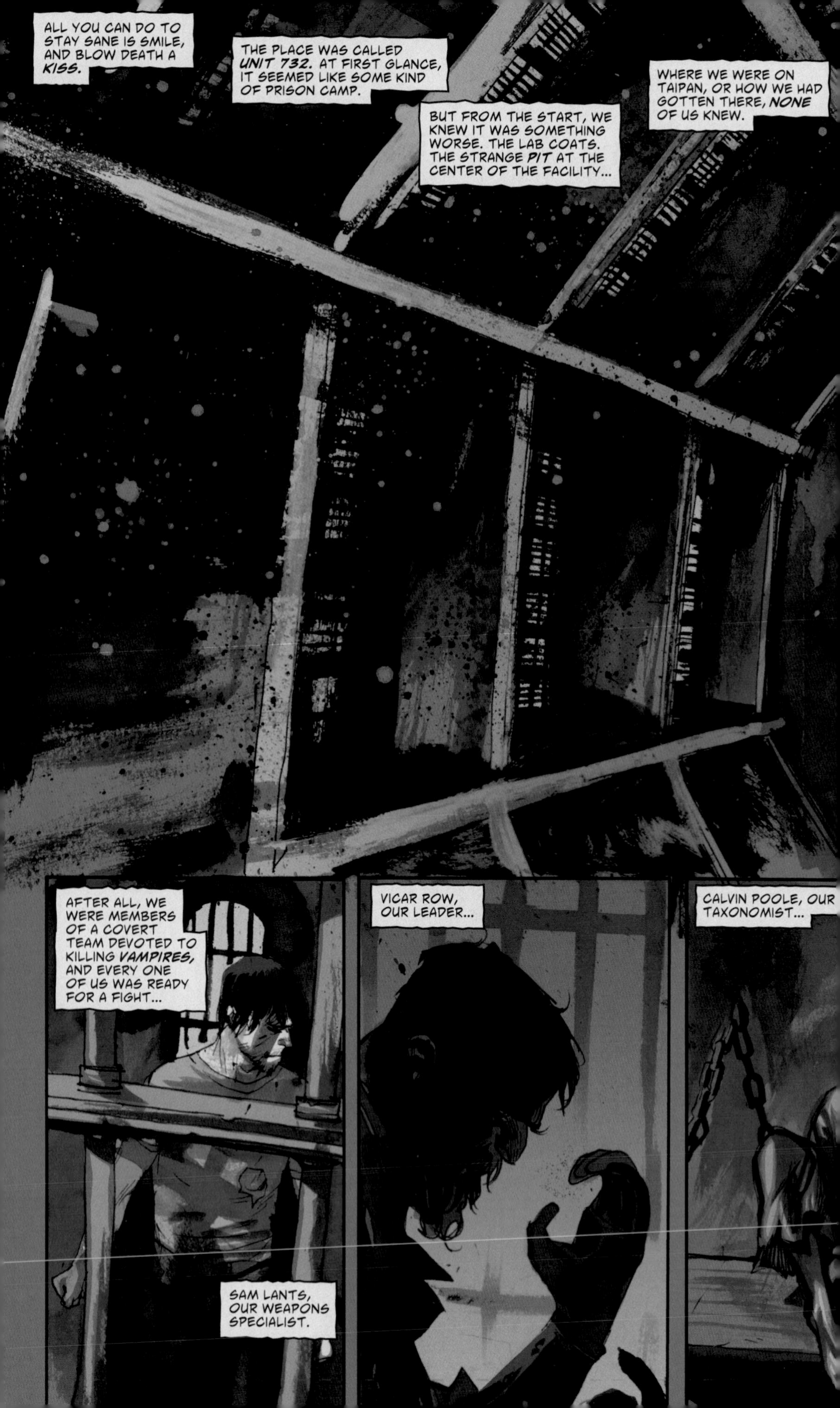
ALL YOU CAN DO TO STAY SANE IS SMILE, AND BLOW DEATH A *KISS.*
THE PLACE WAS CALLED *UNIT 732.* AT FIRST GLANCE, IT SEEMED LIKE SOME KIND OF PRISON CAMP.
BUT FROM THE START, WE KNEW IT WAS SOMETHING WORSE. THE LAB COATS. THE STRANGE *PIT* AT THE CENTER OF THE FACILITY...
WHERE WE WERE ON TAIPAN, OR HOW WE HAD GOTTEN THERE, *NONE* OF US KNEW.
AFTER ALL, WE WERE MEMBERS OF A COVERT TEAM DEVOTED TO KILLING *VAMPIRES,* AND EVERY ONE OF US WAS READY FOR A FIGHT...
SAM LANTS, OUR WEAPONS SPECIALIST.
VICAR ROW, OUR LEADER...
CALVIN POOLE, OUR TAXONOMIST...

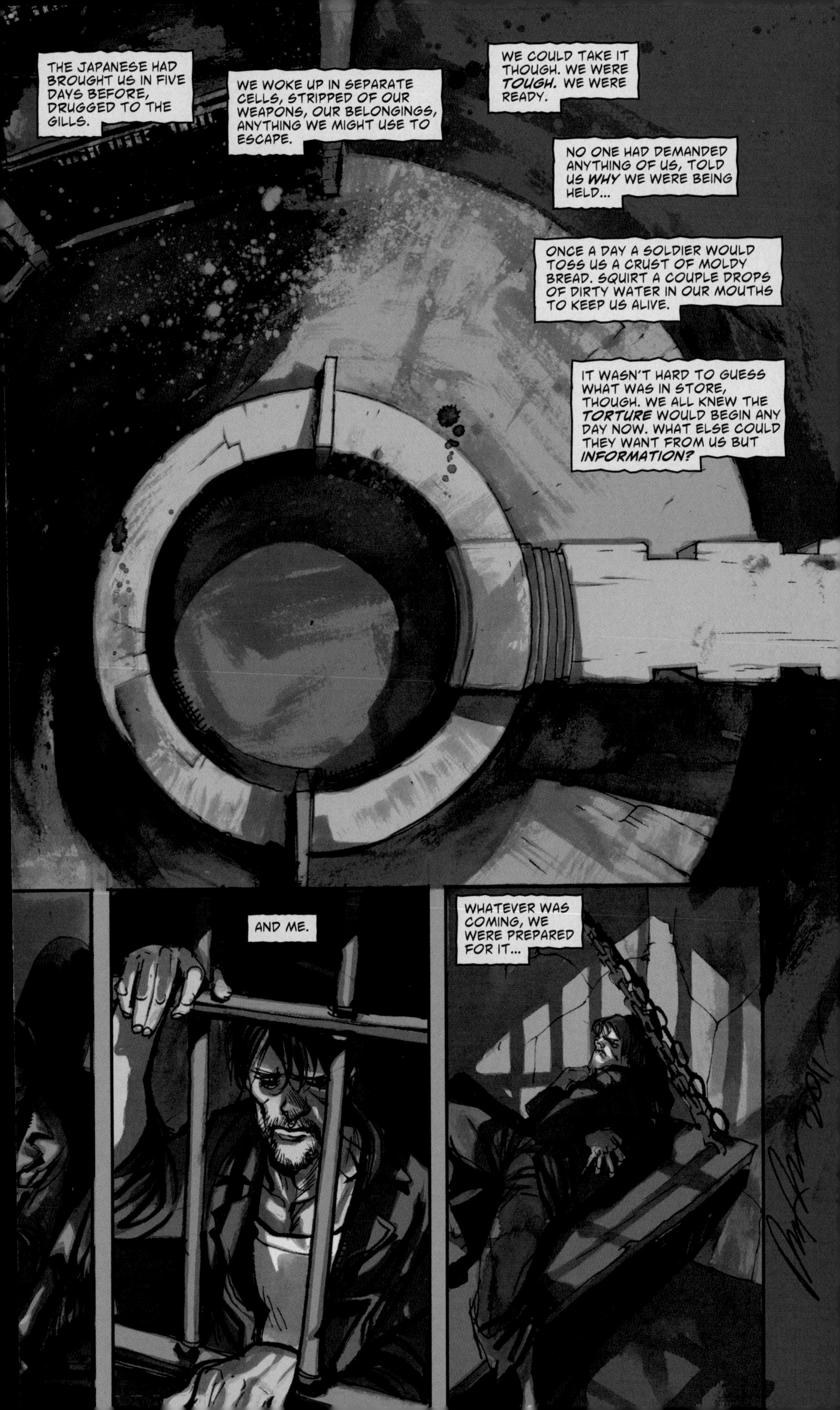
THE JAPANESE HAD BROUGHT US IN FIVE DAYS BEFORE, DRUGGED TO THE GILLS.
WE WOKE UP IN SEPARATE CELLS, STRIPPED OF OUR WEAPONS, OUR BELONGINGS, ANYTHING WE MIGHT USE TO ESCAPE.
WE COULD TAKE IT THOUGH. WE WERE TOUGH. WE WERE READY.
NO ONE HAD DEMANDED ANYTHING OF US, TOLD US WHY WE WERE BEING HELD...
ONCE A DAY A SOLDIER WOULD TOSS US A CRUST OF MOLDY BREAD. SQUIRT A COUPLE DROPS OF DIRTY WATER IN OUR MOUTHS TO KEEP US ALIVE.
IT WASN'T HARD TO GUESS WHAT WAS IN STORE, THOUGH. WE ALL KNEW THE TORTURE WOULD BEGIN ANY DAY NOW. WHAT ELSE COULD THEY WANT FROM US BUT INFORMATION?
AND ME.
WHATEVER WAS COMING, WE WERE PREPARED FOR IT...

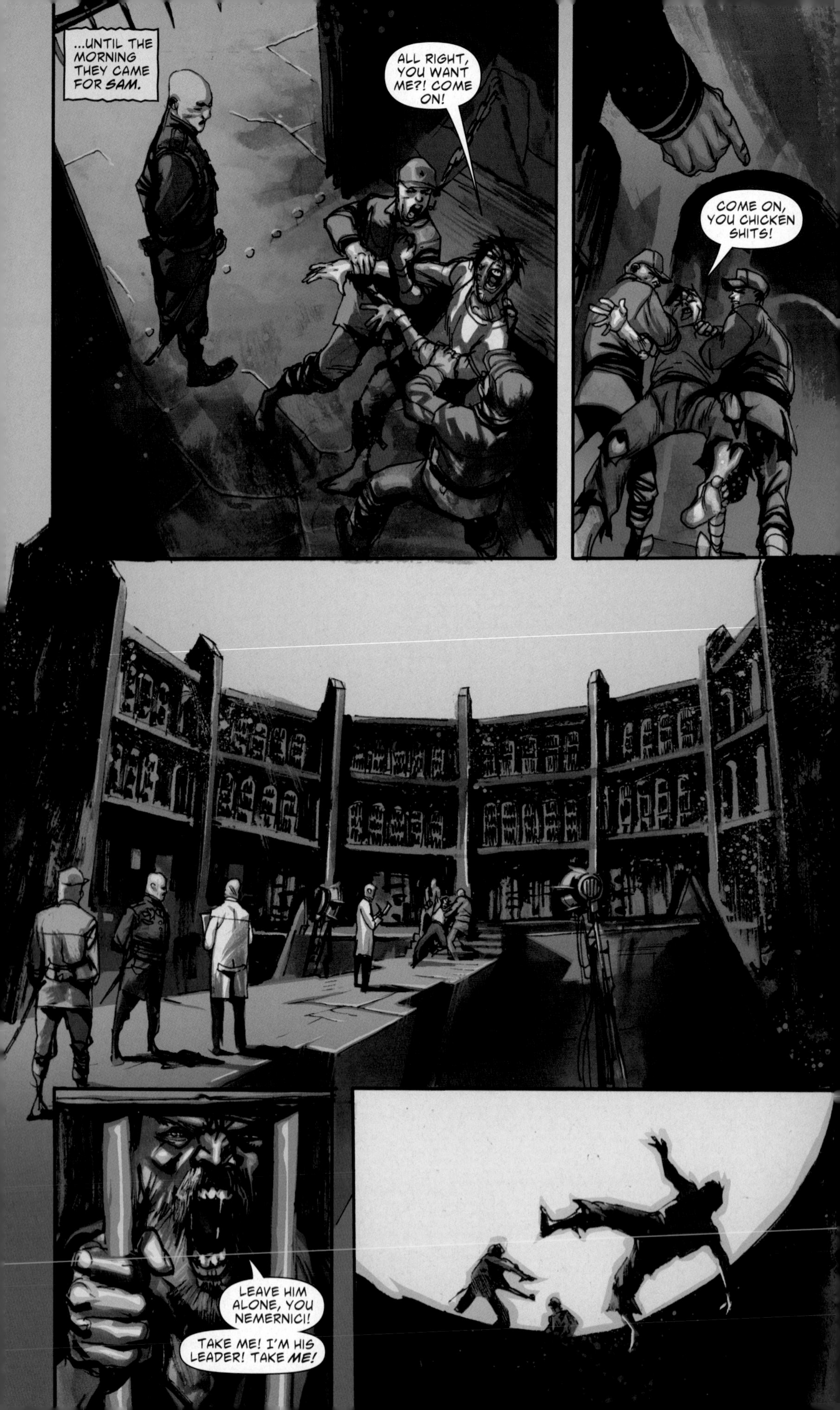
...UNTIL THE MORNING THEY CAME FOR SAM.
ALL RIGHT, YOU WANT ME?! COME ON!
COME ON, YOU CHICKEN SHITS!
LEAVE HIM ALONE, YOU NEMERNICI!
TAKE ME! I'M HIS LEADER! TAKE ME!

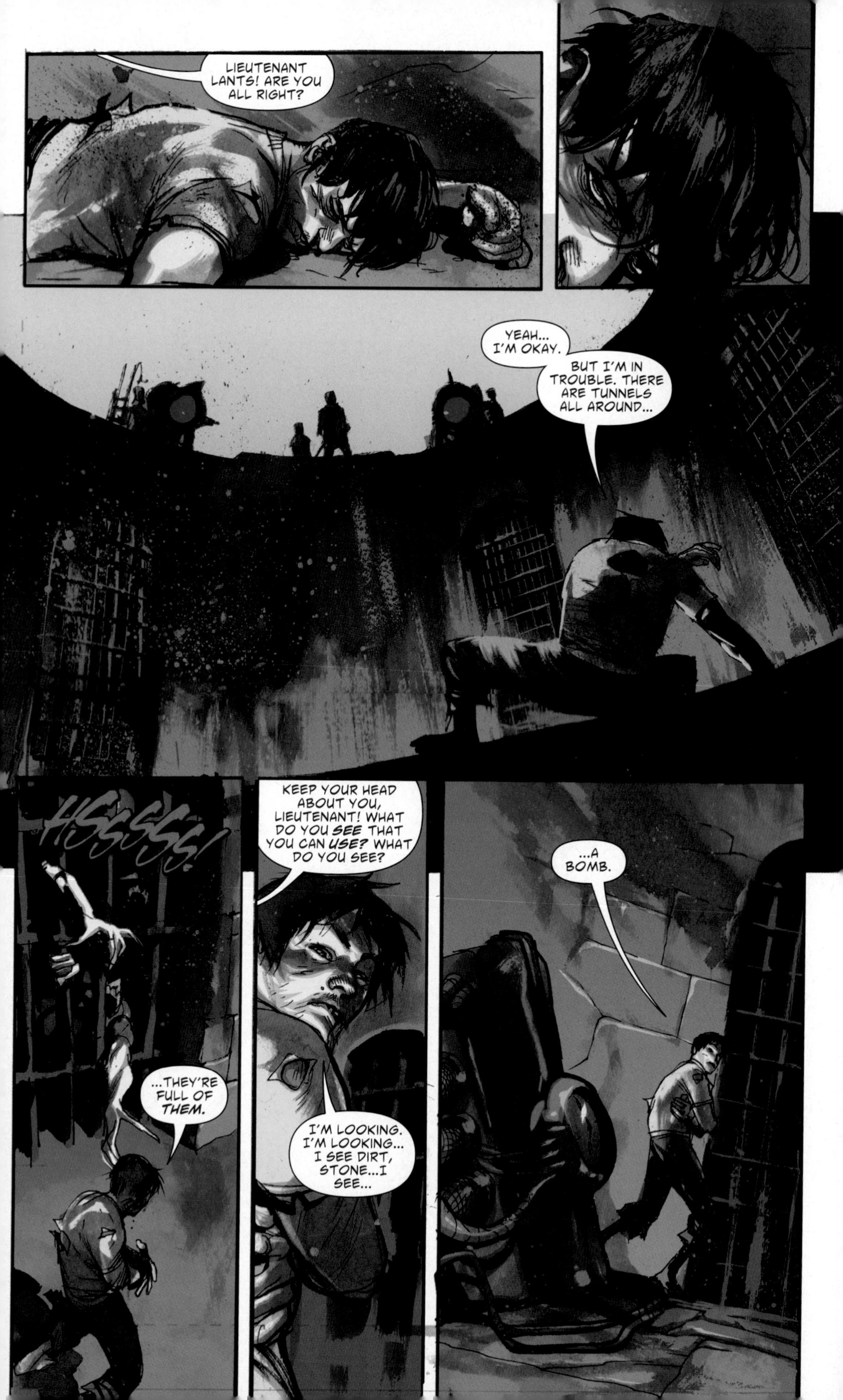
LIEUTENANT LANTS! ARE YOU ALL RIGHT?
YEAH... I'M OKAY.
BUT I'M IN TROUBLE. THERE ARE TUNNELS ALL AROUND...
HSSSSS!
...THEY'RE FULL OF THEM.
KEEP YOUR HEAD ABOUT YOU, LIEUTENANT! WHAT DO YOU SEE THAT YOU CAN USE? WHAT DO YOU SEE?
I'M LOOKING. I'M LOOKING... I SEE DIRT, STONE...I SEE...
...A BOMB.

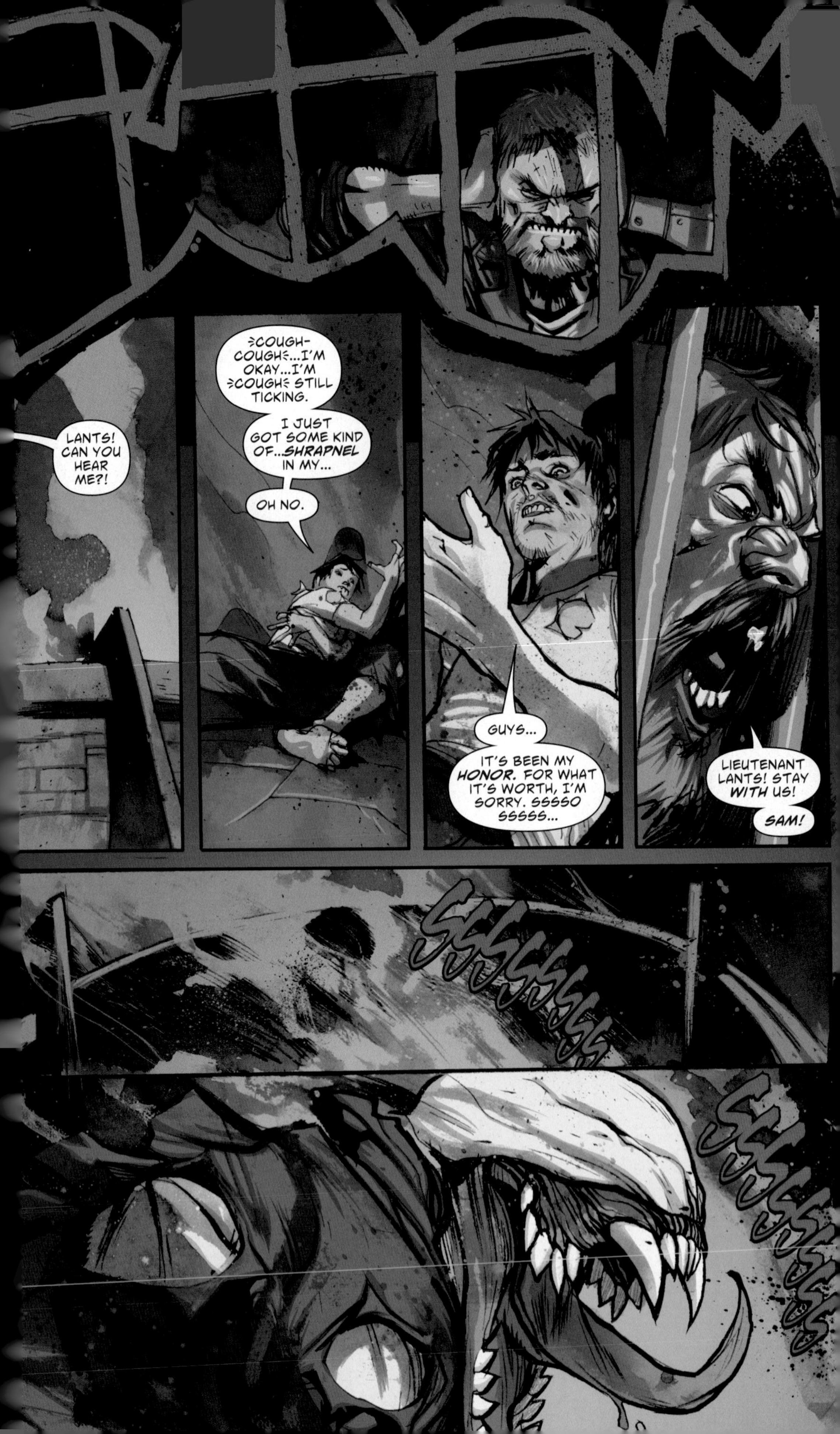
LANTS! CAN YOU HEAR ME?!
COUGH-COUGH ...I'M OKAY...I'M COUGH STILL TICKING.
I JUST GOT SOME KIND OF...SHRAPNEL IN MY...
OH NO.
GUYS...
IT'S BEEN MY HONOR. FOR WHAT IT'S WORTH, I'M SORRY. SSSSO SSSSS...
LIEUTENANT LANTS! STAY WITH US!
SAM!

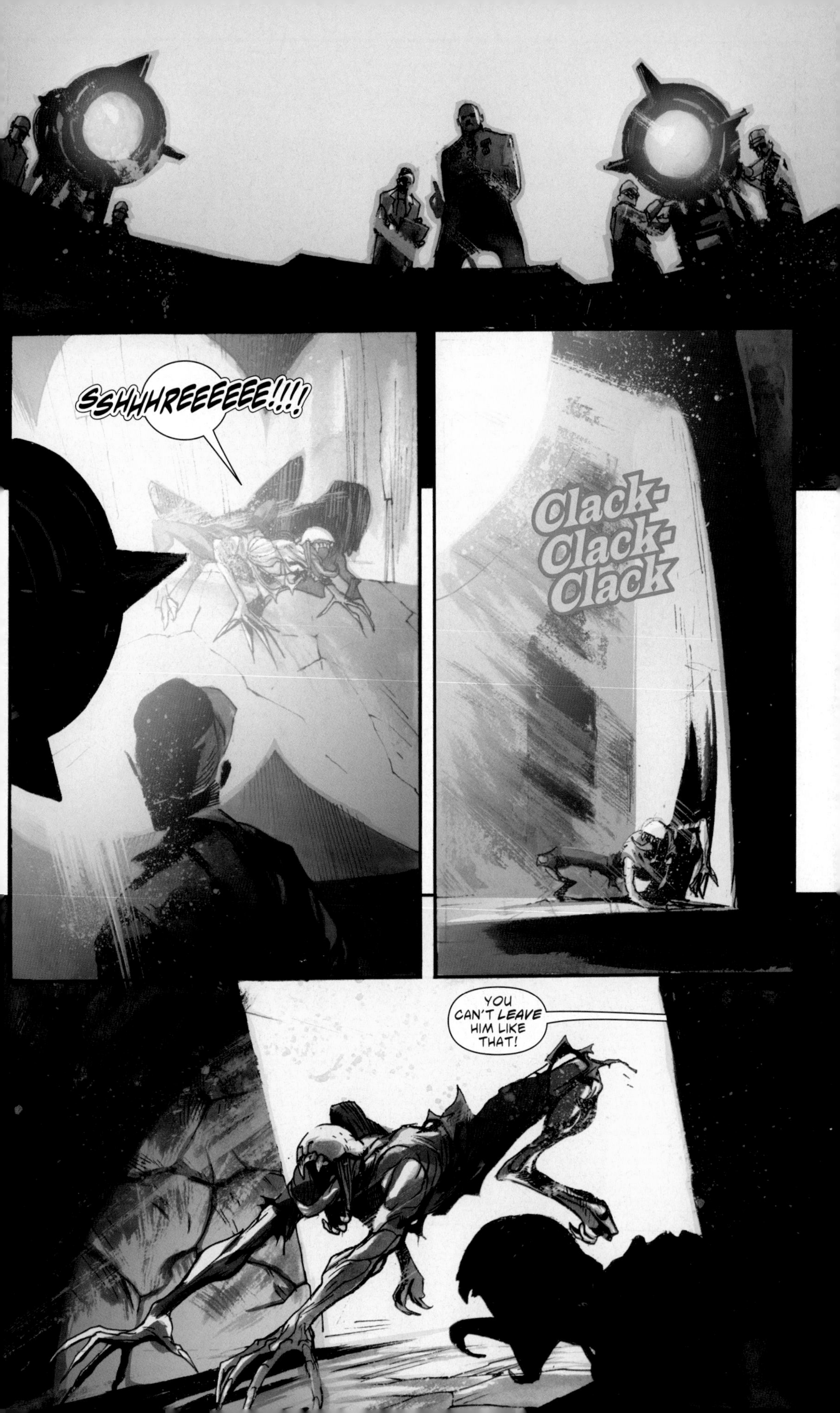
SSHHHREEEEEEE!!!!
Clack-
Clack-
Clack
YOU CAN'T LEAVE HIM LIKE THAT!

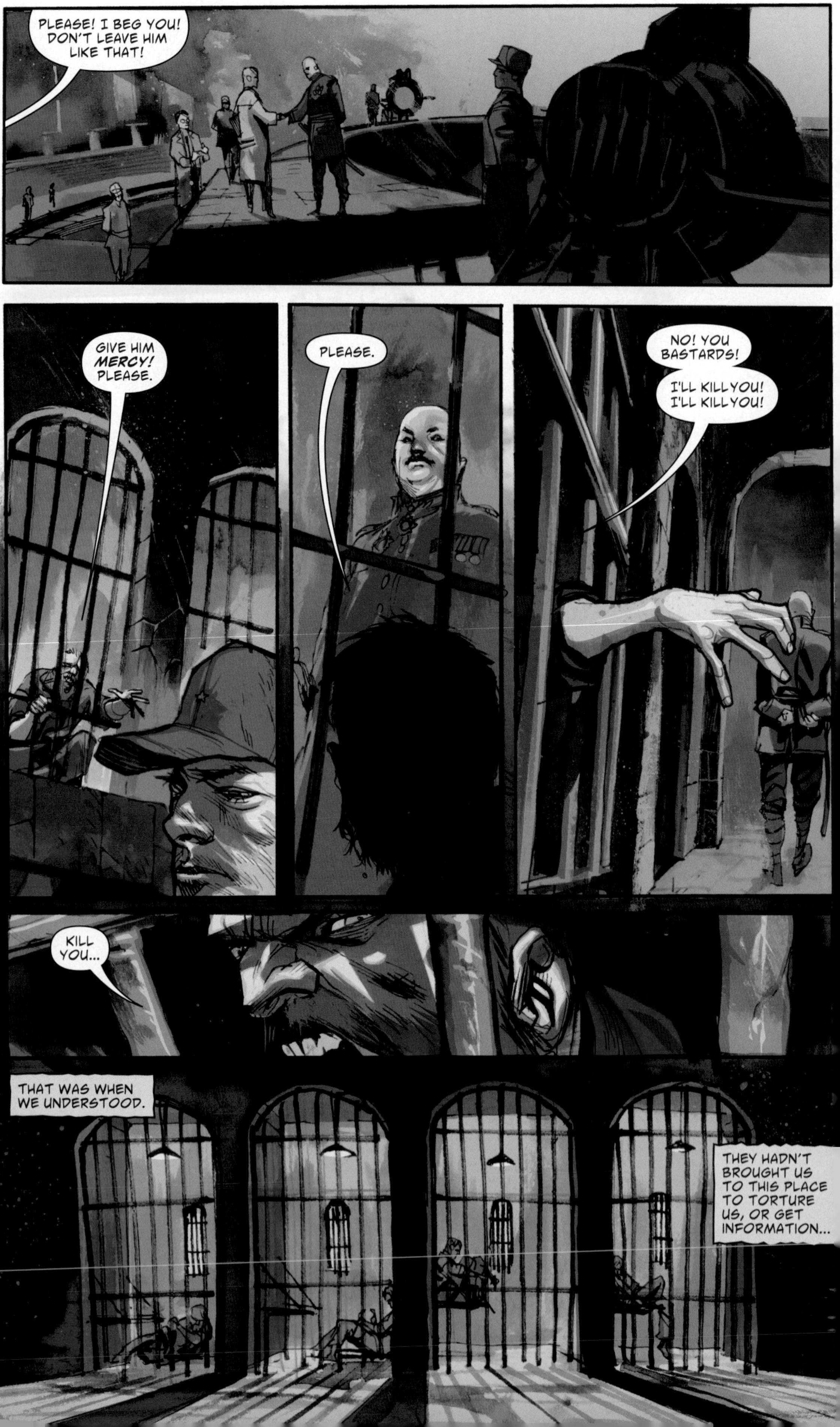
PLEASE! I BEG YOU! DON'T LEAVE HIM LIKE THAT!
GIVE HIM *MERCY!* PLEASE.
PLEASE.
NO! YOU BASTARDS!
I'LL KILLYOU! I'LL KILLYOU!
KILL YOU...
THAT WAS WHEN WE UNDERSTOOD.
THEY HADN'T BROUGHT US TO THIS PLACE TO TORTURE US, OR GET INFORMATION...

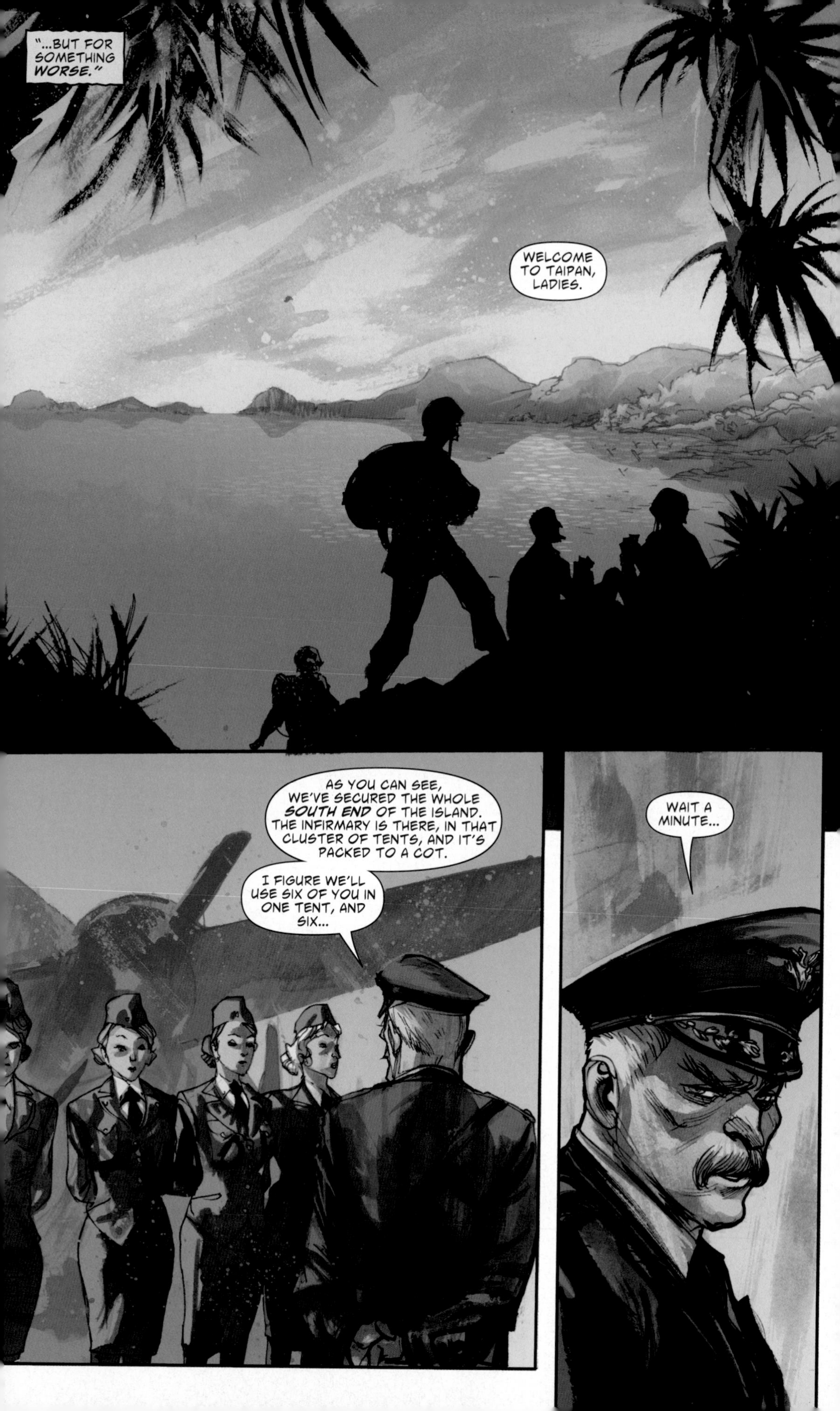
"...BUT FOR SOMETHING *WORSE*."
WELCOME TO TAIPAN, LADIES.
AS YOU CAN SEE, WE'VE SECURED THE WHOLE *SOUTH END* OF THE ISLAND. THE INFIRMARY IS THERE, IN THAT CLUSTER OF TENTS, AND IT'S PACKED TO A COT.
I FIGURE WE'LL USE SIX OF YOU IN ONE TENT, AND SIX...
WAIT A MINUTE...

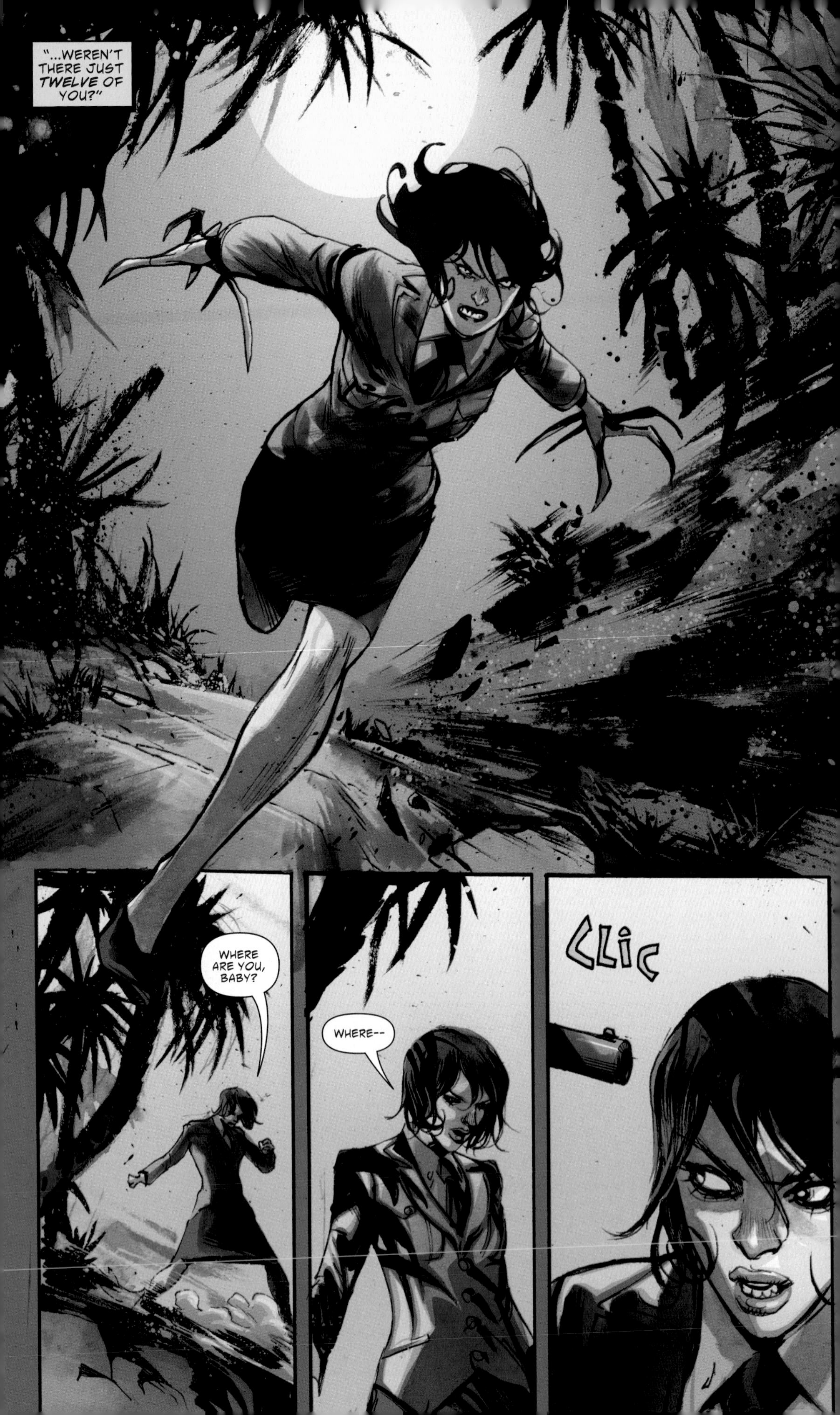
"...WEREN'T THERE JUST *TWELVE* OF YOU?"
WHERE ARE YOU, BABY?
WHERE--
CLIC

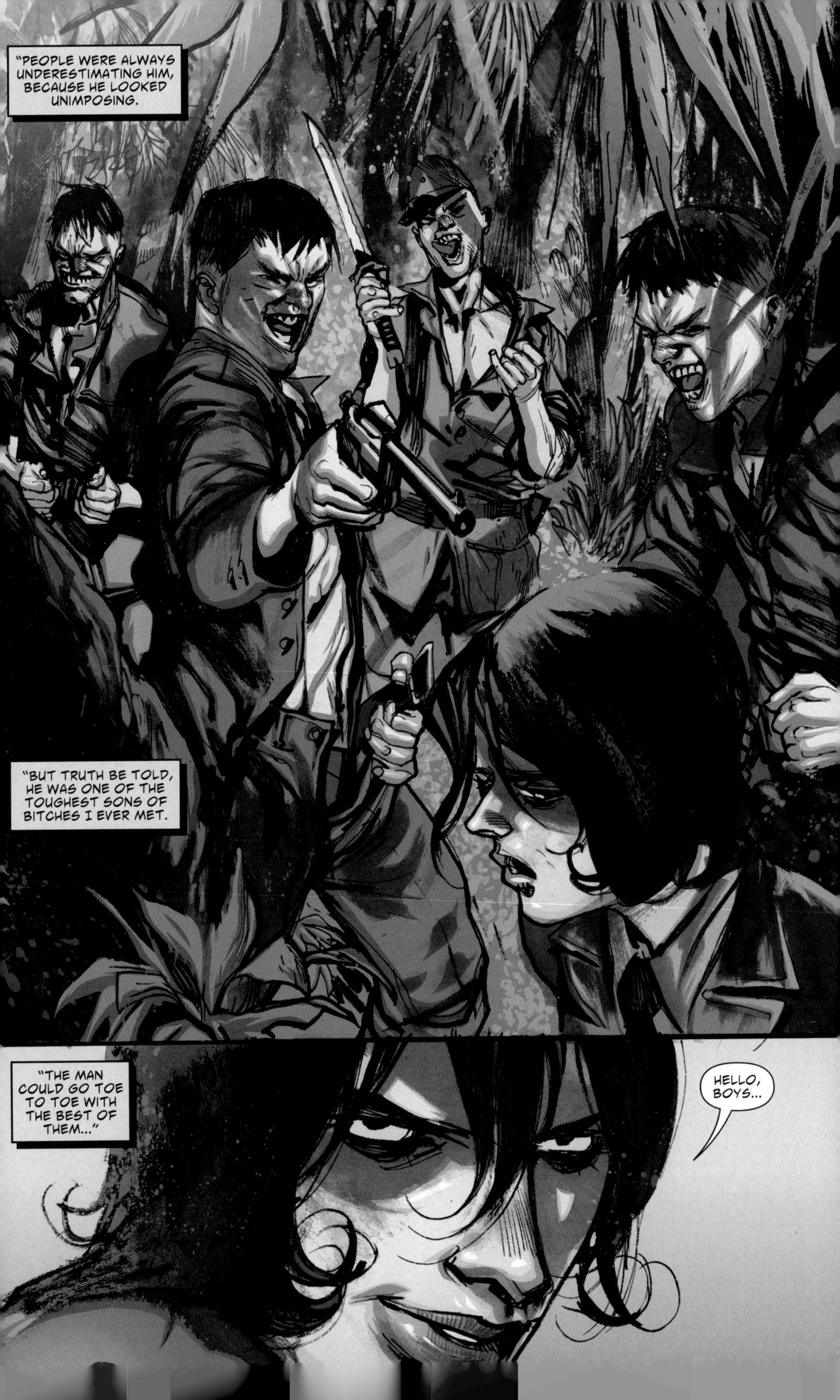
"PEOPLE WERE ALWAYS UNDERESTIMATING HIM, BECAUSE HE LOOKED UNIMPOSING.
"BUT TRUTH BE TOLD, HE WAS ONE OF THE TOUGHEST SONS OF BITCHES I EVER MET.
"THE MAN COULD GO TOE TO TOE WITH THE BEST OF THEM..."
HELLO, BOYS...

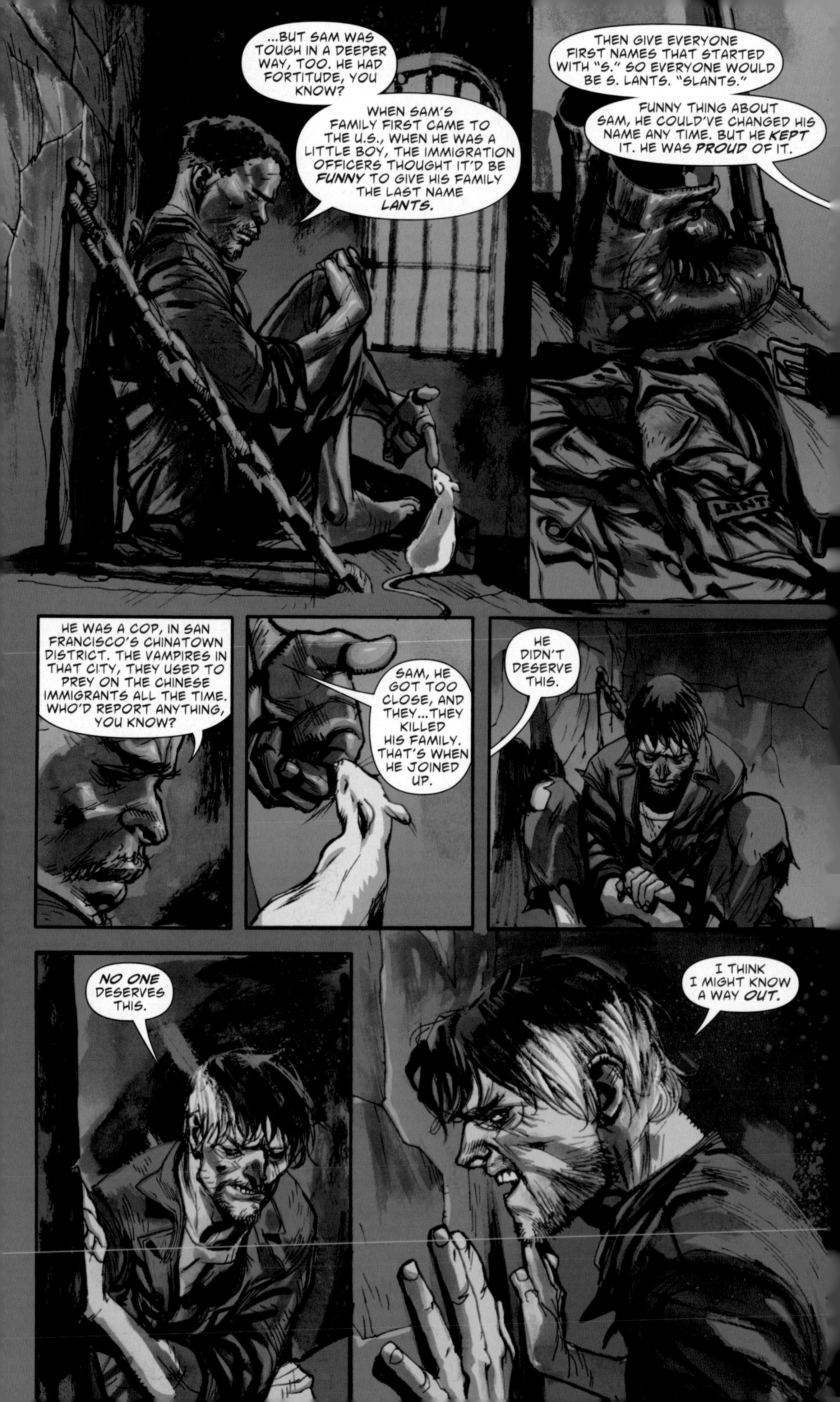
...BUT SAM WAS TOUGH IN A DEEPER WAY, TOO. HE HAD FORTITUDE, YOU KNOW?
WHEN SAM'S FAMILY FIRST CAME TO THE U.S., WHEN HE WAS A LITTLE BOY, THE IMMIGRATION OFFICERS THOUGHT IT'D BE FUNNY TO GIVE HIS FAMILY THE LAST NAME LANTS.
THEN GIVE EVERYONE FIRST NAMES THAT STARTED WITH "S." SO EVERYONE WOULD BE S. LANTS. "SLANTS."
FUNNY THING ABOUT SAM, HE COULD'VE CHANGED HIS NAME ANY TIME. BUT HE KEPT IT. HE WAS PROUD OF IT.
LANT
HE WAS A COP, IN SAN FRANCISCO'S CHINATOWN DISTRICT. THE VAMPIRES IN THAT CITY, THEY USED TO PREY ON THE CHINESE IMMIGRANTS ALL THE TIME. WHO'D REPORT ANYTHING, YOU KNOW?
SAM, HE GOT TOO CLOSE, AND THEY...THEY KILLED HIS FAMILY. THAT'S WHEN HE JOINED UP.
HE DIDN'T DESERVE THIS.
NO ONE DESERVES THIS.
I THINK I MIGHT KNOW A WAY OUT.

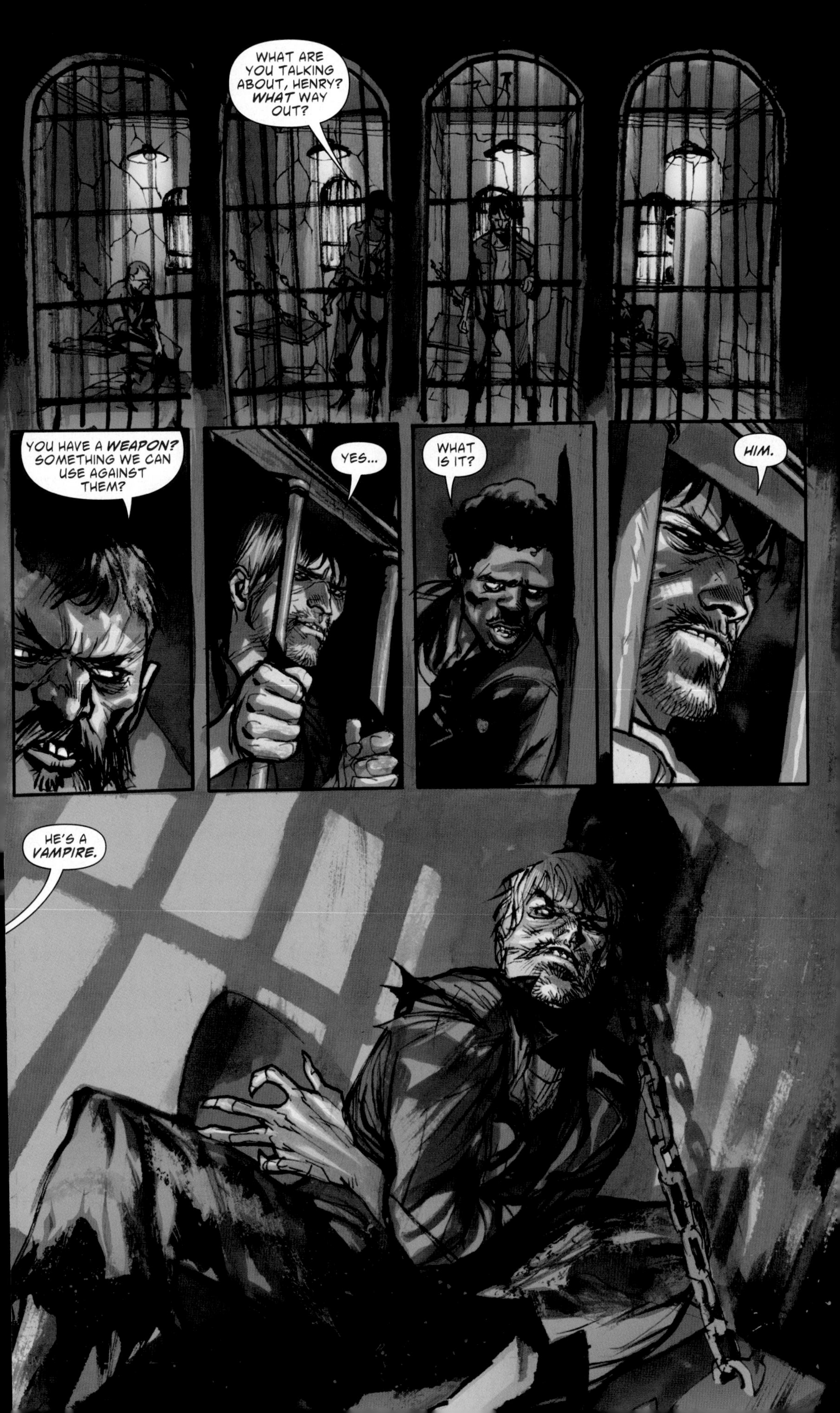
WHAT ARE YOU TALKING ABOUT, HENRY? WHAT WAY OUT?
YOU HAVE A WEAPON? SOMETHING WE CAN USE AGAINST THEM?
YES...
WHAT IS IT?
HIM.
HE'S A VAMPIRE.

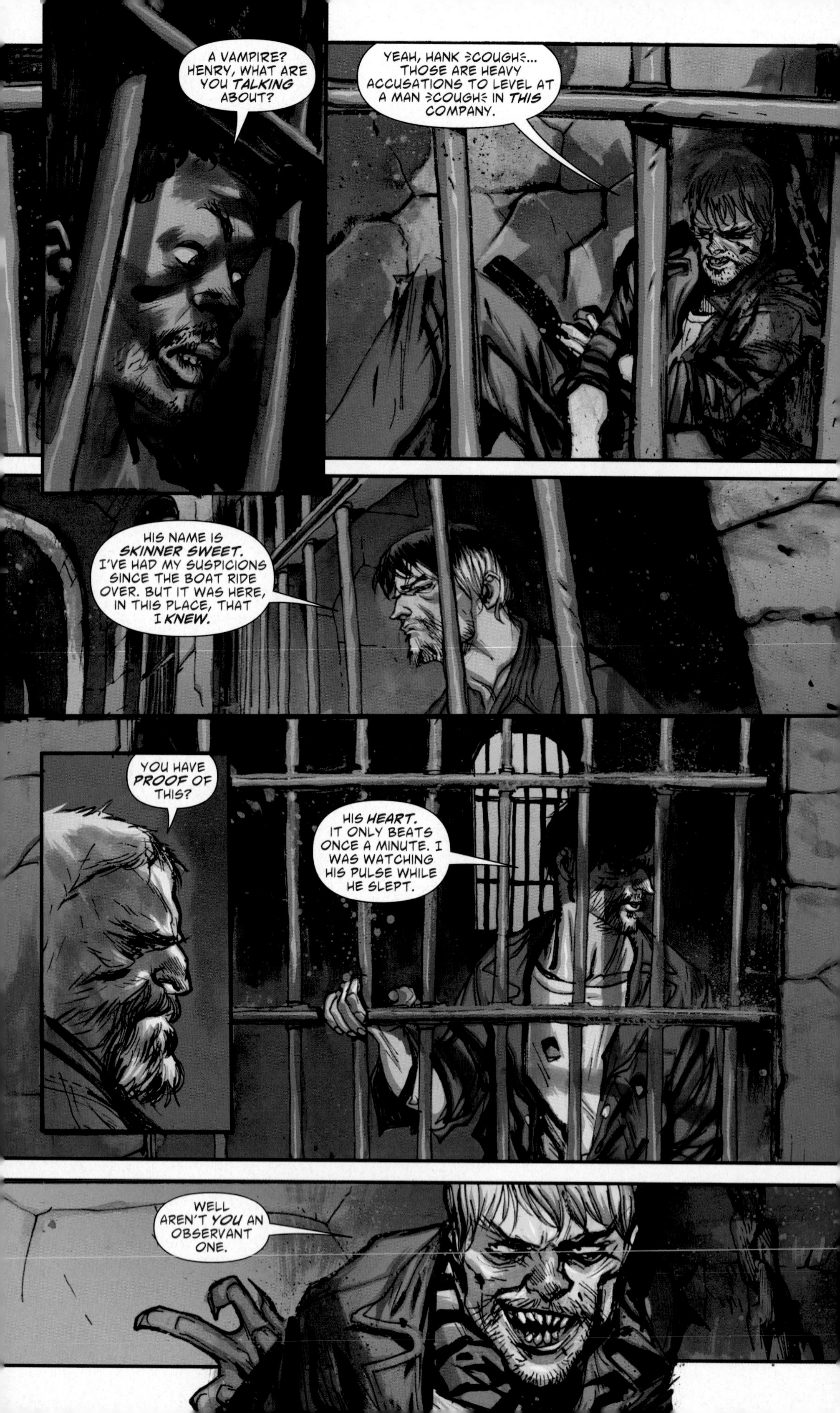
A VAMPIRE? HENRY, WHAT ARE YOU TALKING ABOUT?
YEAH, HANK ≥COUGH≤... THOSE ARE HEAVY ACCUSATIONS TO LEVEL AT A MAN ≥COUGH≤ IN THIS COMPANY.
HIS NAME IS SKINNER SWEET. I'VE HAD MY SUSPICIONS SINCE THE BOAT RIDE OVER. BUT IT WAS HERE, IN THIS PLACE, THAT I KNEW.
YOU HAVE PROOF OF THIS?
HIS HEART. IT ONLY BEATS ONCE A MINUTE. I WAS WATCHING HIS PULSE WHILE HE SLEPT.
WELL AREN'T YOU AN OBSERVANT ONE.

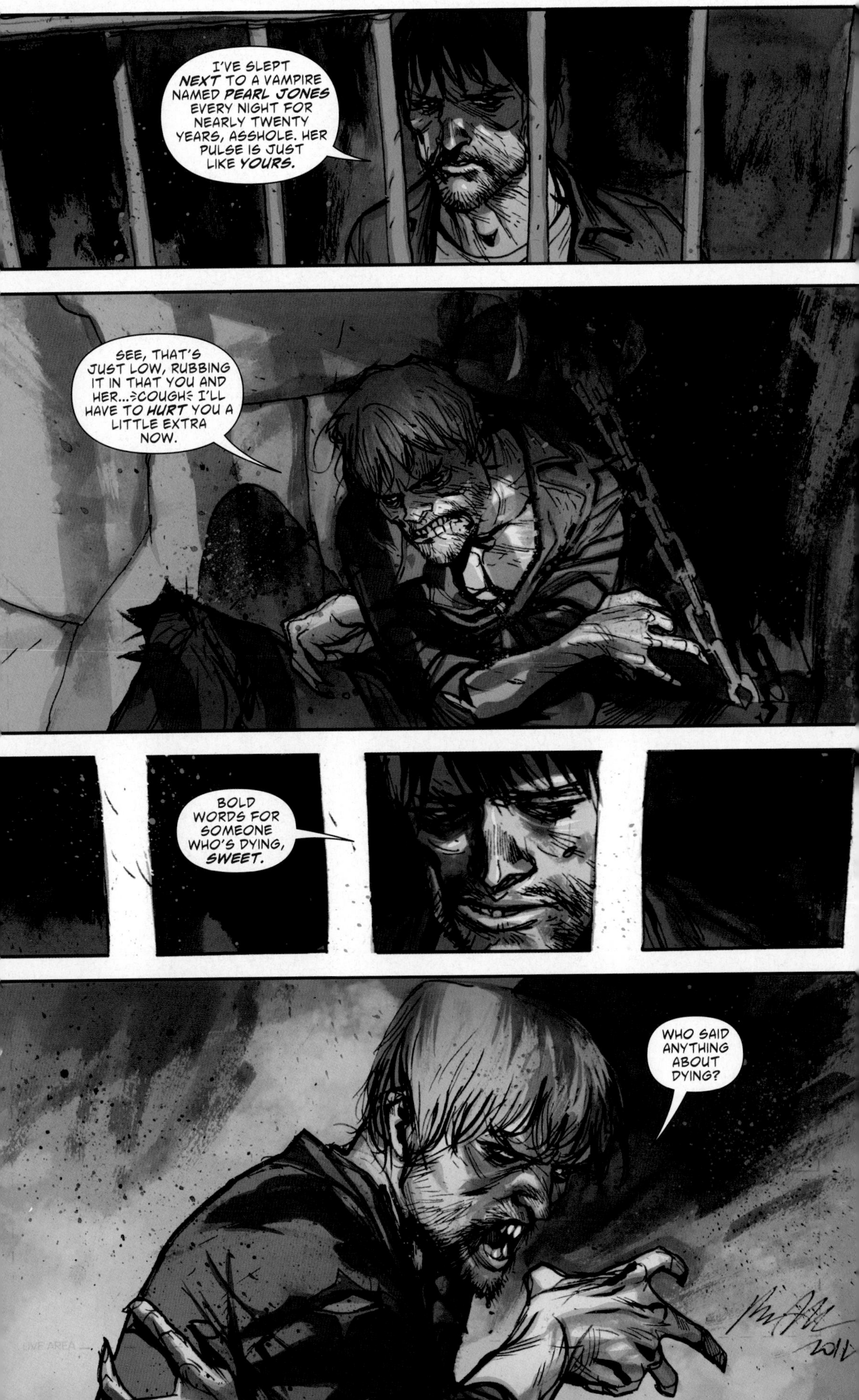
I'VE SLEPT NEXT TO A VAMPIRE NAMED PEARL JONES EVERY NIGHT FOR NEARLY TWENTY YEARS, ASSHOLE. HER PULSE IS JUST LIKE YOURS.
SEE, THAT'S JUST LOW, RUBBING IT IN THAT YOU AND HER... COUGH I'LL HAVE TO HURT YOU A LITTLE EXTRA NOW.
BOLD WORDS FOR SOMEONE WHO'S DYING, SWEET.
WHO SAID ANYTHING ABOUT DYING?

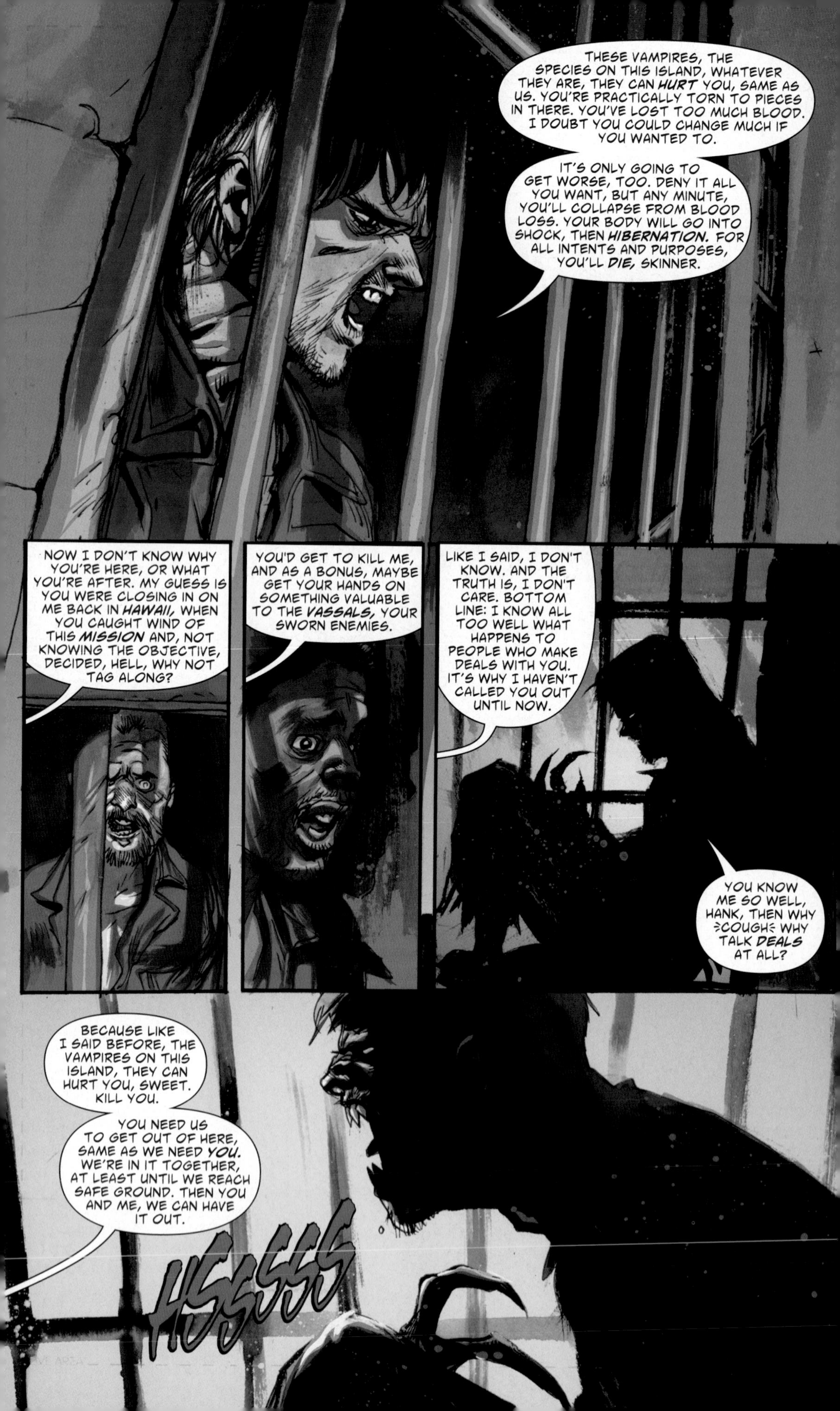
THESE VAMPIRES, THE SPECIES ON THIS ISLAND, WHATEVER THEY ARE, THEY CAN HURT YOU, SAME AS US. YOU'RE PRACTICALLY TORN TO PIECES IN THERE. YOU'VE LOST TOO MUCH BLOOD. I DOUBT YOU COULD CHANGE MUCH IF YOU WANTED TO.
IT'S ONLY GOING TO GET WORSE, TOO. DENY IT ALL YOU WANT, BUT ANY MINUTE, YOU'LL COLLAPSE FROM BLOOD LOSS. YOUR BODY WILL GO INTO SHOCK, THEN HIBERNATION. FOR ALL INTENTS AND PURPOSES, YOU'LL DIE, SKINNER.
NOW I DON'T KNOW WHY YOU'RE HERE, OR WHAT YOU'RE AFTER. MY GUESS IS YOU WERE CLOSING IN ON ME BACK IN HAWAII, WHEN YOU CAUGHT WIND OF THIS MISSION AND, NOT KNOWING THE OBJECTIVE, DECIDED, HELL, WHY NOT TAG ALONG?
YOU'D GET TO KILL ME, AND AS A BONUS, MAYBE GET YOUR HANDS ON SOMETHING VALUABLE TO THE VASSALS, YOUR SWORN ENEMIES.
LIKE I SAID, I DON'T KNOW. AND THE TRUTH IS, I DON'T CARE. BOTTOM LINE: I KNOW ALL TOO WELL WHAT HAPPENS TO PEOPLE WHO MAKE DEALS WITH YOU. IT'S WHY I HAVEN'T CALLED YOU OUT UNTIL NOW.
YOU KNOW ME SO WELL, HANK, THEN WHY *COUGH* WHY TALK DEALS AT ALL?
BECAUSE LIKE I SAID BEFORE, THE VAMPIRES ON THIS ISLAND, THEY CAN HURT YOU, SWEET. KILL YOU.
YOU NEED US TO GET OUT OF HERE, SAME AS WE NEED YOU. WE'RE IN IT TOGETHER, AT LEAST UNTIL WE REACH SAFE GROUND. THEN YOU AND ME, WE CAN HAVE IT OUT.
HSSSSS

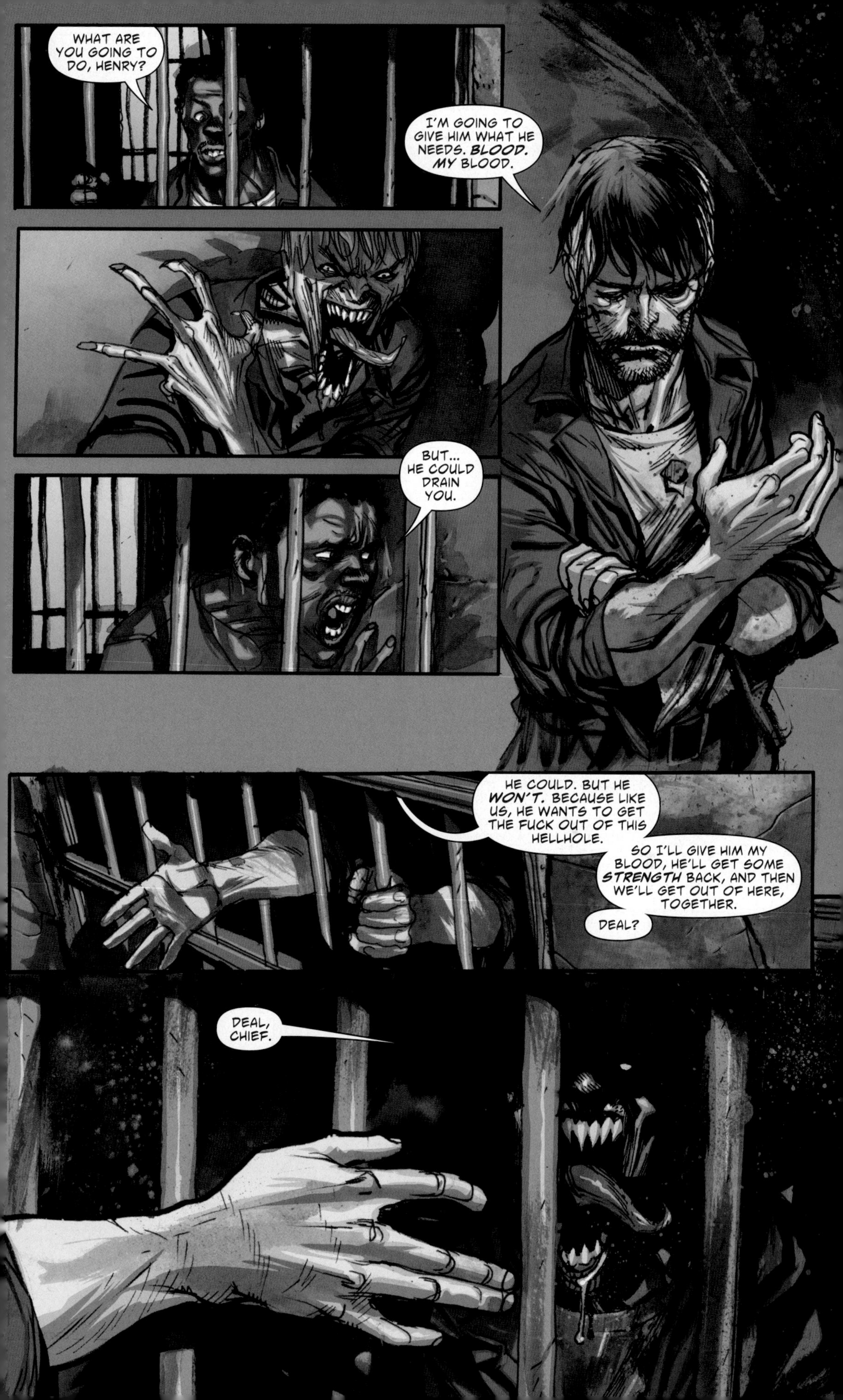
WHAT ARE YOU GOING TO DO, HENRY?
I'M GOING TO GIVE HIM WHAT HE NEEDS. **BLOOD. MY** BLOOD.
BUT... HE COULD DRAIN YOU.
HE COULD. BUT HE **WON'T.** BECAUSE LIKE US, HE WANTS TO GET THE FUCK OUT OF THIS HELLHOLE.
SO I'LL GIVE HIM MY BLOOD, HE'LL GET SOME **STRENGTH** BACK, AND THEN WE'LL GET OUT OF HERE, TOGETHER.
DEAL?
DEAL, CHIEF.

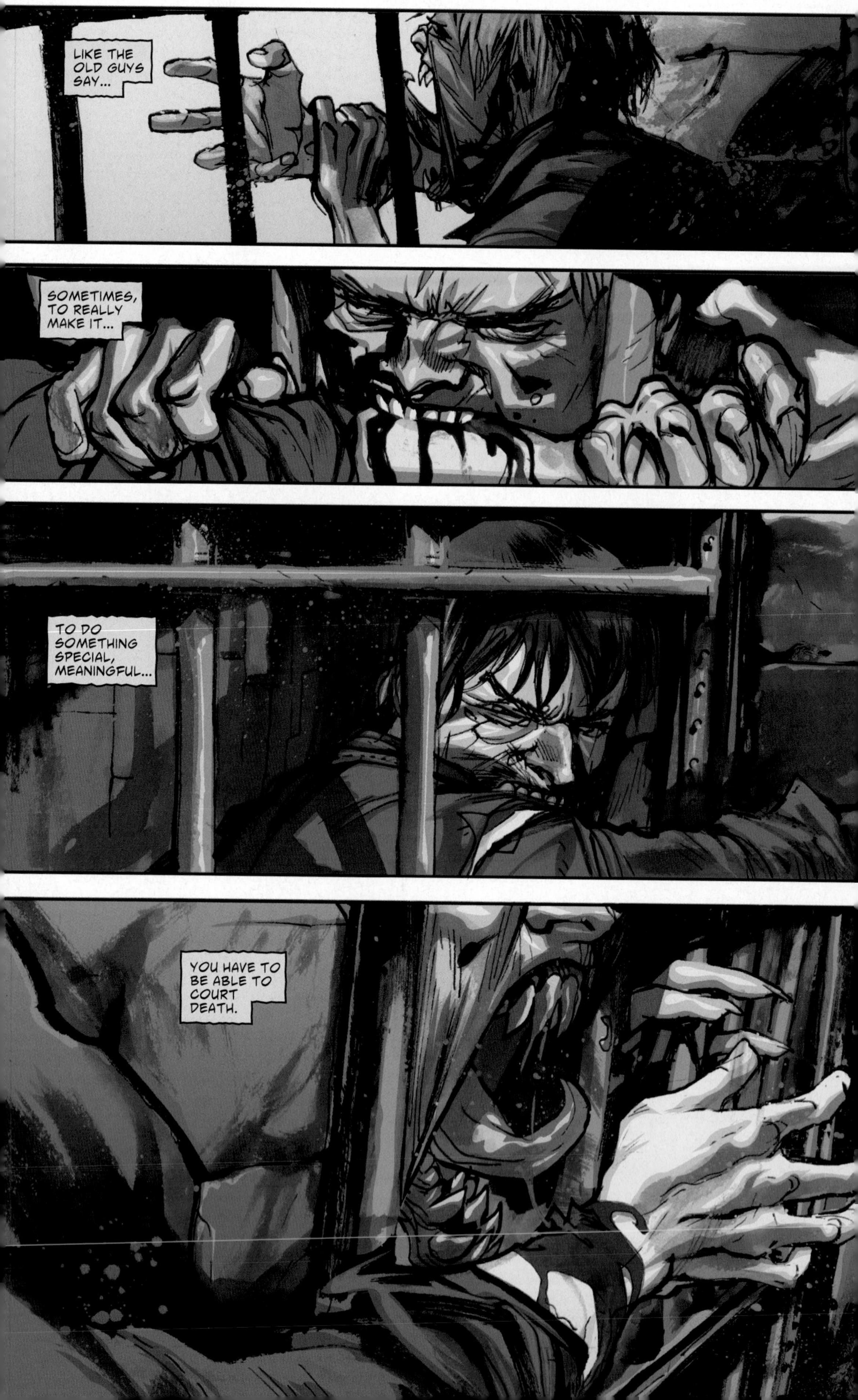
LIKE THE OLD GUYS SAY...
SOMETIMES, TO REALLY MAKE IT...
TO DO SOMETHING SPECIAL, MEANINGFUL...
YOU HAVE TO BE ABLE TO COURT DEATH.

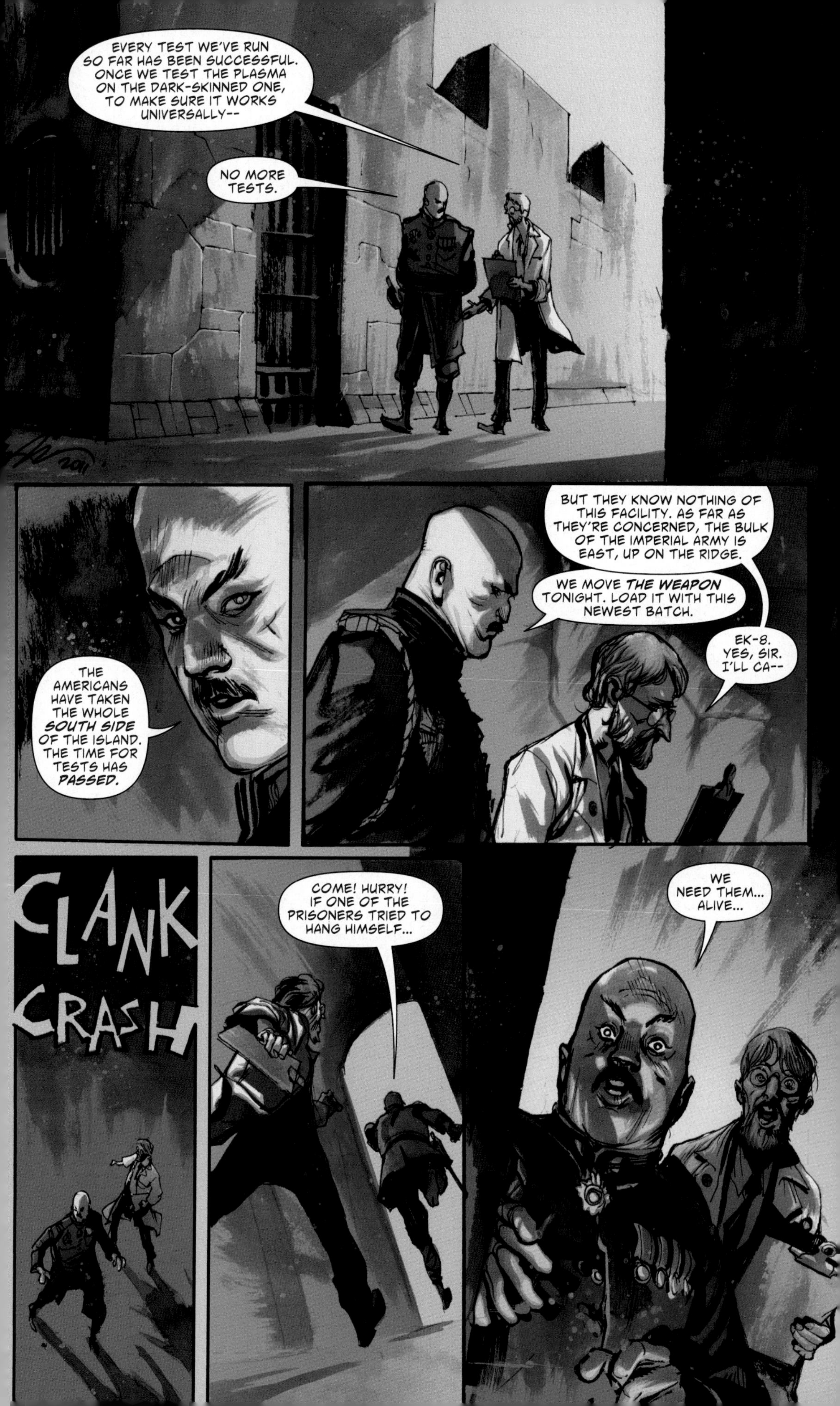
EVERY TEST WE'VE RUN SO FAR HAS BEEN SUCCESSFUL. ONCE WE TEST THE PLASMA ON THE DARK-SKINNED ONE, TO MAKE SURE IT WORKS UNIVERSALLY--
NO MORE TESTS.
THE AMERICANS HAVE TAKEN THE WHOLE *SOUTH SIDE* OF THE ISLAND. THE TIME FOR TESTS HAS *PASSED.*
BUT THEY KNOW NOTHING OF THIS FACILITY. AS FAR AS THEY'RE CONCERNED, THE BULK OF THE IMPERIAL ARMY IS EAST, UP ON THE RIDGE.
WE MOVE ***THE WEAPON*** TONIGHT. LOAD IT WITH THIS NEWEST BATCH.
EK-8. YES, SIR. I'LL CA--
CLANK
CRASH
COME! HURRY! IF ONE OF THE PRISONERS TRIED TO HANG HIMSELF...
WE NEED THEM... ALIVE...

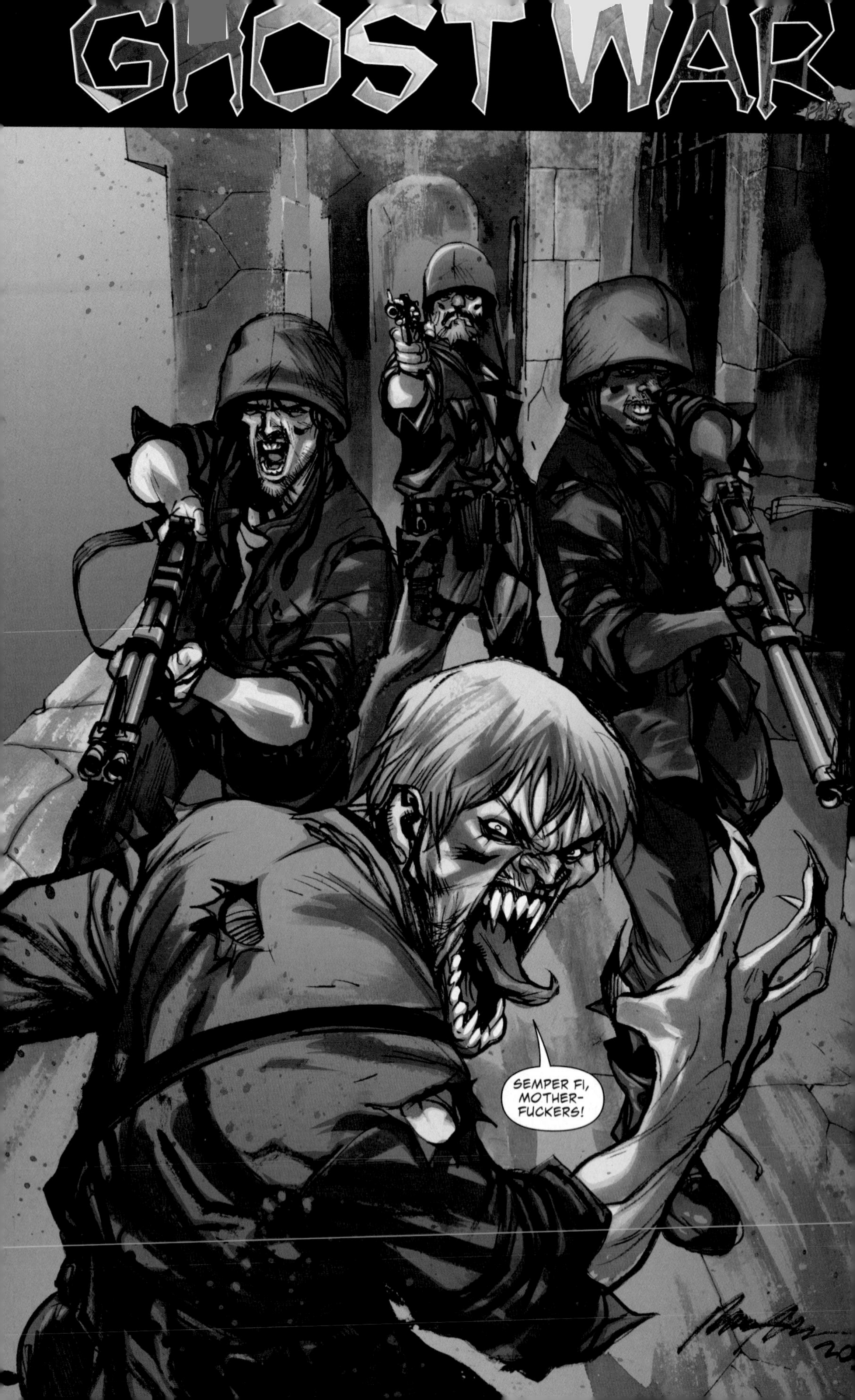
GHOST WAR
PART
SEMPER FI, MOTHER-FUCKERS!

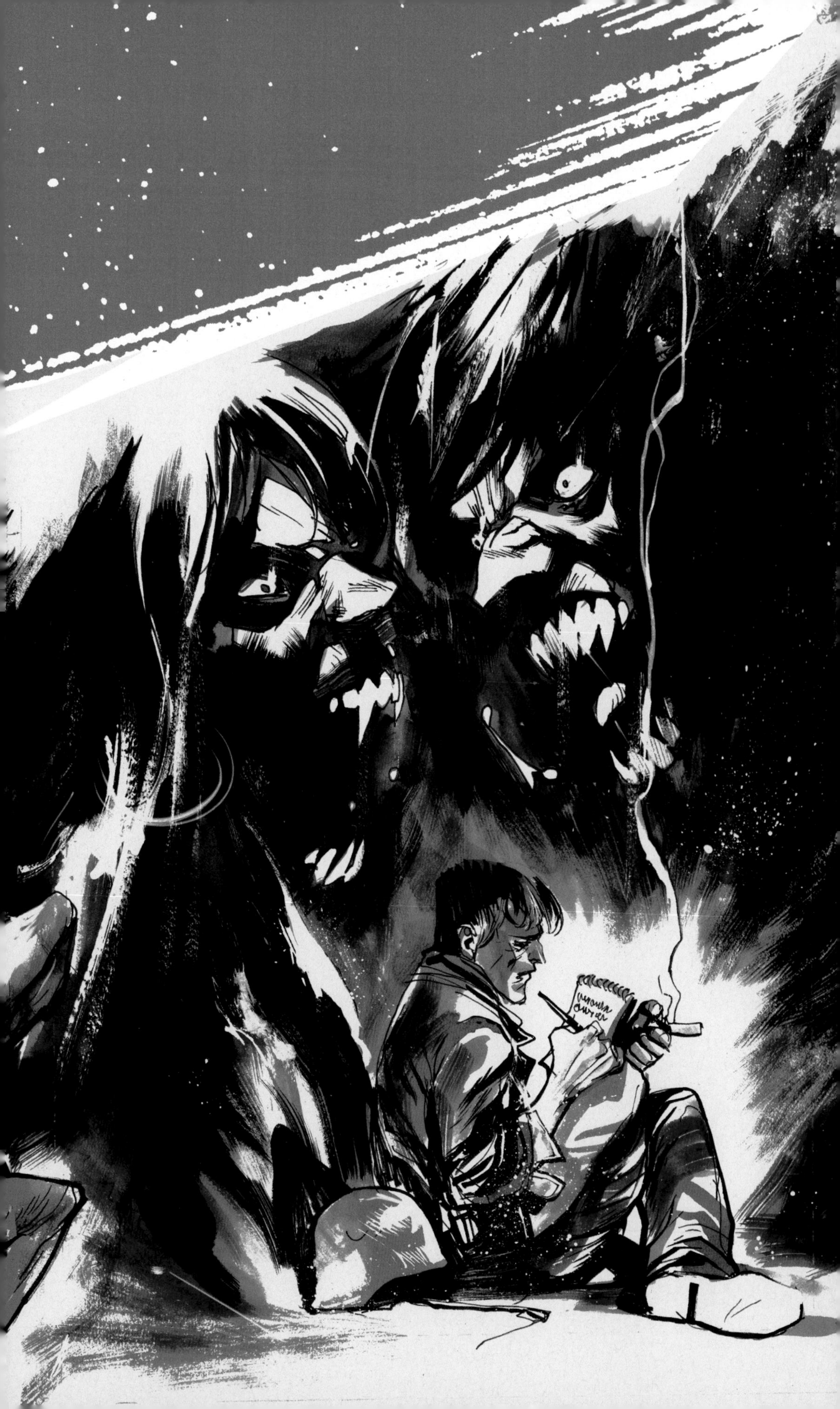

Ghost War

Part Five

Rafael Albuquerque
Artist and cover

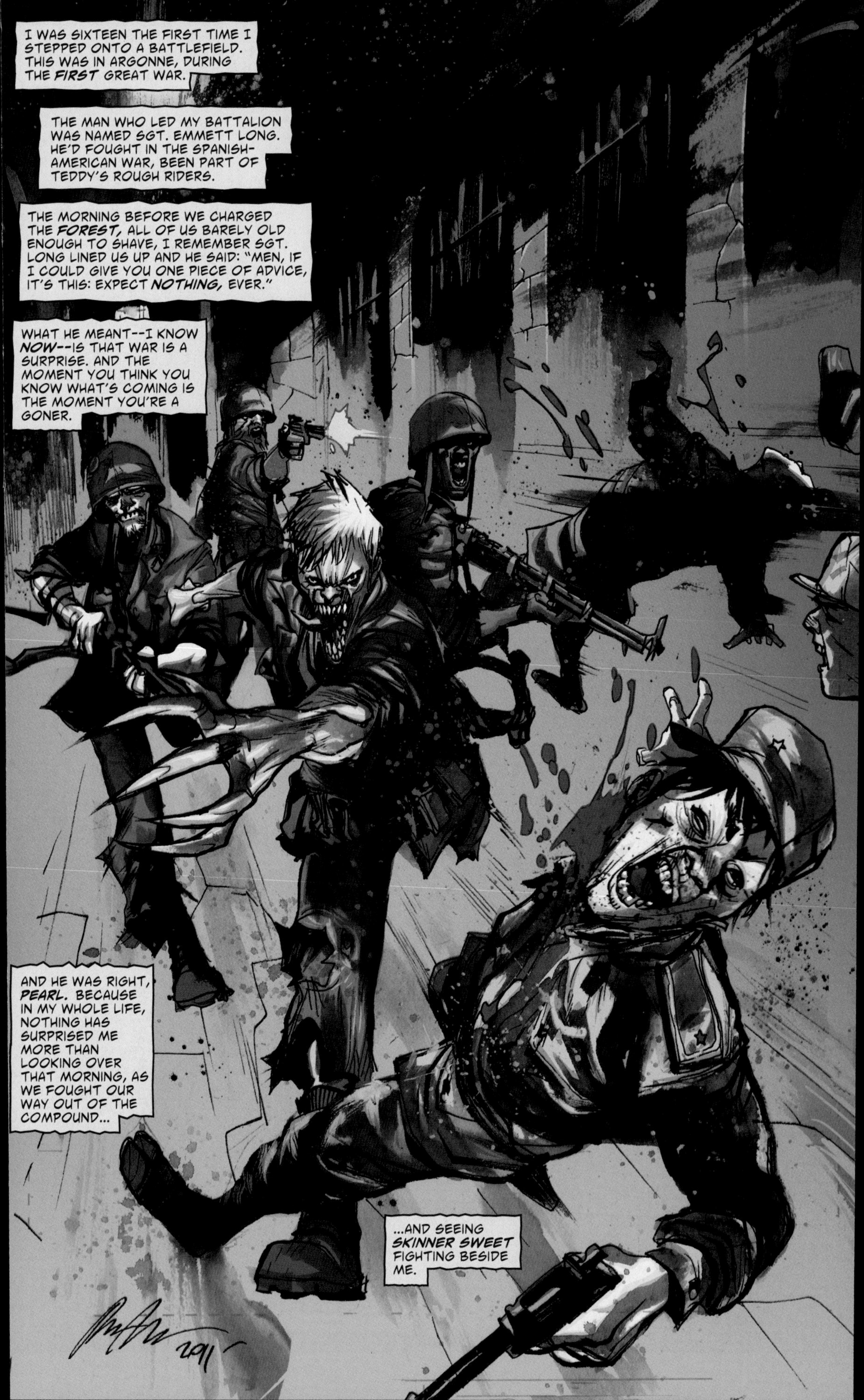
I WAS SIXTEEN THE FIRST TIME I STEPPED ONTO A BATTLEFIELD. THIS WAS IN ARGONNE, DURING THE FIRST GREAT WAR.
THE MAN WHO LED MY BATTALION WAS NAMED SGT. EMMETT LONG. HE'D FOUGHT IN THE SPANISH-AMERICAN WAR, BEEN PART OF TEDDY'S ROUGH RIDERS.
THE MORNING BEFORE WE CHARGED THE FOREST, ALL OF US BARELY OLD ENOUGH TO SHAVE, I REMEMBER SGT. LONG LINED US UP AND HE SAID: "MEN, IF I COULD GIVE YOU ONE PIECE OF ADVICE, IT'S THIS: EXPECT NOTHING, EVER."
WHAT HE MEANT--I KNOW NOW--IS THAT WAR IS A SURPRISE. AND THE MOMENT YOU THINK YOU KNOW WHAT'S COMING IS THE MOMENT YOU'RE A GONER.
AND HE WAS RIGHT, PEARL. BECAUSE IN MY WHOLE LIFE, NOTHING HAS SURPRISED ME MORE THAN LOOKING OVER THAT MORNING, AS WE FOUGHT OUR WAY OUT OF THE COMPOUND...
...AND SEEING SKINNER SWEET FIGHTING BESIDE ME.
2011

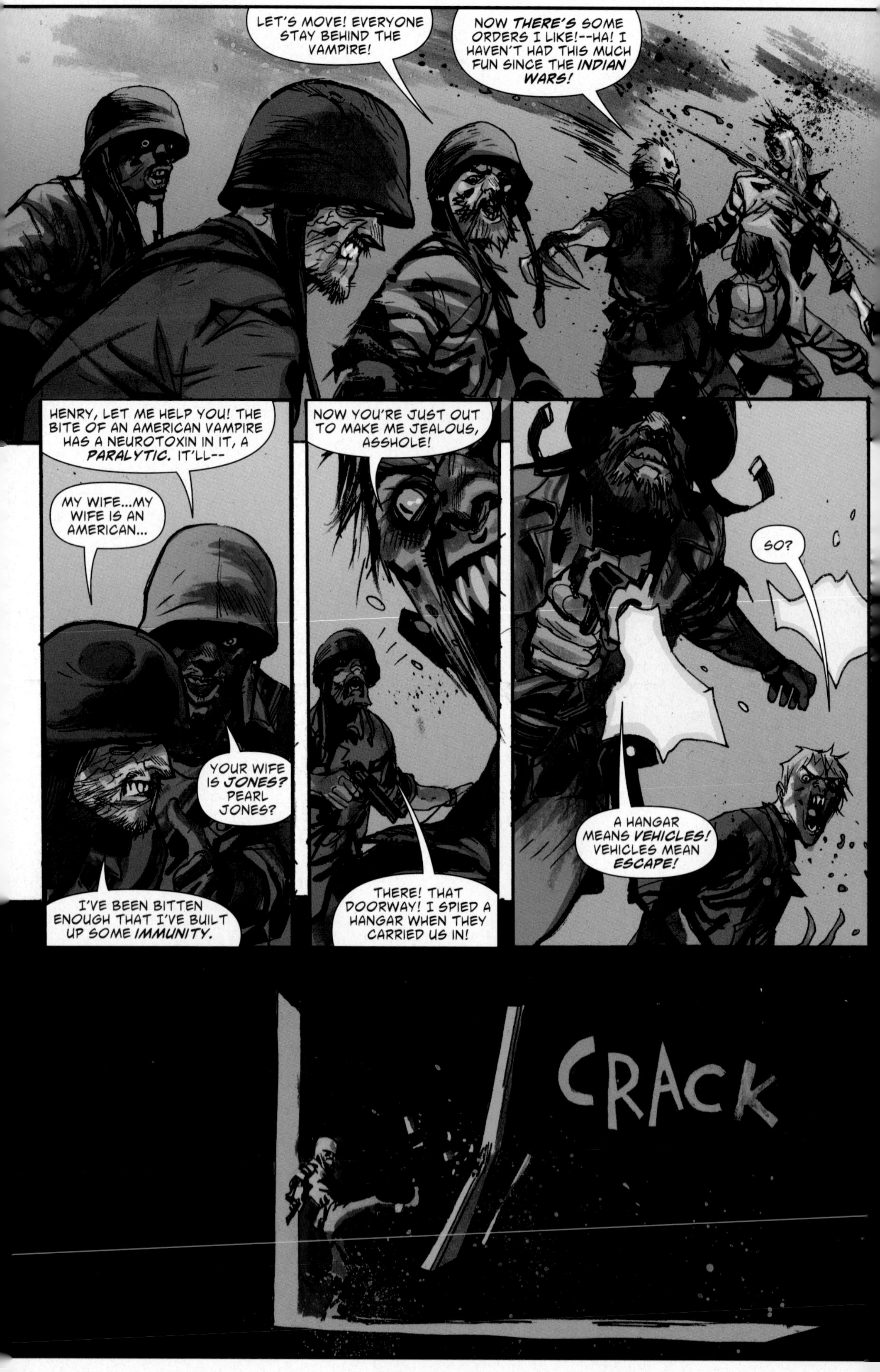
LET'S MOVE! EVERYONE STAY BEHIND THE VAMPIRE!
NOW THERE'S SOME ORDERS I LIKE!--HA! I HAVEN'T HAD THIS MUCH FUN SINCE THE INDIAN WARS!
HENRY, LET ME HELP YOU! THE BITE OF AN AMERICAN VAMPIRE HAS A NEUROTOXIN IN IT, A PARALYTIC. IT'LL--
MY WIFE...MY WIFE IS AN AMERICAN...
YOUR WIFE IS JONES? PEARL JONES?
I'VE BEEN BITTEN ENOUGH THAT I'VE BUILT UP SOME IMMUNITY.
NOW YOU'RE JUST OUT TO MAKE ME JEALOUS, ASSHOLE!
THERE! THAT DOORWAY! I SPIED A HANGAR WHEN THEY CARRIED US IN!
SO?
A HANGAR MEANS VEHICLES! VEHICLES MEAN ESCAPE!
CRACK

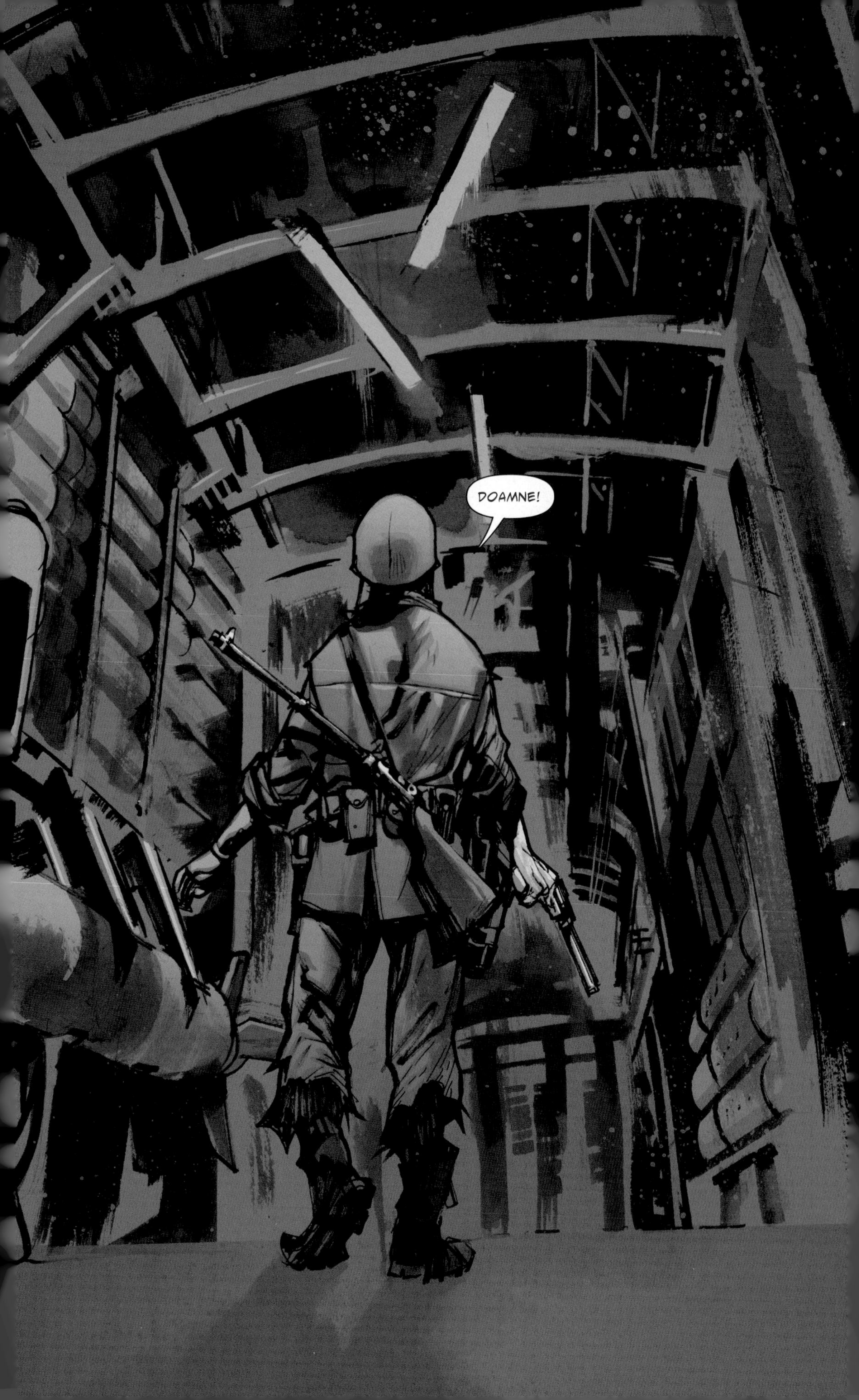
DOAMNE!

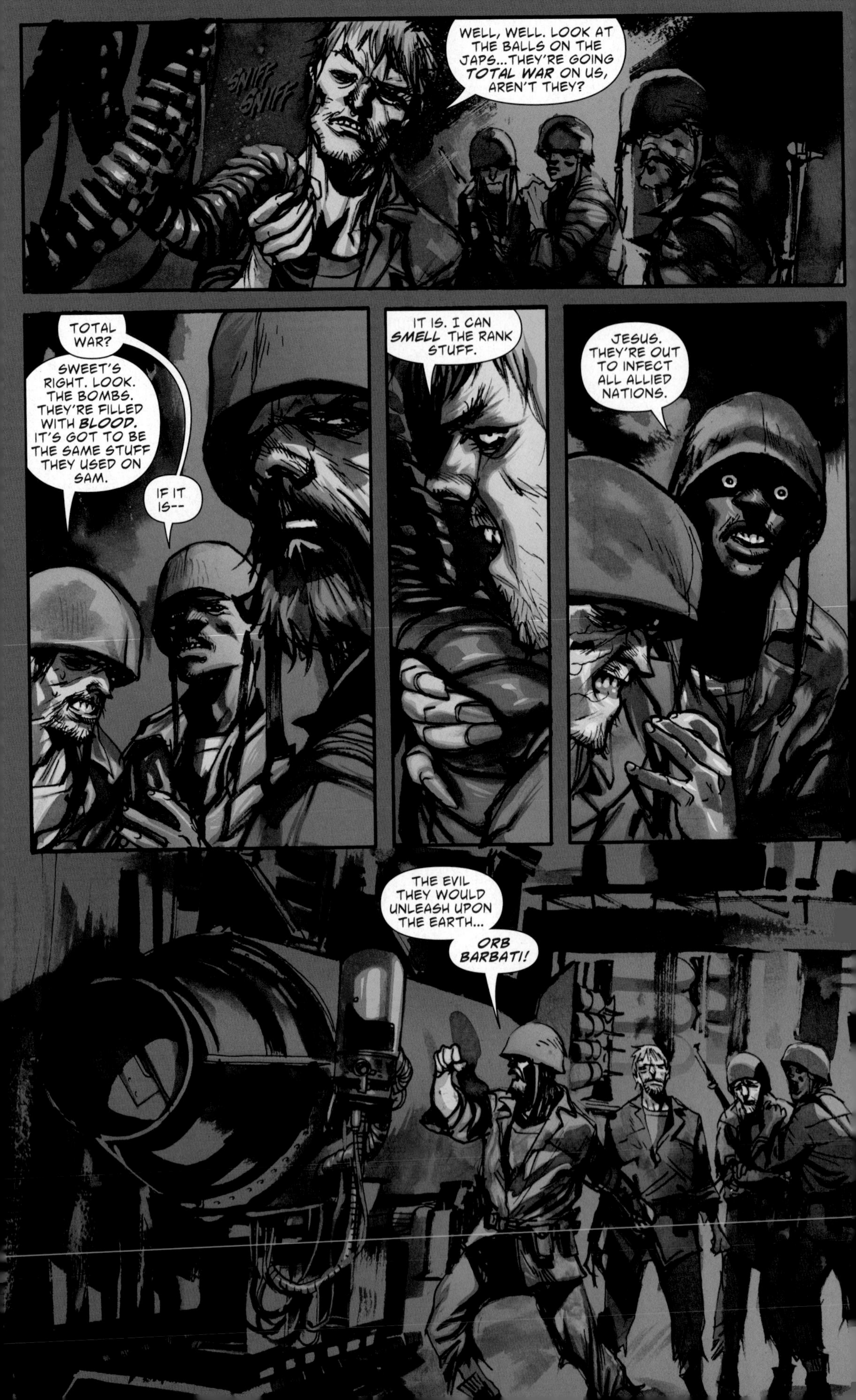
SNIFF SNIFF
WELL, WELL. LOOK AT THE BALLS ON THE JAPS...THEY'RE GOING *TOTAL WAR* ON US, AREN'T THEY?
TOTAL WAR?
SWEET'S RIGHT. LOOK. THE BOMBS. THEY'RE FILLED WITH *BLOOD*. IT'S GOT TO BE THE SAME STUFF THEY USED ON SAM.
IF IT IS--
IT IS. I CAN *SMELL* THE RANK STUFF.
JESUS. THEY'RE OUT TO INFECT ALL ALLIED NATIONS.
THE EVIL THEY WOULD UNLEASH UPON THE EARTH...
ORB BARBATI!

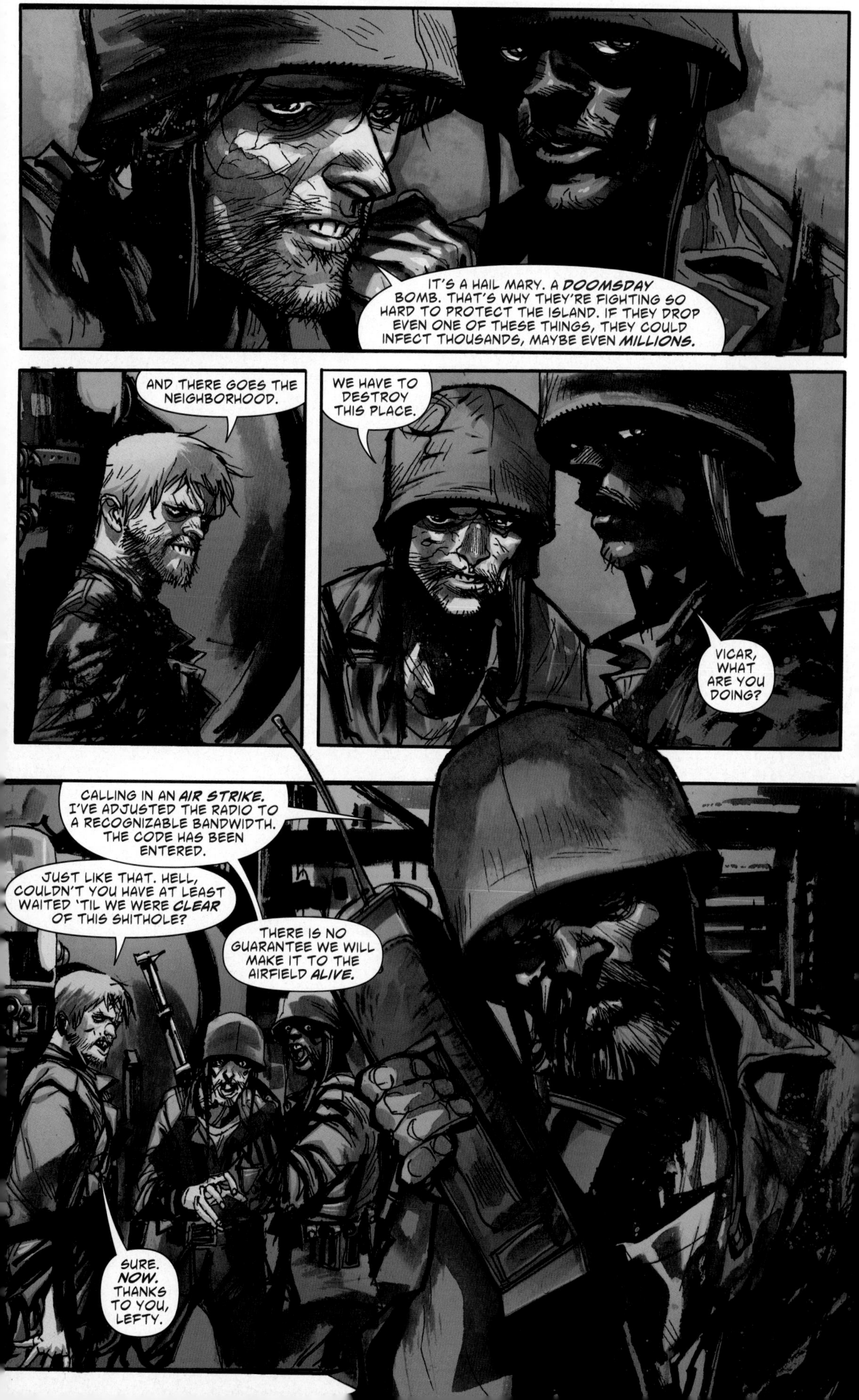
IT'S A HAIL MARY. A DOOMSDAY BOMB. THAT'S WHY THEY'RE FIGHTING SO HARD TO PROTECT THE ISLAND. IF THEY DROP EVEN ONE OF THESE THINGS, THEY COULD INFECT THOUSANDS, MAYBE EVEN MILLIONS.
AND THERE GOES THE NEIGHBORHOOD.
WE HAVE TO DESTROY THIS PLACE.
VICAR, WHAT ARE YOU DOING?
CALLING IN AN AIR STRIKE. I'VE ADJUSTED THE RADIO TO A RECOGNIZABLE BANDWIDTH. THE CODE HAS BEEN ENTERED.
JUST LIKE THAT. HELL, COULDN'T YOU HAVE AT LEAST WAITED 'TIL WE WERE CLEAR OF THIS SHITHOLE?
THERE IS NO GUARANTEE WE WILL MAKE IT TO THE AIRFIELD ALIVE.
SURE. NOW. THANKS TO YOU, LEFTY.

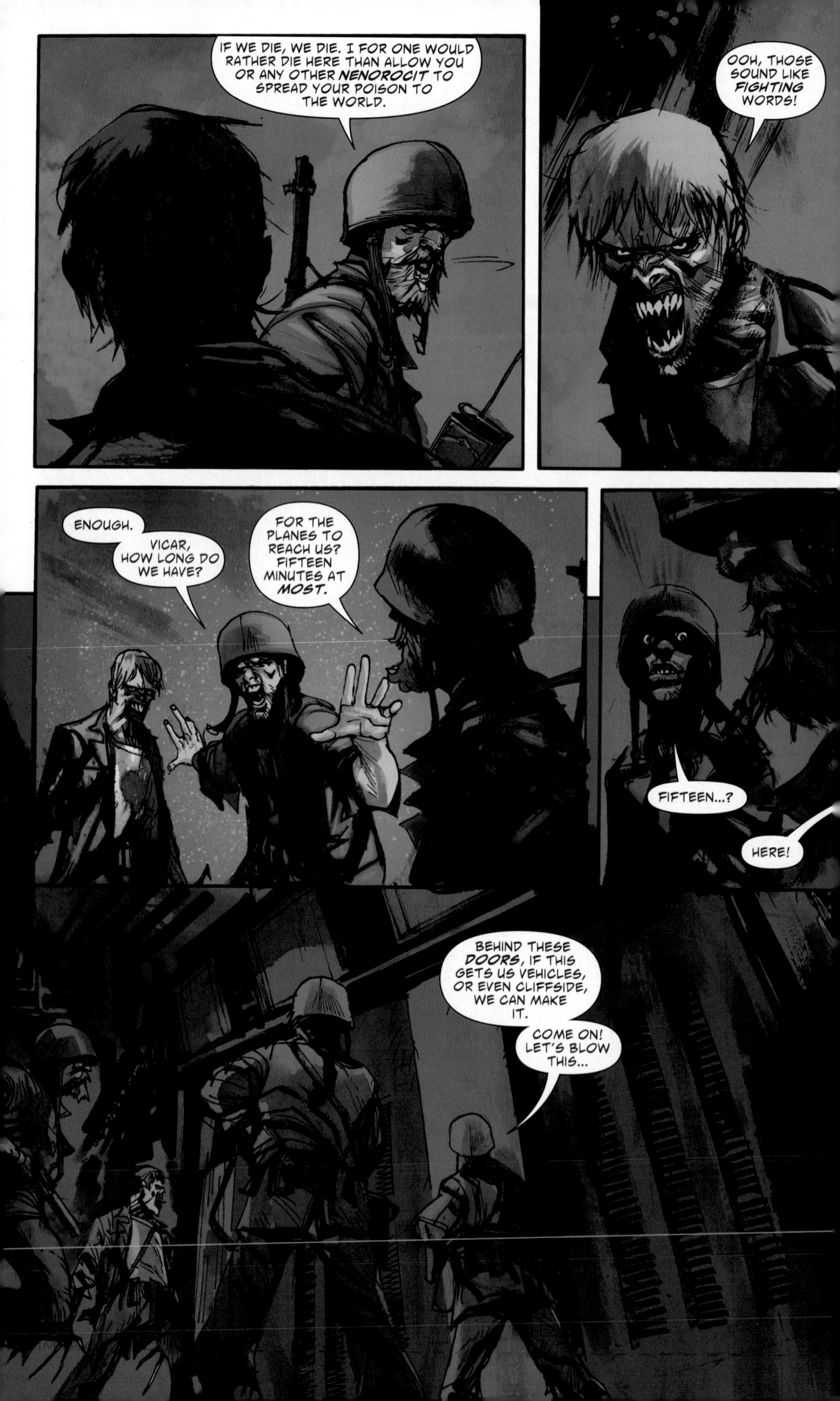
IF WE DIE, WE DIE. I FOR ONE WOULD RATHER DIE HERE THAN ALLOW YOU OR ANY OTHER NENOROCIT TO SPREAD YOUR POISON TO THE WORLD.
OOH, THOSE SOUND LIKE FIGHTING WORDS!
ENOUGH.
VICAR, HOW LONG DO WE HAVE?
FOR THE PLANES TO REACH US? FIFTEEN MINUTES AT MOST.
FIFTEEN...?
HERE!
BEHIND THESE DOORS, IF THIS GETS US VEHICLES, OR EVEN CLIFFSIDE, WE CAN MAKE IT.
COME ON! LET'S BLOW THIS...

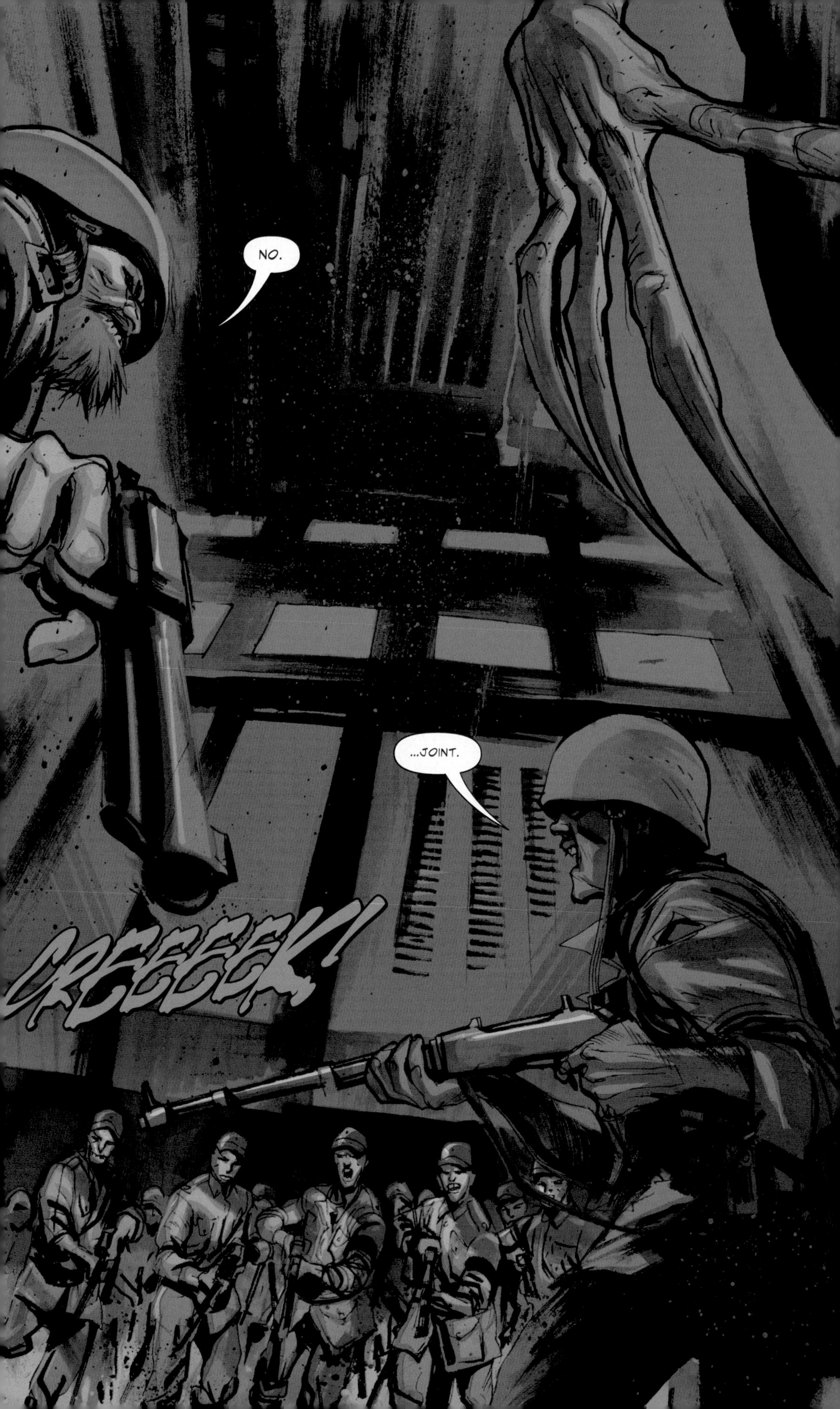
NO.
...JOINT.
CREEEEK!!

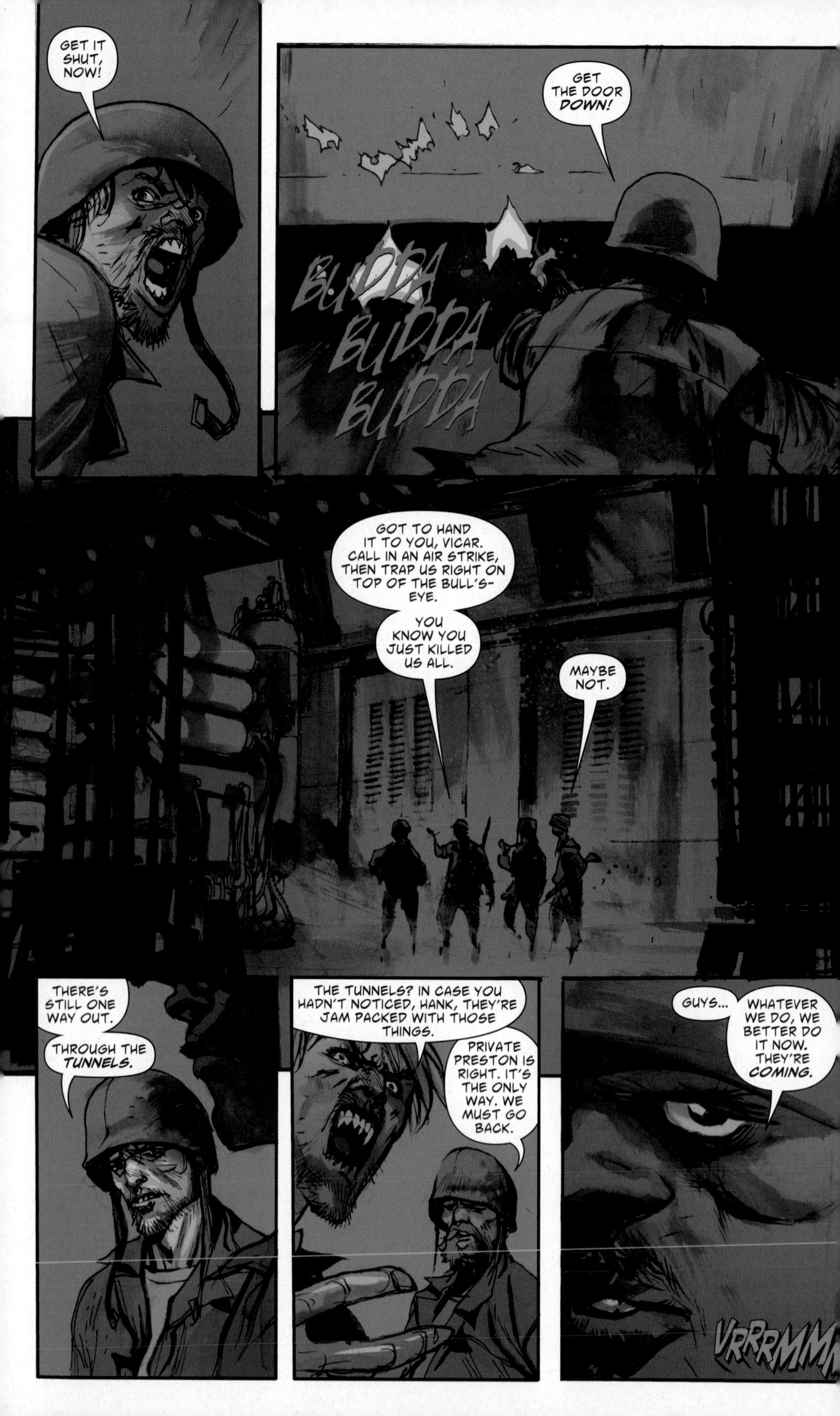
GET IT SHUT, NOW!
GET THE DOOR DOWN!
BUDDA BUDDA BUDDA
GOT TO HAND IT TO YOU, VICAR. CALL IN AN AIR STRIKE, THEN TRAP US RIGHT ON TOP OF THE BULL'S-EYE.
YOU KNOW YOU JUST KILLED US ALL.
MAYBE NOT.
THERE'S STILL ONE WAY OUT.
THROUGH THE TUNNELS.
THE TUNNELS? IN CASE YOU HADN'T NOTICED, HANK, THEY'RE JAM PACKED WITH THOSE THINGS.
PRIVATE PRESTON IS RIGHT. IT'S THE ONLY WAY. WE MUST GO BACK.
GUYS...
WHATEVER WE DO, WE BETTER DO IT NOW. THEY'RE COMING.
VRRRMMM

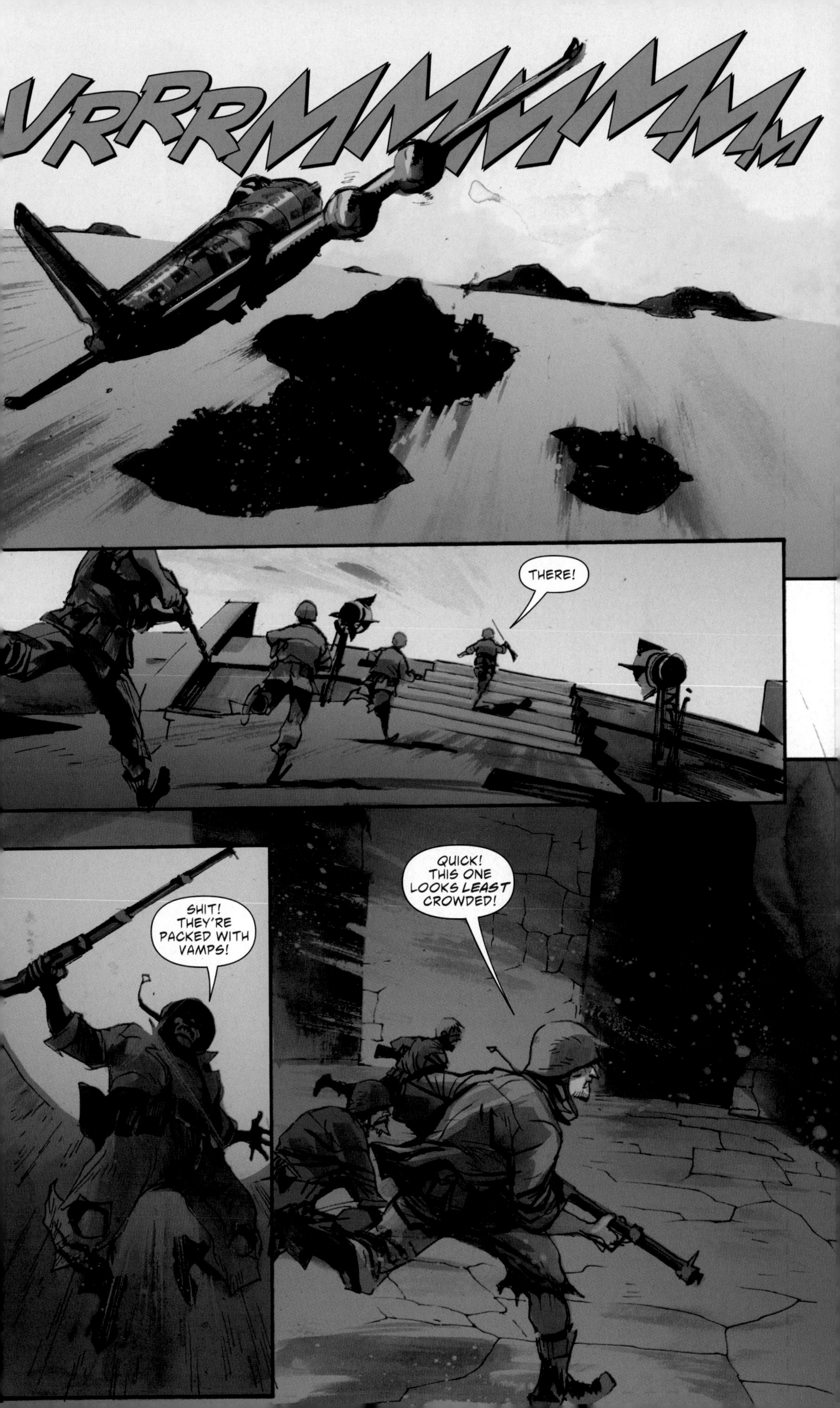
VRRRMMMMMMMMM
THERE!
SHIT! THEY'RE PACKED WITH VAMPS!
QUICK! THIS ONE LOOKS LEAST CROWDED!

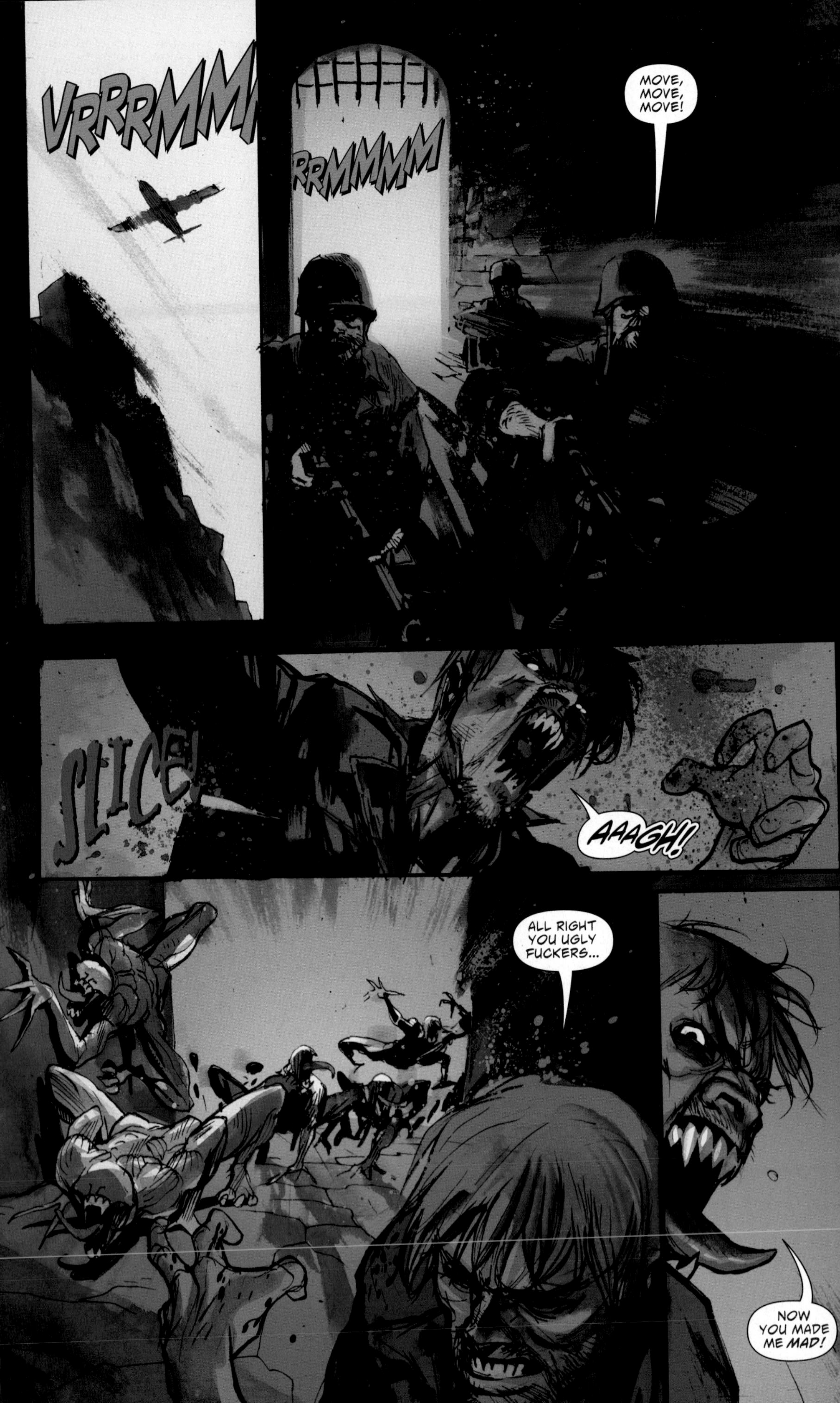
VRRRMMM
RRMMMMM
MOVE, MOVE, MOVE!
SLICE!
AAAGH!
ALL RIGHT YOU UGLY FUCKERS...
NOW YOU MADE ME MAD!

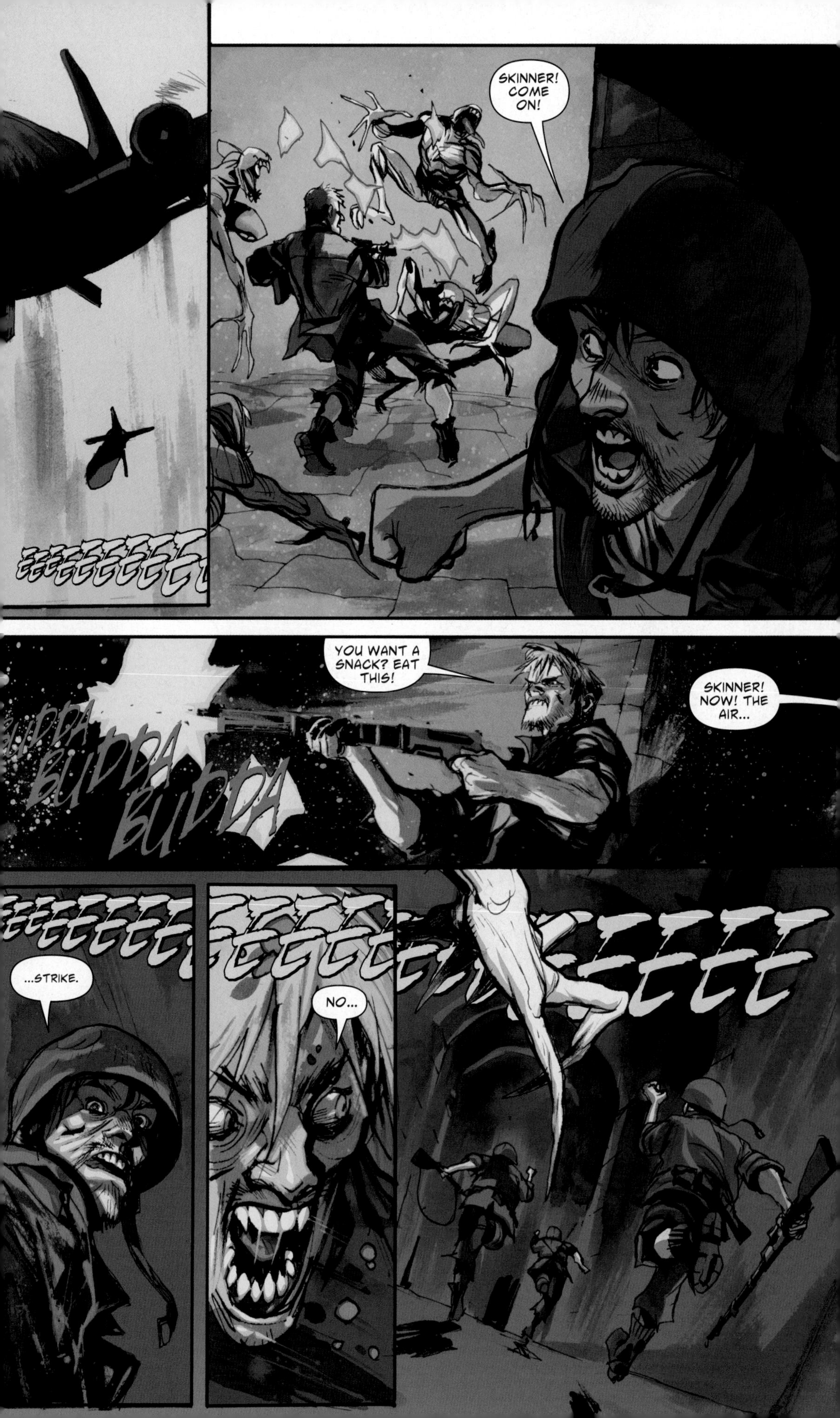
SKINNER! COME ON!
EEEEEEEEEEE
YOU WANT A SNACK? EAT THIS!
BUDDA BUDDA BUDDA
SKINNER! NOW! THE AIR...
EEEEEEEEEEEEEEEEEEEEEEEEEEEE
...STRIKE.
NO...

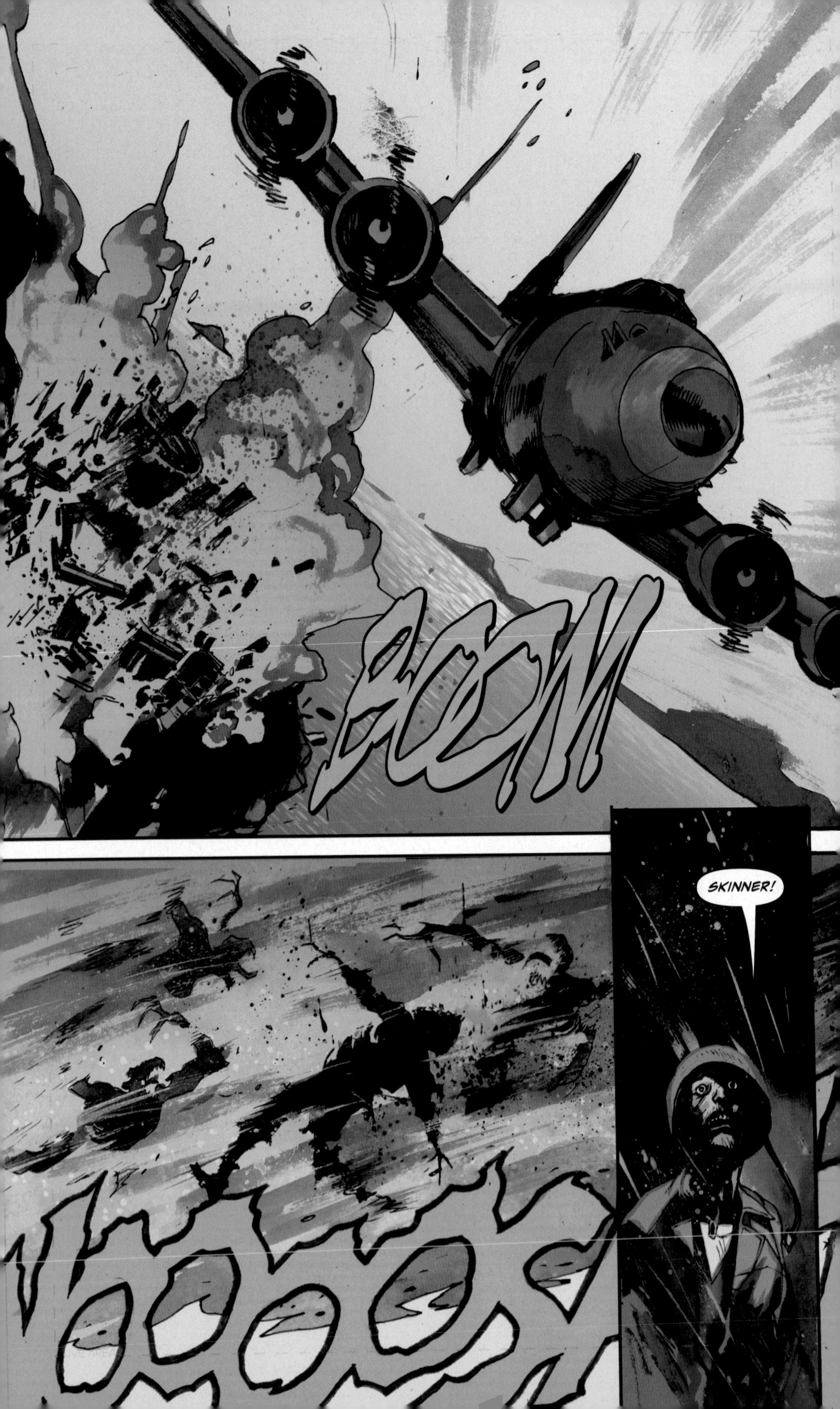
BOOM
SKINNER!
BOOOOOM

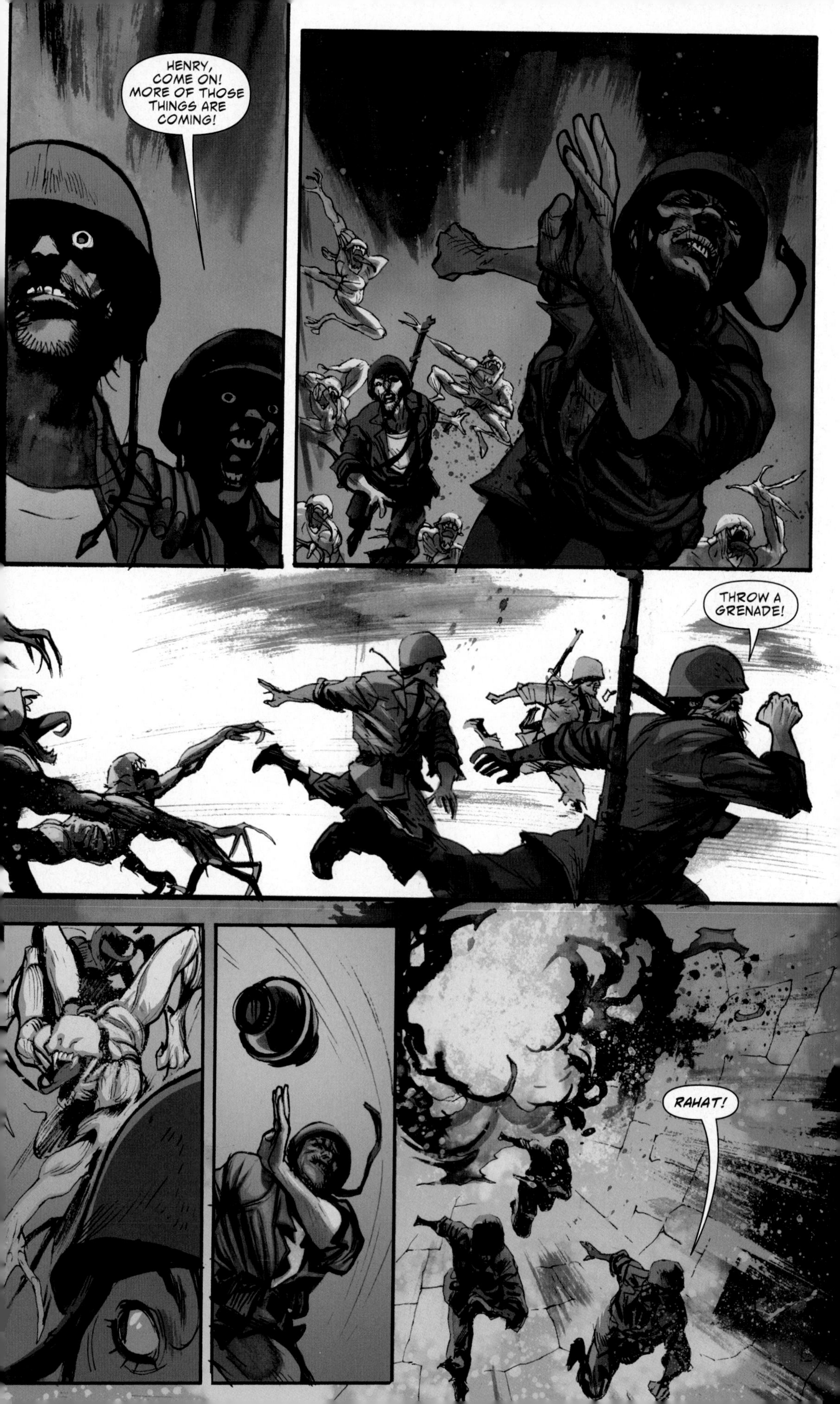
HENRY, COME ON! MORE OF THOSE THINGS ARE COMING!
THROW A GRENADE!
RAHAT!

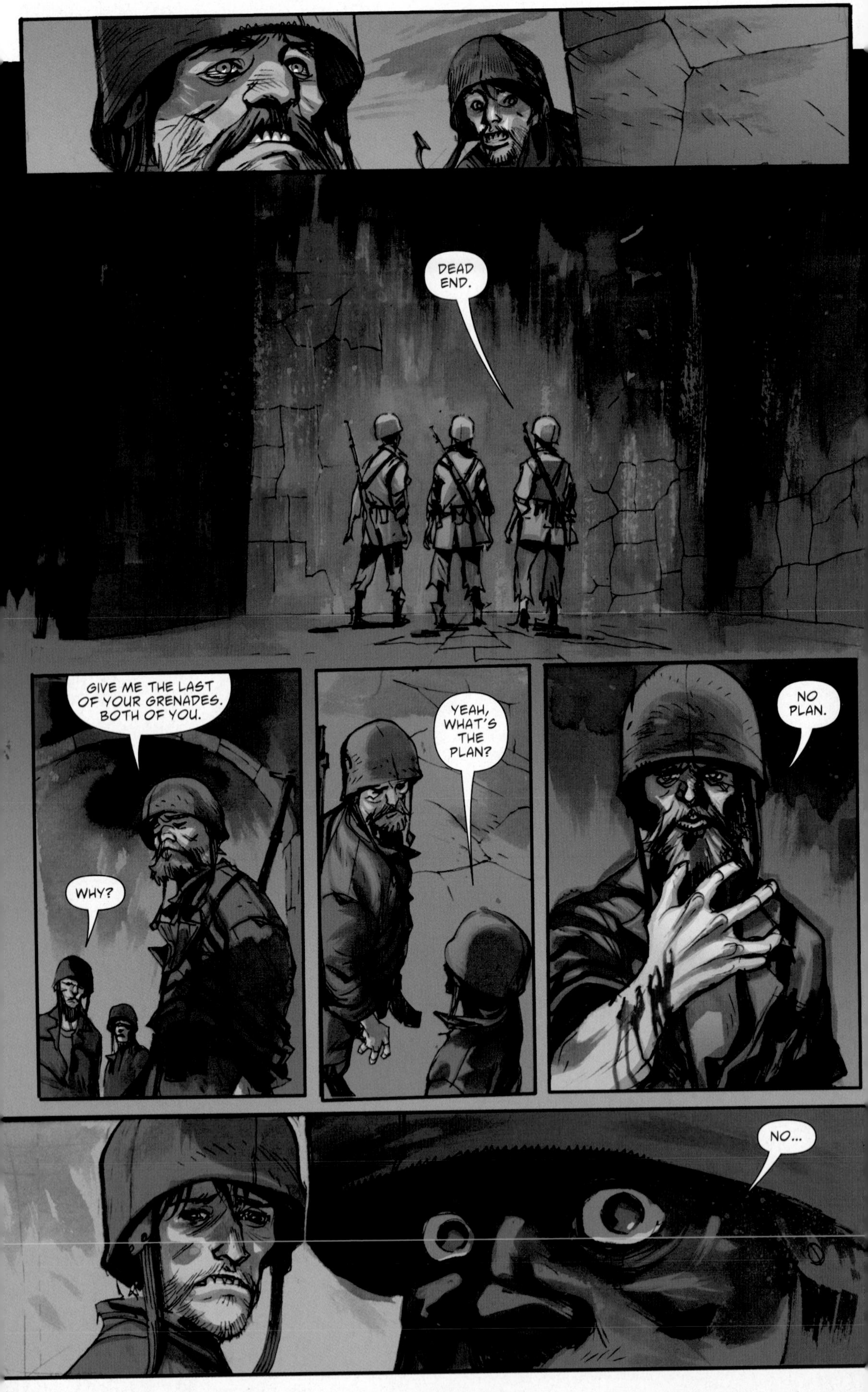
DEAD END.
GIVE ME THE LAST OF YOUR GRENADES. BOTH OF YOU.
WHY?
YEAH, WHAT'S THE PLAN?
NO PLAN.
NO...

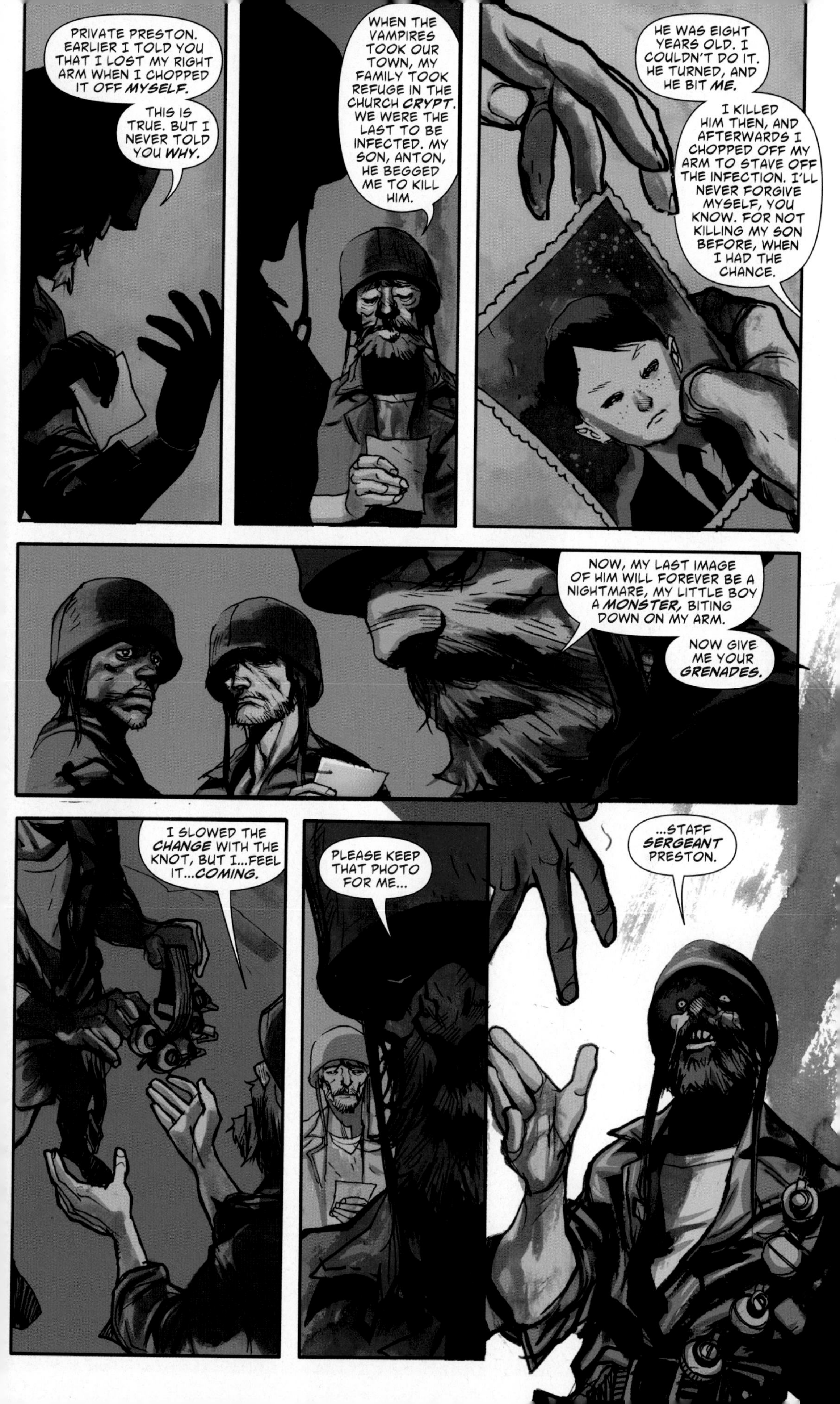
PRIVATE PRESTON. EARLIER I TOLD YOU THAT I LOST MY RIGHT ARM WHEN I CHOPPED IT OFF MYSELF.
THIS IS TRUE. BUT I NEVER TOLD YOU WHY.
WHEN THE VAMPIRES TOOK OUR TOWN, MY FAMILY TOOK REFUGE IN THE CHURCH CRYPT. WE WERE THE LAST TO BE INFECTED. MY SON, ANTON, HE BEGGED ME TO KILL HIM.
HE WAS EIGHT YEARS OLD. I COULDN'T DO IT. HE TURNED, AND HE BIT ME.
I KILLED HIM THEN, AND AFTERWARDS I CHOPPED OFF MY ARM TO STAVE OFF THE INFECTION. I'LL NEVER FORGIVE MYSELF, YOU KNOW. FOR NOT KILLING MY SON BEFORE, WHEN I HAD THE CHANCE.
NOW, MY LAST IMAGE OF HIM WILL FOREVER BE A NIGHTMARE, MY LITTLE BOY A MONSTER, BITING DOWN ON MY ARM.
NOW GIVE ME YOUR GRENADES.
I SLOWED THE CHANGE WITH THE KNOT, BUT I...FEEL IT...COMING.
PLEASE KEEP THAT PHOTO FOR ME...
...STAFF SERGEANT PRESTON.

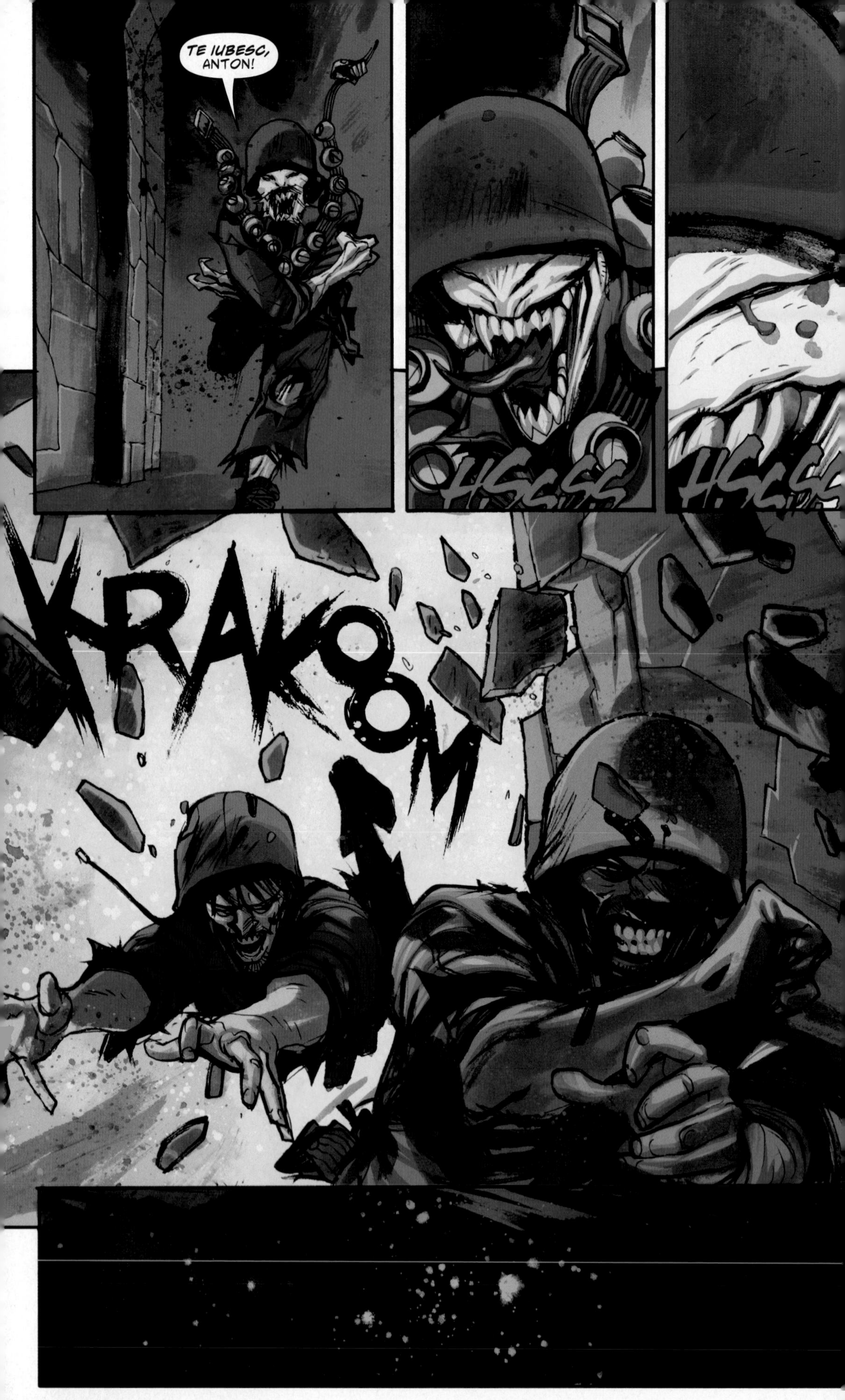
TE IUBESC, ANTON!
HSSSS
HSSSS
KRAKOOM

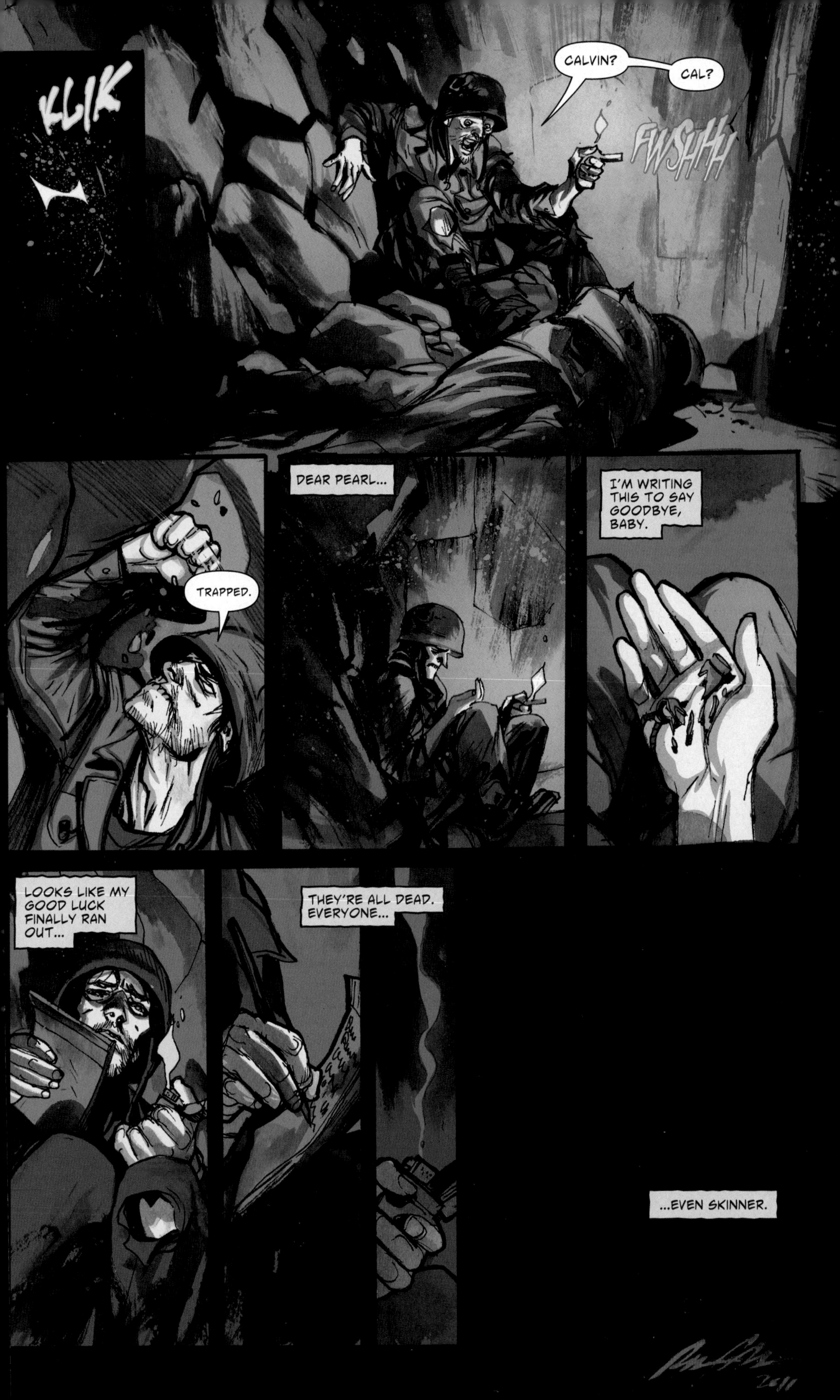
KLIK
CALVIN?
CAL?
FWSHHH
TRAPPED.
DEAR PEARL...
I'M WRITING THIS TO SAY GOODBYE, BABY.
LOOKS LIKE MY GOOD LUCK FINALLY RAN OUT...
THEY'RE ALL DEAD. EVERYONE...
...EVEN SKINNER.

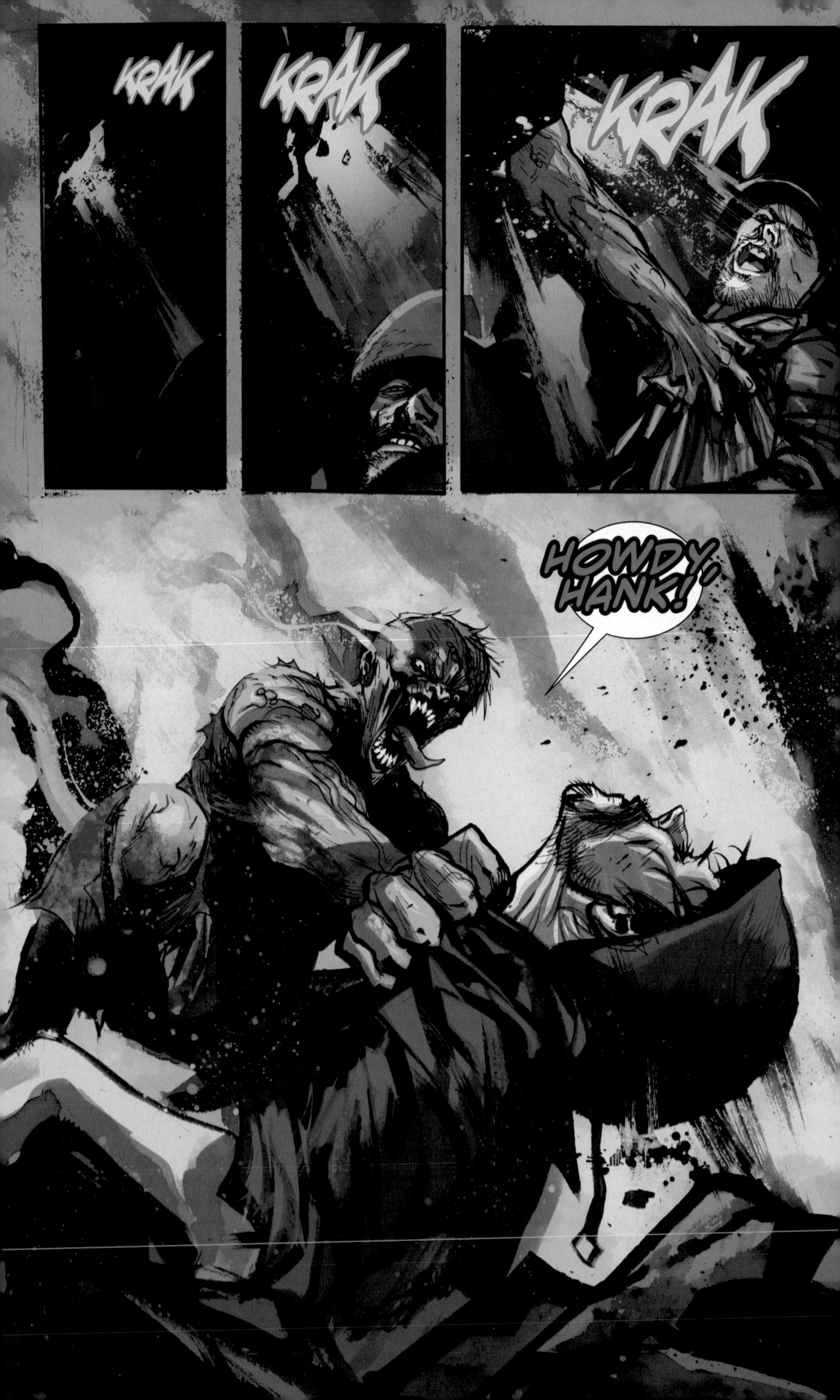
KRAK
KRAK
KRAK
HOWDY, HANK!

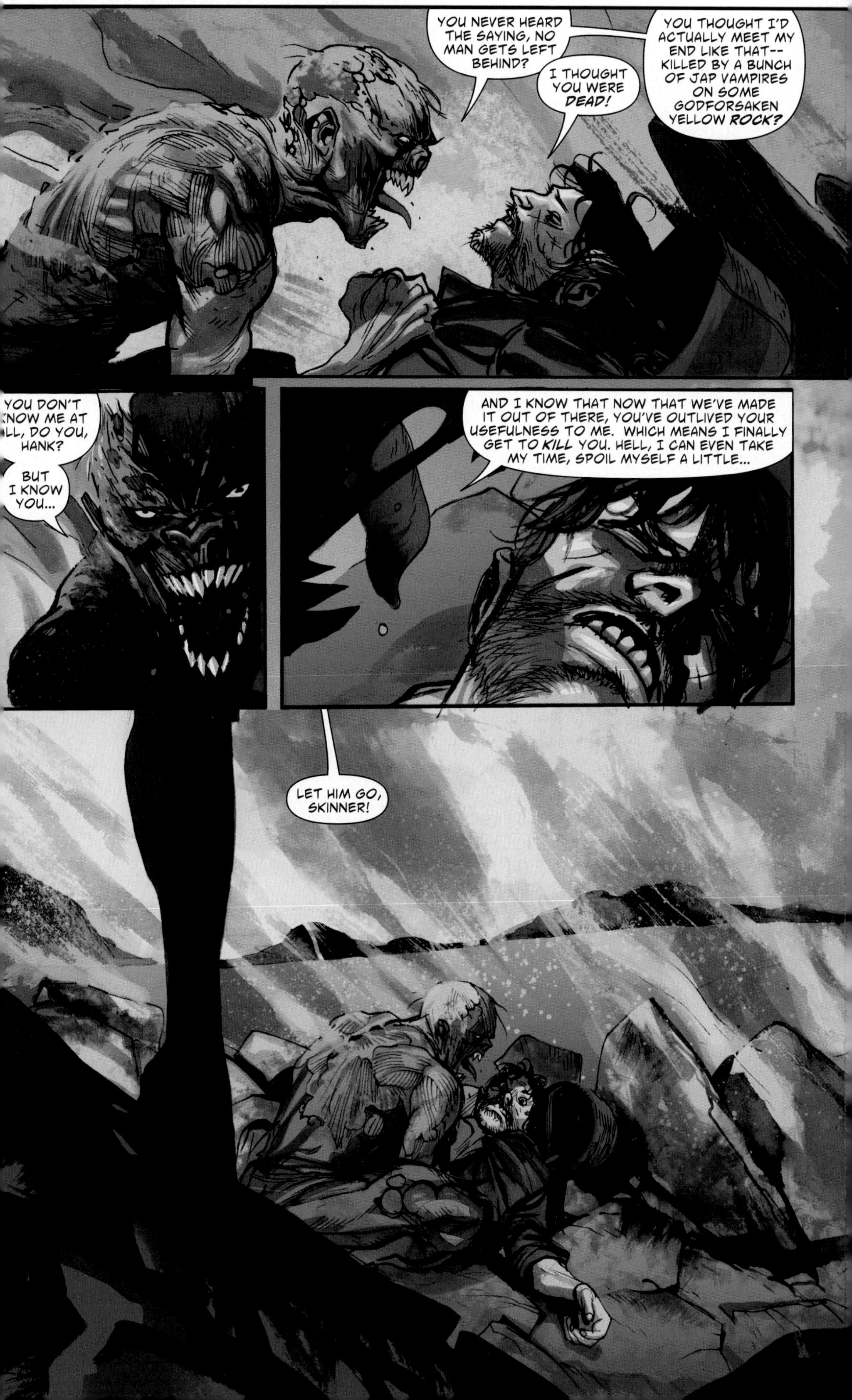

YOU NEVER HEARD THE SAYING, NO MAN GETS LEFT BEHIND?
I THOUGHT YOU WERE DEAD!
YOU THOUGHT I'D ACTUALLY MEET MY END LIKE THAT-- KILLED BY A BUNCH OF JAP VAMPIRES ON SOME GODFORSAKEN YELLOW ROCK?
YOU DON'T KNOW ME AT ALL, DO YOU, HANK?
BUT I KNOW YOU...
AND I KNOW THAT NOW THAT WE'VE MADE IT OUT OF THERE, YOU'VE OUTLIVED YOUR USEFULNESS TO ME. WHICH MEANS I FINALLY GET TO KILL YOU. HELL, I CAN EVEN TAKE MY TIME, SPOIL MYSELF A LITTLE...
LET HIM GO, SKINNER!

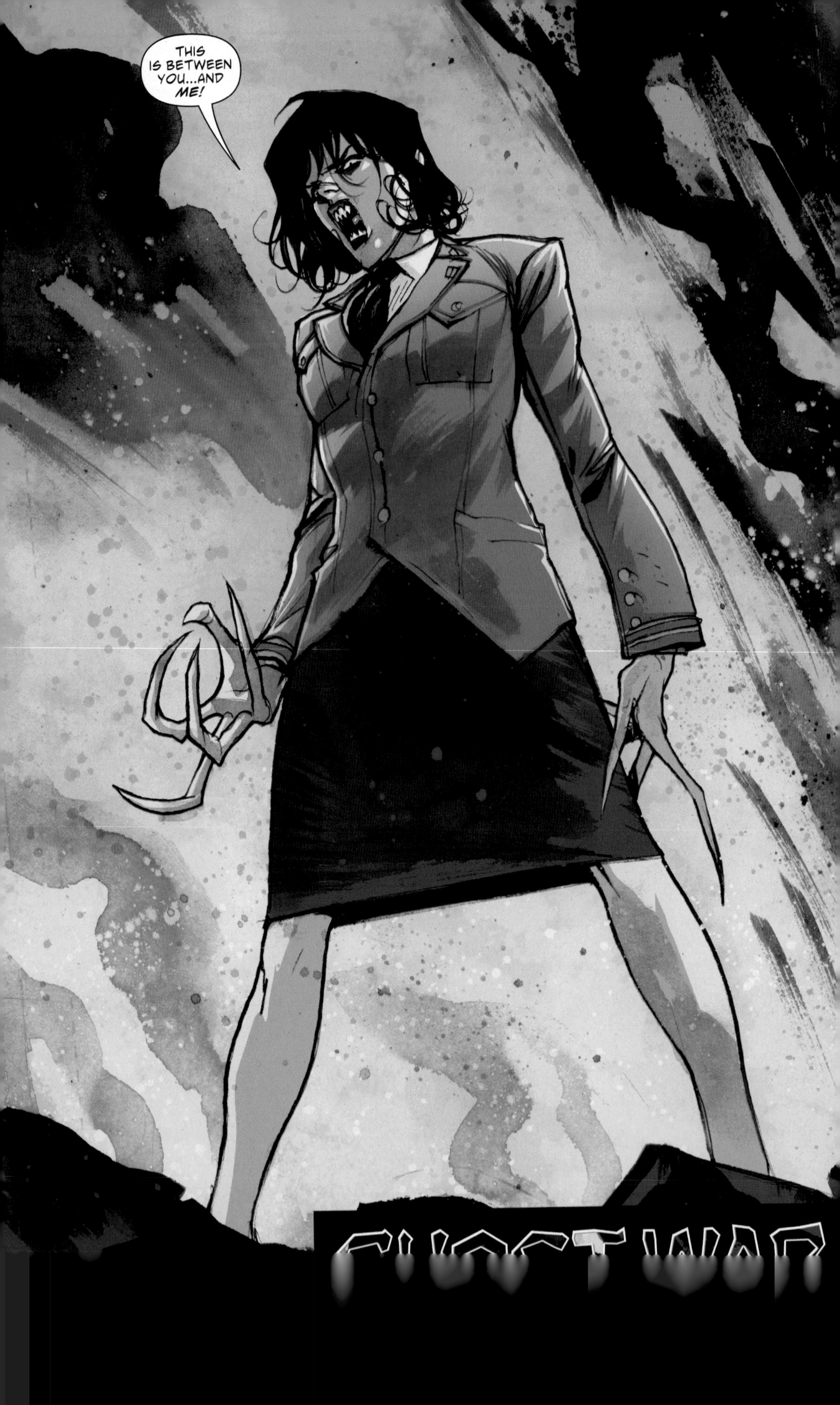
THIS IS BETWEEN YOU...AND ME!

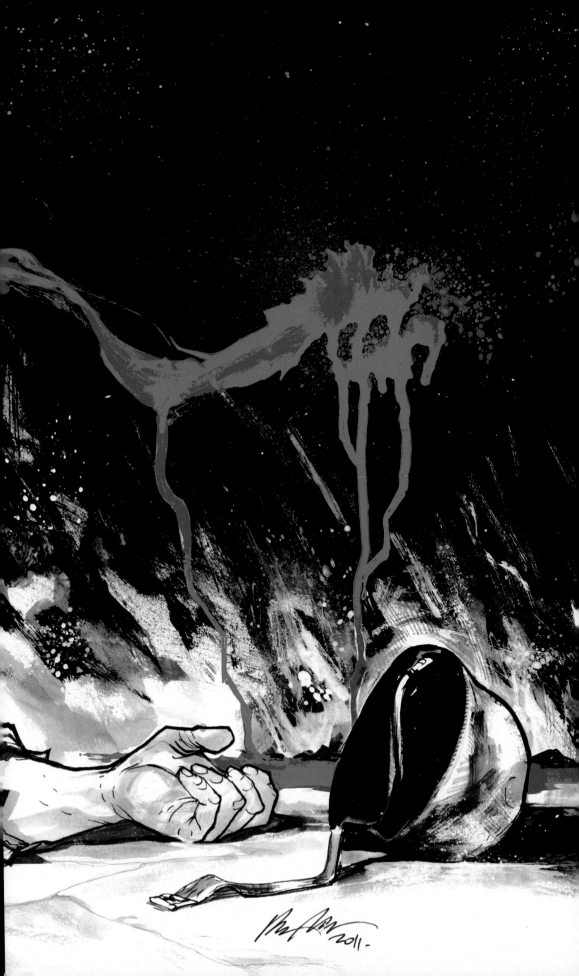

Ghost War
Conclusion

Rafael Albuquerque
Artist and cover

GHOST WAR
CONCLUSION

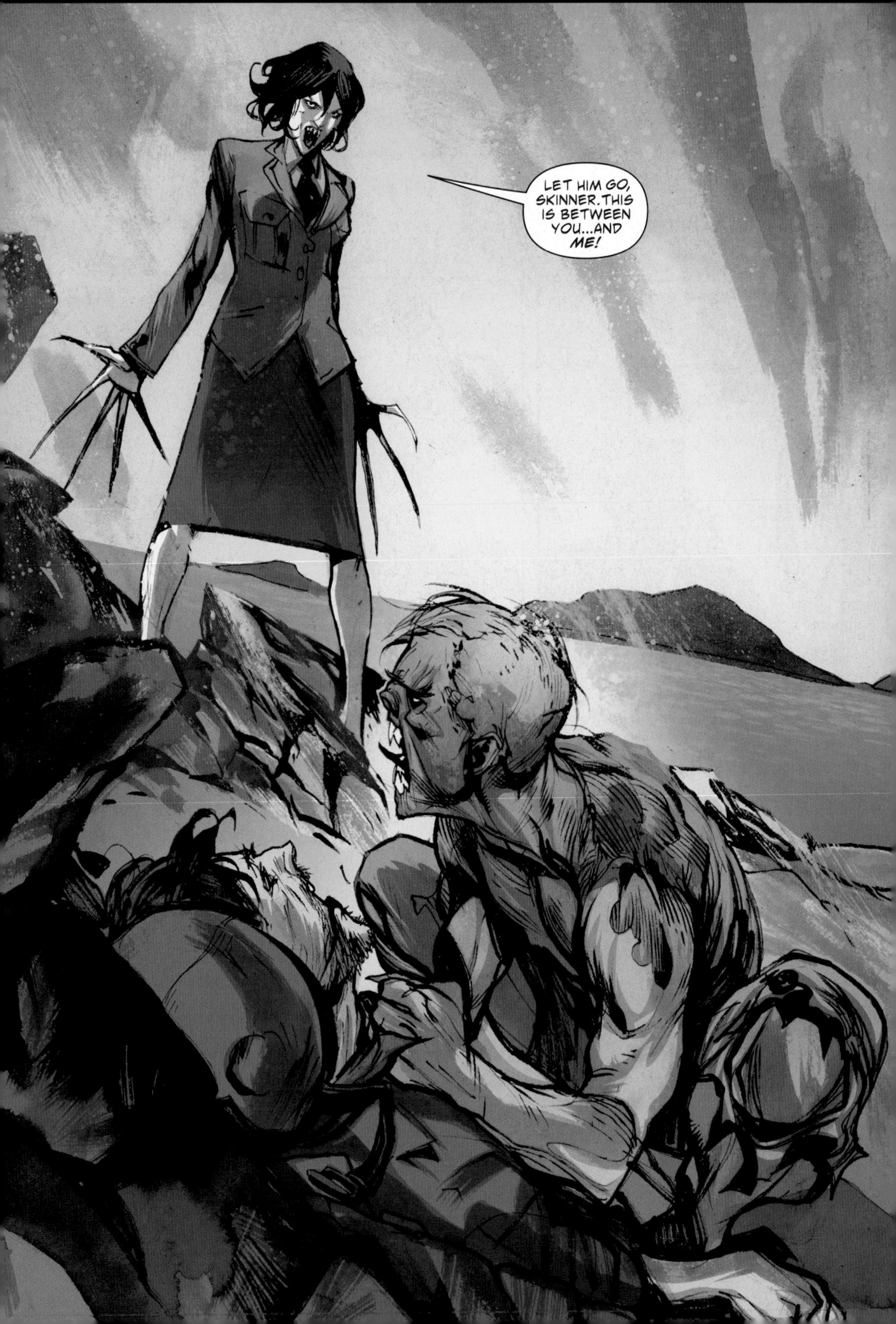
LET HIM GO, SKINNER. THIS IS BETWEEN YOU...AND *ME!*

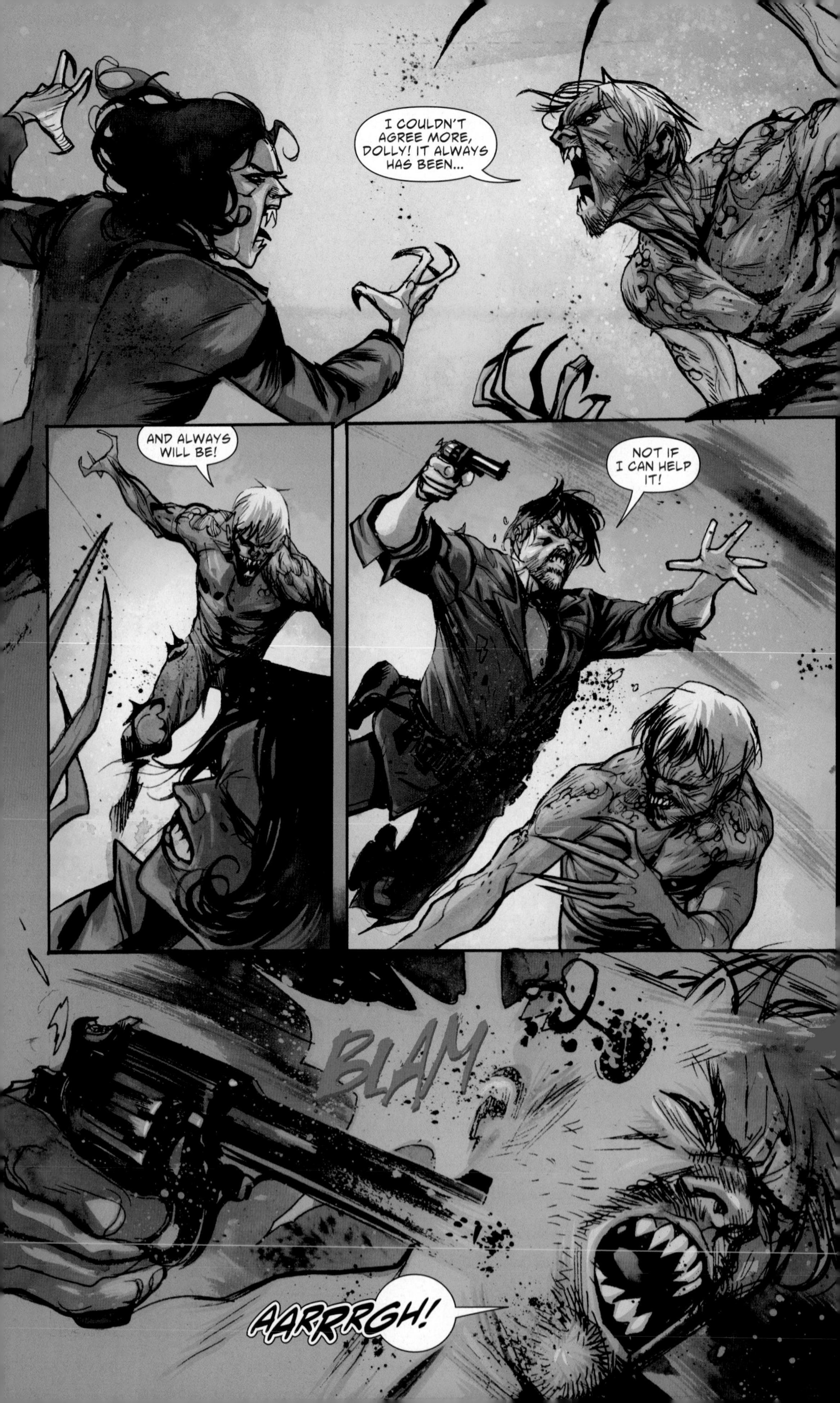

I COULDN'T AGREE MORE, DOLLY! IT ALWAYS HAS BEEN...
AND ALWAYS WILL BE!
NOT IF I CAN HELP IT!
BLAM
AARRRGH!

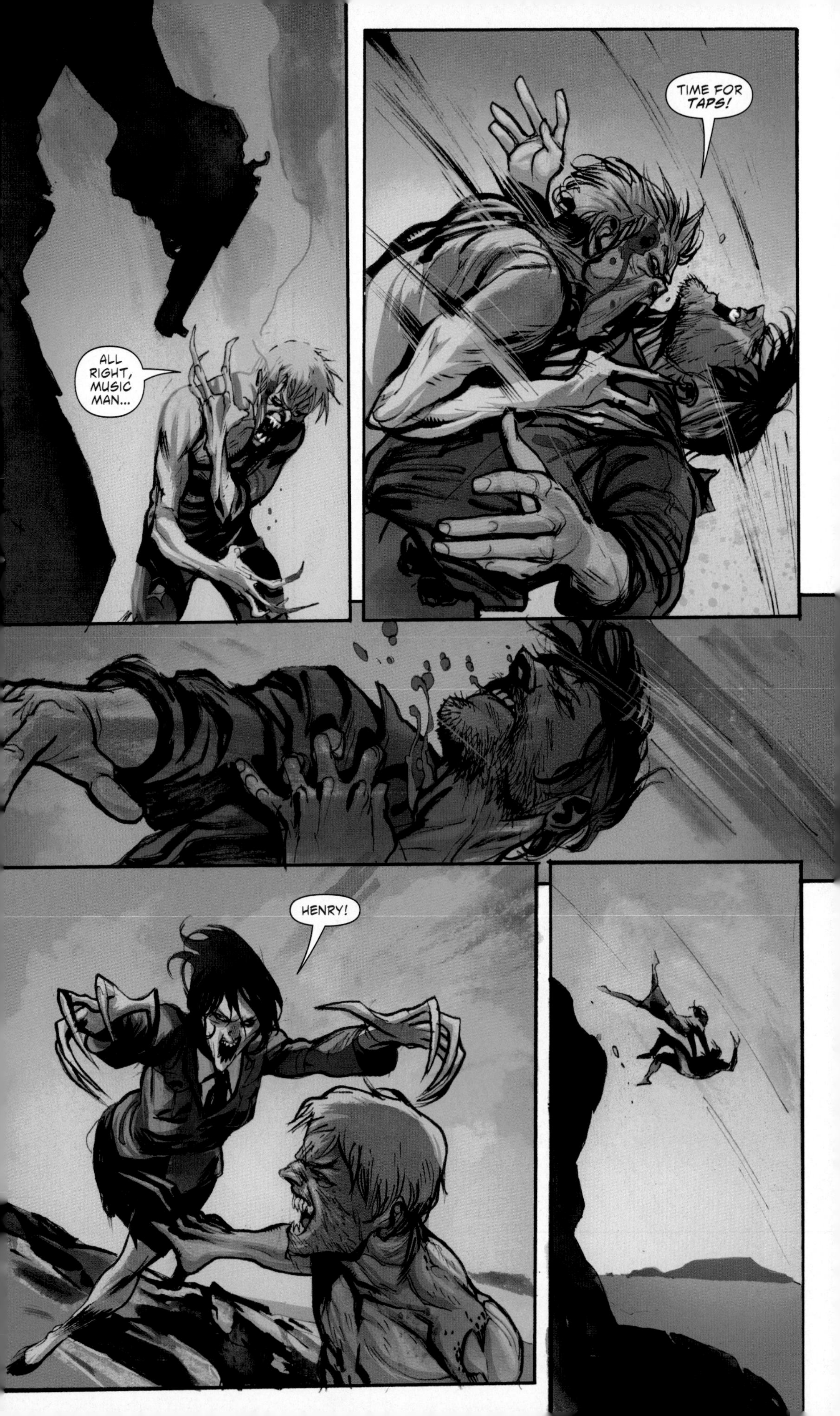
ALL RIGHT, MUSIC MAN...
TIME FOR TAPS!
HENRY!

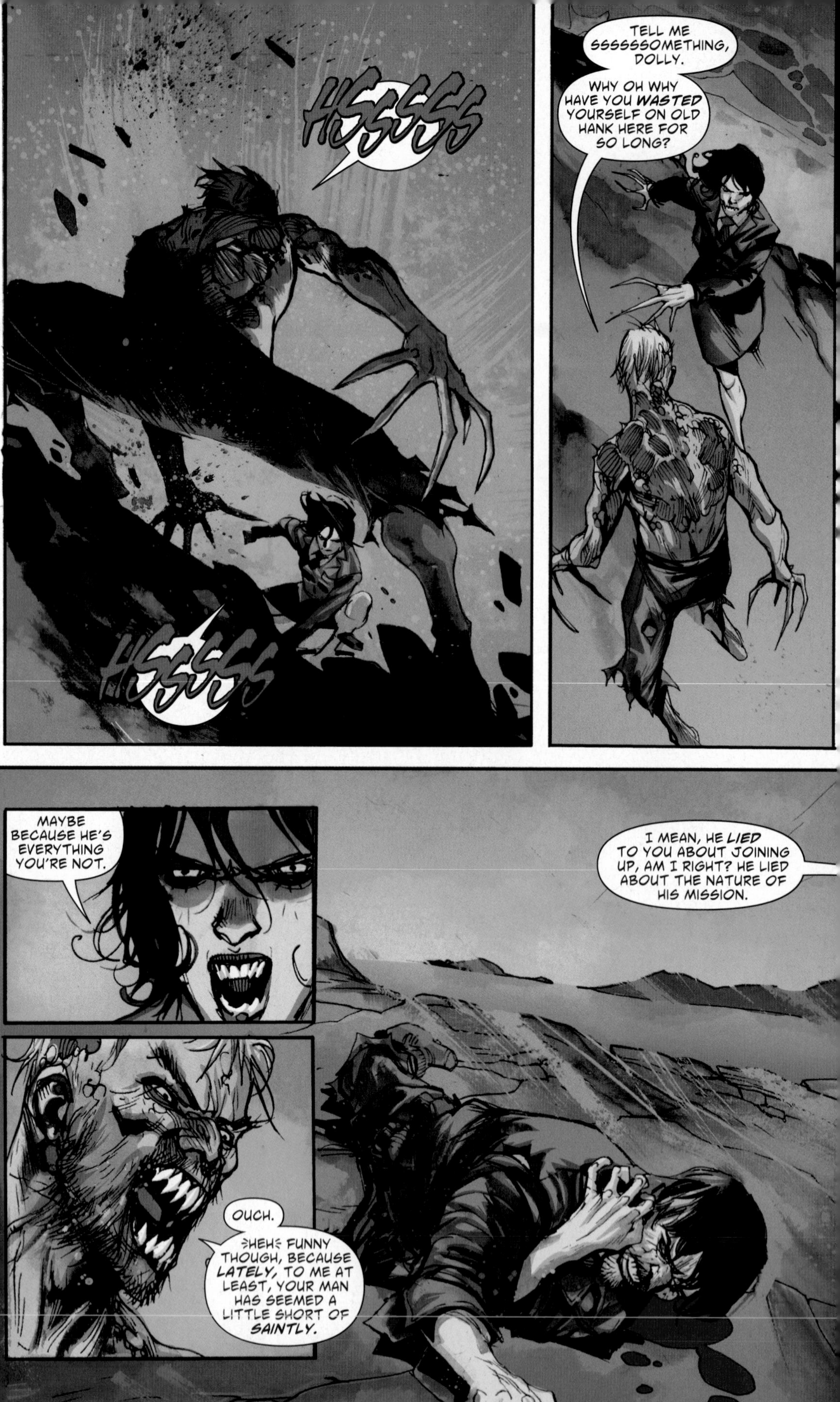
HSSSSS
HSSSSS
TELL ME SSSSSSOMETHING, DOLLY.
WHY OH WHY HAVE YOU *WASTED* YOURSELF ON OLD HANK HERE FOR SO LONG?
MAYBE BECAUSE HE'S EVERYTHING YOU'RE NOT.
I MEAN, HE *LIED* TO YOU ABOUT JOINING UP, AM I RIGHT? HE LIED ABOUT THE NATURE OF HIS MISSION.
OUCH.
HEH FUNNY THOUGH, BECAUSE *LATELY*, TO ME AT LEAST, YOUR MAN HAS SEEMED A LITTLE SHORT OF *SAINTLY*.

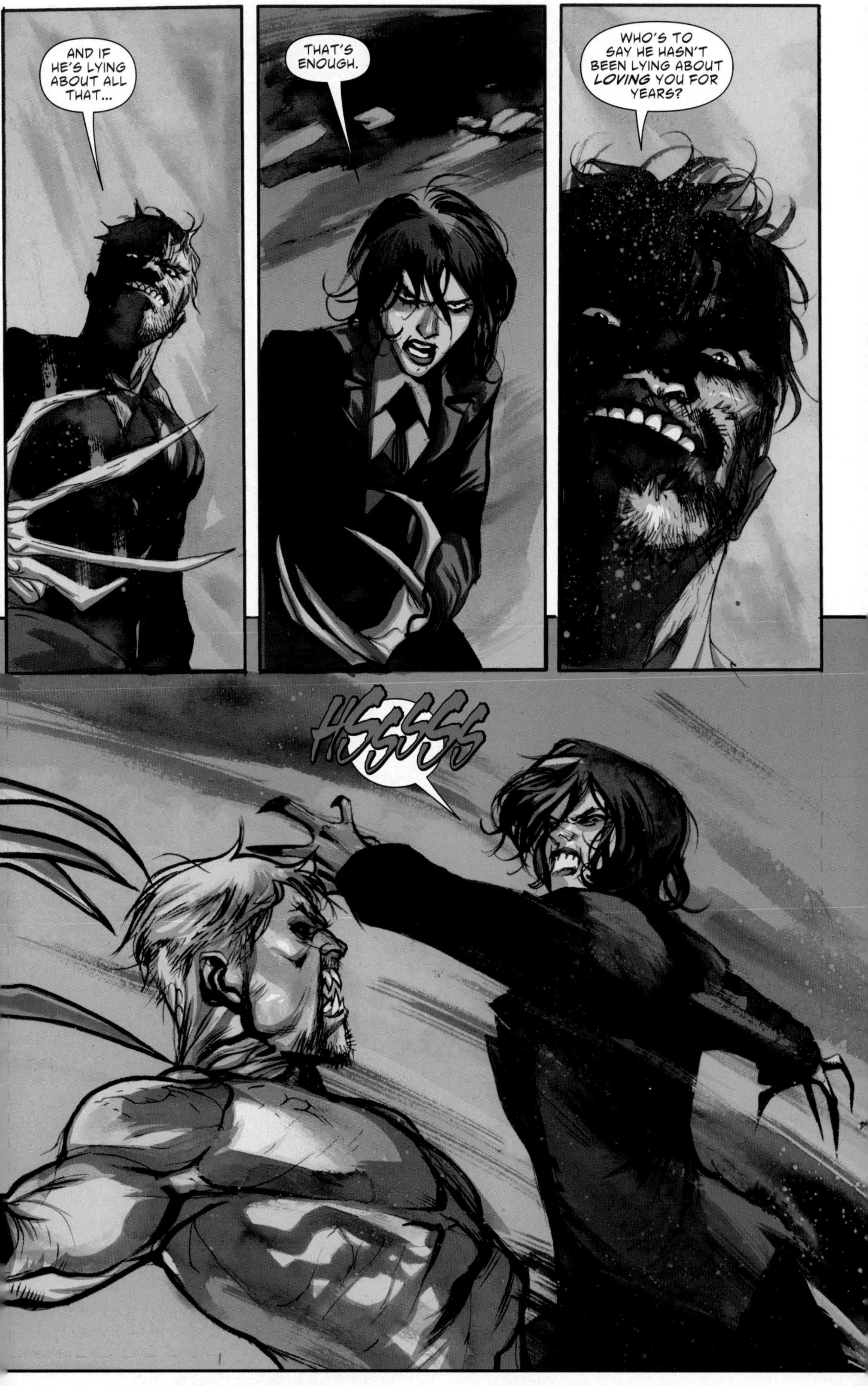
AND IF HE'S LYING ABOUT ALL THAT...
THAT'S ENOUGH.
WHO'S TO SAY HE HASN'T BEEN LYING ABOUT LOVING YOU FOR YEARS?
HSSSSS

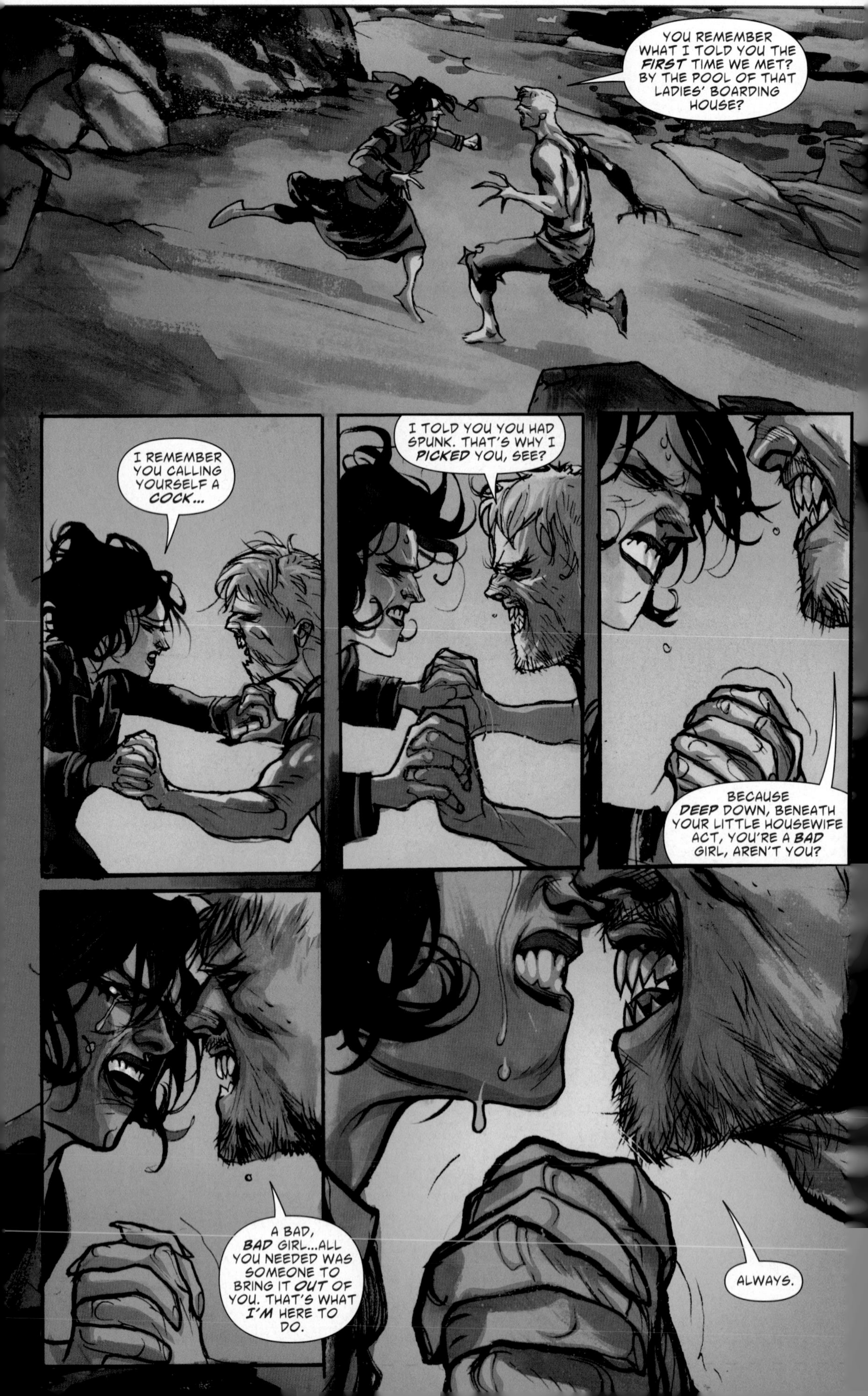
YOU REMEMBER WHAT I TOLD YOU THE FIRST TIME WE MET? BY THE POOL OF THAT LADIES' BOARDING HOUSE?
I REMEMBER YOU CALLING YOURSELF A COCK...
I TOLD YOU YOU HAD SPUNK. THAT'S WHY I PICKED YOU, SEE?
BECAUSE DEEP DOWN, BENEATH YOUR LITTLE HOUSEWIFE ACT, YOU'RE A BAD GIRL, AREN'T YOU?
A BAD, BAD GIRL...ALL YOU NEEDED WAS SOMEONE TO BRING IT OUT OF YOU. THAT'S WHAT I'M HERE TO DO.
ALWAYS.

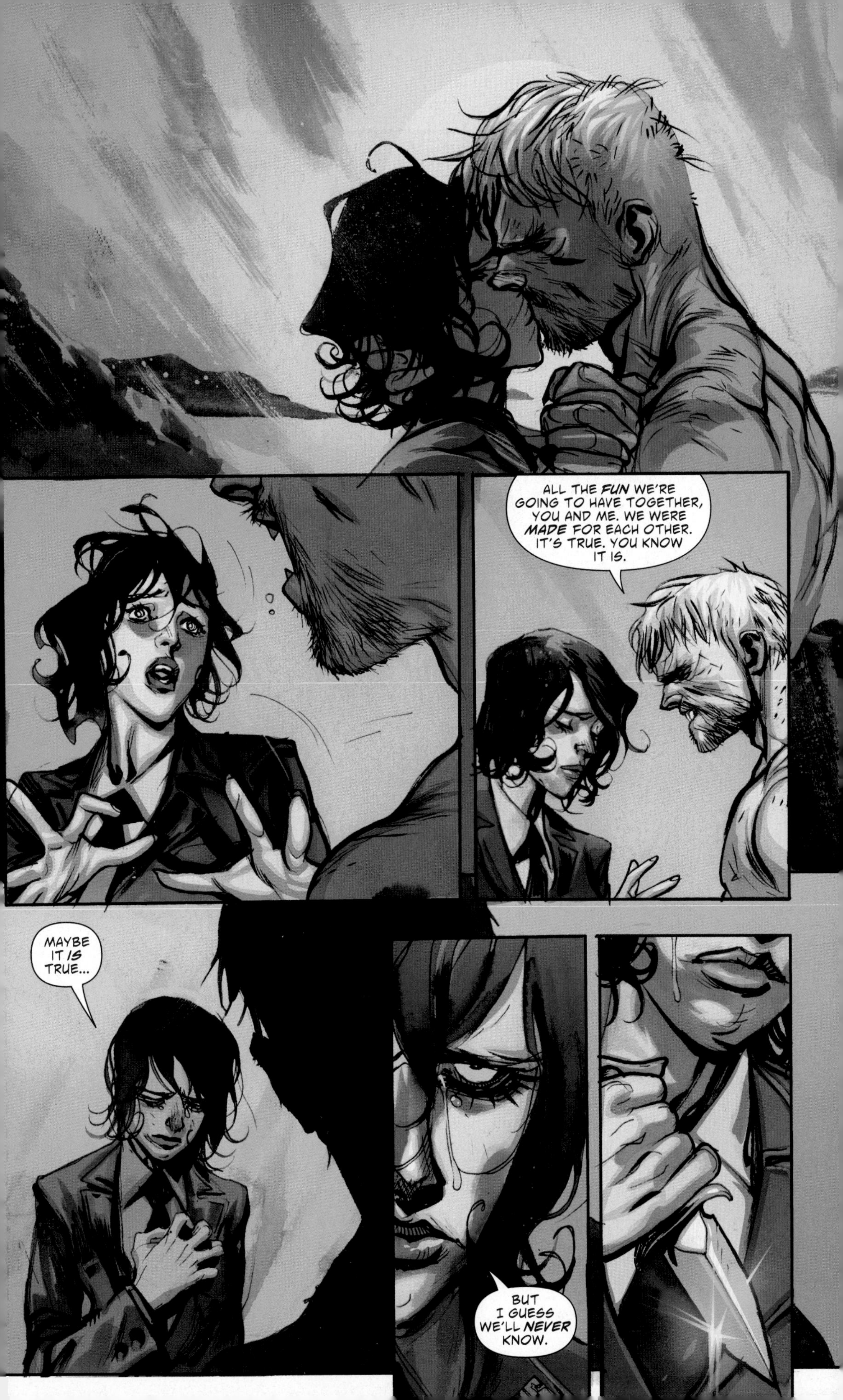
ALL THE FUN WE'RE GOING TO HAVE TOGETHER, YOU AND ME. WE WERE MADE FOR EACH OTHER. IT'S TRUE. YOU KNOW IT IS.
MAYBE IT IS TRUE...
BUT I GUESS WE'LL NEVER KNOW.

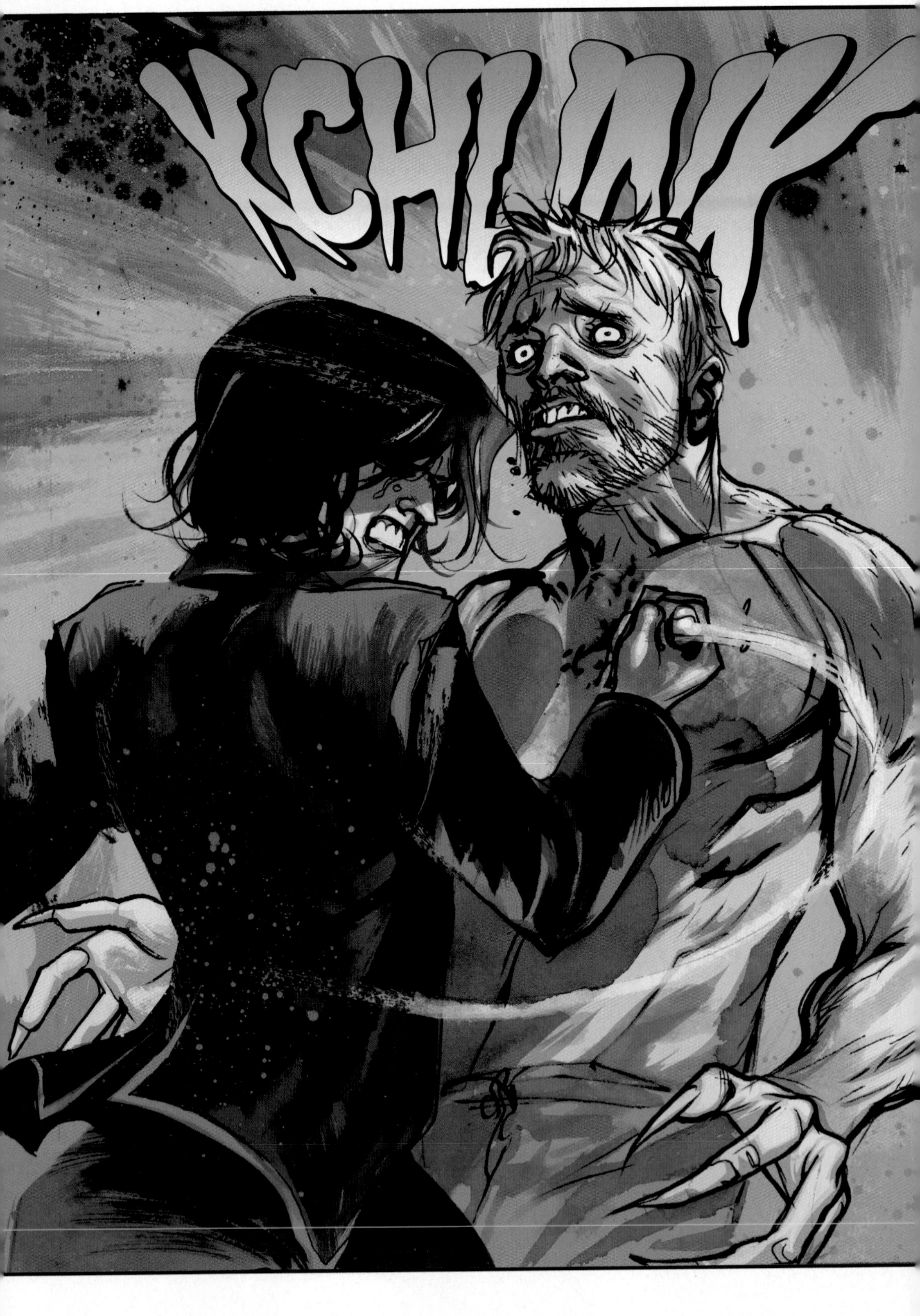
XCHLNK

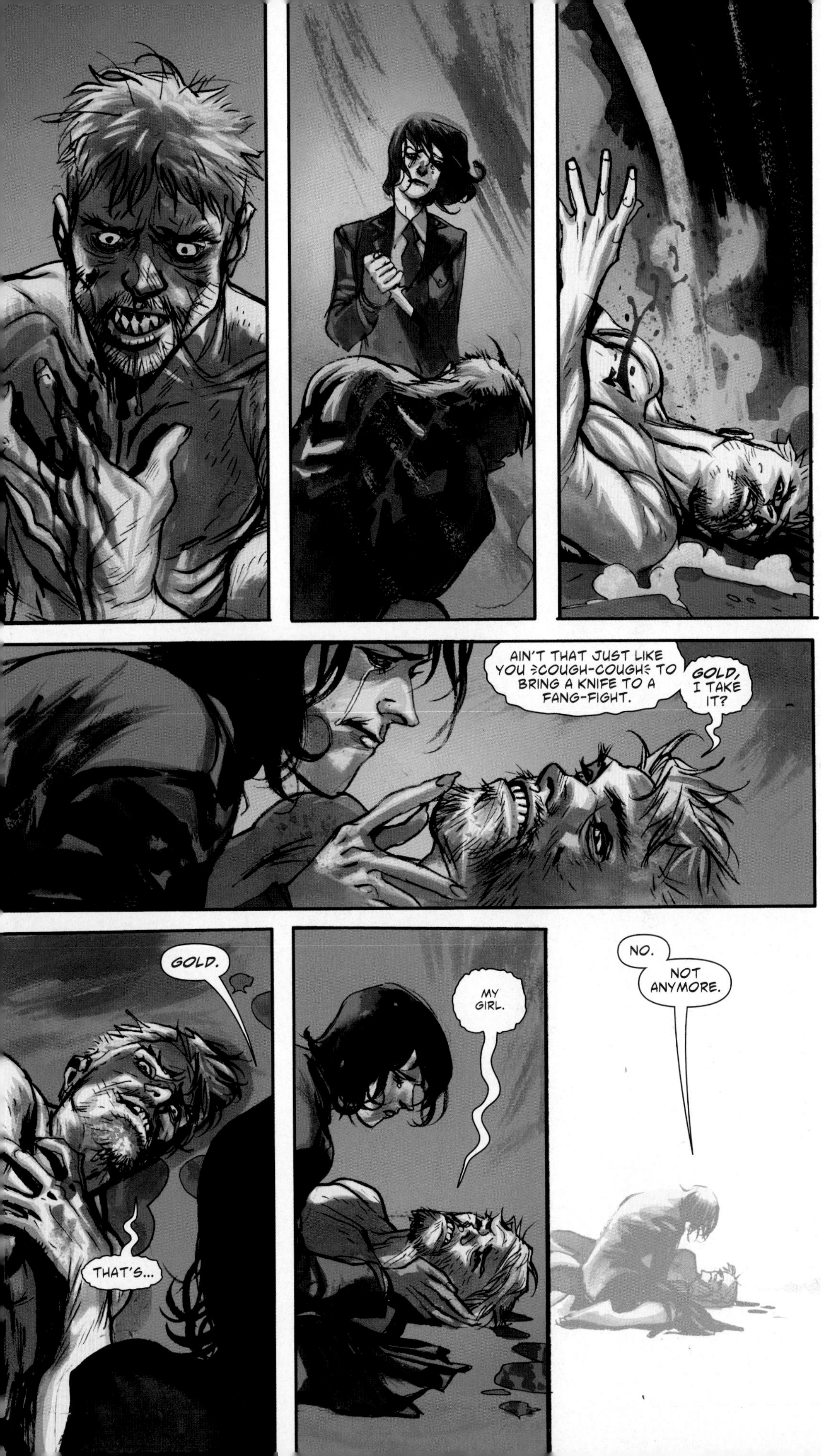
AIN'T THAT JUST LIKE YOU =COUGH-COUGH= TO BRING A KNIFE TO A FANG-FIGHT.
GOLD, I TAKE IT?
GOLD.
THAT'S...
MY GIRL.
NO.
NOT ANYMORE.

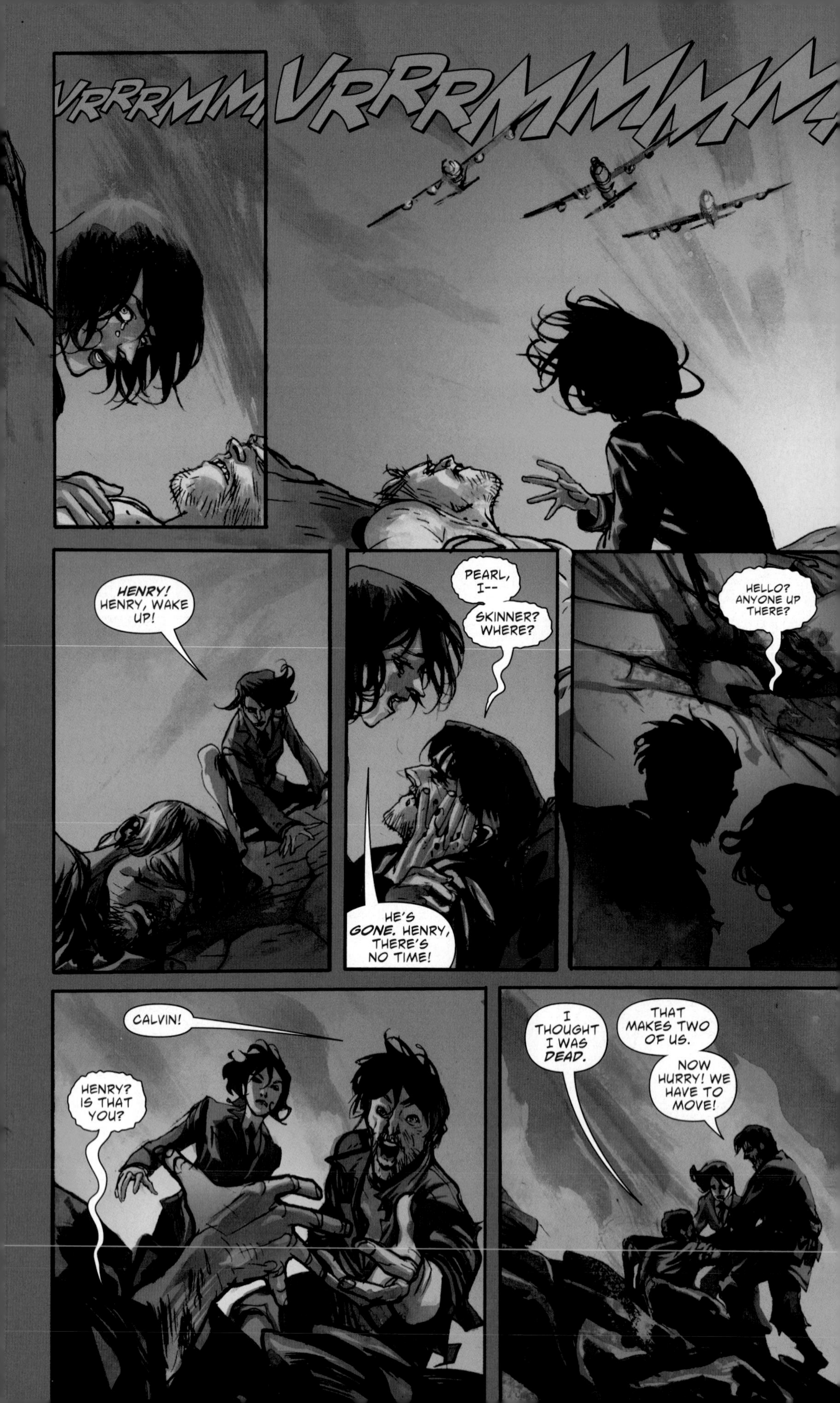
VRRRMM VRRRMMMMMM
HENRY! HENRY, WAKE UP!
PEARL, I--
SKINNER? WHERE?
HE'S GONE. HENRY, THERE'S NO TIME!
HELLO? ANYONE UP THERE?
CALVIN!
HENRY? IS THAT YOU?
I THOUGHT I WAS DEAD.
THAT MAKES TWO OF US.
NOW HURRY! WE HAVE TO MOVE!

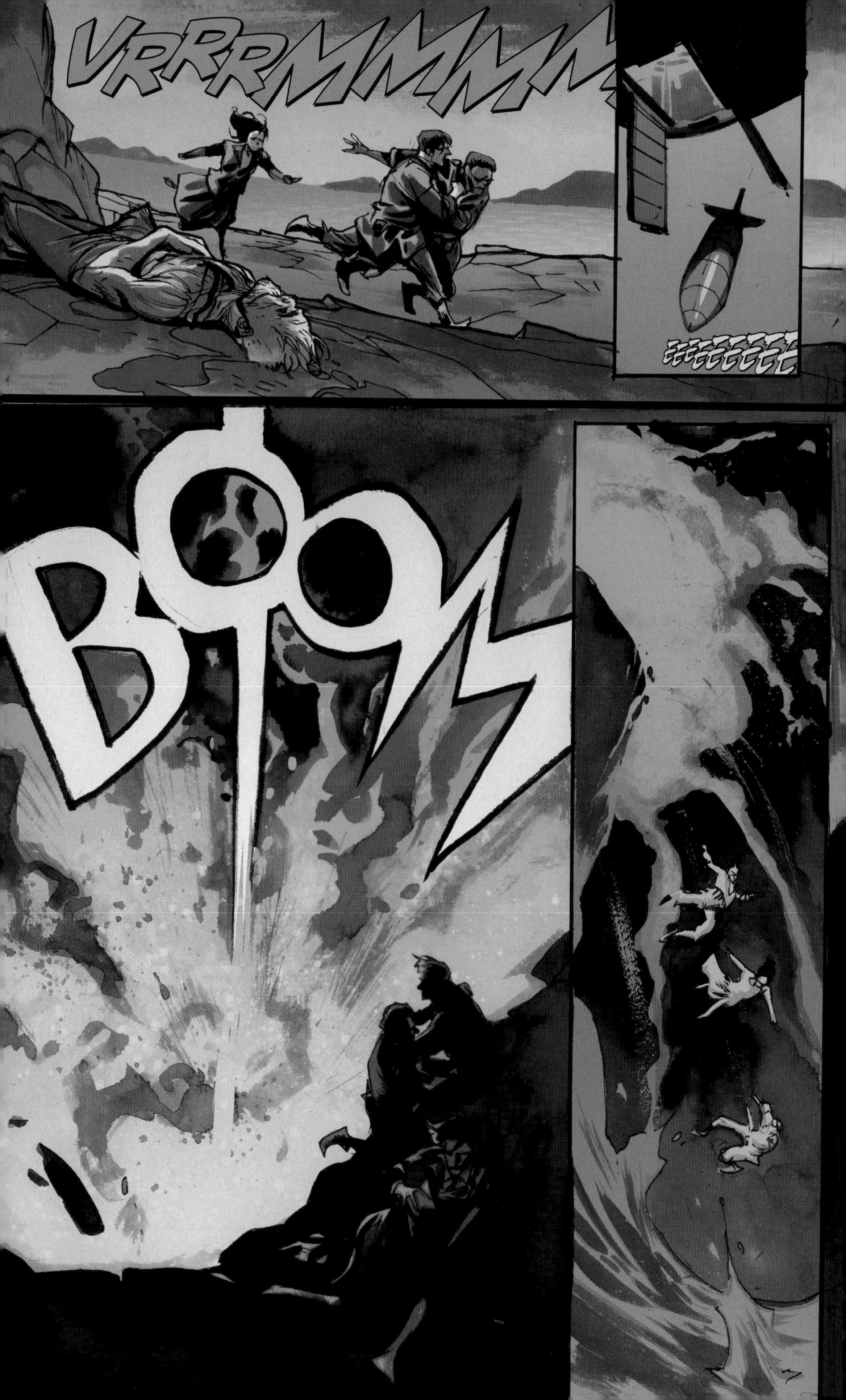
VRRRMMMMM
EEEEEEEEEEE
BOOM

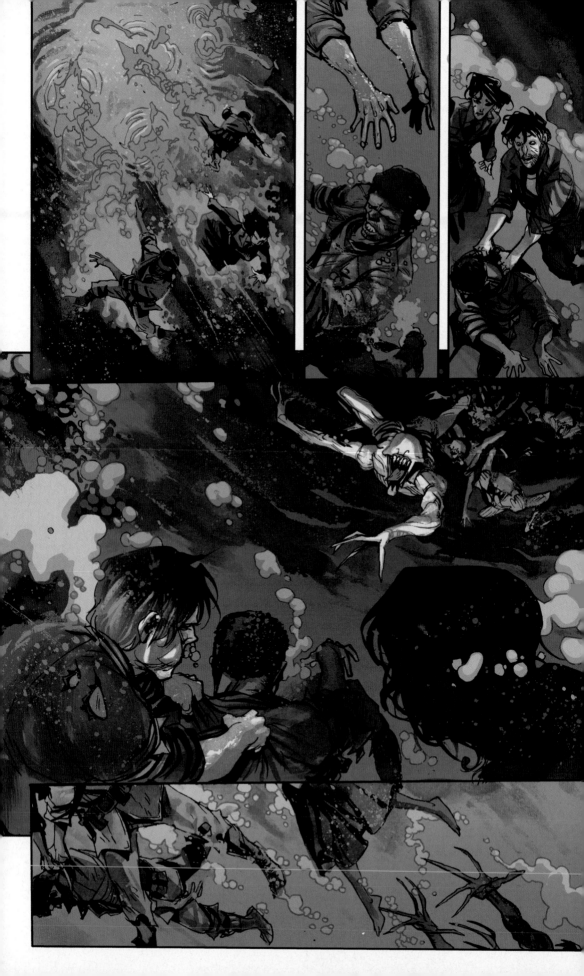

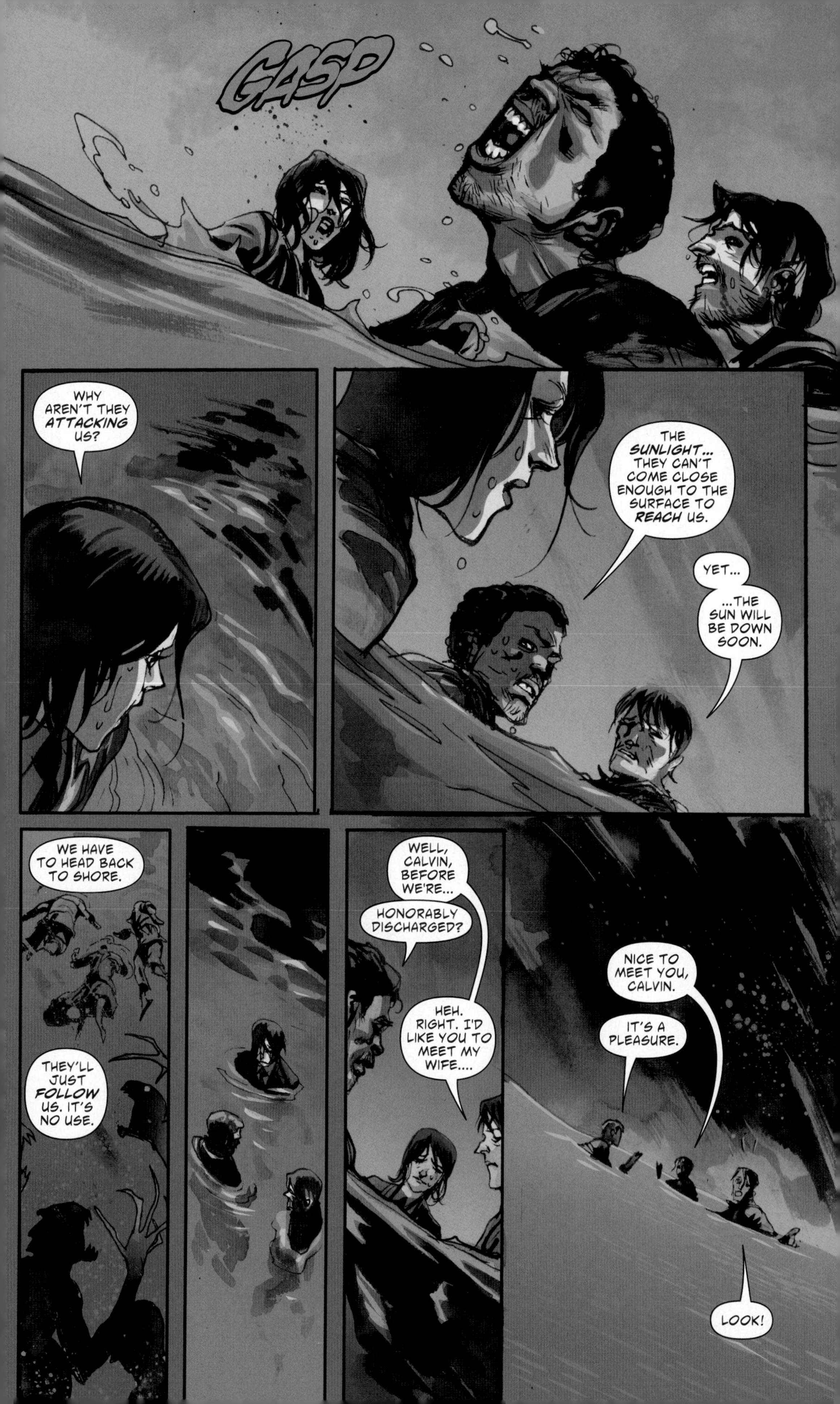
GASP
WHY AREN'T THEY ATTACKING US?
THE SUNLIGHT... THEY CAN'T COME CLOSE ENOUGH TO THE SURFACE TO REACH US.
YET...
...THE SUN WILL BE DOWN SOON.
WE HAVE TO HEAD BACK TO SHORE.
THEY'LL JUST FOLLOW US. IT'S NO USE.
WELL, CALVIN, BEFORE WE'RE...
HONORABLY DISCHARGED?
HEH. RIGHT. I'D LIKE YOU TO MEET MY WIFE....
NICE TO MEET YOU, CALVIN.
IT'S A PLEASURE.
LOOK!

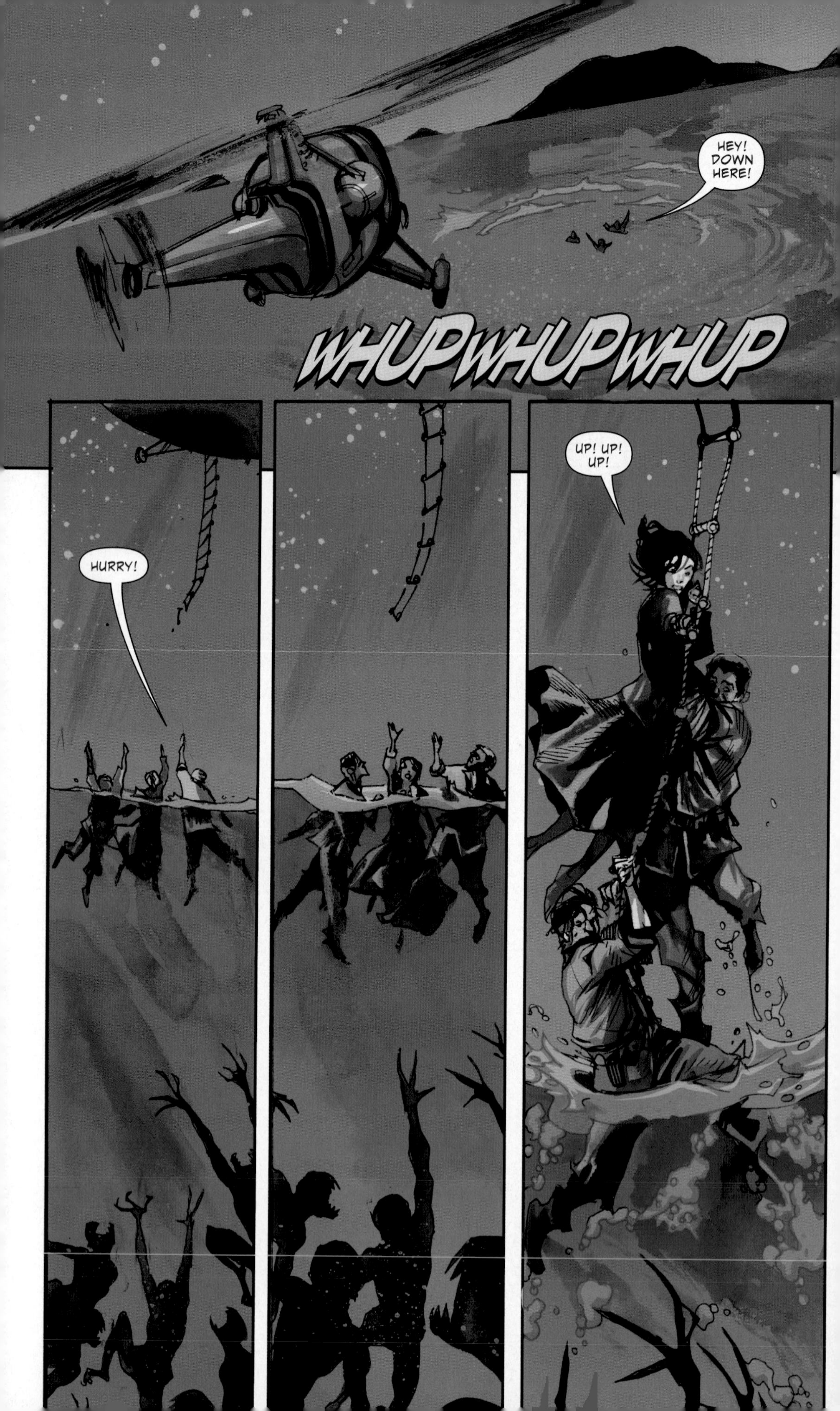
HEY! DOWN HERE!
WHUPWHUPWHUP
HURRY!
UP! UP! UP!

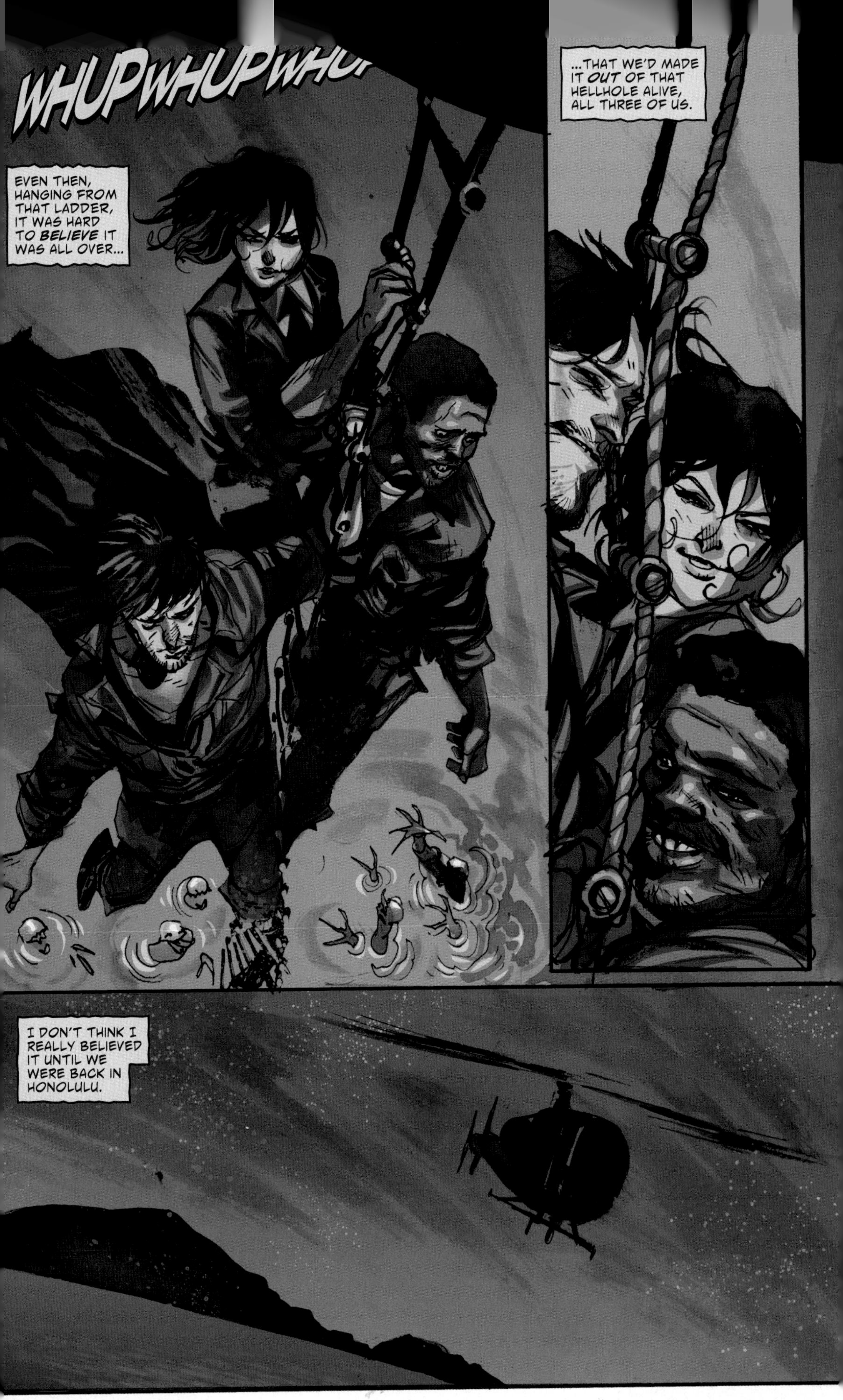
WHUPWHUPWHU
EVEN THEN, HANGING FROM THAT LADDER, IT WAS HARD TO BELIEVE IT WAS ALL OVER...
...THAT WE'D MADE IT OUT OF THAT HELLHOLE ALIVE, ALL THREE OF US.
I DON'T THINK I REALLY BELIEVED IT UNTIL WE WERE BACK IN HONOLULU.

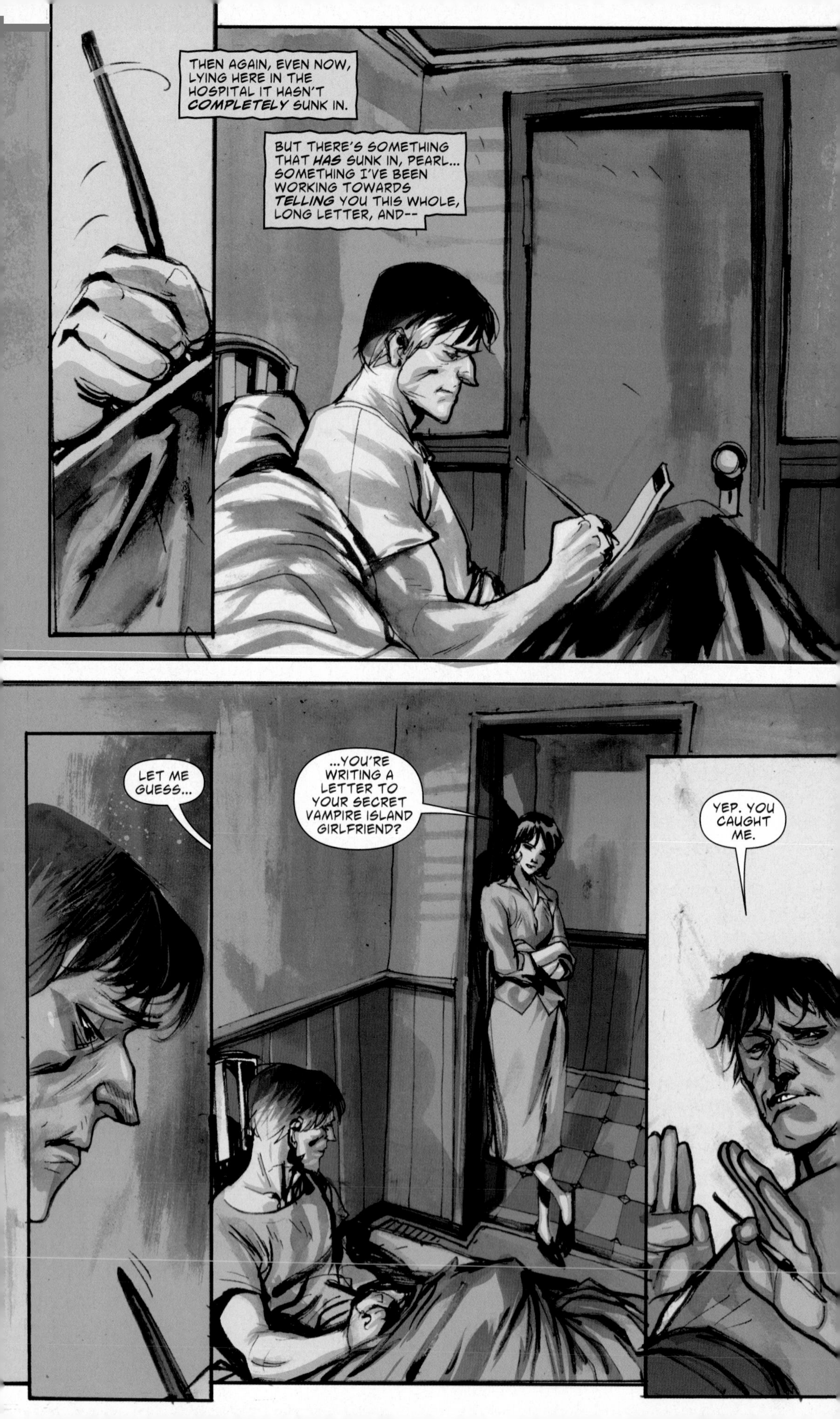

THEN AGAIN, EVEN NOW, LYING HERE IN THE HOSPITAL IT HASN'T COMPLETELY SUNK IN.
BUT THERE'S SOMETHING THAT HAS SUNK IN, PEARL... SOMETHING I'VE BEEN WORKING TOWARDS TELLING YOU THIS WHOLE, LONG LETTER, AND--
LET ME GUESS...
...YOU'RE WRITING A LETTER TO YOUR SECRET VAMPIRE ISLAND GIRLFRIEND?
YEP. YOU CAUGHT ME.

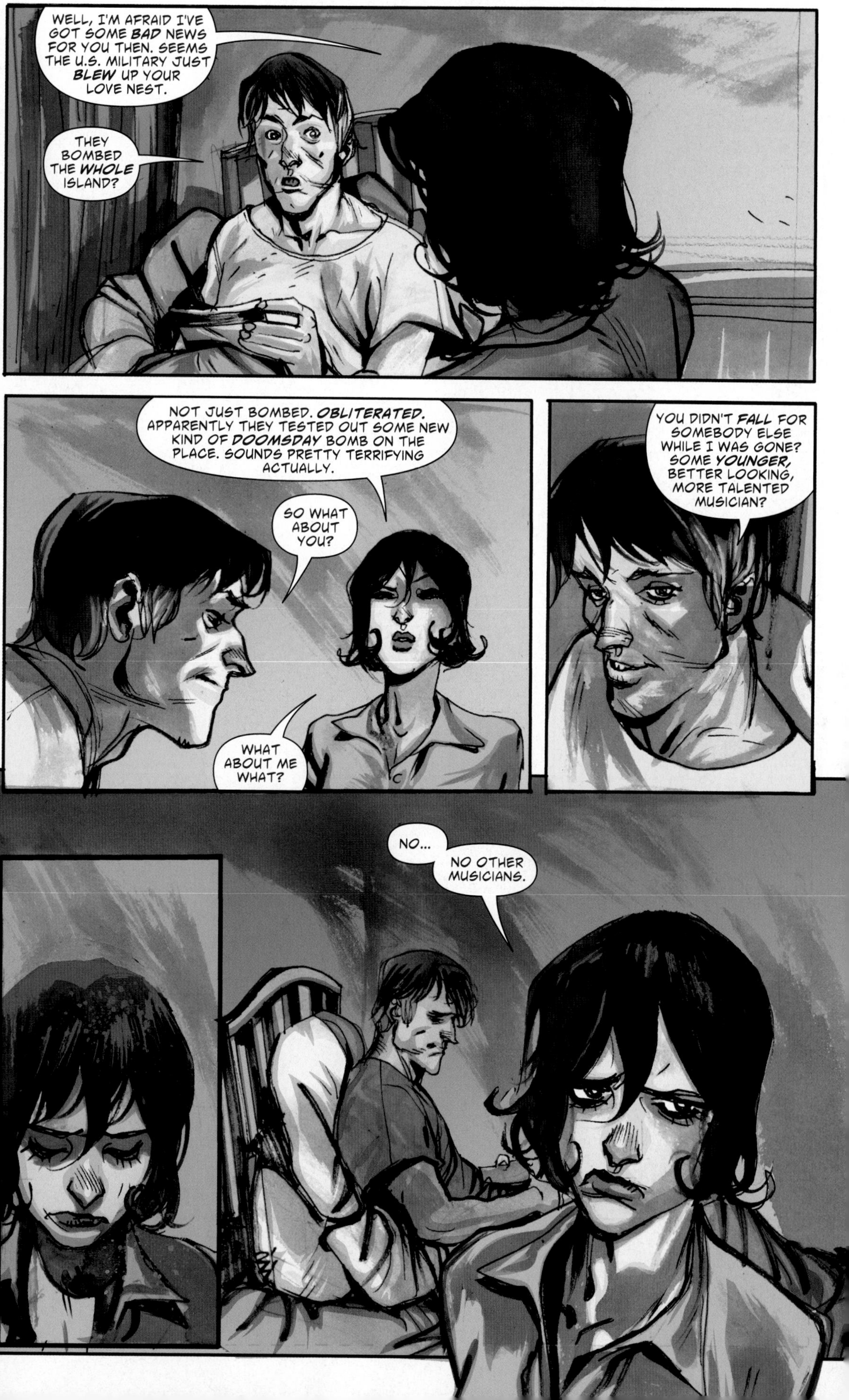
WELL, I'M AFRAID I'VE GOT SOME BAD NEWS FOR YOU THEN. SEEMS THE U.S. MILITARY JUST BLEW UP YOUR LOVE NEST.
THEY BOMBED THE WHOLE ISLAND?
NOT JUST BOMBED. OBLITERATED. APPARENTLY THEY TESTED OUT SOME NEW KIND OF DOOMSDAY BOMB ON THE PLACE. SOUNDS PRETTY TERRIFYING ACTUALLY.
SO WHAT ABOUT YOU?
WHAT ABOUT ME WHAT?
YOU DIDN'T FALL FOR SOMEBODY ELSE WHILE I WAS GONE? SOME YOUNGER, BETTER LOOKING, MORE TALENTED MUSICIAN?
NO...
NO OTHER MUSICIANS.

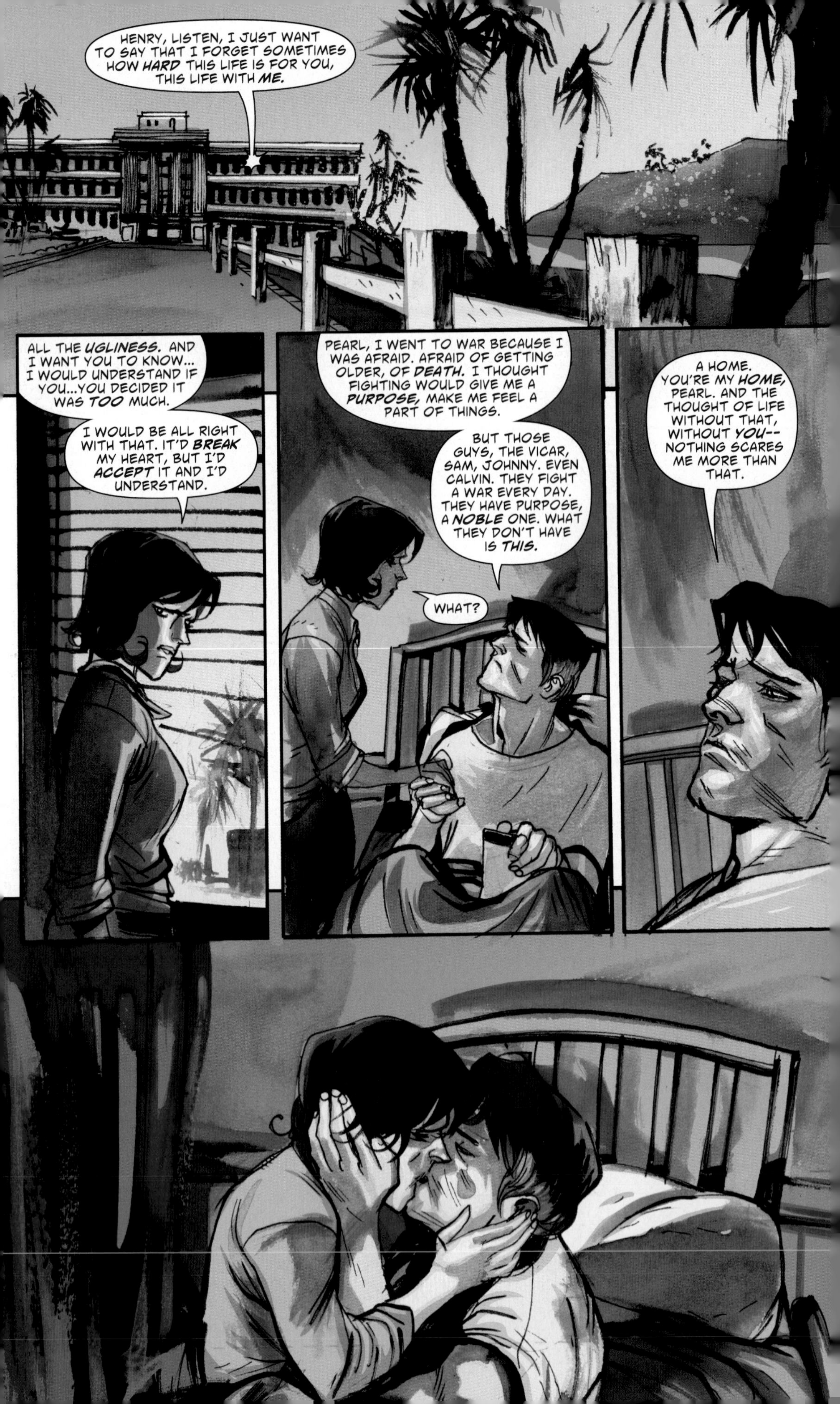

HENRY, LISTEN, I JUST WANT TO SAY THAT I FORGET SOMETIMES HOW *HARD* THIS LIFE IS FOR YOU, THIS LIFE WITH *ME.*
ALL THE *UGLINESS.* AND I WANT YOU TO KNOW... I WOULD UNDERSTAND IF YOU...YOU DECIDED IT WAS *TOO* MUCH.
I WOULD BE ALL RIGHT WITH THAT. IT'D *BREAK* MY HEART, BUT I'D *ACCEPT* IT AND I'D UNDERSTAND.
PEARL, I WENT TO WAR BECAUSE I WAS AFRAID. AFRAID OF GETTING OLDER, OF *DEATH.* I THOUGHT FIGHTING WOULD GIVE ME A *PURPOSE,* MAKE ME FEEL A PART OF THINGS.
BUT THOSE GUYS, THE VICAR, SAM, JOHNNY. EVEN CALVIN. THEY FIGHT A WAR EVERY DAY. THEY HAVE PURPOSE, A *NOBLE* ONE. WHAT THEY DON'T HAVE IS *THIS.*
WHAT?
A HOME. YOU'RE MY *HOME,* PEARL. AND THE THOUGHT OF LIFE WITHOUT THAT, WITHOUT *YOU*-- NOTHING SCARES ME MORE THAN THAT.

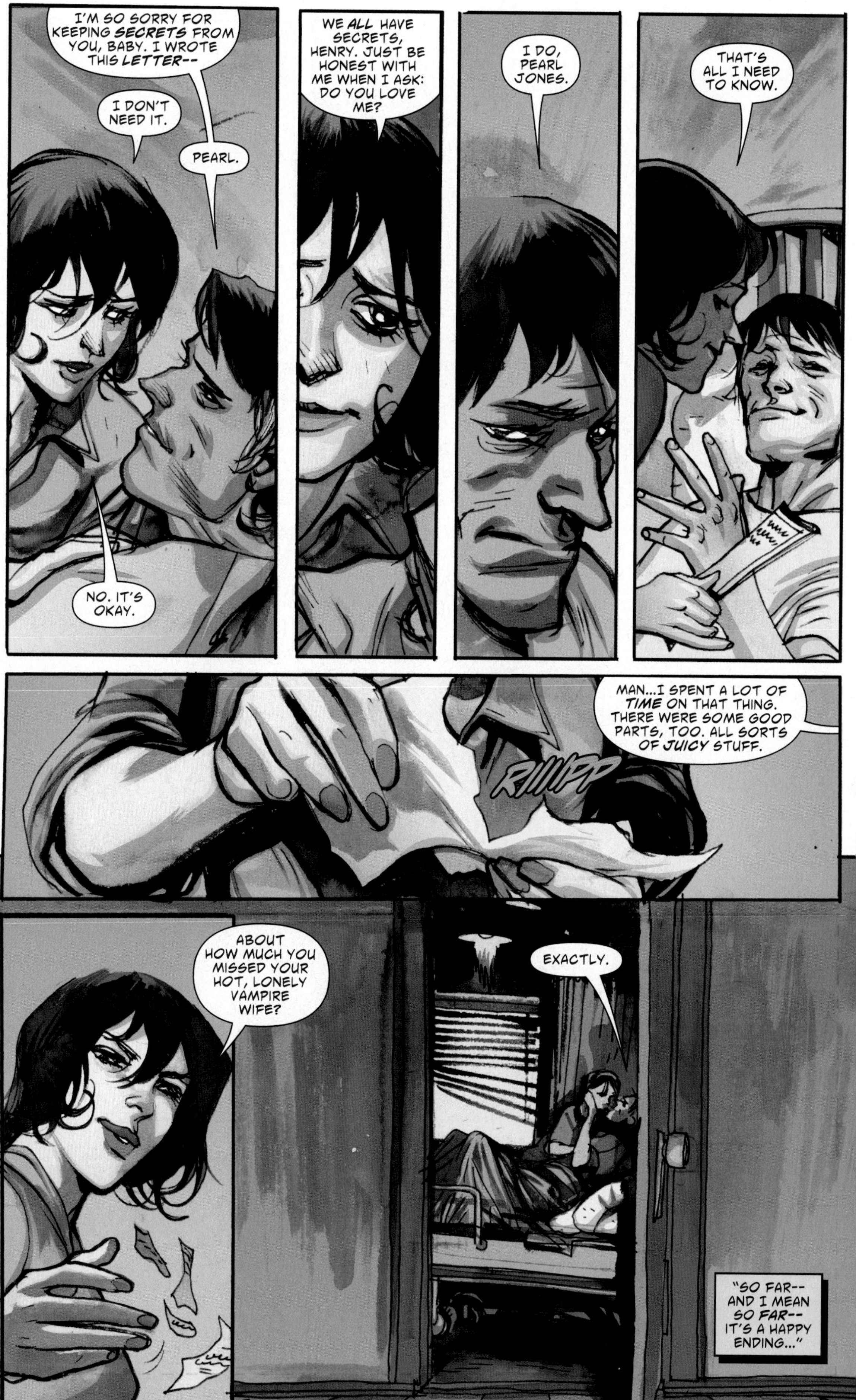

I'M SO SORRY FOR KEEPING SECRETS FROM YOU, BABY. I WROTE THIS LETTER--
I DON'T NEED IT.
PEARL.
NO. IT'S OKAY.
WE ALL HAVE SECRETS, HENRY. JUST BE HONEST WITH ME WHEN I ASK: DO YOU LOVE ME?
I DO, PEARL JONES.
THAT'S ALL I NEED TO KNOW.
MAN...I SPENT A LOT OF TIME ON THAT THING. THERE WERE SOME GOOD PARTS, TOO. ALL SORTS OF JUICY STUFF.
RIIIPP
ABOUT HOW MUCH YOU MISSED YOUR HOT, LONELY VAMPIRE WIFE?
EXACTLY.
"SO FAR-- AND I MEAN SO FAR-- IT'S A HAPPY ENDING..."

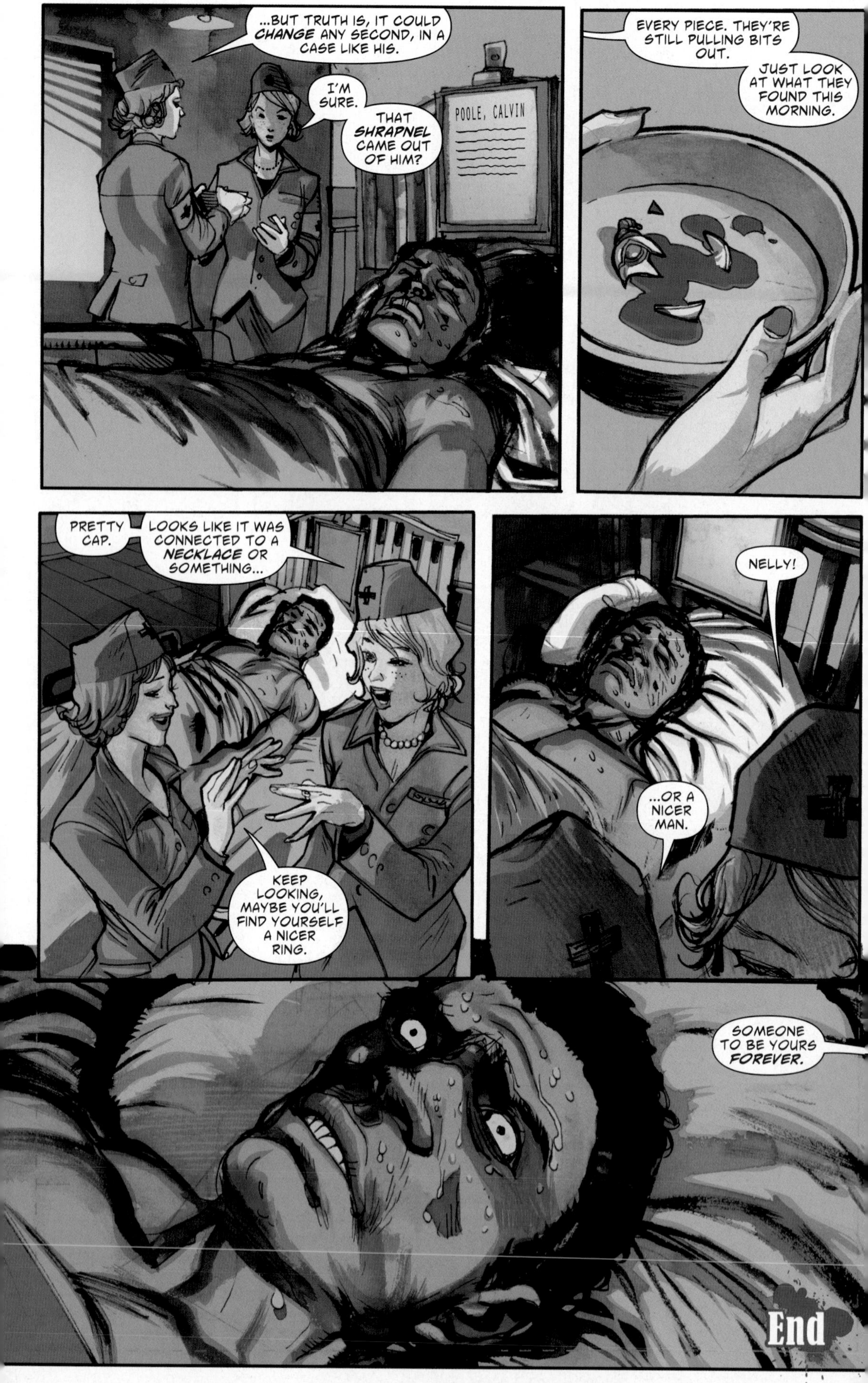
...BUT TRUTH IS, IT COULD *CHANGE* ANY SECOND, IN A CASE LIKE HIS.
I'M SURE.
THAT *SHRAPNEL* CAME OUT OF HIM?
POOLE, CALVIN
EVERY PIECE. THEY'RE STILL PULLING BITS OUT.
JUST LOOK AT WHAT THEY FOUND THIS MORNING.
PRETTY CAP.
LOOKS LIKE IT WAS CONNECTED TO A *NECKLACE* OR SOMETHING...
KEEP LOOKING, MAYBE YOU'LL FIND YOURSELF A NICER RING.
NELLY!
...OR A NICER MAN.
SOMEONE TO BE YOURS *FOREVER*.
End

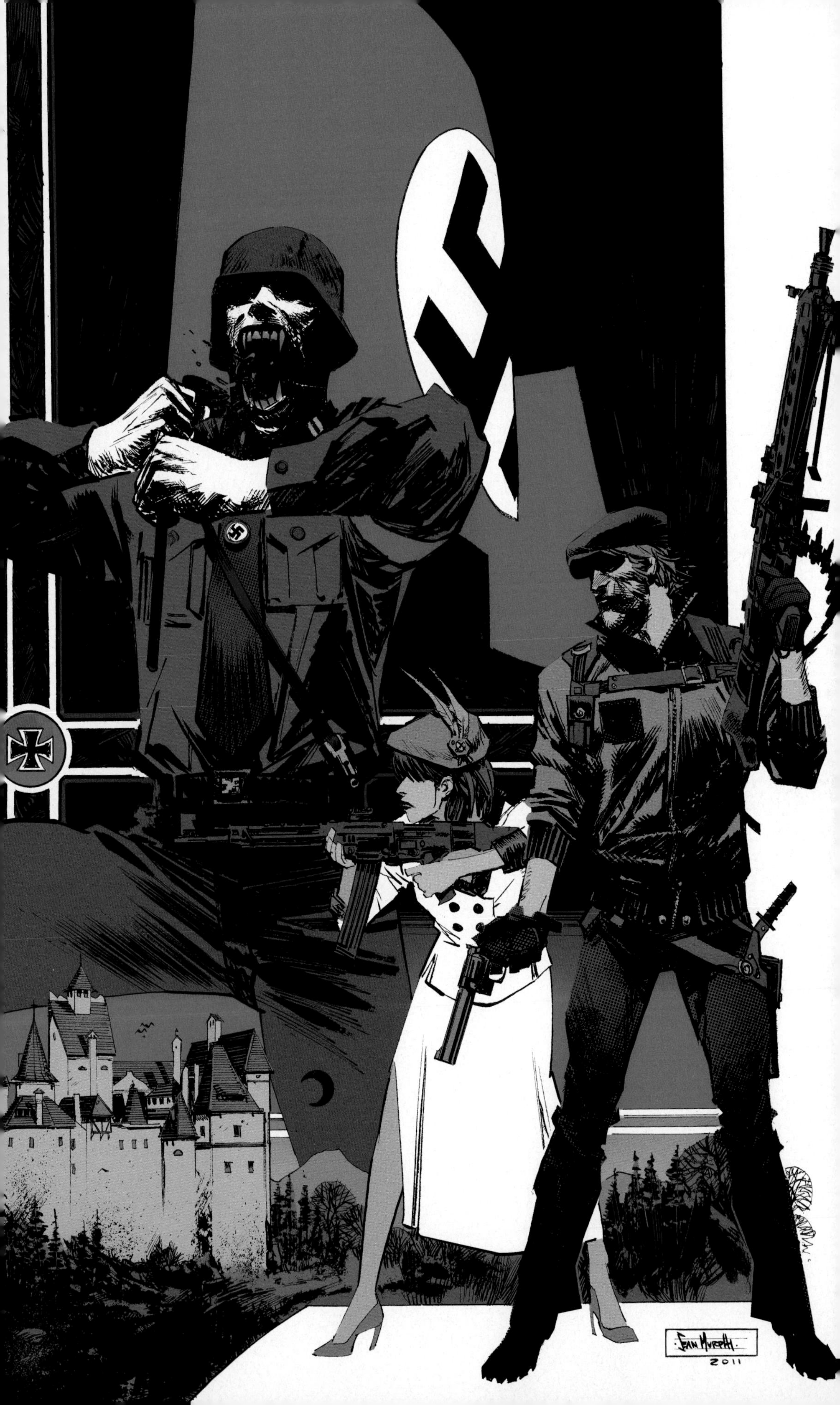
SEAN MURPHY
2011

Survival
of the Fittest
Part One

Sean Murphy
Artist and cover

Dave Stewart
cover color

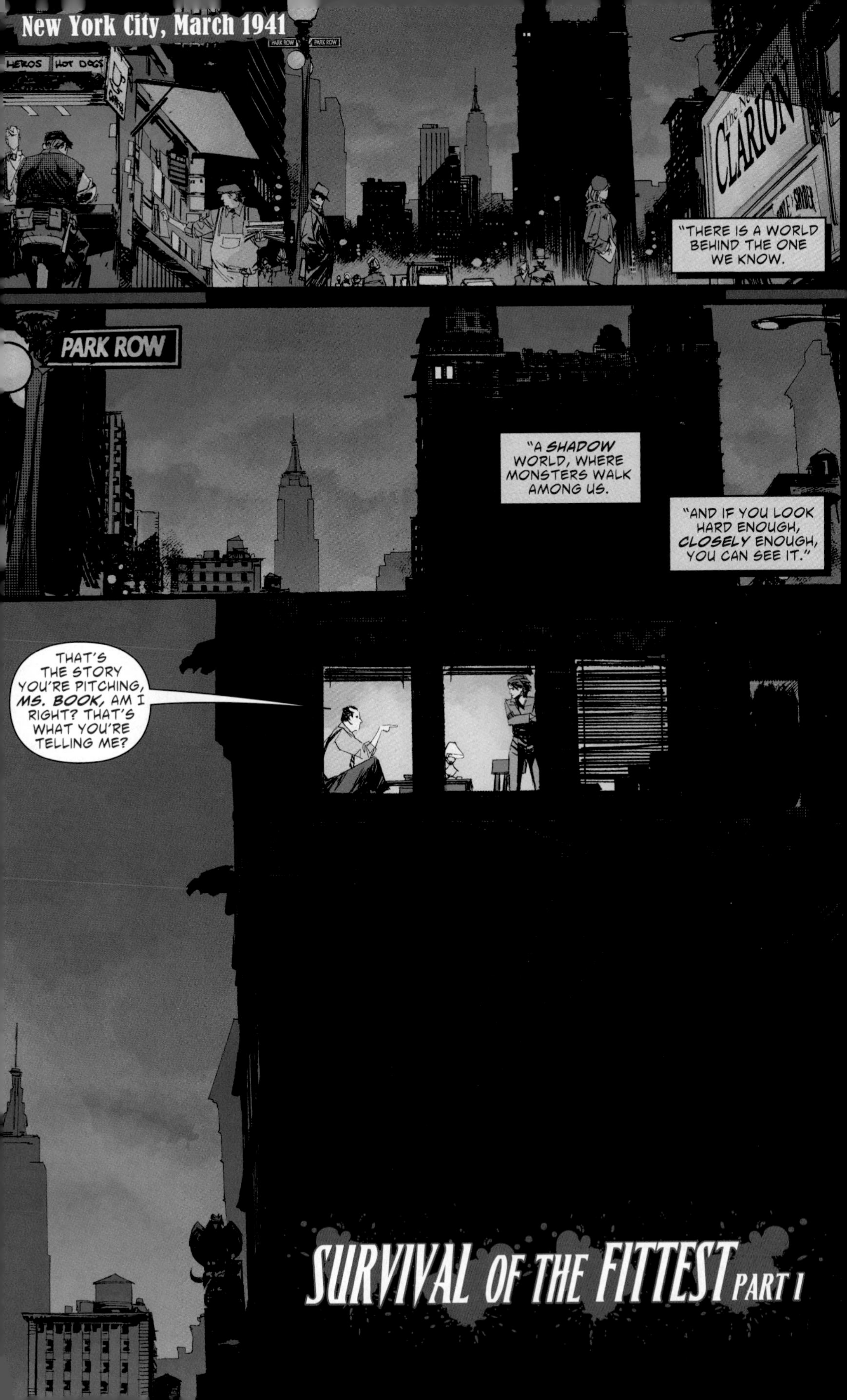
New York City, March 1941
HEROS
HOT DOGS
PARK ROW
PARK ROW
The New York CLARION
"THERE IS A WORLD BEHIND THE ONE WE KNOW.
PARK ROW
"A SHADOW WORLD, WHERE MONSTERS WALK AMONG US.
"AND IF YOU LOOK HARD ENOUGH, CLOSELY ENOUGH, YOU CAN SEE IT."
THAT'S THE STORY YOU'RE PITCHING, MS. BOOK, AM I RIGHT? THAT'S WHAT YOU'RE TELLING ME?
SURVIVAL OF THE FITTEST PART 1

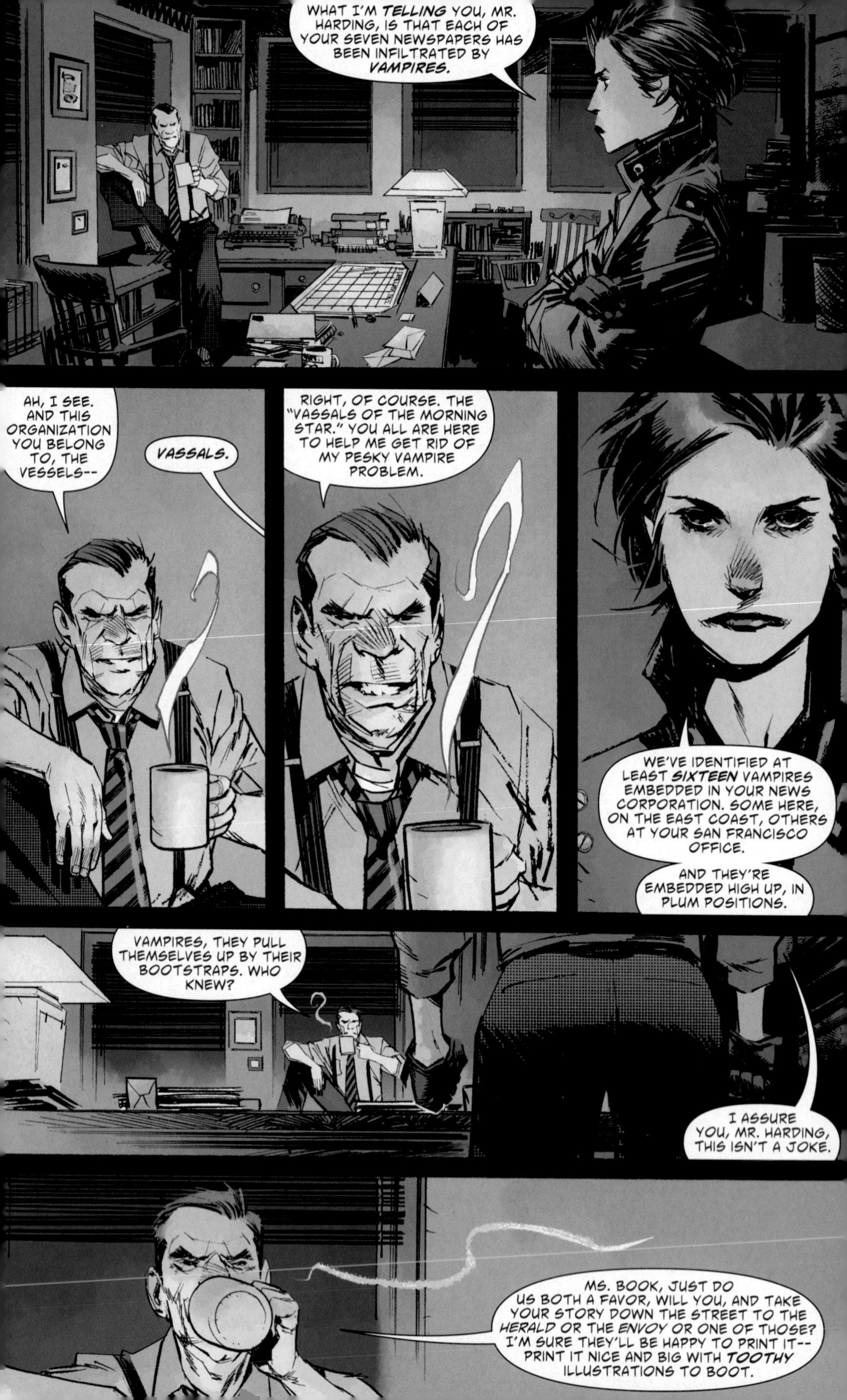
WHAT I'M *TELLING* YOU, MR. HARDING, IS THAT EACH OF YOUR SEVEN NEWSPAPERS HAS BEEN INFILTRATED BY *VAMPIRES.*
AH, I SEE. AND THIS ORGANIZATION YOU BELONG TO, THE VESSELS--
VASSALS.
RIGHT, OF COURSE. THE "VASSALS OF THE MORNING STAR." YOU ALL ARE HERE TO HELP ME GET RID OF MY PESKY VAMPIRE PROBLEM.
WE'VE IDENTIFIED AT LEAST *SIXTEEN* VAMPIRES EMBEDDED IN YOUR NEWS CORPORATION. SOME HERE, ON THE EAST COAST, OTHERS AT YOUR SAN FRANCISCO OFFICE.
AND THEY'RE EMBEDDED HIGH UP, IN PLUM POSITIONS.
VAMPIRES, THEY PULL THEMSELVES UP BY THEIR BOOTSTRAPS. WHO KNEW?
I ASSURE YOU, MR. HARDING, THIS ISN'T A JOKE.
MS. BOOK, JUST DO US BOTH A FAVOR, WILL YOU, AND TAKE YOUR STORY DOWN THE STREET TO THE *HERALD* OR THE *ENVOY* OR ONE OF THOSE? I'M SURE THEY'LL BE HAPPY TO PRINT IT-- PRINT IT NICE AND BIG WITH *TOOTHY* ILLUSTRATIONS TO BOOT.

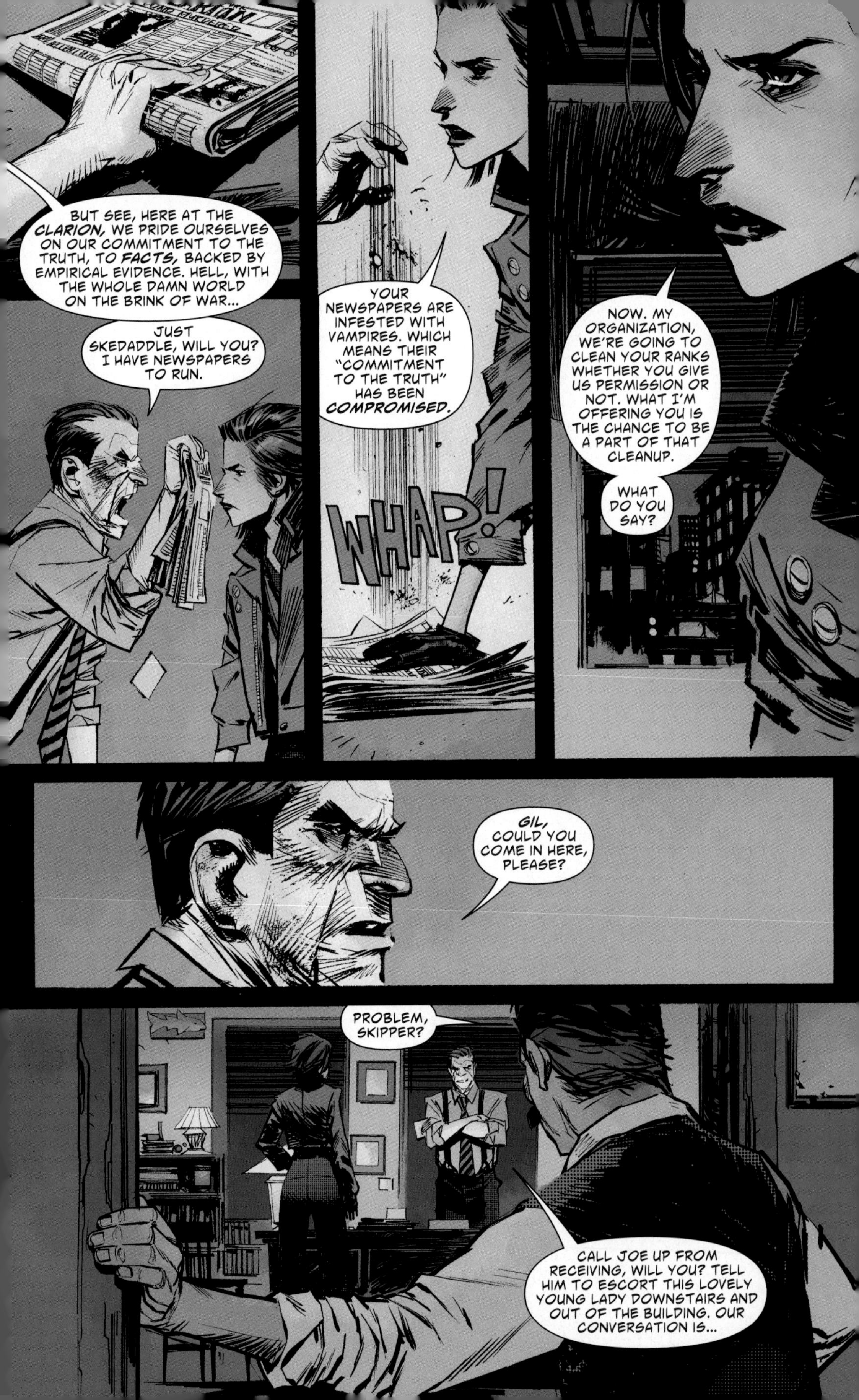
BUT SEE, HERE AT THE CLARION, WE PRIDE OURSELVES ON OUR COMMITMENT TO THE TRUTH, TO FACTS, BACKED BY EMPIRICAL EVIDENCE. HELL, WITH THE WHOLE DAMN WORLD ON THE BRINK OF WAR...
JUST SKEDADDLE, WILL YOU? I HAVE NEWSPAPERS TO RUN.
YOUR NEWSPAPERS ARE INFESTED WITH VAMPIRES. WHICH MEANS THEIR "COMMITMENT TO THE TRUTH" HAS BEEN COMPROMISED.
WHAP!
NOW. MY ORGANIZATION, WE'RE GOING TO CLEAN YOUR RANKS WHETHER YOU GIVE US PERMISSION OR NOT. WHAT I'M OFFERING YOU IS THE CHANCE TO BE A PART OF THAT CLEANUP.
WHAT DO YOU SAY?
GIL, COULD YOU COME IN HERE, PLEASE?
PROBLEM, SKIPPER?
CALL JOE UP FROM RECEIVING, WILL YOU? TELL HIM TO ESCORT THIS LOVELY YOUNG LADY DOWNSTAIRS AND OUT OF THE BUILDING. OUR CONVERSATION IS...

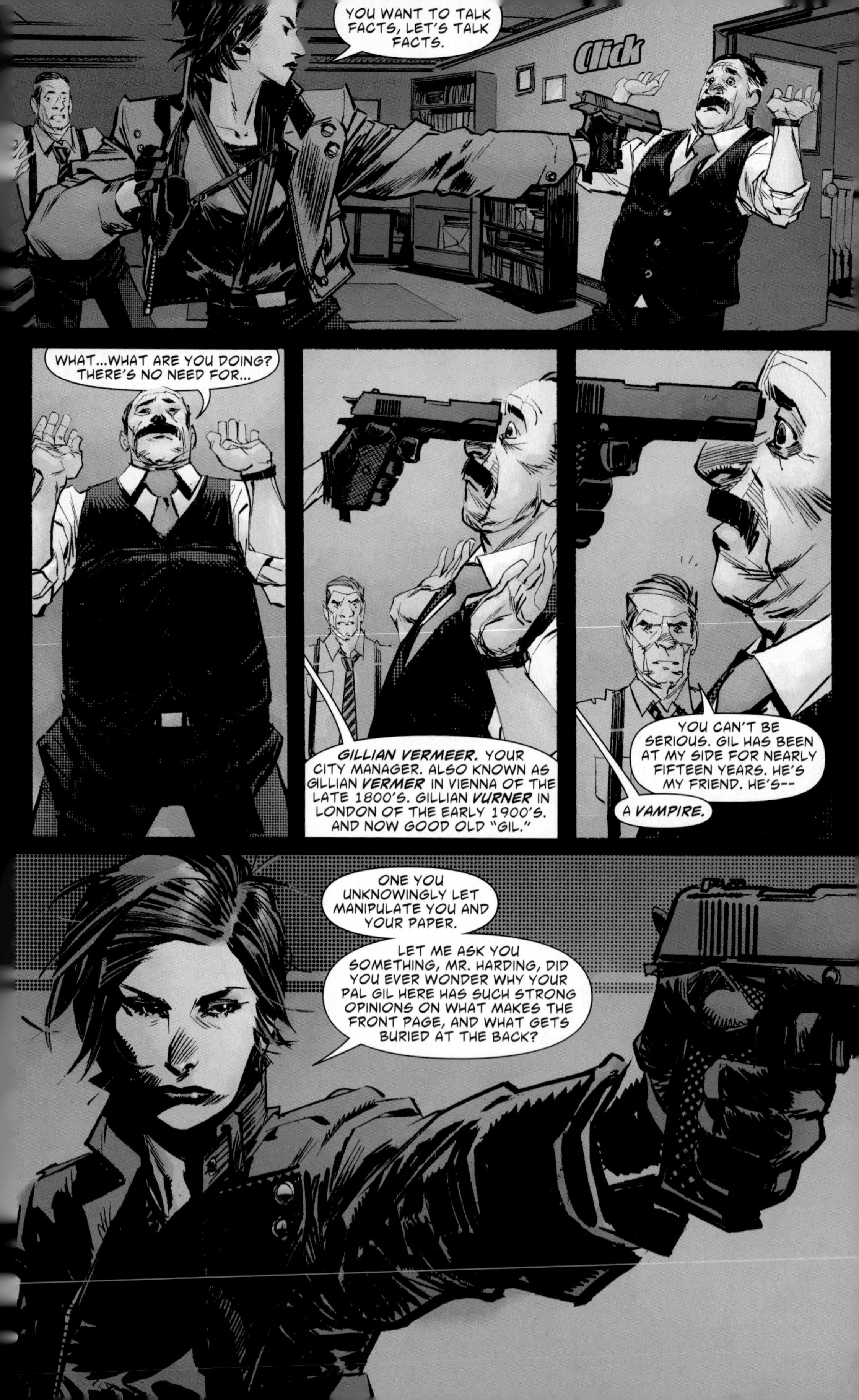
YOU WANT TO TALK FACTS, LET'S TALK FACTS.
Click
WHAT...WHAT ARE YOU DOING? THERE'S NO NEED FOR...
GILLIAN VERMEER. YOUR CITY MANAGER. ALSO KNOWN AS GILLIAN VERMER IN VIENNA OF THE LATE 1800'S. GILLIAN VURNER IN LONDON OF THE EARLY 1900'S. AND NOW GOOD OLD "GIL."
YOU CAN'T BE SERIOUS. GIL HAS BEEN AT MY SIDE FOR NEARLY FIFTEEN YEARS. HE'S MY FRIEND. HE'S--
A VAMPIRE.
ONE YOU UNKNOWINGLY LET MANIPULATE YOU AND YOUR PAPER.
LET ME ASK YOU SOMETHING, MR. HARDING, DID YOU EVER WONDER WHY YOUR PAL GIL HERE HAS SUCH STRONG OPINIONS ON WHAT MAKES THE FRONT PAGE, AND WHAT GETS BURIED AT THE BACK?

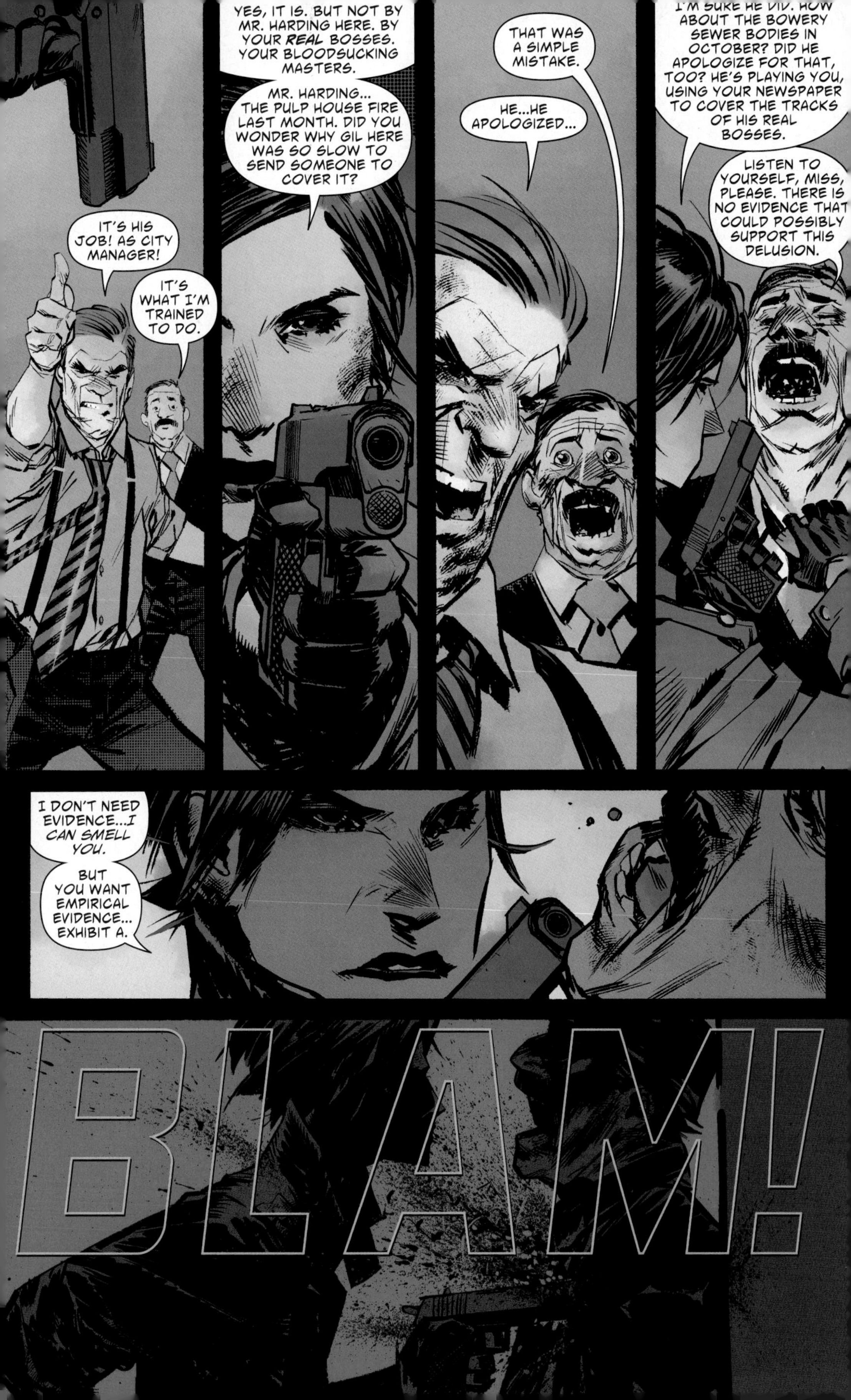
IT'S HIS JOB! AS CITY MANAGER!
IT'S WHAT I'M TRAINED TO DO.
YES, IT IS. BUT NOT BY MR. HARDING HERE. BY YOUR REAL BOSSES. YOUR BLOODSUCKING MASTERS.
MR. HARDING... THE PULP HOUSE FIRE LAST MONTH. DID YOU WONDER WHY GIL HERE WAS SO SLOW TO SEND SOMEONE TO COVER IT?
HE...HE APOLOGIZED...
THAT WAS A SIMPLE MISTAKE.
I'M SURE HE DID. HOW ABOUT THE BOWERY SEWER BODIES IN OCTOBER? DID HE APOLOGIZE FOR THAT, TOO? HE'S PLAYING YOU, USING YOUR NEWSPAPER TO COVER THE TRACKS OF HIS REAL BOSSES.
LISTEN TO YOURSELF, MISS, PLEASE. THERE IS NO EVIDENCE THAT COULD POSSIBLY SUPPORT THIS DELUSION.
I DON'T NEED EVIDENCE...I CAN SMELL YOU.
BUT YOU WANT EMPIRICAL EVIDENCE... EXHIBIT A.
BLAM!

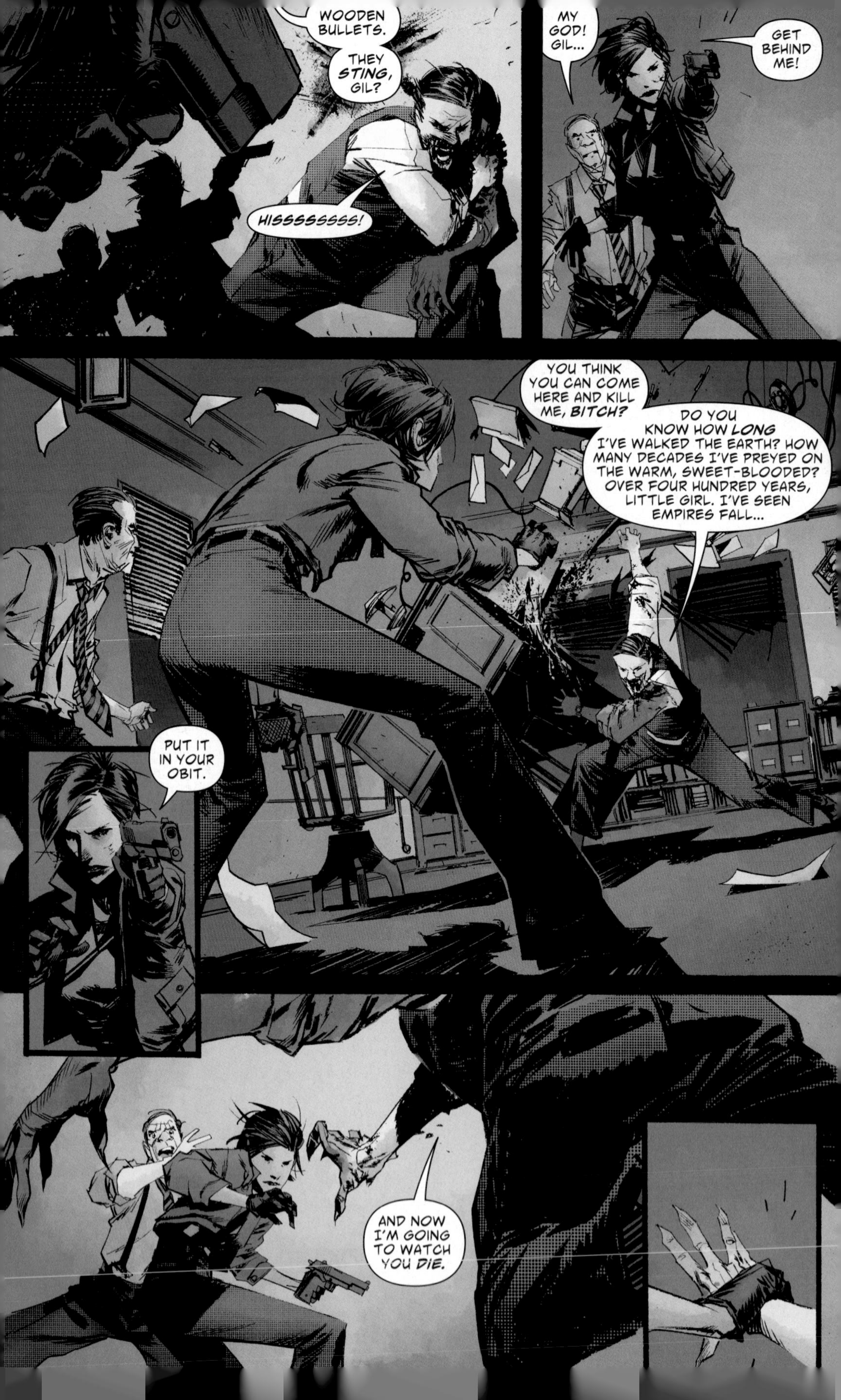
WOODEN BULLETS.
THEY STING, GIL?
HISSSSSSSS!
MY GOD! GIL...
GET BEHIND ME!
YOU THINK YOU CAN COME HERE AND KILL ME, BITCH?
DO YOU KNOW HOW LONG I'VE WALKED THE EARTH? HOW MANY DECADES I'VE PREYED ON THE WARM, SWEET-BLOODED? OVER FOUR HUNDRED YEARS, LITTLE GIRL. I'VE SEEN EMPIRES FALL...
PUT IT IN YOUR OBIT.
AND NOW I'M GOING TO WATCH YOU DIE.

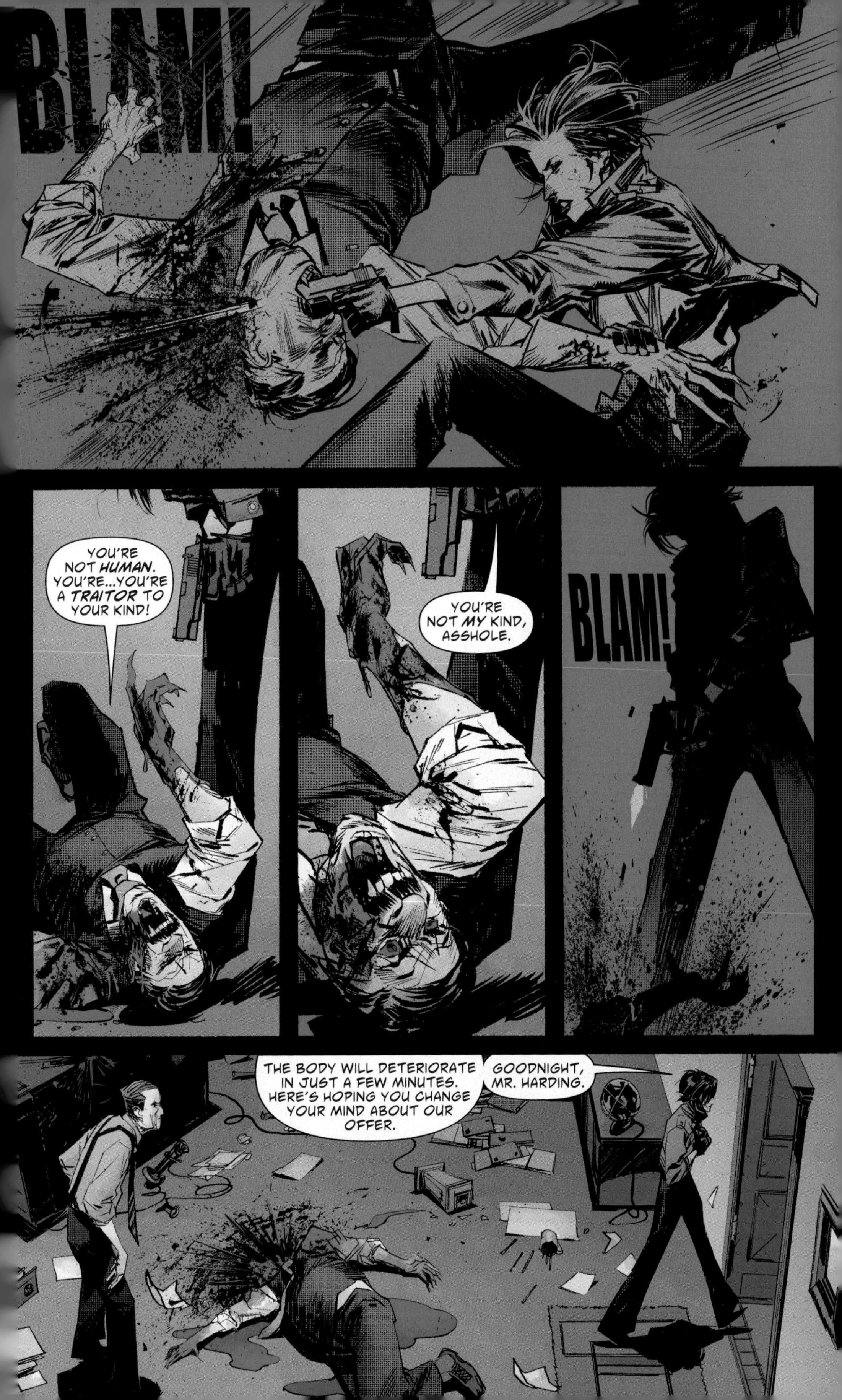
BLAM!
YOU'RE NOT HUMAN. YOU'RE...YOU'RE A TRAITOR TO YOUR KIND!
YOU'RE NOT MY KIND, ASSHOLE.
BLAM!
THE BODY WILL DETERIORATE IN JUST A FEW MINUTES. HERE'S HOPING YOU CHANGE YOUR MIND ABOUT OUR OFFER.
GOODNIGHT, MR. HARDING.

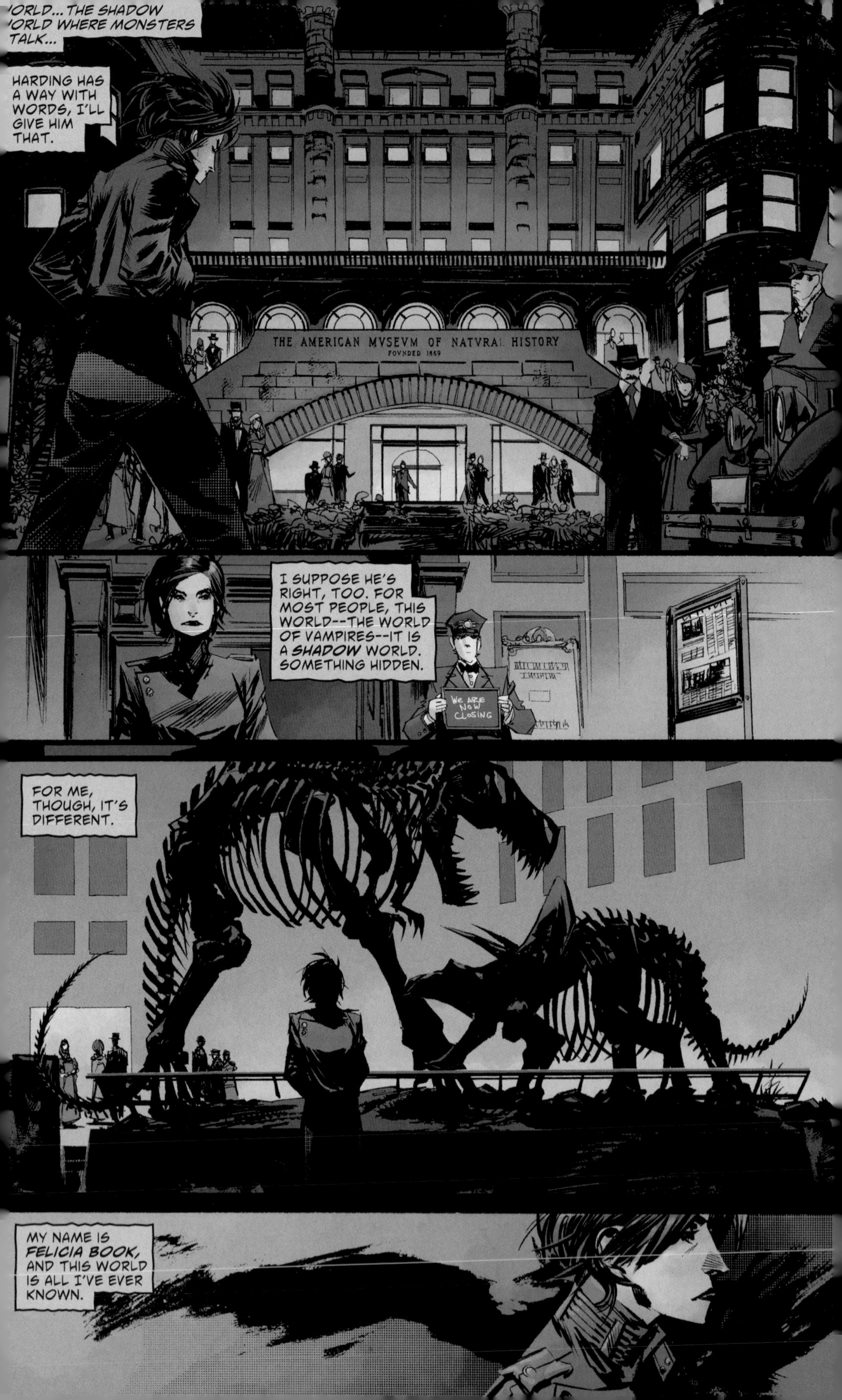
WORLD... THE SHADOW WORLD WHERE MONSTERS TALK...
HARDING HAS A WAY WITH WORDS, I'LL GIVE HIM THAT.
THE AMERICAN MVSEVM OF NATVRAL HISTORY
FOVNDED 1869
I SUPPOSE HE'S RIGHT, TOO. FOR MOST PEOPLE, THIS WORLD--THE WORLD OF VAMPIRES--IT IS A SHADOW WORLD. SOMETHING HIDDEN.
We ARE NOW CLOSING
FOR ME, THOUGH, IT'S DIFFERENT.
MY NAME IS FELICIA BOOK, AND THIS WORLD IS ALL I'VE EVER KNOWN.

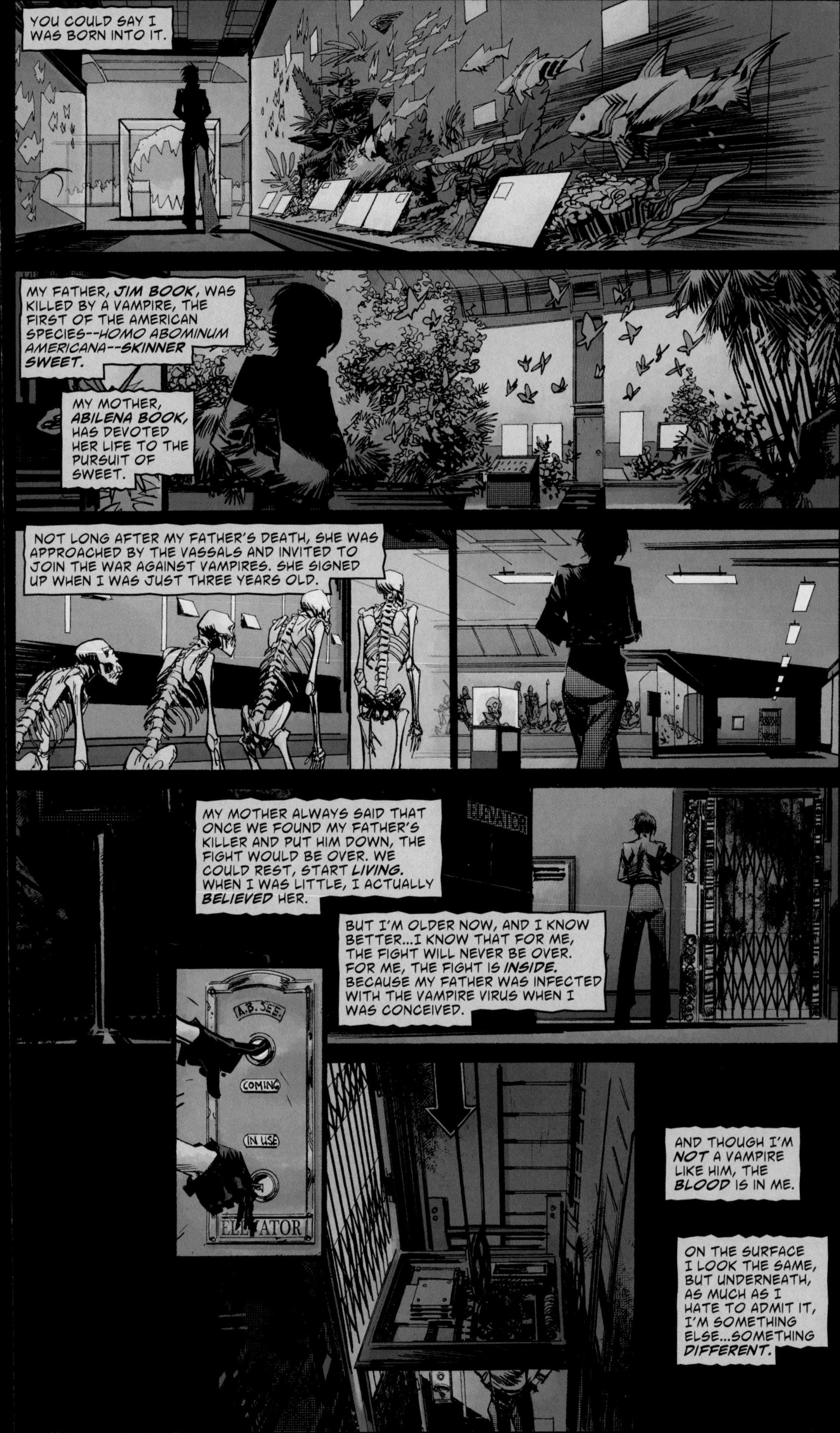
YOU COULD SAY I WAS BORN INTO IT.
MY FATHER, JIM BOOK, WAS KILLED BY A VAMPIRE, THE FIRST OF THE AMERICAN SPECIES--HOMO ABOMINUM AMERICANA--SKINNER SWEET.
MY MOTHER, ABILENA BOOK, HAS DEVOTED HER LIFE TO THE PURSUIT OF SWEET.
NOT LONG AFTER MY FATHER'S DEATH, SHE WAS APPROACHED BY THE VASSALS AND INVITED TO JOIN THE WAR AGAINST VAMPIRES. SHE SIGNED UP WHEN I WAS JUST THREE YEARS OLD.
MY MOTHER ALWAYS SAID THAT ONCE WE FOUND MY FATHER'S KILLER AND PUT HIM DOWN, THE FIGHT WOULD BE OVER. WE COULD REST, START LIVING. WHEN I WAS LITTLE, I ACTUALLY BELIEVED HER.
BUT I'M OLDER NOW, AND I KNOW BETTER...I KNOW THAT FOR ME, THE FIGHT WILL NEVER BE OVER. FOR ME, THE FIGHT IS INSIDE. BECAUSE MY FATHER WAS INFECTED WITH THE VAMPIRE VIRUS WHEN I WAS CONCEIVED.
A.B. SEE.
COMING
IN USE
ELEVATOR
AND THOUGH I'M NOT A VAMPIRE LIKE HIM, THE BLOOD IS IN ME.
ON THE SURFACE I LOOK THE SAME, BUT UNDERNEATH, AS MUCH AS I HATE TO ADMIT IT, I'M SOMETHING ELSE...SOMETHING DIFFERENT.

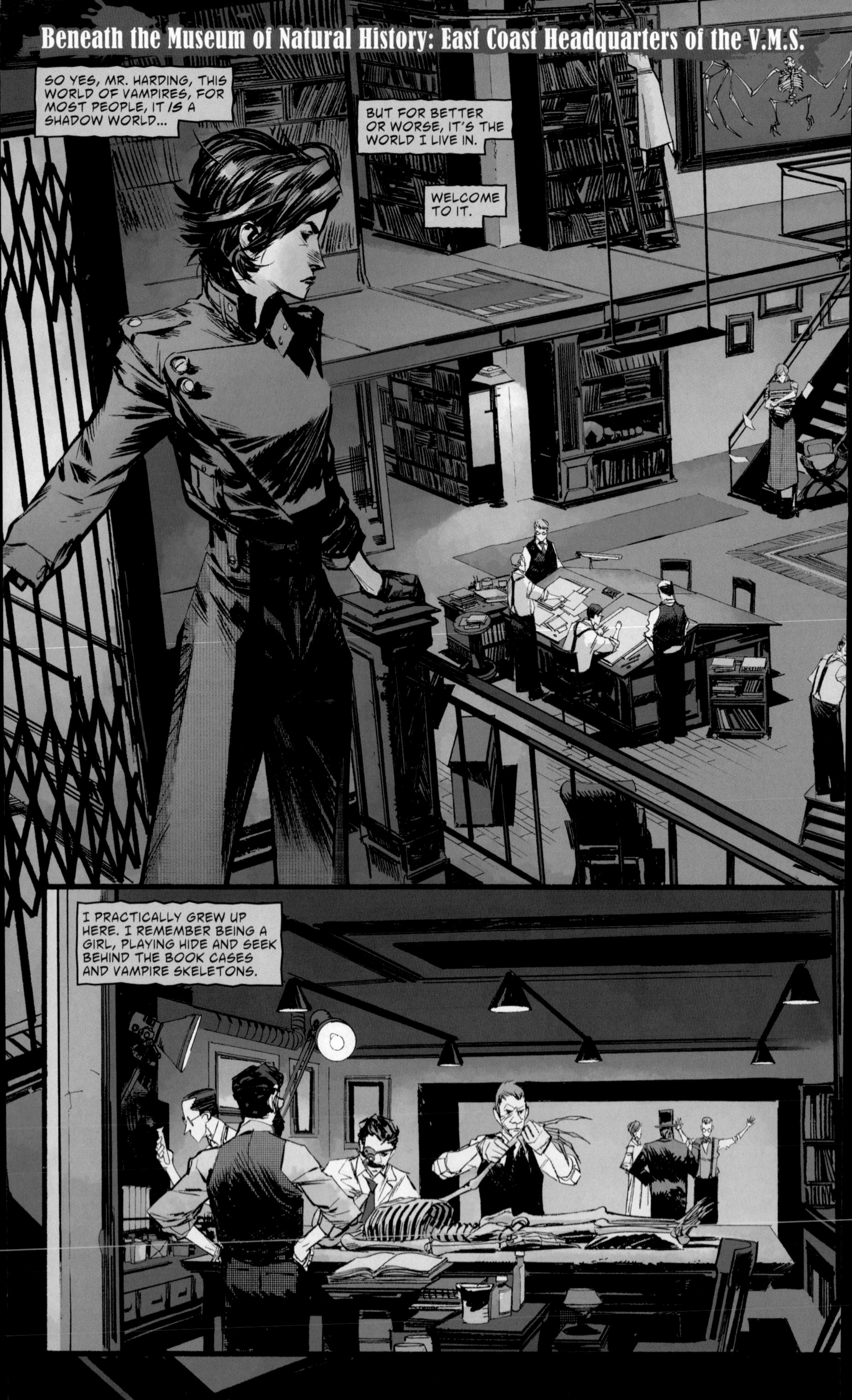
Beneath the Museum of Natural History: East Coast Headquarters of the V.M.S.
SO YES, MR. HARDING, THIS WORLD OF VAMPIRES, FOR MOST PEOPLE, IT IS A SHADOW WORLD...
BUT FOR BETTER OR WORSE, IT'S THE WORLD I LIVE IN.
WELCOME TO IT.
I PRACTICALLY GREW UP HERE. I REMEMBER BEING A GIRL, PLAYING HIDE AND SEEK BEHIND THE BOOK CASES AND VAMPIRE SKELETONS.

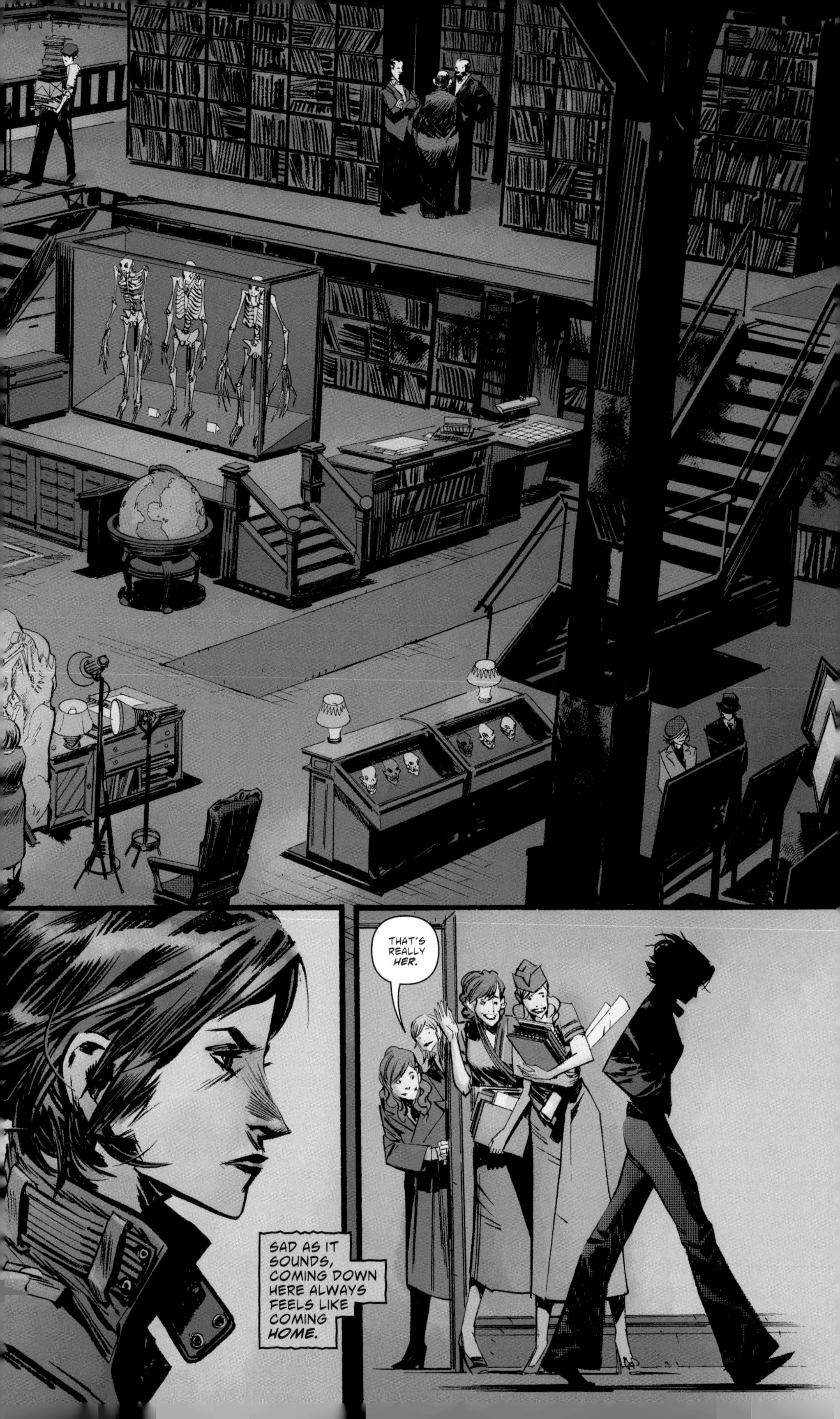
THAT'S REALLY HER.
SAD AS IT SOUNDS, COMING DOWN HERE ALWAYS FEELS LIKE COMING HOME.

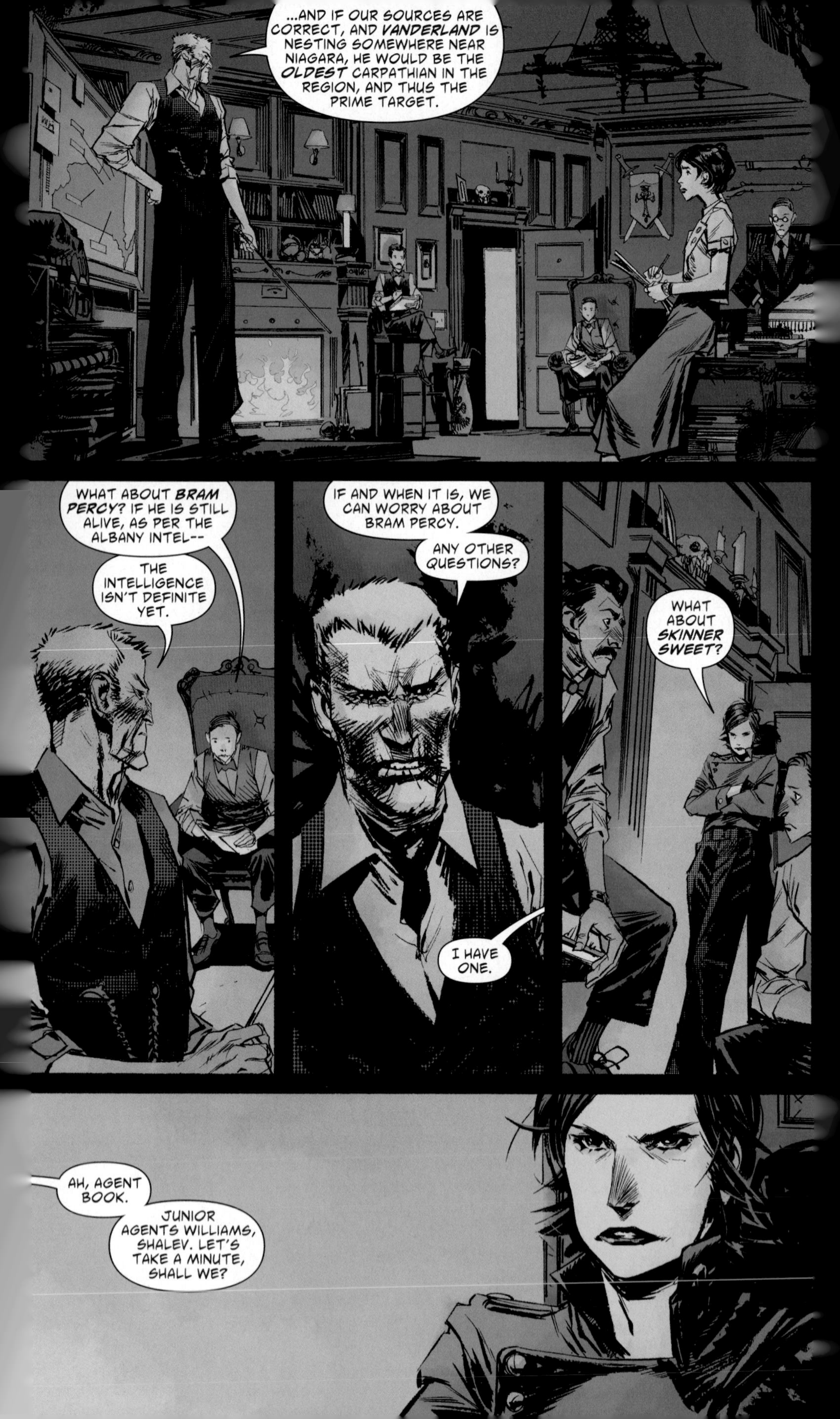
...AND IF OUR SOURCES ARE CORRECT, AND VANDERLAND IS NESTING SOMEWHERE NEAR NIAGARA, HE WOULD BE THE OLDEST CARPATHIAN IN THE REGION, AND THUS THE PRIME TARGET.
WHAT ABOUT BRAM PERCY? IF HE IS STILL ALIVE, AS PER THE ALBANY INTEL--
THE INTELLIGENCE ISN'T DEFINITE YET.
IF AND WHEN IT IS, WE CAN WORRY ABOUT BRAM PERCY.
ANY OTHER QUESTIONS?
I HAVE ONE.
WHAT ABOUT SKINNER SWEET?
AH, AGENT BOOK.
JUNIOR AGENTS WILLIAMS, SHALEV. LET'S TAKE A MINUTE, SHALL WE?

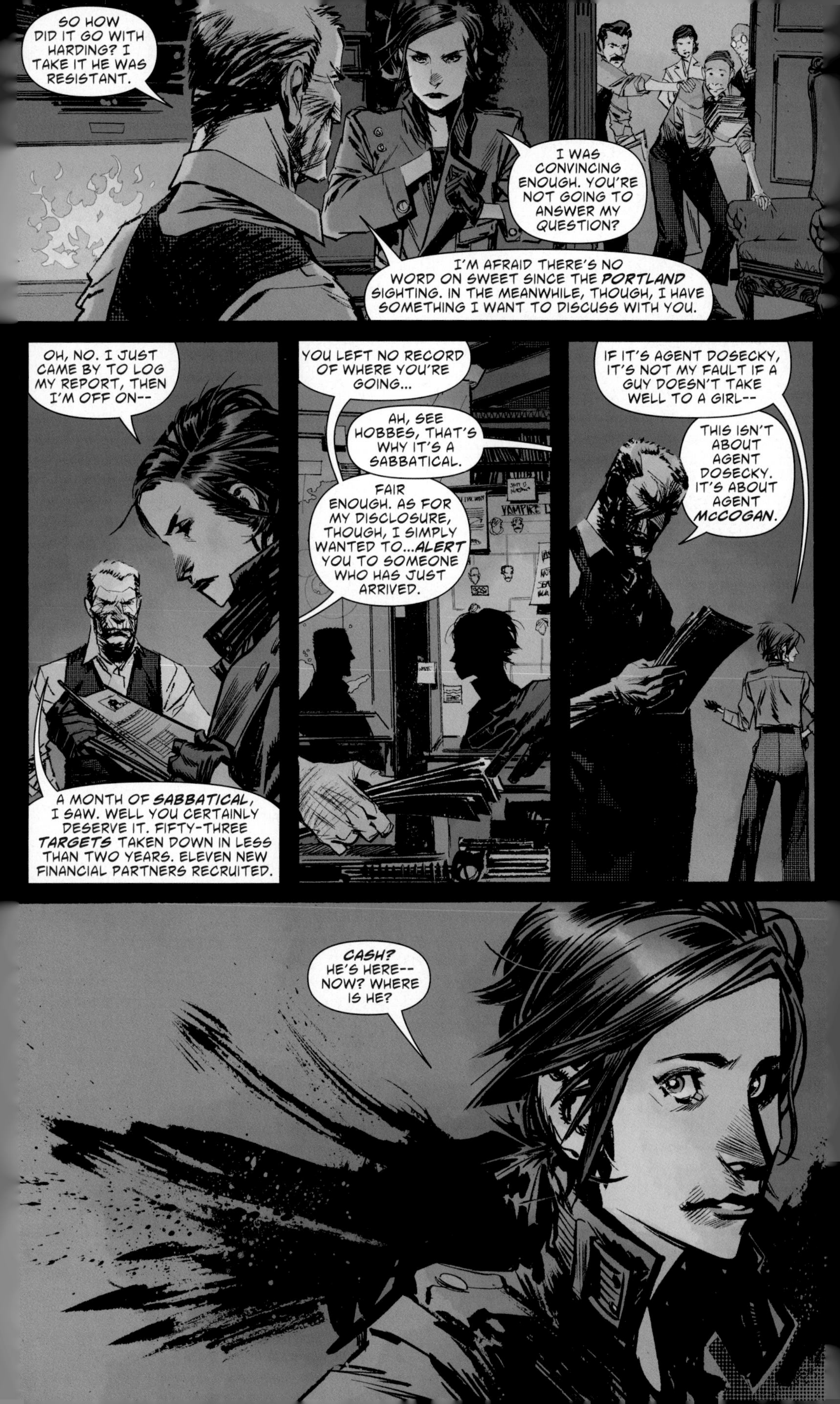

SO HOW DID IT GO WITH HARDING? I TAKE IT HE WAS RESISTANT.
I WAS CONVINCING ENOUGH. YOU'RE NOT GOING TO ANSWER MY QUESTION?
I'M AFRAID THERE'S NO WORD ON SWEET SINCE THE PORTLAND SIGHTING. IN THE MEANWHILE, THOUGH, I HAVE SOMETHING I WANT TO DISCUSS WITH YOU.
OH, NO. I JUST CAME BY TO LOG MY REPORT, THEN I'M OFF ON--
A MONTH OF SABBATICAL, I SAW. WELL YOU CERTAINLY DESERVE IT. FIFTY-THREE TARGETS TAKEN DOWN IN LESS THAN TWO YEARS. ELEVEN NEW FINANCIAL PARTNERS RECRUITED.
YOU LEFT NO RECORD OF WHERE YOU'RE GOING...
AH, SEE HOBBES, THAT'S WHY IT'S A SABBATICAL.
FAIR ENOUGH. AS FOR MY DISCLOSURE, THOUGH, I SIMPLY WANTED TO...ALERT YOU TO SOMEONE WHO HAS JUST ARRIVED.
IF IT'S AGENT DOSECKY, IT'S NOT MY FAULT IF A GUY DOESN'T TAKE WELL TO A GIRL--
THIS ISN'T ABOUT AGENT DOSECKY. IT'S ABOUT AGENT McCOGAN.
CASH? HE'S HERE-- NOW? WHERE IS HE?

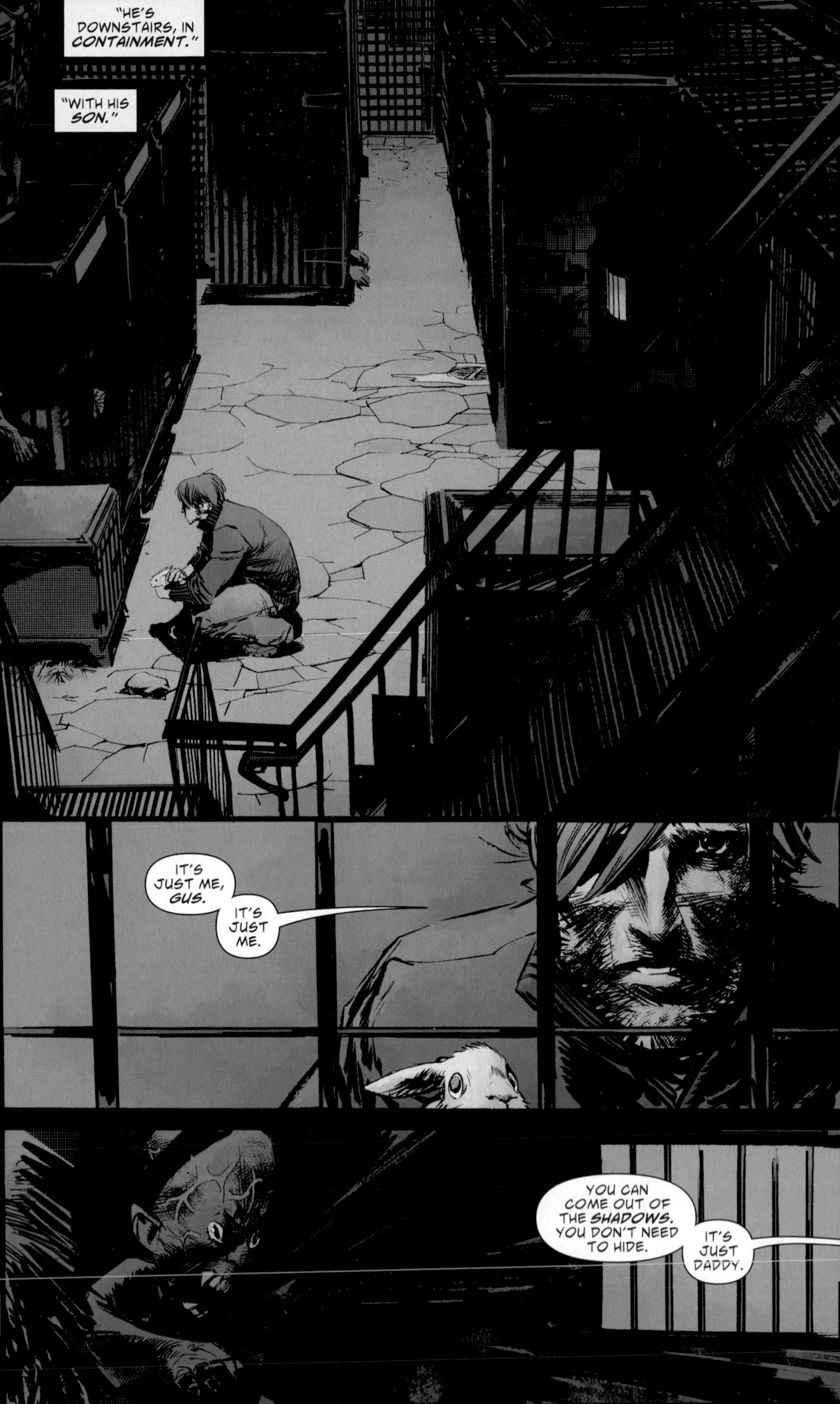
"HE'S DOWNSTAIRS, IN CONTAINMENT."
"WITH HIS SON."
IT'S JUST ME, GUS.
IT'S JUST ME.
YOU CAN COME OUT OF THE SHADOWS. YOU DON'T NEED TO HIDE.
IT'S JUST DADDY.

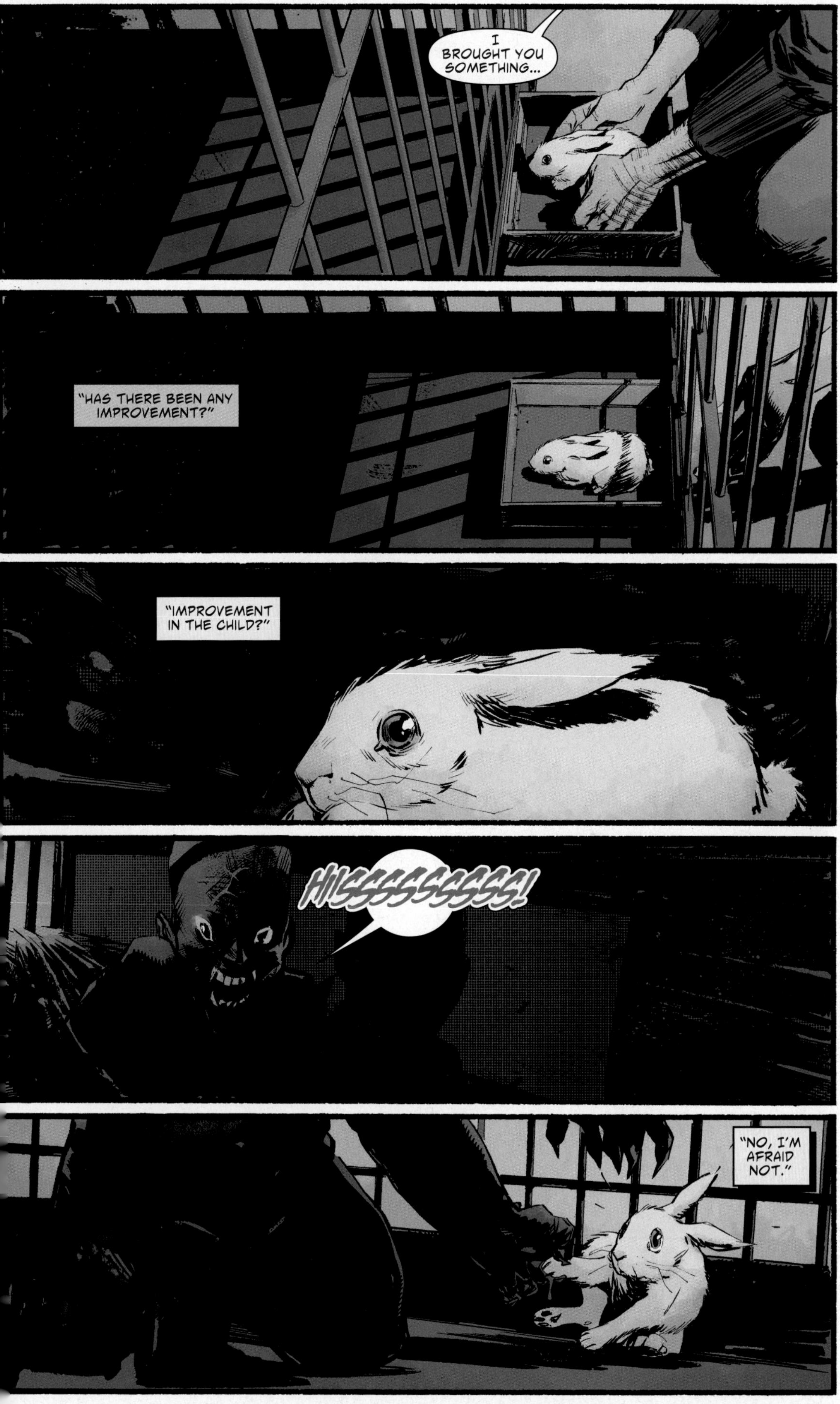
I BROUGHT YOU SOMETHING...
"HAS THERE BEEN ANY IMPROVEMENT?"
"IMPROVEMENT IN THE CHILD?"
HIISSSSSSSSS!
"NO, I'M AFRAID NOT."

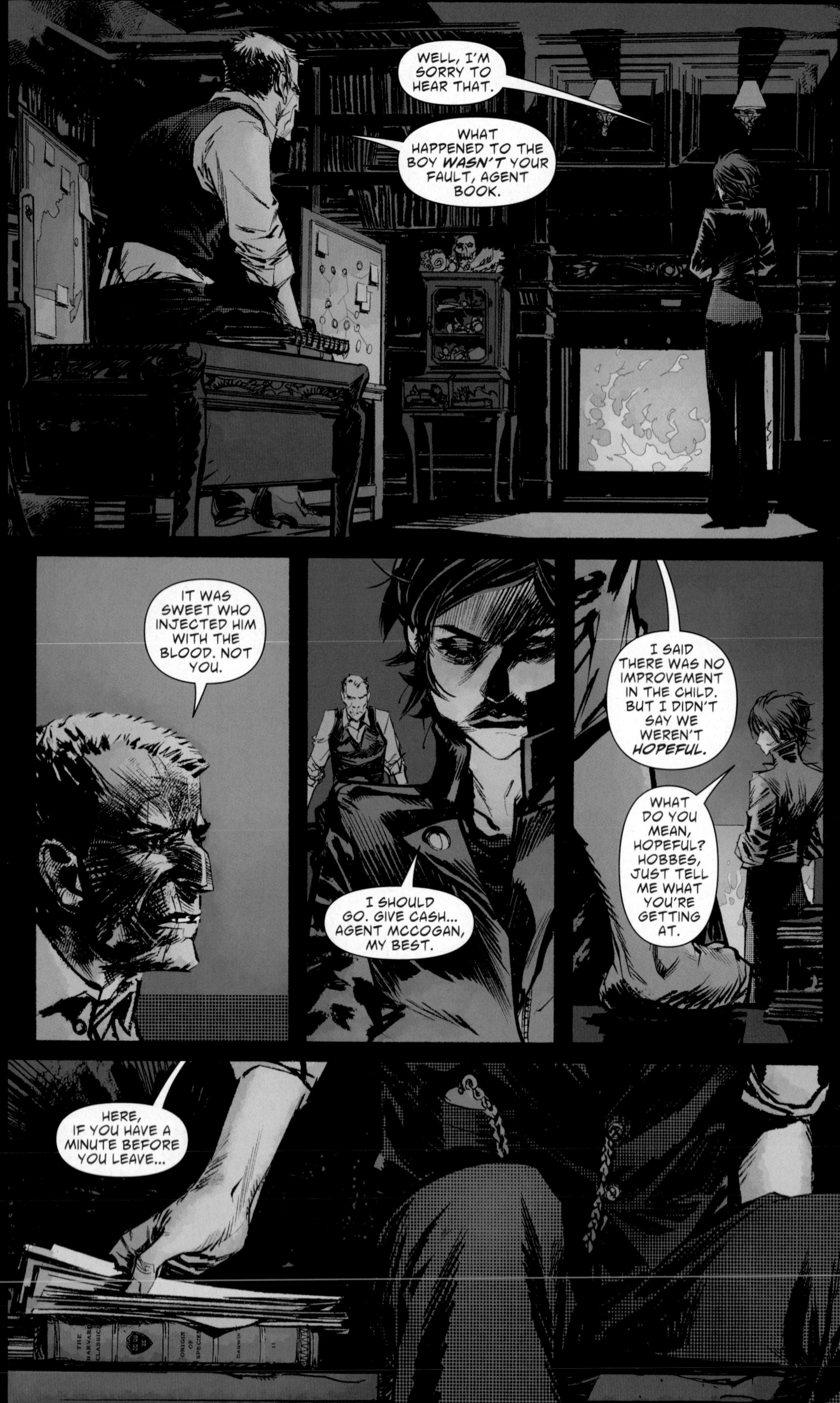

WELL, I'M SORRY TO HEAR THAT.
WHAT HAPPENED TO THE BOY WASN'T YOUR FAULT, AGENT BOOK.
IT WAS SWEET WHO INJECTED HIM WITH THE BLOOD. NOT YOU.
I SHOULD GO. GIVE CASH... AGENT MCCOGAN, MY BEST.
I SAID THERE WAS NO IMPROVEMENT IN THE CHILD. BUT I DIDN'T SAY WE WEREN'T HOPEFUL.
WHAT DO YOU MEAN, HOPEFUL? HOBBES, JUST TELL ME WHAT YOU'RE GETTING AT.
HERE, IF YOU HAVE A MINUTE BEFORE YOU LEAVE...
THE HARVARD CLASSICS
ORIGIN OF SPECIES
DARWIN

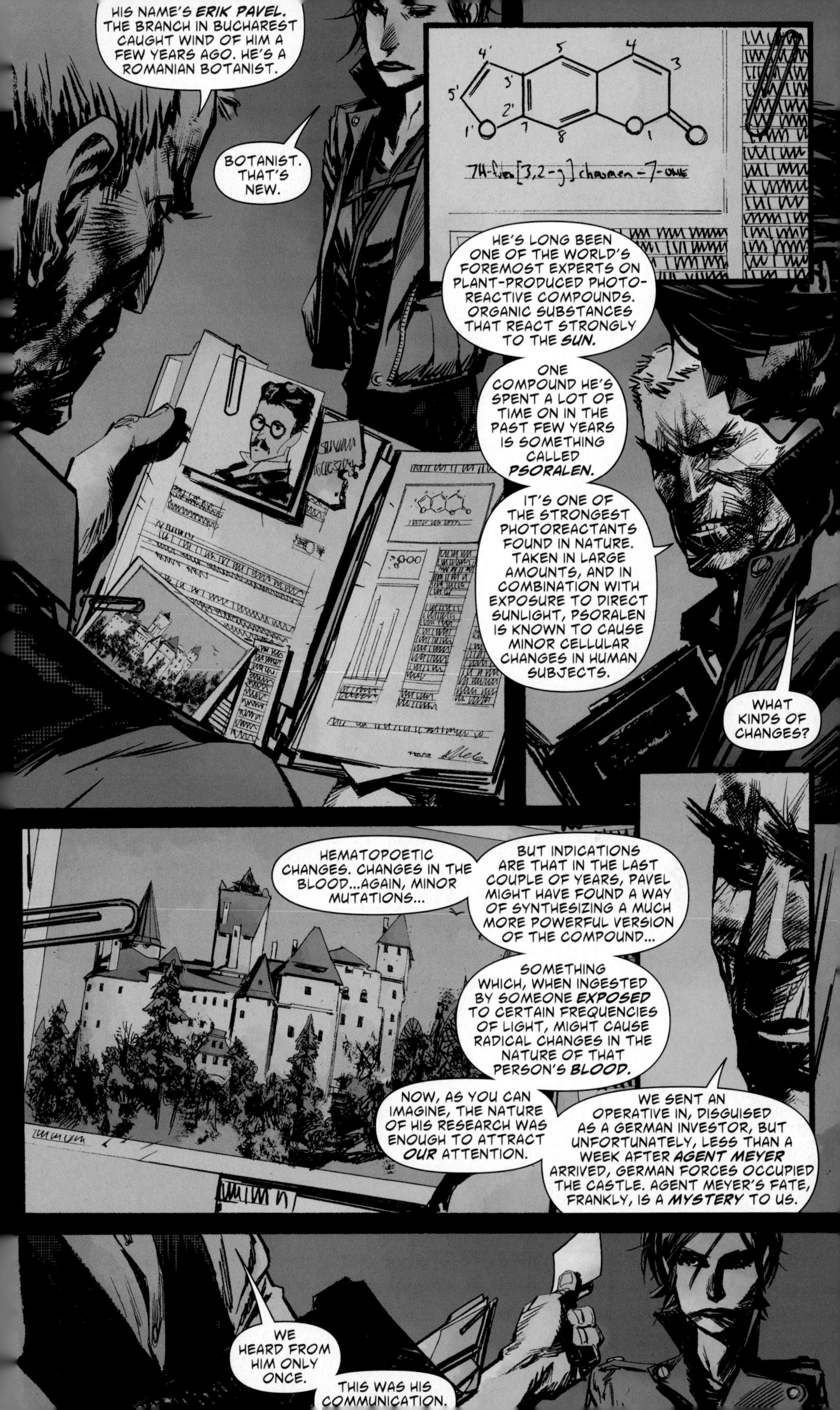
HIS NAME'S ERIK PAVEL. THE BRANCH IN BUCHAREST CAUGHT WIND OF HIM A FEW YEARS AGO. HE'S A ROMANIAN BOTANIST.
BOTANIST. THAT'S NEW.
7H-furo[3,2-g]chromen-7-one
HE'S LONG BEEN ONE OF THE WORLD'S FOREMOST EXPERTS ON PLANT-PRODUCED PHOTO-REACTIVE COMPOUNDS. ORGANIC SUBSTANCES THAT REACT STRONGLY TO THE SUN.
ONE COMPOUND HE'S SPENT A LOT OF TIME ON IN THE PAST FEW YEARS IS SOMETHING CALLED PSORALEN.
IT'S ONE OF THE STRONGEST PHOTOREACTANTS FOUND IN NATURE. TAKEN IN LARGE AMOUNTS, AND IN COMBINATION WITH EXPOSURE TO DIRECT SUNLIGHT, PSORALEN IS KNOWN TO CAUSE MINOR CELLULAR CHANGES IN HUMAN SUBJECTS.
WHAT KINDS OF CHANGES?
HEMATOPOETIC CHANGES. CHANGES IN THE BLOOD...AGAIN, MINOR MUTATIONS...
BUT INDICATIONS ARE THAT IN THE LAST COUPLE OF YEARS, PAVEL MIGHT HAVE FOUND A WAY OF SYNTHESIZING A MUCH MORE POWERFUL VERSION OF THE COMPOUND...
SOMETHING WHICH, WHEN INGESTED BY SOMEONE EXPOSED TO CERTAIN FREQUENCIES OF LIGHT, MIGHT CAUSE RADICAL CHANGES IN THE NATURE OF THAT PERSON'S BLOOD.
NOW, AS YOU CAN IMAGINE, THE NATURE OF HIS RESEARCH WAS ENOUGH TO ATTRACT OUR ATTENTION.
WE SENT AN OPERATIVE IN, DISGUISED AS A GERMAN INVESTOR, BUT UNFORTUNATELY, LESS THAN A WEEK AFTER AGENT MEYER ARRIVED, GERMAN FORCES OCCUPIED THE CASTLE. AGENT MEYER'S FATE, FRANKLY, IS A MYSTERY TO US.
WE HEARD FROM HIM ONLY ONCE.
THIS WAS HIS COMMUNICATION.

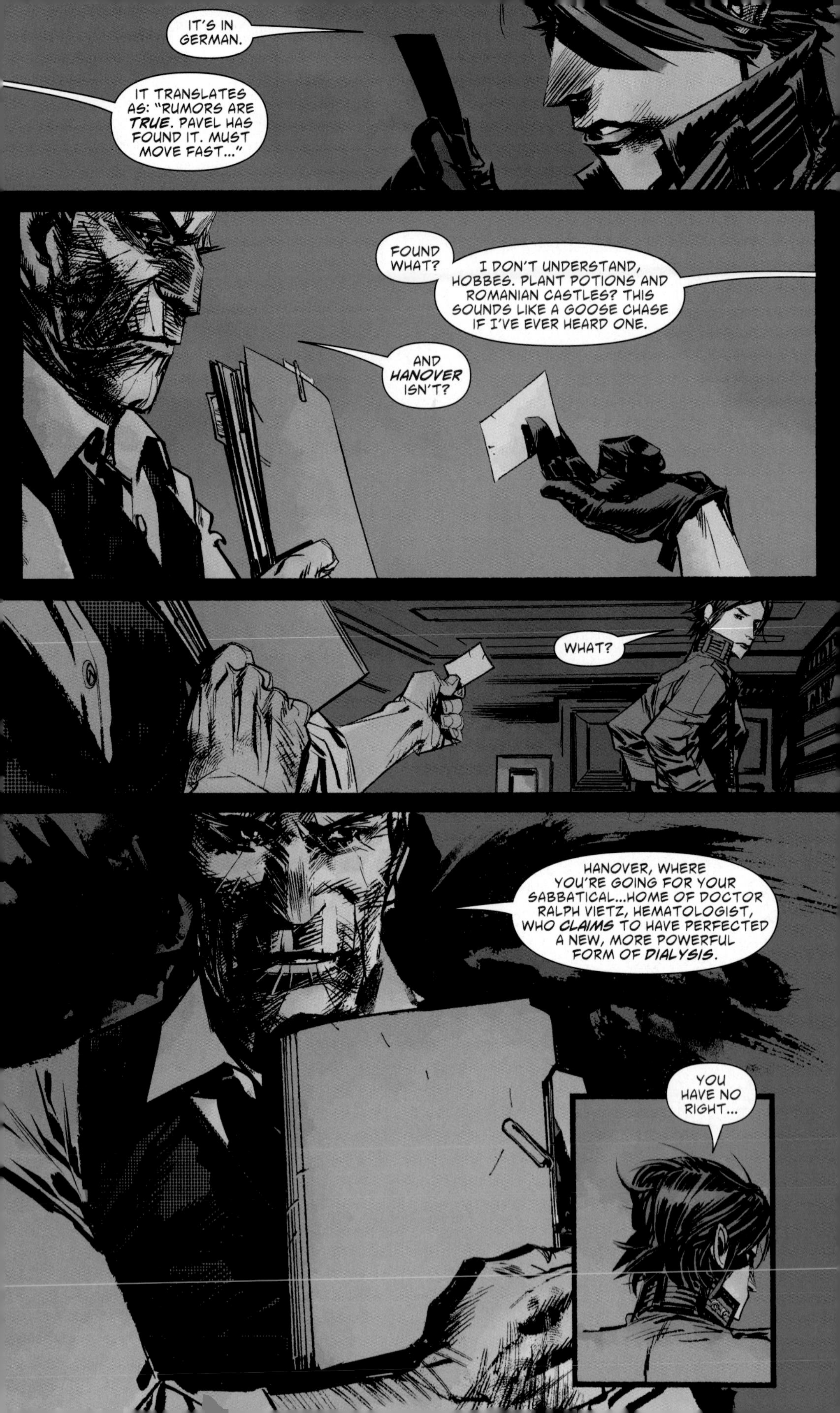
IT'S IN GERMAN.
IT TRANSLATES AS: "RUMORS ARE TRUE. PAVEL HAS FOUND IT. MUST MOVE FAST..."
FOUND WHAT?
I DON'T UNDERSTAND, HOBBES. PLANT POTIONS AND ROMANIAN CASTLES? THIS SOUNDS LIKE A GOOSE CHASE IF I'VE EVER HEARD ONE.
AND HANOVER ISN'T?
WHAT?
HANOVER, WHERE YOU'RE GOING FOR YOUR SABBATICAL...HOME OF DOCTOR RALPH VIETZ, HEMATOLOGIST, WHO CLAIMS TO HAVE PERFECTED A NEW, MORE POWERFUL FORM OF DIALYSIS.
YOU HAVE NO RIGHT...

ELICIA. LISTEN TO ME. OU ARE, HANDS DOWN, HE BEST AGENT WE HAVE. YOUR INNATE ABILITIES TO TRACK ARGETS, TO SENSE BERRATIONS IN THE LOOD, MAKE YOU A CELESS ADDITION TO OUR ORGANIZATION.

WHICH IS TO SAY, FROM A SELFISH STANDPOINT, I HAVE EVERY REASON TO LIKE YOU JUST THE WAY YOU ARE.

NOW, I AM NOT GOING TO PRETEND TO BE A CARING MAN. I AM NOT. AND YET, I HAVE KNOWN YOU SINCE YOU WERE A *CHILD*, AND I HAVE WATCHED YOU *SUFFER*...

WE'RE SENDING IN A TEAM TO INVESTIGATE FOUR DAYS FROM NOW. WE'D LIKE YOU TO BE ON IT.

OUR AGENTS HAVE ALREADY BEEN SOLD TO THE GERMAN FORCES OCCUPYING CASTLE VRAN AS WEALTHY AMERICAN SYMPATHIZERS LOOKING TO INVEST IN THE FUTURE OF THE REICH.

ONCE INSIDE THE CASTLE, YOU'LL CONDUCT YOUR OWN SECRET INVESTIGATION, SEE IF THERE'S ANY TRUTH TO THE CLAIMS ABOUT PAVEL--

WHAT *CLAIMS?*
WHAT IS IT YOU THINK THIS PAVEL GUY HAS *FOUND?*

WHAP!

HE'S TALKING ABOUT *THE CURE.*

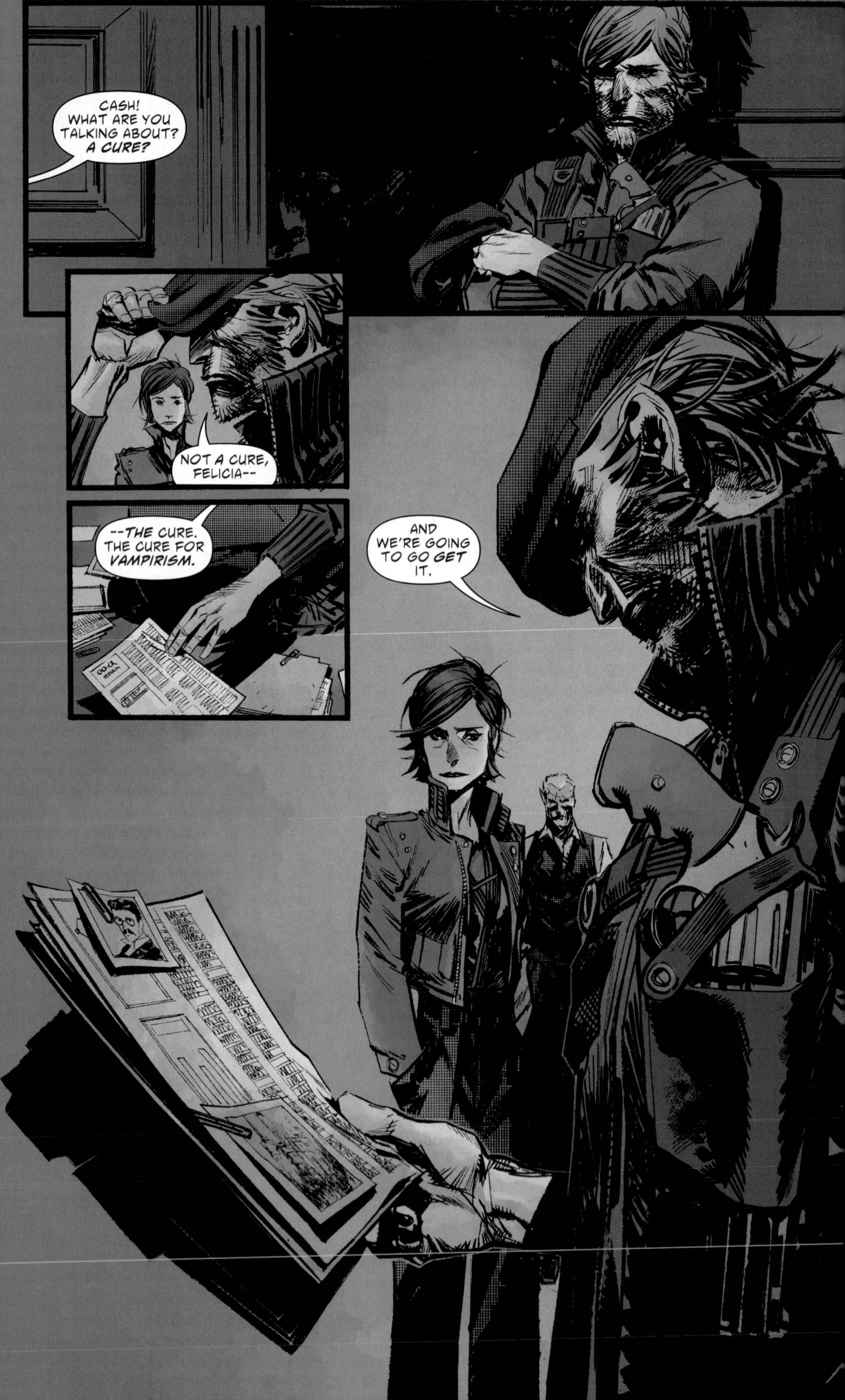
CASH! WHAT ARE YOU TALKING ABOUT? A CURE?
NOT A CURE, FELICIA--
--THE CURE. THE CURE FOR VAMPIRISM.
AND WE'RE GOING TO GO GET IT.

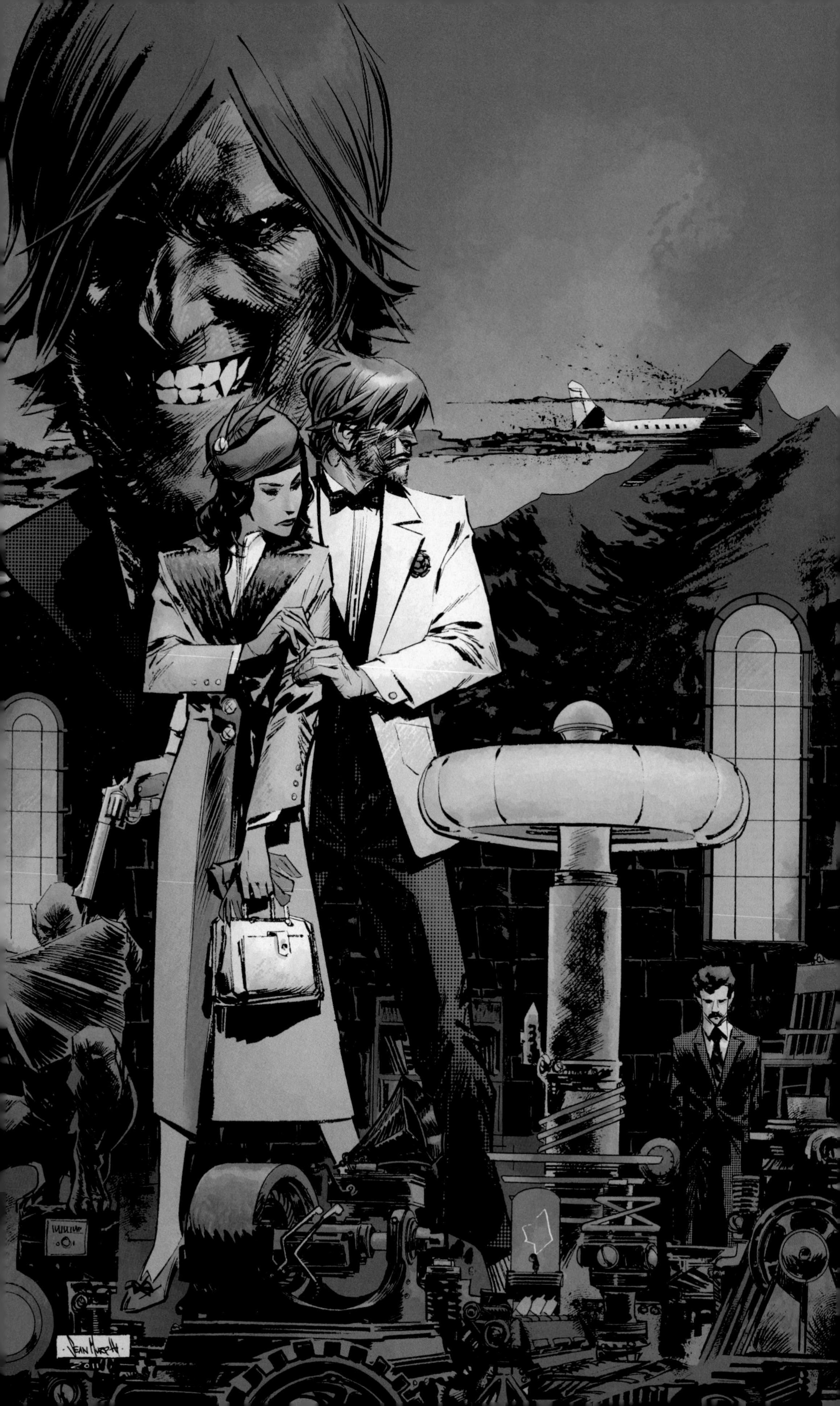

Survival
of the Fittest
Part Two

Sean Murphy
Artist and cover

Dave Stewart
cover color

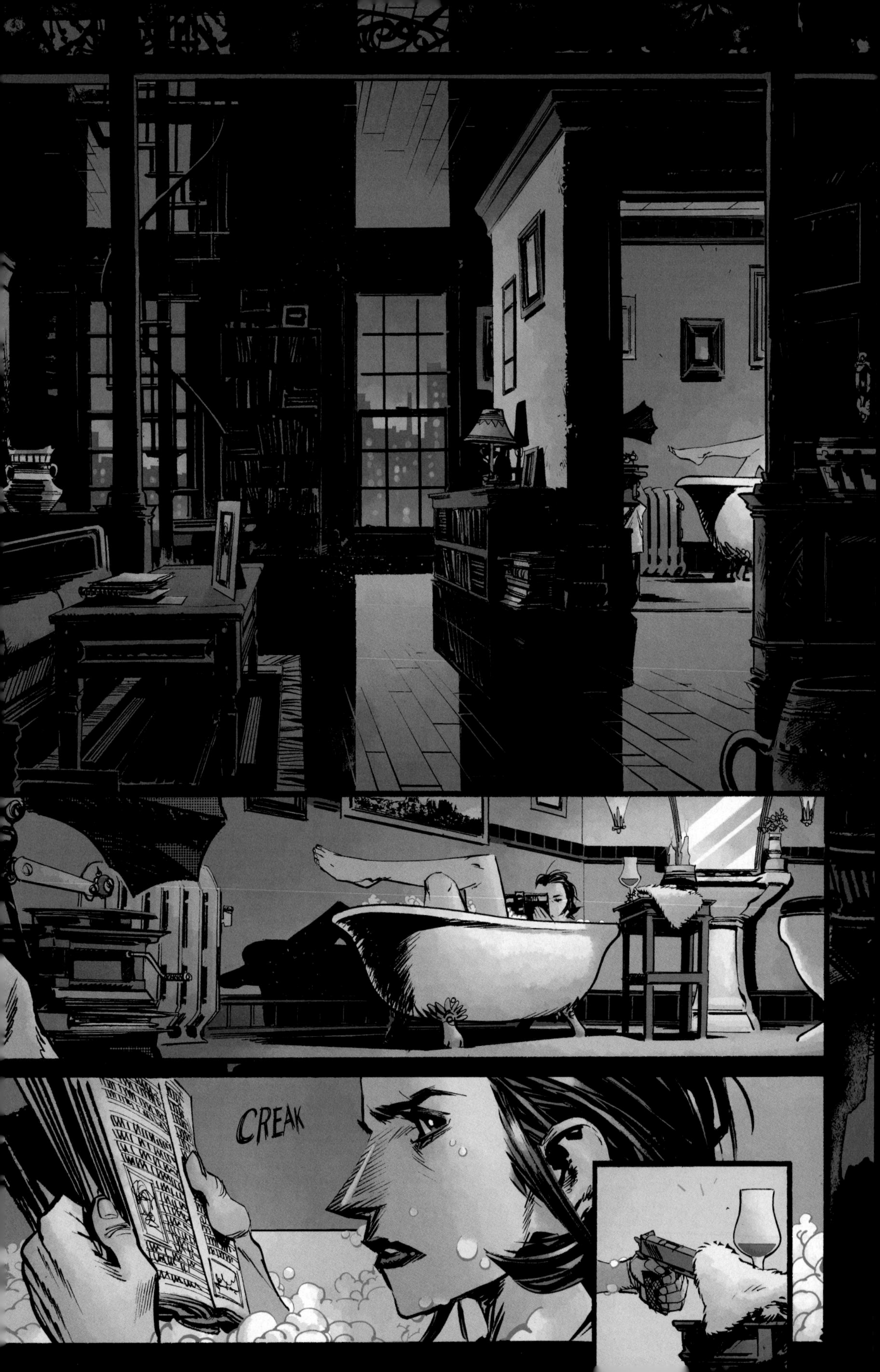
CREAK

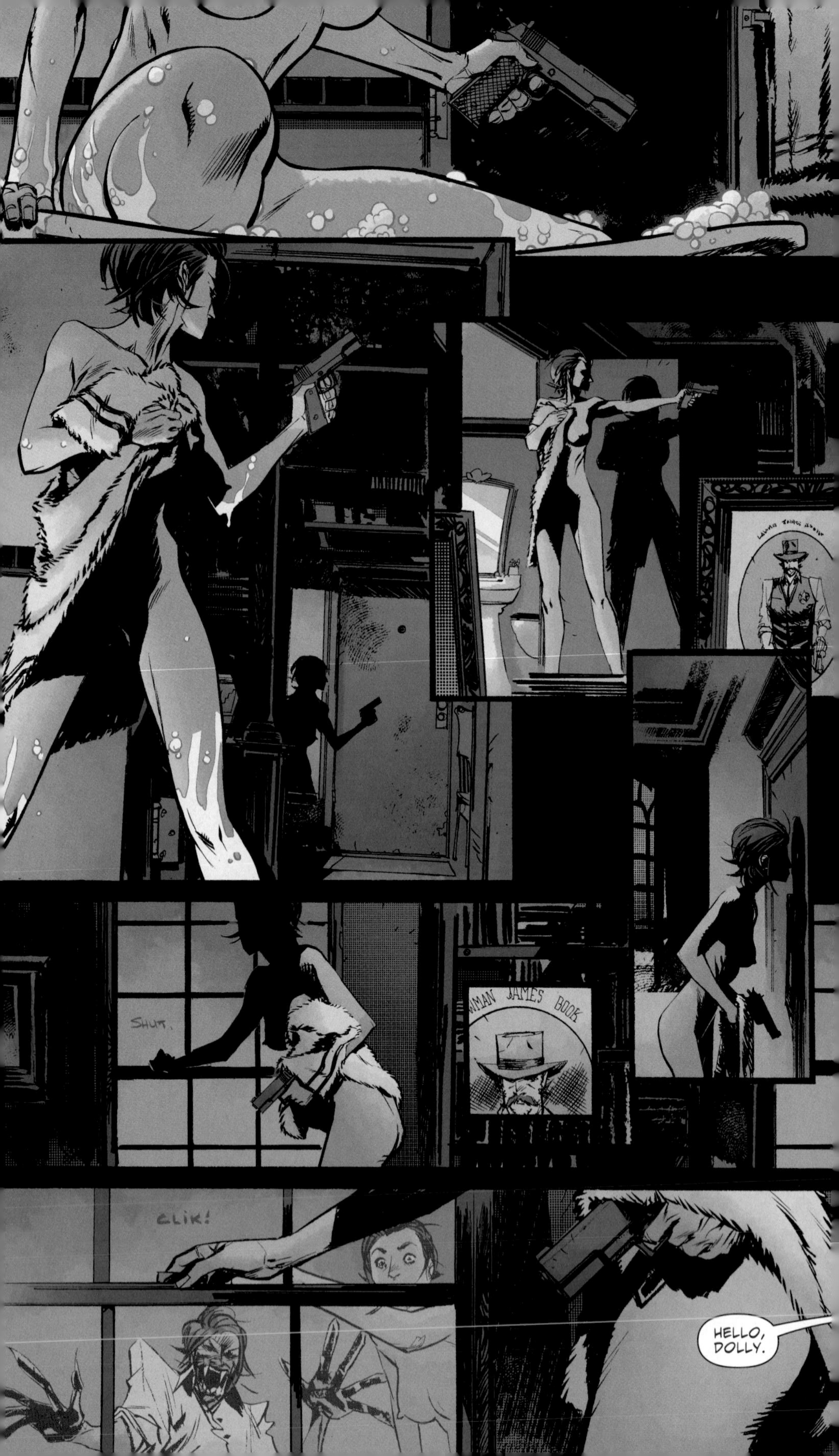
SHUT.
CLIK!
HELLO, DOLLY.

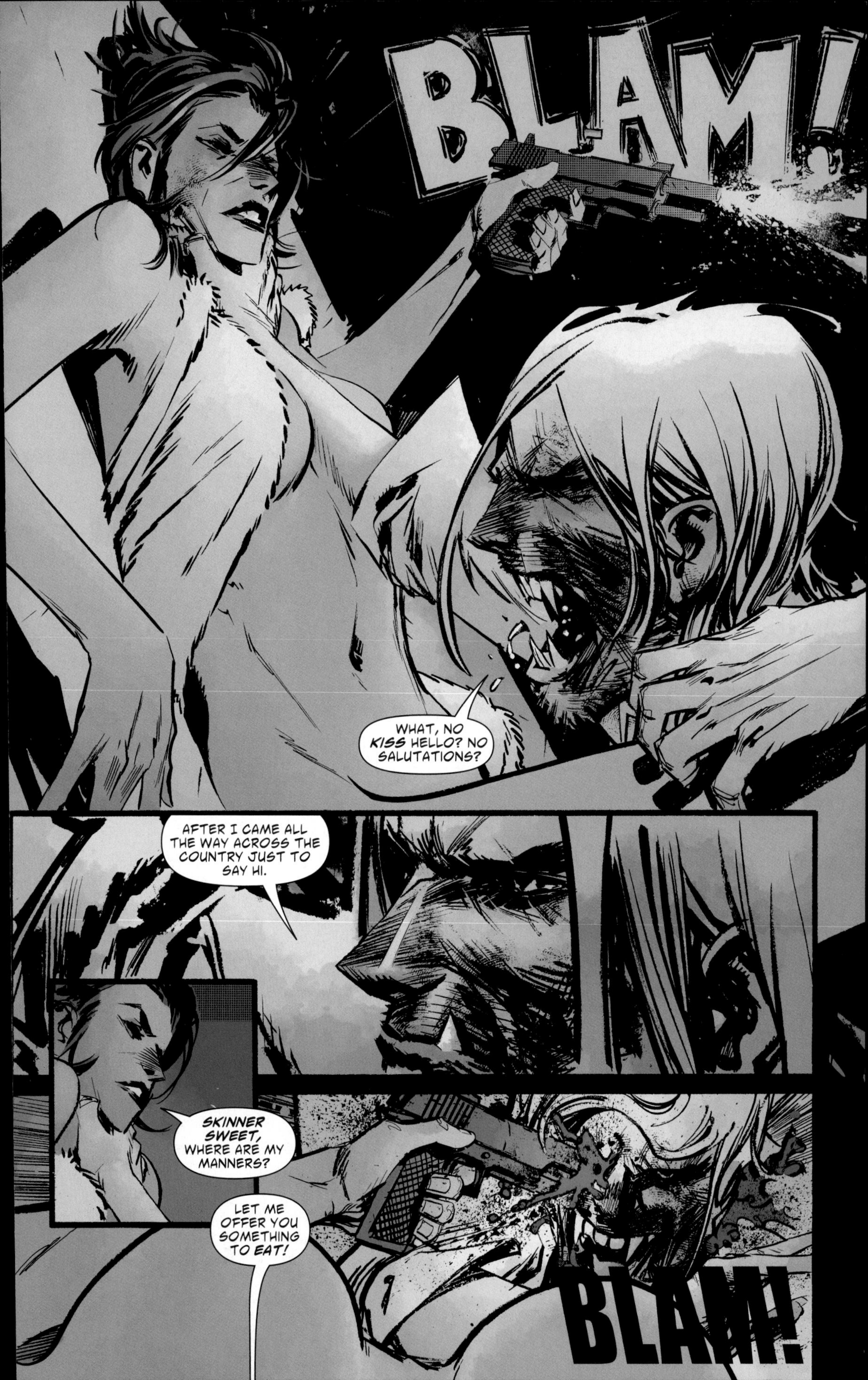
BLAM!
WHAT, NO KISS HELLO? NO SALUTATIONS?
AFTER I CAME ALL THE WAY ACROSS THE COUNTRY JUST TO SAY HI.
SKINNER SWEET, WHERE ARE MY MANNERS?
LET ME OFFER YOU SOMETHING TO EAT!
BLAM!

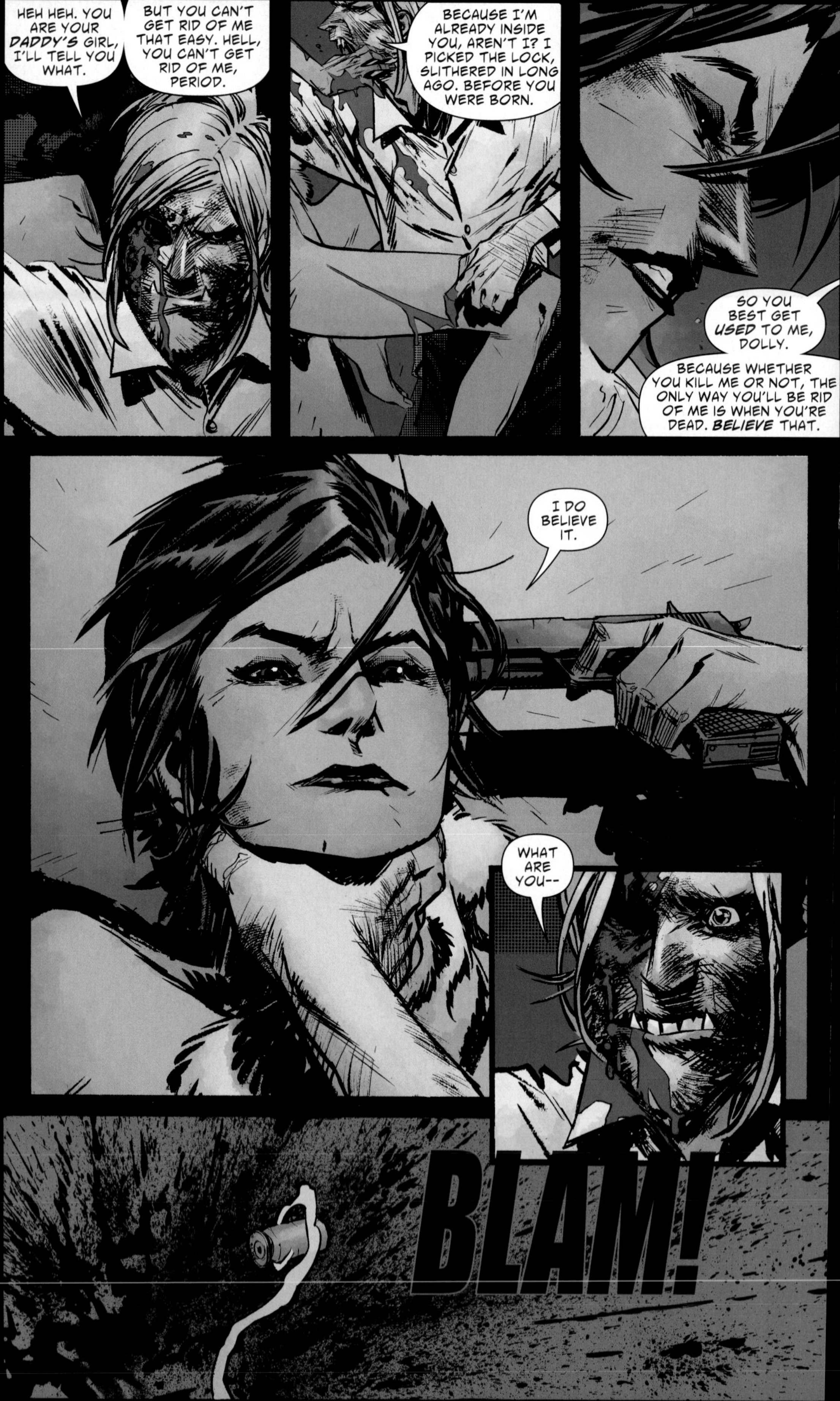
HEH HEH. YOU ARE YOUR DADDY'S GIRL, I'LL TELL YOU WHAT.
BUT YOU CAN'T GET RID OF ME THAT EASY. HELL, YOU CAN'T GET RID OF ME, PERIOD.
BECAUSE I'M ALREADY INSIDE YOU, AREN'T I? I PICKED THE LOCK, SLITHERED IN LONG AGO. BEFORE YOU WERE BORN.
SO YOU BEST GET USED TO ME, DOLLY.
BECAUSE WHETHER YOU KILL ME OR NOT, THE ONLY WAY YOU'LL BE RID OF ME IS WHEN YOU'RE DEAD. BELIEVE THAT.
I DO BELIEVE IT.
WHAT ARE YOU--
BLAM!

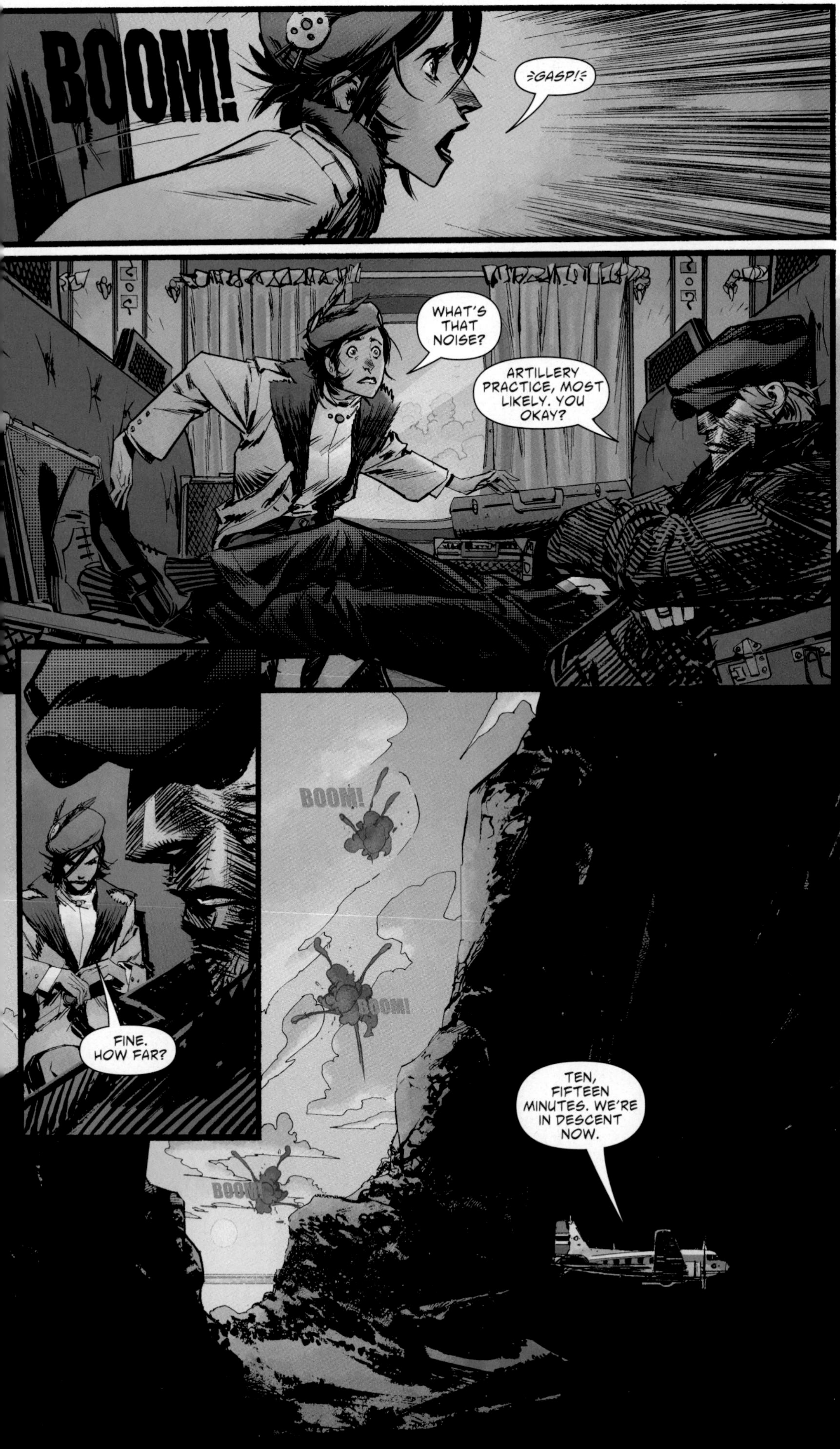
BOOM!
≈GASP!≈
WHAT'S THAT NOISE?
ARTILLERY PRACTICE, MOST LIKELY. YOU OKAY?
FINE. HOW FAR?
BOOM!
BOOM!
BOOM!
TEN, FIFTEEN MINUTES. WE'RE IN DESCENT NOW.

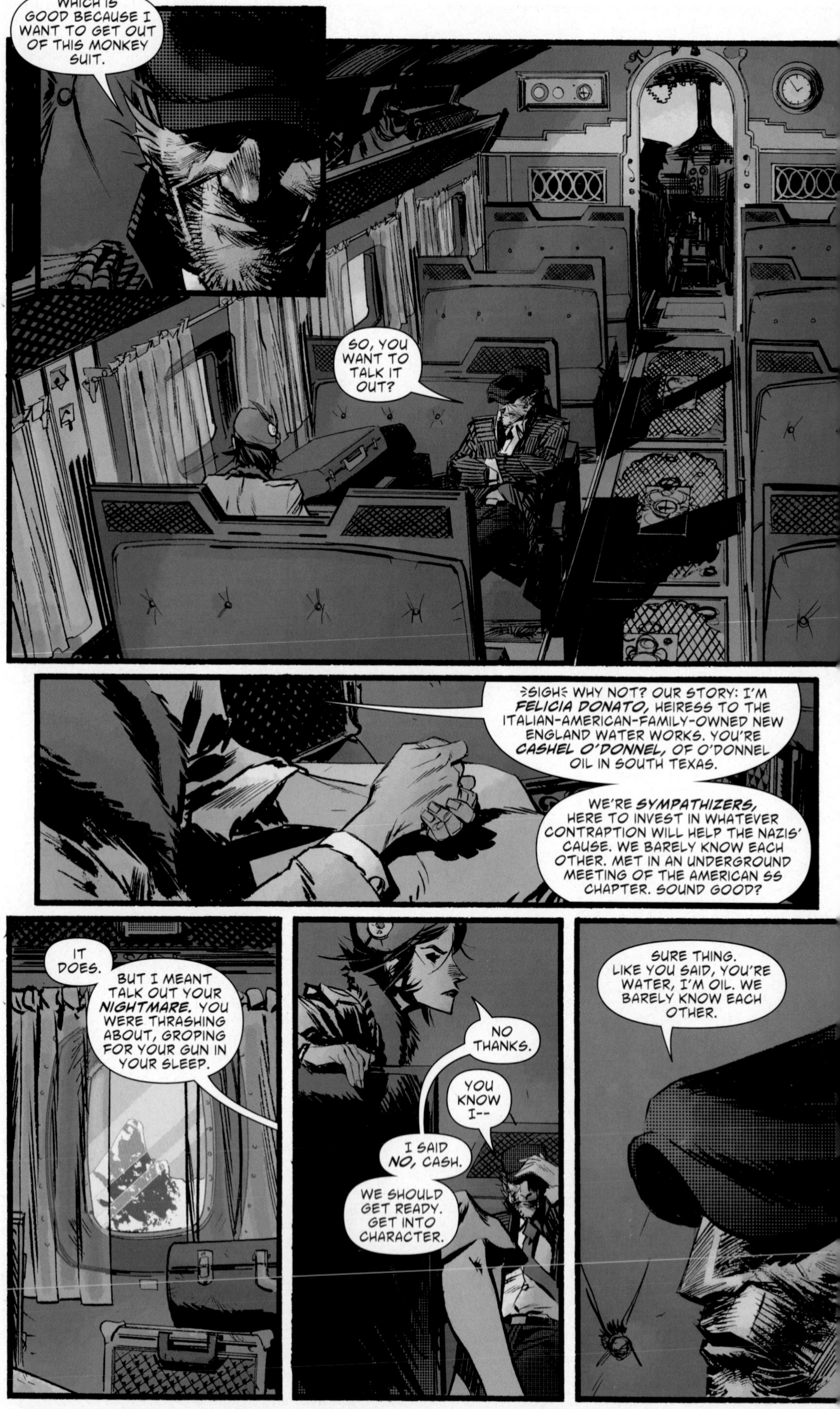
WHICH IS GOOD BECAUSE I WANT TO GET OUT OF THIS MONKEY SUIT.
SO, YOU WANT TO TALK IT OUT?
≥SIGH≤ WHY NOT? OUR STORY: I'M FELICIA DONATO, HEIRESS TO THE ITALIAN-AMERICAN-FAMILY-OWNED NEW ENGLAND WATER WORKS. YOU'RE CASHEL O'DONNEL, OF O'DONNEL OIL IN SOUTH TEXAS.
WE'RE SYMPATHIZERS, HERE TO INVEST IN WHATEVER CONTRAPTION WILL HELP THE NAZIS' CAUSE. WE BARELY KNOW EACH OTHER. MET IN AN UNDERGROUND MEETING OF THE AMERICAN SS CHAPTER. SOUND GOOD?
IT DOES.
BUT I MEANT TALK OUT YOUR NIGHTMARE. YOU WERE THRASHING ABOUT, GROPING FOR YOUR GUN IN YOUR SLEEP.
NO THANKS.
YOU KNOW I--
I SAID NO, CASH.
WE SHOULD GET READY. GET INTO CHARACTER.
SURE THING. LIKE YOU SAID, YOU'RE WATER, I'M OIL. WE BARELY KNOW EACH OTHER.

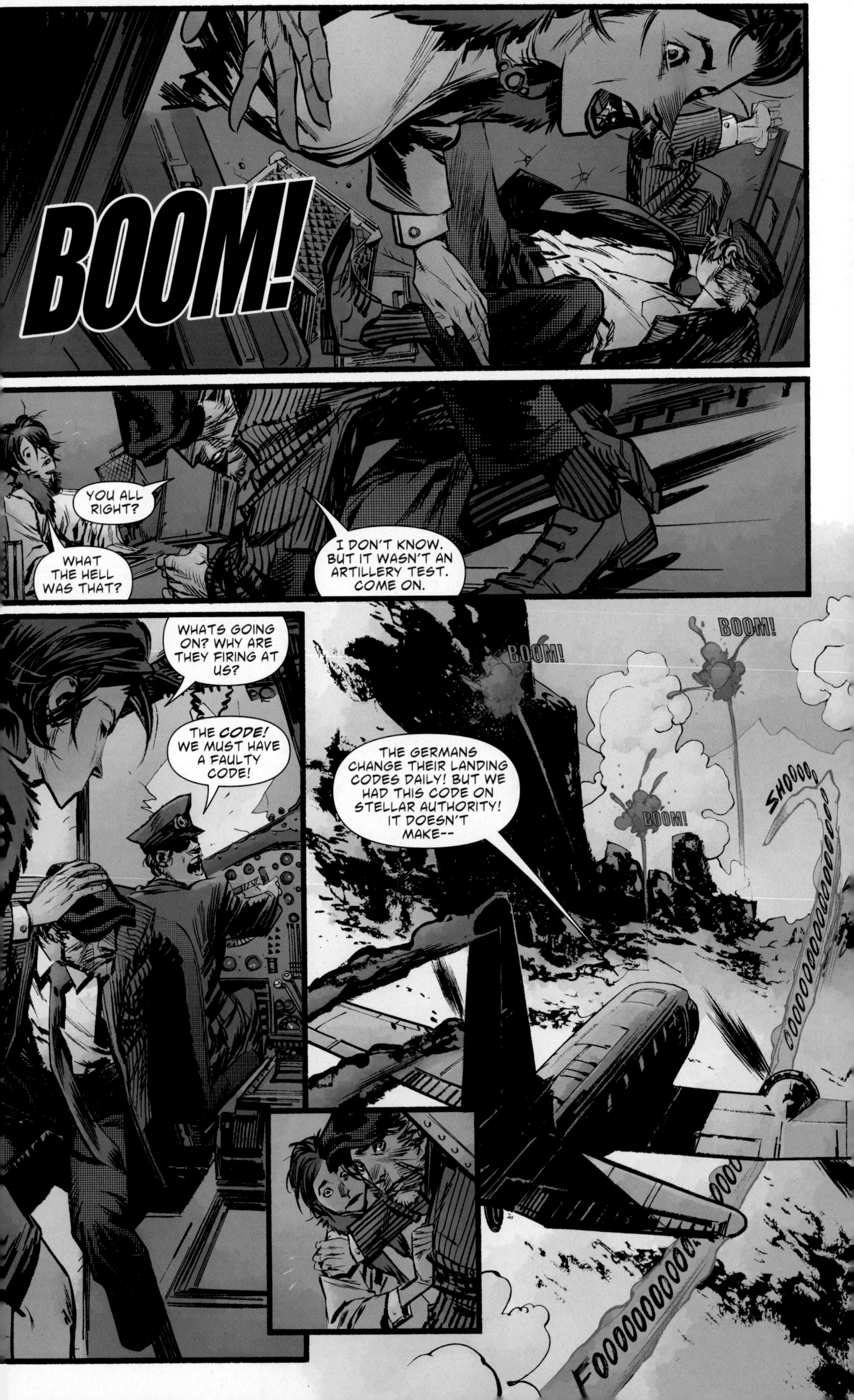
BOOM!
YOU ALL RIGHT?
WHAT THE HELL WAS THAT?
I DON'T KNOW. BUT IT WASN'T AN ARTILLERY TEST. COME ON.
WHATS GOING ON? WHY ARE THEY FIRING AT US?
THE CODE! WE MUST HAVE A FAULTY CODE!
BOOM!
BOOM!
THE GERMANS CHANGE THEIR LANDING CODES DAILY! BUT WE HAD THIS CODE ON STELLAR AUTHORITY! IT DOESN'T MAKE--
BOOM!
SHOOOO
FOOOOOOOOOO

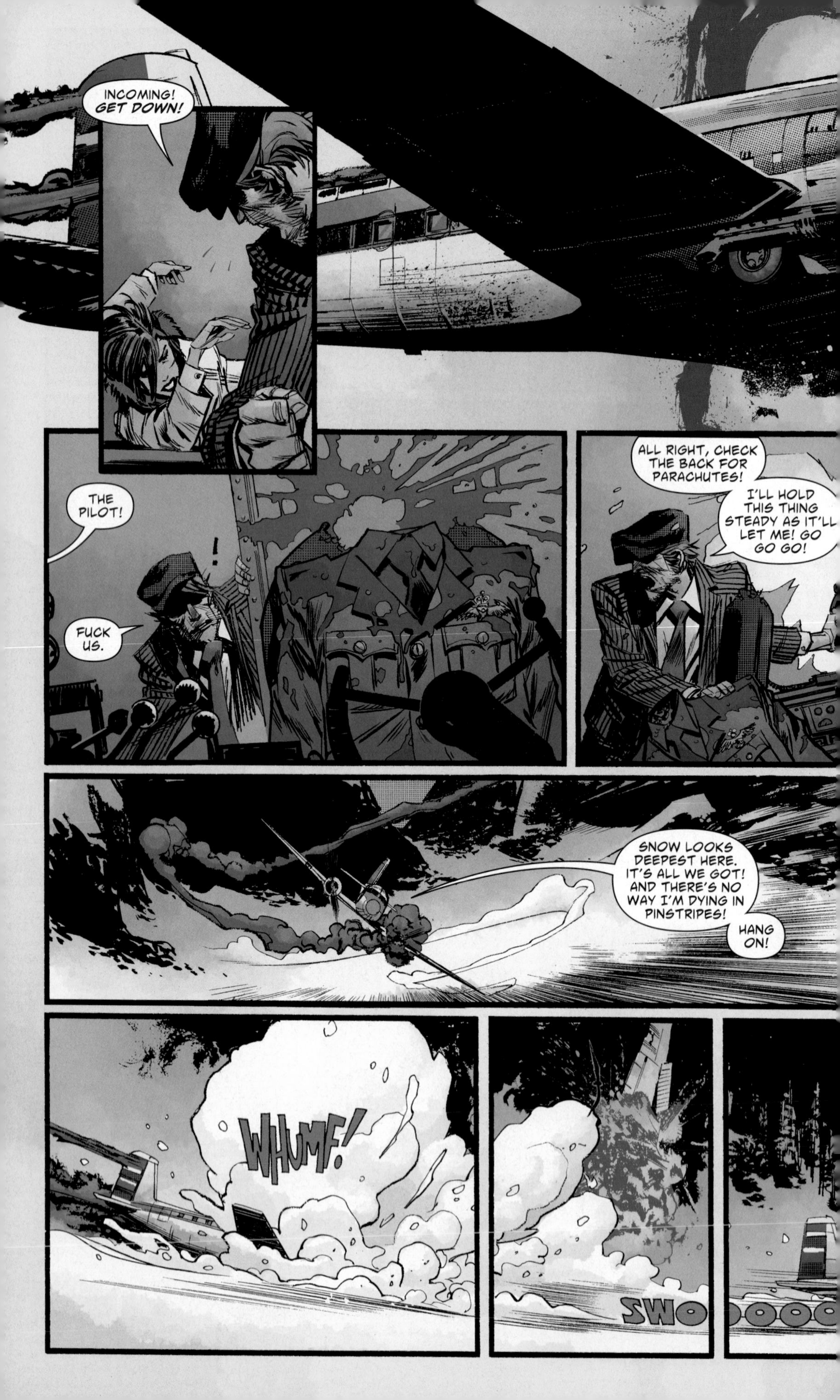
INCOMING! GET DOWN!
THE PILOT!
FUCK US.
ALL RIGHT, CHECK THE BACK FOR PARACHUTES!
I'LL HOLD THIS THING STEADY AS IT'LL LET ME! GO GO GO!
SNOW LOOKS DEEPEST HERE. IT'S ALL WE GOT! AND THERE'S NO WAY I'M DYING IN PINSTRIPES!
HANG ON!
WHUMF!
SWOOOOO

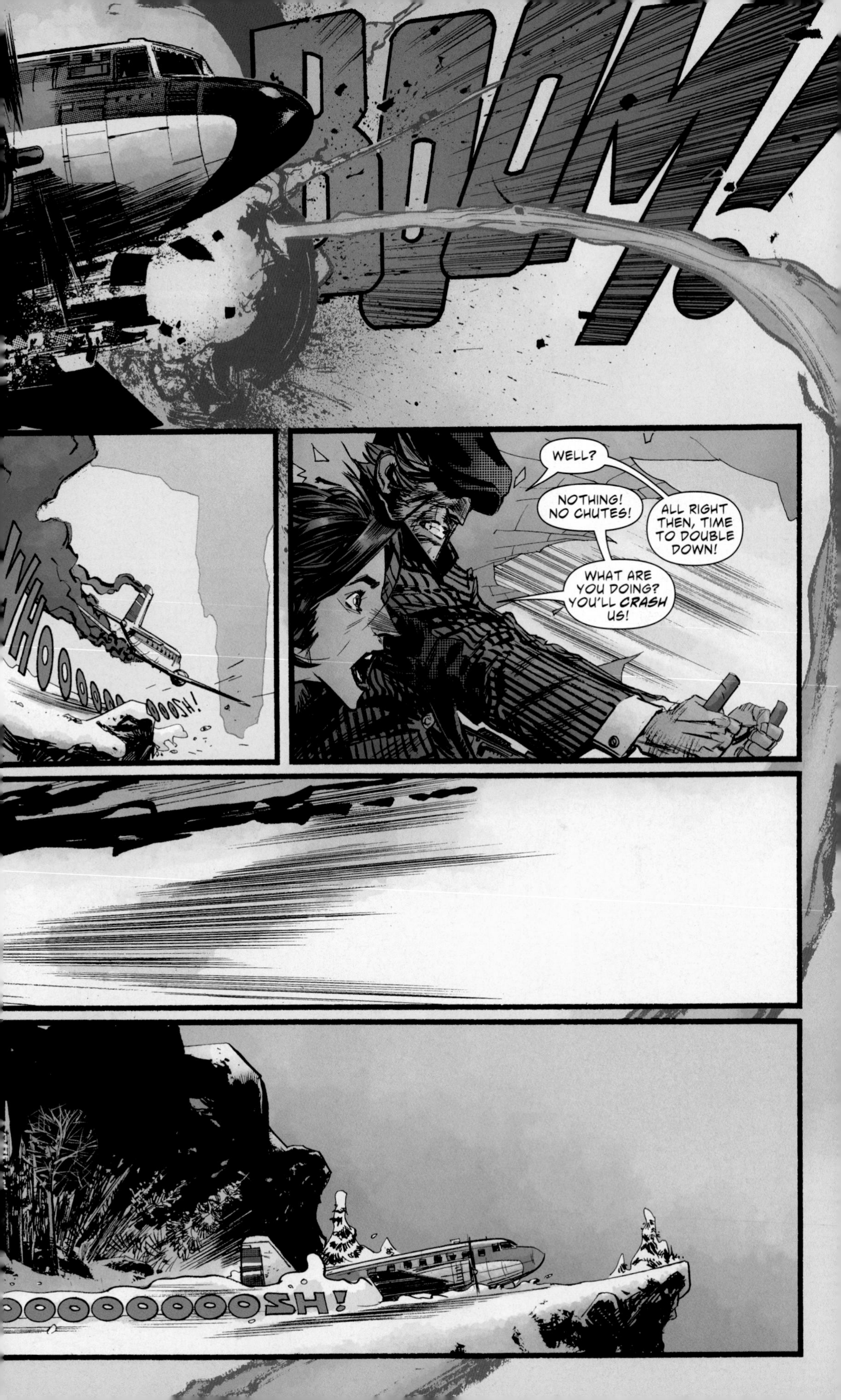
BOOM!
WELL?
NOTHING! NO CHUTES!
ALL RIGHT THEN, TIME TO DOUBLE DOWN!
WHAT ARE YOU DOING? YOU'LL *CRASH* US!

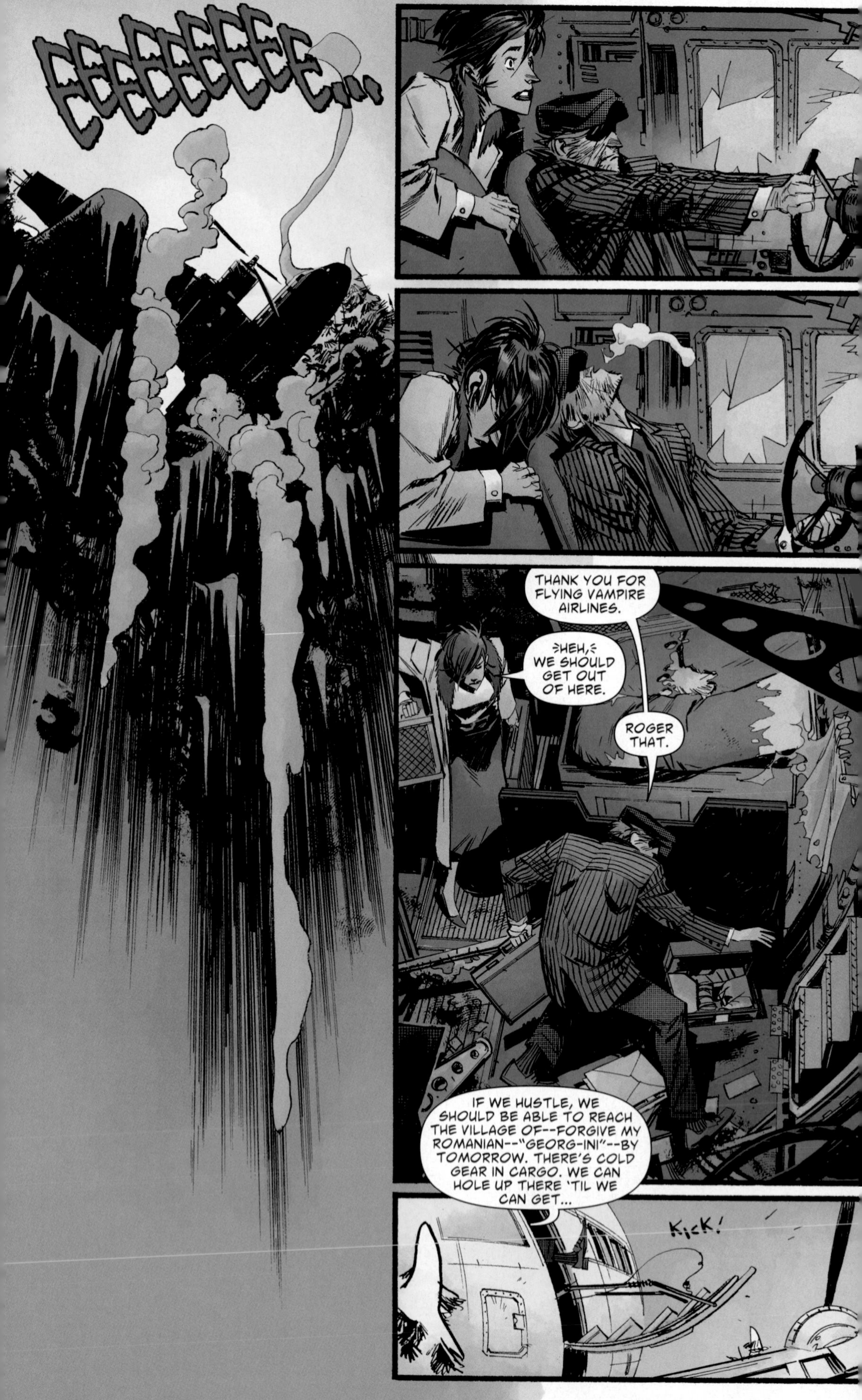
EEEEEEEEEE...
THANK YOU FOR FLYING VAMPIRE AIRLINES.
HEH, WE SHOULD GET OUT OF HERE.
ROGER THAT.
IF WE HUSTLE, WE SHOULD BE ABLE TO REACH THE VILLAGE OF--FORGIVE MY ROMANIAN--"GEORG-INI"--BY TOMORROW. THERE'S COLD GEAR IN CARGO. WE CAN HOLE UP THERE 'TIL WE CAN GET...
KICK!

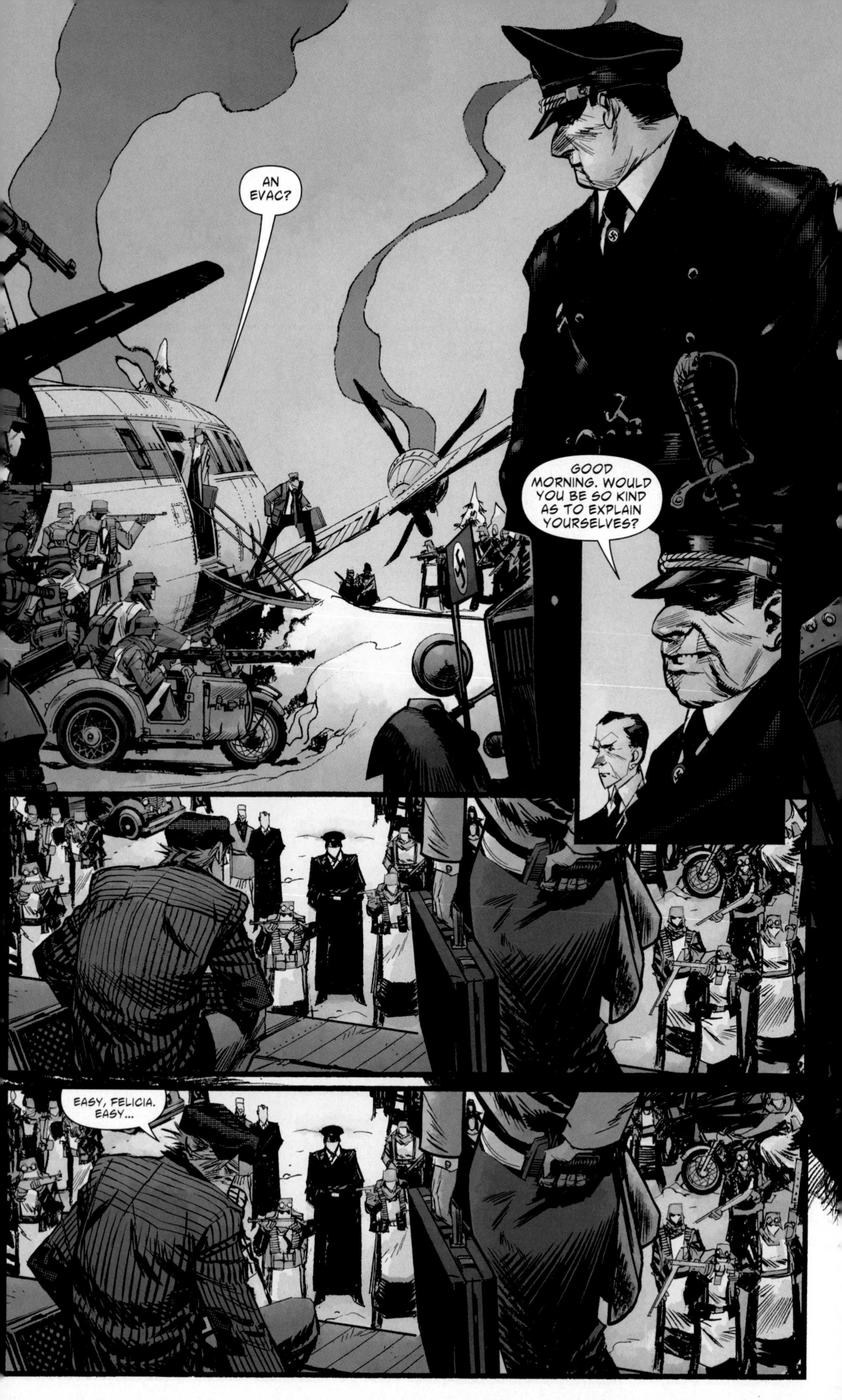
AN EVAC?
GOOD MORNING. WOULD YOU BE SO KIND AS TO EXPLAIN YOURSELVES?
EASY, FELICIA. EASY...

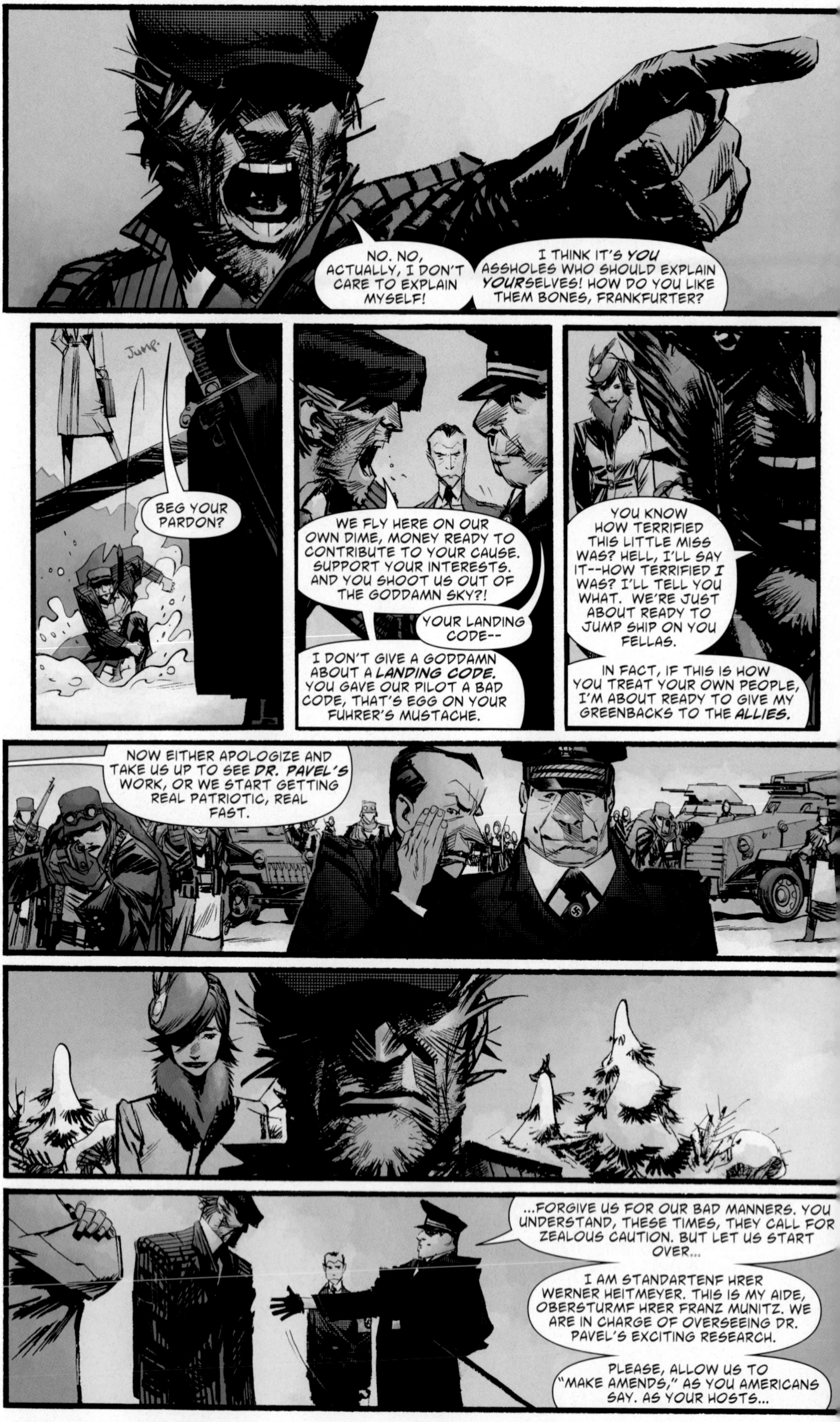
NO. NO, ACTUALLY, I DON'T CARE TO EXPLAIN MYSELF!
I THINK IT'S YOU ASSHOLES WHO SHOULD EXPLAIN YOURSELVES! HOW DO YOU LIKE THEM BONES, FRANKFURTER?
JUMP.
BEG YOUR PARDON?
WE FLY HERE ON OUR OWN DIME, MONEY READY TO CONTRIBUTE TO YOUR CAUSE. SUPPORT YOUR INTERESTS. AND YOU SHOOT US OUT OF THE GODDAMN SKY?!
YOUR LANDING CODE--
I DON'T GIVE A GODDAMN ABOUT A LANDING CODE. YOU GAVE OUR PILOT A BAD CODE, THAT'S EGG ON YOUR FUHRER'S MUSTACHE.
YOU KNOW HOW TERRIFIED THIS LITTLE MISS WAS? HELL, I'LL SAY IT--HOW TERRIFIED I WAS? I'LL TELL YOU WHAT. WE'RE JUST ABOUT READY TO JUMP SHIP ON YOU FELLAS.
IN FACT, IF THIS IS HOW YOU TREAT YOUR OWN PEOPLE, I'M ABOUT READY TO GIVE MY GREENBACKS TO THE ALLIES.
NOW EITHER APOLOGIZE AND TAKE US UP TO SEE DR. PAVEL'S WORK, OR WE START GETTING REAL PATRIOTIC, REAL FAST.
...FORGIVE US FOR OUR BAD MANNERS. YOU UNDERSTAND, THESE TIMES, THEY CALL FOR ZEALOUS CAUTION. BUT LET US START OVER...
I AM STANDARTENF HRER WERNER HEITMEYER. THIS IS MY AIDE, OBERSTURMF HRER FRANZ MUNITZ. WE ARE IN CHARGE OF OVERSEEING DR. PAVEL'S EXCITING RESEARCH.
PLEASE, ALLOW US TO "MAKE AMENDS," AS YOU AMERICANS SAY. AS YOUR HOSTS...

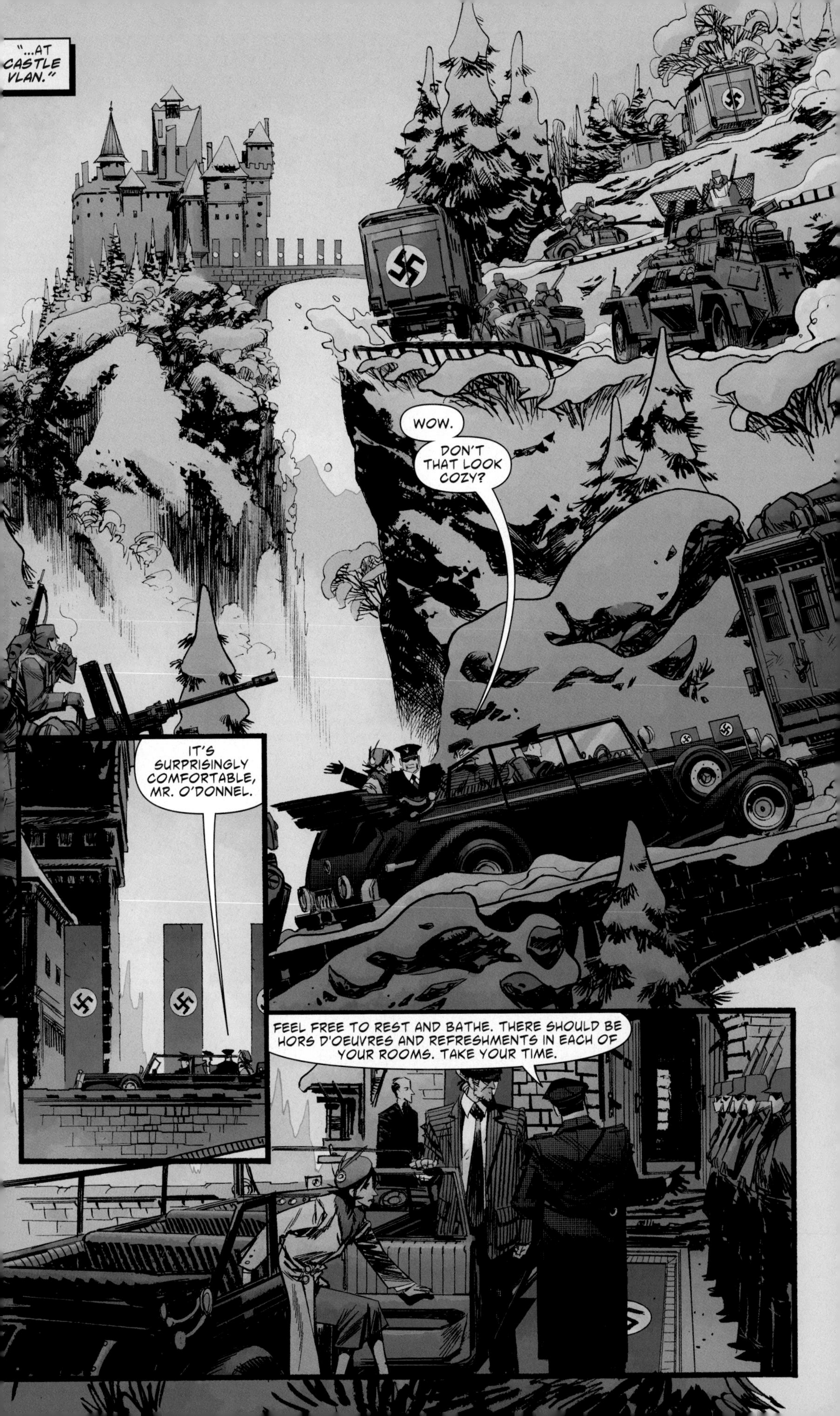
"...AT CASTLE VLAN."
WOW.
DON'T THAT LOOK COZY?
IT'S SURPRISINGLY COMFORTABLE, MR. O'DONNEL.
FEEL FREE TO REST AND BATHE. THERE SHOULD BE HORS D'OEUVRES AND REFRESHMENTS IN EACH OF YOUR ROOMS. TAKE YOUR TIME.

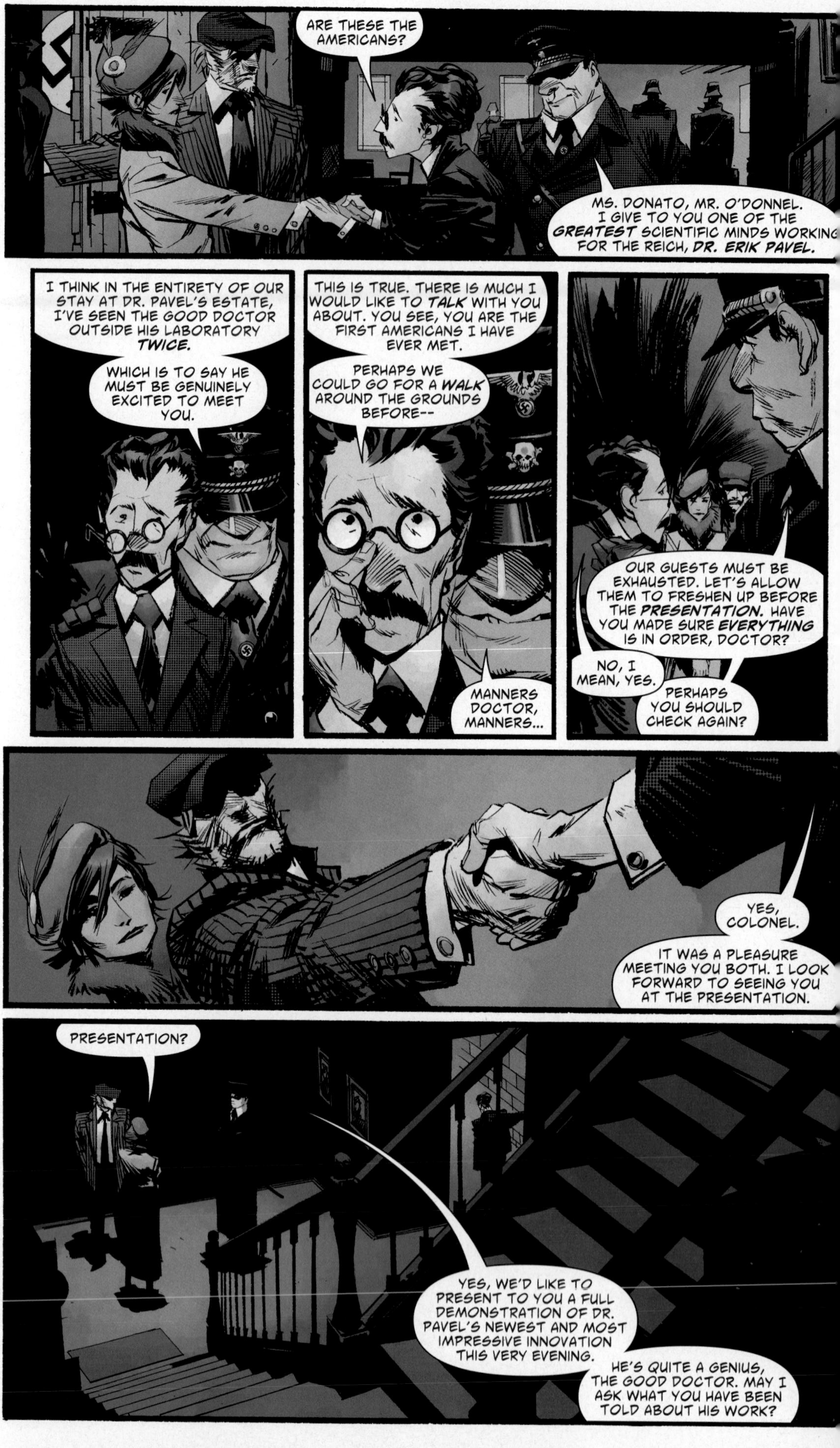

ARE THESE THE AMERICANS?
MS. DONATO, MR. O'DONNEL. I GIVE TO YOU ONE OF THE GREATEST SCIENTIFIC MINDS WORKING FOR THE REICH, DR. ERIK PAVEL.
I THINK IN THE ENTIRETY OF OUR STAY AT DR. PAVEL'S ESTATE, I'VE SEEN THE GOOD DOCTOR OUTSIDE HIS LABORATORY TWICE.
WHICH IS TO SAY HE MUST BE GENUINELY EXCITED TO MEET YOU.
THIS IS TRUE. THERE IS MUCH I WOULD LIKE TO TALK WITH YOU ABOUT. YOU SEE, YOU ARE THE FIRST AMERICANS I HAVE EVER MET.
PERHAPS WE COULD GO FOR A WALK AROUND THE GROUNDS BEFORE--
MANNERS DOCTOR, MANNERS...
OUR GUESTS MUST BE EXHAUSTED. LET'S ALLOW THEM TO FRESHEN UP BEFORE THE PRESENTATION. HAVE YOU MADE SURE EVERYTHING IS IN ORDER, DOCTOR?
NO, I MEAN, YES.
PERHAPS YOU SHOULD CHECK AGAIN?
YES, COLONEL.
IT WAS A PLEASURE MEETING YOU BOTH. I LOOK FORWARD TO SEEING YOU AT THE PRESENTATION.
PRESENTATION?
YES, WE'D LIKE TO PRESENT TO YOU A FULL DEMONSTRATION OF DR. PAVEL'S NEWEST AND MOST IMPRESSIVE INNOVATION THIS VERY EVENING.
HE'S QUITE A GENIUS, THE GOOD DOCTOR. MAY I ASK WHAT YOU HAVE BEEN TOLD ABOUT HIS WORK?

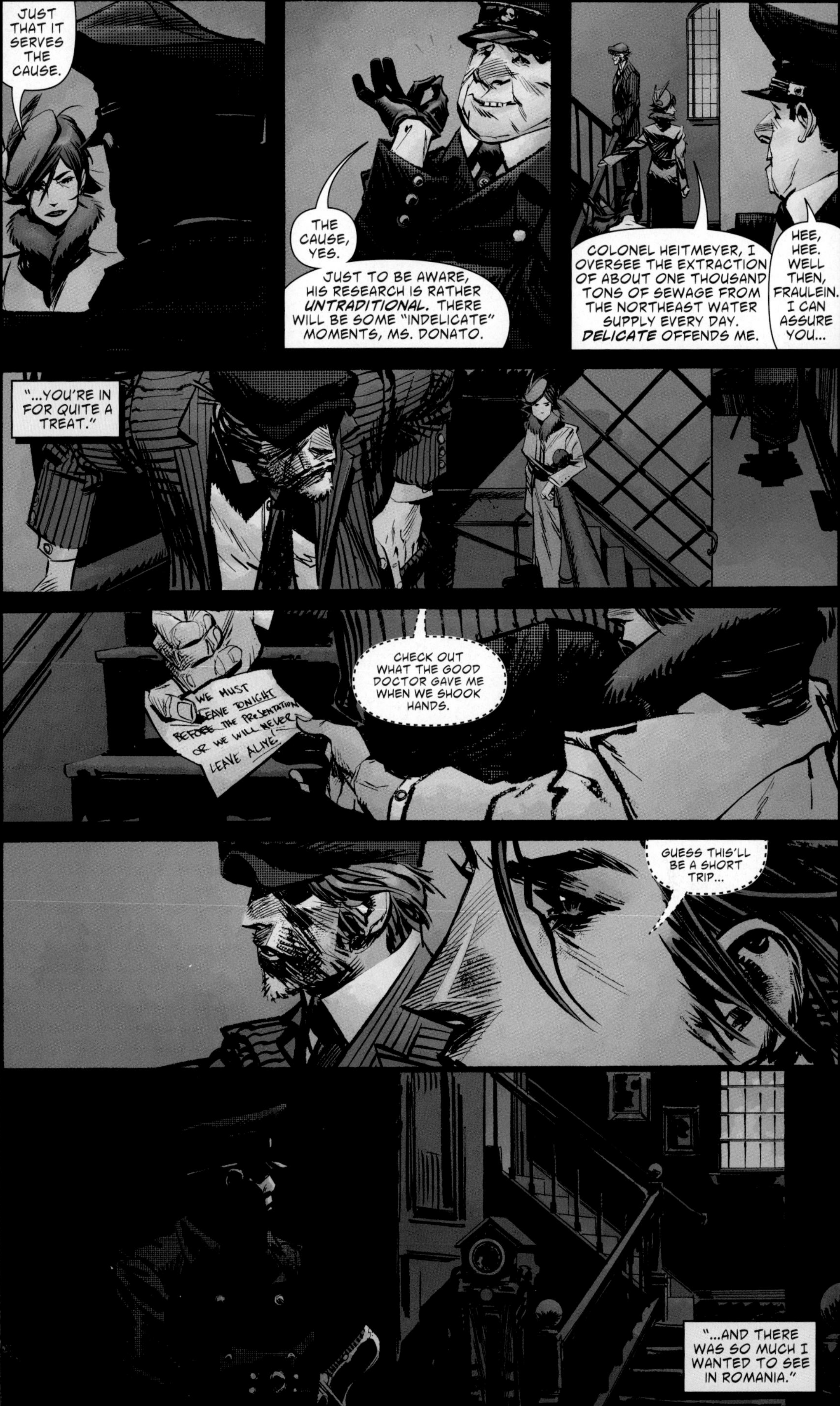
JUST THAT IT SERVES THE CAUSE.
THE CAUSE, YES.
JUST TO BE AWARE, HIS RESEARCH IS RATHER UNTRADITIONAL. THERE WILL BE SOME "INDELICATE" MOMENTS, MS. DONATO.
COLONEL HEITMEYER, I OVERSEE THE EXTRACTION OF ABOUT ONE THOUSAND TONS OF SEWAGE FROM THE NORTHEAST WATER SUPPLY EVERY DAY. DELICATE OFFENDS ME.
HEE, HEE. WELL THEN, FRAULEIN. I CAN ASSURE YOU...
"...YOU'RE IN FOR QUITE A TREAT."
WE MUST LEAVE TONIGHT BEFORE THE PRESENTATION OR WE WILL NEVER LEAVE ALIVE!
CHECK OUT WHAT THE GOOD DOCTOR GAVE ME WHEN WE SHOOK HANDS.
GUESS THIS'LL BE A SHORT TRIP...
"...AND THERE WAS SO MUCH I WANTED TO SEE IN ROMANIA."

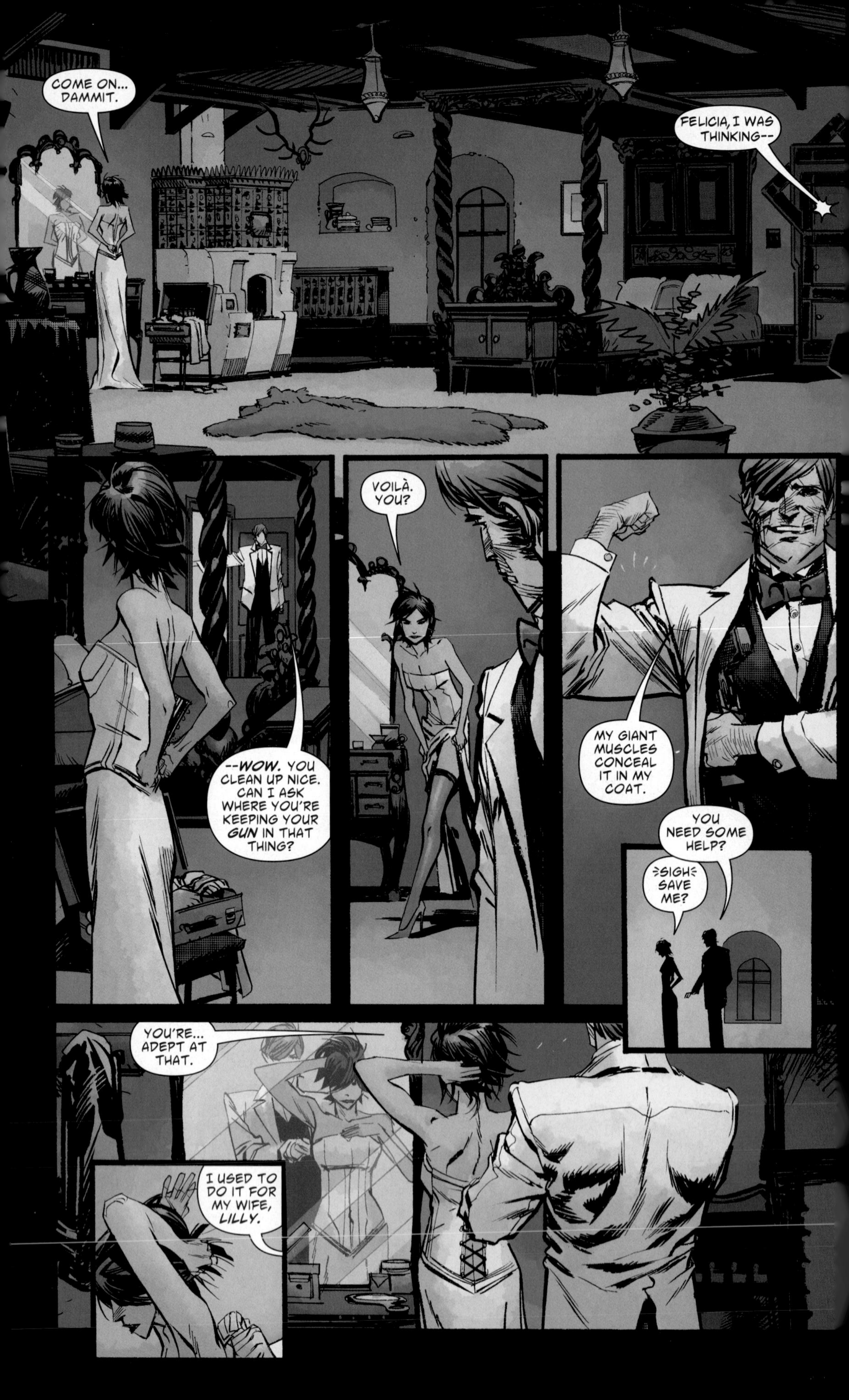

COME ON... DAMMIT.
FELICIA, I WAS THINKING--
--WOW. YOU CLEAN UP NICE. CAN I ASK WHERE YOU'RE KEEPING YOUR GUN IN THAT THING?
VOILÀ. YOU?
MY GIANT MUSCLES CONCEAL IT IN MY COAT.
YOU NEED SOME HELP?
SIGH SAVE ME?
YOU'RE... ADEPT AT THAT.
I USED TO DO IT FOR MY WIFE, LILLY.

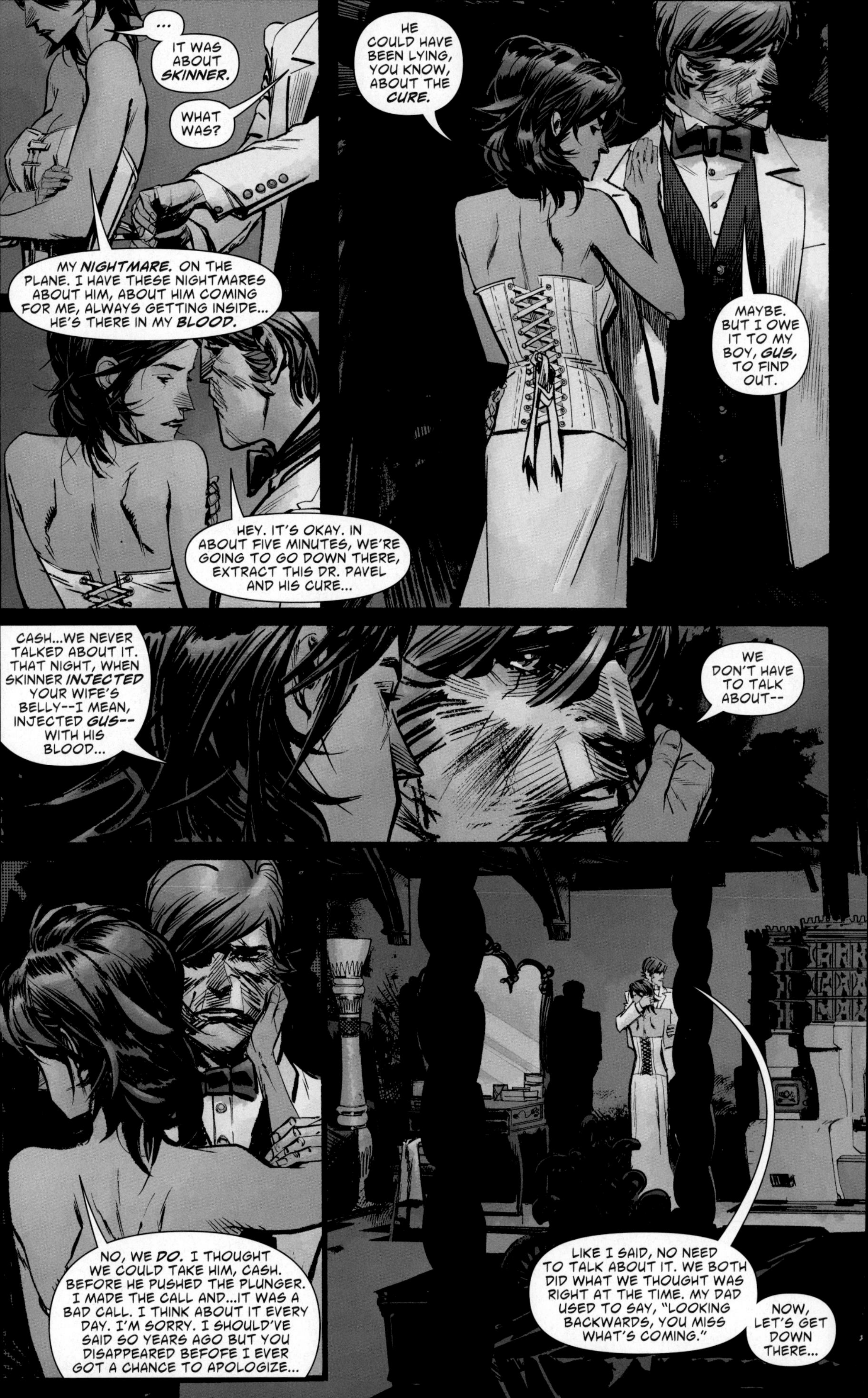
...
IT WAS ABOUT SKINNER.
WHAT WAS?
MY NIGHTMARE. ON THE PLANE. I HAVE THESE NIGHTMARES ABOUT HIM, ABOUT HIM COMING FOR ME, ALWAYS GETTING INSIDE... HE'S THERE IN MY BLOOD.
HEY. IT'S OKAY. IN ABOUT FIVE MINUTES, WE'RE GOING TO GO DOWN THERE, EXTRACT THIS DR. PAVEL AND HIS CURE...
HE COULD HAVE BEEN LYING, YOU KNOW, ABOUT THE CURE.
MAYBE. BUT I OWE IT TO MY BOY, GUS, TO FIND OUT.
CASH...WE NEVER TALKED ABOUT IT. THAT NIGHT, WHEN SKINNER INJECTED YOUR WIFE'S BELLY--I MEAN, INJECTED GUS--WITH HIS BLOOD...
WE DON'T HAVE TO TALK ABOUT--
NO, WE DO. I THOUGHT WE COULD TAKE HIM, CASH. BEFORE HE PUSHED THE PLUNGER. I MADE THE CALL AND...IT WAS A BAD CALL. I THINK ABOUT IT EVERY DAY. I'M SORRY. I SHOULD'VE SAID SO YEARS AGO BUT YOU DISAPPEARED BEFOFE I EVER GOT A CHANCE TO APOLOGIZE...
LIKE I SAID, NO NEED TO TALK ABOUT IT. WE BOTH DID WHAT WE THOUGHT WAS RIGHT AT THE TIME. MY DAD USED TO SAY, "LOOKING BACKWARDS, YOU MISS WHAT'S COMING."
NOW, LET'S GET DOWN THERE...

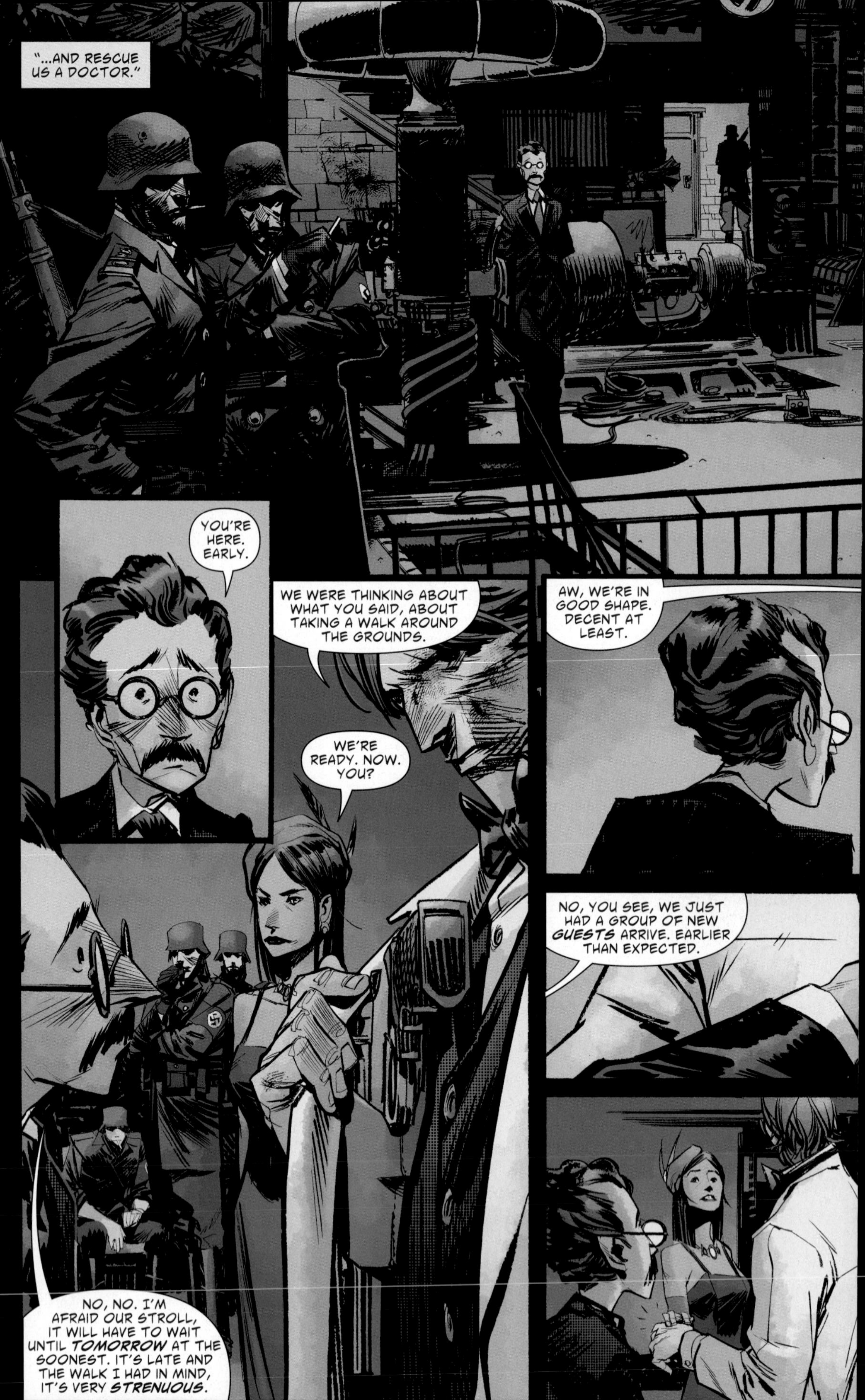
"...AND RESCUE US A DOCTOR."
YOU'RE HERE. EARLY.
WE WERE THINKING ABOUT WHAT YOU SAID, ABOUT TAKING A WALK AROUND THE GROUNDS.
WE'RE READY. NOW. YOU?
AW, WE'RE IN GOOD SHAPE. DECENT AT LEAST.
NO, YOU SEE, WE JUST HAD A GROUP OF NEW GUESTS ARRIVE. EARLIER THAN EXPECTED.
NO, NO. I'M AFRAID OUR STROLL, IT WILL HAVE TO WAIT UNTIL TOMORROW AT THE SOONEST. IT'S LATE AND THE WALK I HAD IN MIND, IT'S VERY STRENUOUS.

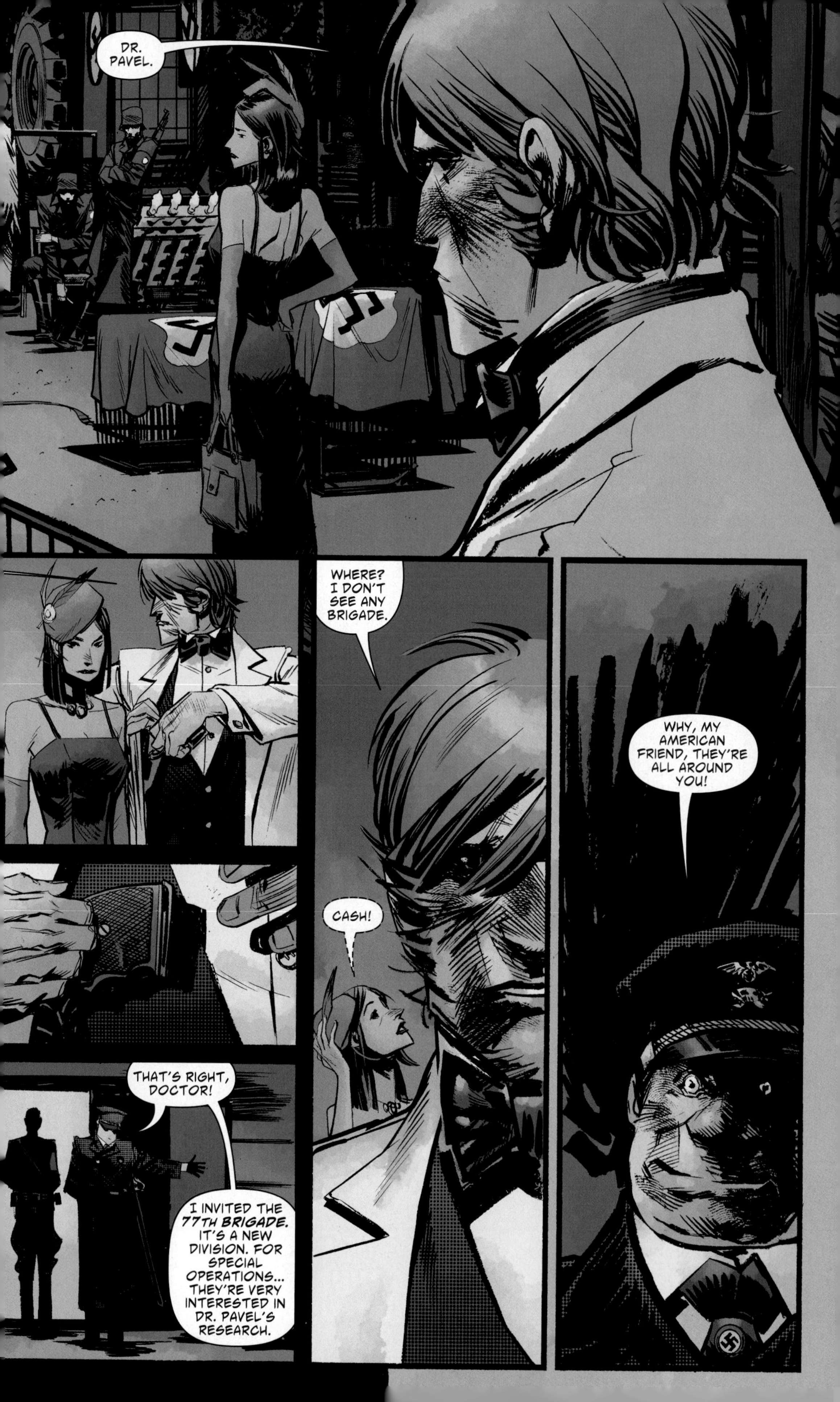

DR. PAVEL.
THAT'S RIGHT, DOCTOR!
I INVITED THE 77TH BRIGADE. IT'S A NEW DIVISION. FOR SPECIAL OPERATIONS... THEY'RE VERY INTERESTED IN DR. PAVEL'S RESEARCH.
WHERE? I DON'T SEE ANY BRIGADE.
CASH!
WHY, MY AMERICAN FRIEND, THEY'RE ALL AROUND YOU!

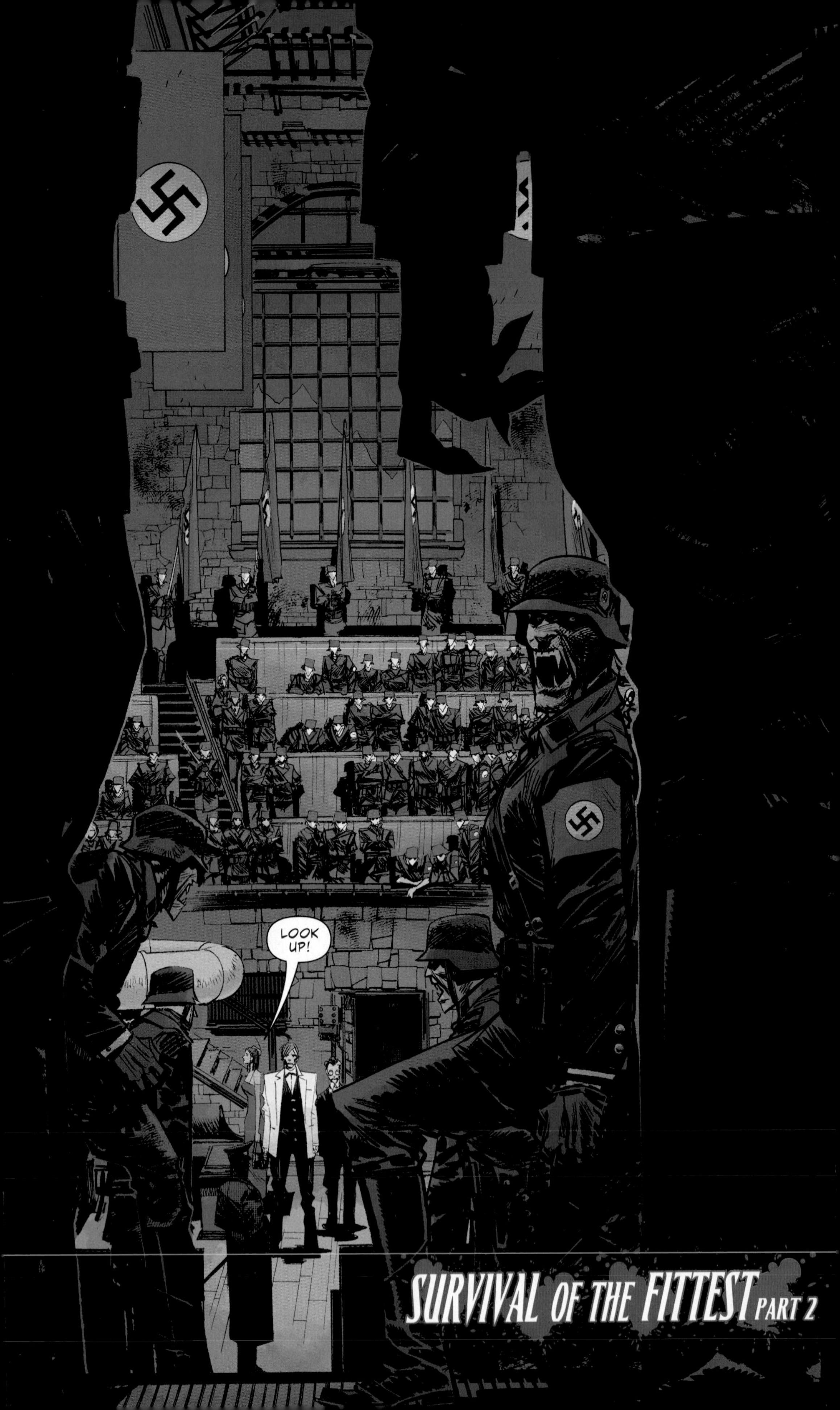
LOOK UP!
SURVIVAL OF THE FITTEST PART 2

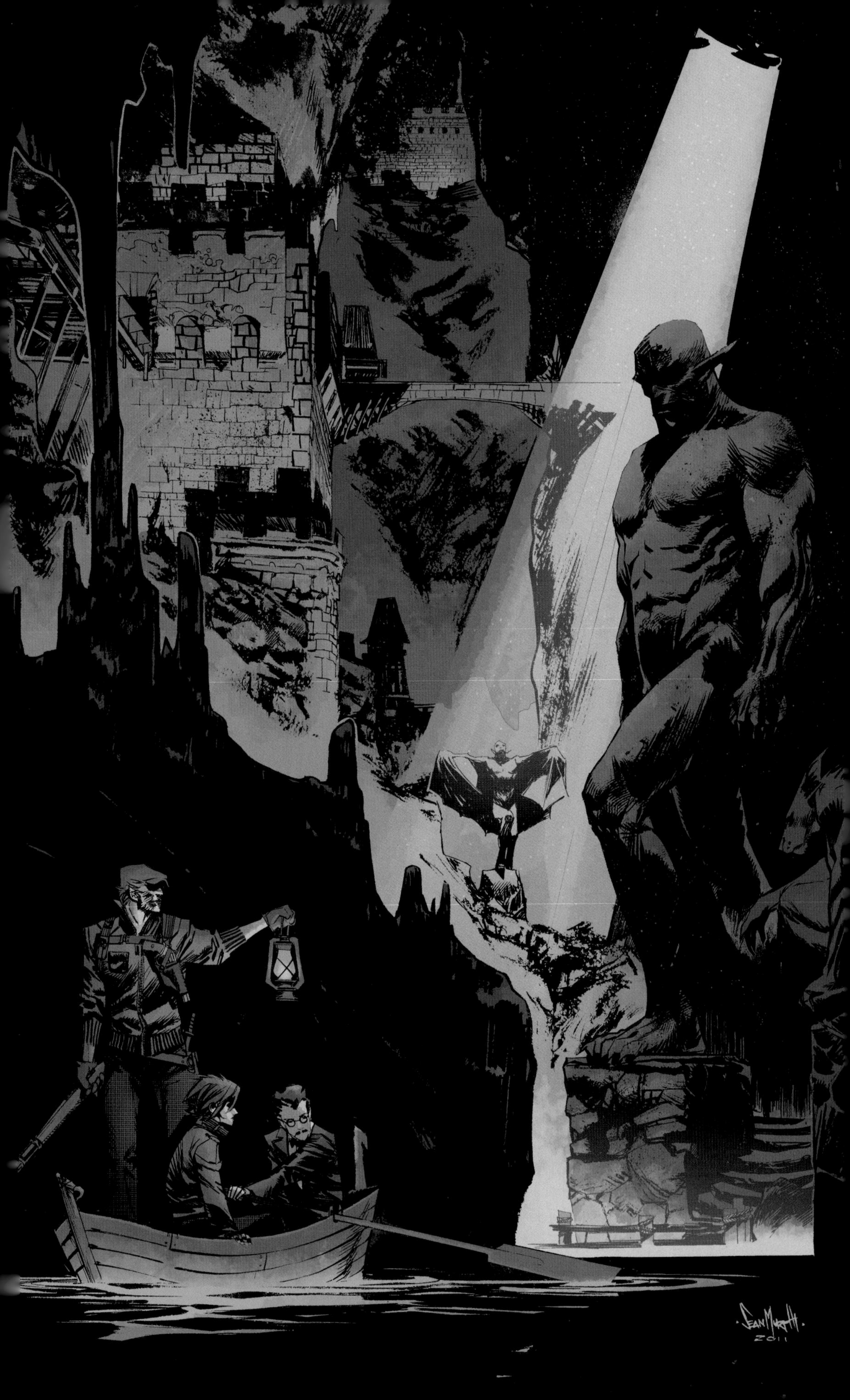
SEAN MURPHY
2011

Survival
of the Fittest
Part Three

Sean Murphy
Artist and cover

Dave Stewart
cover color

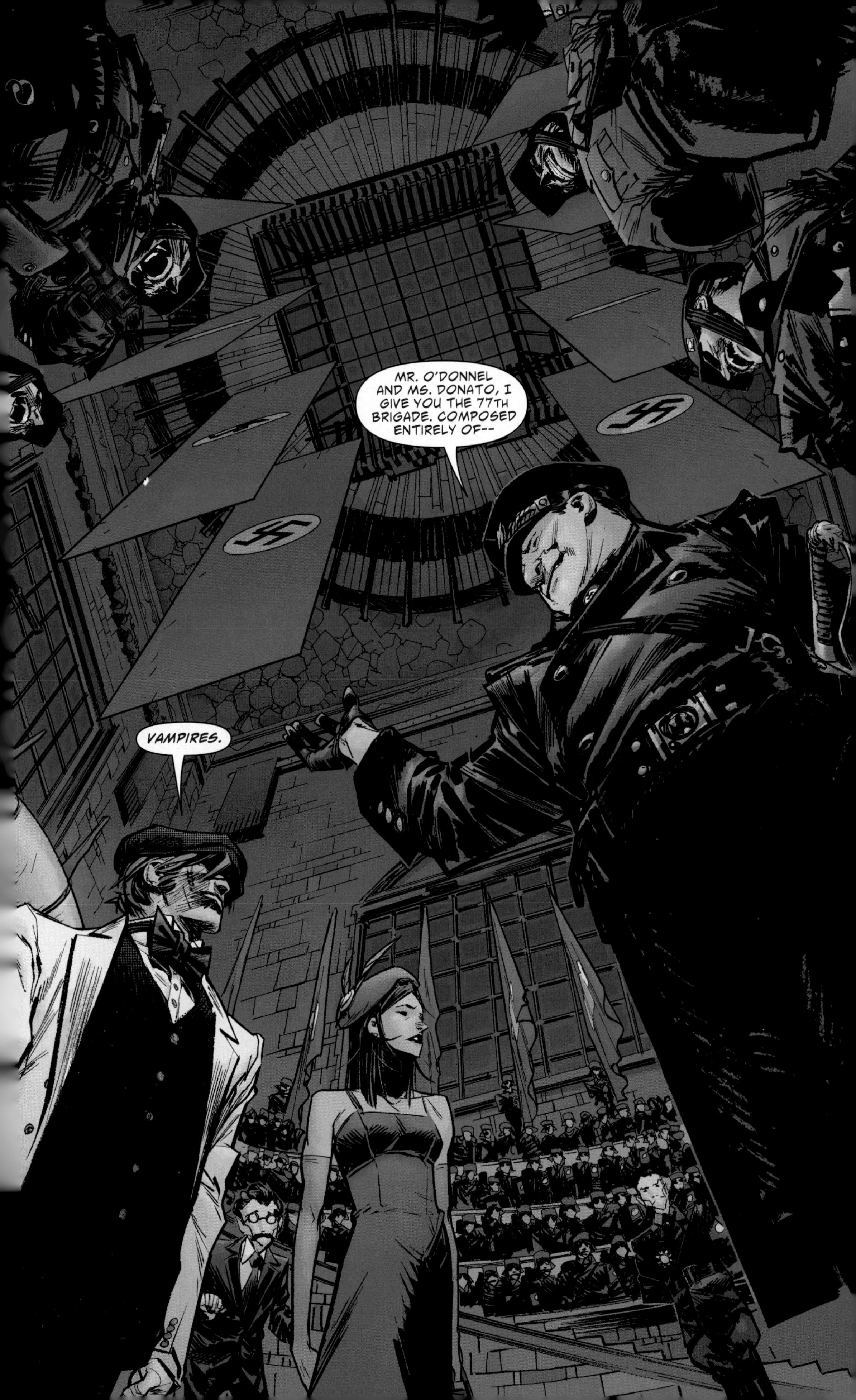
MR. O'DONNEL AND MS. DONATO, I GIVE YOU THE 77TH BRIGADE. COMPOSED ENTIRELY OF--
VAMPIRES.

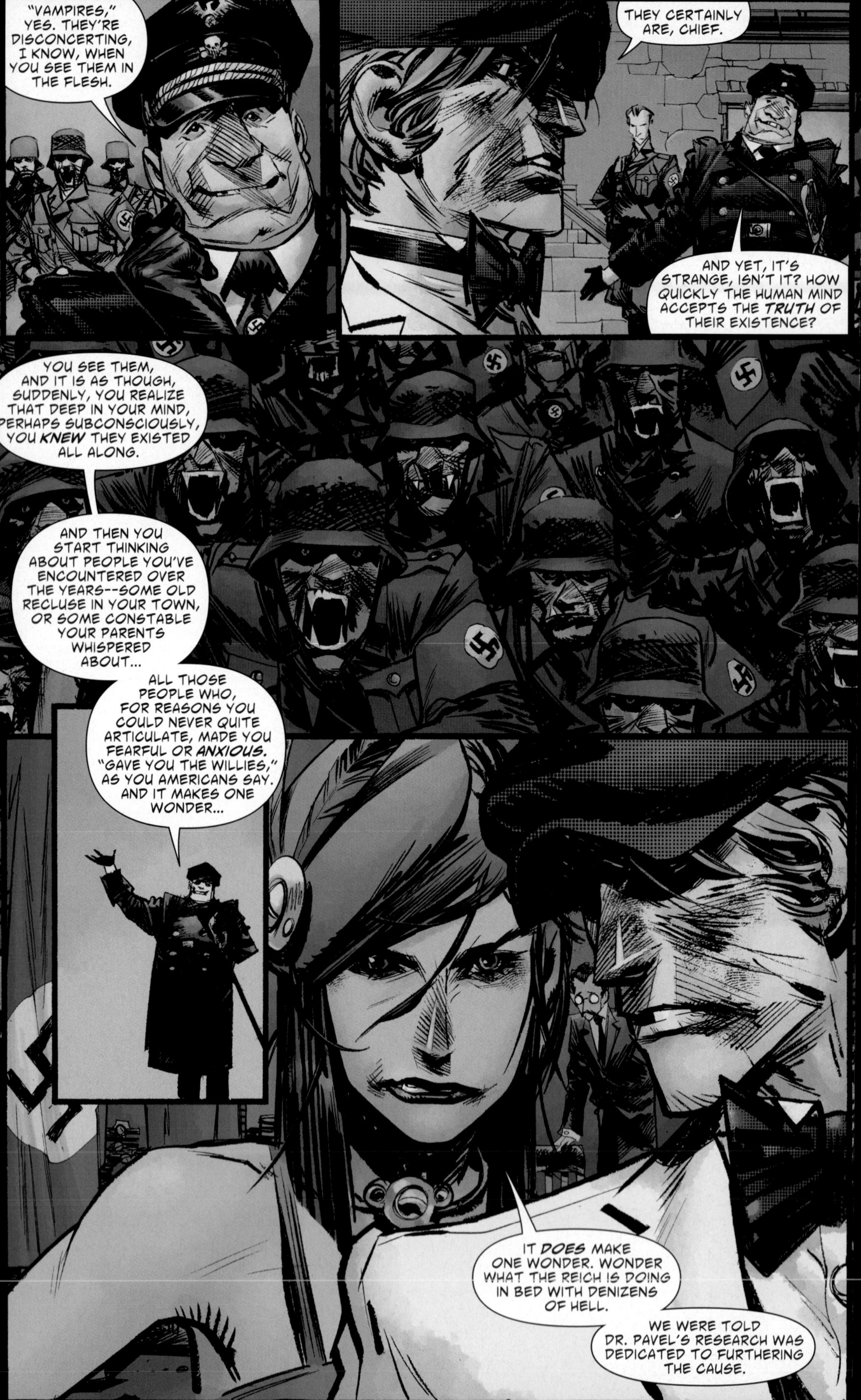
"VAMPIRES," YES. THEY'RE DISCONCERTING, I KNOW, WHEN YOU SEE THEM IN THE FLESH.
THEY CERTAINLY ARE, CHIEF.
AND YET, IT'S STRANGE, ISN'T IT? HOW QUICKLY THE HUMAN MIND ACCEPTS THE TRUTH OF THEIR EXISTENCE?
YOU SEE THEM, AND IT IS AS THOUGH, SUDDENLY, YOU REALIZE THAT DEEP IN YOUR MIND, PERHAPS SUBCONSCIOUSLY, YOU KNEW THEY EXISTED ALL ALONG.
AND THEN YOU START THINKING ABOUT PEOPLE YOU'VE ENCOUNTERED OVER THE YEARS--SOME OLD RECLUSE IN YOUR TOWN, OR SOME CONSTABLE YOUR PARENTS WHISPERED ABOUT...
ALL THOSE PEOPLE WHO, FOR REASONS YOU COULD NEVER QUITE ARTICULATE, MADE YOU FEARFUL OR ANXIOUS. "GAVE YOU THE WILLIES," AS YOU AMERICANS SAY. AND IT MAKES ONE WONDER...
IT DOES MAKE ONE WONDER. WONDER WHAT THE REICH IS DOING IN BED WITH DENIZENS OF HELL.
WE WERE TOLD DR. PAVEL'S RESEARCH WAS DEDICATED TO FURTHERING THE CAUSE.

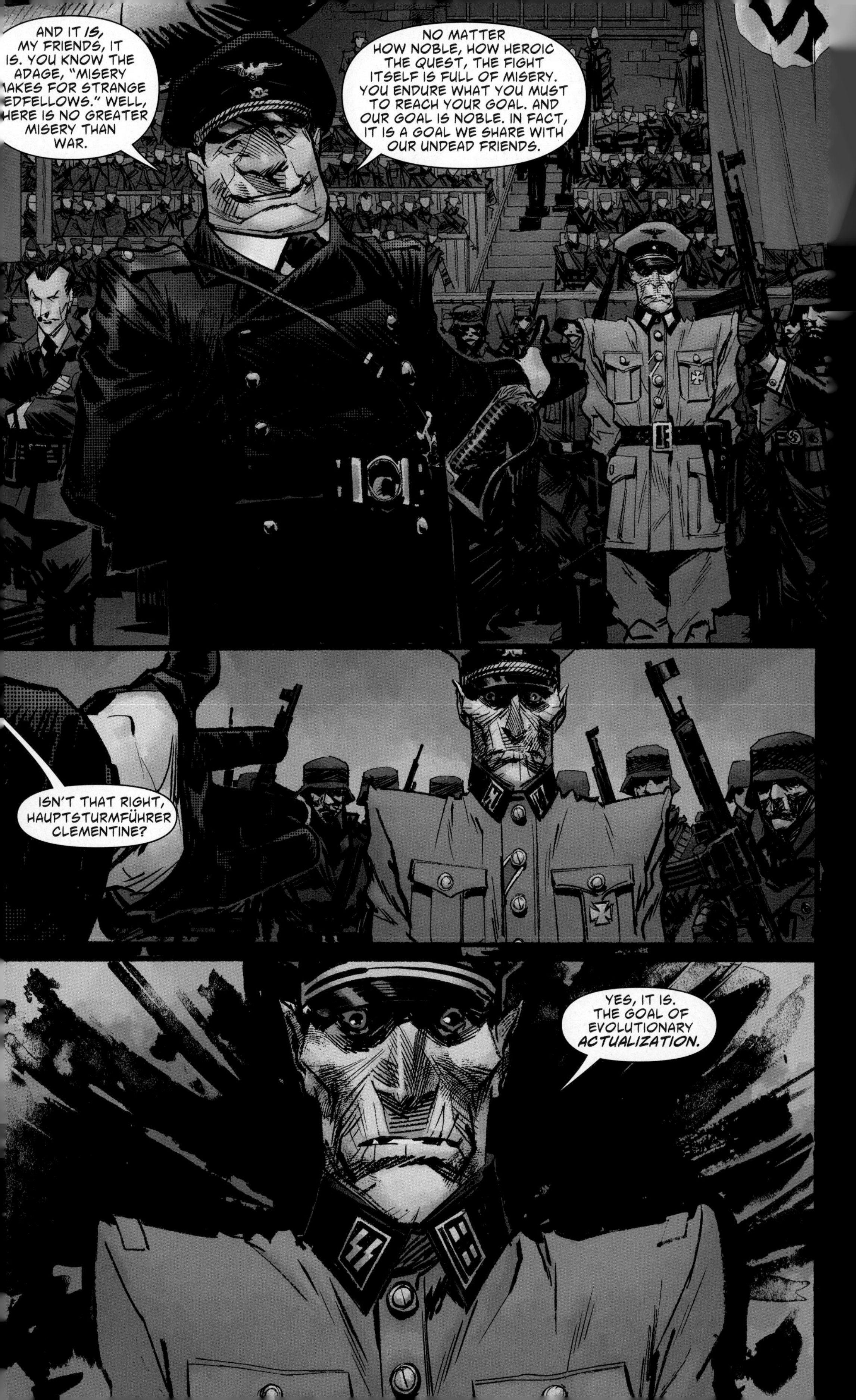
AND IT *IS*, MY FRIENDS, IT IS. YOU KNOW THE ADAGE, "MISERY IAKES FOR STRANGE EDFELLOWS." WELL, HERE IS NO GREATER MISERY THAN WAR.
NO MATTER HOW NOBLE, HOW HEROIC THE QUEST, THE FIGHT ITSELF IS FULL OF MISERY. YOU ENDURE WHAT YOU MUST TO REACH YOUR GOAL. AND OUR GOAL IS NOBLE. IN FACT, IT IS A GOAL WE SHARE WITH OUR UNDEAD FRIENDS.
ISN'T THAT RIGHT, HAUPTSTURMFÜHRER CLEMENTINE?
YES, IT IS. THE GOAL OF EVOLUTIONARY ***ACTUALIZATION.***

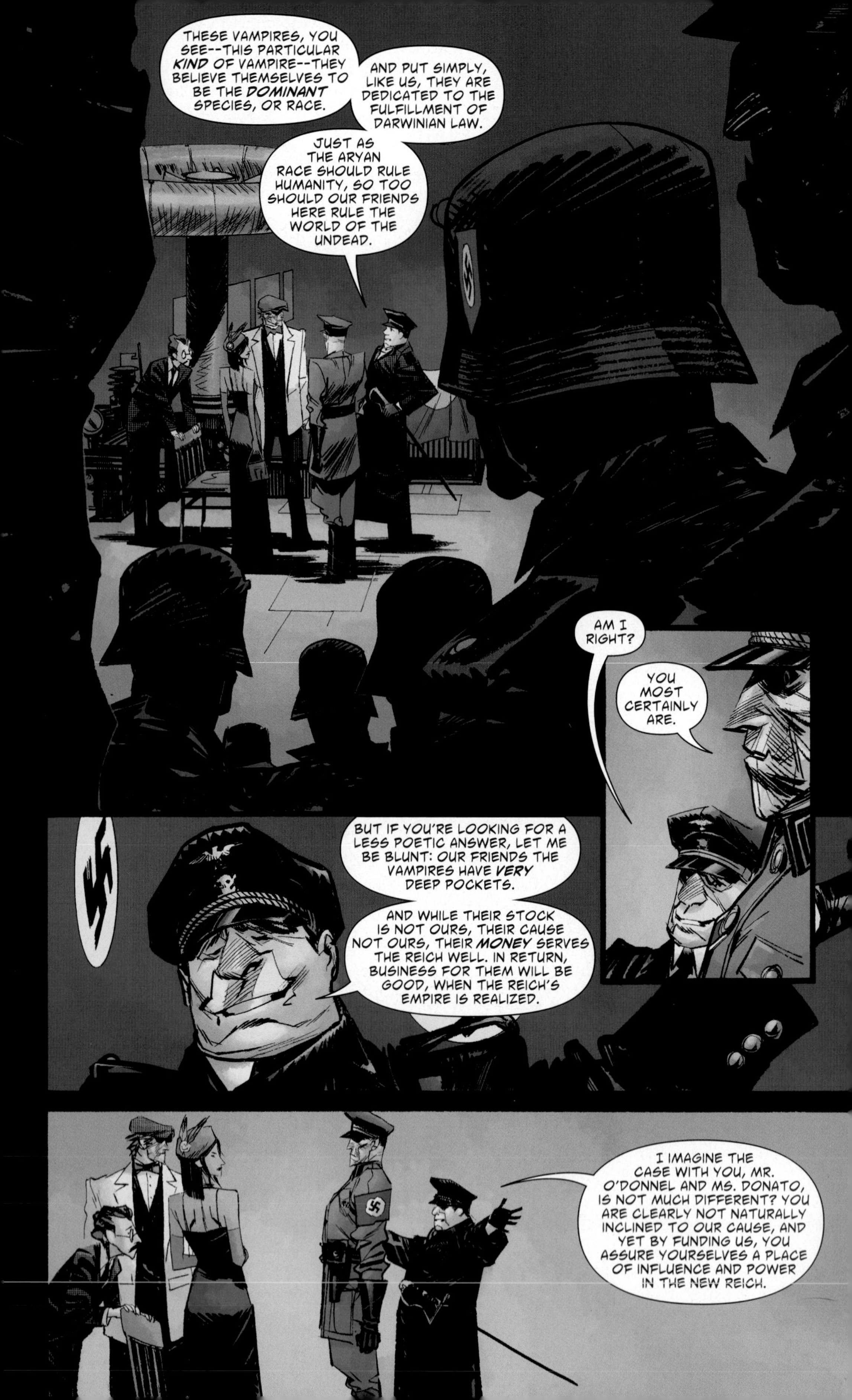
THESE VAMPIRES, YOU SEE--THIS PARTICULAR *KIND* OF VAMPIRE--THEY BELIEVE THEMSELVES TO BE THE *DOMINANT* SPECIES, OR RACE.
AND PUT SIMPLY, LIKE US, THEY ARE DEDICATED TO THE FULFILLMENT OF DARWINIAN LAW.
JUST AS THE ARYAN RACE SHOULD RULE HUMANITY, SO TOO SHOULD OUR FRIENDS HERE RULE THE WORLD OF THE UNDEAD.
AM I RIGHT?
YOU MOST CERTAINLY ARE.
BUT IF YOU'RE LOOKING FOR A LESS POETIC ANSWER, LET ME BE BLUNT: OUR FRIENDS THE VAMPIRES HAVE *VERY* DEEP POCKETS.
AND WHILE THEIR STOCK IS NOT OURS, THEIR CAUSE NOT OURS, THEIR *MONEY* SERVES THE REICH WELL. IN RETURN, BUSINESS FOR THEM WILL BE GOOD, WHEN THE REICH'S EMPIRE IS REALIZED.
I IMAGINE THE CASE WITH YOU, MR. O'DONNEL AND MS. DONATO, IS NOT MUCH DIFFERENT? YOU ARE CLEARLY NOT NATURALLY INCLINED TO OUR CAUSE, AND YET BY FUNDING US, YOU ASSURE YOURSELVES A PLACE OF INFLUENCE AND POWER IN THE NEW REICH.

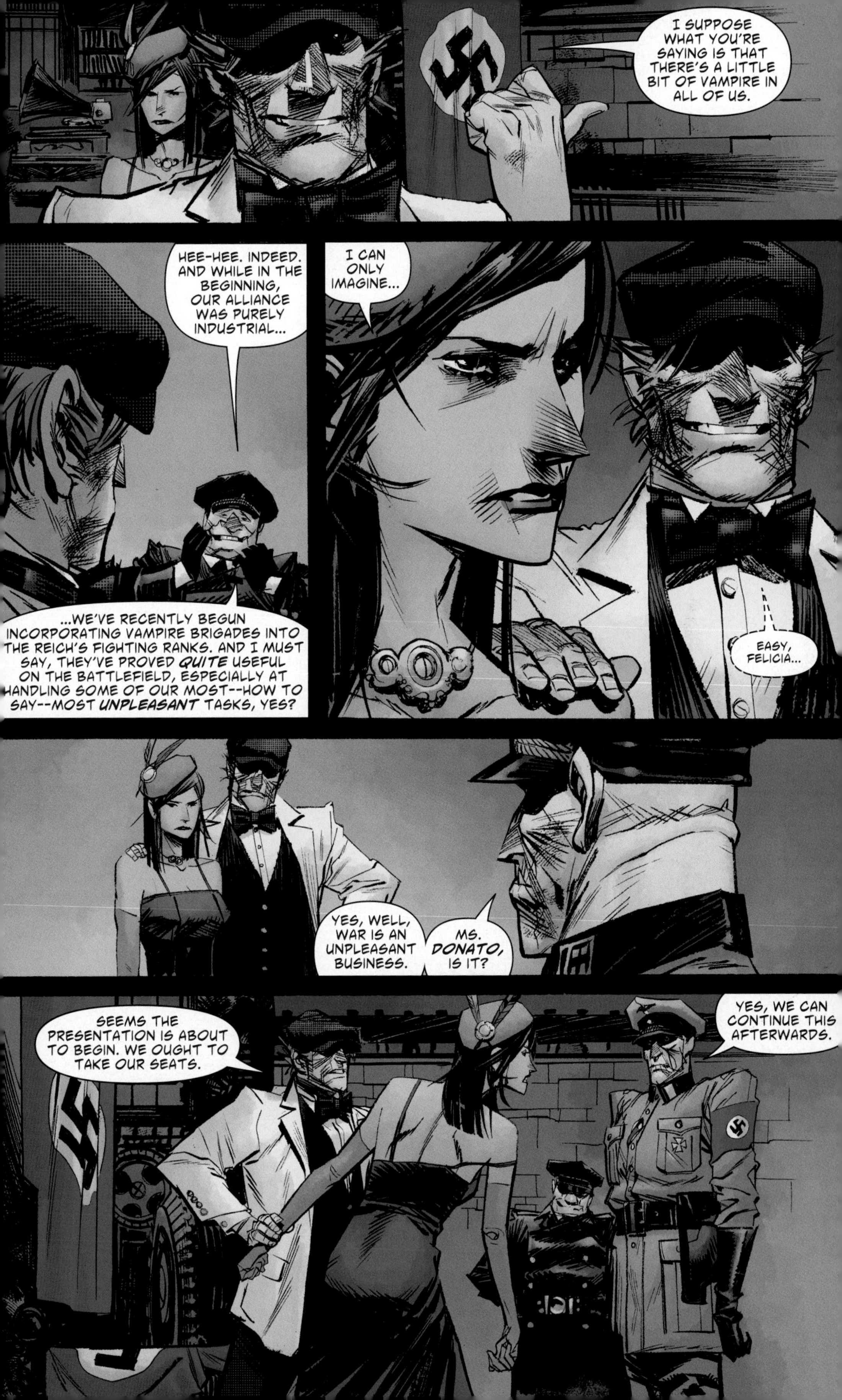
I SUPPOSE WHAT YOU'RE SAYING IS THAT THERE'S A LITTLE BIT OF VAMPIRE IN ALL OF US.
HEE-HEE. INDEED. AND WHILE IN THE BEGINNING, OUR ALLIANCE WAS PURELY INDUSTRIAL...
I CAN ONLY IMAGINE...
...WE'VE RECENTLY BEGUN INCORPORATING VAMPIRE BRIGADES INTO THE REICH'S FIGHTING RANKS. AND I MUST SAY, THEY'VE PROVED QUITE USEFUL ON THE BATTLEFIELD, ESPECIALLY AT HANDLING SOME OF OUR MOST--HOW TO SAY--MOST UNPLEASANT TASKS, YES?
EASY, FELICIA...
YES, WELL, WAR IS AN UNPLEASANT BUSINESS.
MS. DONATO, IS IT?
SEEMS THE PRESENTATION IS ABOUT TO BEGIN. WE OUGHT TO TAKE OUR SEATS.
YES, WE CAN CONTINUE THIS AFTERWARDS.

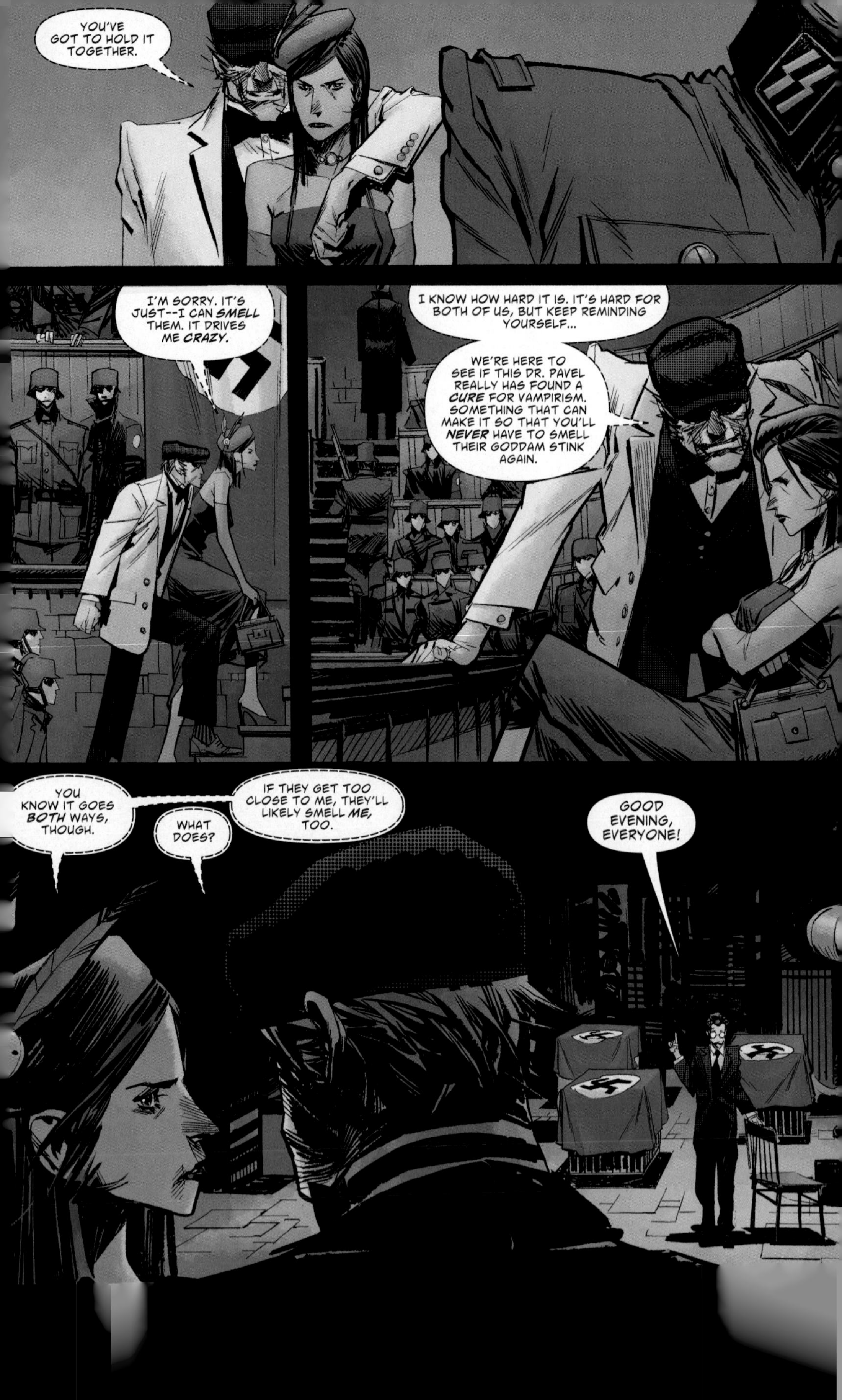
YOU'VE GOT TO HOLD IT TOGETHER.
I'M SORRY. IT'S JUST--I CAN SMELL THEM. IT DRIVES ME CRAZY.
I KNOW HOW HARD IT IS. IT'S HARD FOR BOTH OF US, BUT KEEP REMINDING YOURSELF...
WE'RE HERE TO SEE IF THIS DR. PAVEL REALLY HAS FOUND A CURE FOR VAMPIRISM. SOMETHING THAT CAN MAKE IT SO THAT YOU'LL NEVER HAVE TO SMELL THEIR GODDAM STINK AGAIN.
YOU KNOW IT GOES BOTH WAYS, THOUGH.
WHAT DOES?
IF THEY GET TOO CLOSE TO ME, THEY'LL LIKELY SMELL ME, TOO.
GOOD EVENING, EVERYONE!

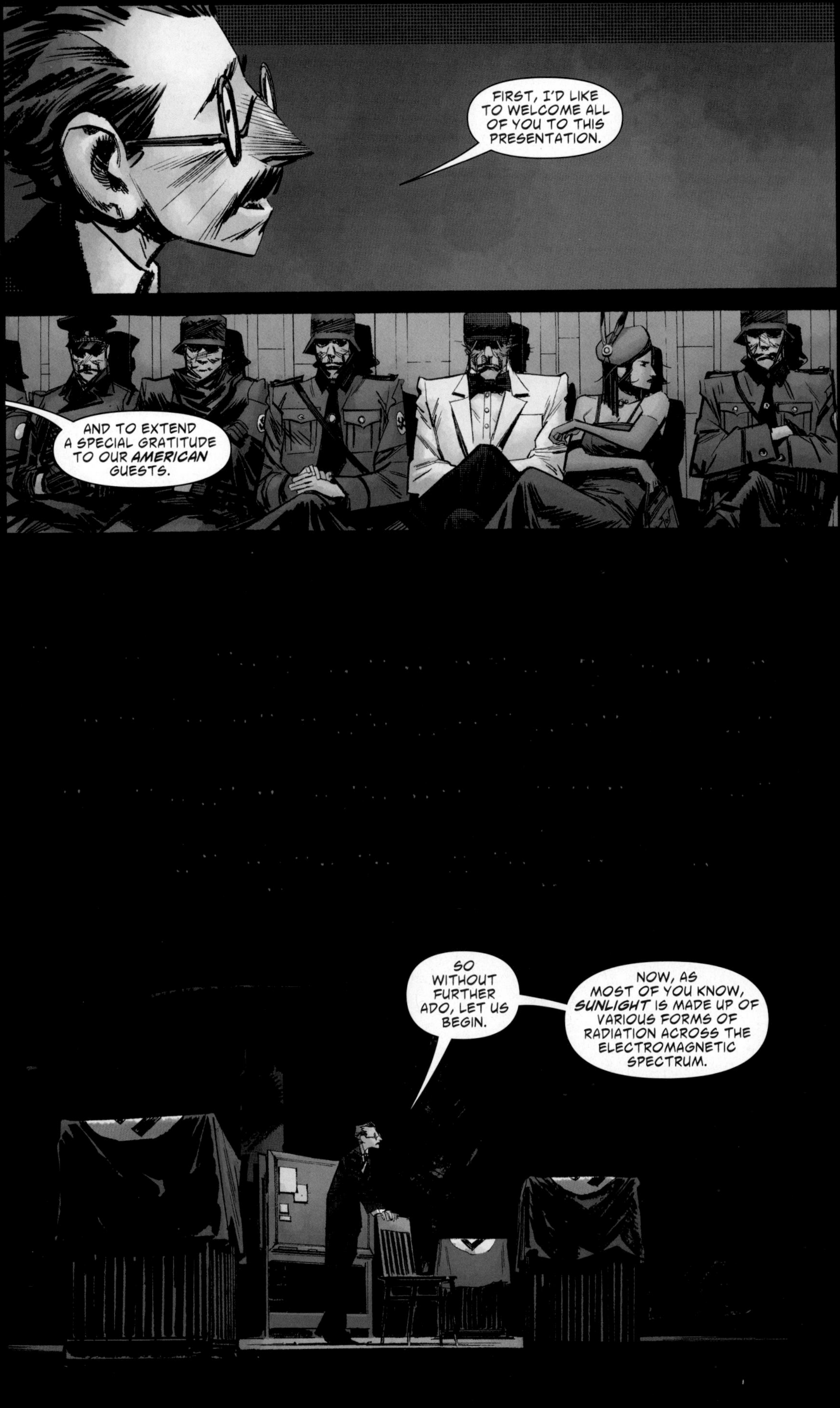
FIRST, I'D LIKE TO WELCOME ALL OF YOU TO THIS PRESENTATION.
AND TO EXTEND A SPECIAL GRATITUDE TO OUR AMERICAN GUESTS.
SO WITHOUT FURTHER ADO, LET US BEGIN.
NOW, AS MOST OF YOU KNOW, SUNLIGHT IS MADE UP OF VARIOUS FORMS OF RADIATION ACROSS THE ELECTROMAGNETIC SPECTRUM.

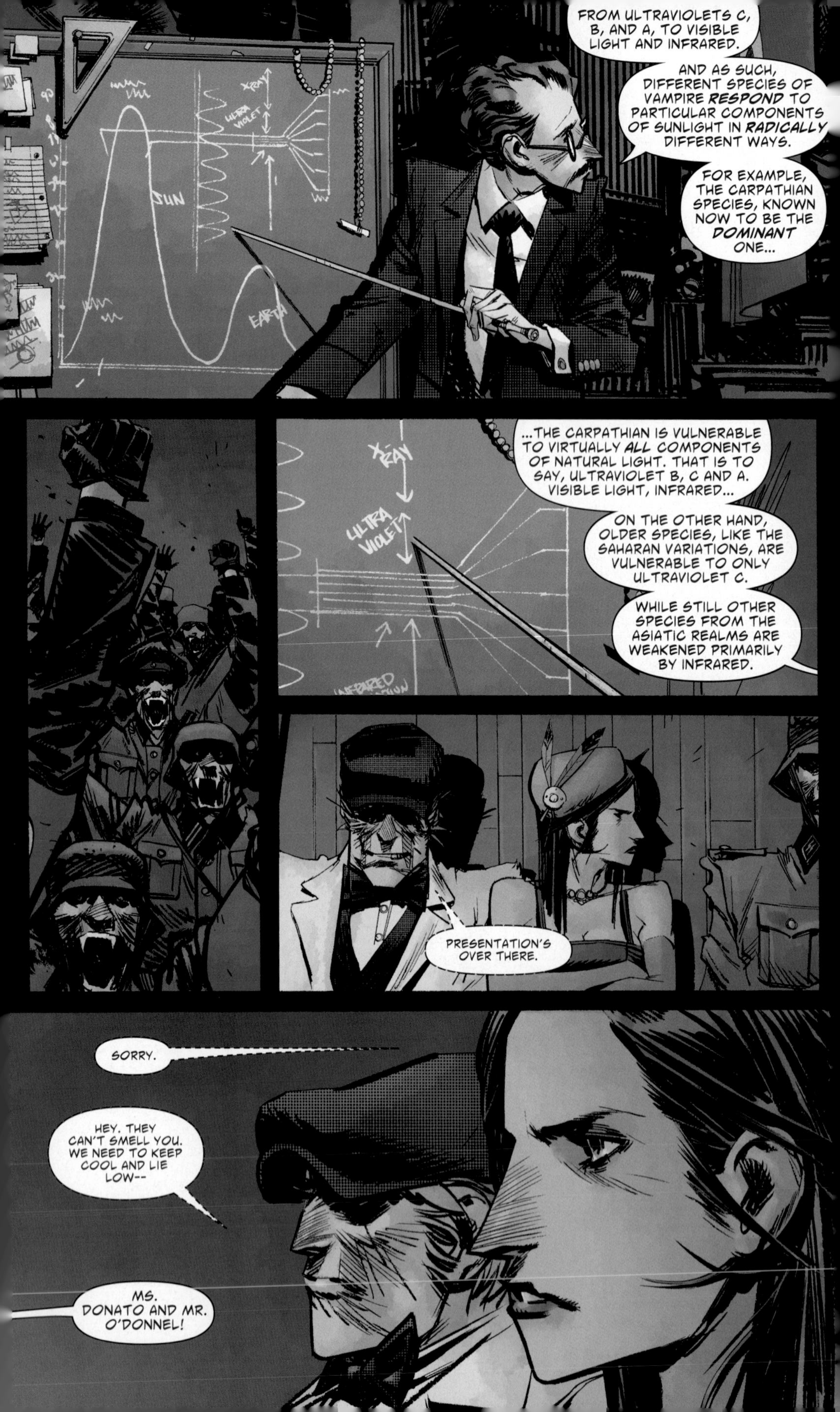
FROM ULTRAVIOLETS C, B, AND A, TO VISIBLE LIGHT AND INFRARED.
AND AS SUCH, DIFFERENT SPECIES OF VAMPIRE RESPOND TO PARTICULAR COMPONENTS OF SUNLIGHT IN RADICALLY DIFFERENT WAYS.
FOR EXAMPLE, THE CARPATHIAN SPECIES, KNOWN NOW TO BE THE DOMINANT ONE...
X-RAY
ULTRA VIOLET
SUN
EARTH
...THE CARPATHIAN IS VULNERABLE TO VIRTUALLY ALL COMPONENTS OF NATURAL LIGHT. THAT IS TO SAY, ULTRAVIOLET B, C AND A. VISIBLE LIGHT, INFRARED...
ON THE OTHER HAND, OLDER SPECIES, LIKE THE SAHARAN VARIATIONS, ARE VULNERABLE TO ONLY ULTRAVIOLET C.
WHILE STILL OTHER SPECIES FROM THE ASIATIC REALMS ARE WEAKENED PRIMARILY BY INFRARED.
PRESENTATION'S OVER THERE.
SORRY.
HEY. THEY CAN'T SMELL YOU. WE NEED TO KEEP COOL AND LIE LOW--
MS. DONATO AND MR. O'DONNEL!

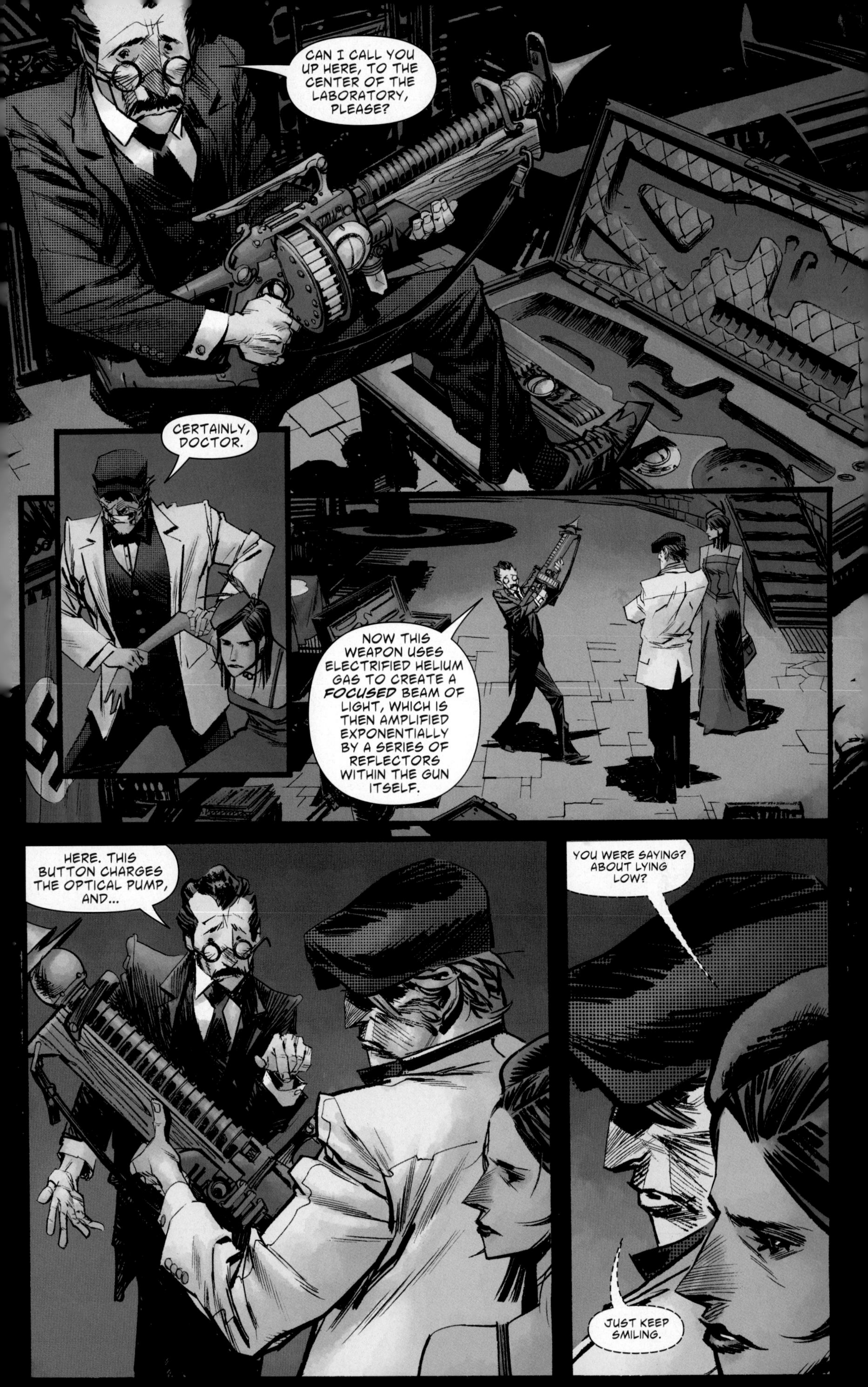
CAN I CALL YOU UP HERE, TO THE CENTER OF THE LABORATORY, PLEASE?
CERTAINLY, DOCTOR.
NOW THIS WEAPON USES ELECTRIFIED HELIUM GAS TO CREATE A *FOCUSED* BEAM OF LIGHT, WHICH IS THEN AMPLIFIED EXPONENTIALLY BY A SERIES OF REFLECTORS WITHIN THE GUN ITSELF.
HERE. THIS BUTTON CHARGES THE OPTICAL PUMP, AND...
YOU WERE SAYING? ABOUT LYING LOW?
JUST KEEP SMILING.

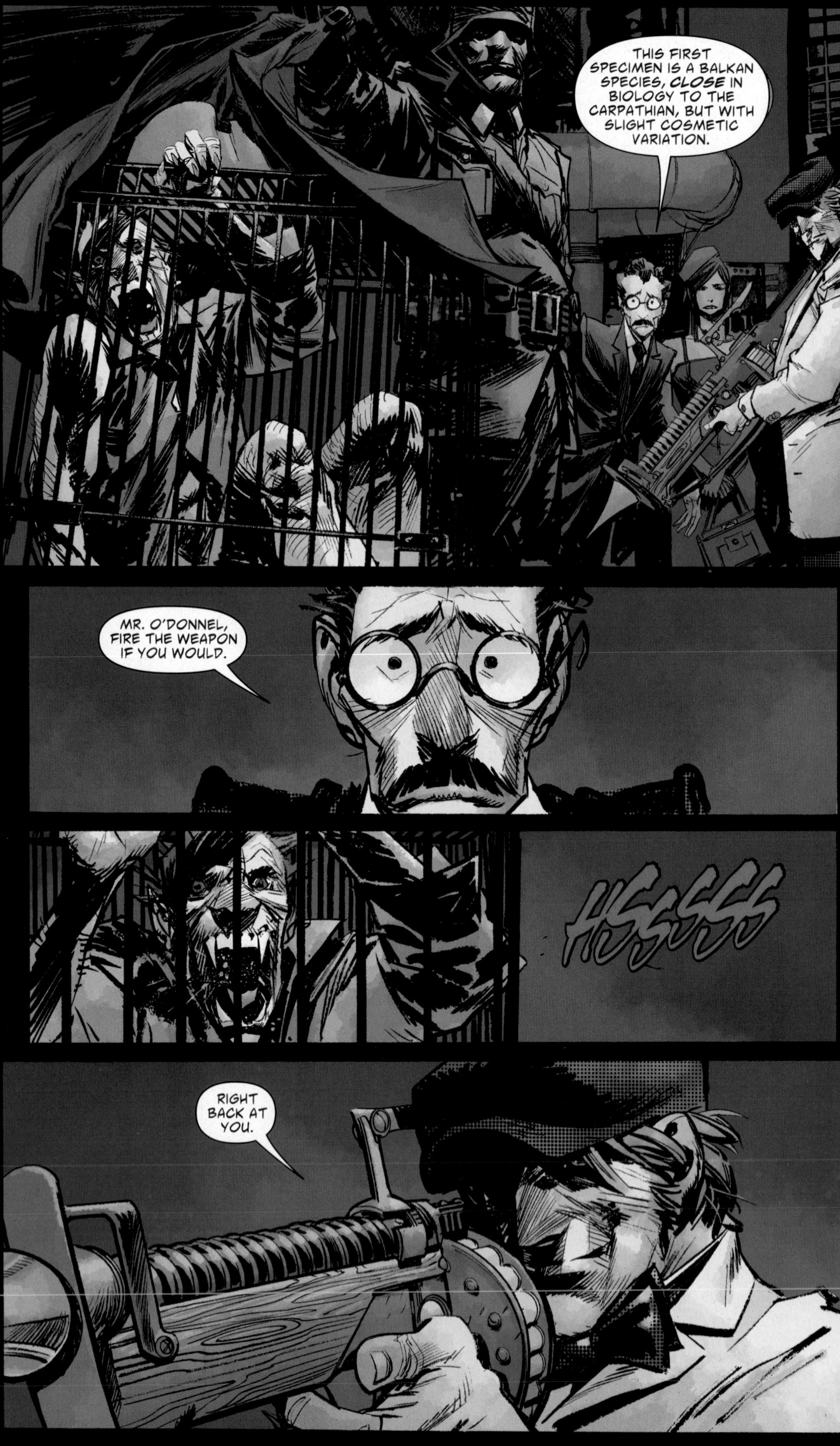
THIS FIRST SPECIMEN IS A BALKAN SPECIES, *CLOSE* IN BIOLOGY TO THE CARPATHIAN, BUT WITH SLIGHT COSMETIC VARIATION.
MR. O'DONNEL, FIRE THE WEAPON IF YOU WOULD.
HSSSSS
RIGHT BACK AT YOU.

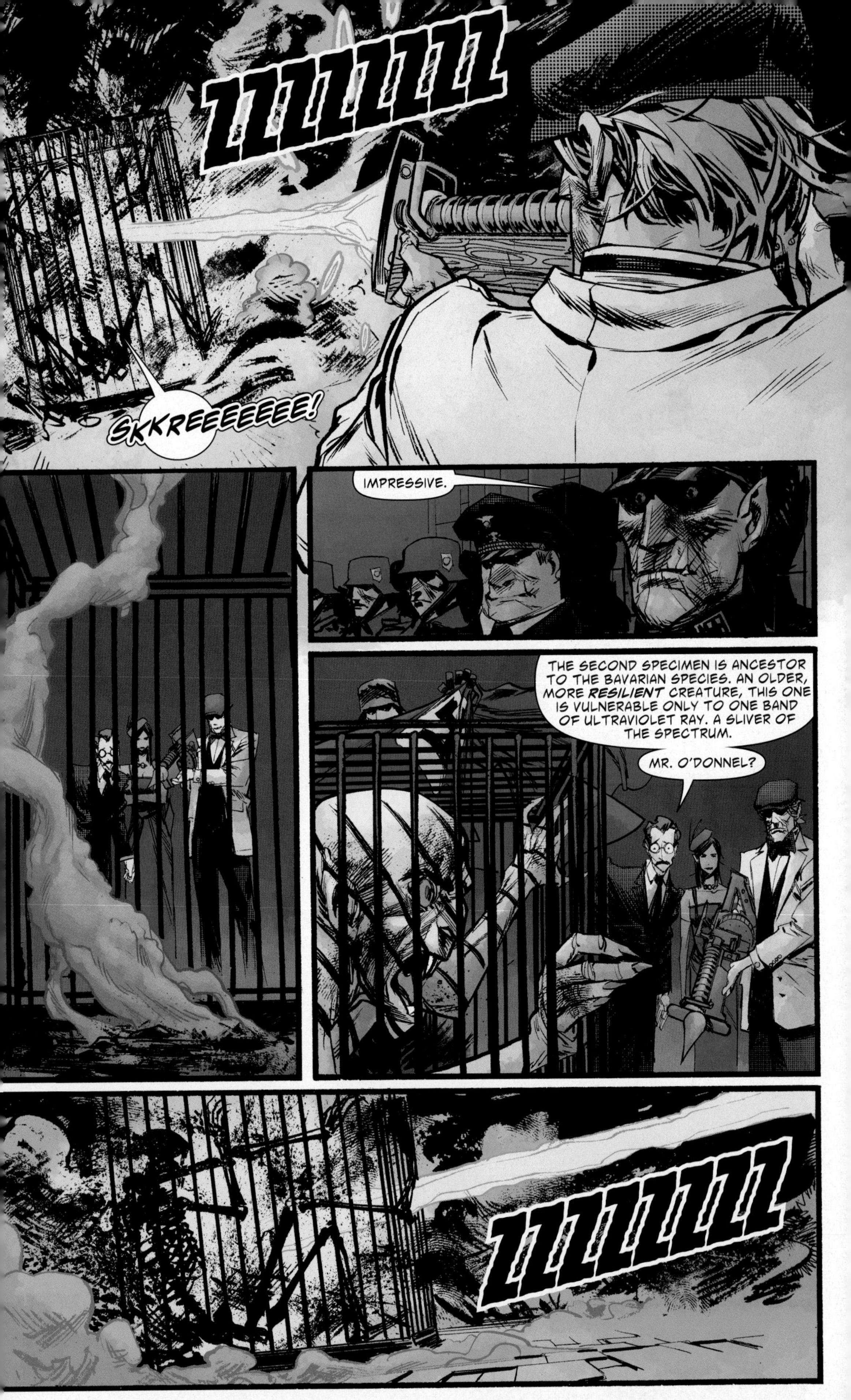

ZZZZZZZZ
SKKREEEEEEEE!
IMPRESSIVE.
THE SECOND SPECIMEN IS ANCESTOR TO THE BAVARIAN SPECIES. AN OLDER, MORE *RESILIENT* CREATURE, THIS ONE IS VULNERABLE ONLY TO ONE BAND OF ULTRAVIOLET RAY. A SLIVER OF THE SPECTRUM.
MR. O'DONNEL?
ZZZZZZZZ

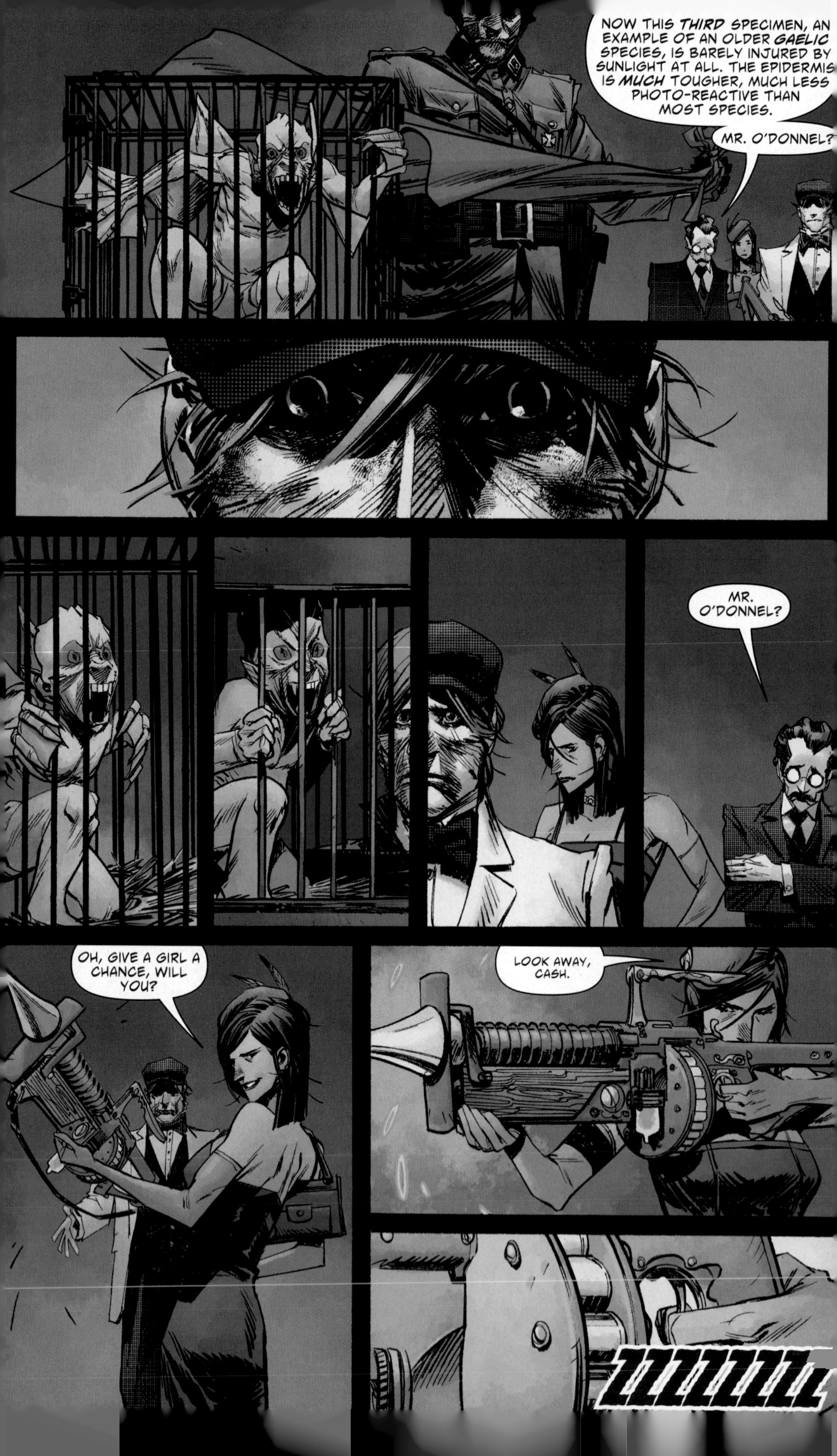
NOW THIS THIRD SPECIMEN, AN EXAMPLE OF AN OLDER GAELIC SPECIES, IS BARELY INJURED BY SUNLIGHT AT ALL. THE EPIDERMIS IS MUCH TOUGHER, MUCH LESS PHOTO-REACTIVE THAN MOST SPECIES.
MR. O'DONNEL?
MR. O'DONNEL?
OH, GIVE A GIRL A CHANCE, WILL YOU?
LOOK AWAY, CASH.
ZZZZZZZ

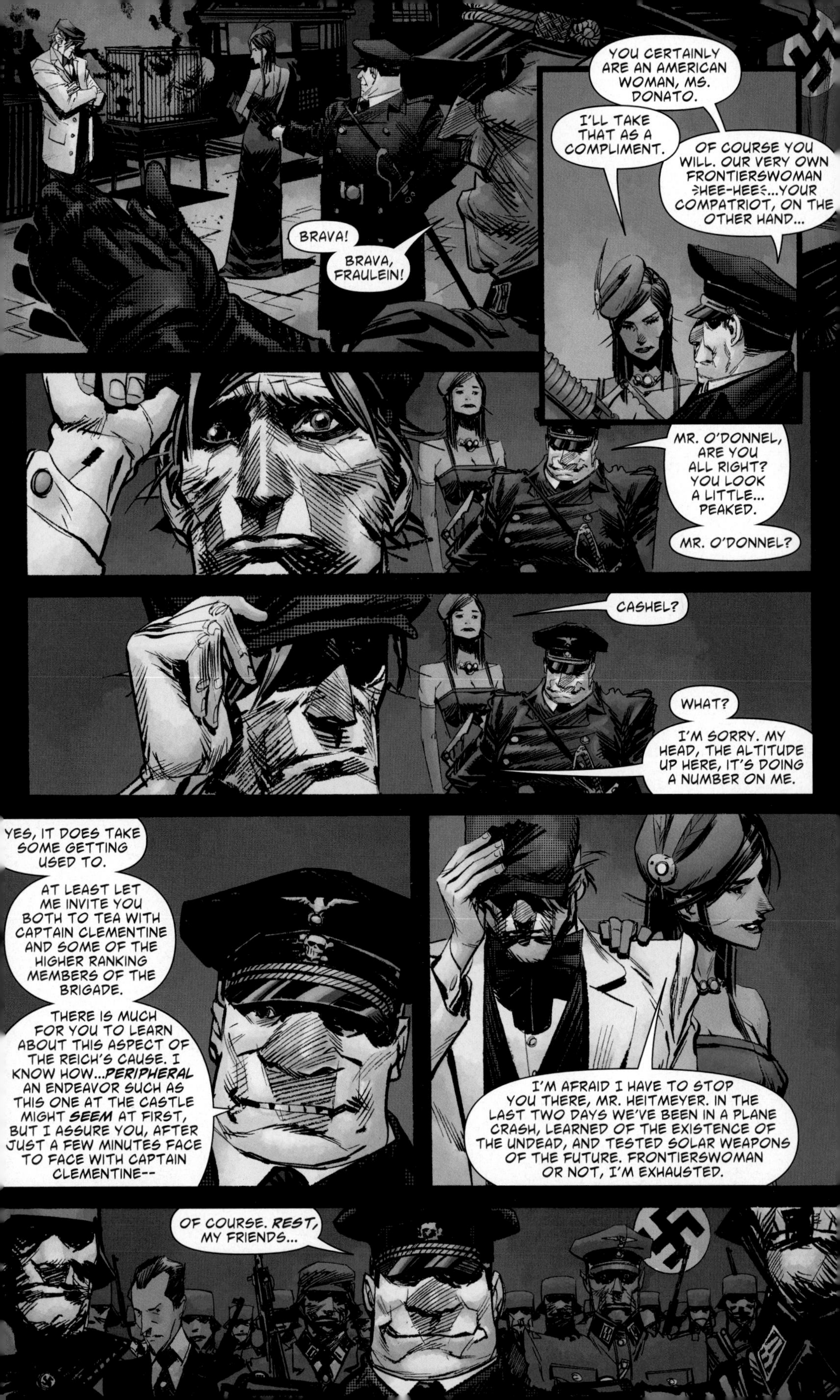
BRAVA!
BRAVA, FRAULEIN!
YOU CERTAINLY ARE AN AMERICAN WOMAN, MS. DONATO.
I'LL TAKE THAT AS A COMPLIMENT.
OF COURSE YOU WILL. OUR VERY OWN FRONTIERSWOMAN ›HEE-HEE‹...YOUR COMPATRIOT, ON THE OTHER HAND...
MR. O'DONNEL, ARE YOU ALL RIGHT? YOU LOOK A LITTLE... PEAKED.
MR. O'DONNEL?
CASHEL?
WHAT?
I'M SORRY. MY HEAD, THE ALTITUDE UP HERE, IT'S DOING A NUMBER ON ME.
YES, IT DOES TAKE SOME GETTING USED TO.
AT LEAST LET ME INVITE YOU BOTH TO TEA WITH CAPTAIN CLEMENTINE AND SOME OF THE HIGHER RANKING MEMBERS OF THE BRIGADE.
THERE IS MUCH FOR YOU TO LEARN ABOUT THIS ASPECT OF THE REICH'S CAUSE. I KNOW HOW...*PERIPHERAL* AN ENDEAVOR SUCH AS THIS ONE AT THE CASTLE MIGHT *SEEM* AT FIRST, BUT I ASSURE YOU, AFTER JUST A FEW MINUTES FACE TO FACE WITH CAPTAIN CLEMENTINE--
I'M AFRAID I HAVE TO STOP YOU THERE, MR. HEITMEYER. IN THE LAST TWO DAYS WE'VE BEEN IN A PLANE CRASH, LEARNED OF THE EXISTENCE OF THE UNDEAD, AND TESTED SOLAR WEAPONS OF THE FUTURE. FRONTIERSWOMAN OR NOT, I'M EXHAUSTED.
OF COURSE. *REST*, MY FRIENDS...

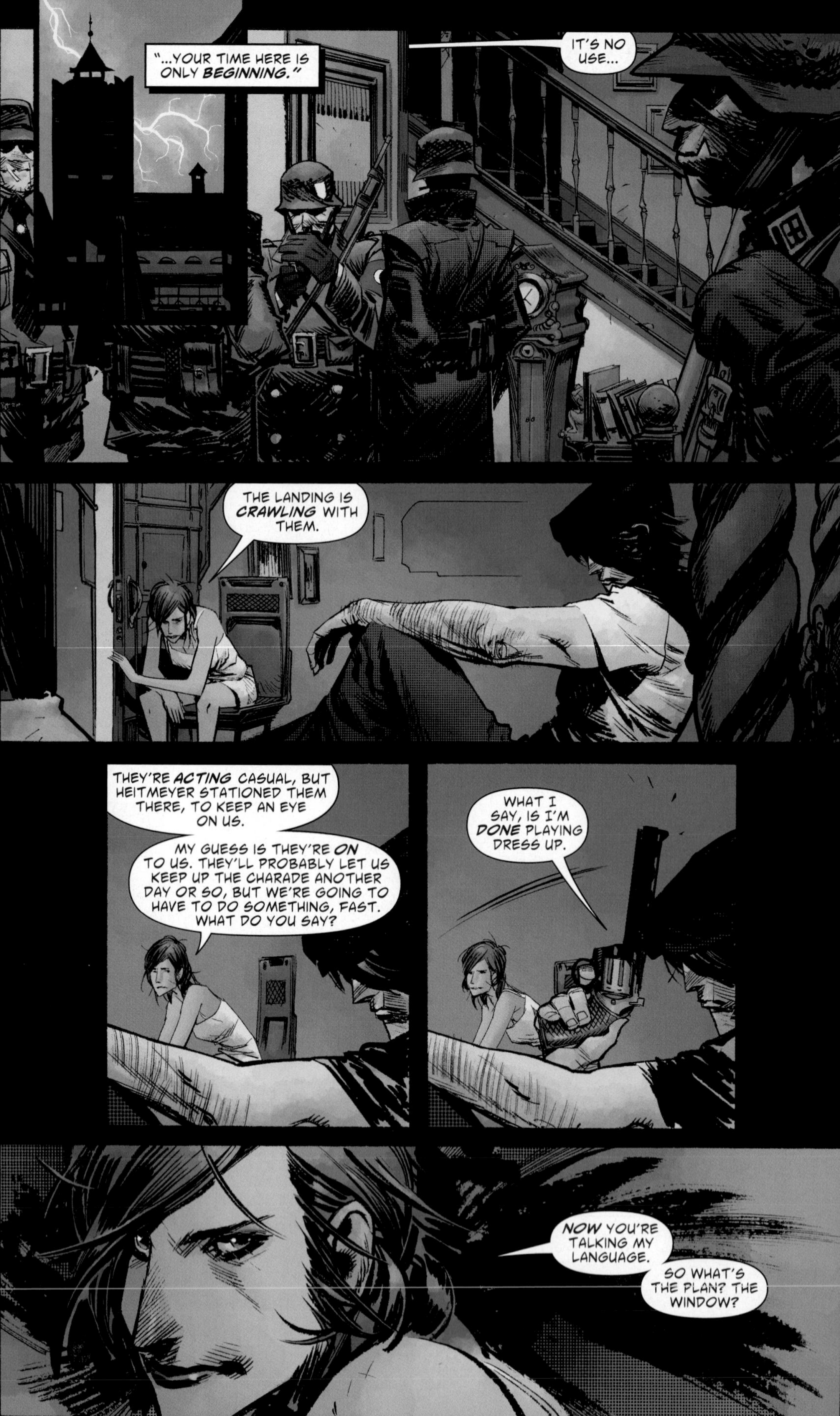
"...YOUR TIME HERE IS ONLY BEGINNING."
IT'S NO USE...
THE LANDING IS CRAWLING WITH THEM.
THEY'RE ACTING CASUAL, BUT HEITMEYER STATIONED THEM THERE, TO KEEP AN EYE ON US.
MY GUESS IS THEY'RE ON TO US. THEY'LL PROBABLY LET US KEEP UP THE CHARADE ANOTHER DAY OR SO, BUT WE'RE GOING TO HAVE TO DO SOMETHING, FAST. WHAT DO YOU SAY?
WHAT I SAY, IS I'M DONE PLAYING DRESS UP.
NOW YOU'RE TALKING MY LANGUAGE.
SO WHAT'S THE PLAN? THE WINDOW?

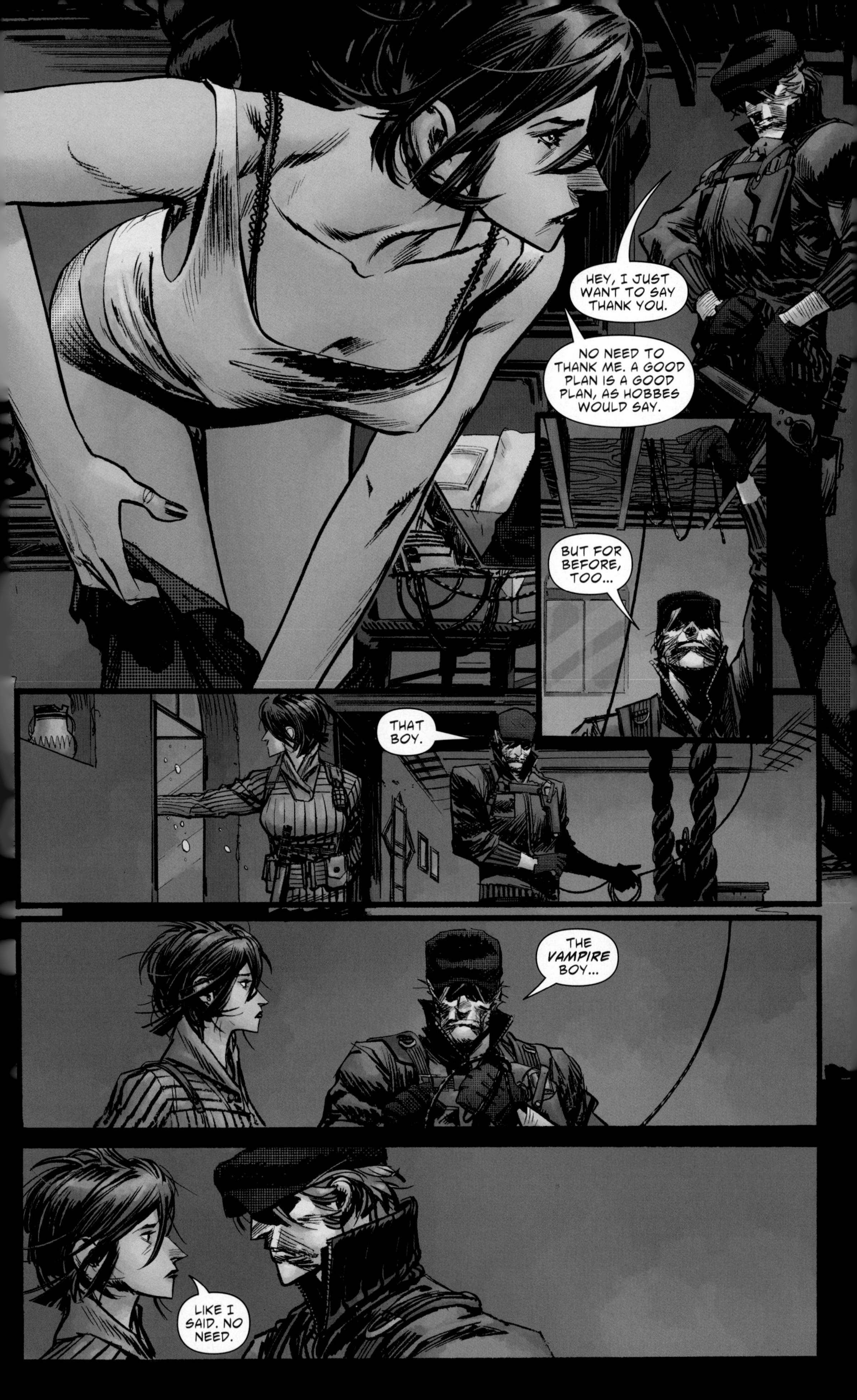
HEY, I JUST WANT TO SAY THANK YOU.
NO NEED TO THANK ME. A GOOD PLAN IS A GOOD PLAN, AS HOBBES WOULD SAY.
BUT FOR BEFORE, TOO...
THAT BOY.
THE *VAMPIRE* BOY...
LIKE I SAID. NO NEED.

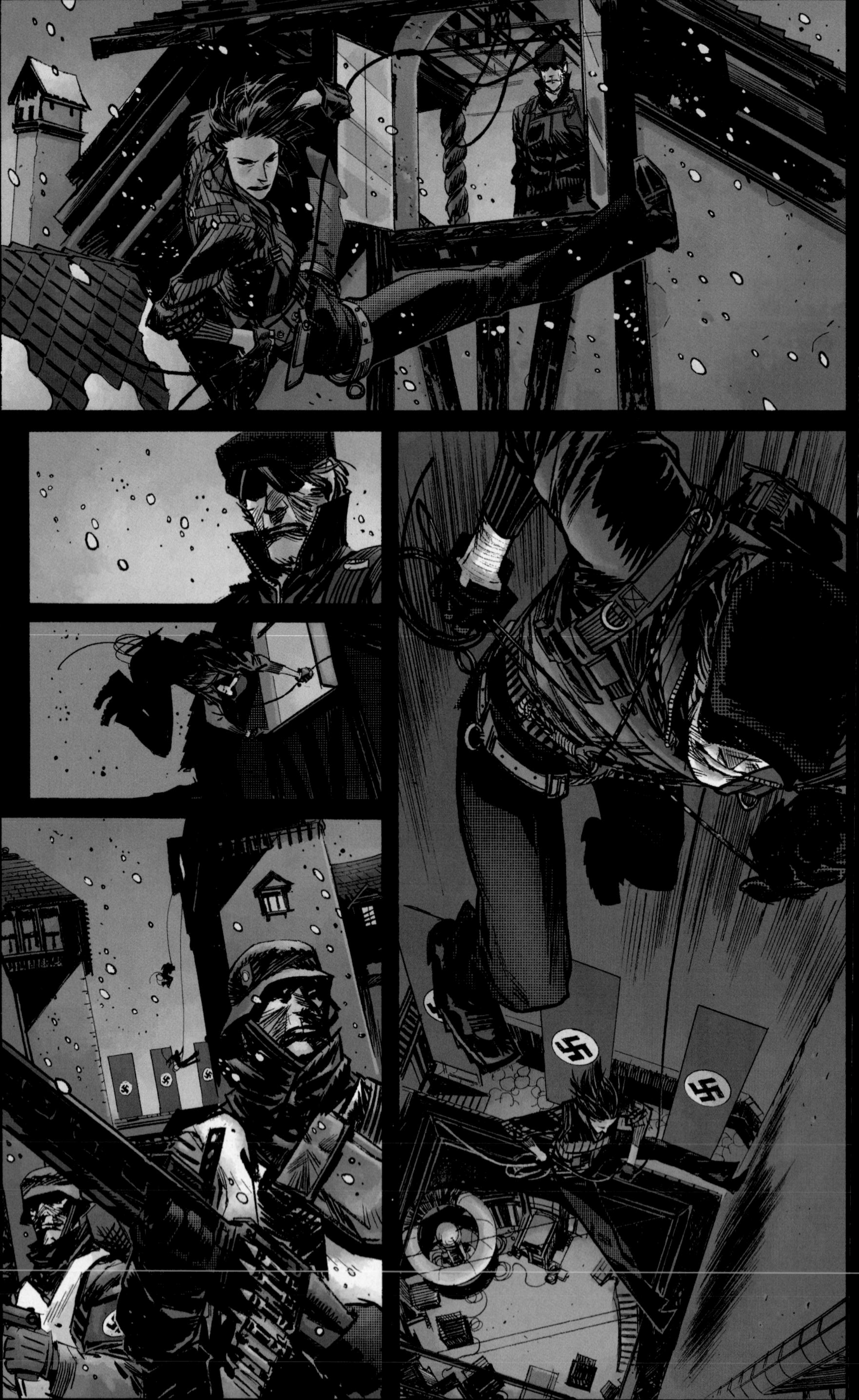

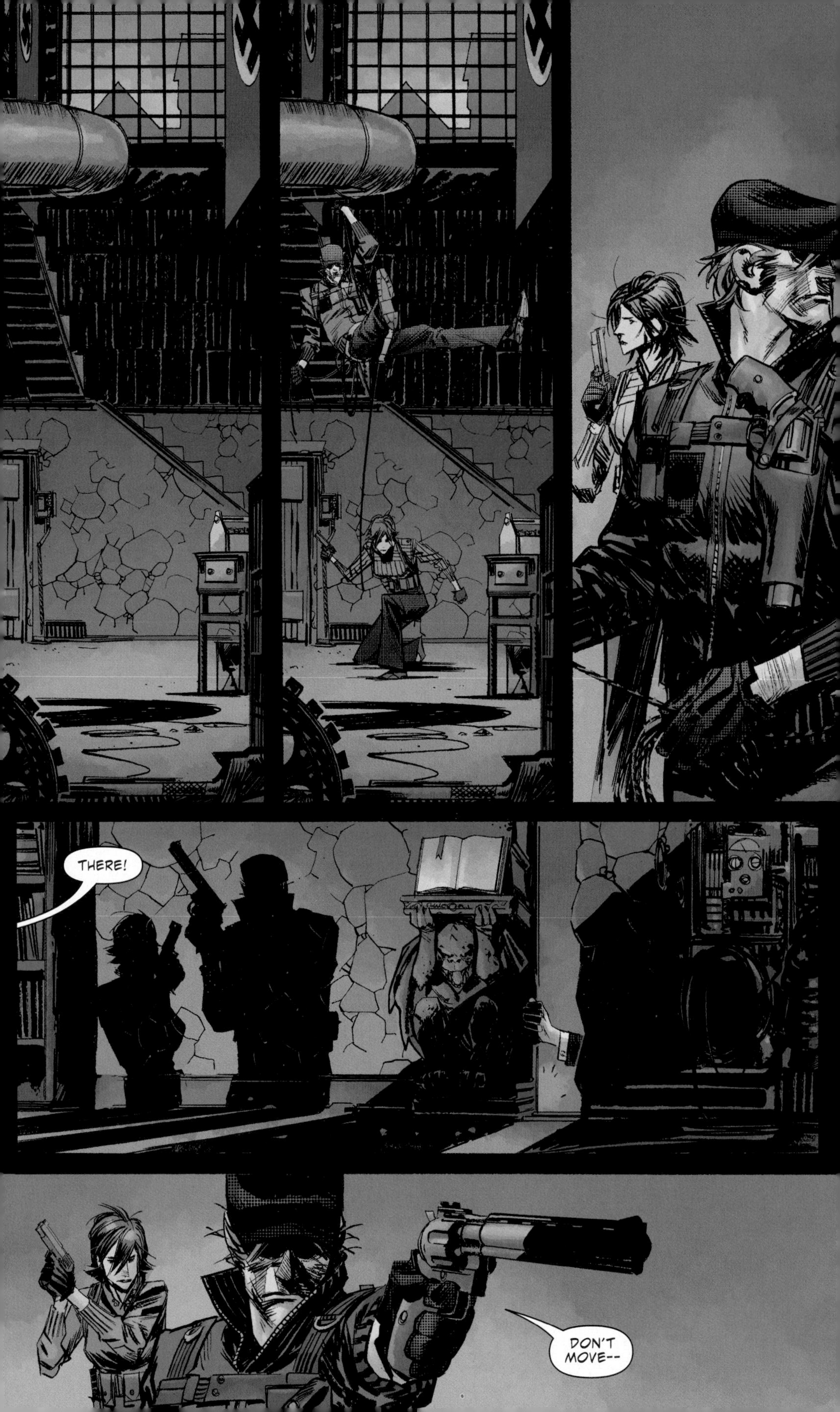
THERE!
DON'T MOVE--

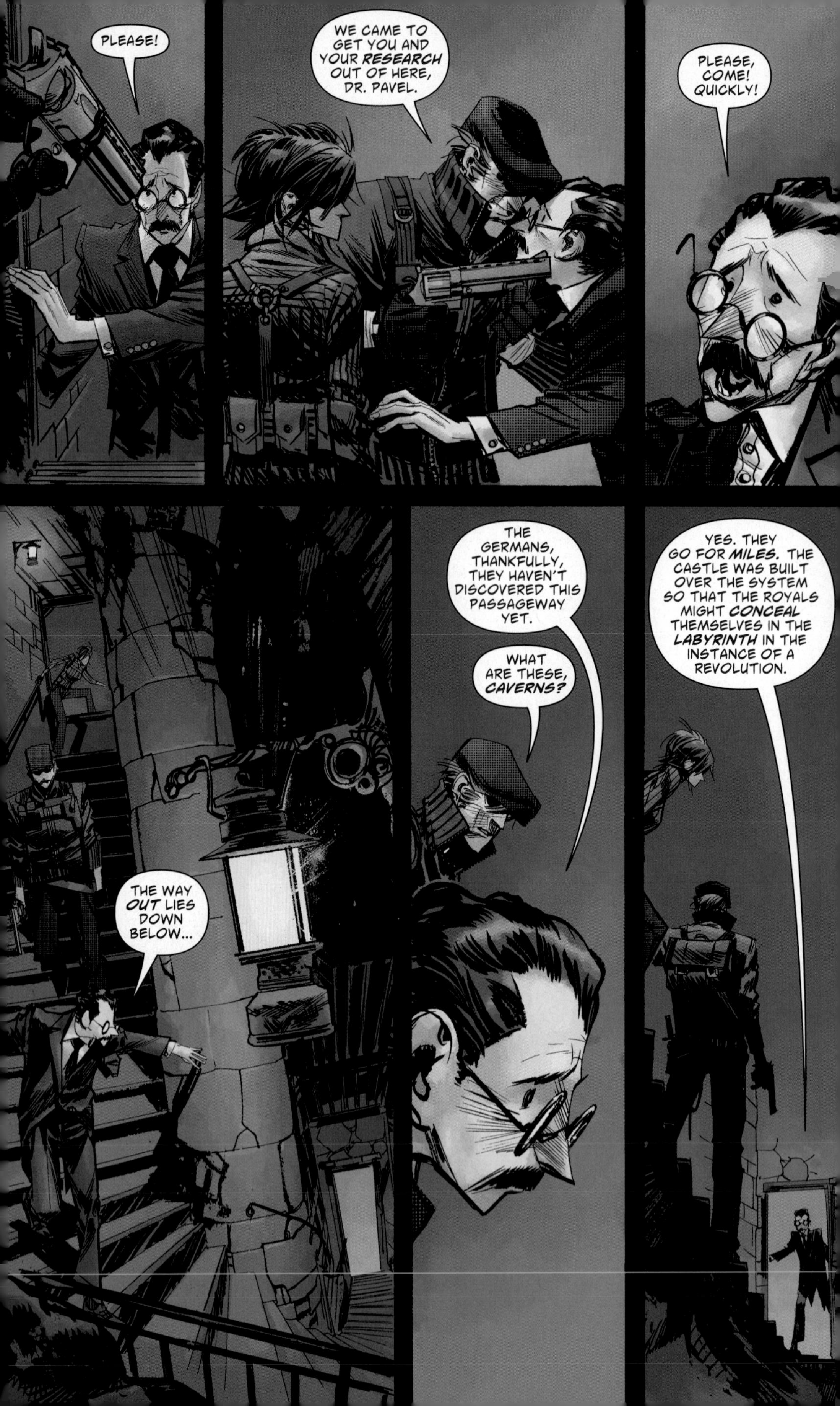
PLEASE!
WE CAME TO GET YOU AND YOUR RESEARCH OUT OF HERE, DR. PAVEL.
PLEASE, COME! QUICKLY!
THE WAY OUT LIES DOWN BELOW...
THE GERMANS, THANKFULLY, THEY HAVEN'T DISCOVERED THIS PASSAGEWAY YET.
WHAT ARE THESE, CAVERNS?
YES. THEY GO FOR MILES. THE CASTLE WAS BUILT OVER THE SYSTEM SO THAT THE ROYALS MIGHT CONCEAL THEMSELVES IN THE LABYRINTH IN THE INSTANCE OF A REVOLUTION.

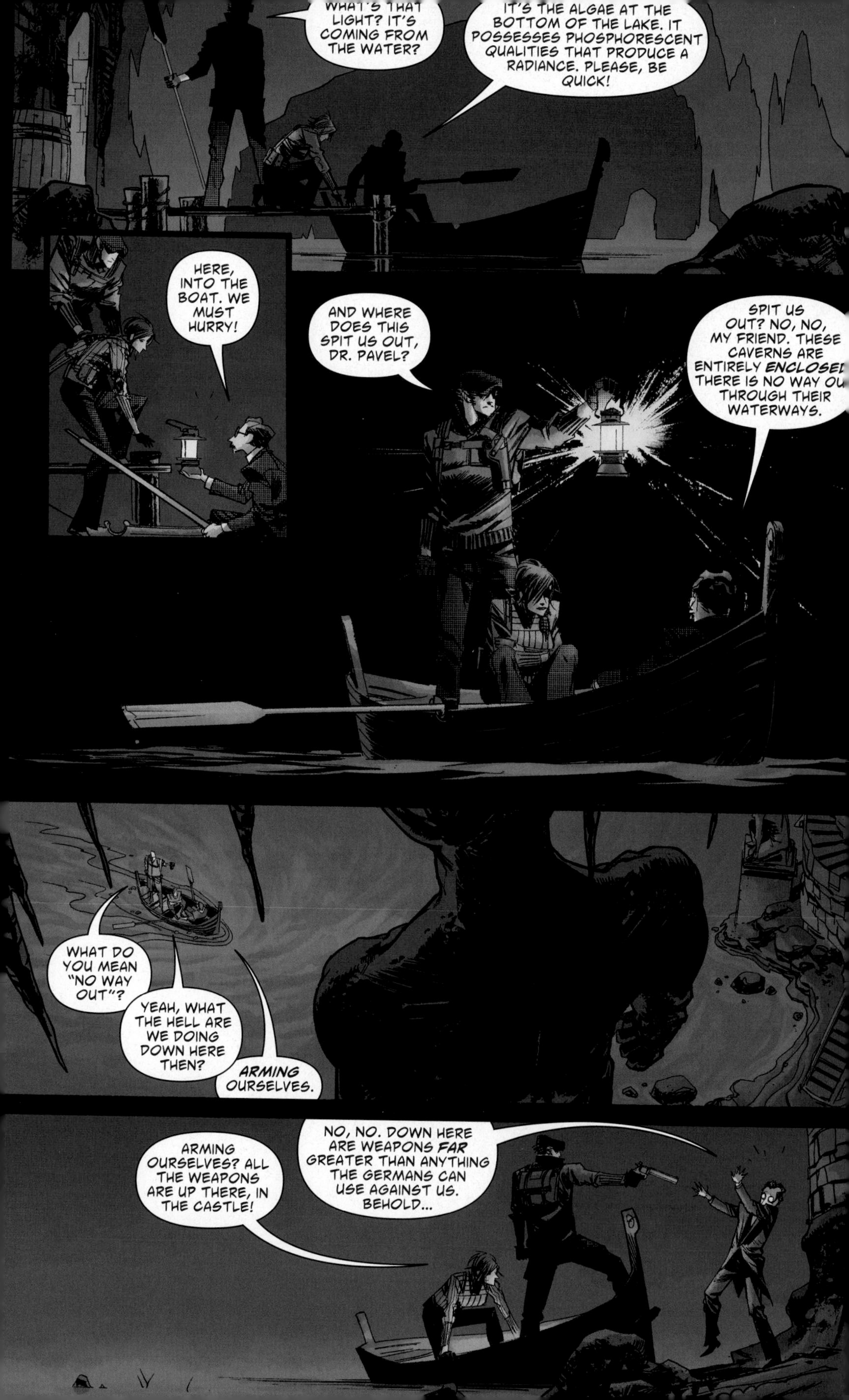
WHAT'S THAT LIGHT? IT'S COMING FROM THE WATER?
IT'S THE ALGAE AT THE BOTTOM OF THE LAKE. IT POSSESSES PHOSPHORESCENT QUALITIES THAT PRODUCE A RADIANCE. PLEASE, BE QUICK!
HERE, INTO THE BOAT. WE MUST HURRY!
AND WHERE DOES THIS SPIT US OUT, DR. PAVEL?
SPIT US OUT? NO, NO, MY FRIEND. THESE CAVERNS ARE ENTIRELY ENCLOSED. THERE IS NO WAY OUT THROUGH THEIR WATERWAYS.
WHAT DO YOU MEAN "NO WAY OUT"?
YEAH, WHAT THE HELL ARE WE DOING DOWN HERE THEN?
ARMING OURSELVES.
ARMING OURSELVES? ALL THE WEAPONS ARE UP THERE, IN THE CASTLE!
NO, NO. DOWN HERE ARE WEAPONS FAR GREATER THAN ANYTHING THE GERMANS CAN USE AGAINST US. BEHOLD...

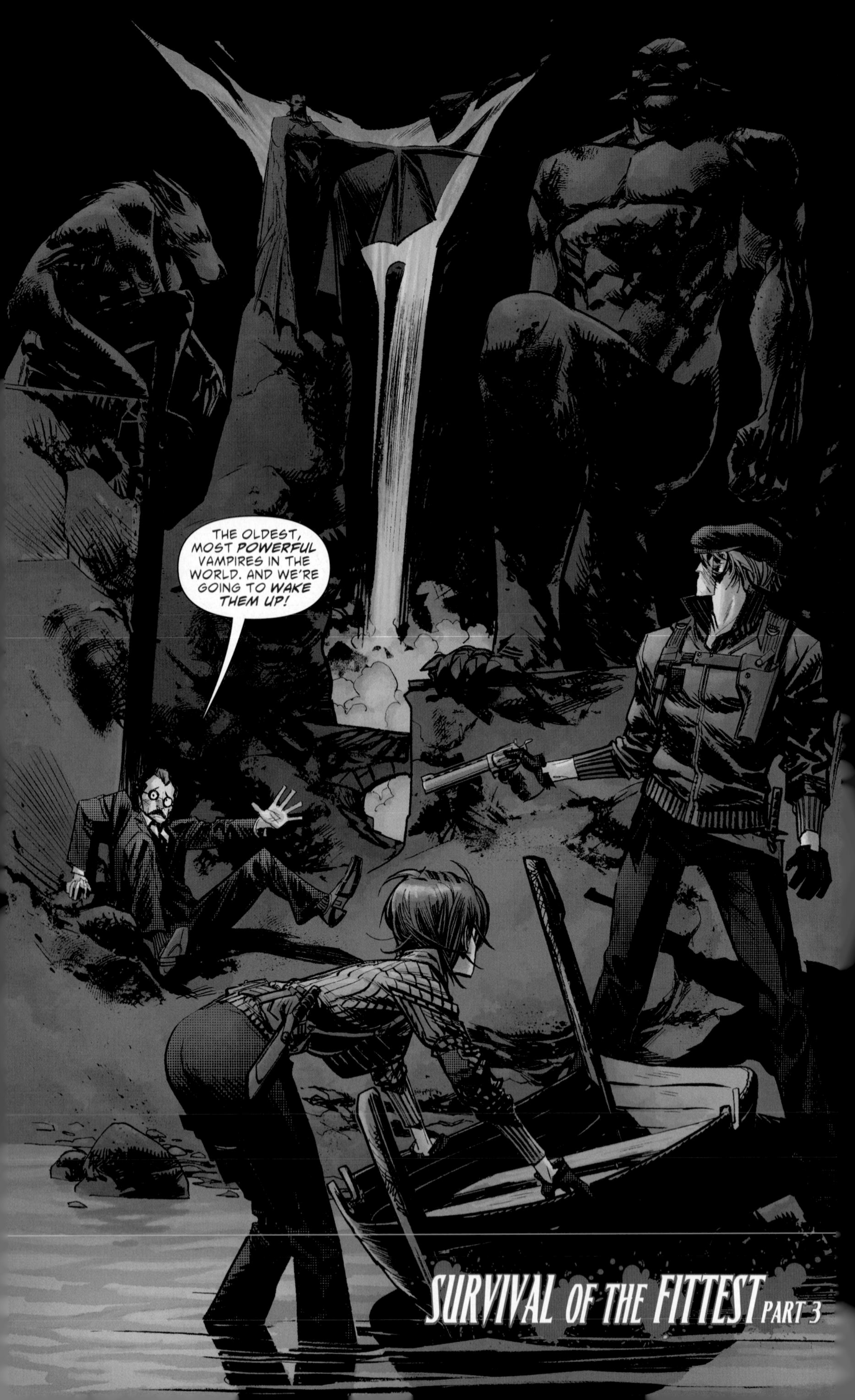

THE OLDEST, MOST POWERFUL VAMPIRES IN THE WORLD. AND WE'RE GOING TO WAKE THEM UP!
SURVIVAL OF THE FITTEST PART 3

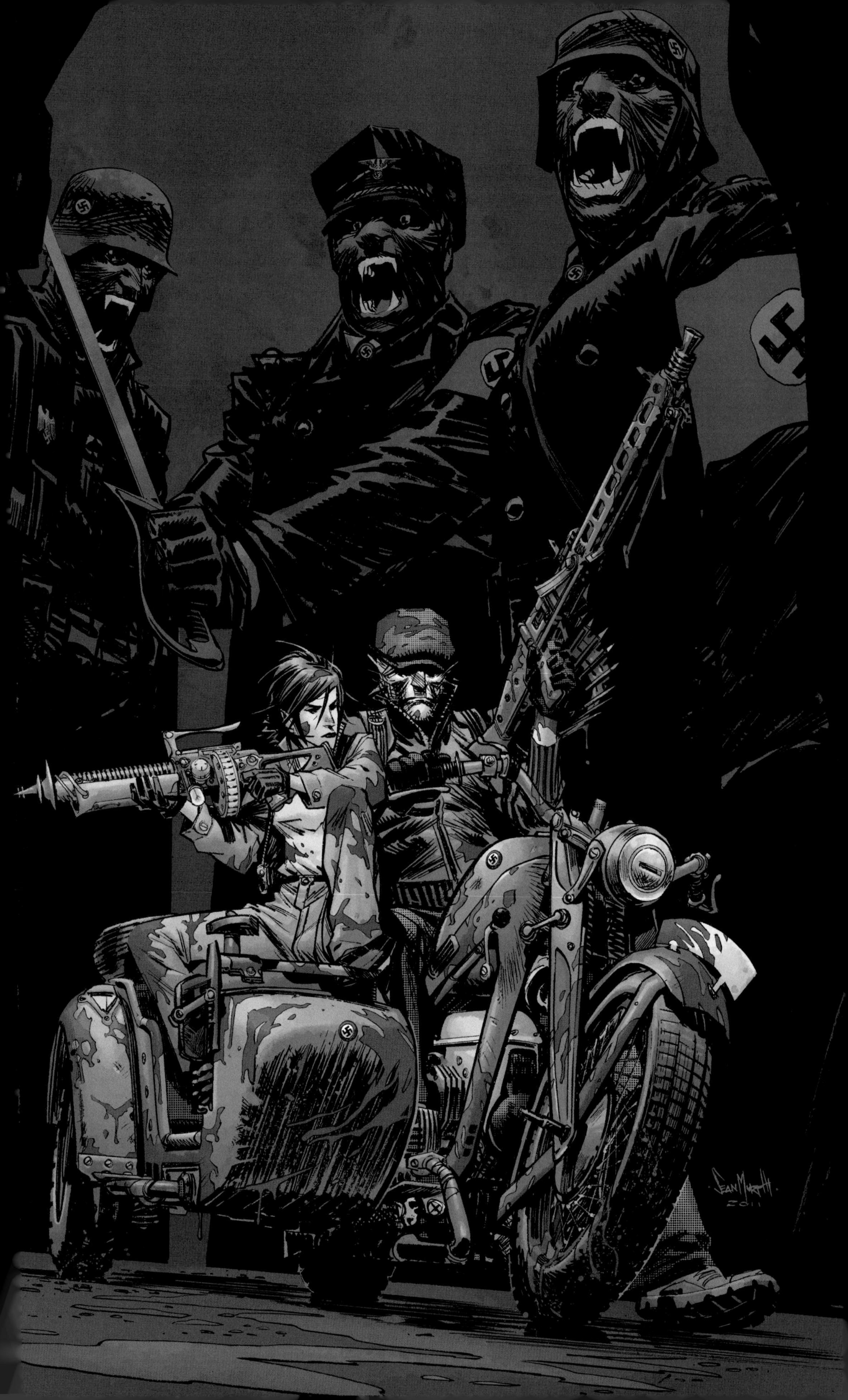

**Survival
of the Fittest**
Part Four

Sean Murphy
Artist and cover

Dave Stewart
cover color

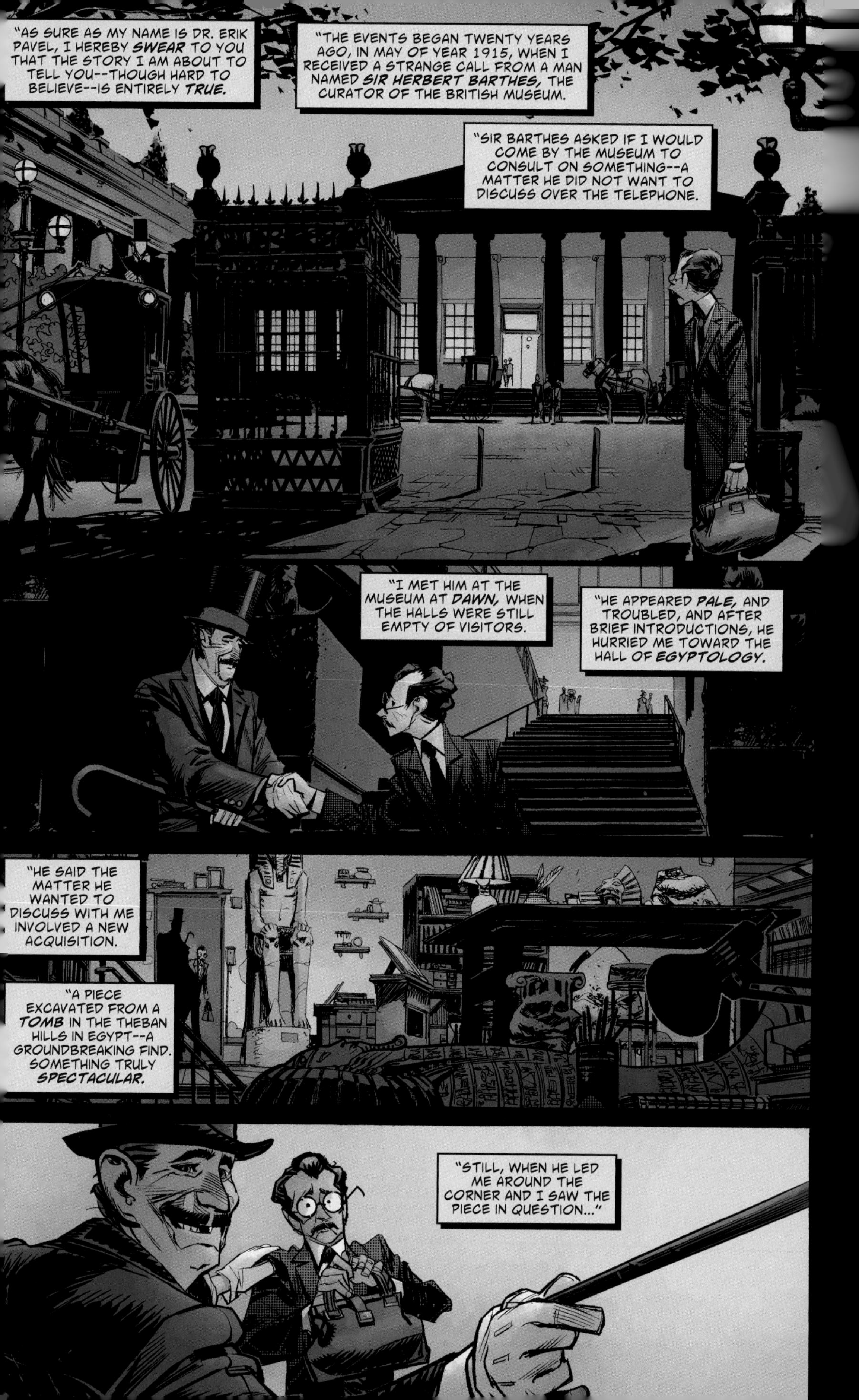
"AS SURE AS MY NAME IS DR. ERIK PAVEL, I HEREBY SWEAR TO YOU THAT THE STORY I AM ABOUT TO TELL YOU--THOUGH HARD TO BELIEVE--IS ENTIRELY TRUE.
"THE EVENTS BEGAN TWENTY YEARS AGO, IN MAY OF YEAR 1915, WHEN I RECEIVED A STRANGE CALL FROM A MAN NAMED SIR HERBERT BARTHES, THE CURATOR OF THE BRITISH MUSEUM.
"SIR BARTHES ASKED IF I WOULD COME BY THE MUSEUM TO CONSULT ON SOMETHING--A MATTER HE DID NOT WANT TO DISCUSS OVER THE TELEPHONE.
"I MET HIM AT THE MUSEUM AT DAWN, WHEN THE HALLS WERE STILL EMPTY OF VISITORS.
"HE APPEARED PALE, AND TROUBLED, AND AFTER BRIEF INTRODUCTIONS, HE HURRIED ME TOWARD THE HALL OF EGYPTOLOGY.
"HE SAID THE MATTER HE WANTED TO DISCUSS WITH ME INVOLVED A NEW ACQUISITION.
"A PIECE EXCAVATED FROM A TOMB IN THE THEBAN HILLS IN EGYPT--A GROUNDBREAKING FIND. SOMETHING TRULY SPECTACULAR.
"STILL, WHEN HE LED ME AROUND THE CORNER AND I SAW THE PIECE IN QUESTION..."

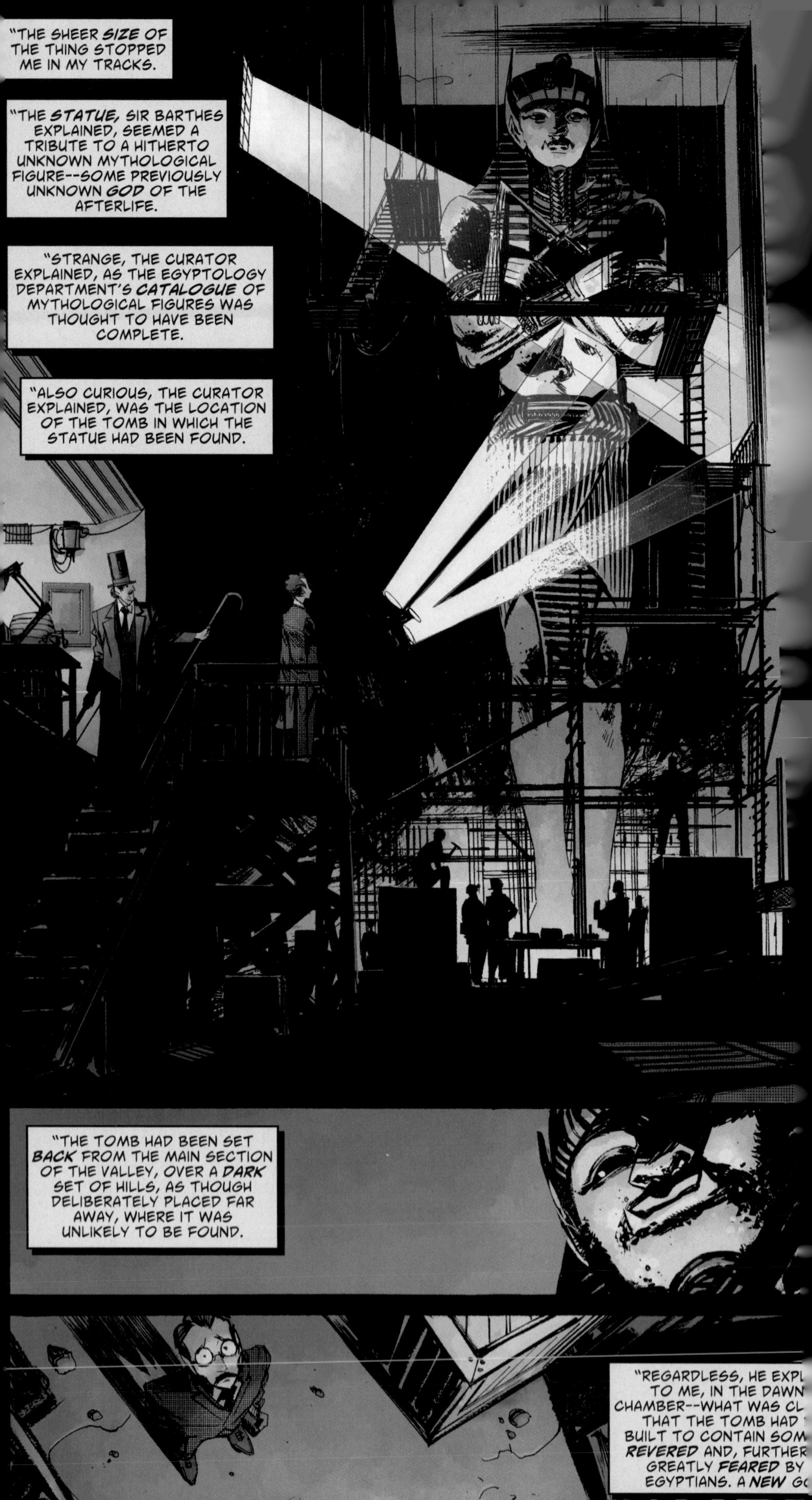
"THE SHEER *SIZE* OF THE THING STOPPED ME IN MY TRACKS.
"THE *STATUE,* SIR BARTHES EXPLAINED, SEEMED A TRIBUTE TO A HITHERTO UNKNOWN MYTHOLOGICAL FIGURE--SOME PREVIOUSLY UNKNOWN *GOD* OF THE AFTERLIFE.
"STRANGE, THE CURATOR EXPLAINED, AS THE EGYPTOLOGY DEPARTMENT'S *CATALOGUE* OF MYTHOLOGICAL FIGURES WAS THOUGHT TO HAVE BEEN COMPLETE.
"ALSO CURIOUS, THE CURATOR EXPLAINED, WAS THE LOCATION OF THE TOMB IN WHICH THE STATUE HAD BEEN FOUND.
"THE TOMB HAD BEEN SET *BACK* FROM THE MAIN SECTION OF THE VALLEY, OVER A *DARK* SET OF HILLS, AS THOUGH DELIBERATELY PLACED FAR AWAY, WHERE IT WAS UNLIKELY TO BE FOUND.
"REGARDLESS, HE EXPL TO ME, IN THE DAWN CHAMBER--WHAT WAS CL THAT THE TOMB HAD BUILT TO CONTAIN SOM *REVERED* AND, FURTHER GREATLY *FEARED* BY EGYPTIANS. A *NEW* G

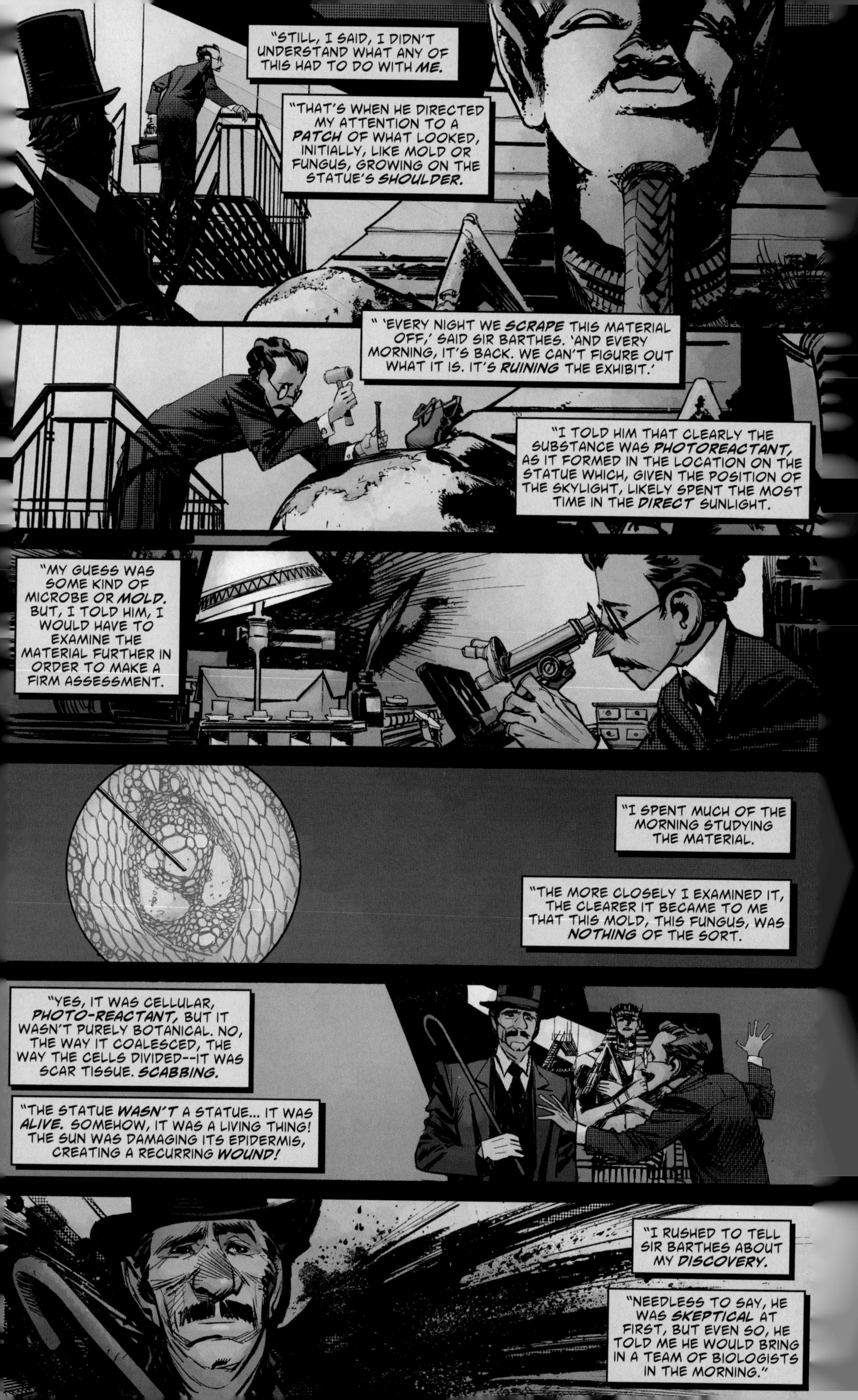
"STILL, I SAID, I DIDN'T UNDERSTAND WHAT ANY OF THIS HAD TO DO WITH ME.
"THAT'S WHEN HE DIRECTED MY ATTENTION TO A PATCH OF WHAT LOOKED, INITIALLY, LIKE MOLD OR FUNGUS, GROWING ON THE STATUE'S SHOULDER.
" 'EVERY NIGHT WE SCRAPE THIS MATERIAL OFF,' SAID SIR BARTHES. 'AND EVERY MORNING, IT'S BACK. WE CAN'T FIGURE OUT WHAT IT IS. IT'S RUINING THE EXHIBIT.'
"I TOLD HIM THAT CLEARLY THE SUBSTANCE WAS PHOTOREACTANT, AS IT FORMED IN THE LOCATION ON THE STATUE WHICH, GIVEN THE POSITION OF THE SKYLIGHT, LIKELY SPENT THE MOST TIME IN THE DIRECT SUNLIGHT.
"MY GUESS WAS SOME KIND OF MICROBE OR MOLD. BUT, I TOLD HIM, I WOULD HAVE TO EXAMINE THE MATERIAL FURTHER IN ORDER TO MAKE A FIRM ASSESSMENT.
"I SPENT MUCH OF THE MORNING STUDYING THE MATERIAL.
"THE MORE CLOSELY I EXAMINED IT, THE CLEARER IT BECAME TO ME THAT THIS MOLD, THIS FUNGUS, WAS NOTHING OF THE SORT.
"YES, IT WAS CELLULAR, PHOTO-REACTANT, BUT IT WASN'T PURELY BOTANICAL. NO, THE WAY IT COALESCED, THE WAY THE CELLS DIVIDED--IT WAS SCAR TISSUE. SCABBING.
"THE STATUE WASN'T A STATUE... IT WAS ALIVE. SOMEHOW, IT WAS A LIVING THING! THE SUN WAS DAMAGING ITS EPIDERMIS, CREATING A RECURRING WOUND!
"I RUSHED TO TELL SIR BARTHES ABOUT MY DISCOVERY.
"NEEDLESS TO SAY, HE WAS SKEPTICAL AT FIRST, BUT EVEN SO, HE TOLD ME HE WOULD BRING IN A TEAM OF BIOLOGISTS IN THE MORNING."

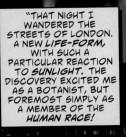

"THAT NIGHT I WANDERED THE STREETS OF LONDON. A NEW *LIFE-FORM*, WITH SUCH A PARTICULAR REACTION TO *SUNLIGHT*. THE DISCOVERY EXCITED ME AS A BOTANIST, BUT FOREMOST SIMPLY AS A MEMBER OF THE *HUMAN RACE!*

"THE NEXT DAY, I WAS AT THE MUSEUM AT FIRST LIGHT...

"WHAT I FOUND WHEN I ENTERED THE MUSEUM'S EGYPTIAN COLLECTION, THOUGH...

"WAS A SIGHT I WILL NEVER FORGET.

"I WAS SPEECHLESS WITH *ANGER.* BUT SIR BARTHES EXPLAINED THAT THE STATUE HAD BEEN FOUND TO BE A FRAUD, AND HAD TO BE DESTROYED IMMEDIATELY.

"DEEP DOWN, THOUGH, IN MY *SOUL,* I KNEW THE TRUTH. I KNEW THAT THE FIGURE I HAD EXAMINED HAD BEEN *ALIVE,* VIBRANTLY, STRANGELY SO.

"AND THAT WAS WHEN I REALIZED, IN MORE WAYS THAN ONE, THAT THE CREATURES YOUR PARENTS TELL YOU ABOUT AT BEDTIME, *MONSTERS* WONDROUS AND TERRIBLE BOTH, DO, IN FACT, WALK THE EARTH."

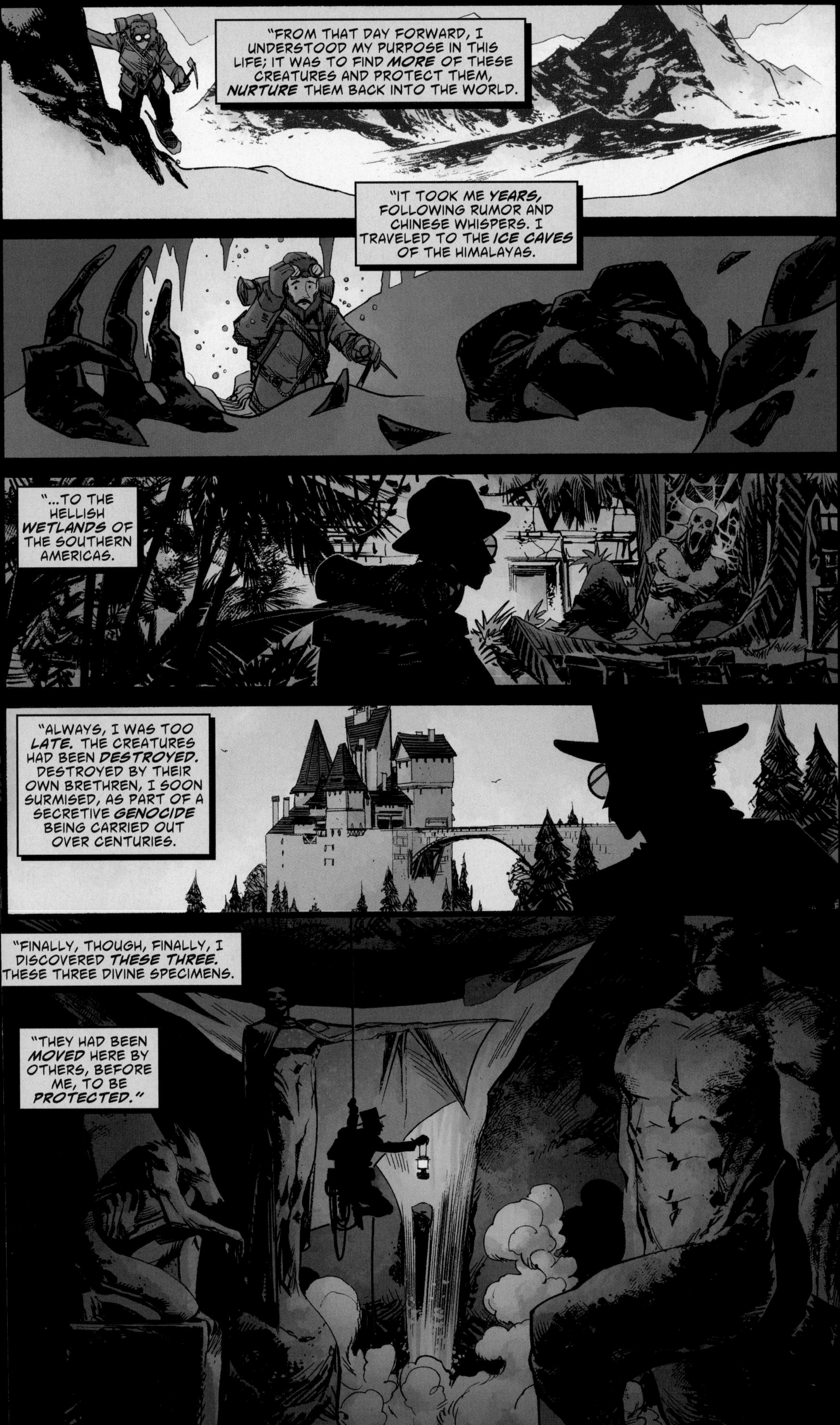
"FROM THAT DAY FORWARD, I UNDERSTOOD MY PURPOSE IN THIS LIFE; IT WAS TO FIND MORE OF THESE CREATURES AND PROTECT THEM, NURTURE THEM BACK INTO THE WORLD.
"IT TOOK ME YEARS, FOLLOWING RUMOR AND CHINESE WHISPERS. I TRAVELED TO THE ICE CAVES OF THE HIMALAYAS.
"...TO THE HELLISH WETLANDS OF THE SOUTHERN AMERICAS.
"ALWAYS, I WAS TOO LATE. THE CREATURES HAD BEEN DESTROYED. DESTROYED BY THEIR OWN BRETHREN, I SOON SURMISED, AS PART OF A SECRETIVE GENOCIDE BEING CARRIED OUT OVER CENTURIES.
"FINALLY, THOUGH, FINALLY, I DISCOVERED THESE THREE. THESE THREE DIVINE SPECIMENS.
"THEY HAD BEEN MOVED HERE BY OTHERS, BEFORE ME, TO BE PROTECTED."

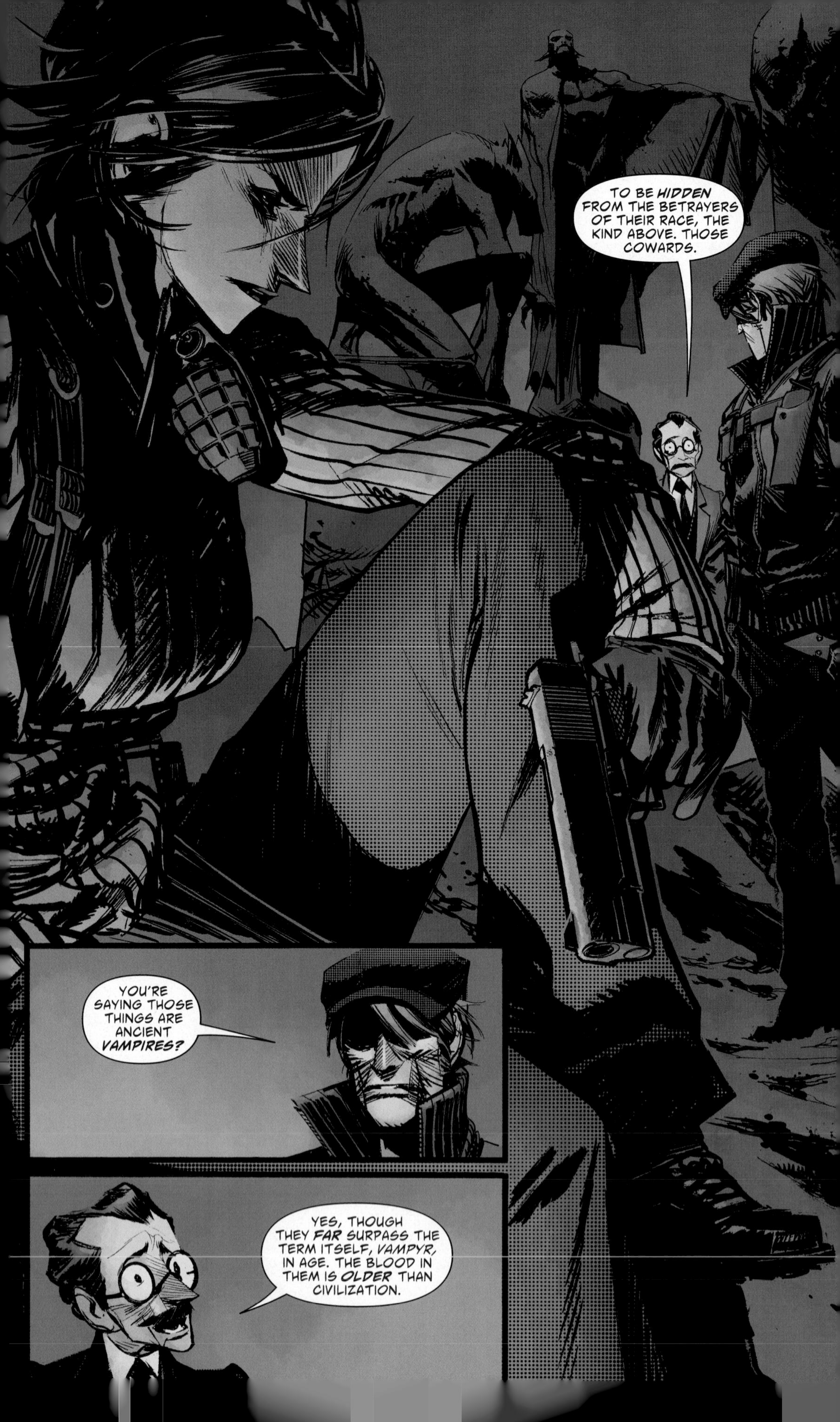
TO BE HIDDEN FROM THE BETRAYERS OF THEIR RACE, THE KIND ABOVE. THOSE COWARDS.
YOU'RE SAYING THOSE THINGS ARE ANCIENT VAMPIRES?
YES, THOUGH THEY FAR SURPASS THE TERM ITSELF, VAMPYR, IN AGE. THE BLOOD IN THEM IS OLDER THAN CIVILIZATION.

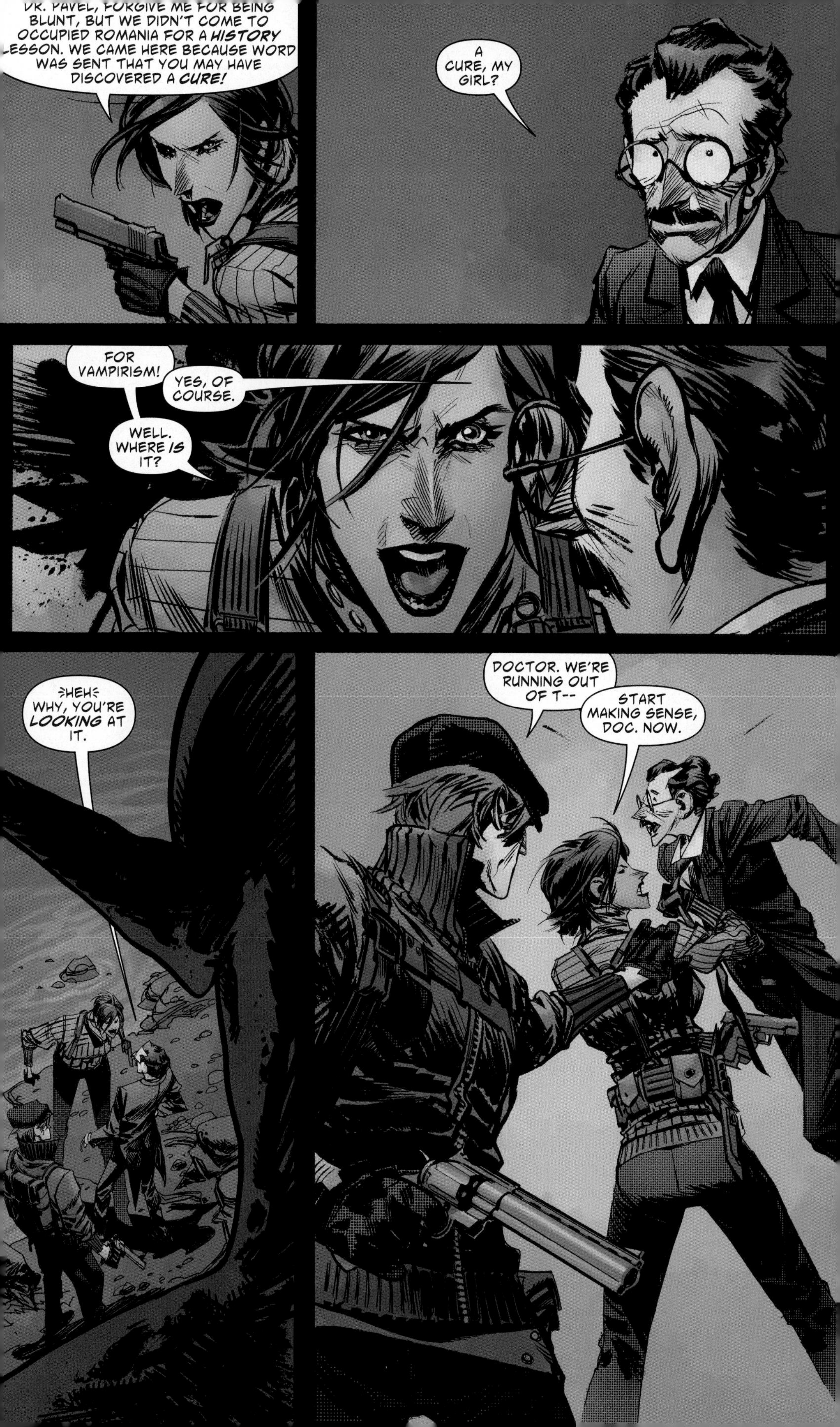
DR. PAVEL, FORGIVE ME FOR BEING BLUNT, BUT WE DIDN'T COME TO OCCUPIED ROMANIA FOR A HISTORY LESSON. WE CAME HERE BECAUSE WORD WAS SENT THAT YOU MAY HAVE DISCOVERED A CURE!
A CURE, MY GIRL?
FOR VAMPIRISM!
YES, OF COURSE.
WELL. WHERE IS IT?
HEH
WHY, YOU'RE LOOKING AT IT.
DOCTOR. WE'RE RUNNING OUT OF T--
START MAKING SENSE, DOC. NOW.

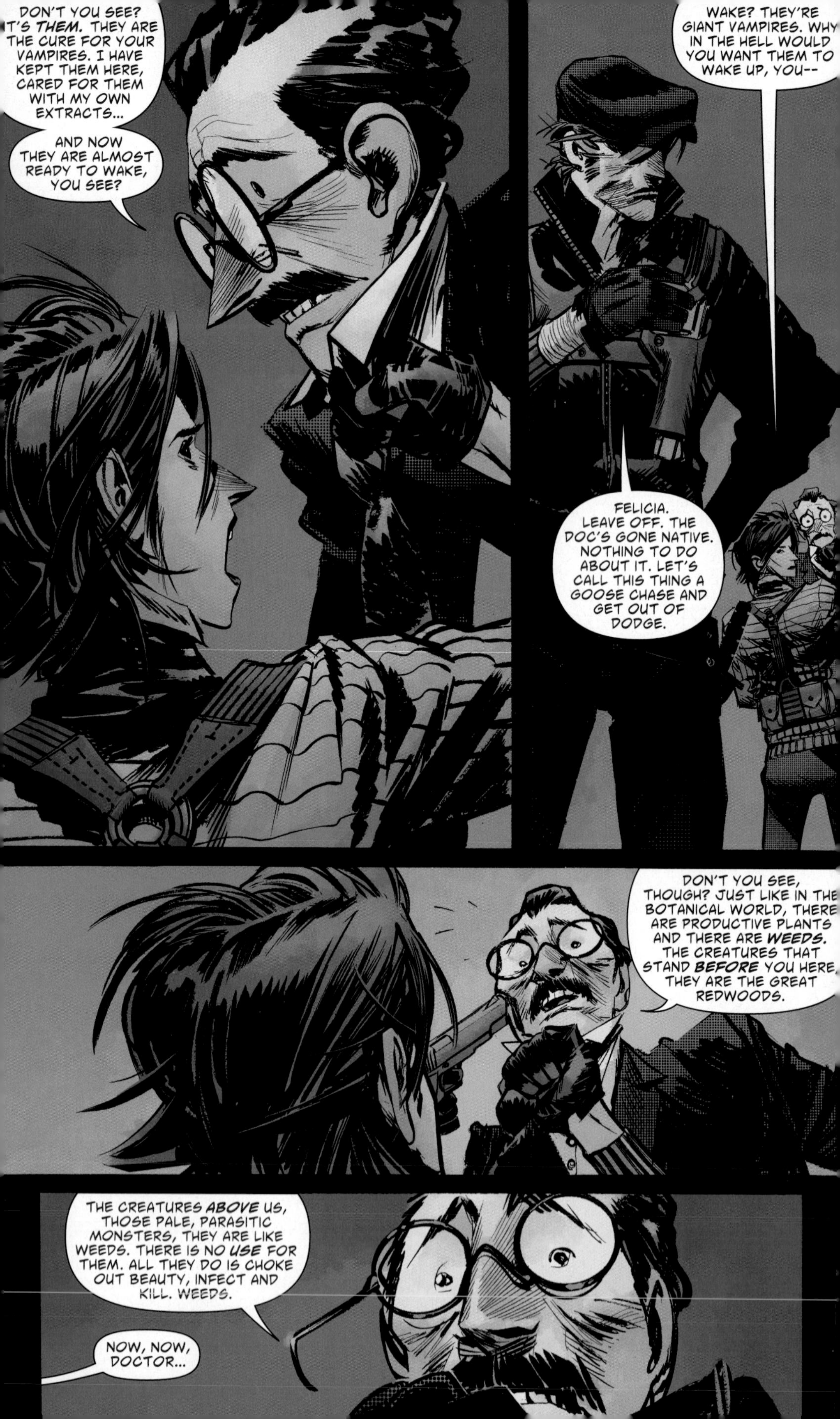
DON'T YOU SEE? IT'S THEM. THEY ARE THE CURE FOR YOUR VAMPIRES. I HAVE KEPT THEM HERE, CARED FOR THEM WITH MY OWN EXTRACTS...
AND NOW THEY ARE ALMOST READY TO WAKE, YOU SEE?
WAKE? THEY'RE GIANT VAMPIRES. WHY IN THE HELL WOULD YOU WANT THEM TO WAKE UP, YOU--
FELICIA. LEAVE OFF. THE DOC'S GONE NATIVE. NOTHING TO DO ABOUT IT. LET'S CALL THIS THING A GOOSE CHASE AND GET OUT OF DODGE.
DON'T YOU SEE, THOUGH? JUST LIKE IN THE BOTANICAL WORLD, THERE ARE PRODUCTIVE PLANTS AND THERE ARE WEEDS. THE CREATURES THAT STAND BEFORE YOU HERE, THEY ARE THE GREAT REDWOODS.
THE CREATURES ABOVE US, THOSE PALE, PARASITIC MONSTERS, THEY ARE LIKE WEEDS. THERE IS NO USE FOR THEM. ALL THEY DO IS CHOKE OUT BEAUTY, INFECT AND KILL. WEEDS.
NOW, NOW, DOCTOR...

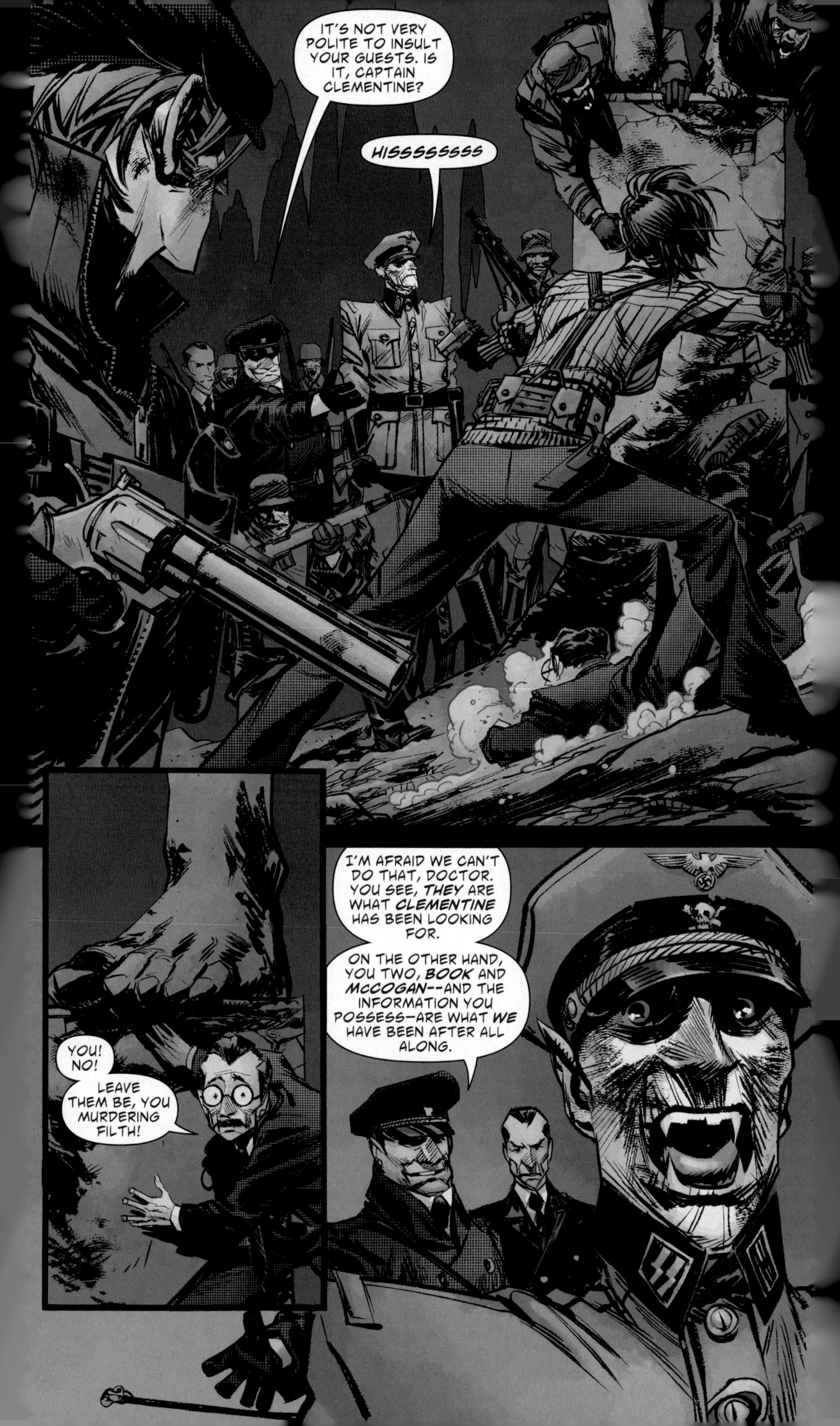
IT'S NOT VERY POLITE TO INSULT YOUR GUESTS. IS IT, CAPTAIN CLEMENTINE?
HISSSSSSSS
YOU! NO!
LEAVE THEM BE, YOU MURDERING FILTH!
I'M AFRAID WE CAN'T DO THAT, DOCTOR. YOU SEE, THEY ARE WHAT CLEMENTINE HAS BEEN LOOKING FOR.
ON THE OTHER HAND, YOU TWO, BOOK AND McCOGAN--AND THE INFORMATION YOU POSSESS—ARE WHAT WE HAVE BEEN AFTER ALL ALONG.

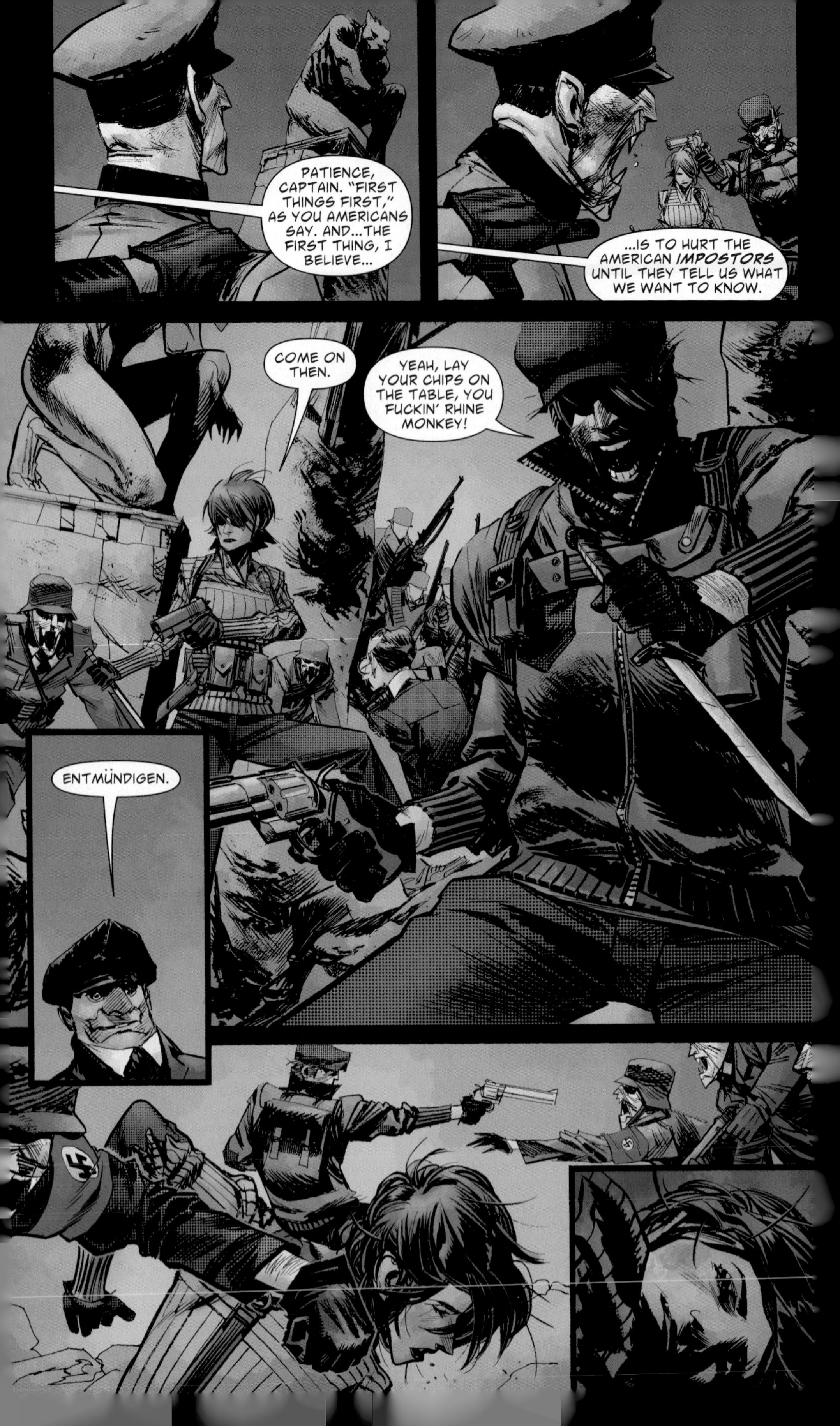
PATIENCE, CAPTAIN. "FIRST THINGS FIRST," AS YOU AMERICANS SAY. AND...THE FIRST THING, I BELIEVE...
...IS TO HURT THE AMERICAN IMPOSTORS UNTIL THEY TELL US WHAT WE WANT TO KNOW.
COME ON THEN.
YEAH, LAY YOUR CHIPS ON THE TABLE, YOU FUCKIN' RHINE MONKEY!
ENTMÜNDIGEN.

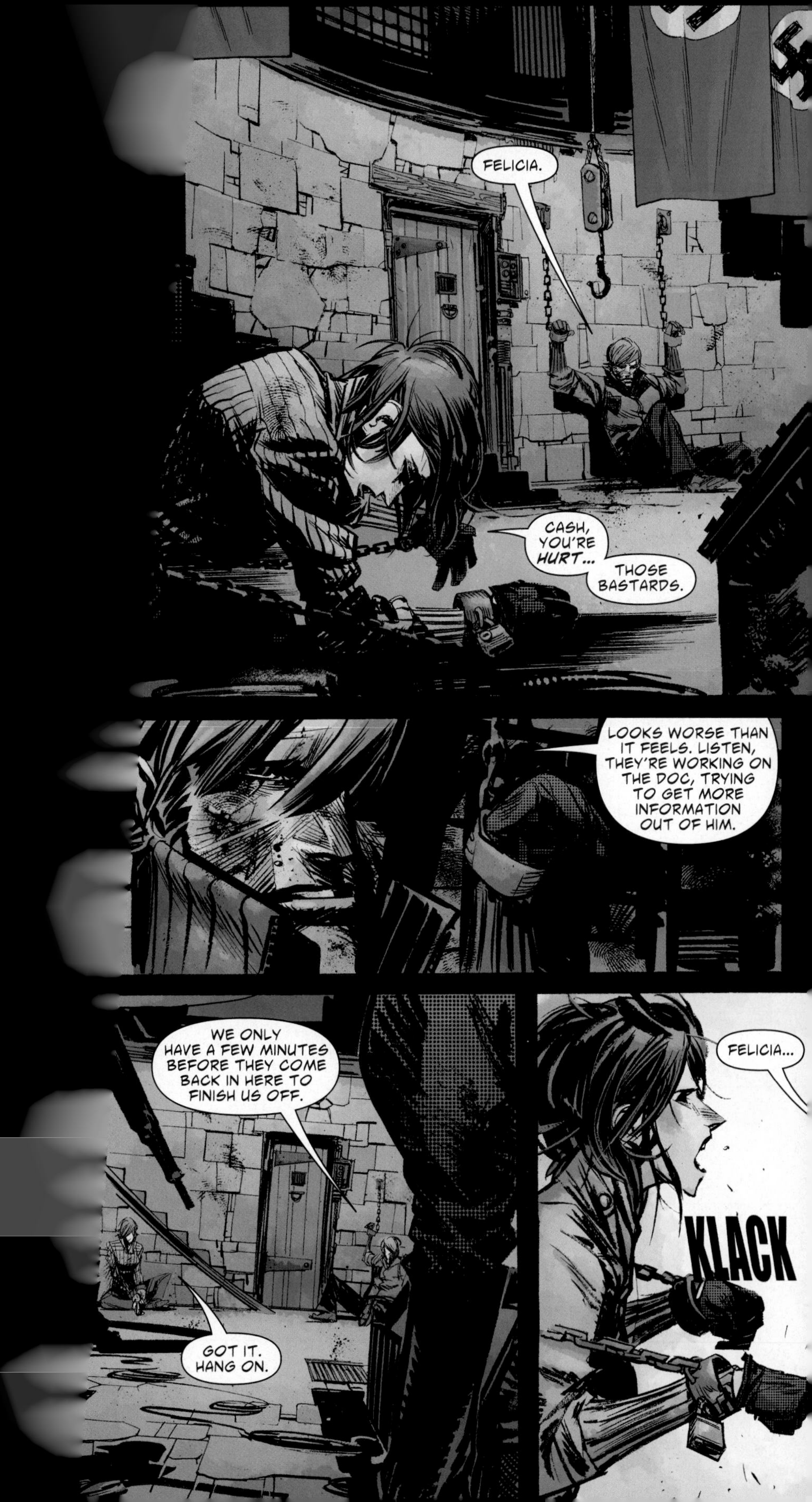
FELICIA.
CASH, YOU'RE *HURT*...
THOSE BASTARDS.
LOOKS WORSE THAN IT FEELS. LISTEN, THEY'RE WORKING ON THE DOC, TRYING TO GET MORE INFORMATION OUT OF HIM.
WE ONLY HAVE A FEW MINUTES BEFORE THEY COME BACK IN HERE TO FINISH US OFF.
GOT IT. HANG ON.
FELICIA...
KLACK

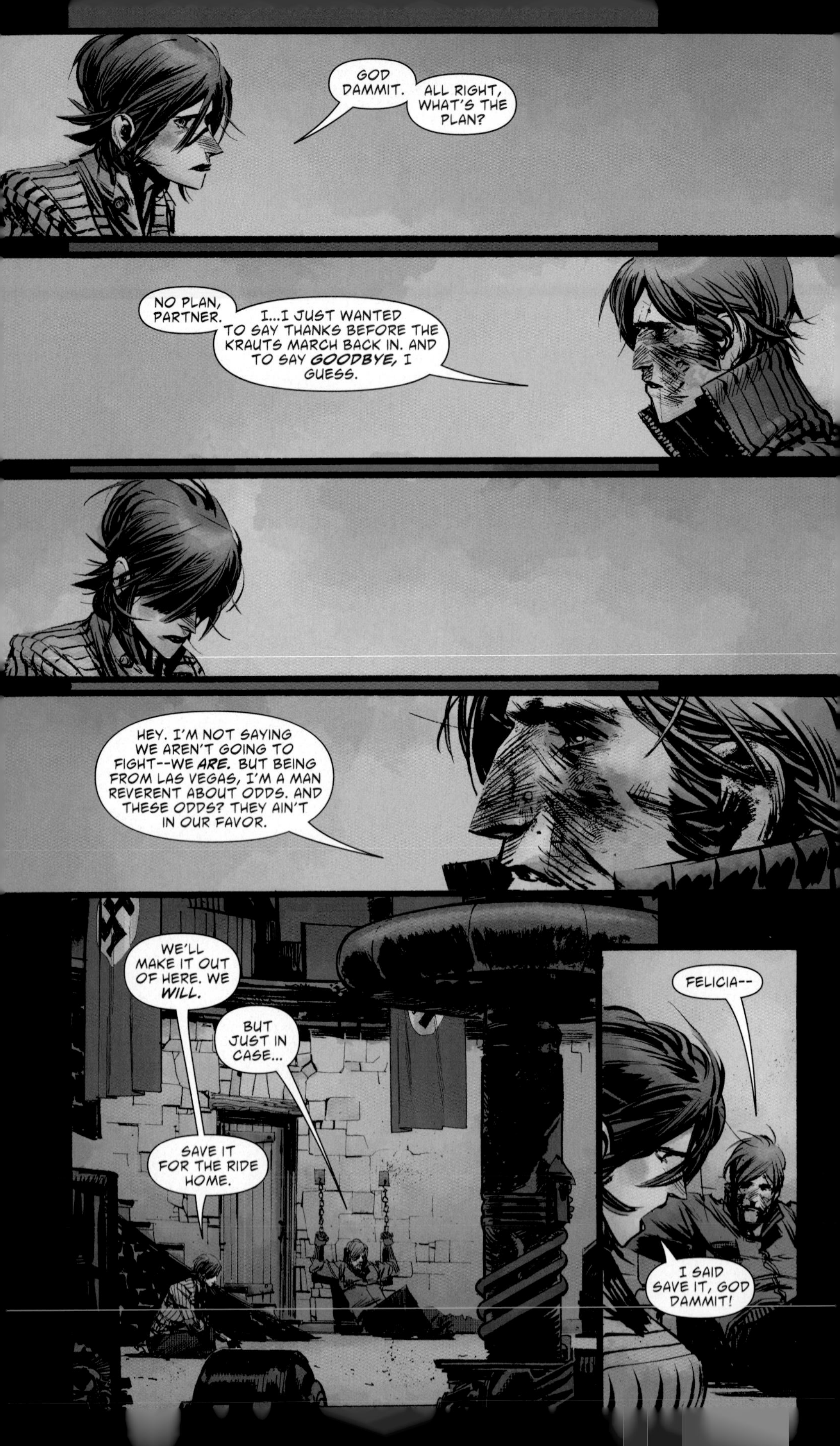
GOD DAMMIT.
ALL RIGHT, WHAT'S THE PLAN?
NO PLAN, PARTNER.
I...I JUST WANTED TO SAY THANKS BEFORE THE KRAUTS MARCH BACK IN. AND TO SAY GOODBYE, I GUESS.
HEY. I'M NOT SAYING WE AREN'T GOING TO FIGHT--WE ARE. BUT BEING FROM LAS VEGAS, I'M A MAN REVERENT ABOUT ODDS. AND THESE ODDS? THEY AIN'T IN OUR FAVOR.
WE'LL MAKE IT OUT OF HERE. WE WILL.
BUT JUST IN CASE...
SAVE IT FOR THE RIDE HOME.
FELICIA--
I SAID SAVE IT, GOD DAMMIT!

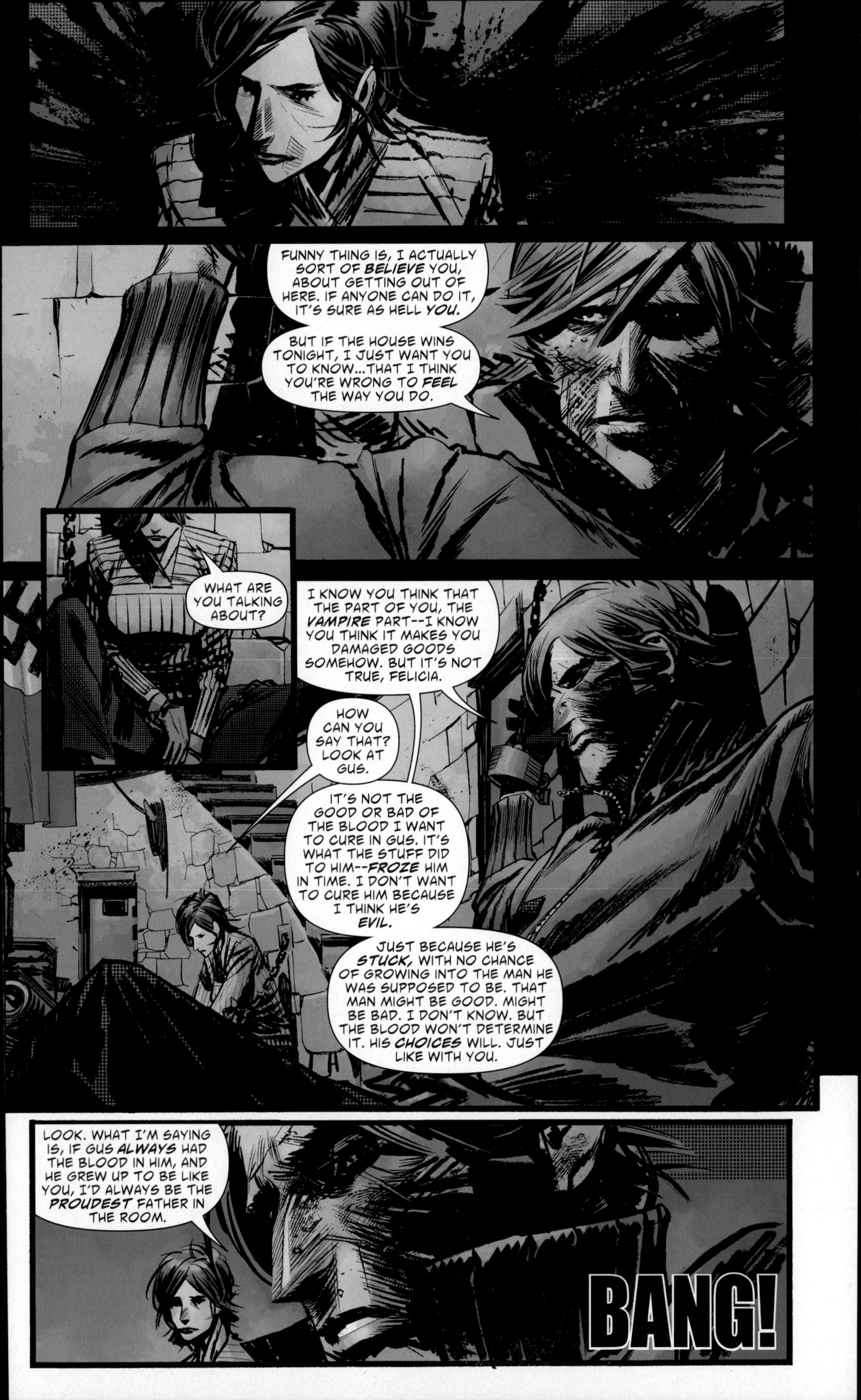

FUNNY THING IS, I ACTUALLY SORT OF BELIEVE YOU, ABOUT GETTING OUT OF HERE. IF ANYONE CAN DO IT, IT'S SURE AS HELL YOU.
BUT IF THE HOUSE WINS TONIGHT, I JUST WANT YOU TO KNOW...THAT I THINK YOU'RE WRONG TO FEEL THE WAY YOU DO.
WHAT ARE YOU TALKING ABOUT?
I KNOW YOU THINK THAT THE PART OF YOU, THE VAMPIRE PART--I KNOW YOU THINK IT MAKES YOU DAMAGED GOODS SOMEHOW. BUT IT'S NOT TRUE, FELICIA.
HOW CAN YOU SAY THAT? LOOK AT GUS.
IT'S NOT THE GOOD OR BAD OF THE BLOOD I WANT TO CURE IN GUS. IT'S WHAT THE STUFF DID TO HIM--FROZE HIM IN TIME. I DON'T WANT TO CURE HIM BECAUSE I THINK HE'S EVIL.
JUST BECAUSE HE'S STUCK, WITH NO CHANCE OF GROWING INTO THE MAN HE WAS SUPPOSED TO BE. THAT MAN MIGHT BE GOOD. MIGHT BE BAD. I DON'T KNOW. BUT THE BLOOD WON'T DETERMINE IT. HIS CHOICES WILL. JUST LIKE WITH YOU.
LOOK. WHAT I'M SAYING IS, IF GUS ALWAYS HAD THE BLOOD IN HIM, AND HE GREW UP TO BE LIKE YOU, I'D ALWAYS BE THE PROUDEST FATHER IN THE ROOM.
BANG!

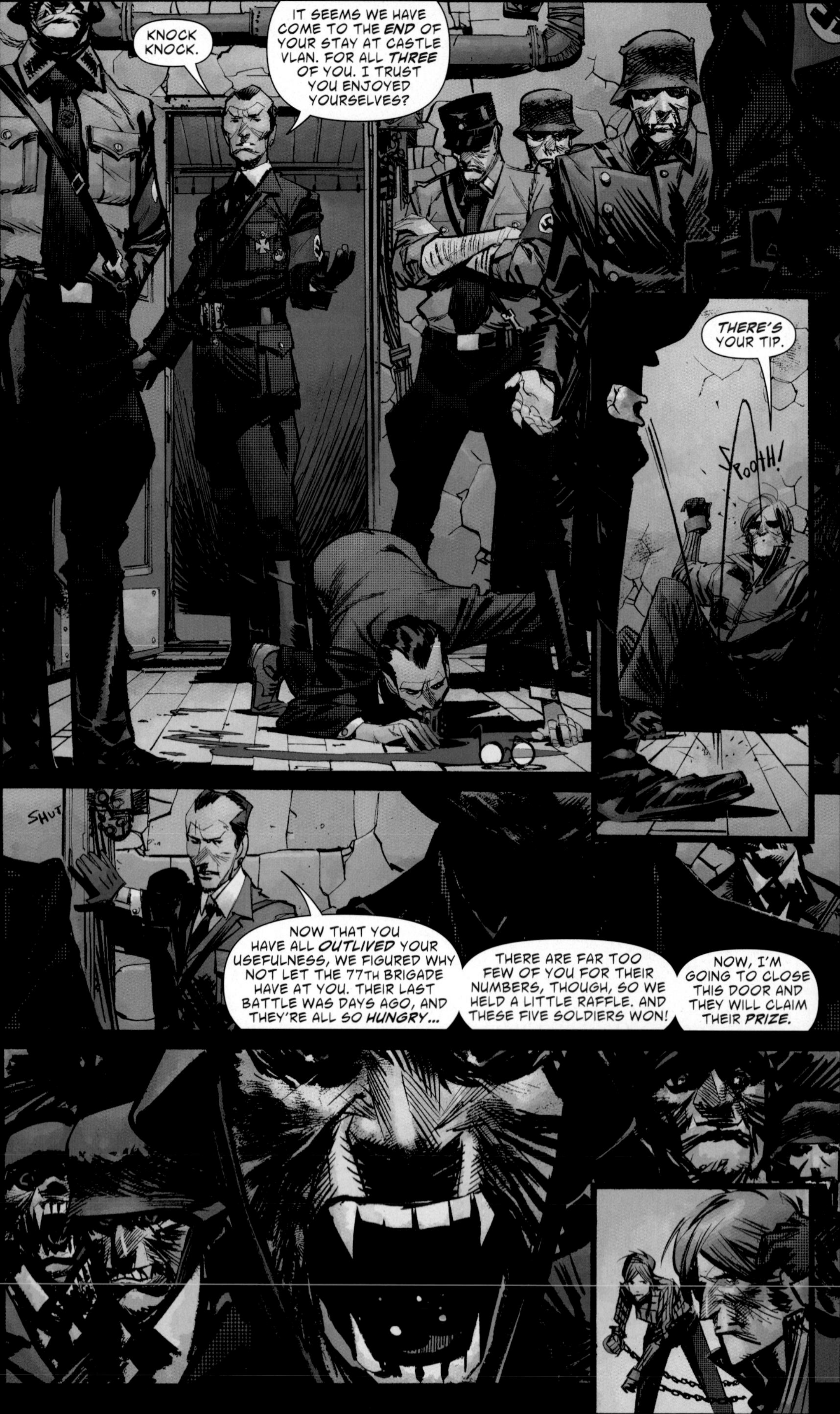
KNOCK KNOCK.
IT SEEMS WE HAVE COME TO THE END OF YOUR STAY AT CASTLE VLAN. FOR ALL THREE OF YOU. I TRUST YOU ENJOYED YOURSELVES?
THERE'S YOUR TIP.
SPOOTH!
SHUT
NOW THAT YOU HAVE ALL OUTLIVED YOUR USEFULNESS, WE FIGURED WHY NOT LET THE 77TH BRIGADE HAVE AT YOU. THEIR LAST BATTLE WAS DAYS AGO, AND THEY'RE ALL SO HUNGRY...
THERE ARE FAR TOO FEW OF YOU FOR THEIR NUMBERS, THOUGH, SO WE HELD A LITTLE RAFFLE. AND THESE FIVE SOLDIERS WON!
NOW, I'M GOING TO CLOSE THIS DOOR AND THEY WILL CLAIM THEIR PRIZE.

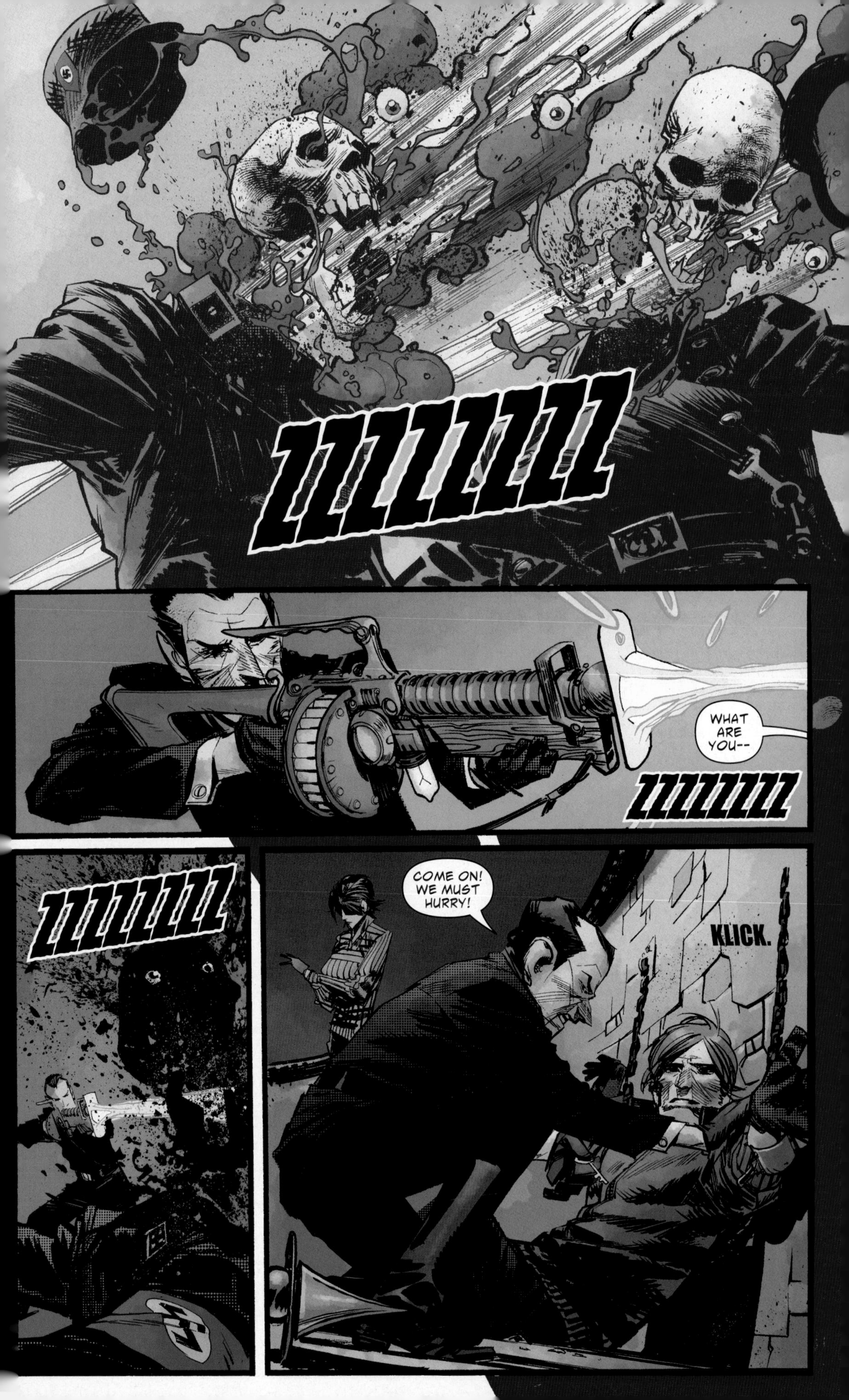
ZZZZZZZZ
WHAT ARE YOU--
ZZZZZZZZ
ZZZZZZZZ
COME ON! WE MUST HURRY!
KLICK.

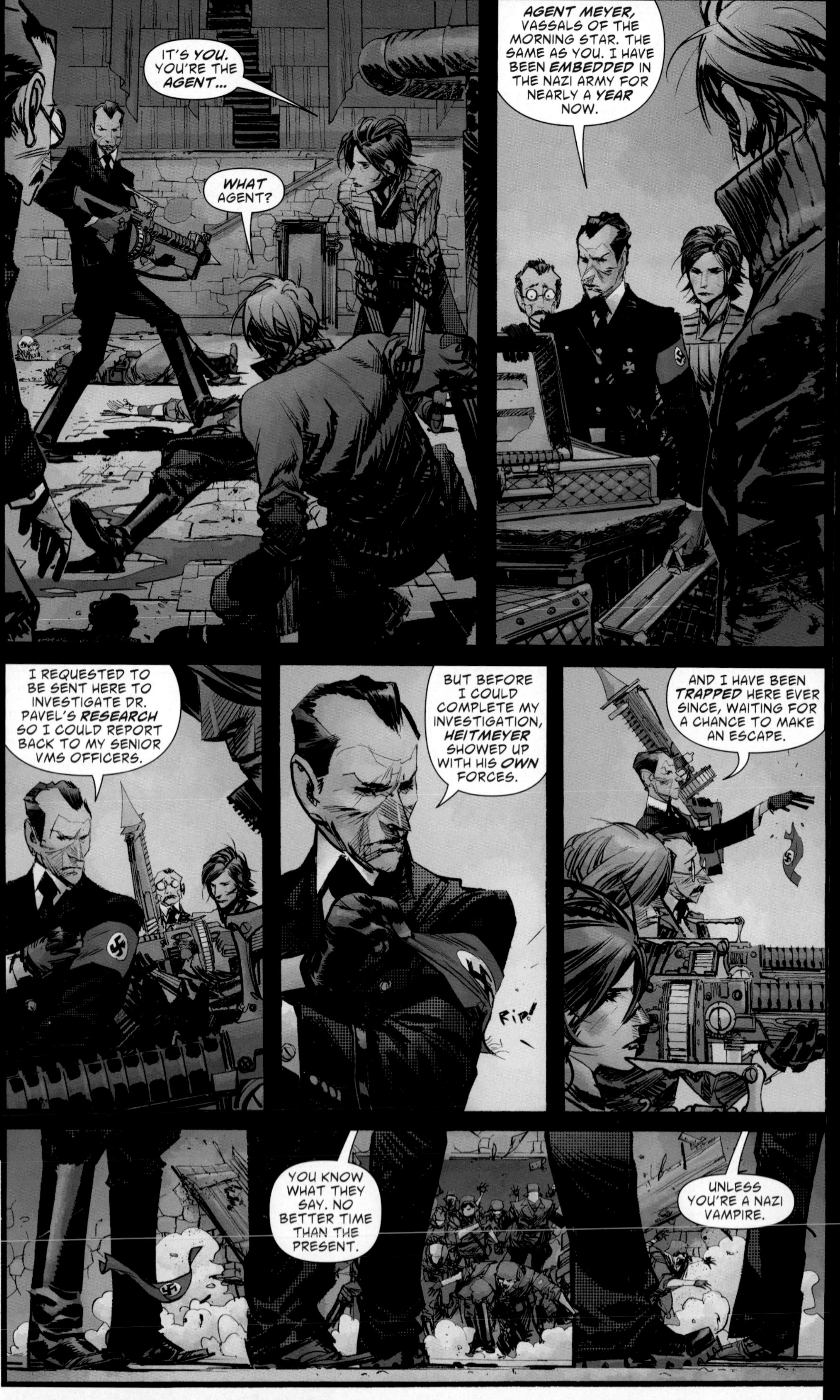
IT'S YOU. YOU'RE THE AGENT...
WHAT AGENT?
AGENT MEYER, VASSALS OF THE MORNING STAR. THE SAME AS YOU. I HAVE BEEN EMBEDDED IN THE NAZI ARMY FOR NEARLY A YEAR NOW.
I REQUESTED TO BE SENT HERE TO INVESTIGATE DR. PAVEL'S RESEARCH SO I COULD REPORT BACK TO MY SENIOR VMS OFFICERS.
BUT BEFORE I COULD COMPLETE MY INVESTIGATION, HEITMEYER SHOWED UP WITH HIS OWN FORCES.
RIP!
AND I HAVE BEEN TRAPPED HERE EVER SINCE, WAITING FOR A CHANCE TO MAKE AN ESCAPE.
YOU KNOW WHAT THEY SAY. NO BETTER TIME THAN THE PRESENT.
UNLESS YOU'RE A NAZI VAMPIRE.

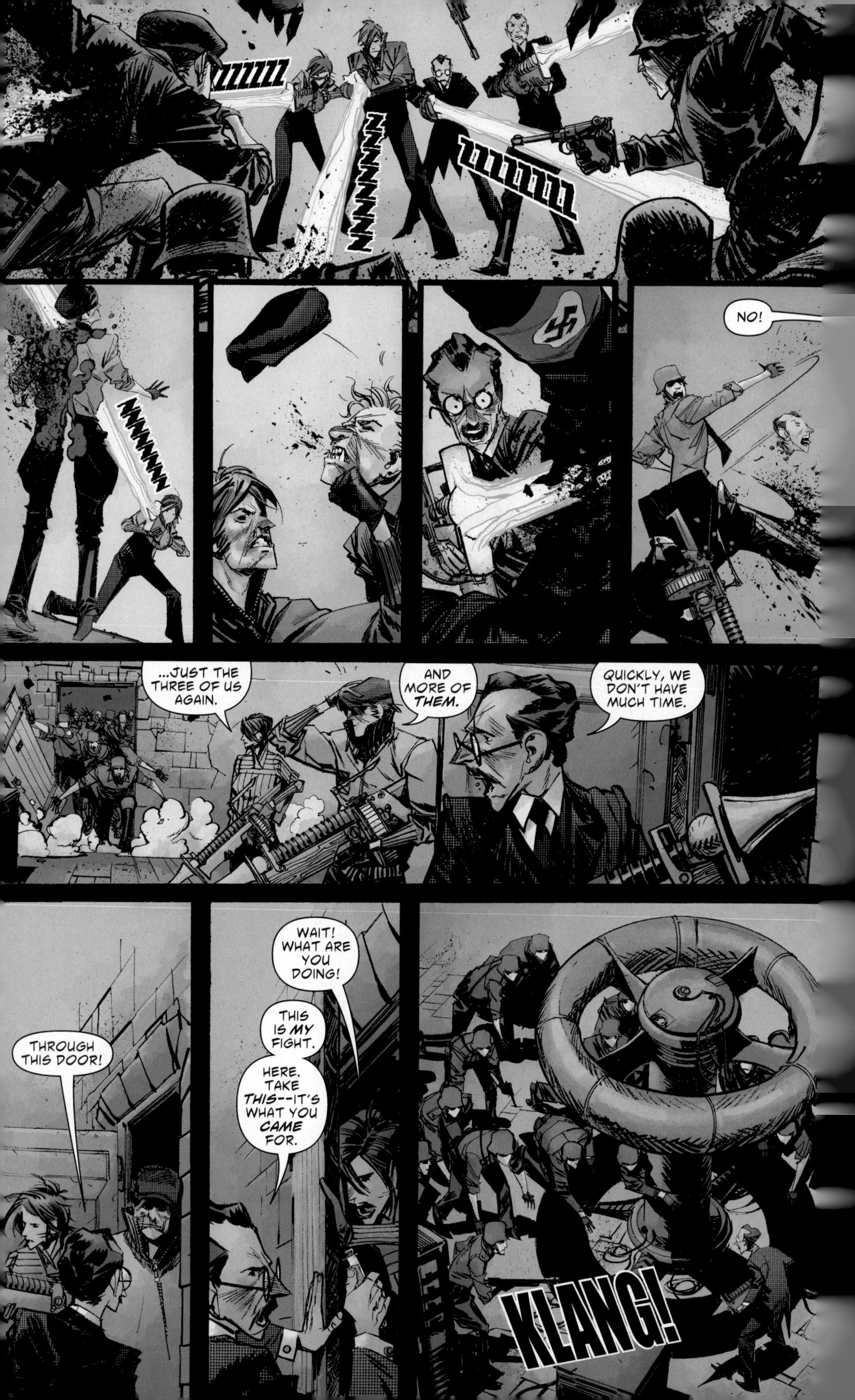

ZZZZZZ
ZZZZZZZZ
ZZZZZZZ
ZZZZZZZZ
NO!
...JUST THE THREE OF US AGAIN.
AND MORE OF THEM.
QUICKLY, WE DON'T HAVE MUCH TIME.
THROUGH THIS DOOR!
WAIT! WHAT ARE YOU DOING!
THIS IS MY FIGHT.
HERE. TAKE THIS--IT'S WHAT YOU CAME FOR.
KLANG!

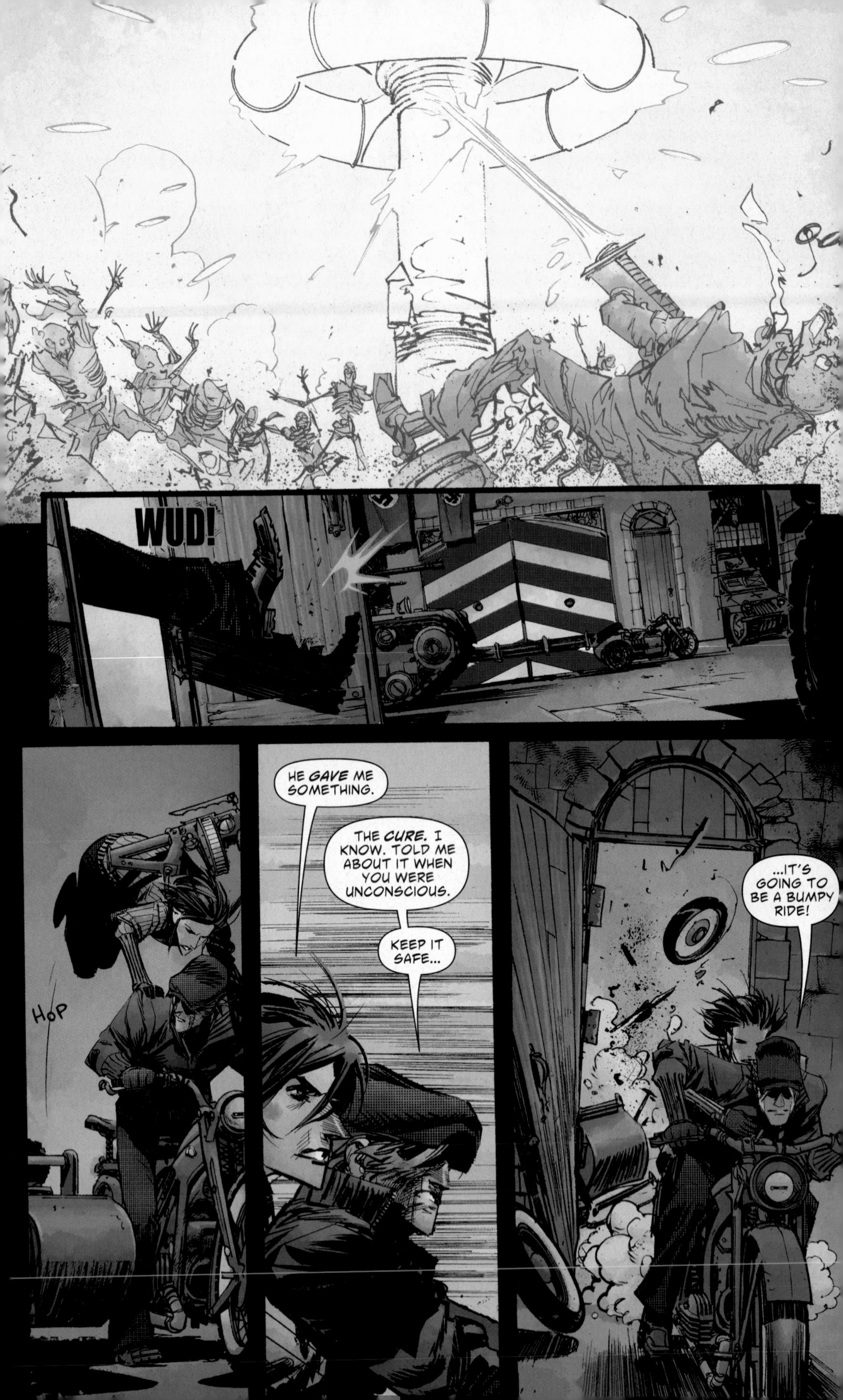
WUD!
HOP
HE GAVE ME SOMETHING.
THE CURE. I KNOW. TOLD ME ABOUT IT WHEN YOU WERE UNCONSCIOUS.
KEEP IT SAFE...
...IT'S GOING TO BE A BUMPY RIDE!

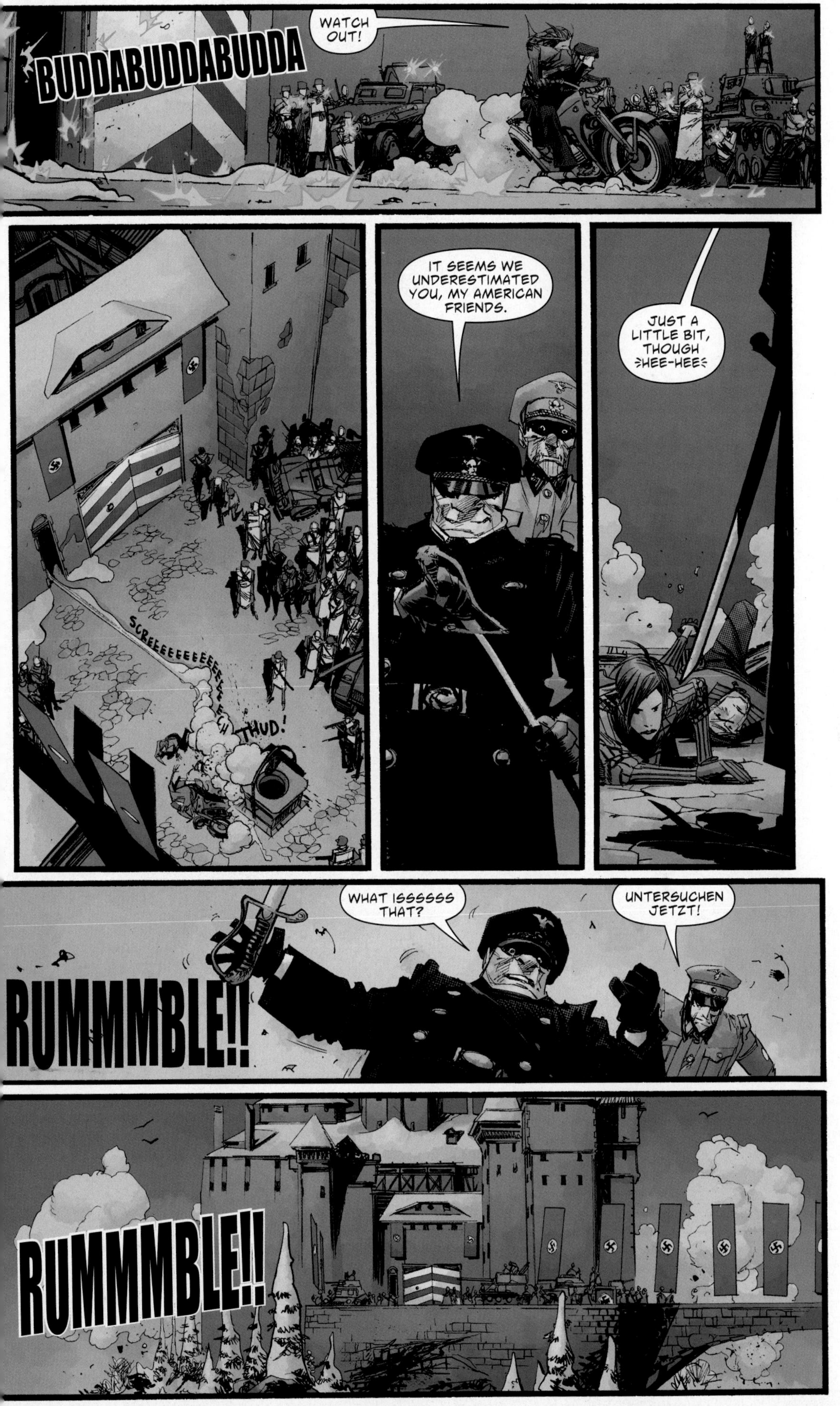
WATCH OUT!
BUDDABUDDABUDDA
SCREEEEEEEEEEEEEECH
THUD!
IT SEEMS WE UNDERESTIMATED YOU, MY AMERICAN FRIENDS.
JUST A LITTLE BIT, THOUGH HEE-HEE
WHAT ISSSSSS THAT?
UNTERSUCHEN JETZT!
RUMMMBLE!!
RUMMMBLE!!

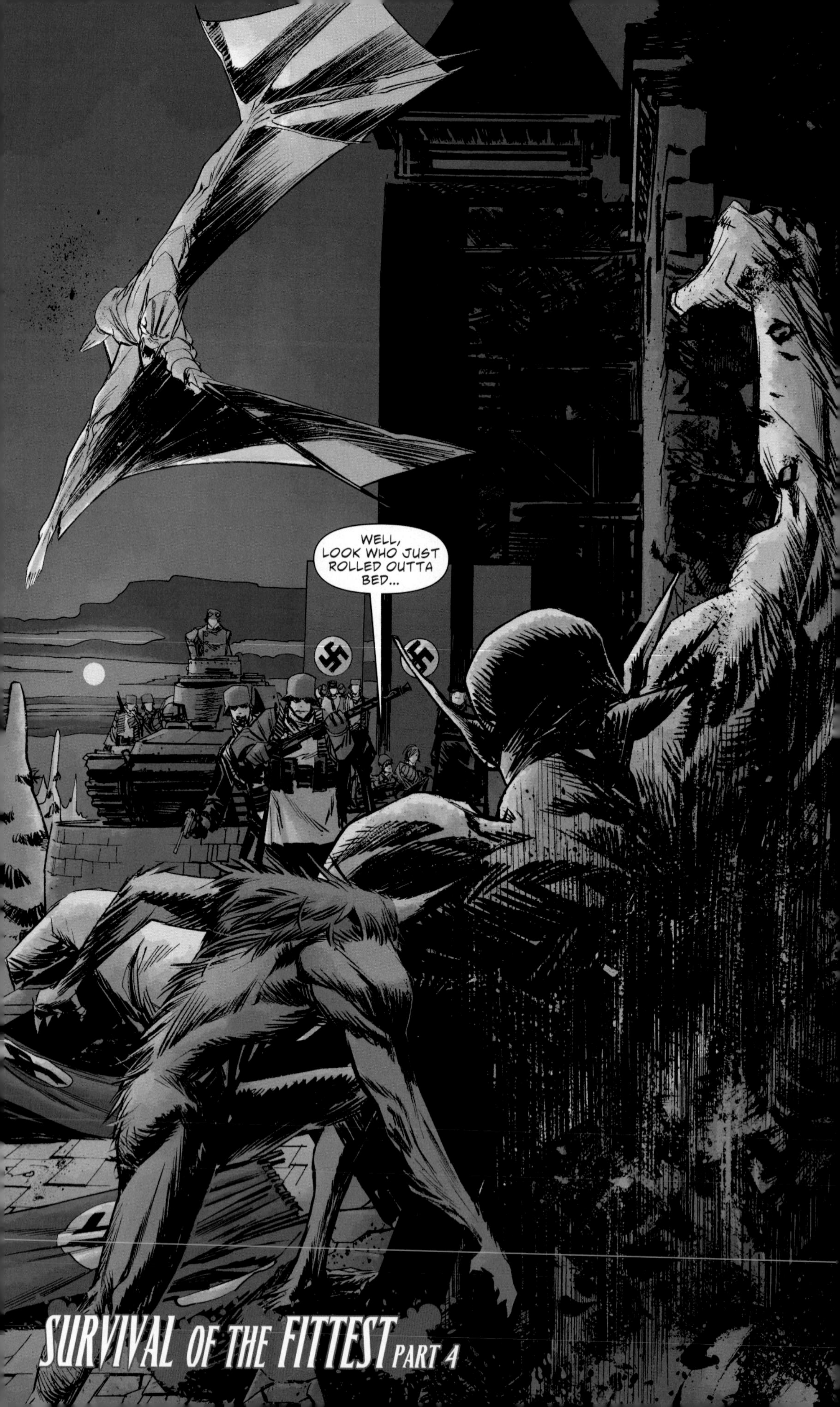
WELL, LOOK WHO JUST ROLLED OUTTA BED...
SURVIVAL OF THE FITTEST PART 4

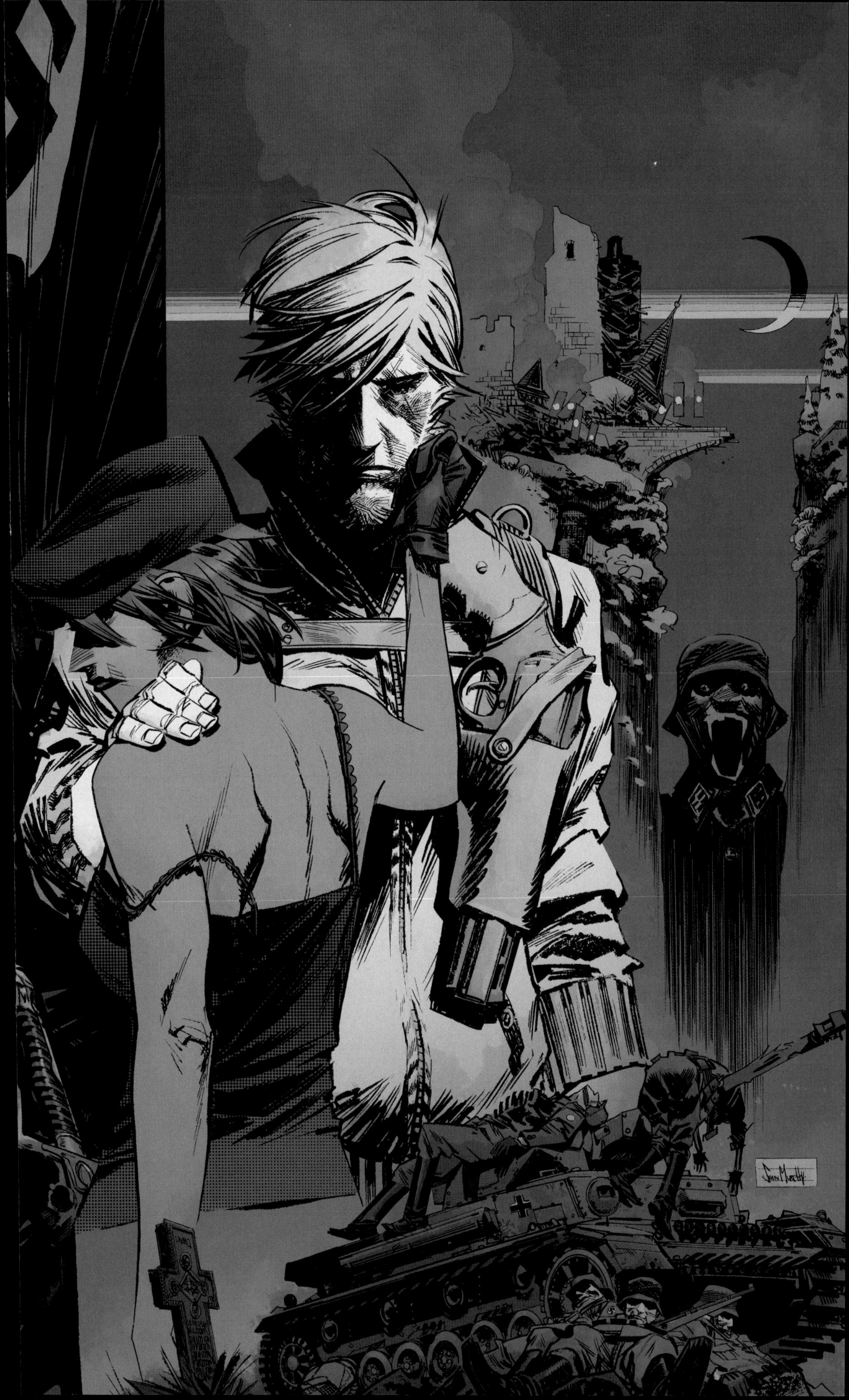

**Survival
of the Fittest**
Conclusion

Sean Murphy
Artist and cover

Dave Stewart
cover color

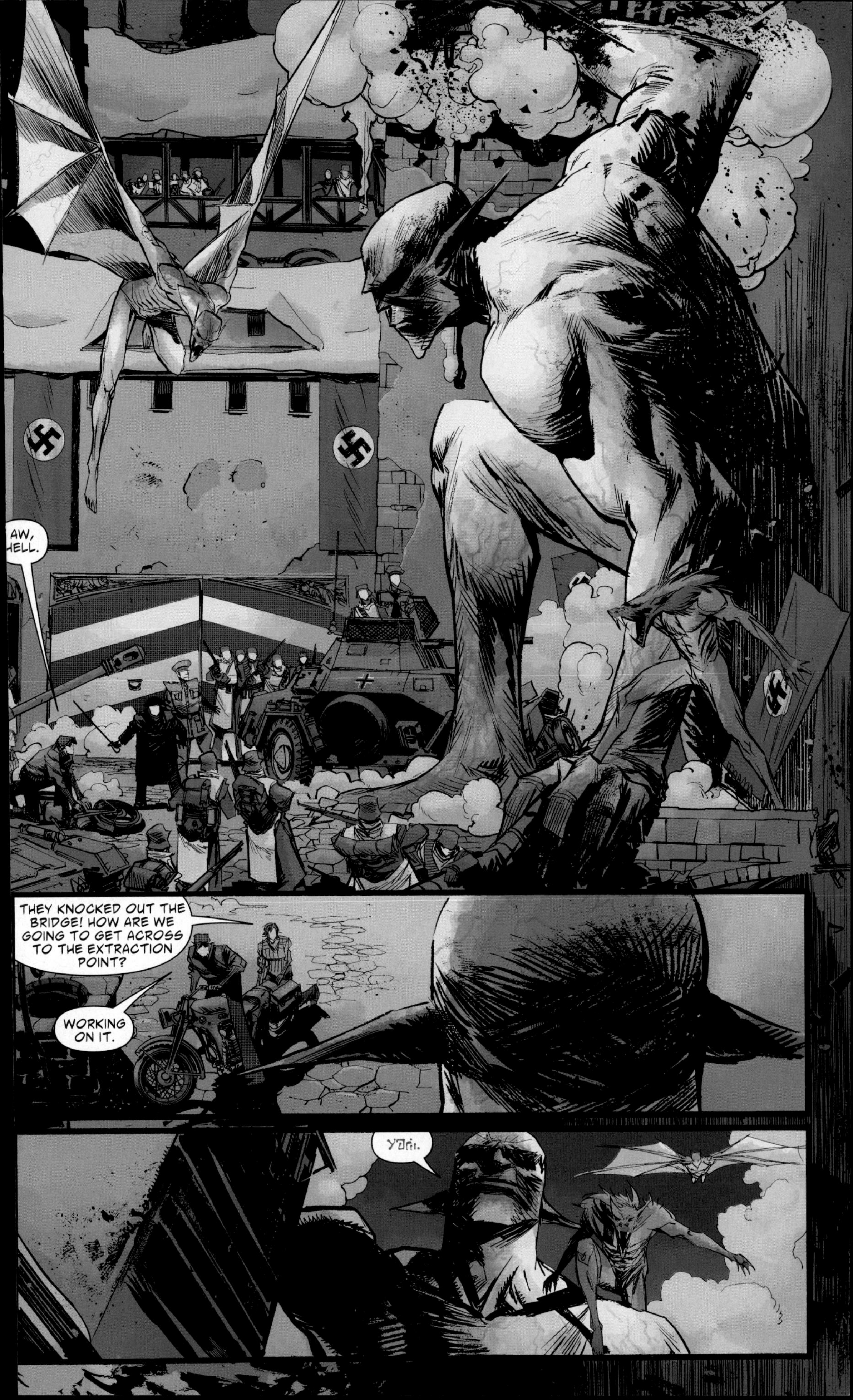
AW, HELL.
THEY KNOCKED OUT THE BRIDGE! HOW ARE WE GOING TO GET ACROSS TO THE EXTRACTION POINT?
WORKING ON IT.

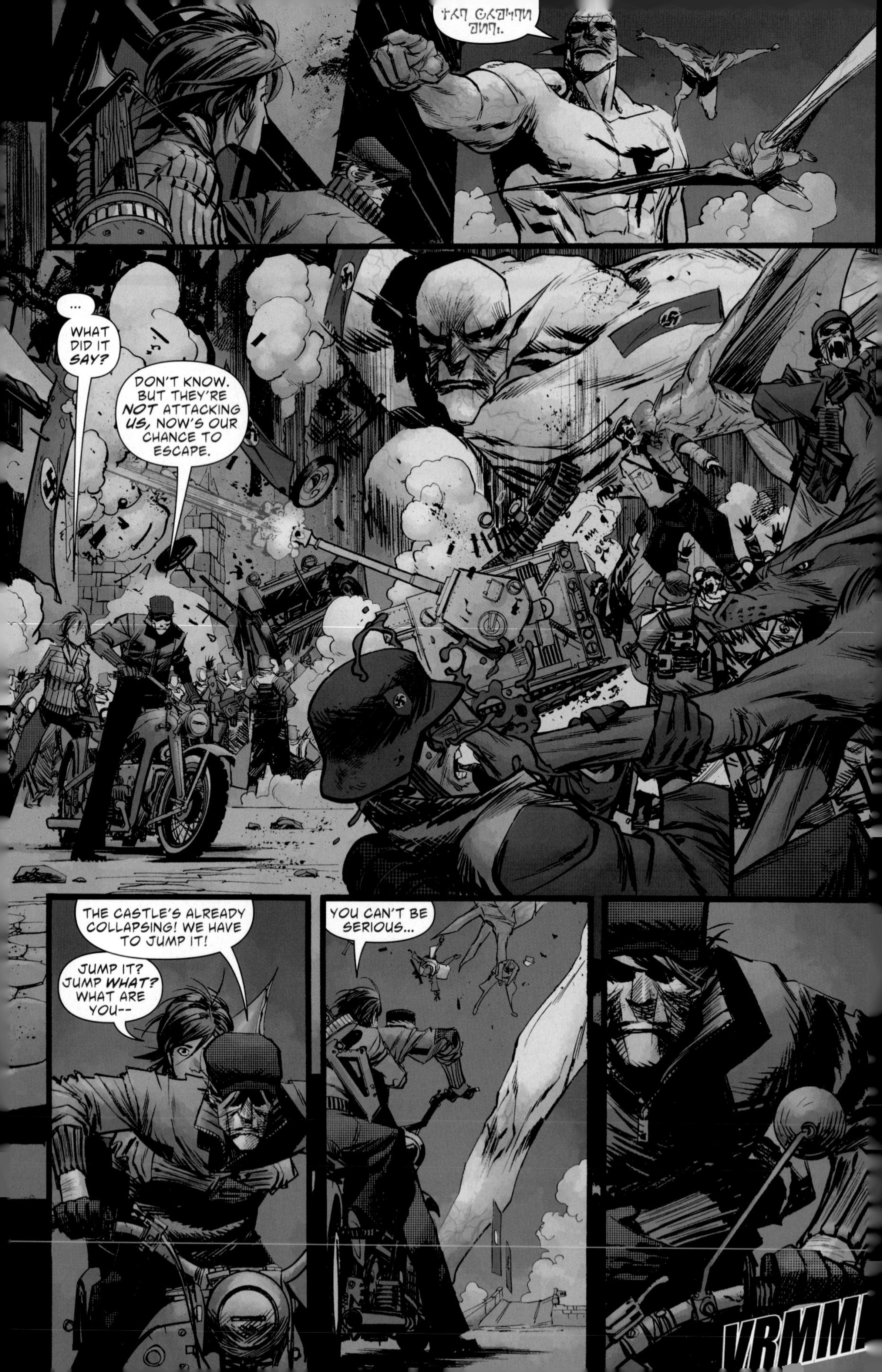
...
WHAT DID IT SAY?
DON'T KNOW. BUT THEY'RE NOT ATTACKING US, NOW'S OUR CHANCE TO ESCAPE.
THE CASTLE'S ALREADY COLLAPSING! WE HAVE TO JUMP IT!
JUMP IT? JUMP WHAT? WHAT ARE YOU--
YOU CAN'T BE SERIOUS...
VRMM

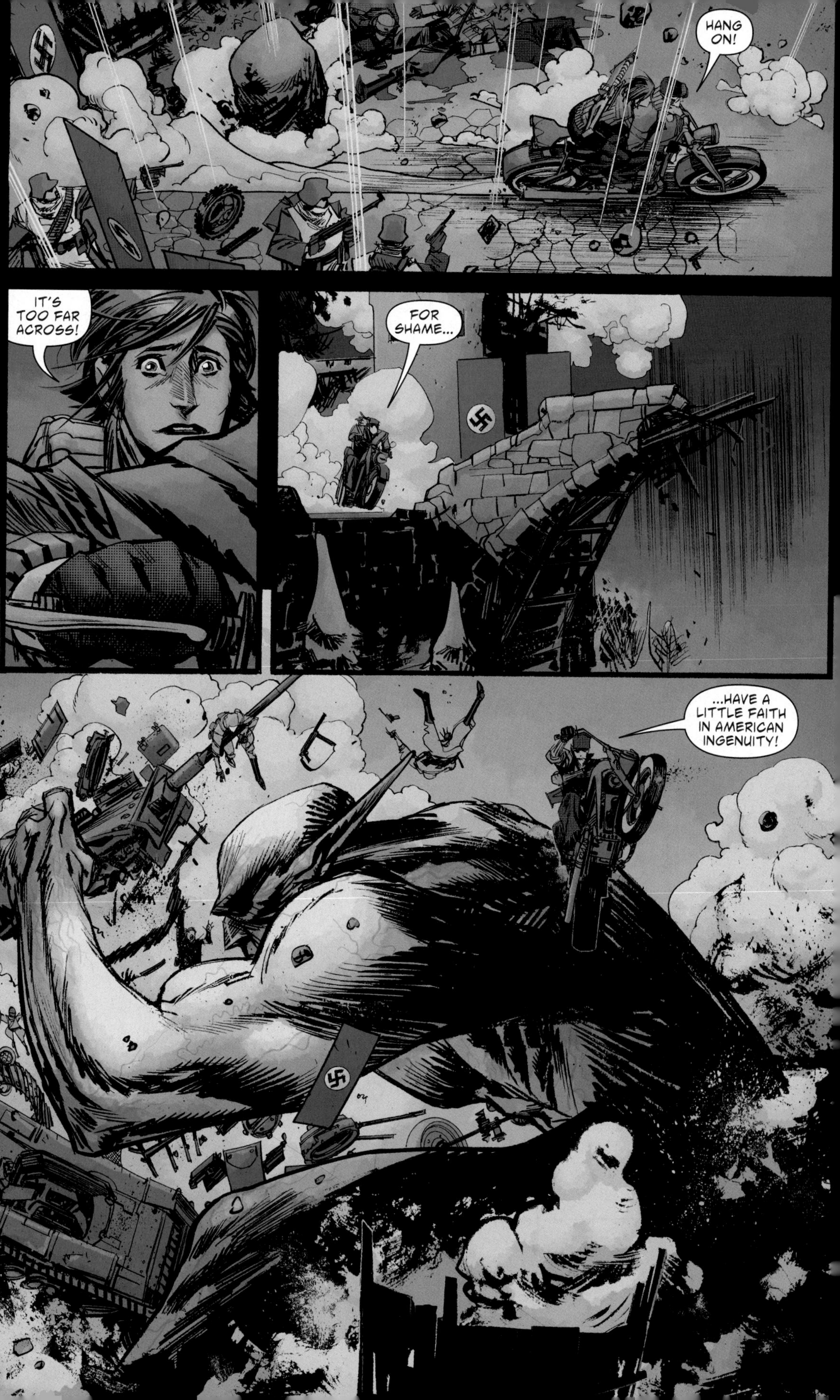
HANG ON!
IT'S TOO FAR ACROSS!
FOR SHAME...
...HAVE A LITTLE FAITH IN AMERICAN INGENUITY!

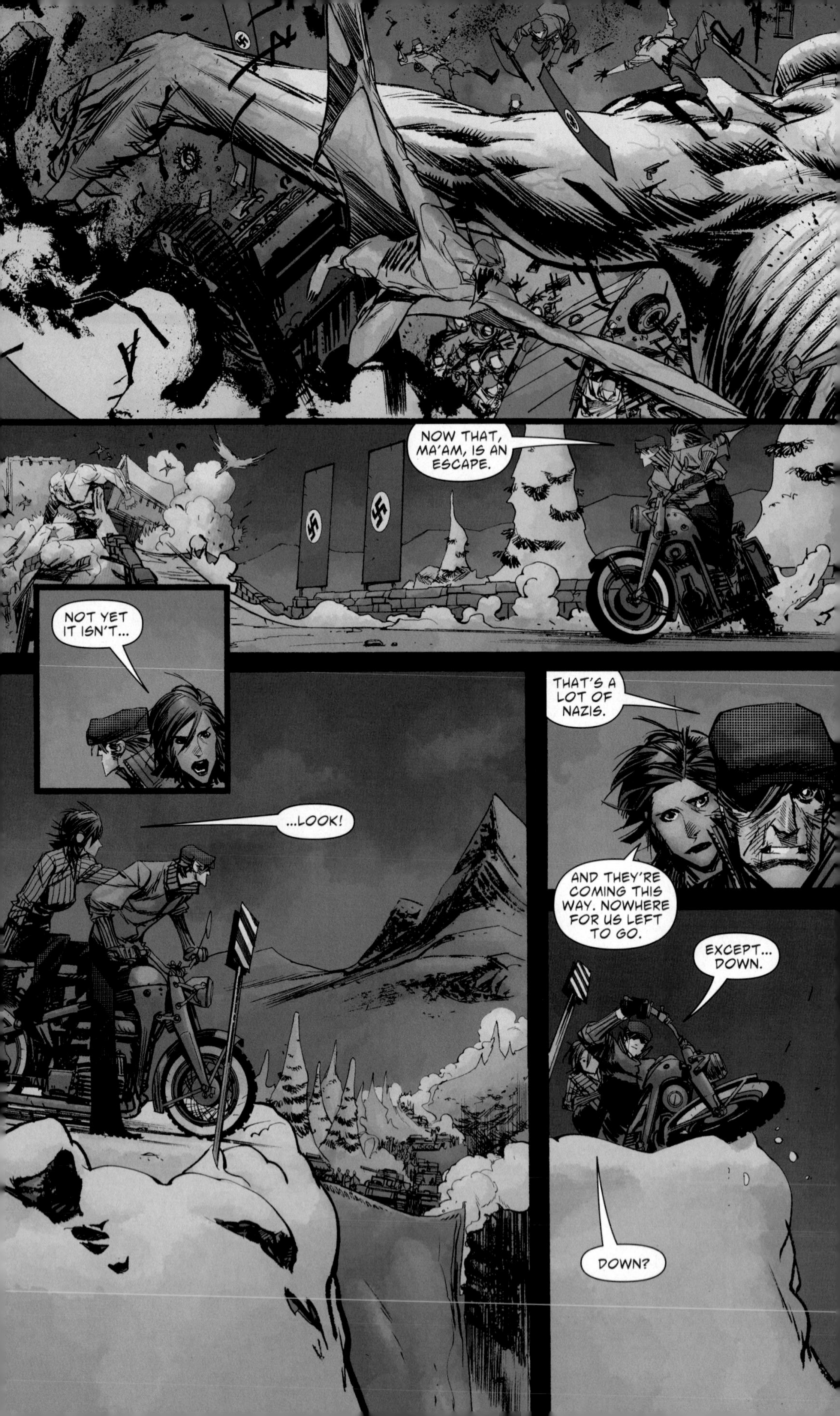
NOW THAT, MA'AM, IS AN ESCAPE.
NOT YET IT ISN'T...
...LOOK!
THAT'S A LOT OF NAZIS.
AND THEY'RE COMING THIS WAY. NOWHERE FOR US LEFT TO GO.
EXCEPT... DOWN.
DOWN?

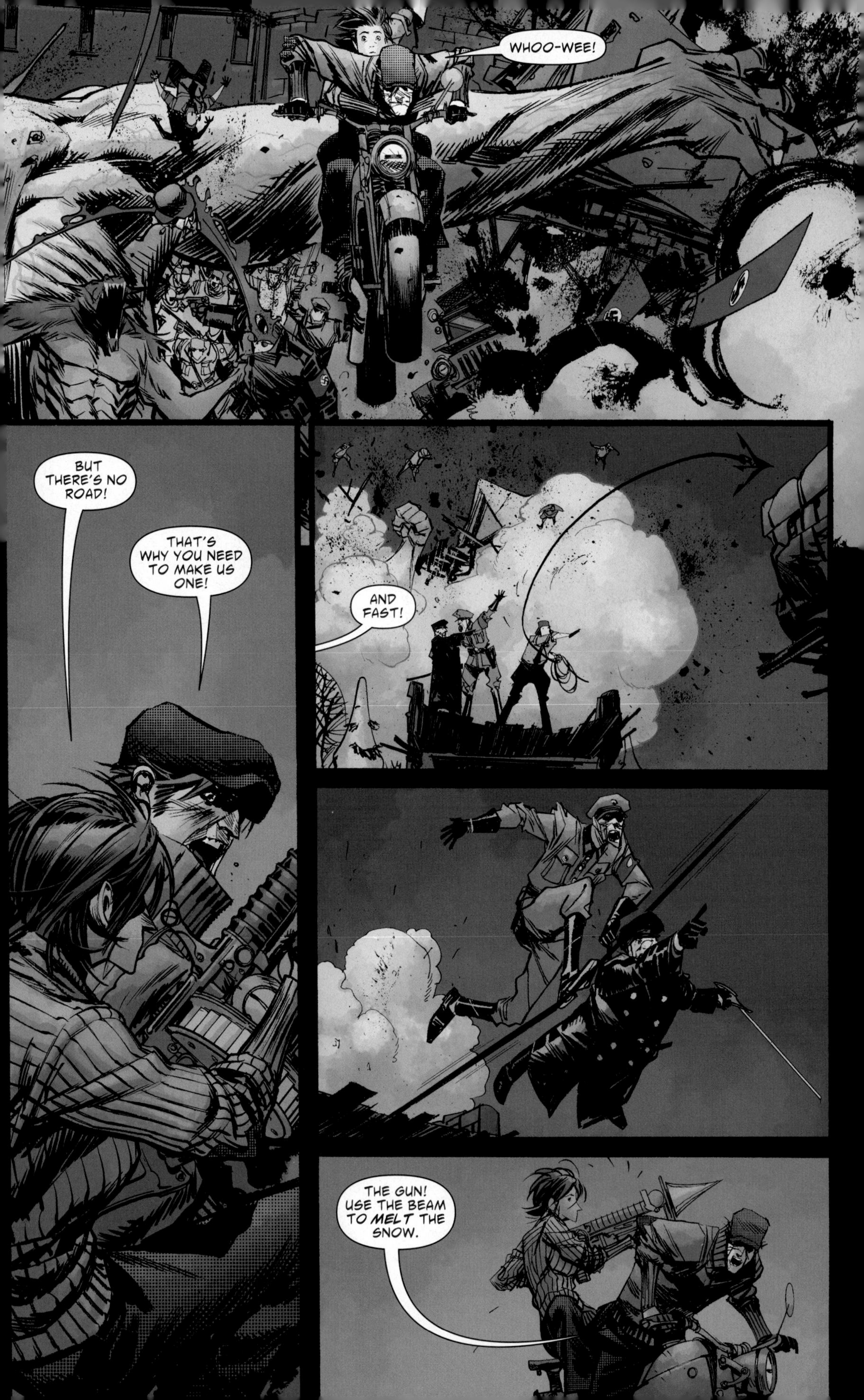
WHOO-WEE!
BUT THERE'S NO ROAD!
THAT'S WHY YOU NEED TO MAKE US ONE!
AND FAST!
THE GUN! USE THE BEAM TO MELT THE SNOW.

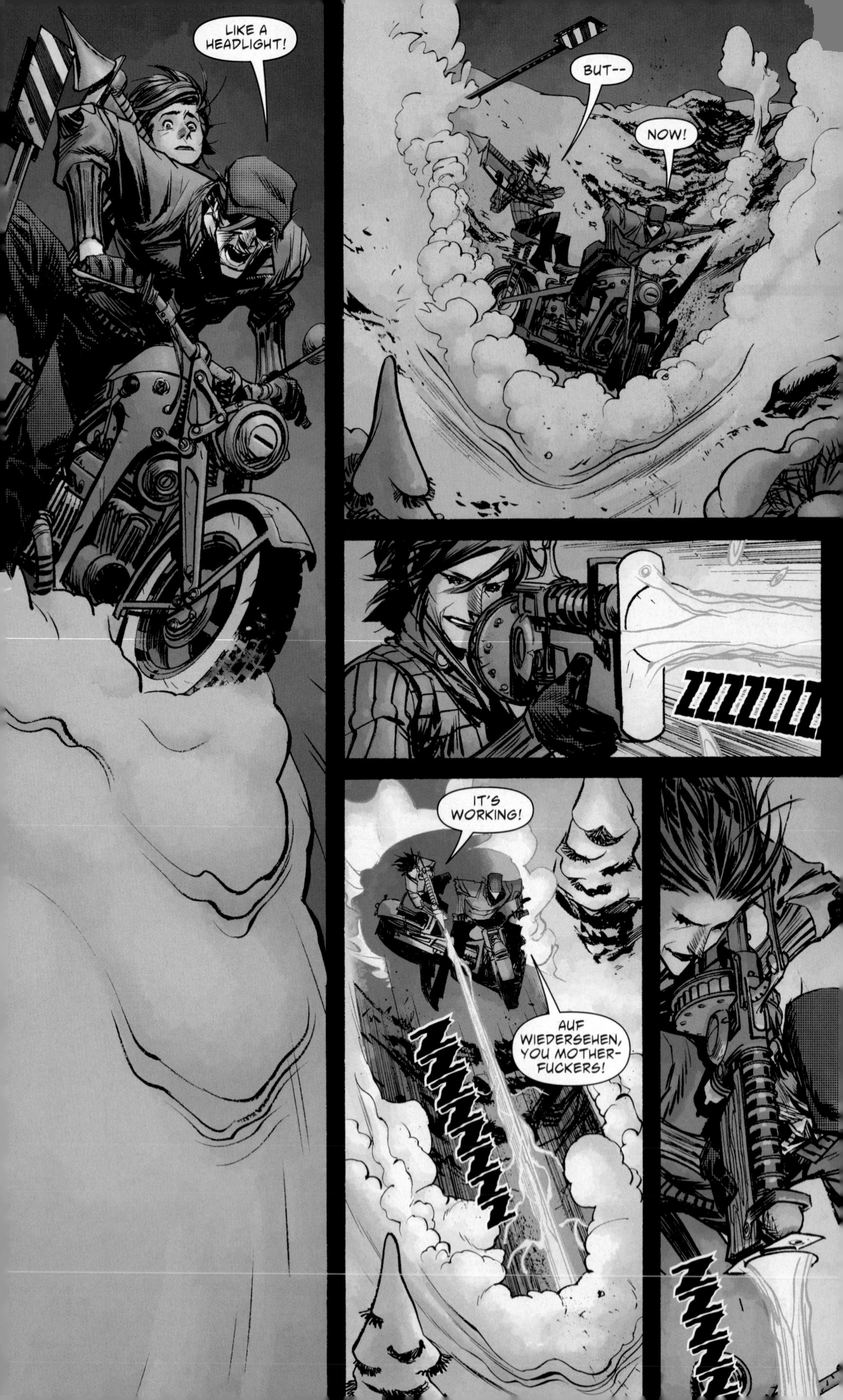
LIKE A HEADLIGHT!
BUT--
NOW!
ZZZZZZZZ
IT'S WORKING!
AUF WIEDERSEHEN, YOU MOTHER-FUCKERS!

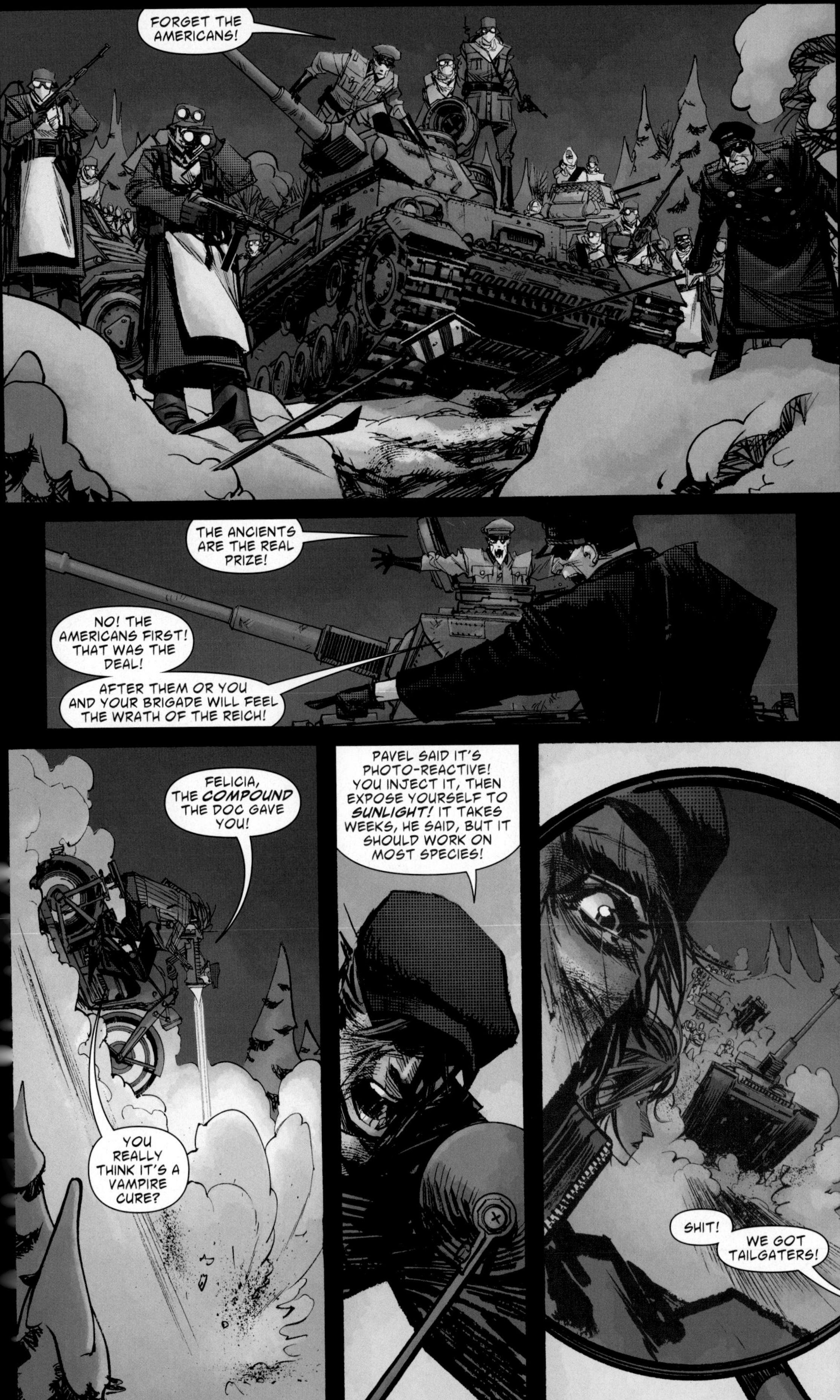
FORGET THE AMERICANS!
THE ANCIENTS ARE THE REAL PRIZE!
NO! THE AMERICANS FIRST! THAT WAS THE DEAL!
AFTER THEM OR YOU AND YOUR BRIGADE WILL FEEL THE WRATH OF THE REICH!
FELICIA, THE COMPOUND THE DOC GAVE YOU!
YOU REALLY THINK IT'S A VAMPIRE CURE?
PAVEL SAID IT'S PHOTO-REACTIVE! YOU INJECT IT, THEN EXPOSE YOURSELF TO SUNLIGHT! IT TAKES WEEKS, HE SAID, BUT IT SHOULD WORK ON MOST SPECIES!
SHIT!
WE GOT TAILGATERS!

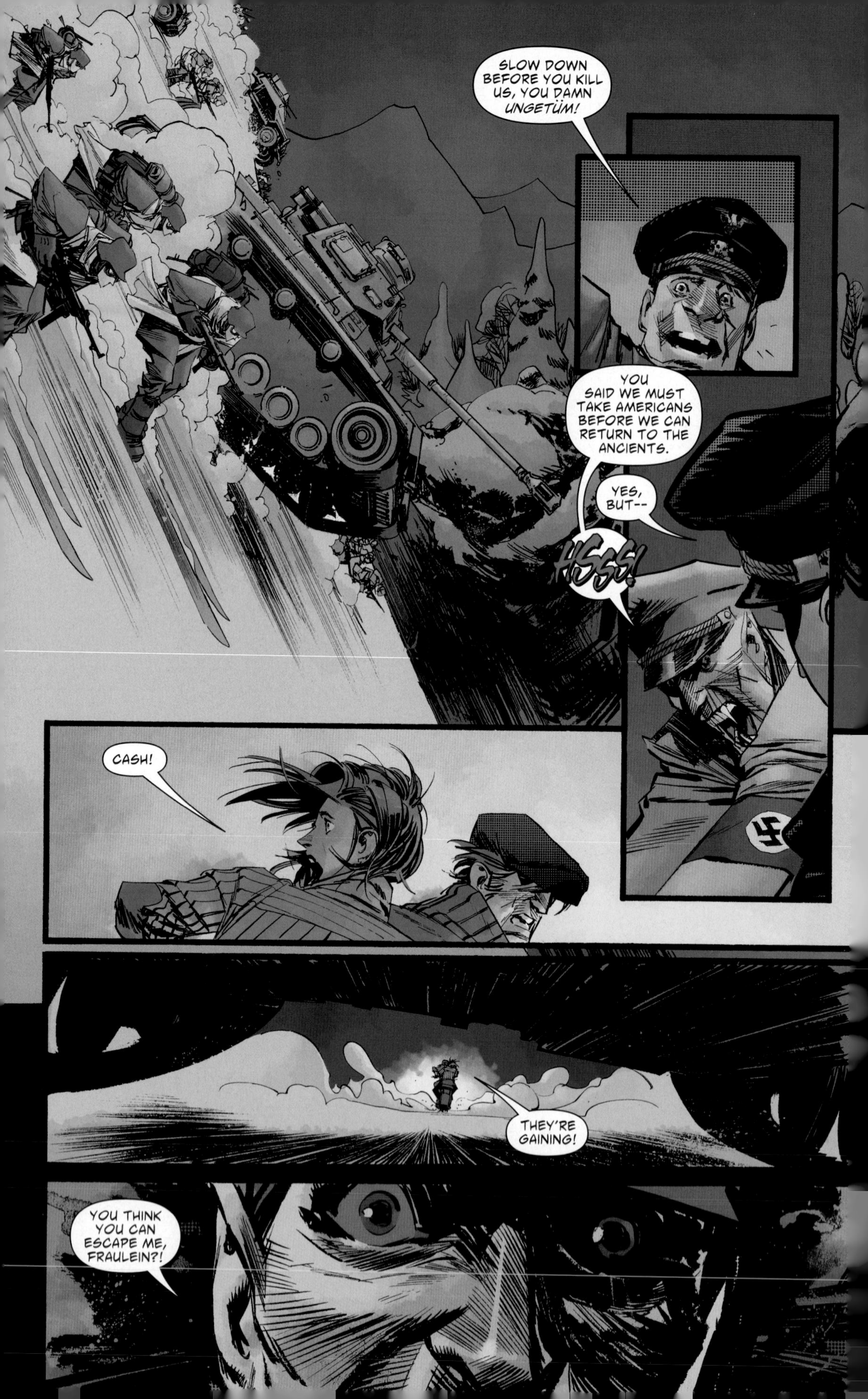
SLOW DOWN BEFORE YOU KILL US, YOU DAMN *UNGETÜM!*
YOU SAID WE MUST TAKE AMERICANS BEFORE WE CAN RETURN TO THE ANCIENTS.
YES, BUT--
HSSS!
CASH!
THEY'RE GAINING!
YOU THINK YOU CAN ESCAPE ME, FRAULEIN?!

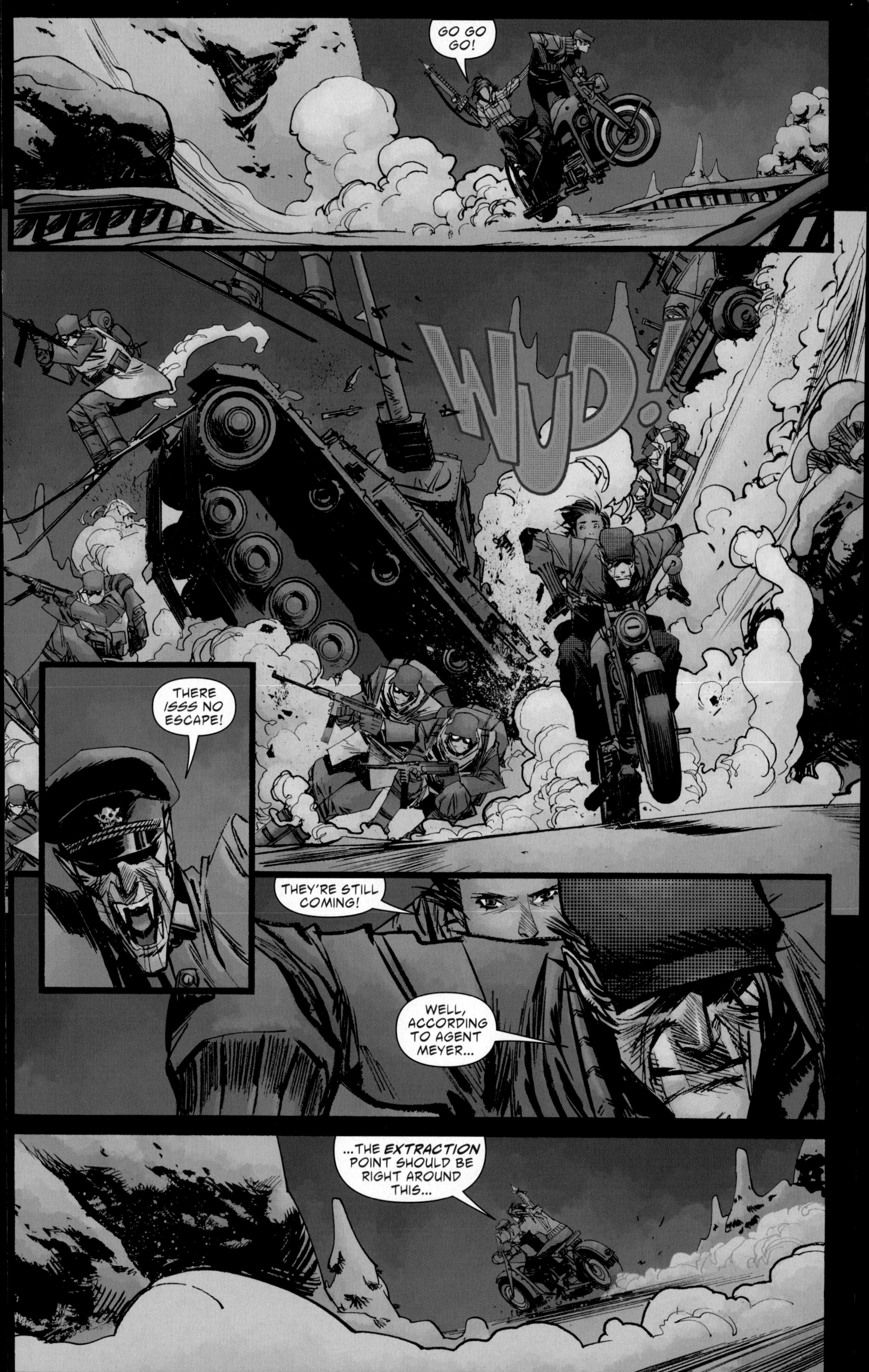
GO GO GO!
WUD!
THERE ISSS NO ESCAPE!
THEY'RE STILL COMING!
WELL, ACCORDING TO AGENT MEYER...
...THE EXTRACTION POINT SHOULD BE RIGHT AROUND THIS...

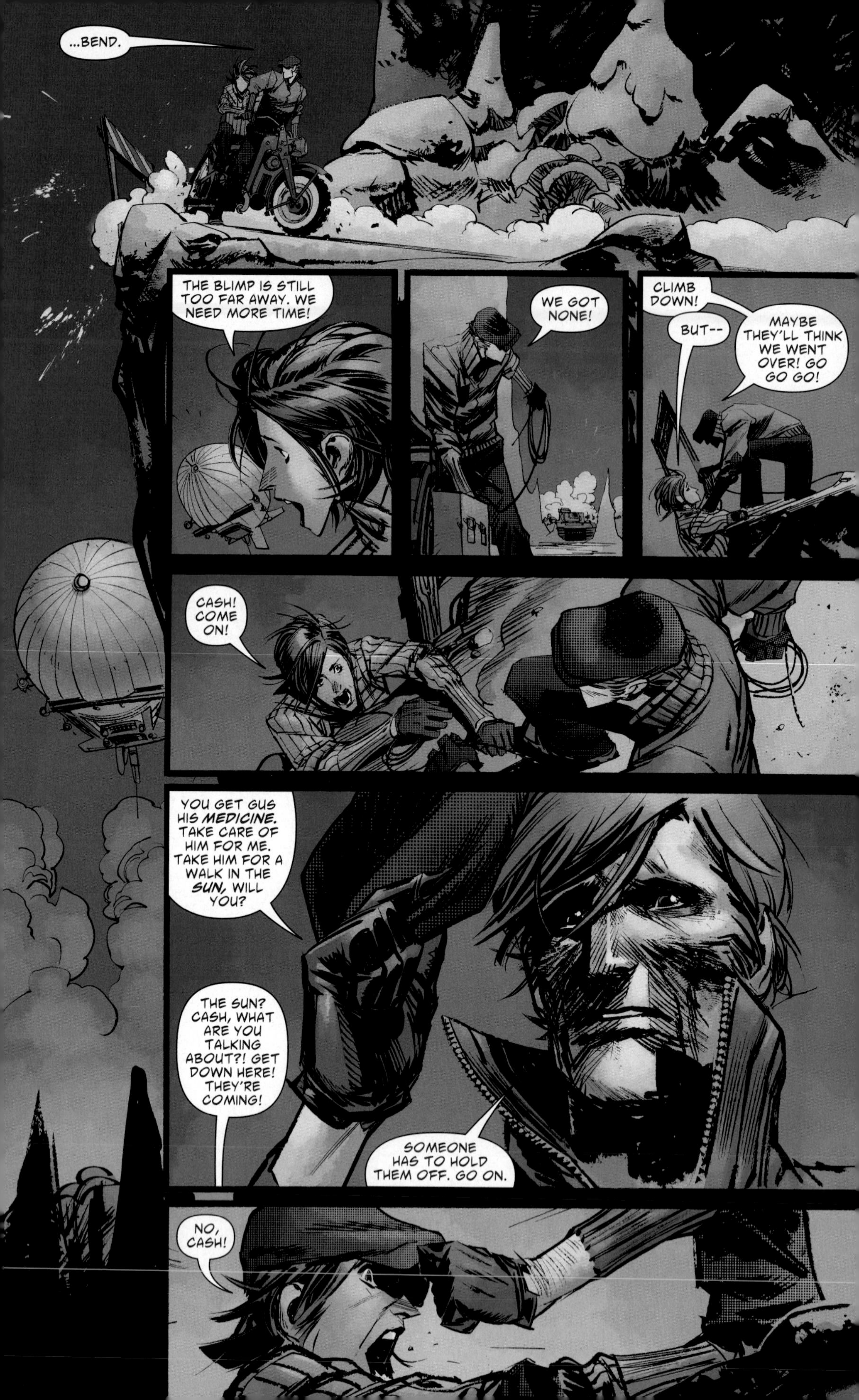
...BEND.
THE BLIMP IS STILL TOO FAR AWAY. WE NEED MORE TIME!
WE GOT NONE!
CLIMB DOWN!
BUT--
MAYBE THEY'LL THINK WE WENT OVER! GO GO GO!
CASH! COME ON!
YOU GET GUS HIS MEDICINE. TAKE CARE OF HIM FOR ME. TAKE HIM FOR A WALK IN THE SUN, WILL YOU?
THE SUN? CASH, WHAT ARE YOU TALKING ABOUT?! GET DOWN HERE! THEY'RE COMING!
SOMEONE HAS TO HOLD THEM OFF. GO ON.
NO, CASH!

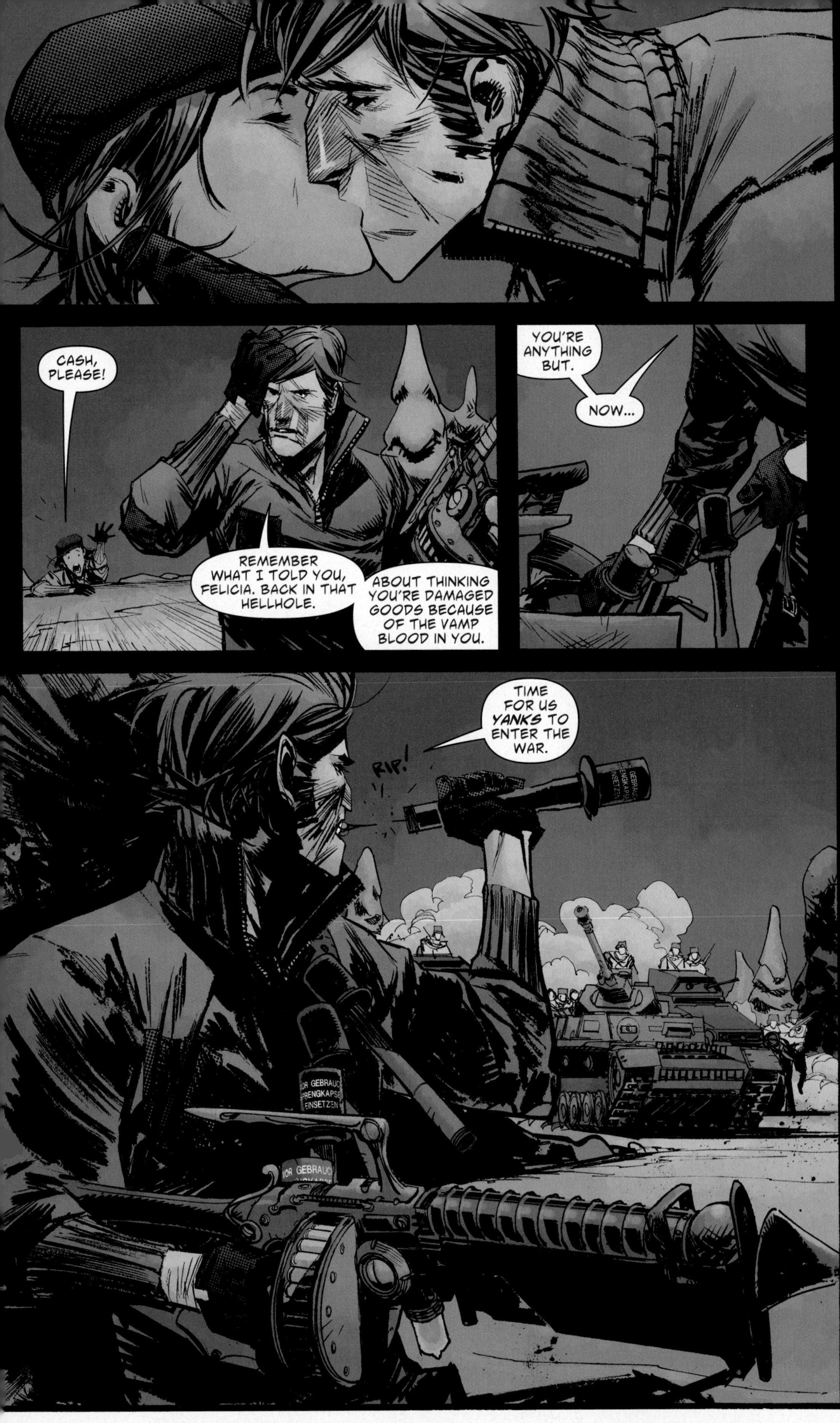
CASH, PLEASE!
REMEMBER WHAT I TOLD YOU, FELICIA. BACK IN THAT HELLHOLE.
ABOUT THINKING YOU'RE DAMAGED GOODS BECAUSE OF THE VAMP BLOOD IN YOU.
YOU'RE ANYTHING BUT.
NOW...
TIME FOR US YANKS TO ENTER THE WAR.
RIP!

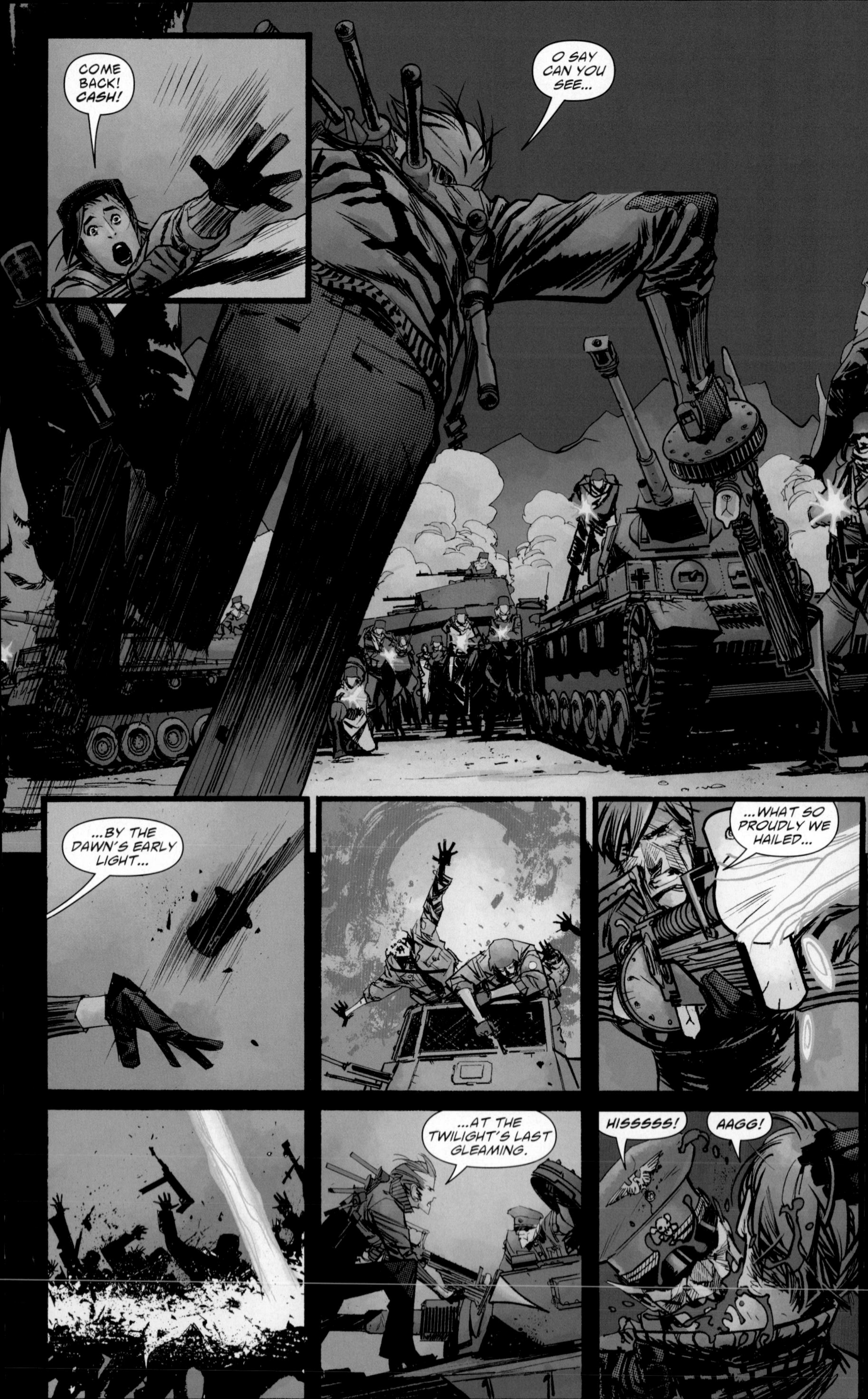
COME BACK! CASH!
O SAY CAN YOU SEE...
...BY THE DAWN'S EARLY LIGHT...
...WHAT SO PROUDLY WE HAILED...
...AT THE TWILIGHT'S LAST GLEAMING.
HISSSSS!
AAGG!

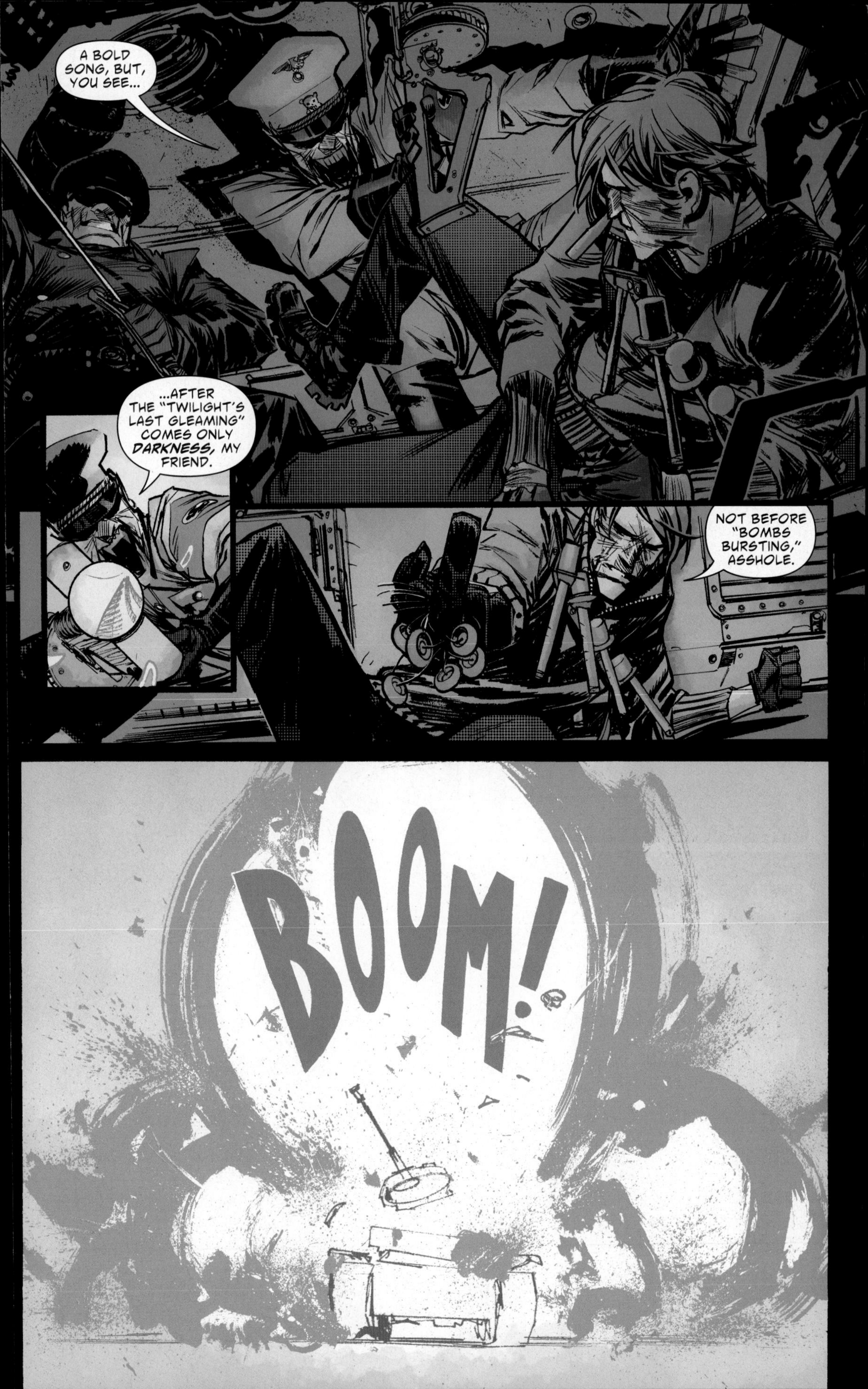
A BOLD SONG, BUT, YOU SEE...
...AFTER THE "TWILIGHT'S LAST GLEAMING" COMES ONLY *DARKNESS,* MY FRIEND.
NOT BEFORE "BOMBS BURSTING," ASSHOLE.
BOOM!

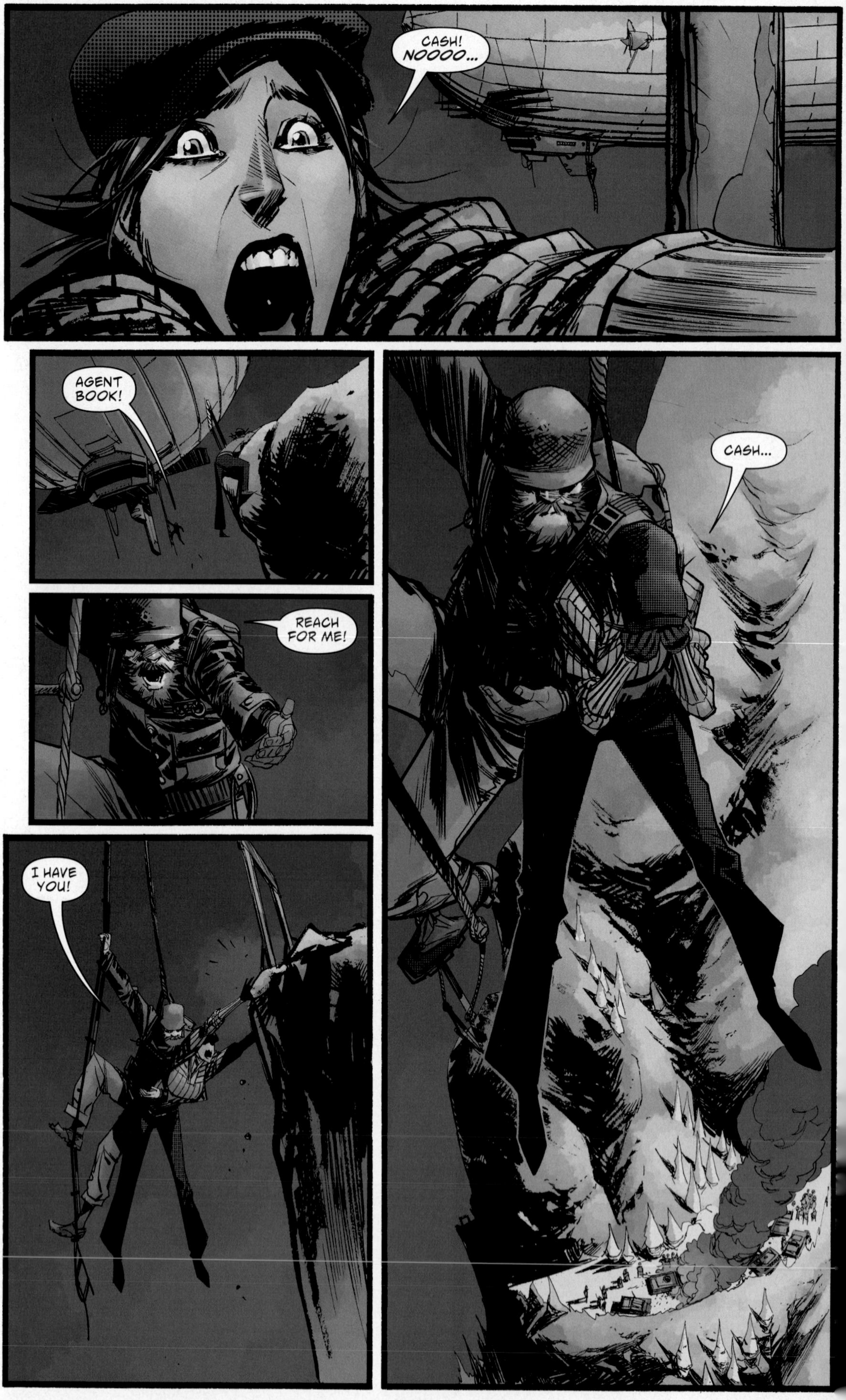
CASH! NOOOO...
AGENT BOOK!
REACH FOR ME!
I HAVE YOU!
CASH...

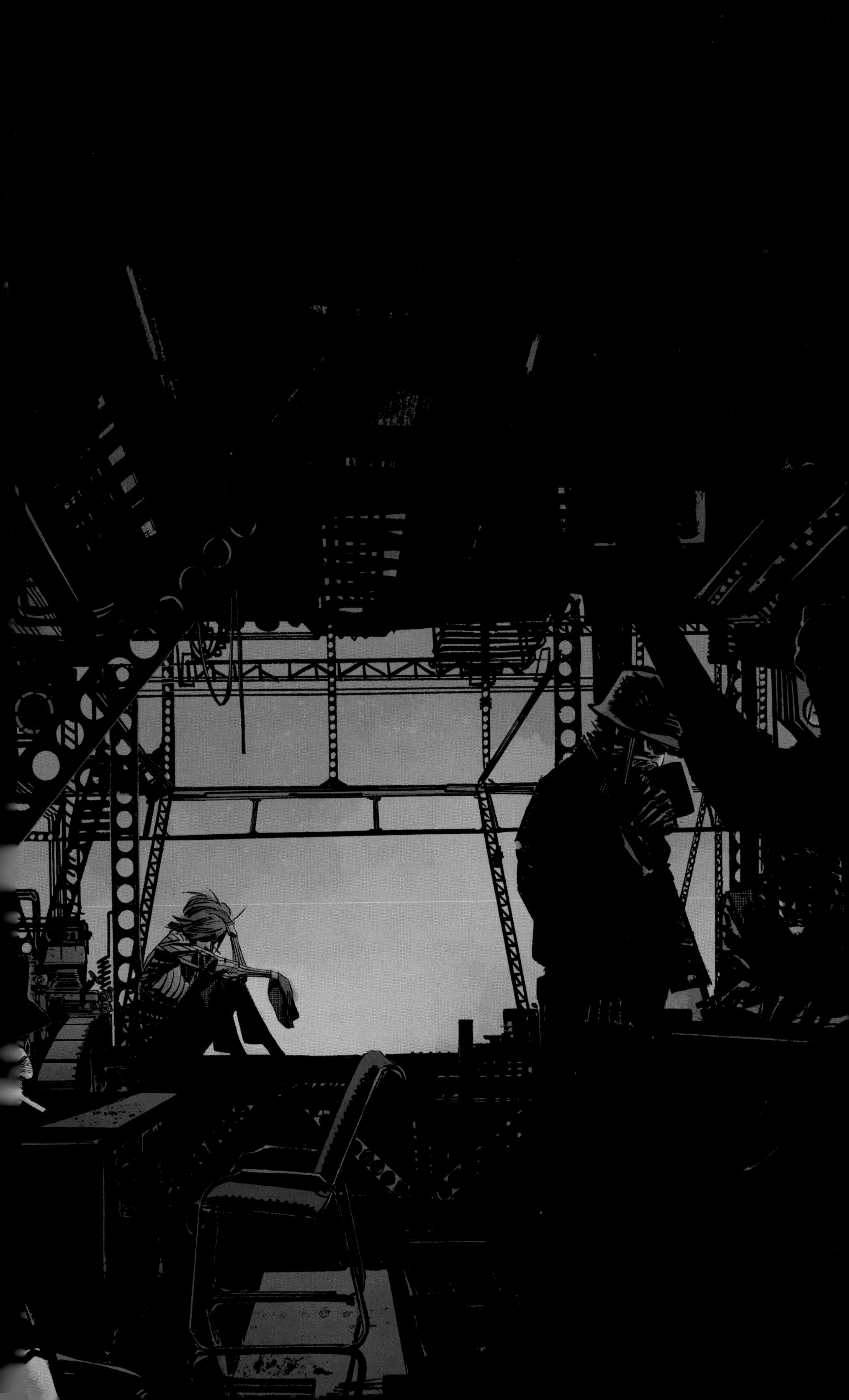

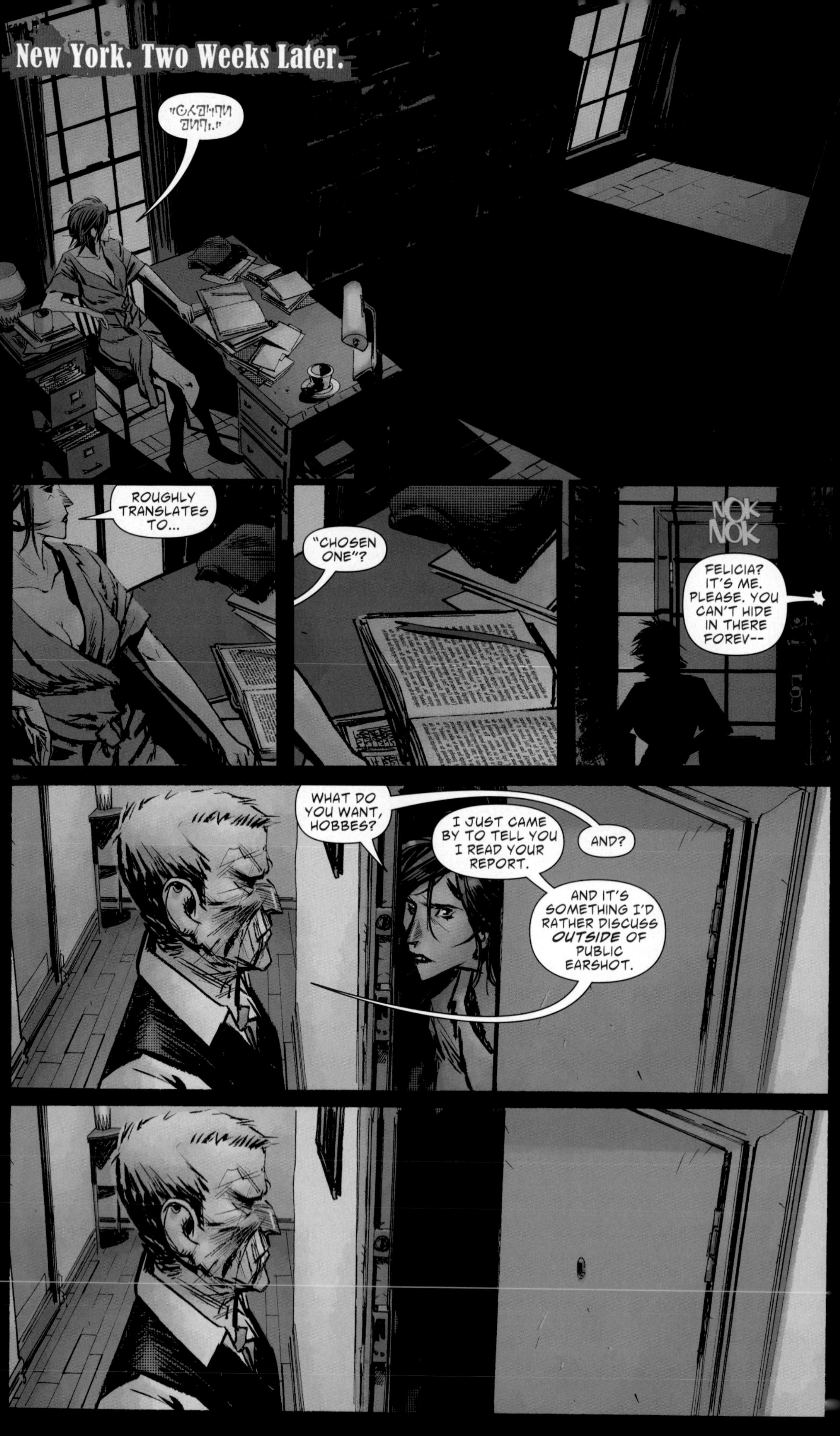
New York. Two Weeks Later.
ROUGHLY TRANSLATES TO...
"CHOSEN ONE"?
NOK NOK
FELICIA? IT'S ME. PLEASE. YOU CAN'T HIDE IN THERE FOREV--
WHAT DO YOU WANT, HOBBES?
I JUST CAME BY TO TELL YOU I READ YOUR REPORT.
AND?
AND IT'S SOMETHING I'D RATHER DISCUSS OUTSIDE OF PUBLIC EARSHOT.

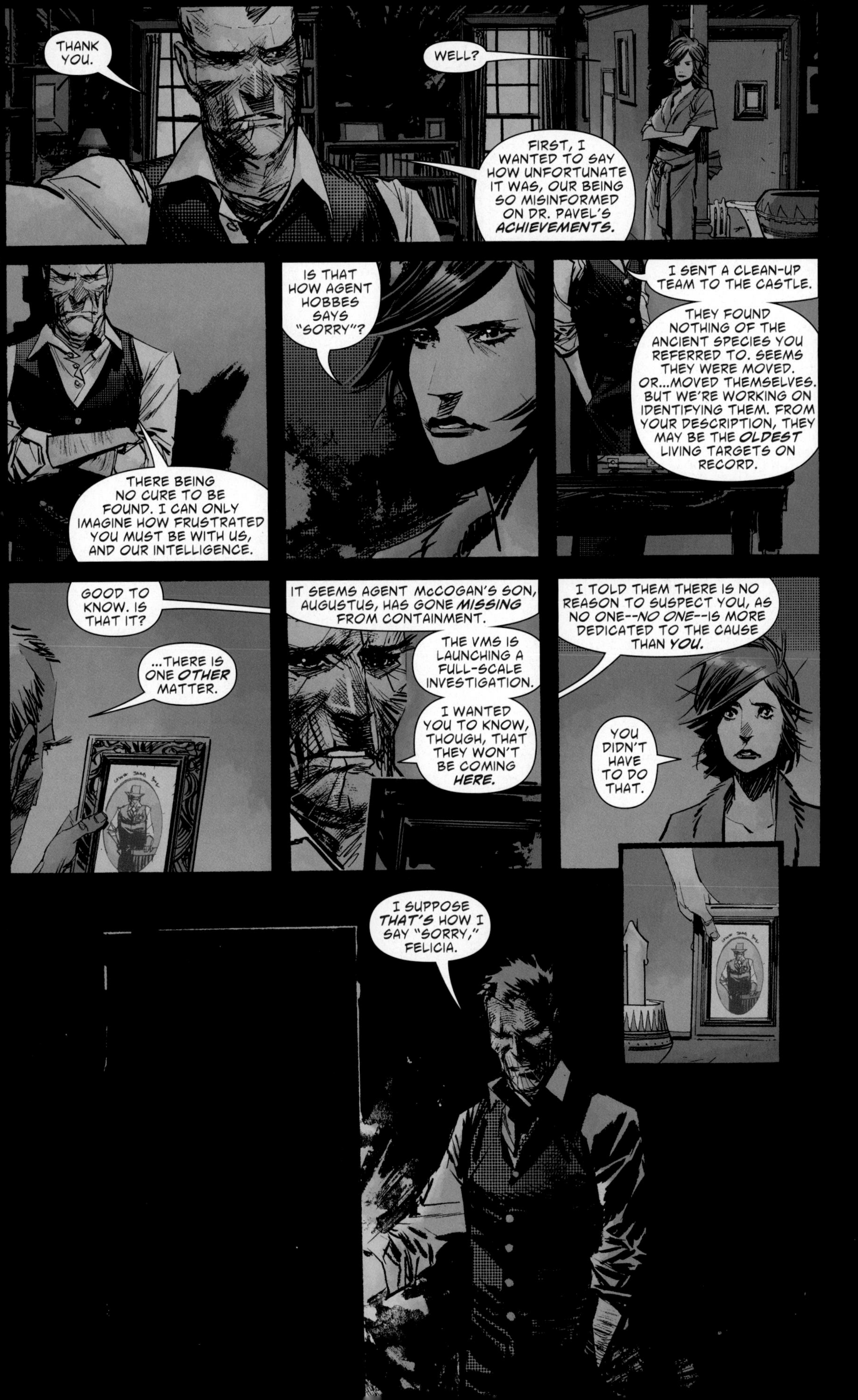

THANK YOU.
WELL?
FIRST, I WANTED TO SAY HOW UNFORTUNATE IT WAS, OUR BEING SO MISINFORMED ON DR. PAVEL'S ACHIEVEMENTS.
THERE BEING NO CURE TO BE FOUND. I CAN ONLY IMAGINE HOW FRUSTRATED YOU MUST BE WITH US, AND OUR INTELLIGENCE.
IS THAT HOW AGENT HOBBES SAYS "SORRY"?
I SENT A CLEAN-UP TEAM TO THE CASTLE.
THEY FOUND NOTHING OF THE ANCIENT SPECIES YOU REFERRED TO. SEEMS THEY WERE MOVED. OR...MOVED THEMSELVES. BUT WE'RE WORKING ON IDENTIFYING THEM. FROM YOUR DESCRIPTION, THEY MAY BE THE OLDEST LIVING TARGETS ON RECORD.
GOOD TO KNOW. IS THAT IT?
...THERE IS ONE OTHER MATTER.
IT SEEMS AGENT McCOGAN'S SON, AUGUSTUS, HAS GONE MISSING FROM CONTAINMENT.
THE VMS IS LAUNCHING A FULL-SCALE INVESTIGATION.
I WANTED YOU TO KNOW, THOUGH, THAT THEY WON'T BE COMING HERE.
I TOLD THEM THERE IS NO REASON TO SUSPECT YOU, AS NO ONE--NO ONE--IS MORE DEDICATED TO THE CAUSE THAN YOU.
YOU DIDN'T HAVE TO DO THAT.
I SUPPOSE THAT'S HOW I SAY "SORRY," FELICIA.

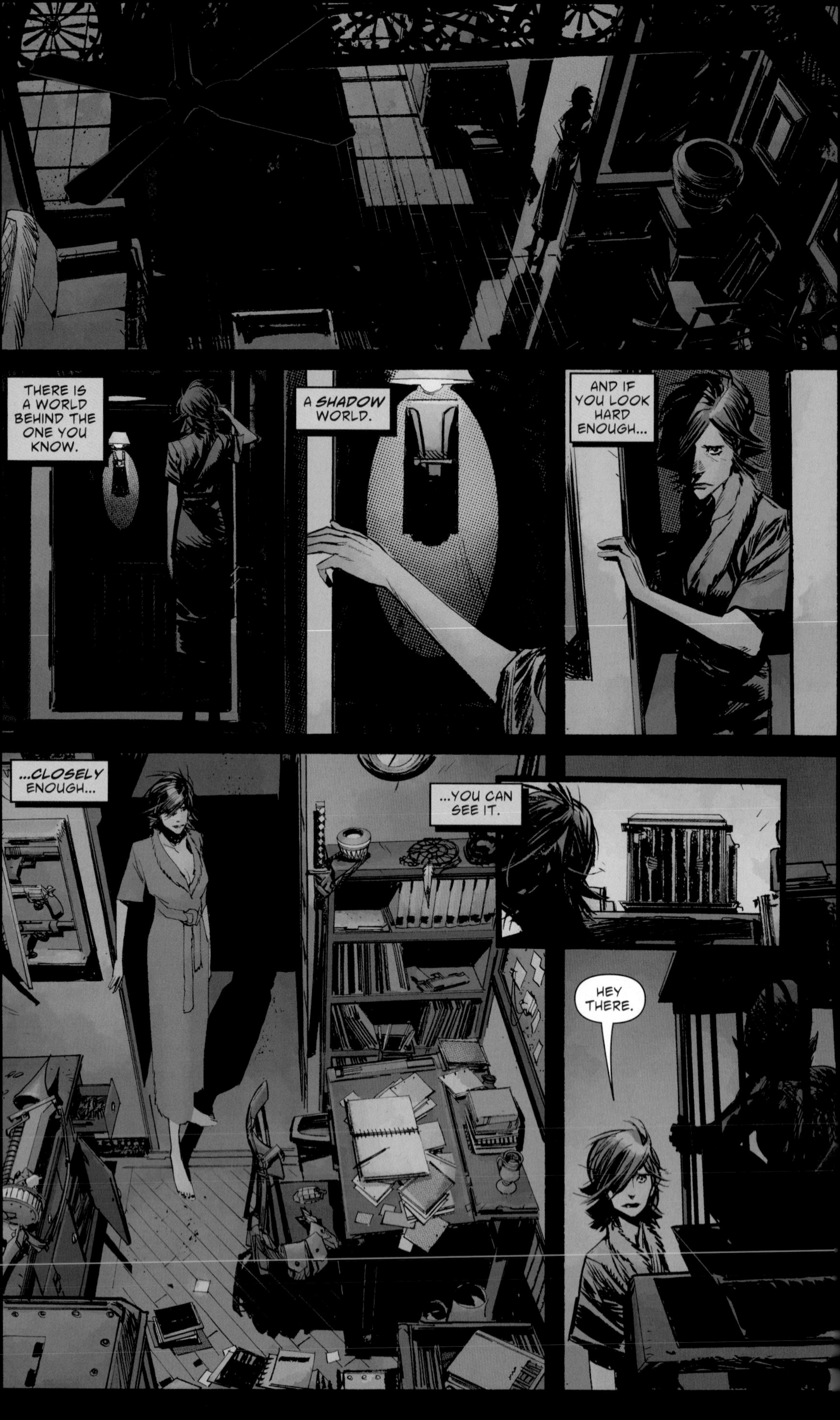

THERE IS A WORLD BEHIND THE ONE YOU KNOW.
A SHADOW WORLD.
AND IF YOU LOOK HARD ENOUGH...
...CLOSELY ENOUGH...
...YOU CAN SEE IT.
HEY THERE.

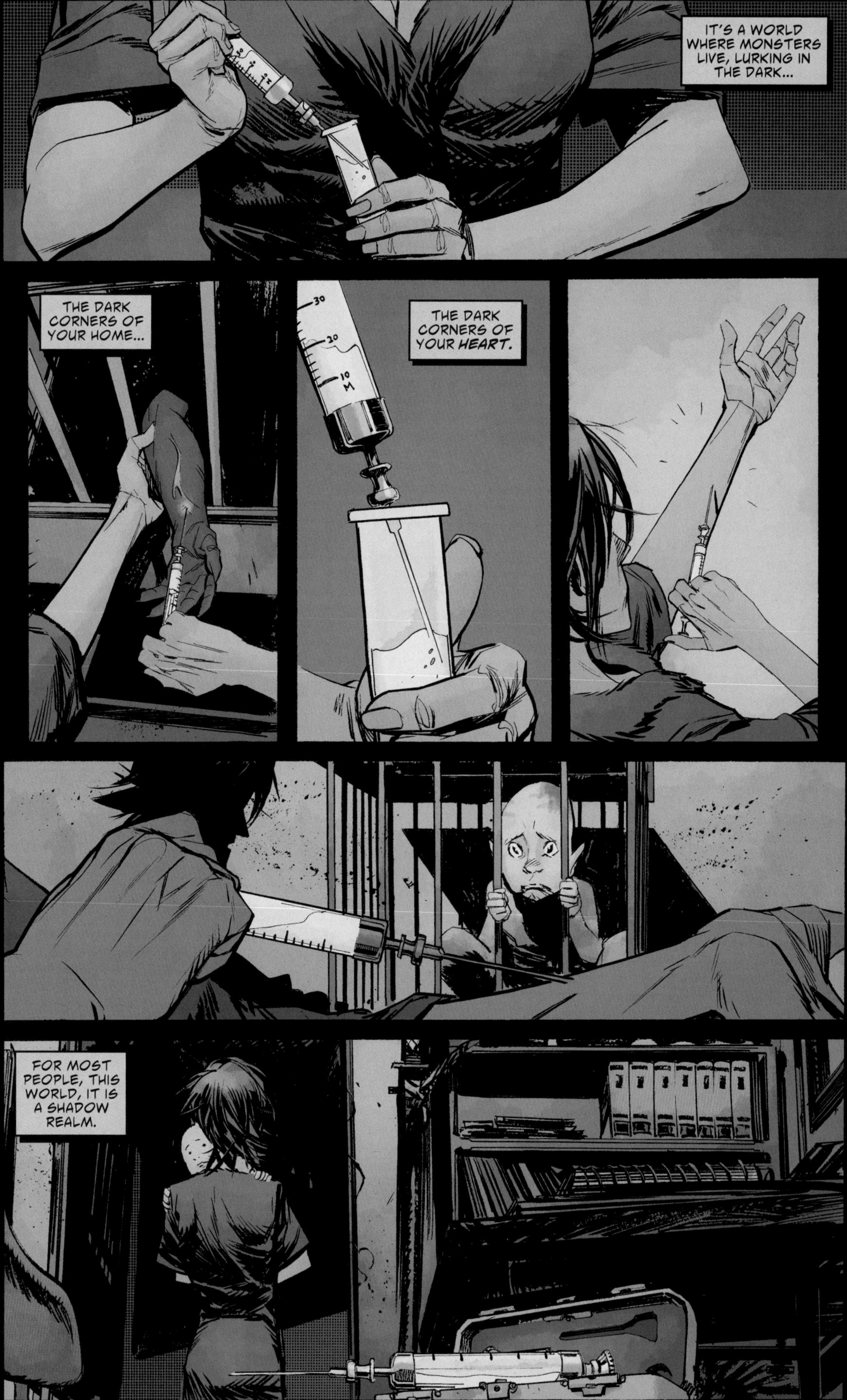
IT'S A WORLD WHERE MONSTERS LIVE, LURKING IN THE DARK...
THE DARK CORNERS OF YOUR HOME...
THE DARK CORNERS OF YOUR HEART.
FOR MOST PEOPLE, THIS WORLD, IT IS A SHADOW REALM.

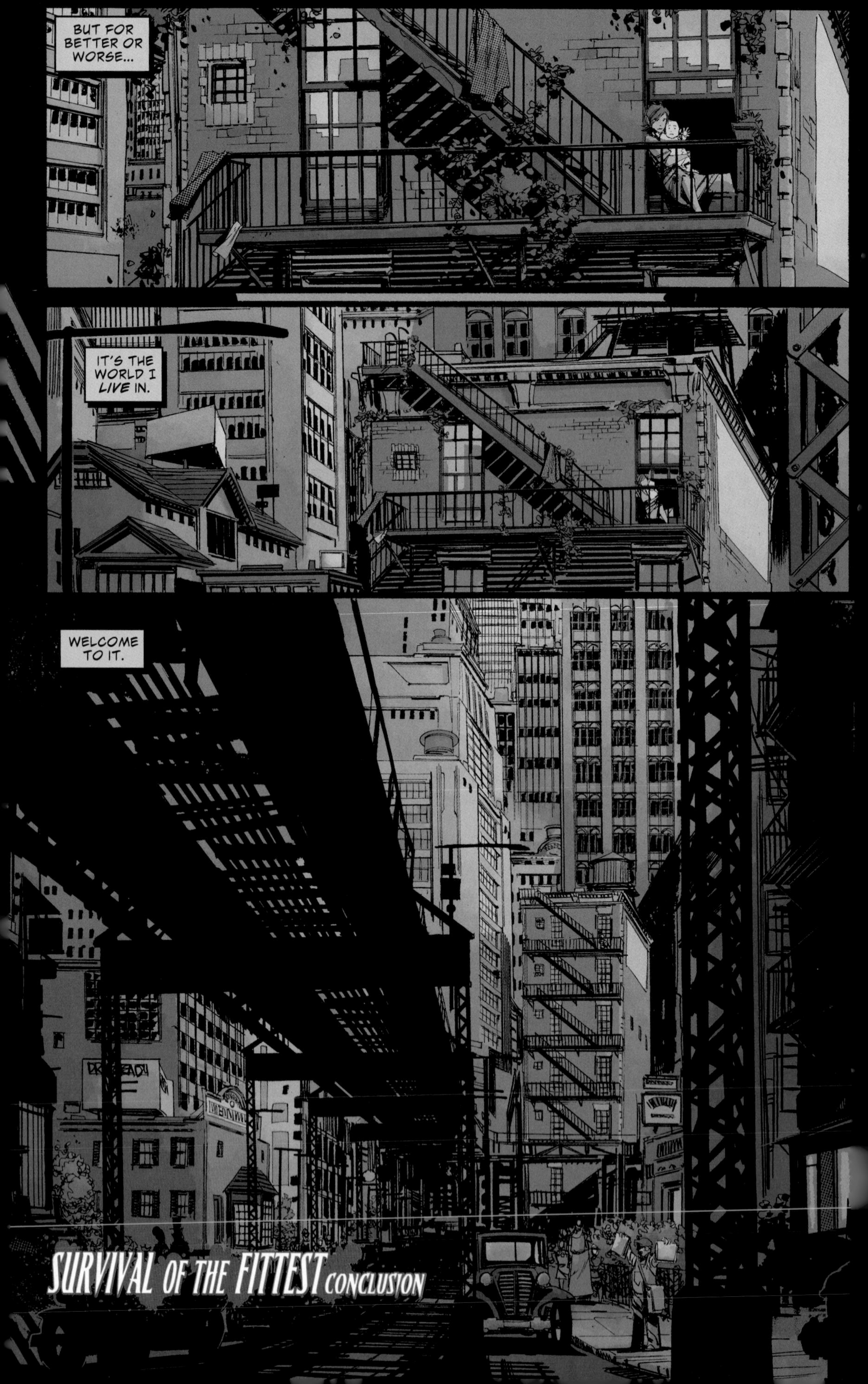

BUT FOR BETTER OR WORSE...
IT'S THE WORLD I *LIVE* IN.
WELCOME TO IT.
SURVIVAL OF THE FITTEST CONCLUSION

Variant to AMERICAN VAMPIRE #13 by Sean Murphy with Dave Stewart

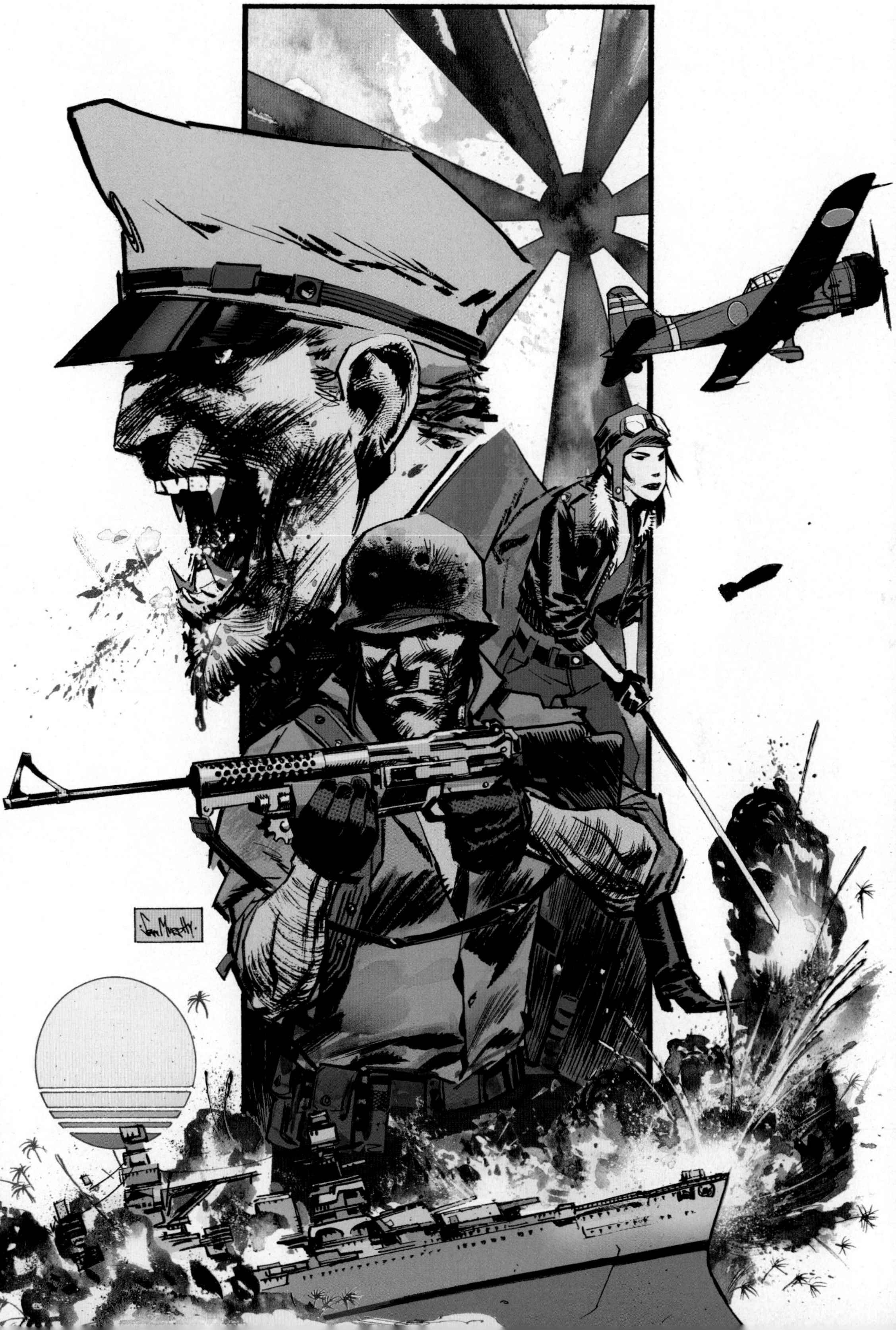

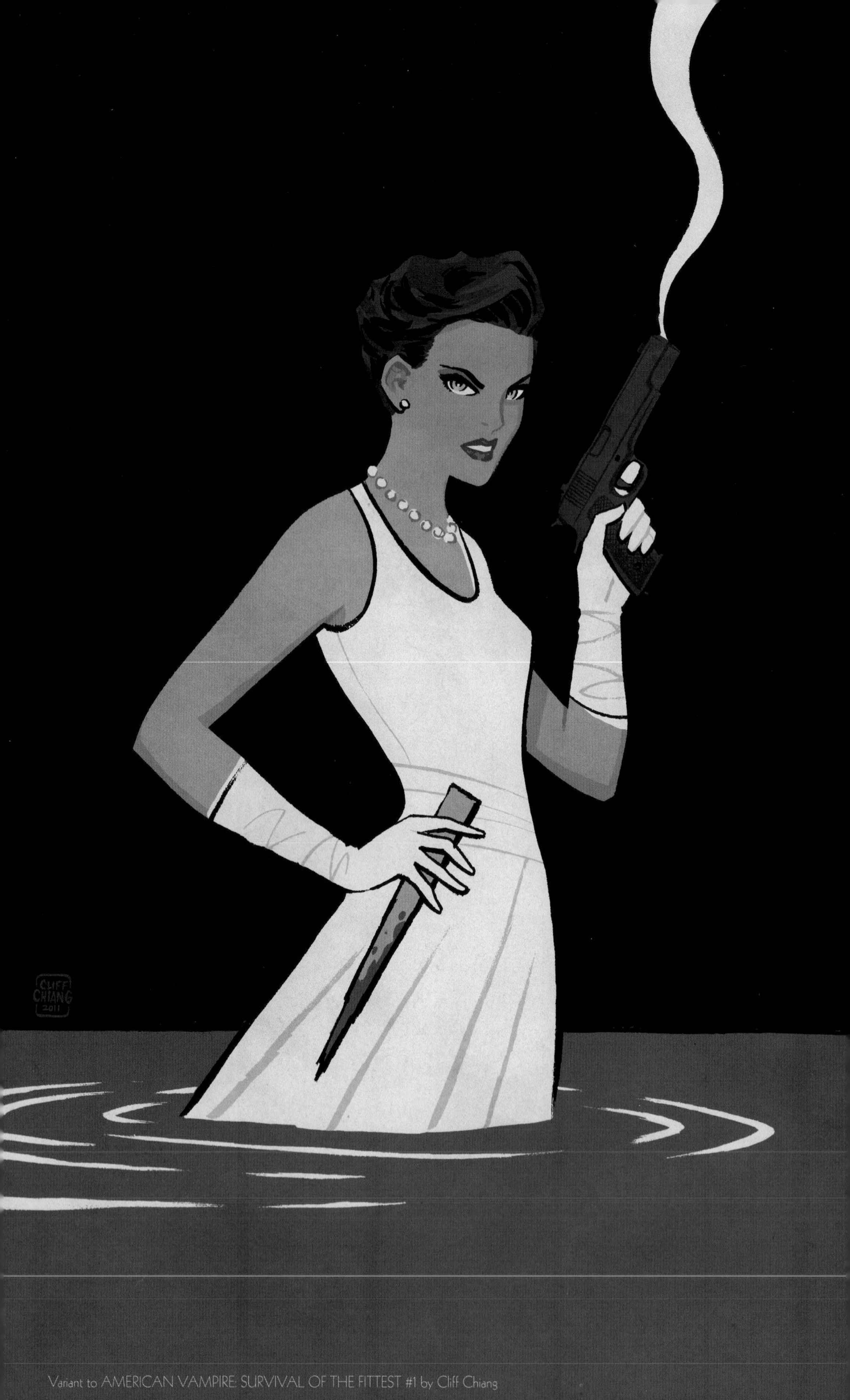
CLIFF
CHIANG
2011

Variant to AMERICAN VAMPIRE: SURVIVAL OF THE FITTEST #1 by Cliff Chiang

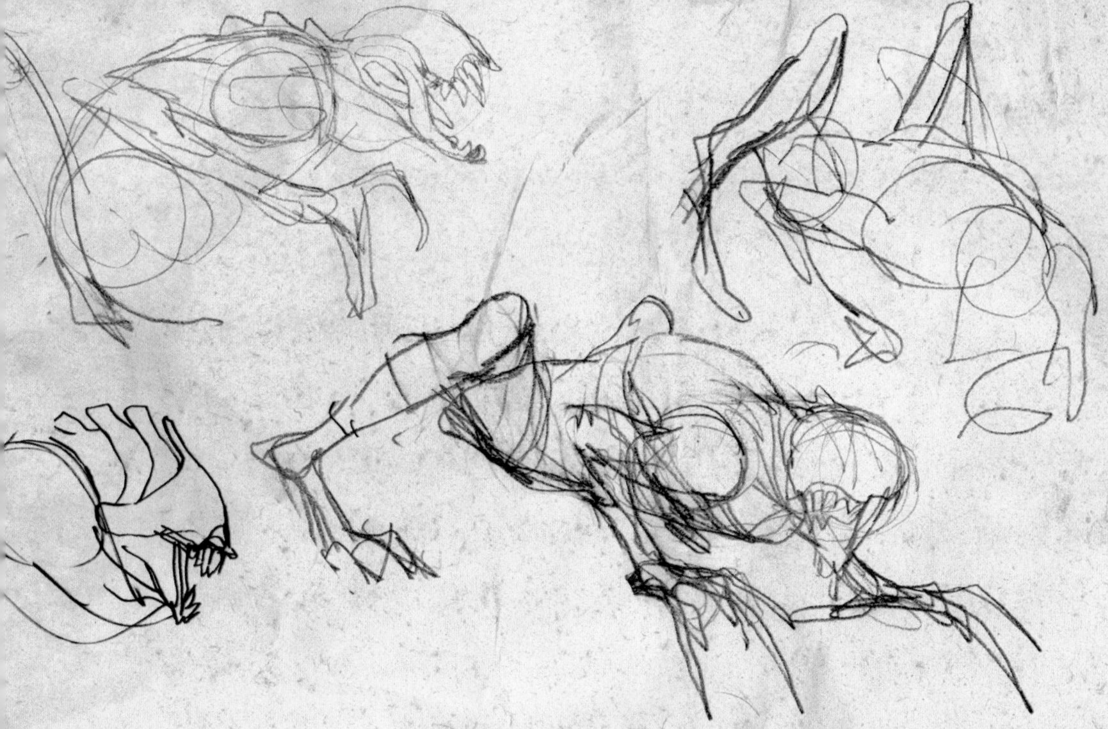

SKETCHES AND DESIGNS BY RAFAEL ALBURQUERQE AND SEAN MURPHY

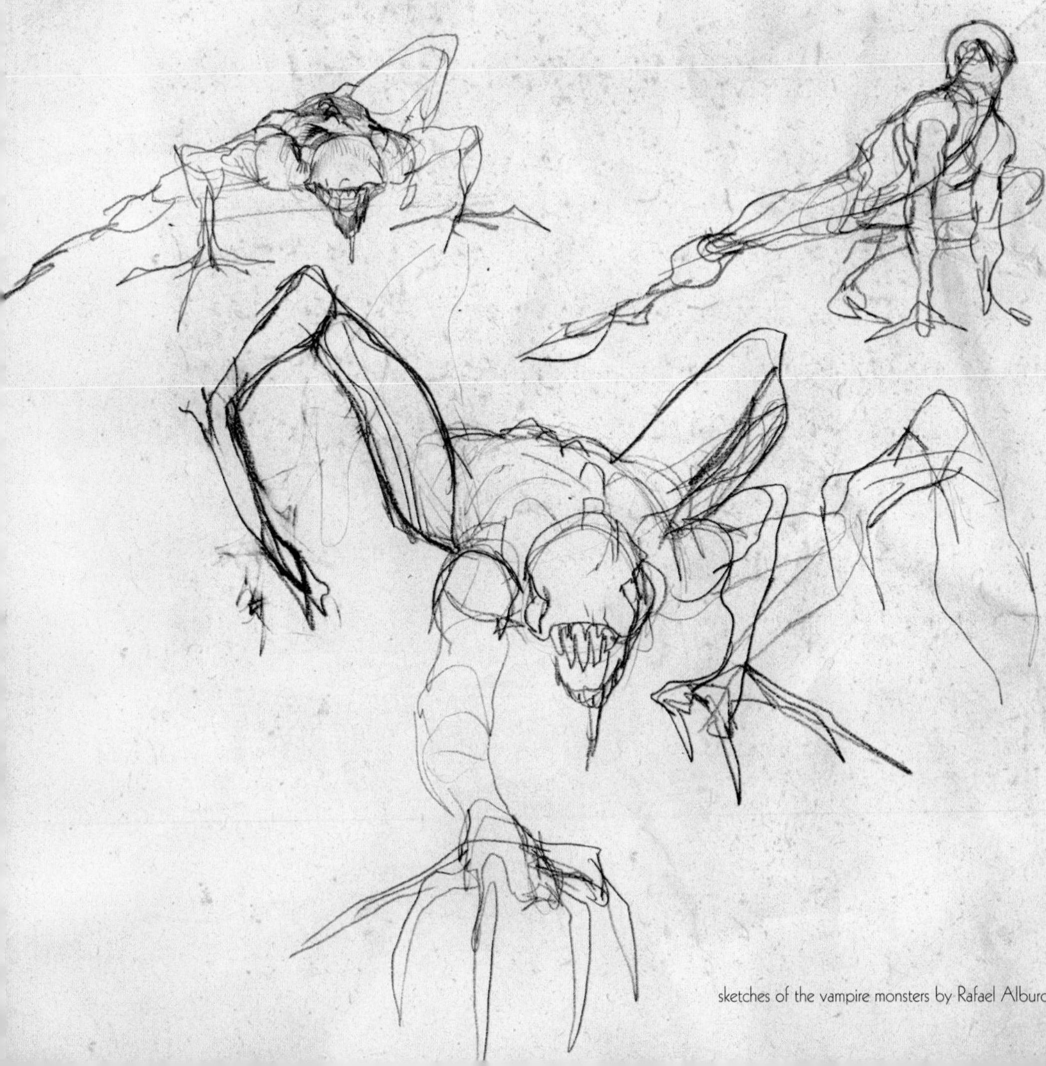

sketches of the vampire monsters by Rafael Alburquerqe

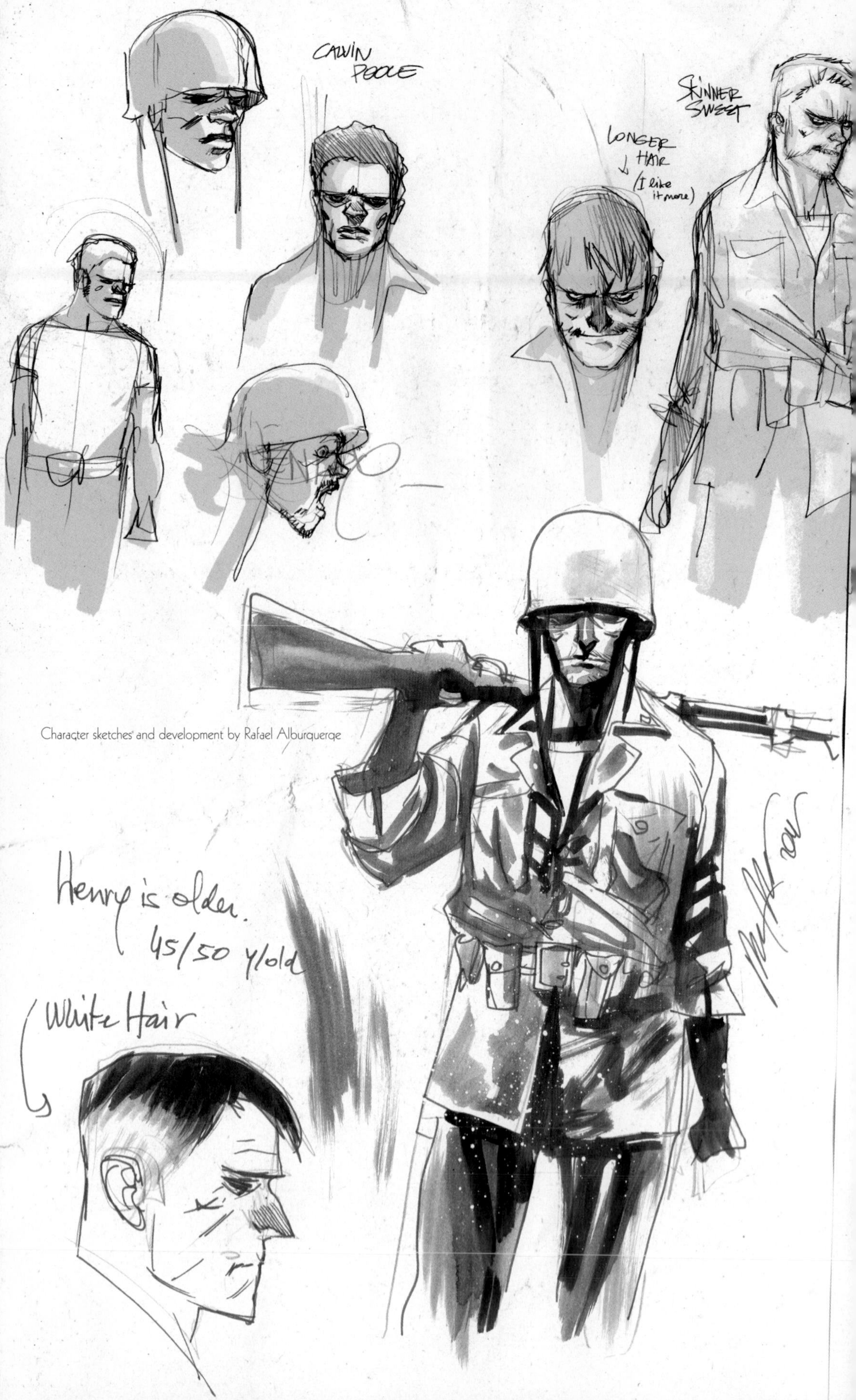

CALVIN
POOLE
SKINNER
SWEET
LONGER
HAIR
(I like it more)
Henry is older.
45/50 y/old
White Hair

Character sketches and development by Rafael Alburquerqe

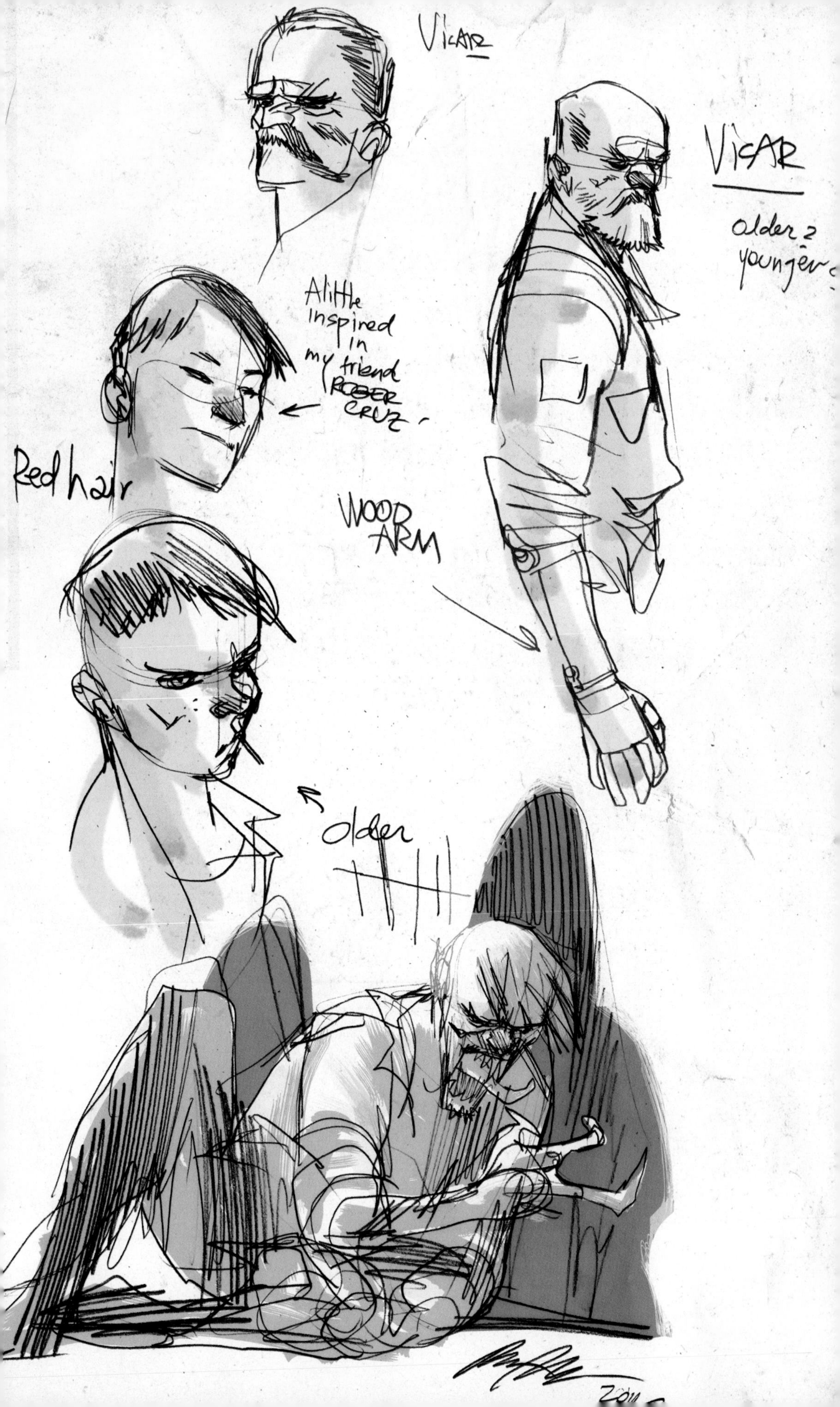

Vicar
Vicar
older & younger
A little inspired in my friend ROBER CRUZ
Red hair
WOOD ARM
older
2011

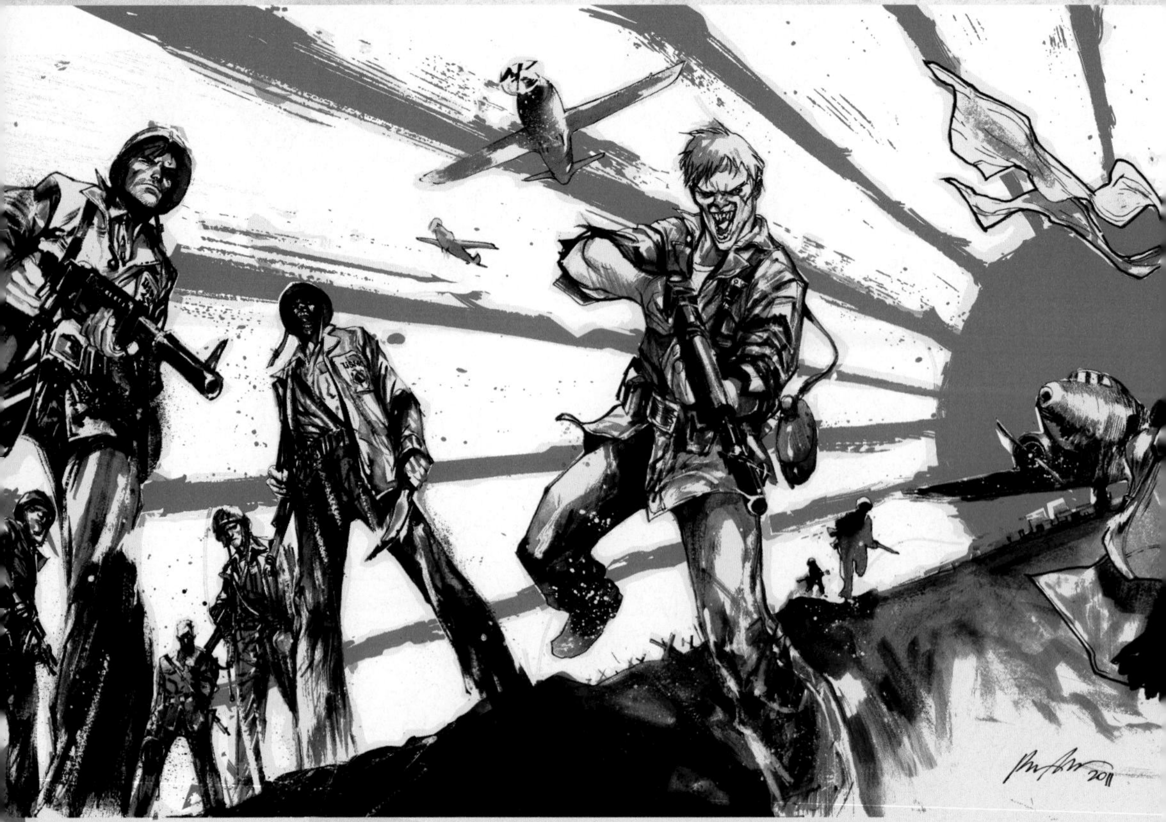

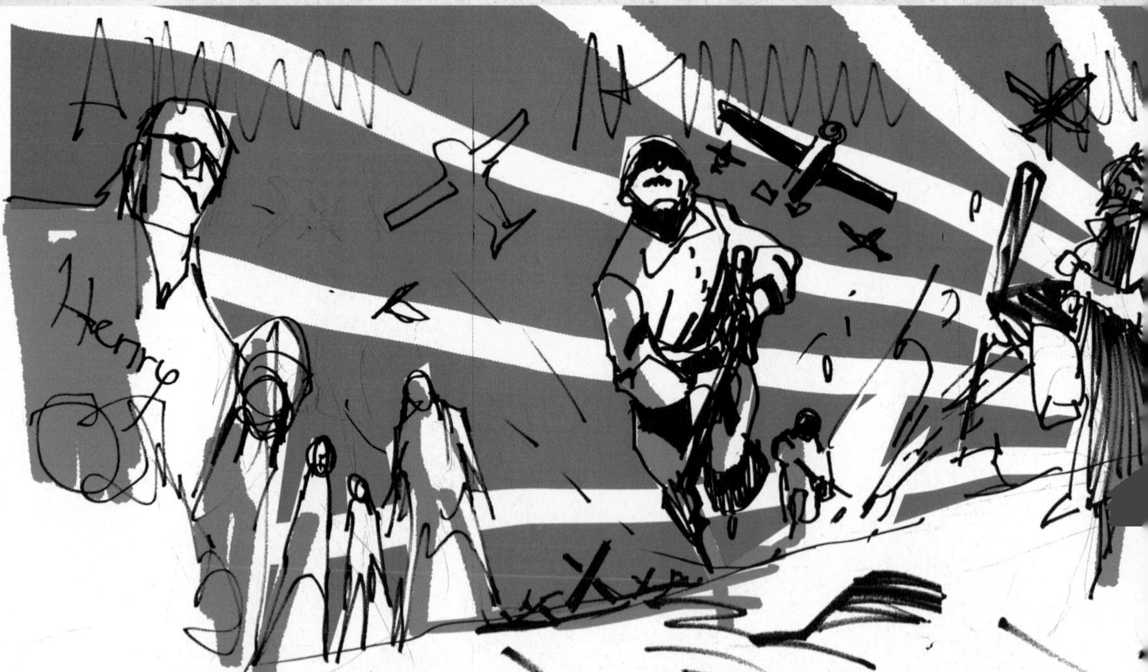
Henry

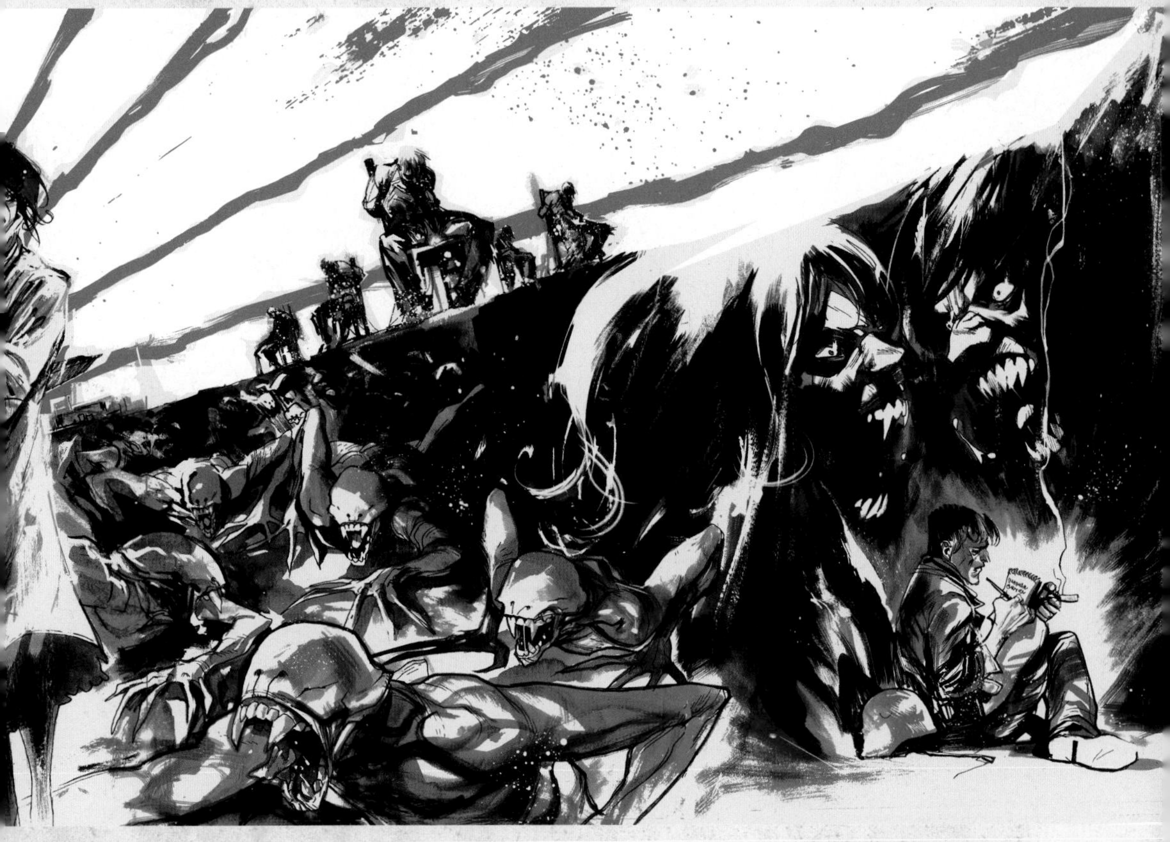

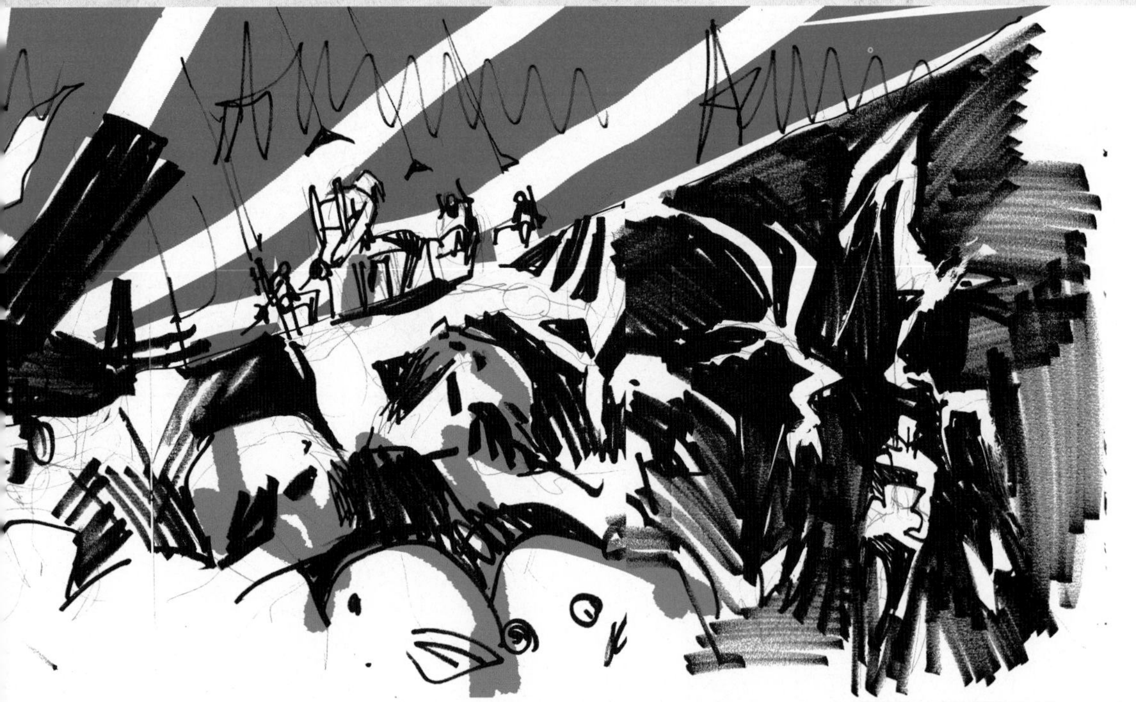

The covers to AMERICAN VAMPIRE #13-17 connect to create one larger image. Here are the sketches and refined layout for the piece by Rafael Alburquerqe. You can see the final images earlier in this collection.

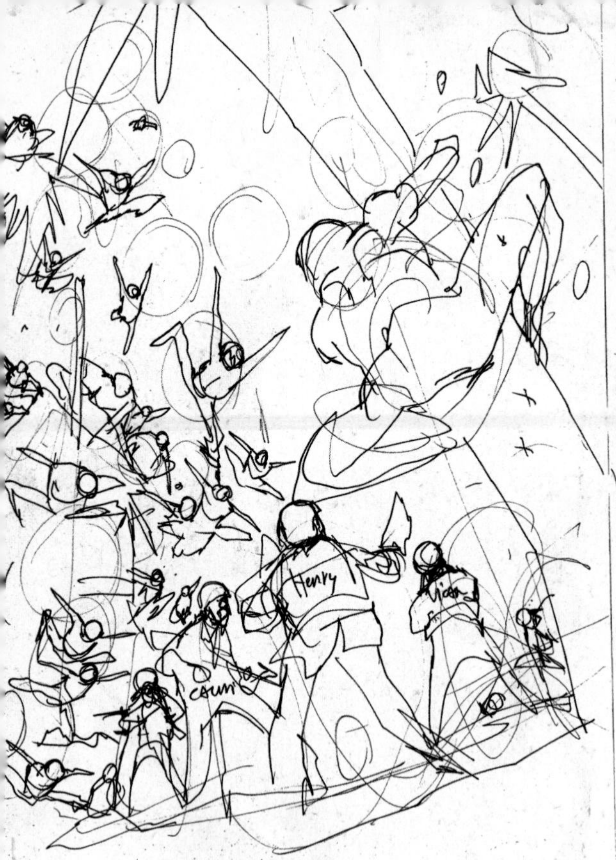
Henry

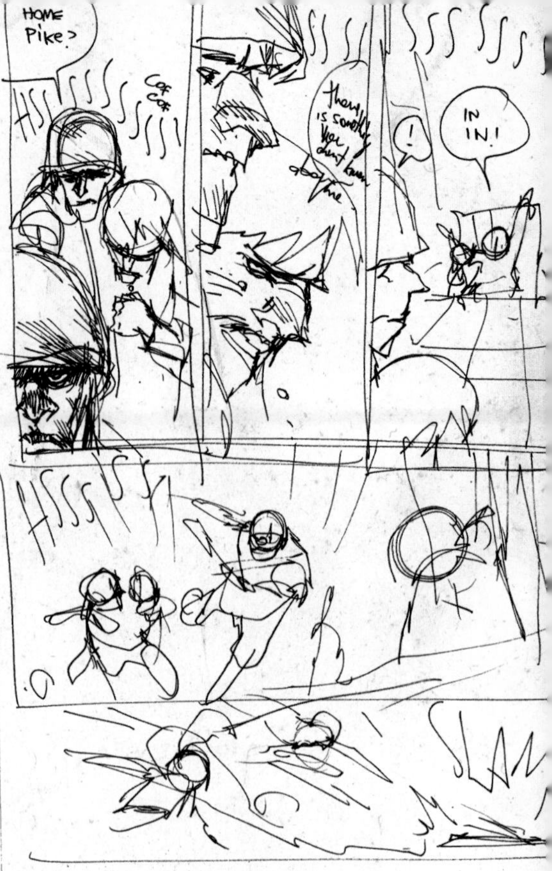
HOME
Pike>
COF COF
!
IN IN!

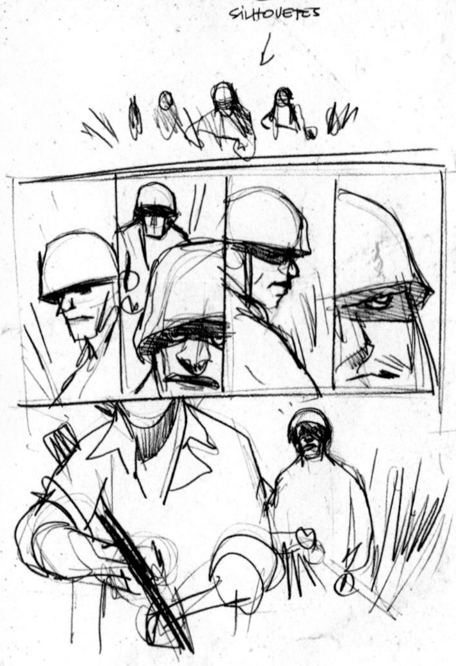
SILHOUETES

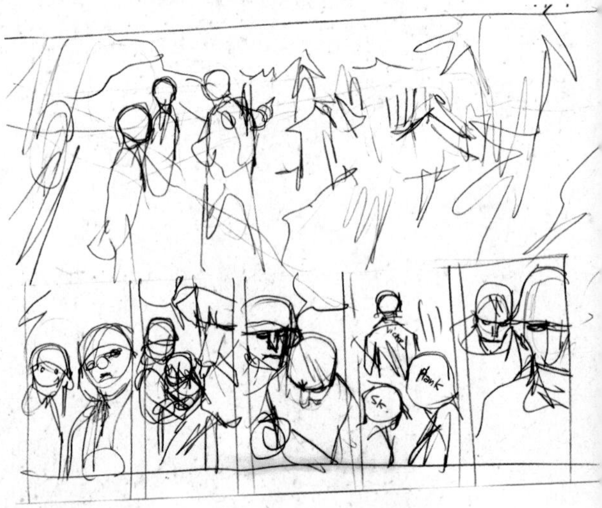

Original page loyouts from AMERICAN VAMPIRE #14 by Rafael Alburquerqe.

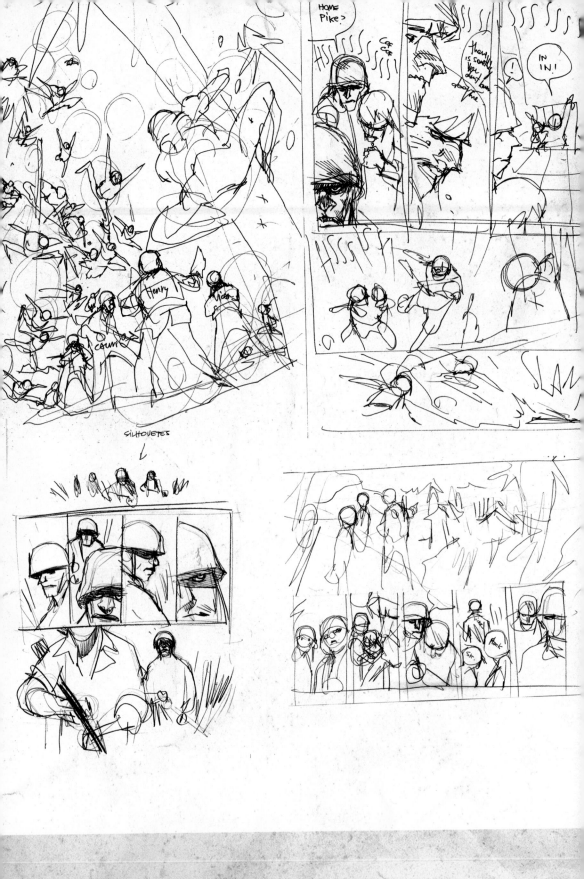

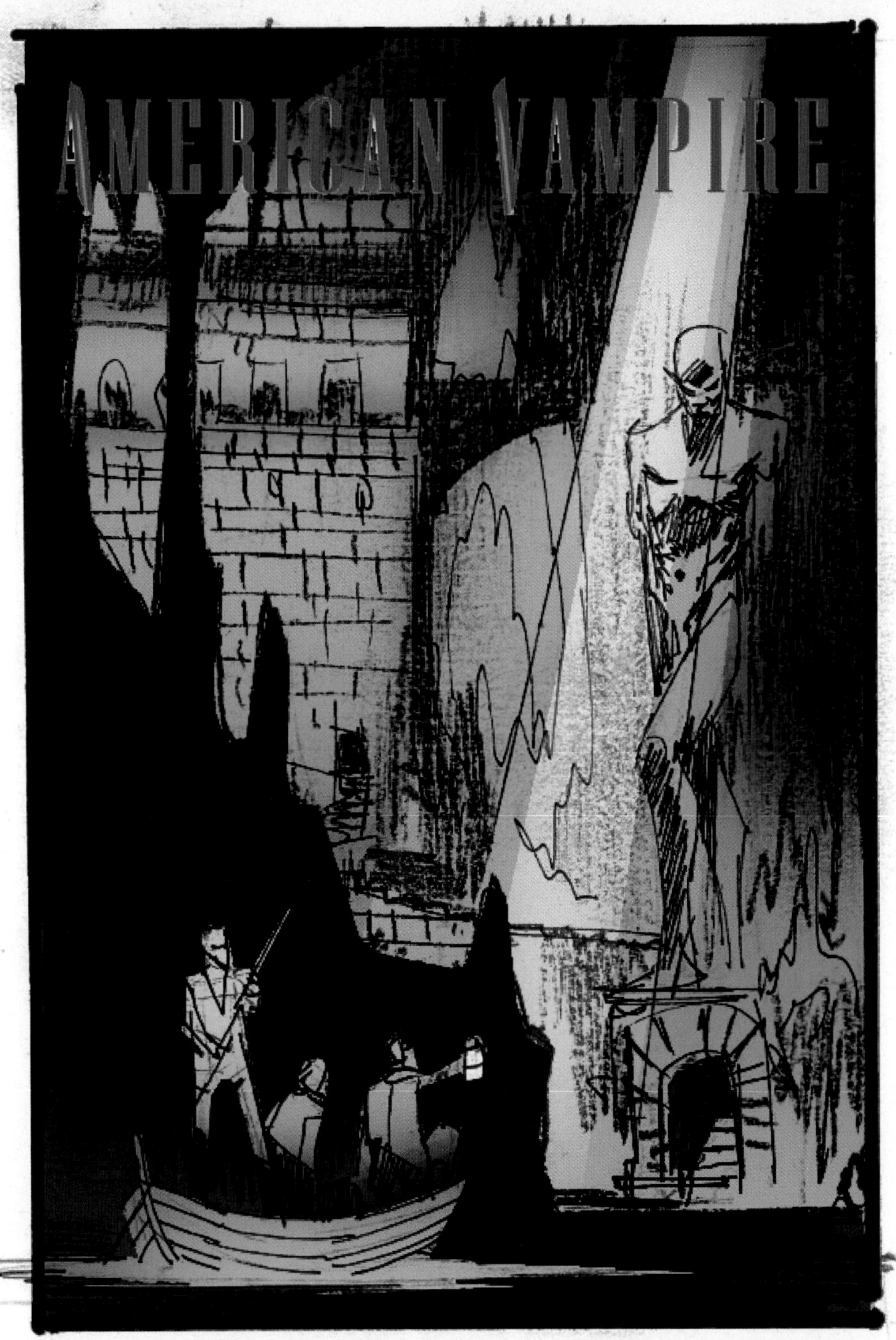
AMERICAN VAMPIRE

Cover 3: Cash, Book and the scientist approach the underground caves beneath the castle. Huge statues of hybernating vampires rest around the stairwell toward the surface.

Original cover sketch to AMERICAN VAMPIRE: SURVIVAL OF THE FITTEST #3 by Sean Murphy.

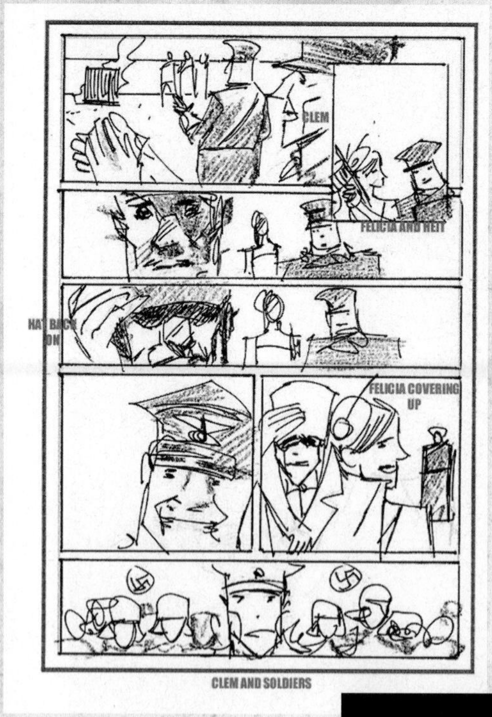
CLEM
FELICIA AND HEIT
HAT BACK ON
FELICIA COVERING UP
CLEM AND SOLDIERS

Page development by Sean Murphy – thumbnails, pencils and inks.

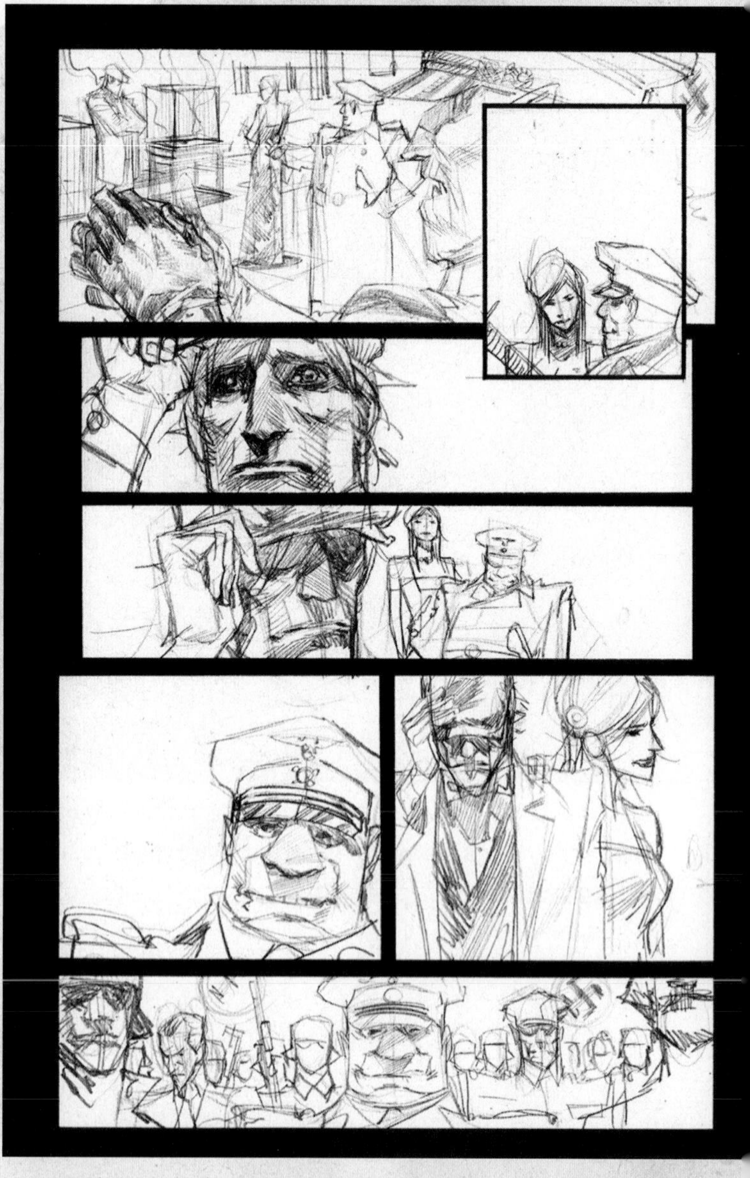

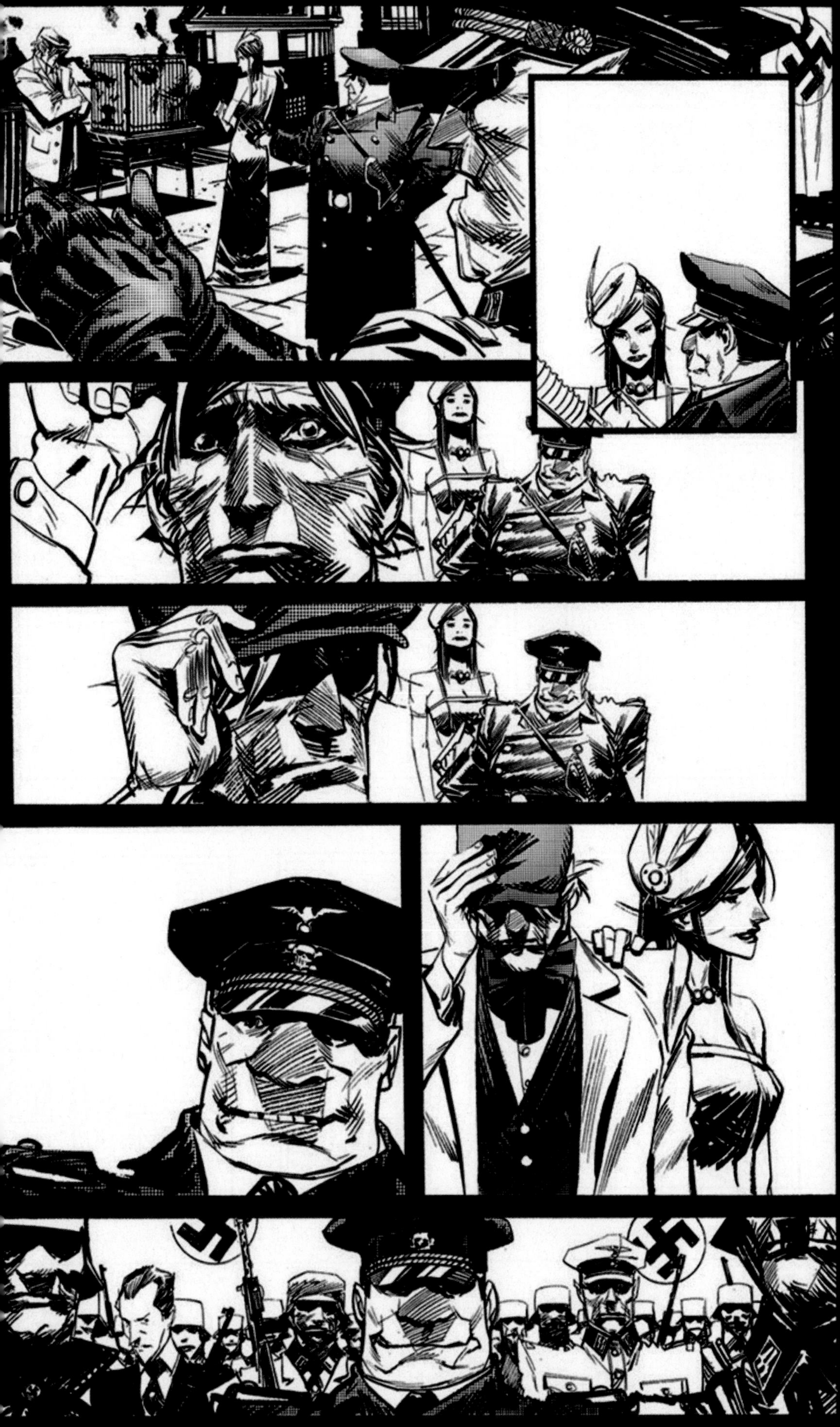

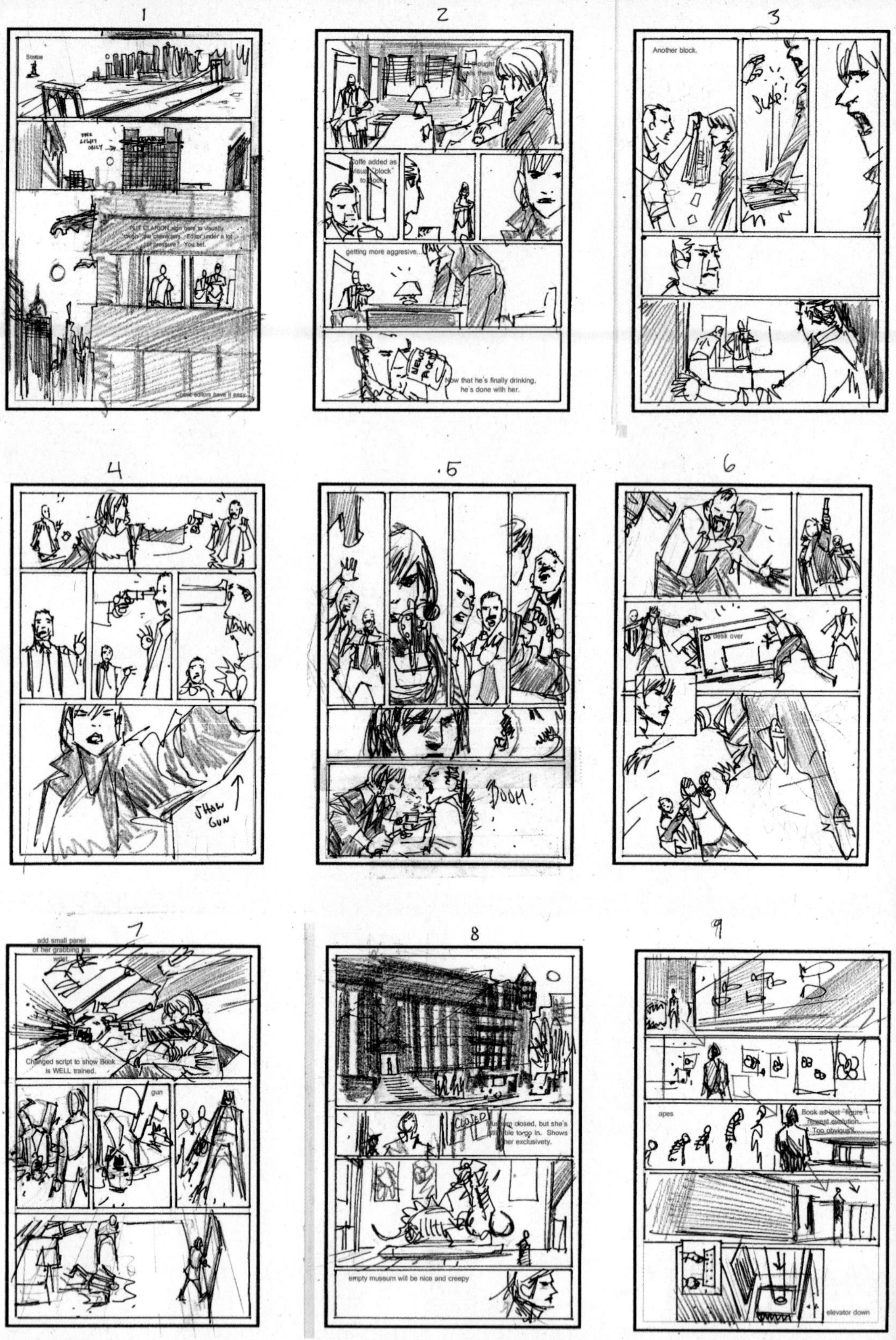
1
Statue
ONE LIGHT ONLY
PUT CLARION sign here to visually crush the characters. Editor under a lot of pressure? You bet.
Comic editors have it easy.
2
Coffe added as visual "block" to Book.
getting more aggresive...
Now that he's finally drinking, he's done with her.
3
Another block.
SLAP!
4
SHOW GUN
5
BOOM!
6
desk over
7
add small panel of her grabbing his wrist.
Changed script to show Book is WELL trained.
gun
8
CLOSED
empty museum will be nice and creepy
9
apes
elevator down

Thumbnail layouts for AMERICAN VAMPIRE: SURVIVAL OF THE FITTEST #1 by Sean Murphy.

library and shit
BOOK
nerds doing nerdy things like reading comics
book
geeking out
B
12
H
H
student
BOOK
doorway
13
charts in BG
14
Cash
15
16
fire
files
17
B
photo
B and H
18
visually space them out.
He's lost her interest.
folder open...
19
"official" vibe
HAND OFF!
knocks folders down
20
Cash--no hat yet
Book
picks up folder
TO BE CONTINUED
Shows that he's already armed. Folder and map will be bigger.

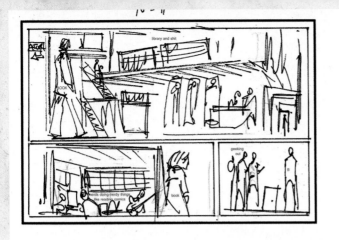

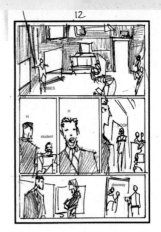

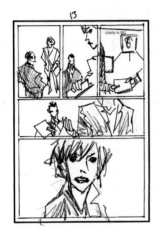

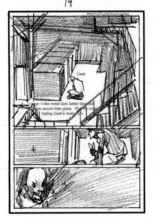

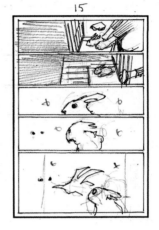

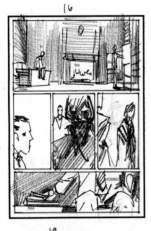

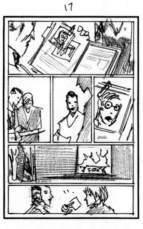

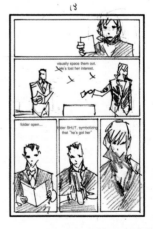

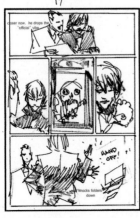

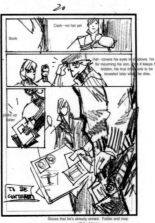

Scott Snyder is the best-selling and award-winning writer of Batman and Swamp Thing as well as the short story collection *Voodoo Heart* (The Dial Press). He teaches writing at Sarah Lawrence College, NYU and Columbia University. He lives on Long Island with his wife, Jeanie, and his sons Jack and Emmett. He is a dedicated and un-ironic fan of Elvis Presley.

Rafael Albuquerque was born in Porto Alegre, Brazil, Rafael Albuquerque has been working in the American comic book industry since 2005. Best known from his work on the *Savage Brothers*, Blue Beetle and Superman/Batman, he has also published the creator-owned graphic novels *Crimeland* (2007) and *Mondo Urbano*, published in 2010.

After breaking into the industry at a young age, **Sean Murphy** made a name for himself in the world of indie comics before joining up with DC for such titles as BATMAN/SCARECROW: YEAR ONE, TEEN TITANS, HELLBLAZER and the miniseries JOE THE BARBARIAN. He also wrote and illustrated the original graphic novel *Off Road*.

Danijel Zezelj is a comic book artist, painter and illustrator of eighteen graphic novels. His comics and illustrations have been published by DC Comics/Vertigo, Marvel Comics, The New York Times Book Review, Harper's Magazine, San Francisco Guardian, Editori del Grifo and Edizioni Charta among others. In 2001 in Zagred, Croatia, he founded the publishing house and graphic workshop Petikat. He currently lives and works in Brooklyn.